THE ARAB CONQUEST OF EGYPT

Map I. Frontispiece.

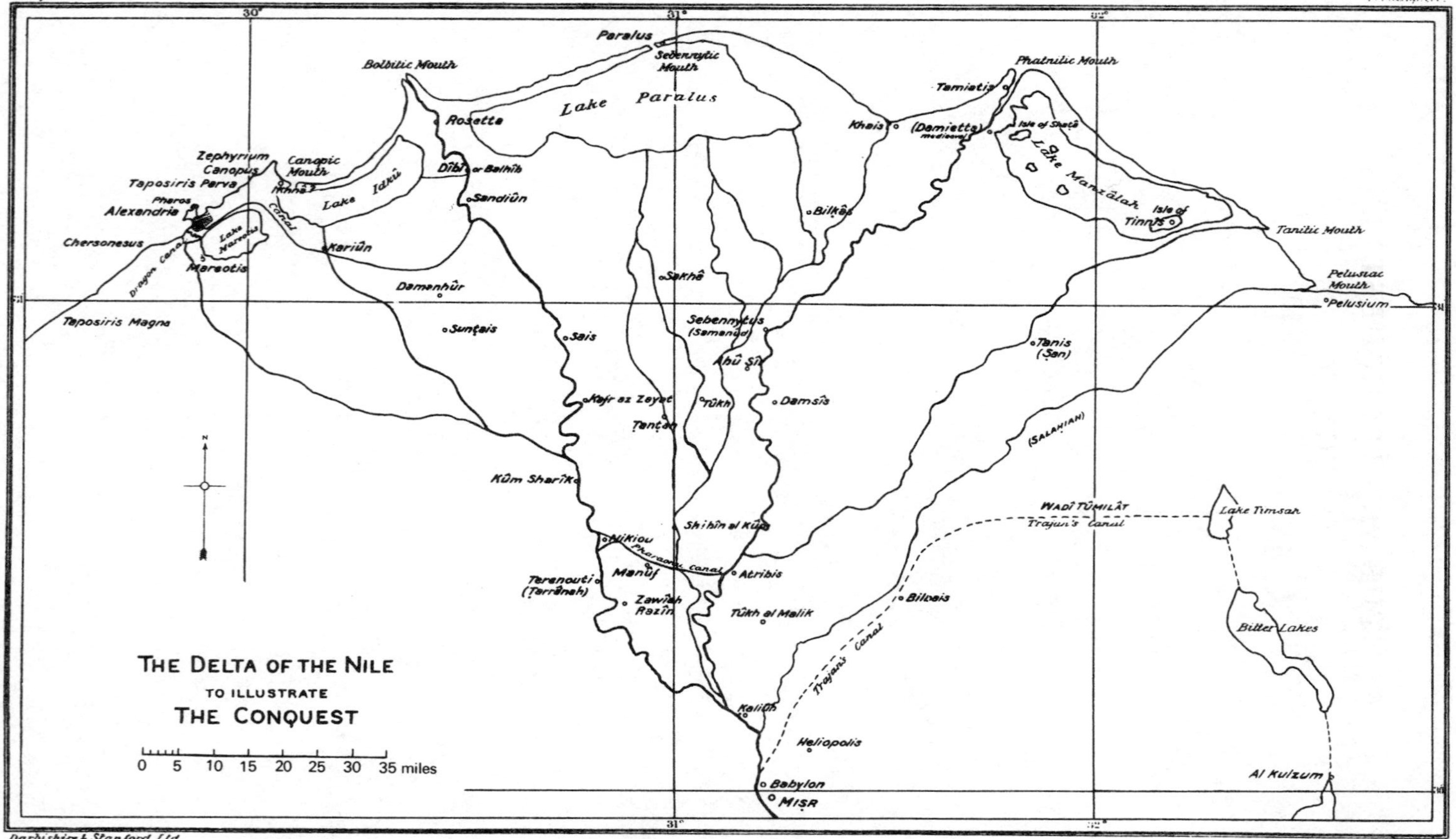

Darbishire & Stanford Ltd. Oxford.

MAP I. The Delta to illustrate the Conquest.

THE ARAB CONQUEST OF EGYPT

AND THE LAST THIRTY YEARS OF THE ROMAN DOMINION

BY

ALFRED J. BUTLER

D.LITT., F.S.A.

Containing also *The Treaty of Miṣr in Ṭabarī* (1913)
and *Babylon of Egypt* (1914)

Edited by

P. M. FRASER

with a critical bibliography and additional documentation

SECOND EDITION

1478
1978

OXFORD
AT THE CLARENDON PRESS

Oxford University Press, Great Clarendon Street, Oxford OX2 6DP
Oxford New York
Athens Auckland Bangkok Bogota Buenos Aires Calcutta
Cape Town Chennai Dar es Salaam Delhi Florence Hong Kong Istanbul
Karachi Kuala Lumpur Madrid Melbourne Mexico City Mumbai
Nairobi Paris São Paolo Singapore Taipei Tokyo Toronto Warsaw
and associated companies in
Berlin Ibadan

Published in the United States by
Oxford University Press Inc., New York

British Library Cataloguing in Publication Data
Data available

ISBN 0-19-821678-5

1 3 5 7 9 10 8 6 4 2

Printed in Great Britain
on acid-free paper by
Bookcraft (Bath) Ltd.,
Midsomer Norton

INTRODUCTION TO THE REVISED EDITION

A. J. Butler's *The Arab Conquest of Egypt*, published in 1902, went out of print in 1945, and has been in steady demand since that time as the most comprehensive and authoritative treatment of its subject. The decision to republish it with some additional matter is therefore fully justified. The conquest of Egypt was but one event in the Arab Conquest of the Middle East and North Africa, and it was not in isolation, but as part of the general history of the reign of Heraclius on the one hand, and, on the other, of the great wave of Muslim conquest that Butler treated it. This gives his work its outstanding value, and that value is heightened by the lively style and robust learning with which it is informed.

Butler brought to his task of writing the history of the Conquest the background of a Classical scholar whom residence in Egypt as tutor to the Prince Tewfik in 1880–1 (to which his reminiscences, *Court Life in Egypt* (1887), bear entertaining witness) had provided with familiarity both with the antiquities of Christian and Muslim Egypt—documented in his early work, *The Ancient Coptic Churches of Egypt* (1884, reprinted by the Clarendon Press, 1970)—and with Arabic sources. The Arab Conquest, the historical link between the two aspects of Egyptian history that most interested Butler, had not previously been the subject of a full critical work, and, as Butler said in his Preface, his work 'needed no apology'.

The Conquest was indeed in need of critical treatment, and this Butler provided with admirable acumen, establishing for the first time, within a wide framework, the true value of the non-Greek sources both for the Conquest and for the preceding Sassanian conquest of the Middle East, and of Heraclius' triumphant but short-lived reconquest. Of these events, no less than of the Conquest, Butler gave a highly individual and independent account, in which he showed himself at once a master of the critical use of sources and of historical writing. The high praise accorded to his treatment of the subject by Ignaz Goldziher in his review in the *Byzantinische Zeitschrift* is in itself a lasting guarantee of its worth.

Nevertheless, our knowledge of the reign of Heraclius, and in particular of his wars with Persia, of the Conquest itself, and, above all, of the nature of early Muslim rule in Egypt, has altered considerably in the last two generations, and a critical reader turning to Butler's narrative today may reasonably expect some guidance as to more recent work in these fields. This I have attempted to provide in the Additional Bibliography (see pp. xliii–lxxxi), which covers in some detail works relating to Egypt in the seventh century A.D. In particular, I have tried to provide fairly full lists of Greek and Arabic papyri of the reign of Heraclius and of the early years of Muslim rule respectively, and also of the very relevant, but slightly later, correspondence of the Ummayad governor of Egypt, Qurrah b. Sharīk, with the pagarch Basilius of

Aphrodito. In general, the reader is referred to these bibliographies, where he will also find some indication of the major points at issue.

In this context one point of general significance in an estimate of Butler's work may be made. Though conversant with the relevant Arabic sources, Butler, as he himself admitted (see p. iv), was in no sense a specialist in Arabic literature and, more particularly, in the vast field of Arabic historiography. It is the burden of the criticism made against Butler by Leone Caetani, Prince of Teano, in his monumental *Annali dell'Islam* (see the bibliography to chs. xiv–xxii, below, p. lxvi) that he had not given due weight to the traditional element, the *ḥadīth*, reaching back in a chain of authorities, the so-called *isnād*, to eye-witnesses of particular historical events, by virtue of which the Traditions recorded by later writers have value only in so far as their source provides it, and must therefore be judged as statements of tradition, frequently of a tendentious nature, and not of an independent inquiry. This criticism, which was also made by K. Vollers in his review of Butler's work in the *Historische Zeitschrift*, must stand—and Butler himself tacitly accepted it, for in his later work, *The Treaty of Miṣr in Ṭabarī*, Clarendon Press, 1913 (reprinted here), he carefully sets out his material in the form of the *isnād*—but since the Arab historians play in any case but a secondary role compared with the narrative of John of Nikiou and some of the Patriarchal and Monastic Coptic and Arabic texts, the defect does not seriously vitiate the narrative. Butler's own major departures from the *fable convenue* of the Conquest—his estimate of the decisive role of Cyrus in facilitating the Conquest, and his defence of the Copts against the charge of betraying Egypt to the Arabs on sectarian and political grounds—derive essentially from his interpretation of John and of Severus Ibn Moqaffaʿ's *History of the Patriarchs*.

I have already mentioned the growth of documentary evidence from Egypt, relating both to the reign of Heraclius and also to the first half-century of Muslim rule, culminating in the richly documented governorship of Qurrah b. Sharīk. Butler could have no knowledge of most of this material, Greek or Arabic, and consequently his picture of Muslim administration is theoretical rather than actual; based, that is to say, on the accounts of the principles of Muslim administration in the conquered territories recorded by the Arab historians and jurists, and not on the contemporary documents which alone indicate the extent of the debt of Muslim to Byzantine in this field. (For an earlier epoch we might compare the picture of the economic regime of Ptolemaic Egypt given by Félix Robiou in his *Mémoire sur l'économie politique, l'administration et la législation de l'Égypte au temps des Lagides* in 1876 with that given by Professor Claire Préaux in her *L'Économie royale des Lagides* in 1939.) The years between 1900 and 1939 saw the publication of a hitherto undreamed-of quantity of documentary material from Egypt—Greek, Arabic, and Coptic—on a scale that is not likely to be repeated—and the present time is not unsuitable for taking stock in this respect.

Butler himself returned to some central issues of the Arab Conquest in two pamphlets which he published on the eve of the First World War, and which have become excessively rare: *The Treaty of Miṣr in Ṭabarī* (Clarendon Press, 1913) and *Babylon of Egypt* (ibid. 1914). In justice to Butler, but at the possible loss of a certain unity of treatment, these two pamphlets are republished after the main text of this edition, with their original pagination and indexes.

In addition to publishing these two pamphlets, Butler's own hand-copy of *The Arab Conquest* contains a large number of additions, corrections, and observations in the light of reviews, subsequently published material, etc., expressly for inclusion in a second edition. Quite apart from considerations of the cost involved in resetting so much material, the incorporation of these scholia into the text would have created major difficulties, since many of them are inconclusive notes of the type any author makes in his hand-copy, and others have themselves been overtaken by still later material; with a few exceptions the additions appear mostly to be earlier than 1918. It may, however, be worth while to indicate the main items, publication of which provoked the major marginalia (often of considerable length); they are (except (v)) included in the Additional Bibliography below, in the relevant place, and the major reviews are noted below, p. x. (i), the publication by F. C. Conybeare, *EHR*, 25, 1910, of his translation of the Armenian translation of the monk Strategios's account of the Persian sack of Jerusalem: see below, p. li, no. E (iii); (ii), the Syriac *Chron. Anon.*, published by Guidi, *CSCO* (1903): below, p. l, no. D (c); (iii), Evetts' edition of Severus's *History of the*

Patriarchs: below, p. xlix, C (g); (iv), corrections on points of fact provided by W. H. Andrew's review, see below; (v), passages in Thomas of Marga's *Book of the Governors*, ed. Budge (2 vols. 1893); (vi), on topographical matters, P. Casanova's *Noms coptes du Caire* (1901): see below, p. liv; (vii), the Arabic text of the Coptic *synaxarion* in *PO* I, etc. Many of the points refer to the Persian campaign, and the most important of those relating to the conquest of Egypt Butler dealt with *in extenso* in the two subsequent pamphlets reprinted here. The last entry of all, on p. 495, *à propos* of the possible location of 'Amr's grave, was prompted by a letter from his Egyptian translator, Abū Hadīd (see below), and Butler's note, written at the age of eighty-five, is dated 'Feb. 1935', that is approximately eighteen months before he died. A list of the more important reviews of the book, in which the reader may find corrections of various minor errors of fact and also some differences of opinion on points of linguistic and historical interpretation, follows. Some minor slips have been tacitly corrected.

I must express my gratitude to my friend and colleague Mr. Rohan Butler, grandson of A. J. Butler, for lending me Butler's copy of *The Arab Conquest*, and also for his encouragement in what has proved to be a complicated editorial operation.

Reviews

The following reviews contain both general appraisals and points of detailed interpretation:

W. H. Andrew, *Rev. Hist. eccl.* 5, 1904, pp. 556–64; I. Goldziher, *Byz. Zeitschr.* 12, 1903, pp. 604–8;

G. Le Strange, *EHR* 18, 1903, pp. 546–8; S. de Ricci, *Rev. Arch.*, 1904, pp. 450–6; K. Vollers, *Hist. Zeitschr.* 56, 1904, pp. 490–2.

An Arabic translation of *The Arab Conquest of Egypt* was published in Cairo in 1933, the work of Muhammad Farīd Abū Hadīd, Inspector of Schools at Ṭanṭa.

I may end on a personal note. I had long hoped that my late colleague Samuel Stern would collaborate with me in this edition, and bring to it his outstanding talents in the field of Islamic studies. That was not to be. It is my hope that this edition may, on a smaller theme and on a smaller scale, contribute, like his masterly re-edition and translation of Ignaz Goldziher's *Muhammedanische Studien* (2 vols., London, 1967–71), to the useful survival of a classic of Islamic studies.

P. M. FRASER

All Souls College,
Oxford

PREFACE

For this book, so far as its purpose is concerned, perhaps no apology is needed. It aims at constructing a history, at once broad and detailed, of the Saracen conquest of Egypt. No such history has yet been written, although scattered essays on the subject may be found from Gibbon onwards—brief sketches or chapters in some wider treatise upon the Roman or the Arab empire. Indeed the fact that no serious and minute study upon the conquest exists in any language is not a little remarkable: but it has been mainly due to two causes—the scantiness of the material accessible to ordinary students, and the total want of agreement among the authorities, familiar or unfamiliar, eastern or western.

The subject consequently has been wrapped in profound obscurity; to enter upon it was to enter a gloomy labyrinth of contradictions. This may seem exaggerated language: but it is no more than the truth, and it is borne out by the opinion of a very well-known writer, Mr. E. W. Brooks, who says: 'There is scarcely any important event in history of which the accounts are so vague and so discrepant as the capture of Alexandria. The whole history of the irruption of the Saracens into the [Roman] empire is indeed dark and obscure: but of all the events of this dark period the conquest of Egypt is the darkest[1].' To render this obscurity in some

[1] *Byzantinische Zeitschrift*, 1895, p. 435.

degree luminous, to bring together the results of recent inquiry, turning to use the mass of fresh material now available, to test the oriental authorities one against another and to set them in comparison with other groups of authorities, and so by the light of research and criticism to place the study of this period on a scientific basis—that at least is the design with which this work has been undertaken. How far the achievement falls short of the design I am fully conscious. In some cases the method failed: it was, in the words of Maeterlinck, 'like turning a magnifying glass on silence and darkness.' In other cases failure has been due to my own shortcomings, such as the slightness of my acquaintance with Arabic, and the difficulty of carrying on in isolated fragments of leisure a work demanding concentration of mind and close and continuous study. Nevertheless the result will, it is hoped, provoke further inquiry. Certainly I have been forced to disagree with nearly all the received conclusions upon the subject of the conquest. Even in the most recent historians it will be found that the outline of the story is something as follows: that before the actual invasion of Egypt the country was laid under tribute to the Arabs by Cyrus for three or more years; that the refusal of the tribute by Manuel occasioned the invasion; that the Muḳauḳas, who was a Copt, sided with the Arabs; that the Copts generally hailed them as deliverers and rendered them every assistance; and that Alexandria after a long siege, full of romantic episodes, was captured by storm. Such is the received account. It may seem presumptuous to say that it is untrue from beginning to end, but to me no other conclusion is possible. Yet every one of these statements, when its foundation is discovered, is seen to rest on a truth or a half-truth; and nothing is more interesting than to trace the manner in which facts have been misplaced or misunderstood, and so used in the construction of false history or legend.

Fault may perhaps be found with the fullness of the notes in places. The answer is that in dealing with a vast mass of controversial and contradictory matter I have felt bound to give both my authorities and my reasons at more length than would have been requisite in dealing with simpler materials. So too of the Appendices, which are very copious. But it was absolutely necessary to construct for oneself the whole framework both of the history and of the chronology. It was impossible, for example, to write about the conquest until one had determined who the Muḳauḳas was, or until one had worked out the scheme of chronology. It would not have done merely to state what are often quite novel conclusions without setting out the data on which they are founded; and those data are exceedingly complex, whether the question be the personality of Al Muḳauḳas, or the chronology of the Persian or of the Arab conquest.

In regard to the scope of the work, it seemed that the mere invasion of Egypt by the Arabs should not be treated as an isolated event, that its historic significance could only be rightly understood in relation to those great movements which brought the ancient empires of Rome and Persia into collision with the rising empire of Arabia. In some such way alone could the conquest be shown in its true perspective. The reign of Heraclius offers an obvious starting-point, and happens to begin with some very vivid but almost unknown pictures from scenes in Egypt. It covers too the downfall of Persia, the active life of Mohammed, the loss of Jerusalem and Syria to the Caesars, and the Persian conquest of Egypt by Chosroes; and it illustrates the political and religious causes which were at work preparing the way for the sword of Islâm and the Ḳurân. At the same time the action of events passing outside the borders of Egypt has for the most part been traced but lightly and kept subordinate to the main purpose of the book.

The sources and authorities for the history of the period chosen require some discussion. Of the short notices in western writers of more modern date Ockley's romantic *History of the Saracens* is almost as well known as Gibbon's *Roman Empire*. Sharpe's *Egypt under the Romans* is not of much value. More recent information is given in Prof. Bury's edition of Gibbon, and the same writer's *Later Roman Empire*; in Mr. Milne's *Egypt under the Romans*; and in Prof. S. Lane-Poole's *Egypt in the Middle Ages* and his *Cairo* in the 'Mediaeval Towns' Series. Weil's *Geschichte der Chalifen* is valuable, even indispensable, but somewhat out of date. Von Ranke's *Weltgeschichte* contains a passage on the conquest and an essay on *Amru in Aegypten*, which rehearse the conventional story. Indeed Von Ranke's opinion may be summed up in his own words: 'The conquest of Egypt resulted from the desertion of a treacherous ruler of the Copts to the Arab standard'[1]—an opinion which can no longer hold the field. Of

[1] Vol. v. pt. i. p. 143; the Essay id., pt. ii. pp. 268 seq.

the larger French histories one must mention de Saint-Martin's edition of Le Beau's *Histoire du Bas Empire*, to which later writers add little or nothing. Thus the passage in Sédillot's *Histoire Générale des Arabes* upon the conquest contains scarcely one accurate sentence. Even C. Diehl can write in his admirable *Afrique Byzantine*, 'Les Coptes embrassèrent presque sans résister le parti de l'envahisseur et assurèrent par leur défection la victoire des Musulmans' (p. 553). But Renaudot's *Historia Patriarcharum Alexandrinorum* is a work of profound scholarship and research, and its importance is undiminished, as far as it goes. The learned works of Quatremère, who was remarkable alike for the range of his knowledge and the acumen of his judgements, have lost little of their value for students of Egyptian history. Yet even if western accounts were less defective, a fresh inquiry of this kind must be based on the original authorities. Of these the Greek writers are very disappointing. *Theophanes*, who wrote in 813, has wholly misunderstood the Arab conquest. His brief and hurried summary confuses the first and second capture of Alexandria—though he mentions neither—invents a treaty with the Arabs previous to the invasion, and is void of all perspective. He is thus responsible for a good deal of false history. *Nicephorus* is somewhat better, but unfortunately there is a blank in his text from 641 to 668: what remains is a 'mere list of defeated generals.' Both writers are fragmentary: they disagree with each other: and in both the chronology is impossible. *John Moschus*, as well as the Patriarchs of Jerusalem, *Zacharias* and *Sophronius*, are religious writers of the late sixth or early seventh century, from whose works some incidental references to events preceding the conquest may be gathered. *Leontius of Neapolis* in Cyprus has left an interesting biography of John the Almoner, Patriarch of Alexandria, which is useful for the Persian conquest and has been admirably edited by Gelzer. The *Chronicon Paschale* or *Alexandrinum* was probably written in the early seventh century in Egypt, but does not go down to the conquest; while the Latin *Chronicon Orientale* of Echellensis is dated 1238 A. D.

The Armenian authorities seem almost useless for the conquest of Egypt, though they deal in great detail with the wars of the Roman Empire against Persia, and the loss of Syria. The bishop *Sebeos* wrote a history, which has appeared in Russian, and which Mr. Conybeare has edited with an English translation, but not yet published: it throws a good deal of light on this period, but little or none on Egypt. *Michael the Syrian*, edited by Langlois, seems to follow Theophanes: Chabot's far better edition is not yet complete. The Syrian *Elijah of Nisibis* exists in MS. in the British Museum, but a portion relating to the Arab conquest has been published by Bäthgen.

Coming now to Egyptian writers, one must place first and foremost *John of Nikiou*, a Coptic bishop who wrote in Egypt towards the end of the seventh century, and was born probably about the time of the conquest. His history of the world was originally written partly in Coptic and partly in Greek, but it seems to have been translated into Arabic at a very early date. On this Arabic was founded the only surviving version of John's Chronicle, which is in Ethiopic, and which Zotenberg has translated and edited. Where the text is clear and uncorrupted, it is of extreme value: but most unhappily it is almost a complete blank from the accession of Heraclius to the arrival of the Arabs before Babylon: thus the story of the Persian conquest and the recovery of Egypt has dropped out, and the history of the later stages of the Arab conquest is in such a tumbled and topsy-turvy state that the true order and meaning of the narrative are almost past the power of criticism to reconstitute. Yet certain cardinal facts are established which, though at variance with later Arab tradition, must be regarded as of absolutely unimpeachable authority, and as furnishing a firm and sure basis for the study of this epoch. Indeed it is the acquisition of John's MS. by the British Abyssinian expedition which has made it possible to write a history of the Arab conquest of Egypt. It is much to be hoped that a Coptic or Arabic version of John of Nikiou, anterior to the Ethiopic, may one day be discovered[1]. Dr. Schäfer has already found in the Berlin Museum a Sa'idic fragment of six leaves showing, as Mr. Crum notes, a remarkably close relation to John's Chronicle. Zotenberg's edition is defective in some points of translation and in the calculation of dates; but scholars are awaiting with much interest the appearance of Dr. Charles' English translation.

[1] M. Amélineau in his *Vie du Patriarche Copte Isaac* (p. xxiv. n.) professes to know of an Arabic MS. of John's Chronicle. In reply to my inquiry asking where this precious document is to be found, he will only say that it is 'au fond d'une province de l'Égypte'—a remark which does not illuminate the mystery. On p. xxvi of the same work is a critique strangely depreciating both John and his history: a critique with which I disagree as decidedly as I disagree with M. Amélineau's chronology of this period.

Of early Coptic MSS. very few are known with any bearing on the subject. The Bodleian fragment of the Life of Benjamin has been edited by Amélineau (*Fragments Coptes pour servir à l'Histoire de la Conquête de l'Égypte* in *Journal Asiatique* for 1888): and the same scholar has published the Life of Samuel of Ḳalamûn in *Monuments pour servir à l'Histoire de l'Égypte Chrétienne aux IVe–VIIe Siècles*. An Ethiopic version of this same Life of Samuel, *Vida do Abba Samuel do Mosteiro do Kalamon*, has been published by F. M. E. Pereira, who has also edited from the Ethiopic a *Vida do Abba Daniel*. To Amélineau also we owe the *Life of Pisentios* and the *Life of the Patriarch Isaac*—both seventh-century Coptic documents with passages of great interest: and the Arabic *Life of Shenoudi*, also edited by Amélineau, is certainly based on a Coptic original. But the historical value of these Coptic documents is not very great. The writers were set upon recording matters of Church interest—the more miraculous the better—and their minds were almost closed to the great movements of the world about them. It is useless lamenting that, where they might have told us so much, they furnish only a few scanty and incidental allusions to contemporary history.

But the regret is all the keener because John of Nikiou and other writers of the seventh century are divided by a great gulf from the Arabic writers—a gulf of nearly two centuries. It is true that there is some hope of bridging the gulf when the immense mass of Fayûm and other papyri comes to be examined. Those at present published by Drs. Grenfell and Hunt and by Mr. Crum are of little avail for the conquest: but the Arabic papyri, which Prof. Karabacek is editing, will certainly throw light upon it, as is proved by his already published catalogue of samples shown at the Vienna Exhibition, in which letters occur from actors in the conquest named both by John of Nikiou and by Arab historians.

Of the Arab historians one cannot pretend to give an exhaustive list, but a brief notice of the principal ones may be useful[1]. One of the earliest and the most esteemed of the Arab writers was *Al Waḳidî* (747–823 A.D.), whose work is lost save for copious extracts and allusions which survive in other historians. Those works, such as *Kitâb Futûḥ Miṣr*, which bear his name, are wrongly attributed to him, but are often for convenience cited as his rather than clumsily ascribed to 'Pseudo-Wakidaeus.'

Al Balâdhurî (806–92) was educated at Baghdad but frequented the court of various caliphs. He wrote circa 868 the *Futûḥ al Buldân*—a book of conquests arranged according to countries or provinces. If not quite the earliest or the fullest, he is certainly among the most valuable authorities: but he makes it clear that even in the ninth century there was great difference of opinion upon the details of the conquest of Egypt. His name is derived from *balâdhur* or *anacardium*, an overdose of

[1] Further information may be found in Mr. E. W. Brooks' articles, (1) *On the Chronology of the Conquest of Egypt by the Saracens*, in *Byzantinische Zeitschrift* for 1895; (2) *The Arabs in Asia Minor*, in *Journal of Hellenic Studies*, vol. xviii, 1898; (3) *Byzantines and Arabs in the time of the Early Abbasids*, in *English Historical Review* for Oct., 1900: see also Mr. Guest's article on the writers quoted by Al Maḳrîzî in *Journal of the Royal Asiatic Society* for Jan. 1902.

which caused his death. Al Balâdhurî was unknown to Weil.

Ibn 'Abd al Ḥakam died at Fusṭâṭ in 870. His work exists only in a unique unpublished MS. at Paris, but arrangements are being made for its publication, to which oriental scholars look forward with keen interest. Copious extracts from this writer are given both by later Arabic historians and by Weil and Quatremère. There is a good deal of romance mingled with history in Ibn 'Abd al Hakam's chronicle; but a critical edition of it would be of very great importance.

There are a number of early geographical writers in Arabic from whom many notes and references of historical value may be gathered. The text of most of them may be found in De Goeje's *Bibliotheca Geographorum Arabicorum*. Among them may be named *Al Iṣṭakhrî* (probably ninth century); *Abû 'l Ḳâsim ibn Ḥauḳal* (flor. circa 960); *Shams ad Dîn al Maḳdasî*; *Ibn Rustah* and *Ibn al Faḳîḥ* (flor. circa 900); *Ibn Wâdhiḥ* or *Al Ya'ḳûbî* (died 874), a very valuable authority, but again unknown to Weil; and *Al Mas'ûdî* (flor. circa 960), a careful observer, and of great importance for the monuments of Alexandria.

Ibn Ḳutaibah (828–89) has left in his *Kitâb al Ma'ârif* a sort of historical and biographical lexicon, as Wüstenfeld says, 'the oldest among all the purely historical works of the Arabs now extant': but he seems to have written entirely from oral tradition without the use of books. His writings are much quoted by later Arab authors, although, as might be expected, his matter is generally meagre and his style sketchy.

We now come to a writer of high repute and, for

the most part, of high importance, *Aṭ Ṭabarî* (839–923). Born in Ṭabaristân, whence his name, after receiving a very good education he travelled in Irak, Syria, and Egypt, studying the Ḳurân, tradition, law and history. Returning he settled at Baghdad and engaged in teaching and writing. His narrative is as a rule painstaking, minute, and circumstantial, but most unfortunately it is singularly wanting for the conquest of Egypt. For not only is the recital exceedingly scanty, but Ṭabarî's ideas of geography and of chronology are confused and confusing, although the fault lies probably less with the historian than with the copyists who cut down the original, and had no knowledge to guide them in their selection and rejection of different passages and versions put side by side in the chronicle. This may explain the curious fact that he seems to place the capture of Alexandria *before* the capture of Memphis or Miṣr.

The Christian writer *Sa'îd ibn Baṭrîḳ* is too well known under his more usual name of *Eutychius* to need many words. He was born at Fusṭâṭ in 876 and died in 940. A distinguished student of medicine, theology, and history, he became Melkite Patriarch from 933 to his death. His annals end in 938. He wove together in a very readable but uncritical story the various threads of narrative found in his authorities, and he has preserved many details of great interest. His chronology has a fixed error of eight years apart from any eccentricity. Another Christian, the Coptic bishop of Ushmûnain, *Severus, ibn Mukaffa'*, has written a *Lives of the Patriarchs* which is unpublished and little known, save for the use which Renaudot has made of the work. There are three known MSS. of this author, one at the British Museum of about fifteenth century, one at the Bibliothèque Nationale of about fourteenth, and one considerably earlier—perhaps twelfth century—in the possession of Marcus Simaikah Bey at Cairo. While for matters of Church history Severus is valuable, his authority upon secular history is slender. He lived in the tenth century, but the exact date of his death has not been ascertained. The Paris MS. has a preface written by Maḥbûb ibn Manṣûr, a deacon of Alexandria in the latter half of the eleventh century, who edited the 'Lives.' In his own preface Severus says that he had recourse to some Copts to get Greek and Coptic documents turned into Arabic, as the two former languages even then were unknown to most Christians. This is interesting both as showing the state of decay reached by Coptic and Greek, and as showing Severus' own ignorance of both languages. Indeed the evidence as regards Coptic is so remarkable as to seem barely credible (see the Paris Catalogue of MSS., ed. de Slane, p. 83).

From the ecclesiastical history of the Egyptian Severus we pass to a treatise on political jurisprudence by *Al Mâwardî* of Baghdad (975–1058) As lawyer, judge, and statesman he attained a very high position, and was no less remarkable for his acumen and learning than for his integrity and independence of character. His *Political Constitutions* is a work of great ability and research, and the main source of our knowledge on the principles of Muslim taxation, as well as upon many other matters of law and custom.

With this exception, from the tenth century we have to leap across another gap to the twelfth, in which we find the geography of *Al Idrîsî*, who was a great traveller, and at the age of about 60 in the year 1154 was an honoured guest at the court of Roger II in Sicily. Idrîsî's writings contain a mass of valuable information. A little later are the annals of *Ibn al Athîr* (1160–1232); those of *Abû Ṣâliḥ* his contemporary, who wrote circa 1200 and may have been born a few years before Ibn al Athîr; and also the biographical dictionary of *Ibn Khallikân*. Ibn al Athîr was a native of Mesopotamia, but studied chiefly at Mauṣil and Baghdad. Most of his life was spent in study or literary work, but he cannot be regarded for our purpose as other than an inferior authority. His account of the conquest seems based on a bad epitome of Ṭabarî, and it only multiplies perplexity: yet, curiously enough, when once the dark passage of the conquest is over, his *Faultless Chronicle*, as he called it, begins to increase in value. It seems as if there were a fate consigning the conquest to oblivion. Ibn Khallikân, who was a personal friend of Ibn al Athîr, has left a most useful work in his *Biographies*, from which I have drawn much information. There is an excellent edition of the book in English by MacGuckin de Slane. Abû Ṣâliḥ's history of the *Churches and Monasteries of Egypt* is now well known owing to Mr. B. T. Evetts' Oxford edition.

The *Short Egyptian History* of '*Abd al Laṭîf* has long been known from White's edition with Latin translation. Born in 1161 at Baghdad, the writer saw a good deal of the war with the Crusaders in the time of Saladin, though he was no soldier. But he travelled all over the Levant, and stayed a great deal in Egypt, where he first went to hear the wisdom of Maimonides. As doctor, philosopher, and historian he won a very great reputation for learning; but his contribution to the history of Egypt is marred both by brevity and by discursiveness.

Yâḳût (1178–1228) is an interesting person and for the most part a sound authority. Born a Roman subject, he was sold as a slave at Baghdad to a merchant and was sent on trading journeys to the Persian Gulf. He parted on some quarrel from his master and took to study, while earning his living as a copyist. By 1200 he had become reconciled to his master, and again was trading to the island of Kis; but upon his return he found the merchant dead. He then turned bookseller, author, and traveller. About 1213 he visited Tabrîz, Syria, Mauṣil, and Egypt: two years later he went eastward from Damascus, and at the well-stocked library of Merv laid the foundation of his *Geographical Dictionary*, the rough draft of which he finished in 1224. But he found it necessary to make a second journey to Alexandria, and his fair copy was not begun till 1227 in Aleppo. In the midst of his labours he died in the following year. It is much to be regretted that he was unable to revise what still remains a work of great historical as well as geographical importance.

The Chronicle of *Al Makîn* or *Ibn al 'Amîd*, called the *History of the Muslims*, is a collection of scanty notes arranged according to chronology. The book is well known from the text and Latin translation published by Erpenius in 1625; and it has been much quoted by Gibbon and others, to whom it was one of the few Arabic authorities accessible. Less well known is Renaudot's judgement: 'qui Elmacinum sequuntur, si Arabice nesciant, non ipsum sed interpretem sequi deprehenduntur, qui, ut in multis saepe falsus est, ita circa annorum Arabicorum cum Romanis comparationem saepissime' (*Hist. Pat. Alex.* p. 172): and again in regard to dates, 'infinitis exemplis constat hallucinari saepissime Elmacinum' (id., ib.). Makîn seems, as Renaudot shows, to have founded his chronicle, or a large part of it, on Severus—a fact which accounts for some of its untrustworthiness. The date of Makîn's birth is circa 1205, but his history stops short of his own time by about a century. Although he was an Egyptian Christian, his work must be regarded as of small value to the student of Egyptian history.

Abû 'l Faraj (1226–86), called also Barhebraeus from his Jewish extraction, was born at Malatia in Armenia. He is well known from the *Historia Dynastiarum*, edited by Pococke with a Latin translation. This history, written in Arabic, is an abridgement by Abû 'l Faraj of a larger work written in Syriac. It contains the first detailed statement of the alleged burning of the Alexandrian library, but adds very little to our knowledge of the Arab conquest. The *Chronicon Ecclesiasticum* in Syriac by the same writer treats rather of the Syrian than the Alexandrian Church, but yields a few facts of value for our period. Abû 'l Faraj was a Jacobite Christian, who became bishop and finally Patriarch of his community.

Another *Biographical Dictionary*—that of *An Nawawî*—contains a good deal which is of general interest, though not much of direct bearing on the conquest. He was born at Nawâ near Damascus in 1234; he devoted his life to study and teaching; and he died of overwork. His tomb is still preserved, and is revered as that of a saint. *Al Kazwînî*, who died in 1283, has left a *Book of the Monuments of the Countries*—a sort of guide to antiquities—which I have found of service in questions of archaeology.

The Geography of Abû 'l Fidâ next claims mention. Valuable in itself, it is further enriched by the excellent edition of Reinaud, the introduction to which contains a very useful essay on the sources of Arab geography in general. Abû 'l Fidâ was a distinguished person. He came of the same family as Saladin and was reared in the same school of chivalry, delighting in battle from his very boyhood. Yet his intellectual side was strongly developed. He ended his life not merely as student and man of letters, but as Sultan of the principality of Hamat, where his court was the resort of men renowned in every branch of art and literature. He was born in 1273 and died in 1331.

It may not be out of place, if, while speaking of geography, I here refer in passing to Amélineau's *Géographie de l'Égypte à l'Époque Copte* as an extremely useful work of reference for place-names both in Coptic and in Arabic, and also to Mr. Le Strange's essay on the Arab geographers in the Introduction to his *Palestine under the Moslems.*

The name of *Ibn Khaldûn* (1332–1405) reminds us of the western extension of the Muslim empire. Though he himself was born at Tunis, his family had long been settled in Spain, and left Seville for Ceuta about a century before his birth. He studied first in Tunis and then in Tilimsân: later he followed the Sultan of Granada back to Spain, and in person negotiated the treaty with Don Pedro the Cruel, King of Castile, which enabled the Sultan to re-enter his capital. Ibn Khaldûn's history, as it survives, is blurred and darkened where it deals with the conquest of Egypt; yet it has passages of great value and striking authenticity.

In *Al Maḳrîzî* (1365–1441) we have an Egyptian authority, a Cairene by birth. His well-known *Al Khiṭaṭ wal Athâr* is a monument of laborious compilation. He was a most voluminous writer, and he had access to a vast number of authorities, the greater part of whose works have absolutely perished. Accordingly he is, in mere point of matter, the most important of our authorities. But among his sources are very many authorities of small value, and obscure or even apocryphal writers. Hence with all his zeal and his labour Maḳrîzî cannot be said to show any real critical or constructive power in dealing with the mass of rough material at his disposal.

To *Ibn Ḥajar al Asḳalânî* (1372–1448) we owe another *Dictionary of Biography*, which is useful for the life of 'Amr and other leaders at the time of the conquest. Born at Ascalon, as his name denotes, he travelled a great deal in Syria, Arabia, and Egypt. He made the pilgrimage when he was ten years old, turned successively merchant, poet, and man of letters, and died at a ripe old age in Cairo.

Abû 'l Maḥâsin (1409–69) was the son of a slave whom the Sultan Barḳûḳ raised to be governor first of Aleppo, then of Damascus: but the historian himself was born in Cairo and there educated, counting Maḳrîzî among his teachers. His history of Egypt is compiled on much the same method as that employed by Maḳrîzî, i. e. he sets out different versions of an event with little or no attempt to criticize or decide between them.

The last of the historians to be named here is *As Suyûṭî* (1445–1505), whose *Ḥusn al Muḥâḍarah* is largely founded upon Maḳrîzî, from whom he borrows whole passages *verbatim*. Suyûṭî was a native of Cairo, though his family, originally of Persian extraction, had been settled for nearly three centuries at Siûṭ in Upper Egypt. His father was a Cadi in Cairo, who taught in the Shaikanîah and preached in the mosque of Ibn Ṭûlûn. He began to write at a very early age, and boasted that his works were known in Asia Minor, Syria, Arabia, North Africa, and even Ethiopia: but his vanity and pugnacity made him very unpopular, and after losing or resigning the various professorships which he held, he retired in dudgeon to the Isle of Rauḍah, where he died. His history shows many signs of degeneracy even in comparison with his immediate predecessors; but it is true of him, as of the others, that his selection of versions or traditions contains points of information or interest overlooked or rejected in other selections.

But there is one other writer of considerable importance, not a historian but a writer on topography and archaeology, whose work was only discovered in 1891. I refer to *Ibn Duḳmâḳ*, who was apparently an Egyptian, and who died in 1406. The Arabic text has been published by Dr. Vollers, whose preface appreciates very justly the remarkable erudition of the author. The main purpose of the work is indicated by its title—*Description of Egypt*—and many of the facts which Ibn Duḳmâḳ preserves, especially in relation to the antiquities of Fusṭâṭ and of Alexandria, are entirely novel and extraordinarily interesting. To give one example, he shows that the original gateway of the Roman fortress under the church of Al Mu'allaḳah was in ordinary daily use in the year 1400. It is to be hoped that Dr. Vollers may publish a translation of this curious work.

These then are the chief oriental authorities which I have drawn upon for this history. Not one of them contains a clear, a connected, or, as I am bound to say, an accurate account of the Arab conquest. Their confusion of dates, of events, and of persons almost passes belief. The confusion of the chronology, and the labour it took to build a scheme both for the Persian and for the Arab conquest, may partly be judged from the Appendices. Theodore, the Roman commander-in-chief, seems unknown to the Arab writers, being confounded with some subordinate leader: Cyrus is confounded with Benjamin: the capture of the town of Miṣr is confounded with the taking of Egypt (Miṣr), and with the capture of Alexandria: the Treaty of Babylon is confounded with the Treaty of Alexandria: and the first surrender of Alexandria under treaty is confounded with the second capture by storm at the time of Manuel's rebellion. Of course I am very far from pretending to have made all this tangle plain; but I have endeavoured to trace the main sources of confusion and to get at the facts underlying the discrepancies of the records. I have also tried to write without bias in favour of either Copts or Arabs. Beginning my study with the prevalent opinion that the Copts sided gladly with the Muslim invaders, I have been forced to the conclusion that history in this has greatly maligned the Copts; and in the same way, beginning with the common belief that the Arabs burned the library of Alexandria, I have been forced to the conclusion that history in this has greatly maligned the Arabs. Both results were equally welcome; for I have much admiration for both peoples; but I hold a brief for neither. My one aim has been to discover and set out the truth, but I may hope that both Copts and Arabs will be interested in this attempt to distinguish fact from falsehood and to throw light upon a very dark chapter in the history of Egypt.

In the spelling of Arabic words I have followed generally the system adopted in the Clarendon Press edition of Abû Ṣâliḥ, and sanctioned by the use of many English scholars: but I have not thought it necessary to transliterate in this manner words which have become naturalized in English, as *Mohammed* or *Omar*, *Mecca* or *Cairo*. In names of persons and places to which the article *Al* is prefixed, I have for the most part omitted the *Al*, as is done by Mr. Le Strange in his scholarly *Baghdad*. In certain cases it has proved far from easy to choose between competing Greek, Coptic, and Arabic forms of the same word: thus while, for example, I have preferred the Graeco-Coptic *Nikiou*, as the form in use at the time of the conquest, to the Arabic *Naḳyûs*, which is practically a dead word to-day, yet in speaking of the *Fayûm* I felt obliged to use the familiar term rather than the Coptic *Piom* or the Graeco-Roman *Arsinoite Nome*. These inconsistencies are often deliberate, therefore, even if wrong, and must not at least be added to the list of unintended errors and imperfections in the book.

My thanks are due to the Rev. Dr. R. H. Charles for the loan of his translation of John of Nikiou; to Mr. F. C. Conybeare for the loan of an English version of Sebeos; to Mr. B. T. Evetts for many translations from Arabic authors; and to Mr. W. E. Crum, Mr. E. W. Brooks, and Professor Vollers of Jena, for valuable suggestions and criticisms. Among those who helped me during a recent visit to Egypt I must mention with gratitude His Eminence the Shaikh Muḥammad 'Abduh, Grand Mufti of Egypt, who presented me with his own notes and extracts relating to the conquest; Marcus Simaikah Bey, who helped me to collate his MS. of Severus and rendered me most useful assistance in many forms unsparingly; Max Hertz Bey, who furnished me with much information concerning the Roman fortress at Babylon and other points of art and archaeology; Capt. Lyons, R.E., of the Public Works Department; Mons. P. Casanova, Director of the Institut Français; and Mr. E. A. Floyer, Head of the Telegraph Department, who aided me freely in questions relating to place-names and topography generally. Above all, my warmest acknowledgements are due to my friend the Very Rev. Dean Butcher of Cairo for the opportunity of revisiting Egypt in connexion with this work, and for the unfailing sympathy and encouragement with which he has followed and lightened it.

A. J. B.

OXFORD, *Sept.* 22, 1902.

CONTENTS

MAPS

PLANS

CHRONOLOGICAL TABLES

A. *General.*

	A.D.
Revolt of Heraclius in Pentapolis	609
Struggle for the possession of Egypt	609–10
Heraclius crowned Emperor	5 Oct. 610
Persian invasion of Syria	614
Capture of Jerusalem by the Persians	end of May, 615
Visit of Athanasius to Alexandria	Oct. 615
Persian advance into Egypt	autumn, 616
Persian capture or surrender of Babylon	spring, 617
Persian capture of Alexandria	end of 617
Subjugation of the whole of Egypt	618
Heraclius' great campaign against Persia opens	spring, 622
Hijrah of Mohammed	16 July, 622
Persian evacuation of Egypt	627
Mohammed's letters to the Rulers	627–8
Final defeat and death of Chosroes	Feb. 628
Exaltation of the recovered Cross at Jerusalem	14 Sept. 629
Cyrus sént as Imperial Patriarch to Alexandria	631
The Great Persecution of the Copts	631–41
Death of Mohammed	632
Arab conquest of Palestine and Syria	629–40
Heraclius' farewell to Syria	636
Surrender of Jerusalem to Omar	637
Invasion of Egypt: 'Amr at 'Arîsh	12 Dec. 639
Capture of Pelusium	Jan. 640
'Amr's raid into the Fayûm	May, 640
Arrival of reinforcements under Zubair	6 June, 640
Battle of Heliopolis and capture of Miṣr	July, 640
Siege of fortress of Babylon begun	Sept. 640
First treaty of Babylon made by Cyrus, Al Muḳauḳas, but repudiated by Heraclius	Oct. 640
Recall of Cyrus	end of 640
Death of Heraclius	11 Feb. 641

	A. D.
Surrender of Babylon under (second) treaty	9 April, 641
Capture of Nikiou	13 May, 641
Alexandria attacked	end of June, 641
Return of Cyrus to Egypt	14 Sept. 641
Capitulation of Alexandria	8 Nov. 641
Excavation of Trajan's Canal / Building of Fusṭâṭ	winter, 641–2
Death of Cyrus	21 March, 642
Enthronement of Cyrus' successor	14 July, 642
Evacuation of Alexandria by the Romans	17 Sept. 642
'Amr's expedition to Pentapolis	winter, 642–3
Restoration of Benjamin	autumn, 644
Revolt of Alexandria under Manuel	end of 645
Second battle of Nikiou	late spring, 646
Recapture of Alexandria by the Arabs	summer, 646
Recall of 'Amr from Egypt	autumn, 646
Reinstatement of 'Amr as Governor of Egypt	Aug. 658
Death of Benjamin	3 Jan. 662
Death of 'Amr	6 Jan. 664

B. *Melkite Patriarchs.*

	DATE OF CONSECRATION.	DATE OF DEATH.
Theodore		609
John the Almoner	609	616 or 617
George	621	630 or 631
Cyrus	631	21 March, 642
Peter	14 July, 642	unknown

C. *Coptic Patriarchs.*

	DATE OF CONSECRATION.	DATE OF DEATH.
Anastasius	June, 604	18 Dec. 616
Andronicus	Dec. 616	3 Jan. 623
Benjamin	Jan. 623	3 Jan. 662
Agatho	Jan. 662	13 Oct. 680
John of Samanûd	Oct. 680	27 Nov. 689
Isaac	4 Dec. 690	5 Nov. 693
Simon	Jan. 694	18 July, 701

CHIEF AUTHORITIES AND EDITIONS

ABD AL LAṬÎF: *Historia Aegypti Compendiosa.* Ed. White, Oxford, 1800. 4to.

ABÛ 'L FARAJ: *Historia Dynastiarum.* Ed. Pococke, Oxon. 1663. 4to.

ABÛ 'L FIDÂ: *Geography.* Ed. J. T. Reinaud. Paris text 1840, trans. 1848 and 1883. 3 vols. 4to.

ABÛ 'L MAḤÂSIN: *An Nujûm az Zahirah,* &c. Ed. Juynboll et Matthes, Lugd. Bat. 1855–61. 2 vols.

ABÛ ṢÂLIḤ: *Churches and Monasteries of Egypt.* Ed. Evetts and Butler. Oxford, 1895. 4to.

AMÉLINEAU, E.: *Vie d'un Évêque de Keft.* Paris, 1887.
Fragments Coptes, &c., in Journal Asiatique, 1888.
Histoire du Patriarche Copte Isaac. Paris, 1890. 8vo.
Vie de Shenoudi in Mém. Miss. Arch. Franç. t. IV. i. p. 340.
Vie de Samuel: id., t. IV. ii. p. 774.
Géographie de l'Égypte à l'Époque Copte. Paris, 1893, &c. 8vo.
Histoire des Monastères de la Basse Égypte. Paris, 1894.

AMMIANUS MARCELLINUS.

BALÂDHURÎ, AL: *Futûḥ al Buldân.* Ed. de Goeje. Lugd. Bat. 1866. 4to.

BARHEBRAEUS (ABÛ 'L FARAJ): *Chronicon Ecclesiasticum.* Ed. Abbeloos et Lamy. Louvain, 1872. 3 parts. 8vo.

BOTTI, G.: *L'Acropole d'Alexandrie et le Sérapeum.* Alexandrie, 1895. 8vo.
Fouilles à la Colonne Théodosienne. Alexandrie, 1897. 8vo.

BROSSET: *Collection d'Historiens Arméniens.* St. Pétersbourg, 1874. 2 tom. 8vo.

BURY, Prof. J. B.: Gibbon's *Decline and Fall.* London, 1896. 7 vols. 8vo.
History of the Later Roman Empire. London, 1889. 2 vols. 8vo.

BUTCHER, E. L.: *Story of the Church of Egypt.* London, 1897. 2 vols. 8vo.

BUTLER, A. J.: *Ancient Coptic Churches of Egypt.* Oxford, 1884. 2 vols. 8vo.

CEDRENUS.

CHAMPOLLION: *L'Égypte sous les Pharaons.* Paris, 1814. 2 vols. 8vo.

Chronicon Orientale.

Chronicon Paschale, ap. Migne, *Patr. Gr.* t. 92.

CRUM, W. E.: *Coptic Ostraka.* London, 1902. 8vo.

D'ANVILLE: *Mémoires sur l'Égypte.* Paris, 1766. 4to.

DE BOCK, W.: *Matériaux pour servir à l'Archéologie de l'Égypte Chrétienne.* St. Pétersbourg, 1901. Fol., with plates.

DE GOEJE, M. J.: v. Balâdhurî and Ṭabarî.

Mémoire sur les Carmathes du Bahrain. Leyde, 1862.

Conquête de la Syrie. Leyde, 1864.

Bibliotheca Geographorum Arabicorum. Lugd. Bat. 1870–79. 8vo.

DIEHL, C.: *L'Afrique Byzantine.* Paris, 1896. 8vo.

Justinien et la Civilisation Byzantine au VIe Siècle. Paris, 1901. 8vo.

DRAPEYRON, L.: *L'Empereur Héraclius.* Paris, 1869. 8vo.

DULAURIER: *Chronologie Arménienne.* Paris, 1859.

EGYPT EXPLORATION FUND REPORTS.

EPIPHANIUS: *De Ponderibus et Mensuris.*

EUNAPIUS: *Vita Aedesii.*

EUSEBIUS: *Historia Ecclesiastica.* Ed. Heinechen. Leipzig, 1828. 3 vols. 8vo.

EUTYCHIUS, Patriarcha Alexandrinus: *Annales:* ap. Migne, *Patr. Gr.*

EVETTS AND BUTLER: v. Abû Ṣâliḥ.

GAYET, A.: *Le Costume en Égypte.* Paris, 1900.

L'Art Copte. Paris, 1902. 8vo.

GELZER, H.: *Leontios' von Neapolis Leben des Heiligen Johannes.* Leipzig, 1893. 8vo.

GEORGE OF PISIDIA: ap. Migne.

GREGOROVIUS, F.: *The Emperor Hadrian*: tr. M. E. Robinson. London, 1898. 8vo.

HAMAKER: *Expugnatio Memphidis*: v. Wakidî.

HOLM, A.: *History of Greece*: tr. F. Clarke. London, 1898. 4 vols. 8vo.

HYVERNAT, H.: *Actes des Martyrs de l'Égypte*. Paris, 1886. Fol.

IBN 'ABD AL ḤAKAM. Paris MS.

IBN AL ATHÎR: *Faultless Chronicle*. Ed. C. J. Tornberg. Leyden, 1868–74.

IBN AL FAḲÎḤ: v. De Goeje, *Bibl. Geog. Arab.*

IBN DUḲMÂḲ: *Description de l'Égypte*. Arabic text. Ed. Dr. K. Vollers. Cairo, 1893. 8vo.

IBN ḤAJAR: *Dict. Biogr.* Ed. A. Sprenger and others. 1856. 4 vols.

IBN ḤAUḲAL: v. De Goeje, *Bibl. Geog. Arab.*

IBN KHALDÛN: *Kitâb al a'bar*, &c. Bûlâḳ, A. H. 1283. 7 parts.

IBN KHALLIKÂN: *Dict. Biogr.* Ed. de Slane. Paris, 1842, &c. 4 vols. 4to.

IBN ḲUTAIBAH: *Kitâb al Ma'ârif.* Ed. Wüstenfeld. Göttingen, 1850.

IBN RUSTAH: v. De Goeje, *Bibl. Geog. Arab.*

IDRÎSÎ, AL: *Geographia Nubiensis*. Paris, 1609. 4to.

IṢṬAKHRÎ, AL: v. De Goeje, *Bibl. Geog. Arab.*

JARRETT, H. S.: *History of the Caliphs*: see Suyûṭî.

KARABACEK, J.: *Mittheilungen aus der Sammlung der Papyrus Erzherzog Rainer*. Wien, 1887, &c. Fol.

Papyrus Erzherzog Rainer: Führer durch die Ausstellung. Wien, 1894. 4to.

KAZWÎNÎ, AL: *Cosmography*. Ed. Wüstenfeld. Göttingen, 1848–9. 8vo.

KOELLE, S. W.: *Mohammed and Mohammedanism*. London, 1889. 8vo.

KYRILLOS II, Mgr.: *Le Temple du Césareum*, in *Bulletin de la Société Khédiviale de Géographie*, Ve Série, No. 6, Fév. 1900 (Le Caire).

LANE-POOLE, Prof. S.: *Art of the Saracens in Egypt*. London, 1886. 8vo.

LANE-POOLE, Prof. S.: *Egypt in the Middle Ages*. London, 1901. 8vo.
The Story of Cairo in 'Mediaeval Towns' Series. London, 1902.

LE BEAU, C.: *Histoire du Bas Empire*. Ed. de Saint-Martin. Paris, 1824–38. 21 vols. 8vo.

LE STRANGE, G.: *Palestine under the Moslems*. London, 1890. 8vo.

LETHABY AND SWAINSON: *St. Sophia, Constantinople*. London, 1894. 8vo.

MAHAFFY, Prof. J. P.: *Empire of the Ptolemies*. London, 1895. 8vo.

MAKÎN, AL: *Historia Saracenica*. Ed. T. Erpenius. Lugd. Bat. 1625. Fol.

MAKRÎZÎ, AL: *Khiṭaṭ*. Bûlâḳ, A. H. 1270. 2 vols. V. also Malan.

MALAN, S. C.: *Original Documents of the Coptic Church*. London, 1874. 8vo.

MAS'ÛDÎ, AL: *Collection d'ouvrages orientaux*. Ed. Barbier de Maynard. Paris, 1863. 8vo.

MATTER, M.: *Histoire de l'École d'Alexandrie*. Paris, 1840. 2 vols. 8vo.

MÂWARDÎ AL: *Kitâb al Aḥkâm as Sulṭaniah*. Ed. M. Enger. Bonn, 1853. 8vo.

MICHEL LE GRAND: *Chronique*. Ed. V. Langlois. Paris, 1866. 4to.

MICHEL LE SYRIEN: *Chronique*. Ed. J.B. Chabot. Paris, 1899, &c. 4to.

MICHELL, R. L.: *Egyptian Calendar*. London, 1900. 8vo.

MILNE, J. G.: *Egypt under Roman Rule*. London, 1898. 8vo.

MOSCHUS, JOHN: *Pratum Spirituale*. Ap. Migne, *Patr. Gr.*

MURTADI: *Egyptian History*. Tr. J. Davies. London, 1672. 12mo.

NÂSIRI KHUSRAU: *Sefer Nameh*. Ed. C. Schefer. Paris, 1881. 8vo.

NAWAWÎ, AN: *Biographical Dictionary*: ed. Wüstenfeld. Göttingen, 1842–7.

NÉROUTSOS BEY: *L'Ancienne Alexandrie*. Paris, 1888. 8vo.

NICEPHORUS.

NICEPHORUS CALLISTUS.

NIEBUHR, C.: *Voyage en Arabie*. Amsterdam, 1776. 4 vols. 4to.

NIKIOU, JEAN DE: *Chronique*. Ed. Zotenberg in t. xxiv of 'Notices et Extraits des MSS. de la Bibl. Nat.' &c. Paris, 1883. 4to.
Also English translation lent by Dr. Charles.

NOURISSON, V.: *La Bibliothèque des Ptolémées*. Alexandrie, 1893. 4to.

OCKLEY, S.: *History of the Saracens.* Ed. Bohn. London, 1847. 8vo.

OROSIUS: *Historiae.*

PALESTINE PILGRIMS TEXT SOCIETY'S PUBLICATIONS.

PAPYRI: *Corpus Papyrorum Raineri.* Ed. J. Krall (Coptische Texte).
Fayûm Towns and their Papyri. Ed. Grenfell and Hunt.
The Amherst Papyri. Ed. P. E. Newberry.
Oxyrhynchus Papyri. Ed. Grenfell and Hunt.

PEREIRA, F. M. E.: *Vida do Abba Samuel do Mosteiro do Kalamon.* Lisboa, 1894. 8vo.
Vida do Abba Daniel do Mosteiro de Scelé. Lisboa, 1897. 8vo.
Historia dos Martyres de Nagran. Lisboa, 1899. 8vo.

QUATREMÈRE, E.: *Recherches sur la Langue et la Littérature de l'Égypte.* Paris, 1808. 8vo.
Mémoires Géographiques et Historiques sur l'Égypte. Paris, 1811. 2 tom. 8vo.

RENAUDOT: *Historia Patriarcharum Alexandrinorum.* Paris, 1713. 4to.

RUFINUS: *Vitae Patrum.*
Historia Ecclesiastica.

SA'ÎD IBN BAṬRÎḲ: v. Eutychius.

SEBEOS: translation lent by Mr. Conybeare.

SEVERUS OF USHMÛNAIN: Brit. Mus. MS. Or. 26,100; Paris MS.; and M. Simaikah Bey's Cairo MS.

SHARPE, S.: *Egypt under the Romans.* London, 1842. 8vo.
History of Egypt. Ed. Bohn. London, 1885. 2 vols.

SIMAIKAH, A.: *La Province Romaine de l'Égypte.* Paris, 1892. 8vo.

SOCRATES: *Historia Ecclesiastica.*

SOPHRONIUS: *Opera*, ap. Migne, *Patr. Gr.*

SOZOMEN: *Historia Ecclesiastica.*

STRZYGOWSKI, J.: *Orient oder Rom.* Leipzig, 1901. 8vo.

SUSEMIHL, F.: *Geschichte der Griechischen Litteratur in der Alexandrinerzeit.* Leipzig, 1891–2. 2 vols. 8vo.

SUYÛṬÎ, AS: *Ḥusn al Muḥâḍarah.* Bûlâk, A. H. 1299.
History of the Caliphs: tr. H. S. Jarrett. Calcutta, 1881. 8vo. (Bibl. Ind. t. 18, series iii.)

ṬABARÎ, AṬ: *Târîkh ar Rusul wal Mulûk.* (1) Ed. Zotenberg. Paris, 1871. 4 vols. 8vo. (2) Ed. De Goeje. Lugd. Bat. 1879–90. 8vo.

TARÎKH JAHAN ARÂ: tr. Sir W. Ouseley. London, 1779. 8vo.

TARÎKH REGUM PERSIAE. Ed. W. Schikard. Tübingen, 1628. 4to.

THEODORET: *Historia Ecclesiastica.*

THEOPHANES.

USENER, H.: *De Stephano Alexandrino.* Bonn, 1880. 8vo. *Acta Martyris Anastasii.* Bonn, 1894. 4to.

VANSLEB: *Histoire de l'Eglise d'Alexandrie.* Paris, 1677. 12mo. *Nouvelle Relation d'un Voyage fait en Égypte.* Paris, 1698. 12mo.

VON GUTSCHMID, A.: *Kleine Schriften.* Leipzig, 1889–94. 8vo.

VON RANKE: *Weltgeschichte.* Leipzig, 1884. Several vols. 8vo.

WAḲIDÎ, AL (so-called), *Kitâb Futûḥ Miṣr* (*Expugnatio Memphidis*). Ed. Hamaker. Leyden, 1825. 4to.

WEIL: *Geschichte der Chalifen.* Mannheim, 1846. 3 vols. 8vo.

WRIGHT, T.: *Christianity in Arabia.* London, 1855. 8vo.

YA'ḲÛBÎ, AL: *Ibn Wâdhiḥ qui dicitur Al Ya'ḳûbî Historiae.* Ed. M. T. Houtsma. Lugd. Bat. 1883. 2 vols. De Goeje, *Bibl. Geog. Arab.*

YÂḲÛT: *Mu'jâm al Buldân,* or *Geographical Dictionary.* Ed. Wüstenfeld. Leipzig, 1866–73. 6 vols.

ZACHARIAH OF MITYLENE: *Chronicle*: tr. Hamilton and Brooks. London, 1889. 8vo.

ZOEGA, G.: *Catalogus Codd. Copticorum MSS.* Romae, 1810. Fol.

Conversion of Hijrah years into Anni Domini.

A TABLE showing every year of the Hijrah from A.H. 1 to A.H. 1000 with the date of commencement for the corresponding year A.D., is given at the end of Professor Stanley Lane-Poole's *Story of Cairo.*

ADDITIONAL BIBLIOGRAPHY

I. RE-EDITIONS ETC. OF SOURCE-MATERIAL

A. Greek; B. Coptic; C. Arabic; D. Syriac; E. Other Languages; F. Pahlavi papyri.

A. Greek

I. Byzantine and Ecclesiastical authors

Butler used chiefly the editions of texts available in the Bonn *Corpus* of Byzantine chroniclers and in Migne's *Patrologia Graeca.* In some cases these have been superseded, but the effect of this on any particular passage, in terms of interpretation, is usually insignificant. I note the following as relevant:

(i) The standard text of Theophanes, the main Byzantine source for the entire subject-matter of the book, is that of De Boor (2 vols., Berlin, 1883–5, repr. 1963), but it is not clear whether Butler used this edition. For Theophanes' sources see A. S. Proudfoot, *Byzantion,* 44, 1974, pp. 367–439, with full bibliography.

For the difficult problem of the conflict between Theophanes' chronological systems see Ostrogorsky, *Byz.-neugr. Jahrb.* 7, 1930, pp. 1–56, 'Die Chronologie des Theophanes im 7. und 8. Jahrhundert'; cf. id., *RE,* s.v. Theophanes (9), cols. 2127–32 (the best general account of T.); and his remarks in *Dumbarton Oaks Papers* 13, 1959, pp. 12 ff. For Grumel's solution of an *annus mundi* beginning (like that used by Syncellus) in March (*Échos d'orient* 33, 1934, pp. 396–408; id., *Chronologie* (Traité d'ét. byz. I (1958), pp. 95–6)) see Proudfoot, op. cit., pp. 374–5.

(ii) George of Pisidia has been re-edited by A. Pertusi with a translation and a very full commentary in which most of the problems relating to the expeditions of Heraclius, for which George is our prime authority, are discussed: *Giorgio di Pisidia, Poemi I, Panegirici Epici* (Stud. Patr. et Byzan., 7, 1960, Ettal). For his relation to Theophanes see Proudfoot, op. cit., pp. 380 ff.

(iii) There is a translation, with a few notes, of the *Life of John the Almoner* by Leontius of Neapolis, by E. Dawes and N. H. Baynes (Blackwell, Oxford, 1948), based on the parallel version of the *Life* published by Delehaye, *Anal. Boll.* 45,

1927, pp. 5–74 (cf. Baynes's note, pp. 195–6, and p. 203, n. to p. 195).

(iv) John Moschus' *Leimonarion* appeared in a French translation as vol. 12 of *Les Sources chrétiennes* (Paris, 1946); see also H. Chadwick, *JTS*, N.S. 25, 1974, pp. 41–74, for a very full analysis of the complex MS. tradition of the *Leimonarion*, and of the lives of Moschus and Sophronius; and P. Pattenden, ibid., N.S. 26, 1975, pp. 38–54. For Sophronius' *Miracula* see N. F. Marcos, *Los Thaumata de Sofronio* (Madrid, 1975).

II. Greek Papyri

Very few Greek papyri of the reign of Heraclius had been published when Butler wrote, and he was able to refer for the most part only to *POxy.*, of which one or two volumes had been published, and to some papyri of the Erzherzog Rainer Collection (see below, on ch. xxviii), especially J. Karabacek's *Papyrus Erzherzog Rainer: Führer durch die Ausstellung* (*CPRF*; Vienna, 1894; cf. Butler, p. xxi, and p. 235 n. 2). The list of dated papyri of his reign below is, I hope, complete; it does not include papyri dated to the seventh century on palaeographic, formulaic, or other grounds, and is intended to serve only as a check-list; cf. the earlier list given by Bell, *BZ* 22, 1913, pp. 395–405.

The documents are almost all receipts and contracts of the conventional types, and I have specified the contents only when they are of particular interest. Much interest naturally attaches to those papyri belonging to the decade of Persian rule between 619 and 628, to which attention was called by E. R. Hardy Jr., *Journ. Soc. Orient. Res.* 13, 1929, pp. 185–9; cf. also below, on chs. vi–vii. The documents seem to show that the final subjection of Egypt to Persia cannot have occurred before early A.D. 619.

A.D. 610: *POxy.* xxiv, 2420

610–11: *POxy.* i, 138

611: *PLond.* v, 1736; *PSI* 611

612: *PAmh.* 157–8 (receipts for money paid by the Alexandrian bank of Mauricius); *PCair.* p. 8, no. 10049; p. 14, no. 10090, no. 10135; *POxy.* i, 139(?), 151; xvi, 1981(?) (undertaking to act in good faith, written on same day as 139); 2045 (list of payments to σύμμαχοι of an ἔνδοξος οἶκος); *PPrinc.* 87; *PSI* 62; *Pklein. Form* (Wessely, *Stud. z. Pal. u. Pap.* iii and viii), 277, 278, 284

613: *POxy.* xvi, 1979; *SB* 4504

614: *BGU* 2208; 2209; *SB* 4669
615: *BGU* 368; *SB* 5271
616: *BGU* 398; *POxy*. xvi, 1991; *SB* 4497, 5328; *PPar*. 21; *PLond*. 483
616–17: *POxy*. vi. 999; *BGU* 2210
618: *BGU* 401; 725; *PCair*. p. 14; nos. 10148, 10149 (=*POxy*. 2010–11); *PEdfu* III; *POxy*. i, 152–3; xvi, 1904 (payments to σύμμαχοι); *Pklein. Form* 285–6; *Stud. Pal. u. Pap*. xx, 220 (*SB* 5269); *PStrass*. 328 (*Bull. fac. lett. Strassb*., Apr. 1964)
619: *SB* 5112 (Jan. 619?)

⟦619–28, PERSIAN OCCUPATION:

619–28: *PIand*. II (L. Eisner, *Epist. graec. priv*. (1913)), 22 (cf. Hardy, loc. cit.); III (L. Spohr, *Instrum. graec. publ. et priv*. I, 1913), 49; *PRoss.-Georg*. iv, pp. 99 ff. (cf. Hardy, loc. cit., and below, p. lxxii; a letter in which the writer describes his torture at τῶ φωσᾶτον by the Persians)
619: *PEdfu* II (*Tell Edfou*, I, pp. 177–8)
621: *POxy*. 1921 (payments, including two λόγῳ τῶν Περσῶν)
[621. The date of an inscription of Egyptian provenance, *JEA* 42, 1956, p. 123 (*SB* 9877=10071), referring to the construction by 'Appa Joseph' of a χαλκευτικὸν ἐργαστήριον within a church, dated Phaophi of the 4th Indiction-year, was assigned by the original editor (*JEA* 30, 1944, p. 76), who read the 10th Indiction-year, to the reign of Heraclius on the ground enunciated by Wilcken, *Archiv* 13, p. 150 (apropos of *PEdfu* II–IV, absence of Emperor's name, indicating Persian occupation); but with the 4th Indiction-year, the date is either 616 or 631, both of which fall outside the years of the Persian occupation.]
625(?): *Stud. Pal. u. Pap*. xx, 209 (cf. H. I. Bell, *Aegypt*. 3, 1922, p. 102; cf. *POxy*. 1829, n. to l. 24); this is the latest papyrus referring to the Apion estate; cf. Hardy, *The Large Estates of Byzantine Egypt*, p. 37
628: *PEdfu* IV (loc. cit., pp. 180–1; cf. Wilcken, *Archiv* 13, p. 150)⟧
630: *BGU* 314; 370
631: *PRoss*. iii, 51

632: *SB* 4662, 9461
633: *PLond.* i, 113, 6(b)
635: *PFlor.* 306 (Impp. Heracl. et Heraclian.); *SB* 4488; *PLond.* 1012
638: *CPRF* 550
639: *PLond.* 113, 10 (cf. below, p. lxxvi)
640: *SB* 6271

I may refer also here to the numerous papyri from Kom Ishqaw (Aphrodito) and elsewhere, of the reigns of Justinian and Maurice, published above all by J. Maspero in *PCair. Masp.* (*Catal. gén., Musée du Caire,* 3 vols., 1911–16), which have been repeatedly used as the basis for reconstructions of the administrative history of the sixth and early seventh centuries in Egypt: see especially Maspero, *BIFAO* 6, 1908, pp. 75–120; 7, 1910, pp. 97–152 and H. I. Bell, *JHS* 64, 1944, pp. 21–36, 'An Egyptian Village in the Age of Justinian'. This 'Archive of Dioscurus' from Kom Ishqaw is also represented in *PLond.* v, nos. 1660 ff.

I leave for notice below (on ch. xxviii) the papyri—Greek, Arabic, and bilingual—of the time of the Conquest and of the following period, especially those of the governorship of Qurrah b. Sharīk. For a Coptic papyrus of the Persian period see below, under 'B. Coptic (v)'.

B. Coptic

(i) The *Life* or *Encomium* of Pisentius of Coptos. In addition to a Bohairic text of this work (by Moses) published by Amélineau, and utilized by Butler (see p. 84. n. 2), a different Sahidic version (by John) was published by Budge, *Coptic Apocrypha in the Dialect of Upper Egypt* (Brit. Mus. 1913), pp. 75–127 (text), 258–334 (transl.); ibid., pp. 331 ff., a fragmentary life from the Ethiopic synaxarium; cf. also P. van Cauwenbergh, *Étude sur les moines d'Égypte* (Paris, 1914), pp. 29–39. For an Arabic version see Lacy O'Leary, *PO* 22, 3 (1930), with collation of other versions (cf. Crum, *ZDMG* 68, 1914, pp. 176 ff.; Polotsky, *OLZ* 38, 1935, pp. 15–18); cf. Graf, *GCAL* i, pp. 279–80, 465–6. An important addition to our knowledge of Pisentius is provided by his correspondence with the hermit Epiphanius of the Theban monastery, published by Crum in Winlock and Crum, *The Monastery of Epiphanius at Thebes* i (Metrop. Mus., Egypt. Expedn.; N.Y., 1926), pp. 209–231, discussion, with ii, Crum and Evelyn White, pp. 33 ff., the texts. Crum's discussion of Pisentius in vol. i is fundamental.

The correspondence supplements that in the Louvre, published by Revillout, *Rev. Égypt.* 9, 1900, pp. 133–79; 10, 1901, pp. 34–47; 14, 1912, pp. 22–32. For Pisentius' chronology (ca. 565–632) see van Cauwenbergh, op. cit., pp. 159–64.

(ii) *Life of Samuel of Kalamūn* by Isaac of Kalamūn: see van Cauwenbergh, op. cit., pp. 39–50, who was able to make use of a complete Sahidic *Life* in the Pierpont Morgan Library (H. Hyvernat's projected catalogue of the Coptic MSS. in the library (see *A Check List of Coptic Manuscripts in the Pierpont Morgan Library* (N.Y., privately printed, 1919), preliminary note), was never published, though the text is reproduced in his photographic album of the entire collection, *Bibliothecae Pierpont Morgan, Codices coptici photographice expressi*, 56 vols., vol. xxxi (1922; repr. 1957; *non vidi*)), while Butler had access only to the fragmentary Sahidic versions and to the Ethiopic translation. Butler's attempt (p. 185, n. 2), to date the *Life*, and therefore Samuel himself, to the period of the Conquest, is refuted by van Cauwenbergh, pp. 49–50, 88–9, who, following the indications given in the full text of the *Life*, assigns Samuel's death to the end of the century. For the *Apocalypse* or *Prophecy* of Ps.-Samuel see Ziadeh, *ROC* 20, 1915–17, pp. 374–92 (text), 392–404 (transl., note by Nau, pp. 405–7); Graf, *GCAL* i, pp. 281–2, and below, p. lxvi.

(iii) *Lives* and works of Shenude: see *CSCO* 41 (Copt. 1), 42 (Copt. 2), 73 (Copt. 5), 96 (8), 108 (12) and cf. Quasten, *Patrology* iii (1960), pp. 185–7.

(iv) T. Orlandi, *Storia della Chiesa di Alessandria*, 2 vols. (Testi e Docum. per lo Studio dell'Antichità, vols. xvii and xxxi, 1968–70), contains text, translation, and commentary of the Coptic *History of the Church*, closely related to the *History* of S. Ibn al-Muqaffaʿ, of which we have only the Arabic text (see below, I.C (g)); but it covers only the period 300–480, i.e. from the Patriarchate of Peter I to Timotheus II.

(v) A Coptic papyrus published by J. Krall, *CPR* ii, pp. 20–3, no. V is dated 12 Athyr of 14 Indict., and records an oath by 'the King of Kings', which clearly indicates the Persian interregnum, i.e. Nov. 626.

C. Arabic

General: D. M. Dunlop's *Arab Civilisation to* A.D. *1500* (London and Beirut, 1971) contains in ch. iii (pp. 70–149) an excellent survey, with notes, of Arabic historical writing; the first part of F. Rosenthal's *A History of Muslim Historiography* (Leiden, ed. 2, 1968) contains a full analysis of the categories of historical writing and of the historians. For the earliest period the introduction to N. Abbott's *Studies in Arabic Literary Papyri* i, Historical Texts (Univ. of Chicago, Orient. Inst. publns., 75, Chicago, 1957) is of especial importance; see also for the early period Sezgin, *Gesch. arab. Schrift.* i (Leiden, 1967), pp. 235–364. [Details will be found in Brockelmann, *GAL*, with its Supplements (*Gesch. arab. Literat.* 2 vols., 1897–1902; Suppbde 1–3, 1936–42; 2te, den Supp. angepasste Aufl., Bde 1, 2 (1943–8), and G. Graf, *GCAL* (*Geschichte der christlichen arabischen Literatur* i (*Studi e Testi* 118; 1944), ii (*S. e T.* 133; 1947), iii (*S. e T.* 146; 1949), iv (*S. e T.* 147; 1951)), v (Register; *S. e T.* 172; 1953).]

Individual authors (selection):

(a) al-Balādhurī's *Kitāb Futūḥ al-Buldān* was translated in two vols. by P. K. Hitti and F. C. Murgotten, *The Origins of the Islamic State* (Columbia Univ. Studies in the Social Sciences (formerly Studies in History, Economics and Public Law), vol. 68, 1916 (repr. A. M. S. Press, N.Y., 1968–9; reprint of vol. 1 only, Khayats, Beirut, 1966); vol. 1 by P. K. H., vol. 2 by F. C. M.); [this translation omits intermediate links in the *isnād* between the first and last sources]. A new edition of the Arabic text was published at Cairo, 1956–7.

(b) Ibn ʿAbd al-Ḥakam, *Futūḥ Miṣr*, known to Butler only from quotations in later writers, notably al-Maqrīzī and as-Suyūṭī, and from quotations from a Paris MS. by Weil and Quatremère (see p. xx; cf., e.g., pp. 429 n. 4; 430 n. 3; 436 n. 1) was edited from MSS. in London, Paris, and Leyden by C. C. Torrey, *Yale Oriental Series*, Researches, III, 1922, 'The History of the Conquest of Egypt, North Africa and Spain, known as the Futūḥ Miṣr of Ibn ʿAbd al-Ḥakam', an outstanding edition; cf. also id. in *Biblical and Semitic Studies* (Crit. and Hist. Essays by the Members of the Sem. and Bibl. Fac. of Yale Univ., 1901), pp. 279–330, 'The Muhammedan Conquest of Egypt and North Africa in the Years 643–705 A.D., translated from the original Arabic of Ibn ʿAbd el-Ḥakem' (events after capture of Egypt). The section relating to the Arab capture of Alexandria and the Conquest is published in a French version, from Torrey's edn. (pp. 37 ff.), by H. E. Omar Toussoun, *Bull. Soc.* [*roy.*] *arch. d'Alex.* 20, 1924, pp. 220-238; and M. Gateau, *Le conquête de l'Afrique du Nord*, etc. (ed. 2 Algiers, 1948) gives a text, translation, and notes of the section (pp. 170 ff. Torrey) dealing with the conquest of Barqa and Ifrīqiyā. The edition of H. Massé, *Le Livre de la Conquête de l'Égypte, du Magreb et de l'Espagne* (Publ. de l'Inst. franç. d'Arch. or., 1914), which contains the Arabic texts of pts. I–II only, is criticized by Torrey, edn. p. 23. Caetani was able to use one of the two Paris MSS. of the *Futūḥ Miṣr*, of which the *Annali* contains translations of substantial extracts (see *Annali* iii, pp. 4–5). For the Egyptian Traditionists cited by Ibn ʿAbd al-Ḥakam see R. A. Guest's introdn. to al-Kindī, *Governors and Judges of Egypt* (Leiden, 1912) and, for his supposed Malikite bias, R. Brunschvig, *Ann. Inst. d'étud. or.* (Univ. of Algiers), 6, 1942, pp. 108–55; cf. below, p. lxvi, on chs. xxvi–xxvii.

(c) al-Maqrīzī, *Kitāb al-Khiṭaṭ*: see the edition by G. Wiet, replacing the Bulaq text of 1270/1853: *Mém. Inst. franç. d'arch. or.* 30 (1911); 33 (1913); 46 (1922); 49 (1924); 53 (1927); and the translation by U. Bouriant, *Maqrizi, Description topogr. et histor. de l'Égypte* (*Mém. Mission archéol. franç. en Égypte* 17, 1900; pts. i–ii), and P. Casanova (*Mém. Inst. franç. d'arch. or.* iii–iv (1), 1906–20; pts. iii–iv).

(d) al-Wāqidī: full text, ed. Marsden Jones, *The Kitāb al-Maghāzī of al-Wāqidī* (3 vols., O.U.P., London, 1966). (For the two works passing under the name of al-Wāqidī, the *Futūḥ Miṣr* and the *Futūḥ al-Bahnasā'* (which forms part of the *Futūḥ ash-Sha'm*), which date from a considerably later period see De Goeje, *Mémoire sur la conquête de la Syrie* (*Mém. d'hist. et de géogr. orient.* ii[2], Brill, 1900 [a revised edition of his *Mémoire sur la conquête de la Syrie*, 1864]), preface; Caetani, *Ann.* iii, pp. 70 ff.; and Dunlop, op. cit., pp. 76–9. The *Futūḥ al-Bahnasā'* was translated by E. Galtier, *Foutouh al Bahnasâ* (*Mém. Inst. franç. d'arch. or.* xxii, 1909).)

(e) al-Māwardī: translation and commentary by E. Fagnan, Algiers, 1915.

(f) al-Masʿūdī: Ch. Pellat has revised Barbier de Meynard and Pavet de Courteille's edn. (Beyrouth, 1966), and also published a translation (Paris, 1962–71; 3 vols.).

(g) Severus ibn al-Muqaffaʿ, *History of the Patriarchs of Alexandria*, which Butler used directly from the MSS. of London, Paris, and Cairo, was edited by B. Evetts with an English translation in *PO* I, 2 (1904) (St. Mark to Theonas (A.D. 300)); I, 4 (1907) (Peter I to Benjamin); V, 1 (1910) (Agathon to Michael I (766)); X, 5 (1915) (Mennas to Joseph (849)). Later parts of the *History* are published by Atiya, Yassa ʿAbd al-Masīḥ, and Burmester, *History of the Patriarchs of the Egyptian*

Church, II, i (A.D. 849–880), ii (880–1066); II, iii (1046–1102); III, i–iii (*non vidi*). (Publ. de la Soc. d'arch. copte, Textes et documents, Cairo, 1948–1970). For other editions, including that of Seybold in *CSCO*, Scr. arab. ser. III, 9, fasc. 1–2, see Graf, op. cit. ii, pp. 301 ff., with much information about versions in MS. (for the superior Hamburg MS., edited by Seybold, and not used by Evetts, see below on chs. xiii, xxvii and Coquin [op. cit. below, p. lxv], pp. 24 ff., 62).

For Butler's later view of Severus see *Treaty*, pp. 68–74.

(h) The *Chronicon Orientale*, a Latin version of which by Abraham Echellensis published in 1651 was used by Butler (see p. xviii); the original Arabic text with a revised version of Abraham's Latin translation was published by I. Cheikho, *CSCO*, Scr. arab. ser. III, 1–2 (1903), *Petrus ibn Rehib, Chronicon Orientale*.

D. Syriac

(a) *Chronicon anonymum ad A.D. 819*: ed. A. Barsaum, *CSCO*, Scr. syr. III, 36 (1920). This chronicle was copied, almost verbatim, by *Chron. anon. ad A.D. 846*, published by E. W. Brooks and translated by J.-B. Chabot, op. cit. (d), below.

(b) *Chron. anon. ad A.D. 1234*: ed. J.-B. Chabot, ibid., vol. 37 (1916).

(c) *Chronica Minora*: I, ed. Guidi, *CSCO*, Scr. syr. III, 4, 1 (pp. 1–39, text; transl., pp. 1–32); (i) the 'Chronicon Edessenum' written shortly after A.D. 540, probably at Edessa, (ii), *Chron. anon. de ult. reg. Pers.*; cf. O. de Urbina, *Patrol. Syr.*² (Rome, 1965), p. 206.

(d) *Chronica Minora*: II, ed. E. W. Brooks, *CSCO*, Scr. syr. III, 4, 2 (text; 1904), pp. 43–242; III, 4, 2, transl. by Chabot: (a) pp. 37–57, '*Chron. Maroniticum*' of post A.D. 664 (pp. 43–155), (b) *Hist. subiect. Syr.* (1 page); (c) *Chron. misc. ad ann. 724*, pp. 61–119; (d) *Chron. ad ann. 846*, pp. 121–80. For the source-relation of the *Chron. ad 846* to Theophanes, see Brooks, *Byz. Zeitschr.* 15, 1906, pp. 578–87; Proudfoot, op. cit., pp. 405–6.

(e) *Chronica Minora*: III, ed. Brooks, Guidi, Chabot, *CSCO*, Scr. syr. III, 4, pp. 243–378 (text), pp. 183–304 (transl.), contains eight minor chronicles.

For further bibliography on these and other chronicles see S. P. Brock, *Byz. & Mod. Gk. Stud.* 2, 1976, pp. 17–23, 'Syriac sources for seventh cent. history'.

E. Other Languages

(i) Armenian: Sebeos: Pt. III translated by F. Macler, *Histoire d'Héraclius par l'Évêque Sebêos* (Leroux, Paris, 1904);

see also id., *JA*, 1905 (X, 6), pp. 121–55, 'Pseudo-Sebêos', which contains an analysis of the relationship of the meagre chronicle and chronological synchronism in pt. II of the published MSS. (pp. 11–21, ed. Patkanian), the 'Pseudo-Sebeos', to pt. III, the chronicle of the 'true' Sebeos; Macler suggests that Pseudo-Seb. and Seb., who cover the same period, i.e. Armenian and Sassanian history down to the caliphate of Muʿāwīya (661), both belong to the seventh century. However, the researches of G. Abgarian, *Rev. ét. armén.* N.S. 1, 1964, pp. 203–15, seem to show that even the 'true' Sebeos (pt. III) is not work of the bishop, who wrote the so-called *History of Heraclius*, but of another Armenian historian, perhaps a Xosrov(ik), and that Sebeos' work has still to be discovered. In the present context the source-value of the work is not greatly affected by this conclusion.

The Armenian text of 'Sebeos' was re-edited by St. Malchassiantz (Malxasian), Erevan, 1939. Conybeare's translation, used by Butler (cf. p. xviii), remained unpublished. The period covered by Heraclius' reign is on pp. 64–103, Macler.

(ii) Ethiopic: John of Nikiou, *Chronicle*, translated from Zotenberg's Ethiopic text by R. H. Charles (London, 1916)—available to Butler before publication. Cf. Crum, *JEA* 4, 1917, pp. 207–9. There is a German translation of John, with notes, in Altheim–Stiehl, *Das Christentum am Roten Meer*, i (Berlin, 1971), pp. 356–89.

(iii) Georgian: the Monk Antiochos Strategios' account, surviving in Georgian from a Greek original, of the Persian capture of Jerusalem in A.D. 615, was published by N. Marr in 1909, and thence in an abbreviated English translation by Conybeare, *EHR* 25, 1910, pp. 502–17. Garitte, *CSCO, Scr. Iber.* 11–12 (vols. 202–3, 1960) has published the Georgian text, based on three MSS. (including that used by Marr), with translation. He has also published, ibid., Scr. Arab. 26–7 (vols. 340–1, 1973), and 28–9 (347–8, 1974) four Arabic accounts of the sack (including that published by Peeters, *Mél. Beyr.* 9, 1923, pp. 3–41).

F. Pahlavi Papyri

Butler knew of the existence of Pahlavi papyri of the period of the Persian occupation of Egypt, especially those in the Erzherzog Rainer collection (see below, on ch. xxviii), but they were almost totally unpublished. Many of these dreadfully obscure and fragmentary documents have now disappeared (see

Menasce, below), but those in Berlin, acquired in the seventies of the last century, and mostly from the Fayyum, were published by Hansen, *Berl. Abh.* 1937 (9), 'Die mittelpersischen Papyrussammlung der Staatlichen Museen zu Berlin', and this remains to the present the basic treatment of Pahlavi papyri. The papyri published by Hansen are mostly unilingual, unlike the Arabic papyri; the Zoroastrian calendar is used, and the correspondence appears to be between Zoroastrians. No. 53 of Hansen's publication has a dating 'Year 2', which may be an era dating from the Persian conquest.

J. Menasce, *JA*, 1953, pp. 185 ff., 'Recherches de papyrologie pehlevie', published a papyrus in Basle which seems to contain a short list of Persian troops, apparently in, or from, Elephantine, Heraclia, Oxyrhynchus, Hermupolis, and other centres. On pp. 186–8 Menasce gives a full list of known Pahlavi papyri, and provides the information that the 525 pieces once in the Vienna collection have been lost.

II. GENERAL BIBLIOGRAPHY

A. Byzantium in the Age of Heraclius

Among general Byzantine histories over-all political and cultural developments are best covered in Vasiliev's *History of the Byzantine Empire*² (1952), pp. 193–233; less satisfactorily in the work of A. N. Stratos, *Byzantium in the 7th Century* (3 vols., Hakkert, Amsterdam, 1968–75), whose discussions and bibliographies are useful and compensate for an amateurish and superficial narrative—vol. i to A.D. 634, vol. ii, added in answer to criticism, covers the Arab conquests to the death of Heraclius, vol. iii, A.D. 642–68. See also the chapter of N. H. Baynes in *CMH*¹ ii, pp. 263–301, and that of E. W. Brooks, ibid., pp. 391–417 (from death of Heraclius); the seventh century in Byzantium is not yet covered in *CMH*². Ostrogorsky, *Dumbarton Oaks Papers* 13, 1959, pp. 1–22, 'The Byzantine Empire in the world of the seventh century', excludes Islam from his consideration. For detailed studies of the reign of Heraclius see below, bibliography to chs. i–iv, ix–x.

B. Byzantine Egypt

For conditions in Egypt and the history of the province between the administrative reforms of Diocletian and the end of the sixth century see the general accounts of H. Munier in *Précis de l'histoire d'Égypte* par divers historiens et archéologues,

2 (Cairo, 1932), covering the period A.D. 284–1517, pp. 64 ff., with, pp. 95–106, an excellent bibliography and, pp. 297 ff., useful appendices (Prefects of Egypt, Patriarchs of Alexandria, Governors of the Caliphate); G. Hanotaux's *Histoire de la nation égyptienne*, 3 (Paris, 1933), by P. Jouguet, V. Chapot, and Ch. Diehl, covering the Ptolemaic, Roman, and Byzantine periods; and vol. 4 (1937) by G. Wiet, covering A.D. 642–1517; detailed narrative (with illustrations) but no documentation. More concise is the old, but excellent, account by Wilcken, *Grundzüge etc. der Papyruskunde*, i, 1 (1912), Einleitung, pp. 66–88. See also G. Rouillard, *L'Administration civile de l'Égypte byzantine*[2] (Paris, 1928).

For the period of Justinian, whose Egyptian reforms (codified in Edict xiii, *Περὶ τῆς Ἀλεξανδρέων καὶ τῶν Αἰγυπτιακῶν Ἐπαρχιῶν*, issued either in August A.D. 538/9 or 553/4—see Rouillard, op. cit., pp. 20 ff.; and for the probability of the former date, see Rémondon, *Chron. d'Ég.* 1955, pp. 112–21) determined the administrative structure of Egypt until the Conquest, see M. Gelzer, *Studien z. die byzantinischen Verwaltung Ägyptens* (diss. Leipzig, 1909; *Leipz. hist. Studien*, 13, 1909); id., *Archiv f. Papyrusforsch.* 5, 1913, pp. 346–77, 'Altes und Neues aus der byzantinisch-ägyptischen Verwaltungsmisère, vornehmlich im Zeitalter Justinians' (apropos of *PCair. Masp.* i, for which see above, I.A. II, p. xlviii); L. Wenger, *Volk und Staat in Ägypten am Ausgang der Römerherrschaft* (Festrede Bayer. Akad., Munich, 1922), which contains some interesting observations on racial mixture etc. in the Byzantine period (pp. 14 ff.); E. R. Hardy Jr., *The Large Estates of Byzantine Egypt* (N.Y., 1931), especially concerning the estates of the Apion family, tenure of which it retained at least during the Persian occupation (see above, under I.A. II Greek Papyri, sub ann. 625); J. Gascon, *Byzantion*, 42, 1972, pp. 60–72; the clear analyses by Nabia Abbott, *The Ḳurrah Papyri* (see on ch. xxviii), pp. 70 ff.; H. I. Bell, *Egypt* (Clarendon Press, 1948), pp. 120–34; more briefly, Jones, *HLRE* i, pp. 281 ff.

Military Organization: see J. Maspero, *Organisation militaire de l'Égypte byzantine* (Bibl. éc. des hautes études, 201, 1912), which remains the standard work for the period; also R. Rémondon, *Rech. de Papyr.* 1, 1961, pp. 41–93, 'Soldats de Byzance d'après un papyrus trouvé à Edfu' (period of Justinian).

Economic and Social Life. The numerous studies of H. I.

(Sir Harold) Bell, arising from his work on the Aphrodito papyri (see below, on ch. xxviii), are fundamental. See *JEA* 4, 1917, pp. 86–106, 'The Byzantine Servile State in Egypt'; ibid. 8, 1922, pp. 139–55, 'Hellenic Culture in Egypt'; id. in *Recueil Champollion* (Bibl. éc. des hautes études, 234, 1922), pp. 261–71, 'An Epoch in the agrarian History of Egypt'. See also E. R. Hardy, *Large Estates, passim;* A. C. Johnson and L. C. West, *Byzantine Egypt; Economic Studies* (Princeton, 1949); A. C. Johnson, *Egypt and the Roman Empire* (Ann Arbor, 1951); and, for currency problems, L. C. West and A. C. Johnson, *Currency in Roman and Byzantine Egypt* (Princeton, 1944).

Geography of Byzantine and post-Conquest Egypt. The following deal especially with the Arabic sources and period: J. Maspero and G. Wiet, *Matériaux pour servir à la géographie de l'Égypte* (*Mém. Inst. franç. d'Arch. or.* xxxvi, 1919)—a gazetteer of the cities mentioned by al-Maqrīzī in his *Kitāb al-Khiṭaṭ*; H.E. Omar Toussoun, *Géographie de l'Égypte à l'époque arabe* (*Mém. Soc. roy. de l'Égypte*, 8, 1926–36; 3 vols.); H. Munier, *Géographie historique de l'Égypte*, II (*Bibliogr. géogr. de l'Égypte, publ. sous la direction de H. Lorin*, 1928); H. Gauthier, *Les Nomes d'Égypte depuis Hérodote jusqu'à la Conquête arabe* (*Mém. Inst. d'Égypte*, 28, 1935); E. Amélineau, *La Géographie de l'Égypte à l'époque copte* (Paris, 1893). See also the studies of Casanova, *BIFAO* 1, 1901, pp. 139–224 'Les noms coptes du Caire et les localités voisines', and R. A. Guest, *JRAS*, 1912, pp. 941 ff., 'The Delta in the Middle Ages'. A. Grohmann, *Studien zur historischen Geographie u. Verwaltung des frühmittelalterlichen Ägypten* (*Wien. Denkschr.* 77 (2), 1959), deals with the Byzantine *nomoi* and the Arab *kuras*. H.E. Youssef Kamal's *Monum. geogr. Afric. et Aegypt.* III (Brill, 1930) contains excerpts of all texts relating to localities in Egypt (including Miṣr!) mentioned in the records of the Conquest.

On the topography of Christian Alexandria see below, on chs. xxiv–xxv. For the Muslim city see P. Kahle *Der Islam*, 12, 1921, pp. 29–83 (walls and canals), and in general Ét. Combe in *Bull. Soc. roy. de Géogr. d'Égypte*, 15, 1928, pp. 201–38 (bibliography of Arab and subsequent descriptions); 16, 1929, pp. 111–71, 269–92, and addenda, added when the articles were reprinted (1933) as a book, *Alexandrie musulmane*, with continuous pagination (to which the addenda refer). See further id., *Bull. Soc. arch. Alex.* 34, 1941, pp. 62–73; ibid., pp. 95–103; ibid. 36, 1946, pp. 120–45. For al-Fusṭāṭ see below, p. lxxi.

For the general topography of Greco-Roman and Byzantine Egypt see the useful topographical work of J. Ball, *Egypt in the Classical Geographers* (Government Press, Bulaq, Cairo, 1942).

III. BIBLIOGRAPHY BY CHAPTERS

Chs. i–iv, ix–x. Reign of Heraclius (for the Sassanian conquests, etc., see below, on chs. vi–vii).

The main single work on the Emperor is that of A. Pernice, *L'imperatore Eraclio* (saggio di Storia bizantina e filologia, 32, Florence, 1905), intended as a general study of social, religious, and political conditions in the Empire in the first half of the seventh century. It was mostly already written before Butler's book appeared, and in his description of the Conquest, Pernice largely follows Butler, of whom he says (p. 297 n.), 'Recentemente A. F. [*sic*] Butler nel suo bel lavoro *The Arab Conquest of Egypt* p. 194 e specialmente nell'appendice D, ha ripreso lo studio della cronologia di questo periodo. . . . Pei fatti che rientrano nel mio racconto, ho seguito il Butler, le cui conclusioni mi sembrano molto serie e fondate; però rimando al suo libro per la critica e la relazione delle fonti bizantine e orientali.' He shared Butler's view of the identity of al-Mukawkas with Cyrus, and in view of his agreement suppressed an appendix containing his own demonstration of the identity.

Pernice's book is of importance for the whole period, and should be considered in the light of the criticisms by E. W. Brooks, *EHR* 21, 1906, pp. 141–3, and of the numerous detailed studies by N. H. Baynes in the articles listed below, especially in the *United Services Magazine*.

The various problems of Heraclius' reign, and in particular the chronological and other difficulties connected with his Persian campaigns, were discussed exhaustively by N. H. Baynes in *United Services Magazine*, 46, 1912, pp. 526–33, 659–666; 47, 1913, pp. 30–8, 195–201, 318–24, 401–12, 532–41, 665–679; see also id., *CQ* 6, 1912, pp. 82–90, 'Some Notes on the Historical Poems of George of Pisidia'; *Byz. Zeitschr.* 21, 1912, pp. 110–28, 'The date of the Avar surprise'; *EHR* 19, 1904, pp. 694–702, 'The first campaign of Heraclius against Persia'; ibid. 27, 1912, pp. 287–99, 'The restoration of the Cross at Byzantium' (on which cf. A. Frolow, *Rev. ét. byz.* 11, 1953, pp. 88–105). Baynes summarized his views in *CMH*[1] ii, pp. 287 ff., to which is appended, pp. 747–57, a remarkable bibliography (the 'Bibliography for the History of the Roman Empire from Anastasius to Heraclius', announced by Baynes as forthcoming on p. 747, was never published); see also W. E. Kaegi, *Byz. Zeitschr.* 66, 1973, pp. 308–30, 'New Evidence on the early reign of Heraclius'. C. Foss, *EHR* 90, 1975, pp. 721–47, 'The Persians in Asia Minor and the End of Antiquity', breaks fresh ground by a study of the archaeological evidence for Persian operations in Asia Minor.

In addition to the above, there are useful summaries of the various problems by Pertusi in his edition of George of Pisidia (see above, I.A (I. ii)), by Stratos, op. cit. above (II.A), and by N. Oikonomides, *Byz. and Mod. Gk. Stud.* 1, 1975, pp. 1–10 (first campaign). I have not been able to see the work of T. Evangelides, *Ἡράκλειος ὁ Αὐτοκράτωρ* (Odessa, 1903), for which see Baynes, *Unit. Serv. Mag.* 46, 1912, p. 529, s.v. ('historically unimportant').

Ch. v. Egypt under Heraclius

See above, II.B, and especially H. Munier in *Préc. de l'hist. d'Ég.*, loc. cit., pp. 64 ff., 95–106. For dated papyri of the reign of Heraclius see above, I.A, II, and for the ecclesiastical history of Egypt at this time see below, ch. xiii.

Chs. vi–vii. Persian Conquest of Syria and Egypt

For the Sassanian background see especially A. Christensen, *L'Iran sous les Sassanides*[2] (Copenhagen, 1944), *passim*; and for the late Sassanian period in general see Nöldeke's translation of, and commentary on, the Persian sections of aṭ-Ṭabarī's *Annals* (*Ta'rīkh ar-Rusul wa'l-Mulūk*), *Geschichte der Perser und Araber zur Zeit der Sasaniden. Aus der arabischen Chronik des Tabari* (Leiden, 1879)—for a summary of the relationship of the Persian version by Balʿamī (trans. Zotenberg, 1869–74) to the original see Dunlop, op. cit., pp. 90–1 (Butler used only Balʿamī in *The Conquest*: see *Treaty*, p. 7 note 2). On Christianity under the Sassanids see Labourt, *Le Christianisme dans l'Empire perse sous la dynastie sassanide* (Paris, 1904); G. Bardy in Fliche–Martin, *Histoire de l'Égl.* iv (1948), pp. 322 ff.; Chaumont, *Rev. Hist. Rel.* 165, 1964, pp. 165–202, 'Les Sassanides et la christianisation de l'Empire iranien au IIIᵉ siècle de notre ère'; also A. Guillaumont, *Dumbarton Oaks Papers*, 23–4, 1969–70, pp. 41–66, 'Justinien et l'Église de Perse'; the account by E. Tisserant, *DTC* s.v. L'Église nestorienne, cols. 163–94 (1930) is a mine of detailed information.

Conquest of Syria: see Pernice, op. cit., pp. 57 ff.; Baynes, locc. citt.; Stratos, I, pp. 63 ff. For the contemporary account of the capture of Jerusalem by the monk Antiochos Strategios, see above, I.E.

Conquest and Occupation of Egypt: see the general works cited above, and in addition E. R. Hardy, *Journ. Soc. Orient. Res.* 13, 1929, pp. 185–9, 'New Light on the Persian occupation of Egypt' (on papyri of the Persian period; cf. above, I.A, II); and for the Pehlevi papyri of the period see above, I.F. There are several references to the Persian invasion or occupation in Upper Egypt in the *Life* of Pisentius, and in the correspondence of Epiphanius published by Crum in Winlock and Crum, *The Monastery of Epiphanius at Thebes* (see above, I.B. (i), p. xlviii); see vol. i, p. 99. Of particular interest are nos. 433 (ii, p. 97 (text), p. 265 (transl.)), which contains a reference to the 'Persians, for they will be coming south'; 324 (ii, p. 81, and p. 239), which apparently contains a reference to a Persian official at Thebes (Nē; cf. no. 151 n. 3); 300 (p. 78, and pp. 233–4). For possible Sassanid bronze emissions in Alexandria see Phillips, *NC*, 1972, pp. 225–41.

Ch. viii. Art and Literature at the time of the Conquest

Butler's very brief sketch of the cultural life of Egypt in the seventh century needs expansion on both the artistic and the literary sides.

Coptic Art. When Butler wrote, little Coptic material had been published or studied systematically. There are now numerous handbooks, and I may note first a few recent general works on the topic. Among the most valuable are those concerned with the exhibition of Coptic art at the Villa Hügel at Essen: see the illustrated catalogue, *Christentum am Nil* (Villa Hügel, Essen, 1963), and the associated volume of studies with the same title (Zürich, 1964; with Nachtrag, n.d.). Among recent publications of museum collections of Coptic art are that of the Coptic Museum at Recklingshausen, K. Wessel, *Koptische Kunst* (Recklingshausen, 1963), and that of the Martin von Wagner Museum at Würzburg, D. Renner, *Die Koptische Stoffe im Martin von Wagner Museum der Universität Würzburg* (Wiesbaden, 1974; good bibliography). Two excellent general works are those of Le R. P. Pierre du Bourguet, *L'Art copte* (Paris, 1968; Eng. trans., *Coptic Art* (London, 1971); originally published as *Die Copten*, Baden-Baden, 1967), with, pp. 204–7, a valuable bibliography, and H. Zaloscer, *Die Kunst im christlichen Ägypten* (Vienna–Munich, 1974).

For Coptic textiles see the recent catalogues of P. du Bourguet for the Louvre, *Catalogue des étoffes coptes*, i (Paris, 1964), and, for the Hermitage, M. Matje (Matthieu; Mate) and K. Lyapunova, *Khudozhestvennye tkani koptskogo Egipta* (Moscow, 1951); and the book of L. Kybalová, *Coptic Textiles* (London, 1967), with excellent photographs of pieces from the former Golenishchev and Bock collections, but with a poor historical introduction; for the Brooklyn Museum, D. Thompson, *Coptic Textiles in the Brooklyn Museum* (Brooklyn, 1971). For a good summary of the long dispute as to Sassanian or Syrian influence on Coptic textiles see Pigulevskaja, *Les Villes de l'État iranien aux époques parthe et sassanide* (Docs. et Recherches sur l'Écon. des pays byz. vi, Paris, 1963, pp. 164–8), in which she discusses the various arguments regarding the different techniques of weaving brought forward by Pfister, Serjeant (see his series of articles in *Ars Islamica* from 1942 to 1951 (Index, 1951, pp. 273–305)), Crowfoot and Griffith, and others. The survival of elements from the pre-Christian period is well illustrated by the two magnificent tapestries, one of which figures Hestia Polyolbos and her attendants and the other Cybele and her followers (Pan, Attis) studied by Friedländer, *Documents of Dying Paganism* (Univ. of California Press, 1945).

For Coptic sculpture see, in addition to the general descriptions of Coptic art noted above, J. Beckwith, *Coptic Sculpture, 300–1300* (London, 1963); and for a comparative study of the architectural sculpture see the important paper of E. Kitzinger, *Archaeologia*, 87, 1938, pp. 181–216 (especially on the fragments from Ahnas al-Madinah and Bahnasa-Oxyrhynchus).

For bone-carvings etc. with representations of classical figures and scenes see now L. Marangou's exhaustive *Benaki Museum, Bone Carvings from Egypt* I (Wasmuth, Tübingen, 1976), with a critical discussion of many aspects of Coptic art. Ead., *Ath. Mitt.* 86, 1971, pp. 163 ff. (cf. op. cit., pp. 71 ff.) published some Ptolemaic bone rings from Cyprus and elsewhere, indicating a Hellenistic origin for such material (cf. D. B. Thompson, *The Athenian Agora* (Agora Picture Book no. 12, 1971), fig. 29). E. Rodziewicz's article on sixth–seventh-century ivories from Alexandria (Kom ed-Dik) in *Acta Conventus XI Congressus Eirene* (Warsaw, 1971), pp. 493–7, discusses their stratigraphical context. For Coptic book-illuminations see J. Leroy, *Les Manuscrits coptes et coptes-arabes illustrés* (IFA, Beyrouth, 1974), and for frescoes id., *Les Peintures des couvents du désert d'Esna* (ibid. 1975).

For small instruments, objects of daily use, etc., see Strzygowski's excellent catalogue of the Cairo Museum, *Koptische Kunst* (Catal. gén., 1904), together with Crum's catalogue of the stelai etc., *Coptic Monuments* (1902), esp. nos. 8318 ff.; and for the parallel Greek stelai see G. Lefebvre, *Recueil des inscriptions grecques chrétiennes d'Égypte* (Cairo, 1907). For documentary evidence for weaving, glass-manufacture, etc., in the Byzantine period see the very useful analysis by Johnson and West, op. cit. II.B above, pp. 107 ff.

Butler's brief account of the Hellenic culture of the capital has something to say of John Moschus and Sophronius (cf. above, I.A i (iv)), Stephanus of Alexandria the polymath and astrologer (see below), and also John Philoponus of the sixth century. But the publication of Greek and Coptic literary papyri had not reached the stage at which both the contemporary knowledge of the pagan classics and the development of the Coptic Biblical tradition could be understood as they can be today. Recent years have brought to light, in addition to much Greek and Coptic Manichaean and Gnostic Literature [see, for the Nag' Hammadi finds (iii–v A.D.), the new facsimile publication of the codices, *The Facsimile Edition of the Nag Hammadi Codices* (Brill, Leiden, 1972– ; published under the auspices of the Dept. of Antiquities of the Arab Republic of Egypt, in conjunction with *UNESCO*), i, Introduction, by James M. Robinson, with good summary of the work on the Codices to date; ii (1974); iii (1976); vi (1972); vii (1972); xi–xiii (1973); also *Nag' Hammadi Studies* (ed. J. M. Robinson et al.), various titles, vols. i–vii (Brill, 1971–) and for a full account of the texts and their discovery, with excellent bibliographies, J. Doresse, *The Secret Books of the Egyptian Gnostics* (London, 1960), *passim*; and for Gnostic texts and beliefs in general, W. Foerster, ed., *Gnosis* (Artemisverlag, 1969; Eng. trans., 2 vols., Oxford, 1973), which contains a study and translation of the transmitted texts (vol. i), and (vol. ii) of the Coptic codices from Nag' Hammadi and of the Mandaean sources; for the Manichaean texts from Madinet Madi, and the new Greek Mani-codex from Oxyrhynchus (*ZPE*, 5, 1970, pp. 97–216) see the excellent bibliography in *Oxf. Dict. Chr. Church*², s.v. Manes; see also the essays in *Gnosis u. Gnostizismus*, ed. K. Rudolph (*Wege der Forschung*, 262, 1975)], and new Greek and Coptic Biblical texts (notably in the Chester Beatty and Bodmer collections; see the list in Turner, *Greek Papyri* (Clarendon Press, 1968), pp. 160–2, s.vv. P.Bodmer and P.Chester Beatty), and a large number of new Coptic martyrologies (see most recently E. A. E. Reymond and J. W. B. Barns, *Four Martyrdoms from the Pierpont Morgan Coptic Codices*, Oxford, Clar. Press, 1973, with bibliography), important fragments of Greek pagan literature, notably Callimachus (see the list of papp. in Pfeiffer's edn., vol. ii (1953), pp. ix ff.), and Menander (see the list in Gomme–Sandbach's commentary (Clarendon Press, 1973), pp. 50–1), including several codices of the sixth and even perhaps of the seventh century. These come from Upper Egypt, but they inevitably reflect in some degree the reading habits of Alexandria in the generations before the Conquest. It is even possible that one or two of these may belong to the years following the Conquest (see on this E. G. Turner, *Ancient Manuscripts* (Clarendon Press, 1971), p. 67, apropos of a papyrus codex of Callimachus (no. 37 in Pfeiffer's list, pp. xxiv–xxv) allegedly of the seventh century; and for the use of the Greek 'Coptic Uncial' at this period see Irigoin, *Jahrb. Österr. byz. Ges.* 8, 1959, pp. 29–51; both Irigoin (p. 40 n. 54) and Turner repeat Lobel's warning (*POxy.* xx, p. 71) regarding the absolute dating of this codex).

Among original works of the century before the Conquest pride of place (if such it is) must be given to the poems of Dioscurus, the official of Aphrodito who composed frigid verses on public occasions and persons. These are largely preserved in the Cairo *PMasp.* (see above, I.B), and were studied by Maspero in *RÉG* 24, 1911, pp. 426–81; see also Heitsch, *Die griech. Dichterfragm. der röm. Kaiserzeit*², no. xlii, pp. 42 ff. (with bibliography) (*Gött. Abh.* 49, 1963). There is an excellent picture of Byzantine poetry in Egypt by A. Cameron, *Historia*, 14, 1965, pp. 470–509.

The developments of science on the eve of the Conquest have been studied in the field of medicine by O. Temkin, *Dumbarton Oaks Papers*, 16, 1962, pp. 97–114, and in the important earlier paper of E. Meyerhof, *SB Berl. Akad.* 1930 (23), 'Von Alexandrien nach Bagdad'; cf. Fraser, *Ptolemaic Alexandria* (Clarendon Press, 1972), ii, p. 538 n. 234. In the physical sciences the work of the later Alexandrian and Athenian commentators on Plato and Aristotle (see for Philoponus and Simplicius, Sambursky, *The Physical World of late Antiquity*, London and N.Y., 1962, pp. 154 ff.) ended with the closing of the philosophical schools by Justinian in 529, and even though some of the neo-Platonists, on their return from residence in Persia, settled in Alexandria where the tradition of Aristotelian interpretation continued (see Westerinck, *Anon. Prolegomena to Platonic Philosophy* (Amsterdam, 1962), pp. xv–xx; Cameron, *Proc. Cambr. Philol. Soc.* 15, 1969, pp. 7–29, esp. p. 9), the last century of Byzantine Alexandria has little to show in the way of speculative thought, pagan or Christian. The most conspicuous figure is the μέγας διδάσκαλος and οἰκουμενικὸς φιλόσοφος, Stephanus of Alexandria (for the title cf. Browning, *Byzant.* 32, 1962, p. 167), for whom see Usener's monograph in his *Kl. Schr.* iii (1914), pp. 247–322, and his second paper (not in *Kl. Schr.*), *De Stephano Alexandrino commentatio altera* (24 pp., Bonn, 1880); but he left Alexandria, being summoned by Heraclius to join the nascent revival of studies in Constantinople (see further R. Vancourt, *Les Derniers Commentateurs alexandrins d'Aristote* (Lille, 1941 [*non vidi*]), pp. 26–42; Westerinck, p. xxiii). His commentaries on Aristotle's *Categories* and the *De Interpretatione* survived to be listed in the *Fihrist* (p. 249, Flügel; pp. 598–9, trans. Bayard Dodge); but the alleged prophecy of the coming of Mohammed, edited by Usener, *Kl. Schr.*, pp. 266 ff., was written in *c.* 775. For the astrological writings passing under his name in numerous manuscripts see *Catal. Cod. Astrol. Graec.*, *passim* (i, p. 20 (F240, the prophecy edited by Usener, loc. cit. above; cf. v, 3, pp. 110 ff., a similar prophecy attributed to Vettius Valens); ii, pp. 181–6; iv, p. 6; v, 1, p. 153; etc.); he also bulks large in *Cat. Man. Alchim. gr.*, e.g. I, pp. 2 ff. = Ideler, *Phys. et Med. gr.* ii, pp. 199 ff. The man himself is hardly recognizable behind the mass of pseudonyma.

Chs. xi–xii. The Rise of Mohammed and the Arab conquest of Syria

1. A bibliography of modern studies of Mohammed (to which a fresh impetus was given by the two works of W. Montgomery Watt, *Muhammad at Mecca* (Clarendon Press, 1953) and *Muhammad at Medina* (Clarendon Press, 1956), and their abridgement, *Muhammad Prophet and Statesman* (Clarendon Press, 1961)) is beyond the scope of this work. A very full bibliographical analysis beyond that date by M. Rodinson will be found in *Rev. hist.* 229, 1963, pp. 169–220, and elsewhere (e.g. the same author's *Mohammad* (Eng. trans. Penguin, 1973), pp. 343–6). Inevitably, little new material has appeared on the early expansion of the Muslim state outside Arabia though numerous modern handbooks exist. An excellent summary, with a balanced discussion of the problems raised in an

assessment of the reasons for the expansion, will be found in F. Gabrieli, *Muhammed and the Conquests of Islam* (London, 1968), with, pp. 242 ff., a critical bibliography, and in the latest edition of Hitti's *History of the Arabs* (ed. 10, 1970), pp. 139–77, with references.

2. The Arab Conquest of Syria. The fullest account, subsequent to Butler, of the events of A.H. 13–16 in Syria is that of Caetani, *Annali*, iii, pp. 3–81 (§§ 7–67), 176–220 (§§ 195–227), 310–440 (§§ 95–441), 493–618 (§§ 4–127), 788–819 (§§ 269–327) (for *Annali* see further below, on chs. xiv–xxii). The account of the conquest of Syria based on Balādhurī's narrative in *Futūḥ al-Buldān* (pp. 110–12) by De Goeje, *Conquête de la Syrie*, which Butler used in its first edn. (1864), appeared in a second edition in 1900: for the full title of the revised work see above, I.C (d); cf. Caetani, op. cit. § 20. For Hitti's translation of Balādhurī see above, I.C (a); id., *History of the Arabs*, pp. 147 ff.

Chs. xiii, xxvii. The Church in Egypt

For general accounts of the history of the Church in Egypt, and of the controversies between the Chalcedonian or Melkite and the Monophysite factions, the rise of nationalism within the Coptic Church, and the history of the varying fortunes of the two patriarchates, Melkite and Monophysite, see the general accounts of Maspero, op. cit. below; of Duchesne, *L'Église au sixième siècle* (Paris, 1925), chs. vii–xi ('Héraclius et Mahomet'); L. Bréhier in Fliche et Martin, *Hist. de l'Égl.* 5 (1947), chs. iii–vi; also E. R. Hardy, *Christian Egypt: Church and People* (Christianity and Nationalism in the Patriarchate of Alexandria) (O.U.P., N.Y., 1952), pp. 177–90, a brief account with excellent bibliography and notes; cf. also id., *Dumbarton Oaks Papers*, 22, 1968, pp. 23–41, 'The Egyptian Policy of Justinian'. See also J. P. van Dieten, *Geschichte Patriarchen von Sergios I bis Johannes VI (610–715)* (Amst., 1972), *passim*, esp. pp. 179–218; W. H. C. Frend, *The Rise of the Monophysite Movement* (Cambr. Univ. Press, 1972), pp. 339 ff. The general account of the Eastern Church by A. S. Atiya, *A History of Eastern Christianity* (London, 1968), which has a long section on the Coptic Church (pp. 13–166) and M. Roncaglia's diffuse and superficial work, *Histoire de l'Église copte* (4 vols. to date, 1966–73) are accounts of Christianity in Egypt from its origins, written from the Coptic point of view.

For the patriarchate in particular see J. Maspero (A. Fortescue,

G. Wiet), *Histoire des Patriarches d'Alexandrie, depuis la mort de l'Empereur Anastase jusqu'à la réconciliation des Églises jacobites (518–616)* (Bibl. éc. des hautes études, 237, 1923); A. Jülicher in *Festgabe Karl Müller* (Tübingen, 1922), pp. 7–23, 'Die Liste der alexandrinischen Patriarchen im 6. und 7. Jahrhundert', the best analysis of the sources (especially for seventh-century accession-dates, discussed by Butler in his Appendix F; J. assigns Benjamin, the Patriarch during the Persian occupation and the early years of the Arab conquest, to 626–66, rather than to 623–62, as Butler; *alii alia*). C. D. G. Müller, *Muséon*, 69, 1956, pp. 313–40 and ibid. 72, 1959, pp. 323–47, 'Benjamin I' gives all the available biographical material, drawn largely from Severus' *History* (see above, I.C (g)); see also id. *Heid. Abh.* (Phil.-hist. Kl.), 1968(1), 'Die Homilie über die Hochzeit zu Kana und weitere Schriften des Patriarchen Benjamin I von Alexandrien', and R.-G. Coquin's important *Livre de la Consécration du Sanctuaire de Benjamin* (IFAO, Bibl. ét. copt. 13, 1975). See also H. Leclercq in *Dict. arch. chrét.* xiii, s.v. Patriarchat, cols. 2456–66; E. R. Hardy, *Church History*, 15, 1946, pp. 81–100. A full list of the two sets of Patriarchs will be found in Maspero's book, and also in Grumel, in Lemerle's *Traité d'études byz.* i, Paris, 1958), pp. 442–5; Bataille, ibid. ii, pp. 70 ff. (Paris, 1955), and in Munier, *Précis de l'hist. d'Égypte* (cf. above, II.B), pp. 297 ff.

For the Coptic and Arabic *Histories of the Patriarchs*, and for the lives of individual Patriarchs (Benjamin, Isaac) see above, I.B and C.

On the problem of the identity of the Coptic Church and faith with the sentiment of Egyptian nationalism see, against the accepted view that such a feeling existed and was a prominent factor in the history of the Church, the discussion by A. H. M. Jones, *JTS*, N.S. 10, 1959, pp. 280–98 (reprinted in Jones, *The Roman Economy*, ed. P. A. Brunt (Blackwell, Oxford, 1974), pp. 309–29, esp. pp. 315–20); see also Hardy, op. cit. above; the discussion in Atiya, loc. cit. naturally stresses the element of nationalism.

On the patriarch-governor of Egypt, Cyrus, and the identity of 'al-Muqawqa(i)s' (المقوقس), discussed at length by Butler, pp. 508–26, and in *Treaty of Miṣr*, pp. 54–83, much has been written, and in general Butler's view that the two are identical—i.e. that the Arabs meant to refer to Cyrus when they spoke of al-Muqawqas—has been upheld (see, by way of contrast, Amélineau, *Rev. Hist.* 119, 1915, pp. 288 ff., who denies that Cyrus was patriarch). On the other hand there is still little agreement as to the meaning of the Arabic word, and the various views discussed and rejected by Butler continue to find adherents. The most detailed subsequent discussion is that of van Cauwenbergh, op. cit., pp. 91–109, who agrees with Butler, both in the identification of al-Mukawkas with Cyrus and also in the explanation of the name as referring to Cyrus' previous appointment as Bishop of Phasis, near the Caucasus, whence he would be known in Greek as *Καυκάσιος*, yielding the presumed Coptic form, **ⲡⲕⲁⲩⲭⲁⲥⲓⲟⲥ** or **ⲡⲕⲁⲩⲭⲓⲟⲥ** (or perhaps **ⲡⲕⲟⲗⲭⲓⲟⲥ**, from the location of Phasis in Colchis), which would then yield the Arabic form المقوقس. Caetani's view, *Annali*, iv, pp. 86–96, 342, that the Arab writers are referring to three different persons, including Cyrus, under the name al-Muqawqas, does not, as Butler pointed out, *Treaty*, p. 82 n. 1, invalidate his theory. There is in fact no doubt that the Arabic term is used of other persons than Cyrus (e.g. the Patriarch Benjamin: see Butler, pp. 475–6), but there seems little room for doubt that the term was originally, and correctly, applied to Cyrus. As Wiet pointed out in a note in Maspero's *Histoire des patriarches* (p. 353 n. 1), 'an Arabic text' (in fact the so-called *Apocalypse of Samuel of Kalamūn* (see I.B (ii) above)) published in *Rev. de l'Orient chrét.* 10 (20), 1915–17, p. 377 calls al-Muqawqas كبيرس المقوقز, which is easily emended to كيرس (cf. F. Nau, op. cit. below, p. 11 n. 4, who himself suggests as an alternative to 'The Caucasian' a derivation from *κακός*!). It is also to be noted that the Hamburg MS. of Severus' *History of the Patriarchs*, separately published by C. F. Seybold, *Severus ibn al Muqaffa', Alexandrinische Patriarchengeschichte* (*Veröff. aus der Hamburger Stadtbibliothek*, Bd. 3, 1912), which is the oldest surviving version, but which was not used by Evetts in his edition of Severus in *PO* (see above, I.C (g)), has at one point (p. 98, line 8) كيرس for the المقوقس of the other MSS. (on p. 489 in the corresponding section in Evetts's edn.); this strongly substantiates the identification, and the bilingual *Livre de la Consécration* (see above, p. lxv) clinches this by giving (p. 110) **ⲕⲩⲣⲟⲥ ⲡⲓⲕⲁⲩⲕⲟⲥ** and كيرس المقوقز(س); cf., id. pp. 57–8. The view of Müller, *Muséon*, 69, 1956, p. 321 n., who follows Caetani in regarding al-Muqawqas as a fusion of many characters: 'Sicher ist, dass die Araber alles auf diese eine Person übertragen haben, die historisch aufgeschlüsselt werden muss und nicht einfach mit Kyros oder Georg identifiziert darf' does not affect the authentic identification. There is an excellent summary of the various views in Grohmann's article in *EI* (1936), s.v. al-Muḳawḳas, pp. 712–13. The study of F. Nau, *Muséon*, 45, 1932, pp. 1–17, 'La politique matrimoniale de Cyrus', apropos of the story told in Nicephorus (p. 24, ed. de Boer) that Cyrus offered ʿAmr the Augusta Eudocia during the siege of Babylon is based on a very uncritical acceptance of this story: see already Butler, p. 264. Graf, *GCAL*, i, p. 281 n. 1, records that a continuous history of al-Muqawqas exists in a Cairo MS. of A.D. 1787.

For monasticism in the period between Shenute and the Arab Conquest see the useful book of van Cauwenbergh, already referred to more than once (see above, p. xlviii); cf. also N. Abbott, *Monasteries of the Fayyum* (below); in addition to the various works noted above.

For the monasteries themselves see van Cauwenbergh, op. cit., pp. 63 ff., *passim*, based on a careful study of the sources; and the works dealing with the architecture and history of the various groups, notably Somers Clarke, *Christian Antiquities of the Nile Valley* (Clarendon Press, 1911); C. C. Walters, *Monastic Archaeology in Egypt* (Warminster, 1974; with, pp. 331 ff., an excellent bibliography); O. F. A. Meinardus, *Christian Egypt, Anc. and Modern* (Cairo, 1965); and the numerous specialized studies of individual monasteries, in particular those of Evelyn White, *The Monasteries of the Wâdi'n Natrûn*; Part II, *The History of the Monasteries of Nitria and Scetis* (N.Y., Metr. Mus., 1932) and Part III, *The Monasteries of the Wâdi'n Natrûn*, (1933), and of Winlock and Crum, *The Monastery of Epiphanius*, I (1926; cf. above, p. xlvi); further details in C. C. Walters. Butler's own early work, *The Ancient Coptic Churches of Egypt* (2 vols., 1884), has been reprinted with corrections (C.P., 1970). There is an excellent account of a visit to the Wadi Natrun in 1883–4 by Butler in *Coptic Churches*, i, pp. 290 ff. There is a useful map published by the Société d'Archéologie copte du Caire, *Carte de l'Égypte chrétienne* (1954; rev. reprint, 1955) which marks monasteries and episcopal seats.

For details of administration and economic life see in general P. Barison, *Aegyptus*, 18, 1938, pp. 29–148, 'Ricerche sui monasteri dell'Egitto bizantino ed arabo secondo i documenti dei papiri greci' (pp. 66–148, a useful 'elenco ragionato dei monasteri secondo i documenti dei papiri greci'); L. Antonini, ibid. 20, 1940, pp. 129–208, 'Le chiese cristiane nell'Egitto del iv al ix secolo' (geographical list of churches, pp. 160 ff.); E. WIPSZYCKA, *Les Ressources et les activités économiques des églises en Égypte du IV au VIIIe siècle* (Papyrolog. Bruxellens. 10, 1972). See also the discussion of monastic administration, based on three Arabic papyri of A.D. 946–7 conveying properties to the monastery of Samuel of Kalamūn, by Nabia Abbott, *The Monasteries of the Fayyūm* (Orient. Instit., Univ. of Chicago, Studies in anc. oriental civilisation, no. 16, 1937). Perhaps the best picture of monastic life of the period is that provided by the Monastery of Epiphanius in the publication of Winlock and Crum (cf. above, I.B (i)); in vol. 1, ch. III, Winlock has an excellent account of 'Trades and Occupations at the Monastery, as shown by the excavations', and in ch. VI Crum describes 'Theban Hermits and their Life' on the basis of the literary material. For the role of the Church in the economic life of Alexandria see G. R. Monks, *Speculum*, 28, 1953, pp. 349–62, 'The Church of Alexandria and the City's economic life in the Sixth century' (based largely on Leontius' *Life of John the Almoner*). For the building of churches in the early Muslim period, in spite of the restrictions imposed by the 'Covenants', see Tritton, *The Caliphs and their non-Muslim subjects* (1930), pp. 37 ff.: a church in al-Fusṭāṭ was built between A.H. 47 and 68 (Abū Ṣāliḥ, p. 86). The shrine of Abū Mīna, between Alexandria and the Wadi Natrūn, with its magnificent church adorned with Arcadius' basilica, which Benjamin visited when he fled from Alexandria, had not been excavated when Butler wrote (see pp. 177–8); its excavation was the work of Mgr. C. M. Kaufmann in 1905–7: see Kaufmann, *Die Menasstadt* I (Leipzig, 1910), and his more popular work, *Die heilige Stadt der Wüste*[2-3] (Kösel Verlag, 1921), and more briefly Breccia, *Alex. ad Aeg.*[2] (Engl. trans.), pp. 345–9; de Cosson, *Mareotis* (London, 1935), pp. 135 ff.; Baedeker, *Egypt*[8] (1929), p. 30; Meinardus, op. cit., pp. 141–6. For over 100 ostraka relating to the vineyards at Abū Mīna see *SB* 10990 (cf. *AA* 1967, pp. 457 ff.).

Chs. xiv–xxii. The Arab Conquest of Egypt and the Coastal towns; xxix, The Revolt of Alexandria under Manuel; its final conquest.

The fullest account of the operations lies in the first four volumes of Caetani's monumental and uniquely diffuse *Annali dell'Islam* (11 vols., 1905–24; all vols. reprinted, 1972), to which every student of the Arab Conquests must admit a great debt. Caetani records in full, in annalistic form (A.H.), all the parallel Traditions of the Arabic writers and of the *isnād* which forms those Traditions, but in spite of the depth and detail of the work (of which Caetani published ten folio volumes of text, with excellent indexes (to vols. i–ii in ii, 2, and to iii–v, in vi), yet only succeeded in covering as far as A.H. 40; a briefer version, in five fascicules, *Chronographia Islamica*, appeared in 1912–22, but this, though intended to cover the period A.D. 622–1517, reached only as far as A.D. 750), it must be said that, though his criticisms of Butler are just in so far as the latter did not sufficiently emphasize either the variety and bias of Arab Traditions, or their tendency to conform to established canons, his criticisms on historical points do no more than emphasize the doubts which are naturally invoked by any imaginative reconstruction of a sadly lacunose tradition. In any event, following E. W. Brooks, *Byz. Zeitschr.* 4, 1895, pp. 431–45, Butler established beyond doubt that (as Leopold von Ranke had already seen, *Weltgeschichte*, V, pp. 140 ff.; cf. also S. Lane Poole, *Egypt, The Middle Ages* (1901), ch. 1) the Arab chroniclers (like the Byzantine) must take second place beside the narratives of John of Nikiou and Severus ibn al-Muqaffa'. The alternative explanations which Caetani offers (iv, pp. 166 ff., 185 ff.) of some of the early military operations of the campaign are reasonable enough in themselves, and may in places be preferable to those of Butler, but they do not, and, in the nature of the case, cannot, go beyond the limited possibilities of interpretation offered by our main source, John of Nikiou. The same is true of his rather captious discussion of the identity of al-Muqawqas (iv, 86–96; see above, p. lxvi). Alongside John of Nikiou, Caetani takes as his main narrative-source of the campaign (iv, 166–81; 232–348; pp. 318–48 contain a clear and full summary of Caetani's view of the campaign) Ibn 'Abd al-Ḥakam's *Futūh Miṣr*, for which see above, I.C (b).

Butler's discussion of the vexed chronology of the campaign, based on that of E. W. Brooks, loc. cit., based in turn on the narrative of John of Nikiou, is to be found on pp. 526–46, and in *Treaty, passim.* His conclusions were challenged at some points by Caetani, Amélineau, and others, but Butler appreciated the uncertainty of the chronological framework, of which he said, *Treaty*, p. 53, 'No historian has yet issued from that inexorable labyrinth which the Arab writers have built around the central facts of the Conquest with a key to its mysteries.' There is in fact still some uncertainty regarding the chronology of events between 639 and 643. In the operations themselves, two main items were challenged by Caetani, and also by Amélineau in his posthumous article, *Rev. Hist.*, 1915 (119), pp. 273–310 (pp. 273–301, analysis of sources; role of Cyrus), (120), 1–25, namely the topography and chronology of the Battle—or Battles—of Umm Dunayn (Tendunias in John, ch. cxii, 10) (identified by Butler with the region of the Ezbekiya Gardens in Cairo, but put by Cresswell, *EMA*, I², p. 35 n. 7, very slightly north of this; cf. Casanova, *BIFAO* I, 1901, pp. 73–6), and the nature and extent of 'Amr's raid into the Fayyūm and Middle Egypt. For both these episodes we are largely dependent upon John of Nikiou's narrative, which at this point is dislocated (see p. 268), and lacks chronological coherence, and therefore does not permit of a firm decision. A final, yet more important point of disagreement lay in the nature of the 'Treaty of Miṣr' recorded by Ṭabarī, for which see below, on chs. xvii–xviii. For the date of the capitulation of Alexandria see below, on ch. xxi.

Chs. xvii–xviii. Topography etc. of Babylon, its siege and surrender.

The surrender of Babylon to 'Amr by the 'Treaty of Miṣr' recorded by Ṭabarī is a crucial problem in the history of the campaign, and Butler dealt first with the question of the topographical identity of Babylon and secondly with that of the Treaty both in *The Conquest* and in the two pamphlets here republished. These are excellently argued, and in spite of obvious inconsistencies in the evidence, he was probably right in accepting its terms as recorded in the usually unreliable Saifite tradition transmitted by Ṭabarī (pp. 2584 ff.) as referring to a surrender of Babylon (cf. Wellhausen, *Skizzen und Vorarb.* vi (1899) pp. 4 ff.; Hill, op. cit. [below; p. lxxiii], pp. 26–7), whereas in *The Conquest*, p. 324, he had applied it to the first surrender of Alexandria. Caetani, iv, pp. 303 ff. rejected the treaty, which is not recorded by Ibn 'Abd al-Ḥakam, *in toto*: see Butler, *Treaty*, pp. 51–3; Hill, pp. 47 ff.

The existence of the city of Babylon-Miṣr within which lay the Trajanic fort of the same name, doubted by Lane Poole, *Proc. Roy. Irish Acad.* 24, Sec. C, no. XIII, 1904, pp. 227–56, who wished to place the fort south of the existing remains on the outlying spur on the Moḳaṭṭam Hills, is argued forcibly by Butler, and is hardly open to doubt. The topography of Babylon-Qaṣr ash-Sham' given by Butler in this chapter, based essentially on the remains of the fort existing before 1882, remains fundamental. The construction of the Coptic Museum in 1908–10 between the Church of Abu Sarga and the al-Mu'allaqa church, and the rebuilding (1909 onwards) of the Orthodox Church of St. George, have altered the appearance of the whole area: see the history of the Museum by its founder, M. Simaika Pasha, *Guide sommaire du Musée Copte* (Cairo, 1937 [Engl. tr. 1938]; dedicated to the memory of Butler, whose *The Coptic Churches of Egypt*, 'a inspiré à l'auteur de ce guide l'idée d'obtenir du Gouvernement de placer les anciennes églises coptes sous le contrôle du Comité de Conservation des Monuments de l'Art Arabe, . . ., et de fonder le Musée Copte'); see Ch. Coquin, *Les Édifices chrét. du Vieux-Caire*, i (*IFAO*, Bull. d'étud. copt. ii, 1974), pp. 86 ff.; 155 ff.

On the topography of the first Arab settlement at al-Fusṭāṭ-Miṣr see Guest, *JRAS*, 1907, pp. 63 ff., 80 ff., 'The foundation of Fusṭāṭ and the Khiṭṭahs of that town' (with map) (cf. Butler, *Babylon, passim*); Caetani, op. cit. iv, pp. 541–95, a complete account (esp. pp. 570 ff.) of the Traditions regarding its foundations and development, based on Ibn 'Abd-al Ḥakam (pp. 91 ff., Torrey); see also Casanova, *Essai de reconstruction topographique de la ville d'Al Fousṭâṭ ou Miṣr* (*MIFAO* 35, 3 parts (I, i–iii), 1913–19), with historical sketch, I, iii, pp. xxiv–xxix; Aly Bay Baghat and A. Gabriel, *Fouilles d'al-Fousṭâṭ* (Paris, 1921); Scanlon, *Journ. Amer. Res. Cent. Egypt*, 4, 1965, pp. 7–30; 5, 1966, pp. 83–112; 6, 1967, pp. 65–86; 10, 1973, pp. 11–25; 11, 1974, pp. 81–91 (renewed excavations; cf. also id. in *The Islamic City*, ed. A. H. Hourani and S. Stern (1970), pp. 179–94). See also the excellent *aperçu* of the whole question by Becker, *EI*[1], s.v. Babylon and s.v. Cairo. For the Mosque of 'Amr see Wiet, *Matériaux pour un Corpus Inscriptionum Arabicarum*, I, ii (1930), pp. 1 ff.; Creswell, *EMA* I[2], pp. 36–8, 149–51 (enlargement of Mosque by Qurrah).

For references to Babylon in papyri of the early Arab period see Bell, *PLond.* iv, Index, p. 585, s.v., and cf. p. xviii (cf. Butler, *Babylon*, pp. 29–31); also Grohmann, *Ét. de Pap.* 8, 1957, pp. 9 ff., no. 2 (*SB* 9749) of A.D. 642 (see below, on ch. xxviii). The papp. use Φοσσάτον and Βαβυλών indifferently (see Bell, op. cit., p. xviii), and φοσ(σ)άτον = *fossatum*, a Roman military camp (see Lampe, *Patr. Gk. Lex.* s.v.; cf. *SEG* ix, 356,

l. 39), remains the most probable etymology of the name al-Fusṭāṭ. The interesting reference in *PRoss.-Georg.* iv, pp. 99 ff. (cf. above, I.A, II, sub ann. 619–28), probably from the Fayyūm, to the torture undergone by the writer of the letter at the hands of the Persians at 'τὸ φωσᾶτον':+*Εἶδεν ὁ ἀγαθός μο(υ) δεσπότηϲ ὅτι πολὰ κόπον ἔπαθα [. . . . . . . α]ὐτὰ ἀλλὰ καὶ τοὺς Πέρσο(υ)ς ἦλθεν ἐν τηνὶ ηει καὶ ἐξένεκέν μοι εἰς τῶ φωσᾶτον καὶ ἐβασάνισέν μοι*, need not refer to the site of the later al-Fusṭāṭ.

Chs. xxi–xxiii. Conquest of Alexandria, and end of Roman dominion

The date of the capitulation and subsequent evacuation of Alexandria depends on a series of associated arguments, of which the pivotal points must be the established date of the death of Heraclius in February 641 and that of Cyrus in March 642: see the detailed exposition in Butler, App. D, pp. 526–46. Butler, developing some arguments already advanced by E. W. Brooks and also (though he does not appear to have consulted him) Wellhausen (op. cit. p. lxx), argues forcibly for 8 Nov. 641 as the date of the capitulation, followed by the evacuation of the Imperial troops some eleven months later, i.e. *c.* Sept./Oct. 642. Caetani, op. cit. iv, pp. 96–103, though differing in some details, also assigns the cardinal events to the same dates. Amélineau, *Rev. Hist.* 120, 1915, pp. 20, 25, adheres to the older chronology (of Zotenberg), and places the capitulation in 642, the death of Cyrus in March 643, and the evacuation of the capital late in 643. As Butler showed, this cannot be right (see Brooks, *Byz. Zeitschr.* 4, 1895, p. 443; Butler, pp. 533 ff.). The second capitulation, of 646, raises no major chronological difficulties (see Butler, pp. 469 ff.).

The terms of the Treaty signed at Babylon by Cyrus and ʿAmr in November 641 (Dölger, *Regesten*, I, p. 25, no. 220), by which, after the capitulation, Arab suzerainty over Egypt was recognized, is recorded by John of Nikiou, chs. cxx, §§ 17–21 (pp. 193–4, trans. Charles). Butler claimed (pp. 334 ff.) that Cyrus, by concluding the treaty, had betrayed the best interests of the Empire and of Egypt, since Alexandria might have held out for a considerable time. Caetani, iv, p. 347, pointed out, rightly, I think, that the approval given to the treaty, both by the Alexandrian populace and authorities (John, ibid. §§ 22–4) and by the Imperial government, as also Cyrus' own subsequent grief for Egypt (cf. John, ibid. §§ 66–7), which is said to have caused his death, argue against this.

The nature of the capitulation and of the final treaty, in terms of the Arab categories of peaceful surrender and forcible conquest (*ṣulḥ, 'anwatan, dhimma*) and of the categories of taxation, *jizya* and *kharāj* (see below, p. lxxxiii) are excellently analysed in the useful monograph of D. R. Hill, *The Termination of Hostilities in the early Arab Conquests*, A.D. 634–56 (London and N.Y., n.d. [1974?]), pp. 34–53; this also contains an analysis of the various Traditions on the Conquest. Cf. above, p. lxx; cf. also Dennett, op. cit. below [p. lxxxii], pp. 72–3.

Chs. xxiv–xxv. Alexandria at the Conquest; the fate of the Library

Butler's two chapters on Alexandria as a city were written when excavations within the city area had hardly begun. Nevertheless, his account of the culture of the last age of Byzantine Alexandria (cf. above, on ch. viii) is a *tour de force*, within its own limits, and his discussion of the dispute concerning the fate of the Library still the best. He was, of course, not primarily concerned with the Ptolemaic and Roman periods of the city's existence, but it is difficult to isolate the evidence chronologically, whether it be literary or archaeological, and the reader should therefore consult the main topographical and archaeological discussions. Of these the most useful are: A. Adriani, *Repertorio d'arte dell'Egitto greco-romano*, Serie C, vols. i–ii (2 vols.; text and plates; 1966), which contains, pp. 201–51, a glossary of Alexandrian topography; A. Calderini, *Dizionario dei nomi geografici e topografici dell'Egitto greco-romano*, I, 1 (Cairo, 1935), which includes, pp. 55–206, an extremely full analysis of all the then available literary and documentary evidence for the city up to the Conquest; pp. 165–78 (an excellent collection of material) deals in detail with the Christian buildings. Cf. also the archaeological notes to Fraser, *Ptolemaic Alexandria* (Clarendon Press, 1972), vol. 1, ch. 1, with the notes in vol. 2; these, though dealing essentially with the Ptolemaic period, also give some indications of the archaeological material for the later periods. There is indeed little evidence that can be specifically referred to the period between Diocletian and the Conquest, except that relating to churches, monasteries, etc., within the city. E. Breccia's *Alexandria ad Aegyptum* (éd. fr. 1913; enlarged Eng. trans., 1922) remains an excellent combination of guide-book and historical narrative. The churches themselves (cf. p. 372) have totally disappeared, not least that of St. Mark (cf. p. 372 and

Add.); see, in addition to the works cited above (p. lxvii, esp. Meinardus), H. Leclercq in *Dict. d'arch. chrét.*, s.v. Alexandrie, cols. 1107–25 (detailed but out of date); L. Antonini, op. cit. above, on chs. xiii, xxvii, pp. 160 ff., s.v. Alessandria; J. Faivre in *Dict. d'hist. et géog. ecclés.*, s.v. Alexandrie (1914), cols. 289–369, an outstanding account of the Christian city. For the Caesarion (pp. 374–7), so called up till the Conquest, though transformed into a cathedral by Constantine, and dedicated to St. Michael, see Calderini, s.v. *Καισάρειον*, and (pp. 171–2) s.v. *Καισαρεία Ἐκκλησία*; Fraser, op. cit. i, p. 24; ii, p. 67 nn. 155 ff., and pp. 70–1 n. 162.

ʿAmr's famous description of the city, recorded by the Arab historians, in an *isnād* that goes back to Ibrahim ibn Saʿīd al-Balawī (in Ibn ʿAbd al-Ḥakam p. 82, ll. 1 ff.) finds a parallel in Michael the Syrian's description of the city, discussed in *JEA*, 37, 1951, pp. 103–8, 'A Syriac Notitia Urbis Alexandrinae', which is ultimately based on a Greek source.

For the *Obelisks* see Fraser, ibid., with n. 160; on the *Museum*, Calderini, s.v. *Μουσεῖον*, and Fraser, ii, p. 30, n. 77 (i, pp. 312–19, on the organization etc. of the Museum). Our knowledge of the *Serapeum* has been revolutionized by archaeological excavation during this century, but Butler's account of the physical structure of the Hill, and the description of the site in the Christian period, based on Rufinus' description, retains its value for the later period. On the archaeological side he was able to make use of Botti's early work, and of the rather drastic excavations carried out when the hill was first cleared of the Arab houses that encumbered it, but it was only with the excavations of A. Rowe during the Second World War that the nature and dimensions of the original Ptolemaic temples and subsequent Roman structures became apparent. See Fraser, op. cit. i, pp. 27–8 and 265–70, with the relevant notes. Butler's view that the Serapeum Hill was *the* Acropolis of Alexandria is irreconcilable with the Ptolemaic evidence: see Fraser, i, pp. 30–1.

Butler's account of the *Pharos* in Arab times may be supplemented by H. Thiersch's very full *Pharos, antike Islam und Occident* (Leipzig and Berlin, 1909), and by the papers by Don Miguel de Asín Palacios, *Al Andalus*, 1, 1933, pp. 241–92, and *Proc. Brit. Acad.* 19, 1933, pp. 277–92; further bibliography in Fraser, ii, pp. 45–6, n. 99. It is of interest that Thiersch's central but untenable contention that the Egyptian minaret derived its form from the Alexandrian pharos was anticipated by Butler (*Athenaeum*, 20 Nov. 1880, p. 681; here, p. 398). Butler does not seem to have known the almost contemporary study by F. Adler, *Zeitschr. f. Bauwesen*, 51, 1901, cols. 170–98, separately published as *Der Pharos von Alexandrien*, Berlin, 1901 (folio), which also deals in detail with the Arabic evidence.

The *Library*. Butler's discussion (pp. 401–26) of the question whether or not the Arabs burnt the Great Library, as the story in Arab sources of the Dialogue between ʿAmr and John Philoponus claims, leaves no room for any compromise solution (cf. already Bury's note on Gibbon, ch. 51, p. 454 n. 141). The story, long discredited, does not emerge until 500 years after the event (in Abū'l-Faraj), and Philoponus was not alive when ʿAmr entered the city (see the clear exposition of the evidence for Philoponus' date, and the history of the old error which assigned him to the seventh century on the basis of precisely the episode under consideration, by Gudeman, *RE*, s.v. Ioannes (21), cols. 1767 ff.; for recent studies on Philoponus see Altaner–Graef, *Patrology*, pp. 612–13, and the summary by H. Chadwick, *OCD*², s.v. Philoponus; Wolska, *Rech. sur la topogr. chrét. de Cosmas Indicopleustes* (Paris, 1962), pp. 147 ff., esp. pp. 161 ff.; W. Böhm, *Johannes Philoponus* (Munich, etc., 1967), pp. 25 ff.). Moreover, the story contains such evident fantasies as that of the books being used to heat the baths. Butler also maintains, on the basis of Orosius vi, 15, 31, who speaks of empty shelves in some of the temples in A.D. 416, and on that of the silence of John Moschus and Sophronius regarding any *public* library in Egypt at the beginning of the seventh century, that no such library then existed. That is perhaps to press the evidence too hard. It is sufficient that the evidence for the Arab conflagration does not withstand scrutiny. The type of 'destruction' is not unfamiliar; we may compare the Sassanian tradition preserved in the *Denkard* (cf. H. W. Bailey, *Zoroastrian Documents*² (Oxford, 1971), pp. 151 ff.) and in some Persian and Arabic texts deriving from Pahlavi originals (*Letter of Tansar*; ath-Thaʿālibī, etc.) of Alexander's destruction of the Avesta. Milman, on Gibbon (1840), ch. 51, p. 298 n. *, pointed out that in due course Muslim writers accused the Crusaders of having destroyed the Muslim library at Tripoli. Casanova, *CRAI* 1923, pp. 163–71, gives a good survey of the various legends, to which he adds that recorded by Landberg, *Arabica*, IV, p. 68 n. 1, that an English sea-captain in the year 1877 held Napoleon to be responsible for the conflagration.

Casanova maintains that the legend derives originally from the refusal of 'Umar to admit any book other than the Qur'ān; the ultimate consequence of this in popular imagination was the destruction of other books such as those in the Alexandrian library

Chs. xxvi–xxvii. Subjugation of Pentapolis, and restoration of Benjamin

For 'Amr's conquest of Pentapolis, John of Nik. ch. cxx, § 34, Ibn 'Abd al-Ḥakam, pp. 170 ff., Balādhurī, pp. 352 ff. Hitti, see the translations by Torrey and Gateau (above, p. l); Caetani, iv, pp. 532 ff.; vii, pp. 180 ff.; Hill, op. cit., pp. 53 ff. (who refutes Brunschvig's attack on the reliability of Ibn 'Abd al-Ḥakam [cf. above, p. li, (b), fin.]). For Benjamin's restoration in 644 by 'Amr see also Coquin, *Livre de la Consécration*, pp. 58–9.

Ch. xxviii. Muslim government of Egypt

This chapter, written before the publication of the large numbers of Greek, Arabic, and Greek–Arabic bilingual papyri of the first century A.H., and particularly those of the time of the governorship of Qurrah b. Sharīk (A.D. 690–714), has to be considered in the light of this material, which, though for the most part not itself of the time of the Conquest, enables us to discern more clearly than Butler could the precise nature of early Arab administration in Egypt. In this process of re-evaluation the labours of C. H. Becker, A. Grohmann, and Nabia Abbott take pride of place on the Arabic side, and those of H. I. (Sir Harold) Bell and R. Rémondon on the Greek. Inevitably, it is to these pioneer studies on the administration of early Muslim Egypt that I must refer the reader. What follows is only a guide through difficult country, not an attempt to rebuild the road.

Greek Papyri

Pride of place among documents of the time of the Conquest belongs to *PLond.* [i], no. cxiii, 10, pp. 222–3 (*WChr.* 8), a receipt of A.D. 639/40, and thus the earliest of all documents attesting the Arab invasion. It was issued by the elders of a Fayyūm village, Kaminoi, to the pagarch for 'payment for supplies furnished by the inhabitants in obedience to a requisition from the government' (Kenyon). This document, which evidently indicates preparations for the invasion, refers to the famous Cyrus as issuing the order: line 14, *διανομὰς γενομένας κατὰ κέλευσιν τοῦ δεσπότου ἡμῶν Κύρου τοῦ ἁγιοτ[άτ]ου καὶ θεοτιμή[του] πάπα*. The most remarkable of the Greek papyri of the period of the Conquest (after the evacuation of Alexandria in September/October 642) is *CPRF* 556 (published, Grohmann, *From the World of Arabic Papyri*, pp. 115–16), an order of ʿAmr to the pagarch of the Heracleopolite nome, Apa Kyros. Other Greek documents of the early Arab period, including that of the Conquest, were published, or republished, by Grohmann, *Étud. de Pap.* 8, 1957, pp. 5–40 (whence *SB* 9748 ff.), with useful notes. I give a list of these (along with their reference-number in Karabacek's *CPRF*, [for the full title see above, p. xlvi):

No. 1 (*SB* 9748; *CPRF* 552), undated, but certainly close to the Conquest, from Kom al-Haryān, Fayyūm, a demand from the Emir Ubeit for repayment of a sum of money by one Kalomenas.

2 (*SB* 9749; *CPRF* 553; cf. Butler, p. 363 n. 1), of 25 Jan.–24 Feb. A.D. 642, a declaration by the Dux of Arcadia, Philoxenus (cf. John of Nikiou, ch. cxx, § 29) regarding the delivery of corn due from the northern division of the Heracleopolite nome to Ἀριγᾶτος (i.e. Khārija b. Hudhafa; cf. Butler, p. 230). Line 1 refers to the seat of the pagarch Apa Kyros *ἐν Βαβυλῶνι*. From Ehnās (Ahnāsya), Heracleopolis Magna. Cf. *CPRF* 551 (published by Grohmann, *Proc. Soc. Hist. Stud. Cairo*, 1, 1951, pp. 52 ff.; cf. Butler, p. 235, n. 1), also an order of Khārija.

3 (*SB* 9755; *CPRF* 564), of 19 July 642, a declaration of receipt of 99 horses delivered to Apa Kyros. Ibid.

4 (*SB* 9750; *CPRF* 554; Butler, ibid.), of 25 Feb. 643, receipt of a loan. Ibid.

5 (*SB* 9751; *CPRF* 559), of 1 June, 643, order of Emir Abdella to pagarchs of Heracleopolite nome, Christophoros and Theodorakios, to provide grain and oil. Ibid.

6 (*SB* 9752; *CPRF* 560), of *c.* 643, order of Emir Jezīt for delivery of goods within five days. Kom al-Haryān.

7 (*SB* 9753; *CPRF* 561), of 29 Nov. 643, order of Emir Abdella to Kosmas, dioecete of Heracleopolite nome. Ehnās.

8 (*SB* 9754; *CPRF* 563), of 4 June 647, declaration of receipt by widow of goods belonging to deceased husband to topoteretes of Heracleopolite nome. Ibid.

9 (*SB* 9756; *CPRF* 565), of 14 Jan. 653, receipt for tax-payments issued by Kaeis, Emir of Heracleopolite nome, for inhabitants of village of Phys. Ibid.

10 (*SB* 9757)–13 (*SB* 9760) of this group are undated, but belong to the seventh century.

Also *CPRF* 555, of 26 Dec. 642, an order of the Emir Abdella to the headman of the village of Pfophtis, to sell fodder to the local Arab commander (= id. *Étud. de Pap.* 1, pp. 42 f.); 558 = Grohmann, *World of Arabic Papyri*, pp. 113–14, no. 1 (cf. Butler, p. 235 n. 1), of 25 Apr., 643 (= *SB* 9576).

Other interesting Greek documents of the early Arab years are those published by H. Zilliacus, *Eranos*, 38, 1940, pp. 78–107, three texts probably from Edfu (*SB* 8986–88), dated *c.* A.D. 640 (2019), 644/5, and 649 (cf. Wilcken, *Archiv* 15 (1953), pp. 120–2). (Note also the *PEdfu* texts of the reign of Heraclius, above, A II, sub ann. 619 and 628.)

The main group of documents of the first period of Arab rule, those from Kom Ishqaw, the ancient Aphrodito (whence came also the documents of the age of Justinian, noted above, pp. xlviii), consists of the correspondence of the Ummayad governor Qurrah b. Sharīk (for whom see Becker, *PSRI* [below, p. lxxxi], pp. 15 ff.). The largest collection of these is that published as *PLond.* iv, by H. I. Bell (1910), a masterpiece of decipherment and interpretation; there are also some pieces of the same archive in *PLond.* i and v. The second large collection of Qurrah documents from Kom Ishqaw is that published as *PRoss.-Georg.* iv by P. Jernstedt (1927). These documents consist largely of Qurrah's correspondence with the pagarch Basilius, in whose archives they were preserved; they belong within the years 698–722, and especially to 708–11. They are either wholly Greek, or Greek documents with Greek, or occasionally Greek and Arabic, protocols (the earliest bilingual protocol is that of the reign of Muʿāwiya I, attached to an ἐντάγιον (order of requisition) of A.H. 54 (Nov. A.D. 674) from Nessana in the Negeb, Grohmann, *Österr. byz. Ges. Jahrb.* 9, 1960, pp. 1 ff., no. 2 = Kraemer, *PColtNessana*, iii, no. 60; Bell, *Proc. Amer. Philos. Soc.* (below), p. 538 f., no. 1). For the purely Arabic papyri from the same archive see below, under 'Arabic Papyri'.

Bell published several valuable historical studies apropos of the Aphrodito papyri, in which he related them to the early history of the Muslim administration, and since significant changes do not seem to have been made until the second century A.H. (see N. Abbott, op. cit. below, pp. 13–14), these documents are valid evidence for the immediate post-Conquest period. In addition to the Introduction to *PLond.* iv, see the following articles by Bell: *JHS* 28, 1908, pp. 97–120, 'The Aphrodito papyri'; *JEA* 12, 1926, pp. 265–81, 'Two official letters of the Arab period' (a firman from the Dux Thebaidis of A.D. 697 or 712; and an improved version of *PLond.* iv, 1393, of interest for the machinery relating to the annual naval κοῦρσον); *Byz. Zeitschr.* 28, 1929, pp. 278–86, 'Organisation of Egypt under the Ummayad Khalifs'; he also published translations of the correspondence in *PLond.* iv in *Der Islam* 2, 1911, pp. 269–83, and 372–84; 3, 1912, pp. 132–40 and 369–73; 4, 1913, pp. 87–96; 17, 1928, pp. 4–8 (the articles from 1912 onwards are translations of some of the accounts in the archive). See also, on the ἐντάγιον, his article in *Proc. Amer. Philos. Soc.* 89, 1945, pp. 531–42, 'The Arabic bilingual entagion', apropos of the bilingual entagia in *PColtNessana*. For the numerous indications in the Qurrah papyri of the obligation of the Arab settlers (*muhājirūn*; μωαγαρῖται) in Egypt to serve in the Saracenic fleet see, in addition to *PLond.* iv, pp. xxxii ff., Bell, *Byz. Zeitschr.* loc. cit., and Kahle, *Der Islam*, 12, 1921, pp. 32 ff., A. M. Fahmy, *Muslim Sea Power in the Eastern Mediterranean from the 7th to the 10th Cent.* ([London], 1950), *passim*, which is essentially an analysis of the relevant material in the papyri; for the *muhājirūn* see especially pp. 103–5. [Another book *by the same author with the same title*, but with a different preface, published in Cairo in 1966 ('First Edition, 1966'), is in fact a different book, and has no reference to papyri or other relevant material, and is concerned mainly with naval operations. I refer here to the London publication only, without attempting to establish the relationship between the two works.]

A further collection of Greek papyri of the first century A.H. (703–14) was published by R. Rémondon, *Papyrus grecs d'Apollônos Anô* (Cairo, 1953, Docs. de fouilles de IFAO du Caire, 19); these were discovered at Edfu in 1921–2, and are letters to and from Papas, pagarch of Apollonos Ano. Though contemporary with the Aphrodito papyri of the time of Qurrah, they are more strictly concerned with local administration, for Papas, unlike Basilius at Aphrodito, communicates only with the Emir of the Thebaid, and not with the governor of Egypt. There are no entagia in this archive. *PColtNessana* III (Princeton, 1958) contains many Greek papyri of the later seventh century: also see the bilingual entagia, nos. 60–6, all of the caliphate of Muʿāwiya I and his immediate successors, and thus earlier than any of the entagia of the Qurrah papyri; for the earliest of the bilingual entagia from Nessana see the publication by Grohmann, noted above (*Österr. byz. Ges. Jahrb.*). Numerous texts in Wessely, *Stud. Pal. u. Pap.* iii, viii (*Pklein. Form* (1908)) and x, and *Wien. Denks.* 37, 1889 (cf. *SB* 4658 ff.), also belong to the seventh and eighth centuries. Other Greek documents of the pre-Qurrah period are *BGU* 312, a μίσθωσις of A.D. 658, *PRoss.-Georg.* iii, no. 52, of A.D. 674, and no. 53, of 674 or 675, and *PWürzb.* 19, an ἐπίσταλμα τοῦ σωματισμοῦ, probably of A.D. 652; cf. also E. Wipszycka, *Byzantion*, 39, 1969, pp. 180 ff. (*SB* 10805).

Finally, I may call attention to the interesting Greek papyrus of A.D. 779 (probably) published by M. Norsa, *Ann. Sc. Norm. Pisa* 19 (N.S. 10), 1941, pp. 164 ff., referring to the perennial problem of the pursuit of fugitives (φυγάδες) (cf. Becker, *Zeitschr. f. Assyr.* 20, 1907, pp. 96–7, no. XIV; Wilcken, *Archiv* 15, p. 122; Fahmy, op. cit., pp. 112–14); and to that published by Préaux, *Chr. d'Ég.* 38, 1963, pp. 268 ff. (*SB* 9868), of the early eighth century, referring to ἀποχώρησις from an οὐσία.

Coptic documents. These, though very numerous, are not usually dated (at most by month and indiction), and though many of them are assignable to the seventh and eighth centuries on palaeographical grounds, they do not provide fixed dates. Coptic documents were included in the Kom Ishqaw archive: see Crum, in *PLond.* iv, pp. 435–525, nos. 1494–1646, several of which (1494–1517) are concerned with conditions of hire etc. of sailors and workmen by the Arab authorities; others are concerned with the problem of fugitives (1518–28; cf. above)—mostly of the time of Qurrah. Other Coptic papyri of the Qurrah period are to be found in Grohmann, *Arab Papyri of the Egyptian Library*, II, nos. 164 ff. The other large collection of Coptic documents is in the Rainer collection: see J. Krall, *CPR* ii, *Rechtsurkunden* (1895), and W. Till, *CPR* iv, *Die koptischen Rechtsurkunden der Papyrussamml. der öst. Nat. Bibl.* (1958). For a Coptic document of the Persian period see above, on I.B (v).

Arabic Papyri. The main publications of Arabic papyri come from the enormous purchases made by Th. Graf in the nineties of the last century, and eventually presented to the Hofsbibliothek (later Nationalbibliothek) in Vienna by the Erzherzog Rainer, and published intermittently, along with the Byzantine papyri from the same source, by J. Karabacek: see Karabacek, *Papyrus Erzherzog Rainer; Führer durch die Ausstellung* (Vienna, 1894; *CPRF*); cf. also A. Grohmann, *CPR* iii, 1, pp. 3–14; id., *Einführ. u. Chrestom.* [see below,

p. lxxxii], pp. 54 ff.; and the correspondence of Graf, Karabacek, and the Erzherzog Rainer published by H. Hunger, *Aus der Vorgeschichte der Papyrussamml. der österr. Nationalbibl.* (*Mitt. Pap.-Samml. der österr. Nationalbibl.* N.S. 7, 1962). Many of these papyri were subsequently lost (including the Pahlavi pieces, for which see above, I.F), but in addition to those published or described by Karabacek many were published by Grohmann, *CPR* iii, Series Arabica, I, 1 (Vienna, 1923/4), 'Allgemeine Einführung in die arabischen Papyri'; I, 2, 'Protokolle' (from different collections including the B.M.), the dated texts of which range from A.D. 705 to 724. A rough idea of the extent of this collection in 1933 is provided by the statistics given by Preisendanz, *Papyrusfunde u. Papyrusforsch.* (Leipzig, 1933), p. 296: 'Inventarisiert: 22000 griech., lat., 1400 hiërogl., hierat., demot., 11000 kopt., 50000 arab. Pap.'; for complete figures see Grohmann, op. cit., p. 10. For other publications by Grohmann of, and relating to, Arabic papyri see below.

The other main collection of Arabic papyri is the Heidelberg collection, of various provenance, published by Becker, *Papyri Schott-Reinhardt* I (*PSR*) (*Veröffentl. aus der Heidelberg. Papyrussamml.* iii, 1 (1906)), which also contains some Qurrah papyri, though most of these were published by Becker separately. The Qurrah Arabic papyri from Kom Ishqaw in the B.M. were published by Becker in *Zeitschr. f. Assyr.* 20, 1907, pp. 68–94, nos. i–xii. The small collection of Qurrah Arabic papyri in the Oriental Institute, Chicago, was published by Nabia Abbott, *The Ḳurrah Papyri from Aphrodito in the Oriental Institute* (Orient. Instit., Univ. of Chicago, Studies in anc. oriental civilisation, no. 15, 1938), to which is prefixed an excellent account of the systems of taxation and administration in Egypt in the last Byzantine age; cf. id., *Ars Islamica*, 8, 1941, pp. 71 ff. For another group of eight Qurrah papyri from the Aphrodito archive, dating from A.D. 708/9–713, acquired by Jouguet at Luxor in 1920, see H. Cadell, *Recherches de Papyrologie*, 4, 1967, pp. 107–60 (*SB* 10453–60). On pp. 138–59 she discusses the chronology of the papyri and gives a chronological list of the known items. On early texts in the Prague collection see Grohmann, *Archiv orientální*, 10, 1938, pp. 149–62, nos. I and II. Those bought by Vogliano in Cairo are published by Grohmann in *PMil.* I (1937), pp. 243–69 (ten Qurrah fragments out of a total of fifty-seven). See also Grohmann, *Arabic Papyri in the Egyptian Library*, I (1934), pp. 1 ff., nos. 1–18 (dated protocols of the time of Qurrah, mostly of unknown provenance), III (1938), nos. 146–66 (letters of Qurrah to Basilius and of pagarchs to Qurrah (nos. 164–6 Coptic)).

Grohmann, in addition to his 'Allgemeine Einführung' (see above) and the other publications mentioned above, published several chrestomathies of Arabic papyrology dealing particularly with the early history of Muslim Egypt, as well as with writing and writing materials. These are in some measure repetitive, but all contain early texts not published elsewhere. They are: (1) *Études de Papyrologie* 1, 1932, pp. 23–95; (2) *From the World of Arabic Papyri* (Roy. Soc. Hist. Stud. Cairo, 1952), with text, translation, and commentary of over 100 select papyri from A.H. 22 onwards; (3) *Einführ. u. Chrestomathie z. arab. Papyruskunde,* I (Monogr. *Archivu orientálního* publ. by Czechoslovak. Orient. Inst. xiii/1, 1955); (4) *Handbuch der Orientalistik,* pt. 1, Ergänz.-Bd. II. 1 (1966), I, Arabische Chronologie, II, Arabische Papyruskunde, the latter containing an expanded version of (1); (5) *Arabische Paläographie* (2 vols.; Österr. Akad. Wiss., Phil.-hist. kl., Denkschr. 94 (1 & 2), 1967, consisting of a first volume on writing-materials, etc., and a second on palaeography).

Becker, like Bell, published important articles on the history of early Muslim Egypt arising from his study of the papyri. See particularly *Der Islam,* 2, 1911, pp. 359–71, 'Historische Studien über das Londoner Aphroditowerk'; also his earlier *Beiträge z. Geschichte Ägyptens unter den Islam* (2 vols., Straßburg, 1902–3), which was published in the same year as *The Arab Conquest.* For his publication of the Arabic papyri of the Aphrodito material see *Zeitschr. f. Assyr.* 20, 1907, pp. 68–104, 'Arabische Papyri des Aphroditofundes'; *Der Islam,* 2, 1911, pp. 245–68, 'Neue arabische Papyri des Aphroditofundes' (Cairo material). His more general articles (e.g. *Klio,* 9, 1909, pp. 206 ff.) are republished in his *Islamstudien,* I (1924; repr. 1967), an essential work (no Index).

On the economic life of early Muslim Egypt in general see the collections of papyri noted above, with their introductions (especially Bell, *PLond.* iv, pp. xxxv ff.), and Grohmann, *Archiv orientální,* 7, 1935, pp. 437–72, 'The economic life of early Arab times'; Casson, *TAPA* 69, 1938, pp. 274–91, 'Tax collection problems in early Arab Egypt'. In the field of taxation, for which Butler used mainly the classic theoretical account in al-Māwardī (see p. 449 n. 1), D. C. Dennett's *Conversion and the Poll Tax in early Islam* (Harvard Historical Monographs, 22, Harvard, 1950) is an important and independent study of the evidence, based both on the literary sources and on the Kom Ishqaw papyri (see pp. 65–115), in which the author argues strongly against the traditional view, as developed by Wellhausen, in *Das arabische Reich*, pp. 168 ff. (Eng. trans., *The Arab Kingdom and its fall* (Calcutta, 1927), pp. 270 ff.), and accepted by Butler (pp. 451 ff.), Becker, Bell, Caetanì, Tritton, and others, that the description of the taxation of the early period by Muslim writers is a reflection of the practice of their own day after the reforms of the 2nd cent. A.H., and does not correspond to the original terms imposed at the Conquest. Dennett's study, which has found general acceptance, shows very clearly that (*a*) the original application of taxation varied from province to province, and (*b*) that in Egypt the papyri (carefully analysed by D.) as well as the historical accounts indicate that the Arab authorities exacted a specified poll-tax (*jizya*) as well as a land-tax (*kharāj*), words which could also mean simply 'tax', and did not restrict themselves to the collection of an over-all tribute by treaty (*'ahd*), as Wellhausen claimed. F. Løkkegarde's *Islamic Taxation in the Classic Period* (Copenhagen, 1950), reaches much the same conclusion as Dennett in his analysis of the Fiqh traditions: see especially pp. 72 ff., 128 ff. Although Dennett's work may need modification in detail (cf. Gibb, *Middle East Journal*, 5, 1951, pp. 117–18; for a lengthy bibliography see Ben Shemesh [below], ii, pp. 78–81), it represents an important advance in the understanding of the nature of the early Muslim taxation, and also in the correct interpretation of this aspect of the Aphrodito texts. (The works of Dennett and Løkkegarde have been reprinted in one volume by the Arno Press, with the title *Islamic Taxation. Two Studies* (N.Y., 1972).) The 3 vols. of the early Taxation texts translated with notes by A. Ben Shemesh as *Taxation in Islam* (Brill, 1958–69 (vol. i, *Yaḥyā ben Ādam's Kitāb al Kharāj*; vol. ii, *Qudāma b. Ja'far's Kitāb al-Kharāj*, pt. VII; vol. iii, *Abu Yusuf's Kitāb al-Kharāj*)) show that already by the second century A.H. *jizya* and *kharāj* had acquired generalized meanings. The Introduction to vol. iii is a valuable study of theoretical and applied taxation. Important evidence on this topic is also provided by Abū 'Ubayd al-Qāsim b. Sallām's *Kitāb al-Amwāl* (Cairo, 1353/1934), analysed by Hill, op. cit., and Ben Shemesh, i, pp. 14 ff.

For the economic activity of the churches and monasteries see above, on chs. xiii, xxvii.

CHAPTER I

REVOLT OF HERACLIUS

Brief sketch of the Emperors from Justinian to Maurice. The Roman Empire in the reign of Phocas. State of Egypt. Revolt of Pentapolis under the leadership of Heraclius. Plan of campaign. The common story, as told by Gibbon, discredited. The Chronicle of John, bishop of Nikiou in the Delta.

AT the opening of the seventh century the Roman Empire seemed passing from decline to dissolution. Sixty years earlier the power of Justinian had spread from the Caucasus and Arabia in the east to the Pillars of Hercules in the west, and his strong personality so filled men's minds that it seemed, as the phrase ran, as if 'the whole world would not contain him[1].' His splendour was equal to his power, and for a while at least his wisdom was equal to his splendour. Moreover his triumphs in the realms of science and art were even more striking than his exploits in war: for of the two foremost achievements by which his name is remembered, the Code and Digest of Justinian still remain the greatest masterpieces of jurisprudence, while the Cathedral of St. Sophia stands to all time as the most splendid monument and model of Byzantine architecture.

But the menace of decay was felt even in Justinian's lifetime. To the mischief, moral and political, which threatened the state, were added physical calamities. The whole of the East was scourged by a plague, which broke out at Pelusium, and swept through

[1] Professor Bury, quoting from Procopius, *History of the Later Roman Empire*, vol. i. pp. 470–1.

Egypt to Libya and through Palestine to Persia and Constantinople. After the plague came an earthquake, which wrought almost as much destruction to the cities as the black death to the peoples of the Empire. The last days of the great lawgiver were clouded by a sense of gloom and foreboding. The government was breaking up, even before his successor Justin closed his brief and nerveless reign in insanity. Tiberius, who came to the throne in 578, gave some promise of better things. He might at least have essayed to arrest the process of decay: but his life was cut short before he could prove his worth, and he bequeathed to Maurice a bankrupt exchequer, a discontented people, and a realm out of joint.

Only a man of the strongest brain and of unerring judgement could have dealt with such a crisis: and Maurice, though well-meaning, was not the man for the task. That blind disregard of changing circumstance which so often ruins the application of wise principles marred and thwarted his policy. His army reforms and his knowledge of military tactics—on which he wrote excellently—could not save his forces from defeat; while his zeal for economy to repair the finances of the state failed in its purpose, and so estranged and wearied his people, that they tossed the crown contemptuously to an illiterate and deformed rebel centurion—Phocas.

It now seemed as if nothing could save the Empire from ruin. The only strength of Phocas was that of a tyrant upheld by a licentious army and a corrupt nobility—a strength which diminished with every mile's distance from the capital. Thus all the provinces of the Empire lay under a kind of agony of misrule, which was probably lightest in the regions torn by war with the Persians or with the northern barbarians.

Certainly no part of the Roman dominion was in worse plight than Egypt. There Justinian's efforts to force the orthodox religion on the nonconforming Copts had been partly balanced by Theodora's open sympathy for their creed [1]: but all such sympathy was recklessly cancelled by Justin. So the ancient and bitter strife between the Melkite and Monophysite parties was more embittered than ever: and for the Copts it filled the whole horizon of thought and hope. Where the two mainsprings of government were the religious ascendency and the material profit of the Byzantine Court, and where the machinery worked out steady results of oppression and misery, it is small wonder that the clash of arms was often heard in Alexandria itself, while not only was Upper Egypt haunted by bands of brigands [2] and harried by raids of Beduins or Nubians, but even the Delta was the scene of riots and feuds little short of civil war [3]. The fact is that the whole country was in a state of smouldering insurrection.

Phocas' reign began on November 22, A. D. 602. On that day he was crowned with all due solemnity by the Patriarch Cyriacus in the church of St. John at Constantinople, and entering the city by the Golden Gate drove in state by the great colonnades and through the principal streets amid crowds that received him with joyful acclamations. By the

[1] See Prof. Bury's *History of the Later Roman Empire*, vol. ii. pp. 8–9, where he quotes from R. Payne Smith's translation of the Syriac *John of Ephesus* a curious account of the conversion of the Nobadae, who occupied a region east of the Nile in Upper Egypt.

[2] See John Moschus, *Pratum Spirituale*, ap. Migne, *Patr. Gr.* c. 143.

[3] John of Nikiou (tr. Zotenberg), pp. 529 seq.

beginning of the year 609 the Empire was ready for revolution. It began at Pentapolis. The common form which the story takes is that Crispus, who had married the daughter of Phocas, incurred the Emperor's furious resentment by setting up his own statue with that of his bride in the Hippodrome: and that having thus quarrelled, he plotted rebellion and invited Heraclius, the Prefect of Africa, to put the scheme in action. The fact however is—and Cedrenus expressly records it—that Heraclius was planning insurrection unbidden of Crispus. Indeed Crispus was not the man to take any initiative: but when he heard of the unrest in Pentapolis, then he ventured to send secret letters of encouragement, and promised help in the event of Heraclius making a movement on Constantinople. Heraclius himself was somewhat old for an adventure of the kind[1]—he cannot have been less than sixty-five—but in his son and namesake, who was now in the prime of life, and in Nicetas his friend and lieutenant-general, he saw at once the fitting instruments of his design.

The plan of campaign has been much misunderstood. Gibbon lends the great weight of his authority to the somewhat childish story that the two commanders agreed upon a race to the capital, the one advancing by sea and the other by land, while the crown was to reward the winner[2]. They were starting, be it remembered, from Cyrene[3]:

[1] He had been commander-in-chief in the Persian wars under Maurice.

[2] Even Diehl adopts this legend: see *L'Afrique Byzantine*, p. 520.

[3] Some authorities make Heraclius start from Carthage: but from John of Nikiou it is fairly clear that the younger Heraclius set out from Cyrene, and that some time after his departure

and given anything like similar forces at starting, surely a more unequal competition was never devised. Heraclius had merely to cross the Mediterranean, coast along Greece and Macedonia, and then to fling his army on the capital: while Nicetas, according to the received theory, marching to Egypt, had to tear that country from the grasp of Phocas, then to make a long and toilsome journey through Palestine, Syria, Cilicia and Asia Minor, under such conditions that even a succession of brilliant victories or the collapse of all resistance would, in mere point of time, put him out of the running for the prize. No: if there was any idea at all of a race for empire, which is extremely doubtful, the course was marked out with far more simplicity and equality. For it must be obvious that the province of Pentapolis could not have furnished material for a very considerable army, still less for two armies: and what the leader of each expedition had to do was not merely to set out for Byzantium, but to raise the standard of revolt as he went, to gather supplies and reinforcements, and then possibly to unite in dealing a crushing blow at the capital. In pursuance of this plan Heraclius was to adventure by sea and Nicetas by land—unquestionably: but what Gibbon and the Greek historians have failed to see clearly is this—that while the immediate objective of Heraclius was Thessalonica, that of Nicetas was Alexandria: and that all depended on the accession or subjugation of these two towns for the success of the enterprise.

It is hardly doubtful that Heraclius had intimate relations with the people of Thessalonica, or at

the elder Heraclius made an expedition against Carthage and after capturing the city took up his residence there.

least with a party among them: while Nicetas calculated on a welcome or a slight resistance in Egypt, though, as will be shown, his calculations were upset by the unforeseen intervention of a formidable enemy. But I must again insist—in opposition to Gibbon—that Nicetas' one aim was the conquest of Egypt: that Egypt was the pivot on which his combinations with Heraclius turned, and the only barrier between him and Constantinople: and that, when once he possessed the recruiting-ground and the granary of the Nile together with the shipping and dockyards of Alexandria, it would have been madness to plunge through Syria and Asia instead of moving straight to the Dardanelles and joining forces with Heraclius.

This then was the plan: Heraclius with his galleys was to make for Thessalonica and there prepare a formidable fleet and army, while Nicetas was to occupy Alexandria—the second city of the Empire—so as at once to cut off the corn supplies from Constantinople, and to secure the strongest base for equipping an armament against Phocas, or at least to prevent his deriving help from that quarter [1].

The whole incident is dismissed by the well-known Byzantine historians in a few lines, and the part played by Egypt in the revolution has hitherto scarcely been suspected. But an entirely new chapter of Egyptian history has been opened since

[1] The nearly contemporary Armenian historian Sebeos justly appreciates the action of Heraclius. He says: 'Then Heraclius the general, with his army which was in the region of Alexandria, revolted from Phocas: and, making himself tyrant, he occupied the land of the Egyptians.' A scanty account, but it hinges the success of the rebellion on the capture of Egypt, as a right estimate of the situation requires.

the discovery—or rather since the translation into a European language—of an Ethiopic MS. version of the Chronicle of John, bishop of Nikiou, an important town in the Delta of Egypt. John himself, who lived in the latter half of the seventh century of our era, must have spoken with many old men who witnessed or remembered the events connected with the downfall of Phocas. His Chronicle, therefore, is of very great importance. In spite of its passage from language to language, where the MS. is not mutilated, its accuracy is often most minute and striking: and though there are errors and inconsistencies, they are balanced by the amount of new knowledge which it discloses. Indeed the work throws all sorts of novel and curious lights on the history of the Eastern Empire, of the Patriarchs of Alexandria, and of Egypt generally during a period of extraordinary interest—a period which has suffered even greater neglect than is warranted by the scantiness and imperfection of the materials; and it supplements and corrects in many curious ways the inadequate and faulty narratives of Theophanes, Cedrenus, and Nicephorus.

CHAPTER II

THE STRUGGLE FOR EGYPT

March on Egypt. Leontius, Prefect of Mareotis, in the plot. The country between Pentapolis and Egypt. Its fertility and population. Phocas alarmed about Alexandria. Nicetas, advancing from the west, wins a battle close to the city. His welcome. Bonôsus, Phocas' general, hurries from Syria. Nikiou surrenders to him. His army reaches Alexandria. Naval assault under Paul repulsed.

FROM the Egyptian bishop's Chronicle we learn that even in Pentapolis there was some fighting. By large expenditure of money Heraclius assembled here a force of 3,000 men and an army of 'barbarians,' i. e. doubtless Berbers, which he placed under the command of 'Bonâkîs' as he is called in the Ethiopic corruption of a Greek name. By their aid he won an easy victory over the imperial generals Mardius, Ecclesiarius, and Isidore, and at one blow put an end to the power of Phocas in that part of Africa. At the same time, 'Kîsîl' the governor of Tripolis sent a contingent which probably passed to the south of Pentapolis. In any case Nicetas now began his advance along the coast towards Alexandria, and was joined at some point by both Kîsîl and Bonâkîs. He was secure of a friendly reception up to the very borders of Egypt: for Leontius, Prefect of Mareotis, the Egyptian province on the western side of Alexandria, had been won over, and had promised a considerable body of troops.

It is thought that nowadays such a march would

lie almost entirely through a waterless desert; but there is abundant evidence to show that in the seventh century of our era there were many flourishing towns, palm groves, and fertile tracts of country, where now little is known or imagined to be but a waste of rocks and burning sands. The subject is one of some interest to scholars and to explorers, and some brief remarks upon it may be pardoned. From Ptolemy we know that the province of Cyrene ceased on the eastern side at a city called Darnis, where the province of Marmarica began. Moving eastward, Nicetas must have passed among other places the city of Axilis, the towns of Paluvius, Batrachus, and Antipyrgus, and the promontory of Cataeonium, all in the nome of Marmarica. The nome of Libya began near Panormus, and included among other towns Catabathmus, Selinus, and Paraetonium [1], or Ammonia as it was also called according to Strabo. Paraetonium was the capital and the seat of government of the Prefect: the name seems to have lingered in the Arabic Al Barṭûn. Still further east in the same nome we come to Hermea, then to Leucaspis; and half way between Leucaspis and Chimovicus began the nome of Mareotis, in which the best known towns were Plinthine in Tainia, Taposiris Magna, the fortress of Chersonesus, and the city of Marea or Mareotis.

Both Ptolemy and Strabo give many other names, and it is certain that in the first century Egyptian territory was regarded as ending where Cyrenaic began, and that there was no break of impassable country between them. Later the nome of Libya suffered some decay, and in the sixth century

[1] It was from Paraetonium that Alexander the Great struck off into the desert on his famous visit to the temple of Ammon.

Justinian compensated the Prefect for the poverty of his province by throwing the nome of Mareotis in with his government. But even then the way from Pentapolis to Alexandria was in well-defined stages, with no serious gaps or breaks: nor had the continuous character of the route changed at the time of which I am writing. This is proved beyond doubt. For we know that early in the seventh century the Persian army, after the subjugation of Egypt, moved on by land to the conquest of Pentapolis, and returned after a successful campaign, in which, according to Gibbon, were finally exterminated the Greek colonies of Cyrene. This, be it remembered, was only eight or nine years after the march of Nicetas. But Gibbon is altogether mistaken in his view of the devastation wrought by Chosroes' troops in that region. Great it was, but in no way fatal or final. On the contrary, less than thirty years later, when 'Amr Ibn al 'Aṣî the Saracen captured Alexandria, his thoughts turned naturally to Pentapolis, and to Pentapolis he went, conquering Barca and Cyrene. There is no record or hint of either march being regarded as a great military achievement or triumph over natural difficulties.

Indeed nothing could be more false than to picture the route as lying across inhospitable deserts. For there is express evidence that practically the whole of the coast provinces west of Egypt continued well populated and well cultivated for some three centuries after they fell under Arab dominion. The Arab writer Al Maḳrîzî mentions the city of Lubîah as the centre of a province between Alexandria and Maraḳîah, showing that the classical names Libya and Marmarica were retained by the Arabs almost unaltered. In another passage he says that, after passing the cities of Lubîah and Maraḳîah, one enters the province of Pentapolis: and Al Kuda'î and Al Mas'ûdî concur in similar testimony. The canton of Lubîah contained twenty-four boroughs besides villages. Maḳrîzî's account of Maraḳîah—taken from Quatremère's version of it—is in substance as follows: 'Maraḳîah is one of the western districts of Egypt, and forms the limit of the country. The city of that name is two stages, or twenty-four miles, distant from Sanṭarîah. Its territory is very extensive and contains a vast number of palm-trees, of cultivated fields, and of running springs. There the fruits have a delicious flavour, and the soil is so rich that every grain of wheat sown produces from ninety to a hundred ears. Excellent rice too grows in great abundance. Even at the present day there are very many gardens in this canton. Formerly Maraḳîah was occupied by tribes of Berbers; but in the year 304 A. H. (916 A. D.) the inhabitants of Lubîah and Maraḳîah were so harried by the Prince of Barca that they withdrew to Alexandria. From that date onwards Maraḳîah steadily declined, and now it is almost in ruins. But it still preserves some remnant of its ancient splendour[1].'

The last words evidently refer to the city, not the province: they are remarkable as showing how much was left even in 1400 A. D. and we may mention, as at any rate curious, the fact that the Portolanos, or Venetian navigation charts, of about the year 1500, show at least an unbroken series of names along this part of the shores of the Mediterranean. But Maḳrîzî has also something to say

[1] *Mém. Géog. et Hist.* ch. i. pp. 374–5.

of Mareotis. Formerly he declares that it was covered with houses and gardens, which at one time were dotted over the whole country westward up to the very frontiers of Barca. In his own time Mareotis was only a town in the canton of Alexandria, and used that city as the market for the abundant produce of its fruit-gardens. Champollion says that under the old Egyptian Empire it was the capital of Lower Egypt, and gradually sank into decay after the foundation of Alexandria. In the time of Vergil and Strabo it was, as they testify, at least renowned for its wine. To-day the ruins that mark the site, twelve miles west of Alexandria, are practically unknown, but the soil beneath the sand is found to be alluvial, in confirmation of its ancient repute for fertility.

It is, then, clear that before the Arab conquest there was a continuous chain of towns, and an almost unbroken tract of cultivated land, stretching from Alexandria to Cyrene, and that the march of Nicetas demanded no great qualities of generalship or endurance. Even at the present time it is probable that the difficulties of the route are greatly exaggerated: for Muslim pilgrims constantly make their way on foot from Morocco, Tunis, and Tripoli along the coast to Egypt. The country abounds in Greek and Roman remains; but the people are fanatics of the lowest type. The wandering Arab keeps out the wandering scholar, and the whole region, though its shores are washed by the Mediterranean and lie almost in sight of Italy and Greece, is more lost to history and to archaeology than if it were in the heart of the Sahara. The fact is, of course, as much due to the rule of the Turk as to the fanaticism of the Beduin: but the two form a combination enough to make travel almost impossible. But if ever the country falls under a civilized power, it will be a splendid field for exploration, and might even, with proper engineering works, resume something of its ancient fertility and prosperity.

This digression, however, has taken long enough. It enables us to follow the movements of Nicetas' army, and to infer that though he met with few perils on the way, yet that the time occupied on the march must have been considerable. Meanwhile in the Egyptian capital plot and counterplot were working. Theodore, son of Menas, who had been Prefect of Alexandria under the Emperor Maurice, and one Tenkerâ (by whom Zotenberg wrongly thinks Crispus may be meant), had engaged together to put Phocas to death and secure the crown for Heraclius. The Melkite Patriarch of Alexandria, another Theodore, who had received his seat from Phocas, knew nothing of this conspiracy; but John, the Governor of the Province and Commander of the Garrison, and yet another Theodore, the Controller of Finance, revealed it to him: whereupon the three addressed a joint letter of warning to Phocas.

The Emperor well knew the uncertain temper of the Egyptians: and, with a view to humour them, he had lately sent from Syria a large consignment of lions and leopards for a wild-beast show, together with a collection of fetters and instruments of torture, as well as robes of honour and money, for just apportionment between his friends and foes. But on receipt of the letter from the Patriarch, while professing to disdain the menace of revolt, yet knowing the supreme necessity of holding Egypt at all costs, he neither faltered in resolve nor paltered in action. Summoning the Prefect of Byzantium, he took from him a solemn oath of allegiance, and dispatched him with large reinforcements both for Alexandria and for the important garrison towns of Manûf and Athrîb in the Delta. At the same time he sent urgent orders to Bonôsus in Syria to hurl all his available troops on Egypt. For Bonôsus was now at Antioch, where he had been sent, with the title of 'Count of the East,' to crush a revolt of the Jews against the Christians—a revolt which seems to have been rather religious than political, although the threads of politics and of religion are often indistinguishable in the tissue of history at this period. Yet so well or so ill did Bonôsus achieve his bloody work by wholesale massacre, by hanging, drowning, burning, torturing, and casting to wild beasts, that he earned a name of execration and terror. Indeed he was a man after Phocas' own heart—a 'ferocious hyena' who revelled in slaughter—and he hailed Phocas' message with delight.

Meanwhile Nicetas was nearing Alexandria on the west. The town of Kabsain (which may possibly be identified with Fort Chersonesus) surrendered, and the garrison were spared, but the prisoners of the revolting faction were released and joined the march. Messengers were sent on ahead to spread the rebellion in the country round the Dragon Canal—so called from its serpentine windings—which was close to the city. But finding that the imperial forces, strong in numbers and well armed, barred his passage here, Nicetas summoned the general to surrender. 'Stand aside from our path,' he said, 'and remain neutral, pending the issue of the war.

If we fail, you will not suffer; if we succeed, you shall be Governor of Egypt. But the reign of Phocas is finished!' The answer was brief—'We fight to the death for Phocas': and the battle began. It is probable that the general was the one under special oath to defend the Emperor, and that he fought with better heart than his soldiers. For Nicetas was completely victorious: the imperial general was killed, and his head set on a pike and borne with the conquering standards through the Moon Gate into the city, where no further resistance was offered. John, the Governor, and Theodore, the Controller of Finance, took refuge in the church of St. Theodore in the eastern part of the town: while the Melkite Patriarch fled to the church of St. Athanasius, which stood by the sea shore. John of Nikiou is silent concerning the Patriarch's fate; but we know from other sources that he perished.

The clergy and people now assembled, and agreed in their detestation of Bonôsus and his wild beasts and in their welcome to Heraclius' general. They set the head of the slain commander on the gate; seized the palace and government buildings, as well as the control of the corn and the exchequer; took possession of all Phocas' treasure; and last, but not least, secured the island and fortress of Pharos and all the shipping. For Pharos, as Caesar saw and said long before, was one key of Egypt, as Pelusium was the other. Thus master of the capital, Nicetas dispatched Bonâkîs to carry the revolution through the Delta. It proved an easy task, for everywhere the native Egyptians hated the rule of Byzantium. Town after town made common cause with the delivering army. Nikiou, with its bishop Theodore, flung open its gates: at Manûf the faction in revolt plundered the house of Aristomachus, the imperial governor, and those of the leading Romans; and nearly every Prefect and every town cast in its lot against Phocas: so that after a triumphant progress Bonâkîs returned to the capital. Only at Sebennytus or Samanûd Paul, the popular Prefect, stood to his colours, and Paul's friend Cosmas, blazing with courage, though crippled with paralysis, was carried about the town to fire the garrison with his own spirit; while at Athrîb[1] another friend of Paul, the Prefect Marcian, equally refused to join the rebellion. The war was not yet over.

[1] Samanûd is still a well-known town on the eastern main of the Nile, about half way between Damietta and the head of the Delta. Athrîb lay on the same branch of the river and flourished as late as the fourteenth century: its site is near where the railway now crosses the Nile by Banhâ al 'Asal. From Athrîb a canal ran westward to Manûf, and thence, following a north-westerly course, to Nikiou, which lay on the western or Bolbitic main. The position of both Manûf and Nikiou is quite wrongly given by D'Anville; but Quatremère, in a learned note, proves by a brilliant piece of demonstration both the identity of Nikiou with Pshati—the one being the Greek, the other the Coptic name of the town—and the position of Nikiou on the Nile. Quatremère's conclusions are entirely borne out by John of Nikiou's Chronicle, which of course he had not seen. They are also confirmed by the MS. of Severus of Ushmûnain, who in the life of the Patriarch Andronicus expressly and explicitly identifies the two places. It may be added that both the forms Naḳyûs and Ibshâdî are found in Arabic. The river or canal passing through Manûf is to-day called 'Baḥr al Fara'ûnîah,' or 'Pharaonic River,' a name which records its great antiquity. Where this stream joins the western Nile, there is an island called Tabshîr, or a place called Tabshîr with an island opposite. About six miles north of Tabshîr, lies the village retaining the ancient Coptic name 'Ash Shâdî' or 'Ibshâdî.' It seems, however, that as not unfrequently has happened, the ancient name does *not* mark the ancient site, but has been transferred to another settlement. For the modern hamlet called Ibshâdî reveals

Bonôsus had reached Caesarea when he heard of the fall of Alexandria. The news only stung him to fiercer action. Shipping his whole force at that port, he sailed swiftly southwards, and either landed his cavalry on the confines of Egypt or was met there by a body of horse from Palestine. His plan was now to relieve Athrîb; and for this purpose he took his fleet in two divisions, one by the main eastern branch of the Nile, and one by the Pelusiac channel, while the cavalry followed by land. Besides the Prefect Marcian there was at Athrîb a redoubtable lady named Christodora, who from motives of private vengeance was a strong supporter of the Emperor's interest. Paul and Cosmas also had come from Manûf to a council of war. In vain the Bishop of Nikiou and the Chancellor Menas wrote urging Marcian and Christodora to throw down the statues of Phocas and acknowledge Heraclius: for

not the slightest trace of antiquity. The name extended to the whole district or 'island of Nikiou' originally, and has lingered on in a village of no importance. Mrs. Butcher in her *Story of the Church of Egypt* identifies the site of Nikiou with the modern Zawîah Razîn. Here are desolate mounds of potsherds, uneven ground, fragments of enormous granite columns, and all the tokens of a vanished Egyptian city. But geographically Zawîah Razîn occupies the wrong position, lying South-east of Manûf, near Ṭarrânah and entirely away from the ancient canal which joined Manûf to the Nile. The place which Quatremère calls Tabshîr is given as Sabsîr or Shabshîr on modern maps, and in the latter form one may well discover an echo of the early Coptic form Pshati. It is a great pity, however, that both Shabshîr and Zawîah Razîn, like so many ancient sites in the Delta, have been totally neglected by archaeologists. But I have no hesitation in pronouncing with Quatremère in favour of Shabshîr. I may add that in using the form Nikiou I am following the Coptic ⲛⲓⲕⲓⲟⲩ rather than the Greek Νίκιον or the Arabic نقيوس. Nikiou was of course a Roman station: it is mentioned in the *Itinerarium Antonini*.

they heard of Bonôsus' arrival on the isthmus, and the report was soon followed by the news of his occupation of Pelusium. His advance was watched in alarm by the Heraclian generals Plato and Theodore (really these Theodores are interminable), who had an army in the neighbourhood of Athrîb. They sent an urgent message for succour to Bonâkîs, who lost no time in moving up the western or Bolbitic branch of the Nile; but he reached Nikiou only to learn of Bonôsus' arrival at Athrîb. Quitting that town, Bonôsus moved by the canal which branched off the main river westwards in the direction of Manûf, and with him were Marcian and Cosmas and the relentless Christodora.

Paul now directed his march to join Bonôsus, and the two imperial forces had hardly united, when the army of Bonâkîs arrived on the scene. The encounter was fierce but decisive. The rebel troops were completely routed—part hurled into the waterway, part slain, part taken prisoner and thrown into irons. Bonâkîs himself was captured alive, but put to death: another general, Leontius, met the same fate: while Plato and Theodore managed to escape, and sought sanctuary in a neighbouring monastery. Nikiou, though a fortified city, was in no position to hold out against the victorious army of Bonôsus. Accordingly Bishop Theodore and the Chancellor Menas went out to the conqueror in solemn procession, carrying gospels and crosses, and threw themselves on his mercy. They might better have thrown themselves from their city walls. Menas was cast into prison, fined 3,000 pieces of gold, tortured with a prolonged bastinade, and set free only to die of exhaustion: while Theodore was taken back to Nikiou by

Bonôsus, who now moved there with his army. At the city gate Bonôsus saw the statues of Phocas lying broken on the ground, the work of the bishop, as Christodora and Marcian testified; and the unfortunate Theodore was instantly beheaded. This execution was followed by that of the generals Plato and Theodore, and of the three elders of Manûf—Isidore, John, and Julian — all of whom had sought asylum in a monastery, and were tamely surrendered by the monks. Of the general body of prisoners Bonôsus merely banished those who had been in Maurice's service, but put to death all who had ever borne arms under the flag of Heraclius.

The tide of war had now fairly turned in favour of the reigning Emperor. Bonôsus was virtually master of the Delta, from all parts of which the rebel forces—afraid to fight and afraid to surrender—streamed towards Alexandria by the vast network of waterways which covered the country. For Bonôsus himself it was an easy passage from Nikiou down the western main of the Nile, and thence by the canal which ran to Alexandria.

Nicetas was well prepared to receive him. Within the city he had organized a large army of regulars and irregulars, sailors and citizens, aided warmly by the Green Faction. The arsenals rang with the din of forging weapons, and the walls were manned and furnished with powerful engines of defence. Paul seems to have been sent on by Bonôsus to attack the city with a fleet of vessels on the south side, probably at the point where the fresh-water canal entered through two enormous gateways of stone, which had been built and fortified by Tatian in the time of Valens. But as soon as Paul's flotilla came within range of the city batteries, the huge stones which they hurled fell crashing among his vessels with such deadly effect that he was unable even to approach the walls, and drew off his ships to save them from being disabled or sunk. Such was the force at that time of the Alexandrian artillery.

CHAPTER III

FAILURE OF BONÔSUS

Route of Bonôsus. He attacks Alexandria. His repulse and defeat. Action of Paul. Attempted assassination of Nicetas. Recapture of Nikiou. Bonôsus driven from Egypt, and the country conquered for Heraclius. State of religious parties in Egypt.

BONÔSUS, who had performed at any rate the last stages of his journey by land, seems nevertheless to have followed Cleopatra's canal, i. e. the principal waterway leading from the Bolbitic branch of the Nile to Alexandria. He first pitched his camp at Miphamômis, and next at Dimkarûni, according to the bishop's Chronicle. Zotenberg has no note on these places, and at first sight they are puzzling. But Miphamômis is called in the text 'the present Shûbrâ.' This must be the Shûbrâ by Damanhûr. Now Champollion speaks of a place called Momemphis[1], which he alleges to have been seven leagues west of Damanhûr, or Timenhôr, as he gives the name of the town in its ancient Egyptian form. We can have no hesitation in identifying Miphamômis with Momemphis and in placing it close to Damanhûr: but then Champollion cannot be right in identifying it with Panouf Khêt, which the Arabs called Manûf as Suflâ, and which the French savant places twenty-one miles—an impossible distance—from Damanhûr.

As to Dimkarûni, one cannot remember any such form elsewhere: but bearing in mind that Dim—or Tim—in ancient Egyptian was a regular prefix de-

[1] Strabo also speaks of the nome of Momemphis.

noting 'town,' it seems beyond doubt that Dimkarûni is merely a Coptic form of Chaereum or Kariûn[1]. This explanation fits accurately with the geography of that region; for Kariûn was not only further west on the canal which Bonôsus was following, as the context requires, but was nearly half-way between Damanhûr and Alexandria, being only thirty-eight kilometres from the latter city and thirty-one from Damanhûr. From Kariûn Bonôsus covered the remaining distance without opposition, and arriving on the eastern side of the capital, he halted his army within view of the walls and resolved to assault them on the following day, Sunday. It would be interesting could we know by what means he hoped to storm the lofty and powerful fortifications which guarded the Great City[2].

But the Alexandrians were in no mood to stand a siege. The story is that a certain saint of Upper Egypt, called Theophilus the Confessor—who lived on the top of a pillar, and there, it seems, acquired practical wisdom—counselled Nicetas to sally out and give battle. Accordingly he marshalled his troops within the 'Gate of Aûn,' where the splendid width of the great street dividing the city lengthwise gave plenty of room for the muster. The name 'Gate of Aûn' is not explained by Zotenberg, and at first sight does not connect with any known feature in Alexandrian topography. But in another

[1] It is strange that this explanation did not occur to Amélineau, who referring to this passage in his *Géographie Copte* (p. 139) conjectures that the place was a village outside Alexandria—a sort of suburb.

[2] It may here be noted that in all the writings of this time Alexandria is almost invariably called the Great City. Constantinople in contrast is sometimes called the Royal City.

passage of the MS. we find Aûn used as a synonym of 'Ain Shams. Now 'Ain Shams is the Arabic name for the town better known as Heliopolis: and the ancient Egyptian for Heliopolis is Ôn or Aôn. The Gate of Aûn is therefore the gate towards Heliopolis, which may further be identified with the well-known Sun Gate closing the eastern end, as the Moon Gate closed the western, of that broad avenue which ran east to west in Alexandria, and was crossed at a sort of Carfax by the other main avenue running north to south. It may be added that the preference for old Egyptian forms shown in this use of Aûn, and in other passages, is a strong indication that John of Nikiou wrote this part of the original in Coptic.

But to resume. The imperial forces were now ordered to advance against the city, a mounted general leading the way. While they were still far out of bowshot, they were harassed by a lively fire from the huge catapults roaring and creaking on the city walls and towers. One of these projectiles struck the general, smashing his jaw, unhorsing and killing him instantly: a second killed another officer: and as the assailants wavered, thrown into confusion by this dreaded artillery, Nicetas gave the order for a sortie. The Sun Gate was thrown open, and his main force issued thence, formed line, and by a brilliant charge broke the enemy's ranks, and after a sharp struggle cut Bonôsus' army in two and turned it to flight. When Nicetas saw that most of the fugitives were streaming northwards, he put himself at the head of his reserve of black troops, and sallied out from another gate by the church of St. Mark on the north or seaward side of the city, near the north-east angle of the walls. He soon headed off the flying soldiers and drove them back either under the ramparts, where they were overwhelmed by volleys of stones and arrows, or else among the prickly hedges which enclosed the suburban gardens, where they were entangled and slain. Those of Bonôsus' men who fled to their left, or southwards, soon found their way barred by the canal in front: behind they saw the swords of their pursuers flashing: and, maddened by the press and panic, they turned their weapons blindly one against another.

The army of Bonôsus was cut to pieces. Marcian. Prefect of Athrîb, Leontius, Valens and many notable persons were among the slain; and such was the effect of the victory that even the Blue Faction abandoned the cause of Phocas. But Bonôsus himself managed to escape and retreat to the fortress of Kariûn, a place which figures again some thirty years later in the advance of the Arabs under ʿAmr on Alexandria. It lay on both banks of the canal which connected the capital with the Nile. Ibn Ḥauḳal describes it in his day as a large and beautiful town surrounded by gardens, and it still survives as a village. What Paul and his flotilla were doing during the battle is uncertain. They may have been making a diversion towards the south-west of the city, but they do not seem to have been near the scene of the encounter either to aid in the fight by land or to rescue survivors.

When at length Paul heard of this crushing defeat, he thought seriously of surrendering and joining Nicetas; but he remained loyal to his party, and secured his retreat by some means to Kariûn, where he joined Bonôsus. That general—whose extraordinary resource and courage challenge our reluctant admiration—had no thought of abandoning the struggle. He passed rapidly by the canal to the western arm of the Nile and ascended the stream to Nikiou, which his troops still garrisoned. There he recruited his fleet, and, after destroying a vast number of Alexandrian vessels, he succeeded in dominating the river. But not being strong enough to confront Nicetas again, he passed down another waterway (probably that called Ar Rûgâshât) towards Mareotis, and entered the Dragon Canal on the west of Alexandria with the intention of seizing Mareotis as a fresh base of operations against the capital. But Nicetas received intelligence of his plan, and defeated it by sending to break down the bridge at a place called Dafashîr, near Mareotis, and so blocking the canal.

Furious with this check, Bonôsus, renouncing the methods of open warfare, resolved to assassinate his rival. He persuaded one of his soldiers to go as an envoy to Nicetas under pretence of arranging terms of surrender. 'Take a short dagger with you,' he said, 'and conceal it under your cloak. When you come close to Nicetas, drive it through his heart, so as to kill him on the spot. You may escape in the confusion; but if not, you will die to save the Empire, and I will take charge of your children at the royal palace and will provide for them for life.' Such was the plot of Bonôsus; but it was betrayed by a traitor. One of his own followers named John sent a message of warning to Nicetas; so that when the assassin appeared, he was at once surrounded by a guard, who searched him and found the hidden dagger. The weapon was used to behead him.

Thus baulked of his vengeance, Bonôsus marched by land to Dafashîr, and wreaked his spite by massacring the inhabitants. Nicetas was hurrying to meet him: but Bonôsus knew the folly of risking a battle with the diminished remnant of his force. He therefore retreated, crossed the Nile, and once more gained the shelter of Nikiou. Instead of passing the river to pursue him, Nicetas remained on the western side, and occupied the town and province of Mareotis with a considerable army. The desperate valour of his foe and the baffling rapidity of his movements still gave the general of Heraclius much cause for anxiety, and he met his daring tactics with calculating prudence. It was not till Nicetas had firmly secured his rear and the western bank of the Nile that he passed over the river and advanced on Manûf. Here there was a very strong fortress—one of the great works of Trajan—which might have held out for an indefinite time if vigorously defended. But it is clear that popular sympathy was with the revolting party, and that the imperial soldiers were losing heart, in spite of the undaunted prowess of their leader. Many of the garrison took to flight, and the citadel itself was taken after a feeble resistance.

Having thus mastered the country on both banks of the Nile, Nicetas advanced on the town of Nikiou, which he had caught in a vice. At length the indomitable spirit of Bonôsus was broken. He fled under cover of darkness, and either slipped past the besieging army eastward and got to Athrîb, or else dropped quickly down the main river, and then crossed by one of the innumerable canals towards Tanis. In either case he reached Pelusium in safety, and took ship to Palestine: whence under the execration of the people he passed on his way to Constantinople, and joined his master Phocas. The fall of Manûf and Nikiou was the signal for the surrender of the other imperial towns and generals. Paul, Prefect of Samanûd, and the vigorous cripple Cosmas were captured, but frankly pardoned by the conqueror: and the Green Faction, who had made the occasion of Nicetas' success an excuse for maltreating the Blues and for open pillage and murder, saw their leaders arrested and solemnly admonished to be on their good behaviour. The two Factions were actually reconciled: new governors were appointed to every town: law and order were re-established: and Heraclius was master of Egypt.

It had been a long and a desperate struggle, with a romantic ebb and flow of fortune. We have seen the country roused from its sullen torpor by the sound of Heraclius' trumpets: Nicetas capturing Alexandria almost without striking a blow, and the revolution triumphant through Egypt: then Bonôsus flinging himself like a tiger on the head of the Delta, sweeping all before him to the walls of Alexandria, and dashing against the city's bulwarks only to recoil crushed and disabled for any further contest save a guerilla warfare, which he maintained for a time with fiery courage; then, brought to bay at last, he cheated the enemies that surrounded him of their vengeance and stole away in the night. It is a remarkable picture, drawn in strong colours, but bearing in every detail the image of reality; it is one entirely unknown to history until revealed in the Chronicle of John of Nikiou.

For not a word of all this dramatic struggle in Egypt occurs in the Byzantine historians, except that the *Chronicon Paschale* speaking of 609 A. D. says, 'Africa and Alexandria revolt.' Gibbon, who knows every page of their writings, thus sums up what he gleaned from them about the revolution: 'The powers of Africa were armed by the two adventurous youths (Heraclius and Nicetas); they agreed that one should navigate the fleet from Carthage to Constantinople, that the other should lead an army through Egypt and Asia, and that the imperial purple should be the reward of diligence and success. A faint rumour of their undertaking was conveyed to the ears of Phocas, and the wife and mother of the younger Heraclius were secured as the hostages of his faith: but the treacherous art of Crispus extenuated the distant peril, the means of defence were neglected or delayed, and the tyrant supinely slept till the African navy cast anchor in the Hellespont.' There is no suspicion here of the part played by Egypt in the revolution. Indeed a few pages later in the same chapter[1], Gibbon, in treating of the Persian invasion of Egypt under Chosroes in 616 A. D., expressly speaks of that country as 'the only province which had been exempt, since the time of Diocletian, from foreign and domestic war': an extraordinary statement, which Gibbon in part demolishes in his own brief but vigorous account of the Copts in the following chapter. The truth is that the more one studies this period, the clearer it becomes that Egypt was one of the most restless and turbulent countries in the whole Empire, and, certainly since the Council of Chalcedon, was in an almost chronic state of disorder. There is abundant evidence of this not only within the wide range of the Chronicle of John of Nikiou but in Renaudot's well-known History of the Patriarchs of Alexandria and in other writings,

[1] Ch. xlvi.

āpart from the particular story of Heraclius, with which we are now dealing.

This is not the place for a discussion upon either the facts or the sources of Egyptian history during the last two centuries of the Empire: but when that record comes to be fully written, it will prove a record of perpetual feud between Romans and Egyptians—a feud of race and a feud of religion—in which, however, the dominating motive was rather religious than racial. The key to the whole of this epoch is the antagonism between the Monophysites and the Melkites. The latter, as the name implies, were the imperial or the Court party in religion, holding the orthodox opinion about the two natures of Christ: but this opinion the Monophysite Copts, or native Egyptians, viewed with an abhorrence and combated with a frenzy difficult to understand in rational beings, not to say followers of the Gospel[1].

[1] Nor were the Monophysites without their own divisions. Witness the curious contest between Theodosius, the man of letters, and Gaian the Copt, for the Jacobite Patriarchate in the early sixth century, when the monks were all for Gaian, and though Theodosius got the start of him in performing the vigil at St. Mark's Cathedral and securing his investiture with the pallium, yet the people rose and drove him from the throne. But no sooner was Gaian seated, than Theodora dispatched Narses to depose him and to restore Theodosius. Popular tumults followed and sanguinary encounters in the streets of Alexandria, as the whole city rose, the very women hurling tiles from the housetops on the head of the alien soldiers battling in the streets.

In the time of Justin I, civil war was waged for years between one party who held that the body of Christ was corruptible and another who held it incorruptible. Justinian's appointment of Zoilus as Patriarch caused a rebellion in which the Roman troops were overpowered: and his device of making Apollinarius at once Prefect and Patriarch of Alexandria occasioned a massacre, for which the bishop in armour gave the word from the altar, so

The spirit of the savage fanatics who tore Hypatia to pieces at the altar was alive and unchanged: only now instead of being directed against the supposed paganism of a young and beautiful woman, it was divided between two sects each of which called itself children of Christ, and called the other sons of Satan. But further, apart from all religious dissensions, though crossed and complicated by them, the strife of the Blue and the Green Factions was as real and as relentless on the banks of the Nile as in any part of the Empire.

So much then for the domestic peace of Egypt at this period: and the alleged freedom from foreign war is disproved at least by the invasion of the Persians in the time of the Emperor Anastasius, when according to Eutychius, a writer born in Egypt, all the suburbs of Alexandria were burnt down, battle after battle was fought between the Persian invaders and the Egyptians, and the country was so harried that it escaped from the sword only to be smitten by a famine which led to insurrection. And what is to be said of the almost perennial persecutions and massacres, such as even Justinian

that the church ran with the blood of his Coptic congregation. And though Justinian issued what was meant to be a reforming edict for Egypt, it was the edict of a tyrant for a people of slaves.

John of Nikiou implies that the Gaianite faction was still in being at the time when he wrote. The Gaianite doctrine of the incorruptibility of Our Lord's body was gradually abandoned by the Copts, and the Theodosian doctrine of the natural body prevailed. Thus Le Quien quotes the superscription of a letter written by Khail, the forty-sixth Patriarch, as follows: 'Khail by the Grace of God Bishop of the city of Alexandria and of the Theodosian people.' This would be in the eighth century of our era. Coptic documents of the seventh century have the same expression, and Severus identifies the Copts with the Theodosians.

must be said to have countenanced? the petty rebellions, like that of Aristomachus under the Emperor Maurice? the outbursts of organized brigandage, the Beduin raids, the continual alarms and incursions of the Sudân tribes, who then as now menaced the frontiers? If war was not often present in act, its phantom was always hovering in the mirage of the Egyptian horizon.

It is clear, then, that many causes contributed to keep the whole province in a state of unrest. And the divisions were at once so fierce and so manifold that almost any determined invader might count on the aid of some party within its borders. What helped Nicetas was a genuine detestation of Phocas: the measure of his crimes was full even in the judgement of the Romans, while to the Copts he was not merely a tyrant and an assassin, but the sign and centre of that foreign power and that accursed creed, the existence of which in Egypt embittered their daily bread. But it is probable that, even after the flight of Bonôsus, Nicetas felt his continued presence necessary to secure his authority. Unfortunately the dates here are somewhat hard to follow. Apparently John of Nikiou makes all the war, previous to the defeat of Bonôsus before Alexandria, take place in the seventh year of Phocas' reign, i.e. before the close of 609: the battle itself then would be about the end of November, 609 [1], and the subsequent events may have occupied a few weeks longer. Still it would follow that Nicetas was in possession of Egypt in the spring of 610.

[1] This agrees with the statement that John the Almoner was elected Patriarch in 609, in the room of Theodorus, who was killed in the revolt of Nicetas. See Le Quien, *Or. Christ.* ii. 444.

On one point the bishop's Chronicle is curiously silent—on the part played in the contest by the powerful fortress of Babylon near Memphis. Next to Alexandria, it was the strongest place in Egypt, and of course it was held by an imperial garrison. In the war of the Arab conquest it was the first objective of the Saracen commander, and its reduction sealed the triumph of the Crescent. This is so fully set forth by the Chronicle, that one can only interpret its silence to mean that Babylon surrendered to Nicetas without a conflict. But if so, and if the war in Egypt was over by the spring of 610, it is more than ever clear that Nicetas had no idea of racing for Constantinople. Else, assuming that he could have drawn an adequate armament from Egypt, which there is no reason to doubt, he might have reached the Byzantine capital and overthrown Phocas six months in advance of Heraclius. It is true that Cedrenus assigns the massacre by Bonôsus at Antioch to 610, which would make the whole Egyptian war fall within that year: but this chronology is not consistent with the rest of Cedrenus: it disagrees with the *Chronicon Paschale*: and it is hopelessly at variance with our Ethiopic MS., in which generally speaking the dates are remarkably trustworthy. The balance of evidence is then strongly in favour of the earlier date, and we may take it that Nicetas, having achieved the object of his mission, when he won the final throw of the die on the Nile, was well content to hold the province pending the advance of Heraclius, to keep centralized and friendly all the imperial forces in the country, and to control its vast resources in corn and shipping on which Constantinople largely depended.

CHAPTER IV

ACCESSION OF HERACLIUS

Heraclius' voyage. His long delay at Thessalonica. He sails for Constantinople. Fighting at the capital, and death of Bonôsus. Naval engagement. Imperial treasure sunk in the sea. Phocas captured and confronted with Heraclius. Sentence of death carried out with barbarity. Coronation of Heraclius. Retrospect.

MEANWHILE how was Heraclius faring? Our information of his progress by sea is scanty enough, nor does John of Nikiou add greatly to the meagre details of the Byzantine historians, who, like him, reserve their descriptions for the closing scenes at Constantinople. But it is clear that the progress was slow, and that like Nicetas he set out with a comparatively small force of vessels, carrying some Roman and African troops on board, and that he had to collect and organize both a fleet and an army with which he might adventure against Phocas. At the islands where he touched, and at the towns on the seaboard, he was welcomed, and recruits—particularly of the Green[1] Faction—flocked to his standard. Of resistance to his arms there is no record: and yet it is certain that Heraclius never dreamt of moving direct on Constantinople with the small force with which he started. On quitting Africa he coasted along Hellas or threaded the islands slowly to Thessalonica, where he fixed his base of operations and spent a considerable time—

[1] There seems some doubt about the part played by the two Factions. The Blue was originally for and the Green against Phocas: but he clearly alienated even the Blue. John of Nikiou's evidence on the whole goes to show that in Egypt it was the Greens, as in Thrace and Constantinople, who favoured Heraclius.

not less than a year—in equipping a fleet and army and in strengthening his connexion with the disaffected party led by Crispus in the capital. Thessalonica was at this time, as we know, strongly fortified, and it was one of the few places in Macedonia which had withstood the hordes of Huns and other barbarians then flooding the country [1]. It was in fact one of the gates of the Eastern Empire: it commanded the trade routes from Carthage, Sicily, and the western Mediterranean to Constantinople. Here then Heraclius established himself presumably without a struggle, and so firmly that one writer, Eutychius, appears to imagine him a native of the town. It must, however, be said that Eutychius' whole account of the revolution is no less imperfect as a record of events than confused in chronology: and on this point he is clearly mistaken.

During the many months which Heraclius spent at Thessalonica, we can only conceive of him as maturing plans, gathering resources, and removing obstacles. What difficulties he had to encounter we cannot say: it is possible that at this period, which is a blank in the annals, he may have displayed that combination of calculating foresight and brilliant activity with which he subsequently astonished the world in his Persian campaigns. But it was not till September, 610, that all was ready,

[1] A very interesting description of Thessalonica is given in *Joannis Cameniatae de Excidio Thessalonicensi Narratio* which may be read in Combefisius' *Historiae Byzantinae Scriptores Post Theophanem* (Paris, 1685, fol. pp. 320 seq.). The general situation of the town is picturesquely sketched, and full details are given of the forts, walls, and harbours. The magnificence of the streets and buildings and the vastness of its trade, wealth, and resources are a tolerable index of the importance of the city to Heraclius. John wrote circa 900.

and the vast armament which he had collected and provisioned weighed anchor from the harbour. On the leading galleys reliquaries were carried, and the banner of the Cross waved at the mast-head: while on Heraclius' own vessel an image of special sanctity, 'the image not made with hands,' formed the figure-head. News of the arrival of the fleet in the Dardanelles spread like wild-fire to the capital; and while Crispus seems for the moment to have kept in the background, Theodore the Illustrious and a large number of senators and officials declared for Heraclius. According to John of Nikiou the city rabble also rose against the Emperor, hurling imprecations on his head.

Phocas, meanwhile, seems to have been ill prepared for the storm that had been so long in breaking. When he first received news of the revolt of Egypt, there was a large fleet of corn-ships from Alexandria in harbour. These he seized, and flung the sailors into prison in the fortress on the harbour of the Hebdomon, where they were kept in long durance. Yet after the failure of Bonôsus' expedition to reconquer Egypt, we read of no further serious efforts on the Emperor's part. But it was the shout of these Alexandrian prisoners, as they acclaimed the sails of Heraclius, that sounded the first note of real alarm which was borne to Phocas. The Emperor was then at the Hebdomon palace[1] near the fortress: but he sprang on his horse and galloped to a palace called the palace of the Archangel

[1] The palace and fortress of the Hebdomon were on the coast about three miles west of the Golden Gate of Constantinople, as Prof. Van Millingen proves in his learned work *Byzantine Constantinople*, pp. 316–41 (London, 1899). The incident in the text is referred to on p. 324.

within the walls. From the *Chronicon Paschale* we know that this was on a Saturday; which must have been the 3rd October. Next day Bonôsus was sent with the imperial chariots and other troops to encounter any force landed by Heraclius: but the charioteers, who had been won over by Crispus, revolted and turned on their leader, who fled back, eating his heart with rage, to the city. There in a fit of savage treachery Bonôsus hurled fire into the quarter round the palace called Caesarion: but, failing to kindle a conflagration, he baffled for a while the pursuing mob, and escaped in a small boat to the quay called Port Julian. Here, however, he was followed and found, and the chase closed about him. He essayed a fierce but vain resistance against overwhelming odds: then in the last extremity of danger he plunged into the sea. As he rose a sword-cut clove his skull, and that indignant spirit fled from the scene where it had wrought so much havoc. The body was taken out of the water and dragged to the Ox Market, where it was burned in public ignominy and execration.

This account of the death of Bonôsus is put together from the records of Cedrenus, John of Nikiou, and the *Chronicon Paschale*. It is curious how well they combine, and how little real disagreement there is between them; for although the stories differ, it is rather by omission or addition than by any discrepancy of fact. Moreover the points of coincidence are often very striking; and as it is rather a coincidence of logic than of detail, it seems to establish at once the independence of the writers and to carry a conviction of their trustworthiness. There is no sign of the three writers relying on any common document.

When the Emperor heard what had befallen Bonôsus, he knew that his own hour had come. He had no intention of resigning the crown, nor indeed any hope of mercy in case he surrendered to his enemy: his only chance lay in fighting to the bitter end, and the defection of his best troops made this chance almost worthless. All he had now to rely upon was the allegiance of the Blue Faction, or rather their furious hostility to the Green and their exasperation at the first successes of the rival colour. Phocas accordingly manned a fleet with the Blues in the harbour of St. Sophia, and prepared to give battle to Heraclius. John of Nikiou is responsible for a curious anecdote which, as far as I am aware, does not occur in any other historian. He relates that Phocas and his chamberlain or treasurer, Leontius the Syrian, knowing that after the death of Bonôsus their own lives were in imminent danger from the mob, took all the hoarded wealth of the imperial treasury and sank it in the sea. All the riches of the Emperor Maurice, all the vast store of gold and jewels which Phocas himself had amassed by confiscating the property of the victims he had murdered, and last but not least all the money and precious vessels which Bonôsus had heaped up by his multiplied iniquities, were now in a moment lost to the world. 'Thus,' as the Egyptian bishop remarks, 'did Phocas impoverish the Eastern Empire.'

It was an act of triumphant spite such as well accords with the character of the Emperor, and apparently it took place when victory declared for Heraclius in the naval engagement. The treasure must have been taken on board the Emperor's galley, to save it from being plundered while the battle was raging, and sunk bodily when the battle was lost. For though the contest may have been stubborn, the issue was not doubtful. The imperial vessels were defeated and driven on the shore or captured. All who could, escaped, and fled for sanctuary to the Cathedral of St. Sophia. Phocas himself seems to have made his way back with Leontius to the palace of the Archangel, where they were followed and seized by Photius (or Photinus) and Probus. The crown was struck off the Emperor's head, and he was dragged with his companion in chains along the quay, his raiment torn to pieces. There he was shown to the victorious fleet and army, and with a storm of curses ringing in his ears, he was haled into the presence of his conqueror in the church of St. Thomas the Apostle.

It is probable that this church was chosen for Heraclius' thanksgiving service rather than St. Sophia, because the latter was too crowded with refugees of the defeated Faction to admit of any large company or solemn pageant. There is no necessity to draw on the imagination for many details of the meeting between Phocas and Heraclius. We may picture a stately basilica thronged with officers, senators and soldiers, priests standing in gorgeous vestments round the altar laden with golden vessels, and the strains of the *Te Deum* dying away as Phocas is brought in chains.

For a moment the fallen Emperor and his victorious vassal stand fronting each other. Their portraits are well known as drawn by Cedrenus. Heraclius was in the prime of life—his age was about thirty-five—of patrician family, of middle stature and muscular build, deep-chested, with well-knit athletic frame: his hair and beard were fair, his complexion bright and clear, his eyes pale blue and singularly handsome. Altogether a man of frank and open presence and aristocratic mien, with a look of power, physical and intellectual: a face denoting courage, insight, ability, and perhaps that unscrupulousness which Eutychius commemorates. Phocas was of the same height: but there the resemblance ended. His person was repulsive from its hideous deformity: his beardless face was crossed by a deep and ugly scar which flushed and blackened in his fits of passion: his jutting eyebrows met on a low forehead under a shock of red hair, and the eyes of a savage glared beneath them. Foul of tongue, besotted in wine and lust, ruthless and remorseless in torture and bloodshed—such was the ex-centurion whose lash had scourged the Eastern Empire for eight years, and who now was called to answer for his deeds. As crime after crime was unfolded, 'Is this,' said Heraclius, 'the way you have governed?' 'Are you the man,' was the retort, 'to govern better?'

Sentence of death was passed, and it is a reproach rather to the manners of the time than to the character of Heraclius that its execution was accompanied by horrible barbarities—though perhaps not much worse than the drawing and quartering which our own law formerly sanctioned. Phocas' body was dismembered: first the hands and feet were cut off, then the arms, and after other mutilations the head at last was severed, put on a pole, and carried about the main streets of the city. Meanwhile the trunk was dragged along the ground to the Hippodrome, and thence to the Ox Market, and burned on the spot where Bonôsus' ashes were hardly cold. The banner of the Blue Faction (not the Green, as Gibbon says) was also burned, and a statue of Phocas was carried through the Hippodrome in mock procession by men clad in white dalmatics and bearing lighted tapers, and was thrown on the fire. 'They burned Phocas, Leontius, and Bonôsus and scattered their ashes to the winds: for all men hated them.'

According to John of Nikiou, Heraclius was crowned—against his own wishes—in the same church of St. Thomas; and after his prayer was ended, he repaired to the palace, where all the dignitaries of the city rendered him homage. Cedrenus makes the imperial coronation take place in the chapel of St. Stephen attached to the palace, while the *Chronicon Paschale* puts it out of order between the burning of Phocas' body and his statue, naming no place. It is curious that the Egyptian chronicle confirms the story of Heraclius' reluctance to accept the crown—a reluctance emphasized by the *Chronicon Paschale* as well as the Byzantine historians. But his scruples were overcome: and on October 5 in the year 610 he was proclaimed Emperor, with Fabia, his betrothed wife, whose name was changed to Eudocia, as Empress.

Nicetas does not seem to have made any effort to join Heraclius before Constantinople: for though John of Nikiou uses language apparently implying his presence in the city at the time of Phocas' fall, Zotenberg must be right in thinking that 'Nicetas' there is a mere slip on the part of writer or copyist for 'Crispus.' The fact of Nicetas leaving Egypt to join forces with Heraclius, and succeeding in his object, would not have been buried, if it were a fact, in the obscurity of a chance allusion. But I must again differ from Gibbon, who says:—

'The voyage of Heraclius had been easy and prosperous, the tedious march of Nicetas was not accomplished before the decision of the contest: but he submitted without a murmur to the fortune of his friend.'

The truth, as I have shown, is just the reverse. It was Nicetas' march which on the whole was easy and prosperous: and in spite of the dangers and delays arising from the intervention of Bonôsus, he reached his final goal, the possession of Egypt, long before Heraclius was able to move from Thessalonica. From which it is fair to argue that Heraclius in his voyage had difficulties and adversities to master, of which we have no record and no measure.

CHAPTER V

EGYPT UNDER THE NEW EMPEROR

Nicetas remains as Governor of Alexandria. His policy. Gap in the history of Egypt. Our dependence on patriarchal biographies. John the Almoner and the great famine. Corn-ships belonging to the Church. Succession of Coptic Patriarchs.

NICETAS was confirmed by the Emperor in the governorship of Alexandria or, as it might be called, the Viceroyalty of Egypt[1]. The adherents of Phocas had now been killed or banished, or had thrown off their allegiance to the lost cause, and the chief work of Nicetas was the resettlement of the Roman civil service and the reorganization of the Roman military service, which between them held Egypt in fee for the Empire. Both these services were filled by the ruling class to the general exclusion of the Copts or natives, and the system was so far analogous to the British administration of India: it differed profoundly and fatally in this, that the whole machinery of government in Egypt was directed to the sole purpose of wringing profit out of the ruled for the benefit of the rulers. There was no idea of governing for the advantage of the governed, of raising the people in the social scale, of developing the moral or even the material resources of the country. It was an alien domination founded on force and making little pretence of sympathy with the subject race. It held the Greek capital of Alexandria and the ancient Egyptian capital of

[1] There is a good note on Nicetas in H. Gelzer's *Leontios' von Neapolis Leben des heiligen Johannes*, p. 129.

Memphis, with its great bulwark the Roman fortress of Babylon on the eastern side of the Nile, and from Syene to Pelusium it occupied a chain of fortress towns. From these its soldiers and tax-gatherers patrolled the country, keeping order and collecting money, while Roman merchants and Jewish traders settled freely under protection of the garrisons, keenly competing with their Coptic rivals.

Alexandria itself was as difficult a city to govern as any in the world with its motley population of Byzantine Greeks, Greeks born in Egypt, Copts, Syrians, Jews, Arabs, and aliens of all nations. Yet Nicetas seems really to have won the respect, if not the affection, of the fickle and turbulent Alexandrians. One of his first measures was to grant a three years' remission of the imperial taxes, an act of singular favour, which heightened the popularity already gained by his record as a brilliant soldier. That he remained at Alexandria is no longer open to question [1]. True, we hear of him at Jerusalem before the Persian advance to that city, where he is said to have saved some of the holy relics—the spear and the sponge—from capture: but as we shall see he returned to Alexandria again.

[1] This is quite clear from Leontius and other sources. But the fact of Nicetas' governorship of Alexandria seems unknown even to Professor Bury, who apparently follows Gibbon in thinking that Nicetas was still bent on marching his hapless forces all the way by land to Constantinople, through Egypt, Palestine, Syria, and Asia Minor; for he says that Nicetas 'did not arrive in Constantinople till about April, 612. We know not what detained him on his journey: but it may be conjectured that he lingered in Syria to operate against the Persians' (*History of the Later Roman Empire*, vol. ii. p. 216, n. 2). The story of the landward race to Constantinople is pure legend. Nicetas' destination was Egypt, and he remained there to govern the country he had conquered for Heraclius.

The fact doubtless is that Heraclius ordered him to Palestine in hope that he might offer an effectual resistance to the Persian armies, whose numbers and strength he greatly under-estimated; and that Nicetas had no alternative but to beat a hasty retreat.

But here most unfortunately the history of Egypt is extremely difficult to recover. The annals of John of Nikiou, which up to this point have furnished a wealth of information, now become totally silent. There is in the MS. a blank of thirty years, just as if some malignant hand had torn out every page on which the record of the reign of Heraclius was written. Some Armenian[1] and other eastern authorities who deal with this period throw much light upon the history of some parts of the Empire: but, like the Byzantine historians, they have little to say on the subject of Egypt. Yet dimly through the gloom one may mark the movement of those great events which at the close of the Emperor's life closed the book of Byzantine overlordship in Egypt.

In tracing the story of Egypt during the thirty years between the accession of Heraclius and the Arab conquest we are mainly dependent on ecclesiastical writers or writers with a strong religious bias. The truth is that in the seventh century in Egypt the interest of politics was quite secondary to the interest of religion. It was opinion on matters of faith, and not on matters of government, which formed and divided parties in the state; and religion itself was valued rather for its requirement of intellectual assent to certain propositions than

[1] For a list of Armenian authorities see *Journal Asiatique*, 6e série, 1866, vol. vii. p. 109.

for its power to furnish the springs of moral action. Love of country was practically unknown, and national or racial antagonisms derived their acuteness mainly from their coincidence with religious differences. Men debated with fury upon shadows of shades of belief and staked their lives on the most immaterial issues, on the most subtle and intangible refinements in the formulas of theology or metaphysics. And the fierce battles which Juvenal describes as turning in his day on the relative merit of cats or crocodiles as objects of worship found their analogue in Christian Egypt:—

> Numina vicinorum
> Odit uterque locus, cum solos credat habendos
> Esse deos quos ipse colit.

Times had changed, but the temper of the people was the same. Inasmuch then as parties and party divisions were essentially sectarian, it is rather the lives of saints and patriarchs than those of warriors or statesmen, which have survived to furnish the sources of Egyptian history.

The resulting difficulties are not lessened by the fact that at this time, as ever since the Council of Chalcedon in 451, each of the two great parties into which the Church was cloven had its own separate Patriarch and administration. These parties, it may be repeated, are distinguished by the familiar names Jacobite or Coptic and Melkite[1] or Royalist. The Jacobites were by creed Monophysites, by race mainly, though not exclusively, native Egyptians[2]:

[1] The root 'melek' signifying king is common to all Semitic languages. The term Melkite as employed in Egypt probably came from the Syriac, so that there is no anachronism in using it before the Arab conquest.

[2] The importance of the Copts even in Alexandria is shown by

while the Melkites were orthodox followers of Chalcedon and for the most part of Greek or European origin. Severus of Ushmûnain and all the authorities agree that, whatever Emperor reigned, the policy of suppressing the Jacobite heresy in Egypt was pursued with relentless intolerance: while the Jacobites aimed no less at extirpating all that stood in the following of Chalcedon.

It has already been shown that the Melkite Patriarch, who was called Theodorus, was slain at the capture of Alexandria by Nicetas in 609[1]. The revolt of Heraclius was directed against the imperial power at Constantinople, and in joining it the Copts doubtless hoped for better treatment than they had received under the iron rule of Phocas.

a story in Procopius (Athens, 1896, p. 221). When Justinian in 538 made Paul bishop of Alexandria, he gave him authority over the governor Rhodon, hoping thus to secure obedience to Chalcedon from the chief men of the city. Paul's first act was to deliver to death the deacon Psoes, a Copt who wrote Coptic and was the main hindrance to the Emperor's policy. Psoes died under torture: the people rose in fury: and to pacify them Justinian recalled Rhodon and had him executed at Constantinople in spite of the thirteen dispatches, ordering him to obey the Patriarch, which he produced in self-defence. Liberius, who succeeded Rhodon as governor of Alexandria, proceeded to crucify one Arsenius who had been a principal agent in the death of Psoes; so that the latter was fully avenged. Le Quien makes out that it was Rhodon who originated the order to murder Psoes: but his bias in favour of the Court party is as clear as Procopius' testimony against the Patriarch Paul.

[1] Sharpe is mistaken in saying that Theodore was bishop 'during the first three years of Heraclius': *History of Egypt under the Romans*, p. 240. The *Chronicon Paschale* says that in this year the Pope of Alexandria 'was slain by his enemies' (σφάζεται ἀπὸ ἐναντίων—which may mean the Copts) i. e. 609, in which year also Zacharias was made Patriarch of Jerusalem.

Nor at first were they greatly disappointed. The Coptic Patriarch Anastasius, who had been on the throne for five years at the time of the rebellion, retained his seat for another six years till his death on 22 Khoiak (18 Dec.), A. D. 616[1]. And although the Melkites remained in possession of power and held the principal churches in Alexandria, yet the Copts were able to build or rebuild several churches of their own, such as those of St. Michael, St. Angelus, SS. Cosmas and Damian, besides various monasteries, to all of which Anastasius appointed priests and ordained bishops[2].

There seems no reason to doubt that Heraclius was genuinely anxious to win over the Coptic party, and at the same time Nicetas felt bound to recompense their services rendered. Hence although the Byzantine Court still appointed a Melkite Patriarch in place of the slain Theodorus, they

[1] This on the whole seems the most probable date, though here as elsewhere the chronology is extremely difficult. Abû 'l Birkat makes Anastasius die in 604: the *Chronicon Orientale* assigns his death to 611, after a primacy of 12 years and 190 days: while Echellensis claims greater accuracy in dating him 607 to 619. But on the one hand the *Chronicon* expressly states that the reception of the Jacobite Patriarch of Antioch by Anastasius occurred in the year in which the Persians devastated Jerusalem, i.e. *in 615*: and on the other hand we know from Severus that the Persian invasion of Egypt (which happened in 616) took place after the death of Anastasius. Both statements may be reconciled with the date given in the text for the death of Anastasius, viz. December, 616, although the *Chronicon* is inconsistent with itself in putting the decease of Anastasius in the year 611. See Appendix B, where all this chronology is discussed at more length.

[2] Severus of Ushmûnain quoted by Le Quien, *Or. Christ.* ii. 444. The *Chronicon Orientale* goes further in saying that Anastasius not only built new churches, but restored to the Copts many of which the Melkites had taken possession. This could only be by the favour of Nicetas and the Emperor.

chose, on the special recommendation of Nicetas[1], a man whose life and character so far commanded the admiration of the Jacobites, that they honoured him during his lifetime and after death enshrined his memory in the Coptic calendar. It is curious to find that Nicetas was at a later date largely instrumental in bringing about the union of the Monophysite Syrian with the Coptic Church, a fact which shows that his abiding attitude to the Copts was one of sympathy rather than mere tolerance.

The new Melkite Archbishop was John the Compassionate, or the Almoner—a name bestowed upon him for his great acts of charity[2]. But his lavishness was not wholly without a method. He told those about him to go through the city and take note of all his 'lords and helpers.' When they questioned his meaning, he explained: 'Those whom you call paupers and beggars I call lords and helpers: for they truly help us and grant us the Kingdom of Heaven.' So a roll of the poor was prepared, and they received daily relief to the number of 7,500. The governor Nicetas, watching with envy the ceaseless flow of wealth from the Patriarch, went to him one day and said, 'The government is hard pressed for money: what you receive is gotten freely without impoverishing anybody: therefore give it to the treasury.' The

[1] Gelzer's *Leontios von Neapolis,* Anhang ii. p. 110 (fragment from Life of John the Almoner by John Moschus and Sophronius).

[2] Gibbon remarks curiously and with curious unfairness: 'The boundless alms of John the Eleemosynary were dictated by superstition *or* benevolence *or* policy': and he seems to say that it was in John's time that 'the churches of Alexandria were delivered to the Catholics and the religion of the Monophysites was proscribed'—a statement which happens to be less true of this time than of almost any other.

Patriarch answered: 'What is offered to the heavenly King must not be given to an earthly. I can give you nothing. But yours is the responsibility, and the store of the Lord is under my bed.' So Nicetas called his retainers, and ordered them to take the money. As they were leaving, they met men carrying in their hands little jars labelled 'Best Honey' and 'Unsmoked Honey,' and Nicetas asked for a jar for his own table. The bearers whispered to the Patriarch that the vessels were full of gold: nevertheless John sent a jar to Nicetas with a message advising him to have it opened in his own presence, and adding that all the vessels he had seen were full of money. Nicetas thereupon went in person to the Patriarch and returned all the money he had taken, together with the jar and a handsome sum besides[1].

Stories of this kind at least show the power and resources of the pontiff at Alexandria, and it is interesting to learn also that the Church had its own fleet of trading vessels. It is related that one such ship with a cargo of 20,000 bushels of corn was driven so far out of its course by storms that it reached Britain, where there happened to be a severe famine. It returned laden with tin, which the captain sold at Pentapolis. In another instance we hear of a flotilla of thirteen ships, each carrying 10,000 bushels of grain, which lost all their burden in a tempest in the Adriatic. They belonged to the Church, and besides corn they carried silver,

[1] These details are given by Leontius (Gelzer, op. cit., and Migne, *Patr. Gr.* t. 93, col. 1618). Another account—and a very probable one—makes Nicetas demand the money by order of Heraclius, who needed it to reorganize his army: see Lebeau's *Histoire du Bas Empire*, ed. de Saint-Martin, vol. xi. pp. 52–3.

fine tissues, and other precious wares[1]. Nor can it be doubted that the Church had its share of the enormous grain trade between Alexandria and Constantinople which Justinian carefully reorganized[2]. And beyond the profits of such traffic and the voluntary offerings of the people, the Church had endowments of land which brought in large revenues. Hence it is not surprising to learn that, while John the Almoner astonished the world by his bounty, Andronicus, who succeeded Anastasius as Coptic Patriarch, and was for some few months at any rate contemporary with John, was scarcely less famed for his wealth and his charity.

Although the double succession of pontiffs was maintained, and although the early policy of Heraclius was to bring about a reconcilement between the two great branches of the Church of Egypt, yet as a rule the Coptic Archbishop was unable to maintain his

[1] It is possible that the Church secured special trading privileges when Hephaestus, governor of Alexandria under Justinian, stopped the public distribution of corn (then amounting to 2,000,000 bushels annually), which had been customary since the days of Diocletian. Hephaestus in a letter to the Emperor criticized the system of distribution as both unjust and impolitic. See Procopius, p. 219 (Athens, 1896).

[2] The corn-stores by the docks at Phiale in Alexandria were liable to attack and plunder in every street riot, till Justinian fortified the granaries in connexion with the service of barges from the Nile with a strong enclosure wall. Moreover the corn-ships were often detained at the mouth of the Dardanelles waiting for a south wind to carry them forward: but to obviate this delay Justinian built large storehouses where the ships could at once deliver their cargoes and clear for return to Egypt, while another service of vessels would carry the corn on to Constantinople when the wind favoured. See Procopius on the *Buildings of Justinian*, Palestine Pilgrims Text Society, vol. ii. p. 152.

seat in the metropolis. The hostility between the two sects, even when smouldering, was ready to burst into a blaze when fanned by the slightest gust of passion; and the government could not in common prudence brook the presence of the rival Archbishops in the capital[1]. When, for example, Anastasius welcomed the Patriarch of Antioch, we find him living at the Ennaton, a famous monastery, which lay near the shore nine miles westward of Alexandria[2], and from there he went forth in solemn

[1] It is fair to state that Maḳrîzî makes Anastasius 'take up his residence at Alexandria.' This may mean no more than that he resided *near* Alexandria, which is not disputed: but Maḳrîzî's whole account of this period is very confused and untrustworthy. See Malan's translation, pp. 67–9.

[2] In Coptic this monastery appears as **πιενατον** (Zoega, *Cat. Cod. Copt.* pp. 89, 93), **πιϩενατον** (id. ib. 337), and **πϩενατον** (Amélineau, *Géographie de l'Égypte à l'époque Copte*, p. 531). The Greek form τὸ Ἔνvατον or Ἔνατον (Cotelerius, *Monumenta Ecclesiae Graecae*, t. i. pp. 460, 520; John Moschus, *Pratum Spirituale*, c. 145, 177, 184) is translated as 'Ennatum' in Latin (Rosweyde, *Vitae Patrum*, pp. 609, 613). The Arabic Maḳrîzî identifies a monastery which he calls that of الزجاج (or the glass-blower) with the Ennaton, الهانطون, and he adds that it is under the invocation of St. George. The Patriarch formerly was obliged after his election in the church of Al Mu'allaḳah in the Roman Fortress of Babylon at Miṣr to visit the Monastery of Al Zûjâj, but the custom fell into disuse, says Maḳrîzî. It certainly points to the very great importance of the Ennaton in the eyes of the Copts—an importance which is emphasized in the history of the sixth and seventh centuries. It was there that, according to the Synaxaria, the body of Severus, Patriarch of Antioch, was preserved, that the work of revising the Syriac version was carried out, and that the union of the Churches of Egypt and Antioch was accomplished at this period. The monastery is mentioned by Abû Ṣâliḥ (*Churches and Monasteries of Egypt*, ed. Evetts and Butler, p. 229 and note), who uses the form هونانادون. Goldschmidt and Pereira, to whose note I am much indebted, conclude that the Ennaton is the same as Al Zûjâj: that it lay nine miles

procession to meet his visitor[1]. Nor did he go to Alexandria, but summoned thence his clergy and held in the monastery that conclave which resulted in the re-establishment of full communion with Antioch.

But Andronicus, the successor of Anastasius, offers a remarkable exception to this rule of non-residence. At the time of his election he was deacon at the Cathedral church of Angelion[2] in Alexandria, and there in the cells attached to the Cathedral he continued to reside during the whole period of his

to the west of Alexandria: and that it was under the invocation of St. George (*Vida do Abba Daniel do Mosteiro de Scetê*, Versão Ethiopica, p. 37 n.). I think it clear that the name comes from the milestone distance, just as at Constantinople the well-known fortress and palace was called the Hebdomon or Seventh: but the dedication is more doubtful. It appears to be called Σαλαμᾶ in John Moschus; it was quite distinct from the monastery which appears in Severus as دير قيرنوس but which should certainly be read as دير قيريوس, or قبريوس, Kyrios or Cyprius. But the fact doubtless is that, as usual in the case of large monasteries, many churches were included within the walls; and as these had their separate dedications, there is ground for some confusion. South-west of Alexandria towards Mareotis there was another called τὸ Πέμπτον, and we read of another called τὸ Ὀκτωκαιδέκατον: see *Revue de l'Orient chrétien*, 1901, no. 1, p. 65, n. 1.

[1] Mrs. E. L. Butcher, in her work *The Story of the Church of Egypt*, represents the Patriarch of Antioch as taking refuge in Egypt at the time of the Persian invasion: but the truth is that he came to confer with the Coptic Patriarch on Church matters, more particularly the Union. At the same time great numbers of Syrian clergy *with their bishops*, as well as laymen of all ranks, are specially recorded to have fled to Alexandria before the Persian invasion. Gelzer's *Leontios von Neapolis*, Anhang ii. p. 112.

[2] It is not clear whether Angelion or Euangelion is the proper title of this church. Both forms are found, but the simple Angelion seems the more common.

primacy, which lasted six years. This immunity from banishment was due to the fact that he belonged to a noble family, and had the support of powerful kinsmen in the government of the city. What the personal relations of the two Patriarchs were is not known; but John the Almoner died a few months after Andronicus came to the Coptic throne, and it is doubtful whether George[1], the successor of John in the Melkite chair, lived in Alexandria at all, so that the personal question may never have become dangerous.

It is useless to regret that these not very interesting details of matters ecclesiastical furnish the chief record that remains of the history of Egypt during the first five or six years following the revolt of Heraclius. But it is time now to pass to those great events with which the eastern part of the Empire was ringing, events which had their instantaneous echo on the banks of the Nile, and which were destined to shake the Byzantine power in Egypt to its foundations and prepare the way for the Arab conquest. But the great conflict between the Empire and Persia took place on a wider stage; and in order to understand its bearing upon the fortunes of Egypt, it is necessary to follow its vicissitudes, if only in rough outline.

[1] Little or nothing is known of George except that he wrote a life of St. John Chrysostom. Theophanes gives fourteen years as the term of his patriarchate, yet inconsistently, though truly perhaps, makes him die in 630, after a period of only ten years on the throne. Eutychius makes a vacancy of seven years between John and George, and this is probably the explanation of the discrepancy in Theophanes.

CHAPTER VI

PERSIAN CONQUEST OF SYRIA

Chosroes established on the throne of Persia. Death of Maurice and rupture between Persia and the Empire. Persian conquest of Syria. Jews and Christians. Fall of Jerusalem and captivity of the Patriarch Zacharias. Flight of refugees to Egypt. John the Almoner's measures of relief. Rebuilding of the churches in Jerusalem. Christian council held by Chosroes. The Almoner's mission to Jerusalem.

WHEN Chosroes, grandson of Anûshîrwân, the great King of Persia, had a few days after his enthronement been driven from his kingdom by the rebel usurper Bahrâm, he fled with his two uncles across the Tigris, cutting the ropes of the ferry behind him to baffle his pursuers [1]. He pushed on to Circesium on the Euphrates, wishing to pray at a Christian shrine for deliverance from his enemies. Thence he is said to have wandered irresolute and despondent; and hesitating whether he should seek protection with the Huns or with the Romans, he threw the reins on his horse's neck and left the decision to chance [2]. His animal carried him to the Roman frontiers, and he became the guest of the nation with whom his country had been waging war for the space of nearly seven centuries.

He was well received by the Emperor Maurice, or rather by his lieutenant, at Hierapolis. The Emperor is said himself to have sent him a treasure

[1] *Journal Asiatique*, 6e série, 1866, p. 192. The uncles, named Bundâwi and Bustam, were put to death in true oriental style by their nephew on his accession to the throne.

[2] *Taríkh Regum Persiae*, ed. W. Schikard, p. 154.

of priceless jewels and to have given him his daughter Mary in marriage[1]. It is of more importance that he espoused the cause of the Persian prince, and sent Narses with a vast army to recover the kingdom from Bahrâm. The issue was decided in a bloody battle on the river Zab in the district of Balarath, where, although the Persian commander fought with his usual adroitness and valour, his army was outnumbered and cut to pieces. Bahrâm fled to Balkh, where the ministers of the King's vengeance soon tracked him down and destroyed him[2]. Chosroes was thus by Roman aid placed on the throne of Persia; a picked regiment of a thousand Romans formed his body-guard; and peace was established between the two Empires. It is even said that Chosroes turned Christian, and his costly offerings at the shrine of St. Sergius and his letters to the Patriarch of Antioch are quoted as evidence of his preference for the Jacobite profession of faith[3].

[1] So Eutychius and Makîn, while other writers merely make the lady of Roman birth. She is apparently identified by Gibbon with Shîrîn; but the Persian romance called *The Loves of Khusrau and Shîrîn* clearly distinguishes Mary as a separate personality. See Sir W. Ouseley's translation in *Oriental Collections*, vol. i. p. 224. Yet Shîrîn also was a Christian. Sebeos, who calls her Queen of Queens, says that she built besides monasteries a church near the royal palace, which she adorned with gold and silver, and to which she appointed priests and deacons, with endowments from the royal exchequer for salaries and vestments.

[2] According to one account he was poisoned by the Queen of the Khakân of Tartary, to whom Chosroes was related. See Sir J. Malcolm's *History of Persia*, vol. i. p. 155 n.

[3] Abû 'l Faraj, who gives in full the letters exchanged between Chosroes and Maurice, adds that after the defeat of Bahrâm the King built two churches for the Christians, one dedicated to the

No doubt his education and his close relations with the Christian Empire, as well as his marriage, softened the traditional hostility of a Magian to the Christian religion. But the Romans claimed as the reward of their alliance an annexation of territory which brought their Empire up to the banks of the Araxes; and while this loss was galling to Chosroes and his people, the King's leanings to an alien religion were equally galling to his priests, and

B.V.M., the other to St. Sergius (ed. Pococke, pp. 96–8). The offerings are mentioned by Evagrius, who says that Chosroes gave to the church a processional cross, a chalice and paten, an altar-cross, and a censer—all of pure gold—besides a curtain of Hunnish embroidery spangled with gold. Theophylact also relates that Chosroes in his hour of dejection vowed a magnificent golden cross set with pearls and sapphires to St. Sergius—a saint whom even the wandering tribes venerated—and he gives the same list of additional offerings made by Chosroes when Sira or Shîrîn showed promise of bearing a son. The great Anûshîrwân himself, for all his persecution of the Christians, is alleged to have been on friendly terms with Uranius, a Nestorian Christian philosopher widely famed for his Aristotelian teaching: see Mosheim's *Ecclesiastical History* eleventh ed., p. 218. 5 (London, W. Tegg, 1880). But the author of this story cannot have read or believed Agathias, who was a contemporary of Uranius, and reports him as a shallow disputatious fellow, given to loafing among the bookstalls of Constantinople. Agathias makes out that Anûshîrwân was no scholar, though a fine soldier, and that Uranius was little better than a drunken parasite at his court (*Hist.* lib. 2, ap. Migne, *Patr. Gr.* t. 88). Zachariah of Mitylene gives some interesting details of the honour shown to Christians at the court of the Persian King, and of the good service wrought by Christian physicians, especially in getting the King to build and endow a hospital—a thing then unknown in Persia (tr. Hamilton and Brooks, p. 331). See also infra, p. 66, n. 2, and p. 135, n. 1. In India even to-day there is a firm tradition that one of Anûshîrwân's sons, called Mushzâd, was a Christian. That very eminent convert from Islâm, the Rev. M. 'Imâd ad Dîn Lalûz, who died in the year 1900, claimed direct descent from this Mushzâd (*Church Missionary Intelligencer*, December, 1900, p. 913).

were doubtless quickly corrected. He was consequently driven by powerful forces, religious and political, to break the pact with Byzantium. He got rid of the Roman guard, and he quarrelled with Narses who was in command at Dara; whereupon Maurice, anxious to soothe the King's enmity, replaced Narses by Germanus [1].

It was at this time that the deformed and ferocious Phocas, having secured the supreme power at Byzantium, had the Emperor Maurice and all his sons and his daughters put to death. Chosroes hardly needed now the pretext his indignation furnished for a declaration of open war. Any doubt he may have felt was removed when Narses set up the standard of revolt at Edessa, dividing the Empire against itself [2]. It is true that Narses, venturing in a fit of foolish confidence to visit his partisans at the capital, was seized by Phocas and burnt at the Hippodrome; but the die was cast. When therefore Lilius, the envoy of Phocas, reached Germanus

[1] The last page or so of Theophylact may be consulted here: he ends with the rupture of peace. But, though a native of Egypt, he is very disappointing as an authority. He only mentions his country twice, and that to record foolish prodigies. The first is, the rise of a monstrous form from the Nile—a story which curiously is recorded also by John of Nikiou in a slightly altered shape (p. 533); the second is the downfall of all the statues of Maurice in Alexandria on the night of his murder. This, says Theophylact, was witnessed by a friend of his own, an illuminator, returning late from a festive party. A natural explanation of the phenomenon is not far to seek.

[2] It appears from the *Tarîkh Regum Persiae* of Schikard (p. 155) that this revolt coincided with and was probably caused by the elevation of Phocas to the throne. John of Nikiou relates that Chosroes tried to poison Narses and his men and horses: but it is not clear in what way the achievement of this purpose would have advantaged him (pp. 528–9).

at Dara and was sent on with every mark of honour to the Persian court, bearing letters and royal gifts for the King, Chosroes flung the Emperor's ambassador into a dungeon and marched his forces into Armenia.

It is not within the scope of this work to follow the campaigns of Chosroes against Phocas. They neither fall within the period under review, nor connect, save by their broad results, with the history of Egypt; and the present writer could add little or nothing to the records already written. Suffice it therefore to say that after overrunning Armenia, which had so often been the battlefield of contending empires, the Persian King divided his forces, and sent one army southward to the conquest of Syria and another westward through the heart of Asia Minor with the design of reaching Constantinople. The order of events is by no means clear; but it is the fortune of the southern force that concerns us here, and so slow was its progress that the fall of Antioch only coincided with the coronation of Heraclius. Had the motive of Chosroes in waging war been merely revenge against Phocas, the death of that tyrant might have ended the strife: but the Great King had proved the weakness of his enemies, and the success of his arms only fired his ambition. He now aimed at nothing less than the total subjugation of the Roman Empire. It was no visionary scheme. In numbers, equipment, and discipline his troops were far superior to those of the enemy; his commanders—now that Bonôsus and Narses were dead—were unrivalled; his treasury was full and his people united, while the Emperor's people were divided, and his exchequer wellnigh exhausted.

Still the Syrian country was difficult: siege

methods were tedious: and a great amount of time was wasted every year in winter quarters. Hence it was not till the fifth year of Heraclius' reign that the Persian general Khorheam [1] after taking Damascus and Caesarea advanced to the capture of Jerusalem. From his head quarters at Caesarea, Khorheam, it seems, sent envoys calling on Jerusalem to surrender to the Great King; and the city was actually delivered up to the Persian officers by the Jews, who had prevailed over the Christian population [2]. Some months later, however, the Christians

[1] Eutychius, ap. Migne, *Patr. Gr.* t. 111, col. 1082, gives the name as Chorawazaih. It is found as Σαρβαραζᾶς and Σαρβαναζᾶς in Theophanes: as Σάρβαρος in the *Chronicon Paschale*: also in the forms Sharawazaih and Shahrbarz: and it is a corruption of the Persian 'Shah-Waraz,' which means 'The King's Wild Boar.' A wild boar, as the emblem of fierce strength, was engraved on the seal of ancient Persia and also on that of Armenia. The designation Shah-Waraz was of course a title of honour, not a name. The same general (who afterwards for a short time usurped the throne of Persia) is known also by another title, which appears in Armenian authors as Erasman, Razman, Rhomizan, or Ramikozan, and in Greek authors as Rasmisas or Romizanes; in the proper form of Rhozmiozan in Moses of Kaghankatouts; and as Ῥουμίαζαν in Theophanes. His name as distinguished from these titles was Khorheam. See *Journal Asiatique*, 6e série, 1866, p. 197. Yet the name Khorheam seems unknown to Persian writers. Mr. Platts tells me that in Persian histories this king is called كراز (kurâz = boar) or شهر برز (shahr-baraz), or شهر يار (shahr-yâr).

[2] The same fierce hostility of Jew to Christian is recorded by Cedrenus, who relates that in the last year of Phocas' reign the Jews fell upon the Christians at Antioch, whereupon Phocas sent Bonôsus against the Jews, on whom he wreaked vengeance with the most revolting barbarity. See above, ch. ii. p. 14. Doubtless in the next year the Jews at Antioch aided the Persian invaders, as they did at Jerusalem. See *Corp. Hist. Byzant. Script.* t. vii. p. 708: also Maḳrîzî (Malan's tr.), p. 68. So also when Shahîn (or Saên) appeared in 610 before Caesarea in Cappadocia, the

rose in revolt, slew the Persian chiefs, overmastered the garrison, and closed the gates. The Shah-Waraz then advanced to beleaguer the town: but aided by the Jews he succeeded in undermining the walls, and on the nineteenth day from their arrival his troops entered by the breach and took the city by storm [1]. Scenes of massacre, rapine, and destruction ensued. The most reasonable estimate, which is that of Sebeos and of Thomas Ardzrouni, places the slain at 57,000 and the captives at 35,000, while the Byzantine historians say loosely that 90,000 perished [2]. The Armenians are probably nearer the truth, but it is certain that many thousand clergy and monks, saints and nuns, were put to the sword. After twenty-one days of plunder and slaughter, the Persians retired outside the walls, and set fire to the city. Thus the church of the Holy Sepulchre and all the famous churches of Constantine [3] were

Christians fled, but the Jews tendered their submission to the Persians. In harmony with all this is the evidence of Sebeos, which is most explicit. 'At this time,' he says, 'all the country of Palestine freely submitted to the rule of the Persian King. Chiefly the remnant of the Hebrews rose against the Christians, and moved by traditional hatred, they wrought much evil in the midst of the faithful. They went over to the Persians, and joined with them in friendly relations.' If further proof of the Jews' intolerant hatred of Christians were wanted, it might be found in the pages of Zachariah of Mitylene, who describes the barbarities wrought by the Homerite Kings of Arabia, who were Jews, upon their Christian subjects: see Hamilton and Brooks' tr., pp. 200 seq.

[1] This account is given by Sebeos and, I think, by him alone among the authorities.

[2] Theophanes, Cedrenus, and Zonaras agree in this number, which is found also in the *Tarîkh Regum Persiae*, p. 155. It tallies closely with Sebeos' number, if we put his slain and captives together. But one MS. of Sebeos gives 17,000 as the number of the slain.

[3] For an account of these beautiful buildings see Palestine

destroyed or dismantled. The Holy Rood, which had been buried in its golden and bejewelled case [1], was unearthed [2] when its hiding-place had been disclosed under torture, and with countless holy vessels of gold and silver was carried away as plunder, while great multitudes, including the Patriarch Zacharias, were driven into captivity. The reliquary of the Holy Cross and the Patriarch were sent as presents to Mary the wife of Chosroes [3]: but of the ordinary captives many were redeemed by the Jews for the mere pleasure of putting them to death, if Cedrenus is to be believed. 'All these things happened not in a year or a month but within a few days' pathetically exclaims the writer of the *Chronicon Paschale*, and the date is accurately fixed to the month of May, 615 [4].

Pilgrims Text Society, vol. i, and the anacreontics of Sophronius in Migne, *Patr. Gr.* t. 87 (3).

[1] Malcolm's *History of Persia*, vol. i. p. 157.

[2] The Cross had been buried in a garden and vegetables planted over it.

[3] Eutychius, ap. Migne, *Patr. Gr.* t. 111, col. 1082.

[4] Theophanes gives the fifth year of Heraclius, A. M. 6106. This A. M.=615 A. D., as is proved by the correspondence of A. M. 6113 with the year of Heraclius' expedition and Mohammed's appearance (A. D. 622). Sebeos gives the year as Chosroes 25, the latter half of which corresponds with the first half of 615. As regards the day of the month, there is some confusion in the Armenian writers. Thomas Ardzrouni says the capture of the city took place ten days after Easter on Margats 28. Dulaurier (*Chronologie Arménienne*, pp. 222–3) shows that the two dates cannot coincide, since Easter in 614, to which year Dulaurier seems to assign the fall of Jerusalem, was March 31, and ten days later=April 10; whereas Margats 28=May 26. Sebeos agrees very closely with Thomas Ardzrouni, but makes the ten days after Easter= Margats 27, which date Mr. Conybeare puts as equivalent to May 20. But Easter in 615 fell upon April 20, and if we suppose that in the MS. the figure 10 is confused with 30, we have in

So the Holy City was smitten with fire and sword. But of the remnant that escaped slaughter and captivity many fled southward to the Christian cities of Arabia[1]—quiet communities whose peace was already disturbed by echoes of the cry of the rising prophet of Islâm. Yet it was probably in connexion with this very triumph of the idolatrous Persians at Jerusalem that Mohammed uttered his famous prophecy: 'The Romans have been overcome by the Persians in the nearest part of the land; but after their defeat they shall be overcome in their turn within a few years[2].' But the main refuge of the scattered Christians was in Egypt, and particularly Alexandria, where the population was already swollen by crowds of refugees who had been flocking thither during the whole course of the Persian invasion of Syria.

The bounty and resources of John the Almoner were already strained by the prevailing destitution, even before the exiles from Jerusalem were thrown upon the city. To add to the troubles of the time, that same summer saw a serious failure of the Nile flood, and the result was a devastating famine[3] throughout the land of Egypt. Gifts nevertheless

May 20 an exact correspondence. Moreover the *Chronicon Paschale* says that the capture took place 'towards the month of June,' and this is quite decisive as between the discrepant dates of the Armenians. It is, however, to be remarked that the *Chronicon* makes the capture of the city take place in the fourth year of Heraclius, and apparently Severus and Cedrenus agree with it in placing the date in 614. The testimony of the *Chronicon Paschale* is difficult to reject, but one must in this particular decide against it on a balance of evidence.

[1] For an account of these communities see Wright's *Christianity in Arabia.*

[2] Al Ḳurân, s. xxx, and Sale's notes.

[3] Leontius, ap. Migne, *Patr. Gr.* t. 93, col. 1625.

poured in to the Church, and few of those who came to John, 'as to a waveless haven,' for refuge were disappointed. Besides the daily dole of food for the needy the good Patriarch provided almshouses and hospitals for the sick and wounded, and scorned even to rebuke those wealthy men who were mean enough to take advantage of his charity. But such lavishness could not last: and as the famine grew fiercer, John found his chest becoming empty. In this strait he was sorely tempted by a layman who had been twice married and was therefore disqualified for orders [1], but who offered a vast sum of money and a great weight of corn as the price of his ordination. John had only two measures of corn remaining in his granary: but in the end he rejected the offer, and was rewarded almost on the moment by the news that two of the Church corn-ships, with large cargoes of grain, had just rounded the Pharos from Sicily, and were moored in the harbour.

Yet the good works of the Patriarch were not bounded by Egypt or confined to feeding the hungry. No sooner had the Holy City been sacked than a certain monk named Modestus, who had escaped the slaughter, wandered through Palestine begging for alms to reinstate the ruined churches. He was successful in his mission, and returning with a great sum of money to Jerusalem, he found that the Jews had now forfeited the special protection of the Persians, which they had at first received as the guerdon of their service to the conquerors. The Christians were again in favour, and Modestus being appointed civil and spiritual head of the community, was suffered to rebuild the churches. Indeed, as

[1] See Mrs. E. L. Butcher's *Story of the Church of Egypt*, vol. i. p. 345.

Sebeos relates, Chosroes had sent special orders to treat the captives kindly, to resettle them, and to restore the public buildings. He also sanctioned the expulsion of the Jews—an order which was carried out with the greatest alacrity.

The same historian gives a letter written by Modestus to Koumitas, Metropolitan of Armenia, after the completion of the work upon the churches. 'God now has made our adversaries friends,' it says, 'and shown us mercy and pity from our captors. But the Jews . . . who presumed to do battle and to burn those glorious places, are driven out from the Holy City, and must not inhabit it nor see the holy places restored to their magnificence.' And again: 'All the churches of Jerusalem have been set in order, and are served by clergy: peace reigns in the City of God and round about it.'

Not less curious is the narrative, given by the same writer, of a kind of council held by the Christians at the suggestion of Chosroes. The story is preserved in a letter sent by the Armenian Catholicus and bishops in reply to a message from Constantine, successor to Heraclius. The latter relates that the Great King ordered all the bishops of the East and of Assyria to assemble at his Court, remarking: 'I hear that there are two parties of Christians, and that the one curses the other: which is to be regarded as in the right? They shall come to a general assembly to confirm the right and reject the wrong.' One Smbat Bagratouni and the King's chief physician were made presidents. It is specially recorded that Zacharias, the Patriarch of Jerusalem, was present, and 'many other wise men who had been carried into captivity from Alexandria.' The council proved very turbulent, and the King had to expel all sects but those who followed the doctrines of Nicaea, Constantinople, Ephesus, and Chalcedon. These several doctrines he ordered the assembled divines to examine and report upon. Memorials representing various opinions were submitted to the King, who discussed and pondered them. Finally, Zacharias and the Alexandrian divines were separately asked to pronounce the truth under oath, and they declared the right faith to be that approved by the Councils of Nicaea, Constantinople, and Ephesus, but not that of Chalcedon: in other words they pronounced for the Monophysites. Thereupon the King ordered a search to be made in the royal treasury or library for the document of the Nicaean faith, which was found, and declared to be in agreement with the faith of the Armenians. Accordingly Chosroes issued an edict that 'All the Christians under my rule shall accept the faith of the Armenians.' Among those who so agreed are named 'the God-loving queen Shîrîn, the brave Smbat, and the chief royal physician.' The instrument embodying the right confession of faith, as the result of the council, was sealed with the Great King's seal, and deposited with the royal archives.

This singular episode, embedded in the letter of the Armenian bishops and so preserved to history, is the most striking evidence we possess of Chosroes' attitude to the Christians. The letter itself has the ring of truth, and there is no reason whatever to question its genuineness. It was written somewhere about the year 638, or some twenty years after the council which it records, and which was assembled not long after the Persian capture of Jerusalem. The Great King is here revealed in a new light. He is no fanatical heathen monarch, persecuting or warring against the believers in the Cross. On the contrary, he acknowledges the right of the Christians to their belief, shows a curious speculative interest in their tenets, is puzzled by their most unchristian fightings and anathemas, and either from kindly wishes for their welfare or from mere motives of state policy he desires to compose their differences. He was present at the debate, put questions, and weighed answers. When his mind was made up and his decision given, he seems to have threatened some of the bishops that he would put them to the sword and pull down their churches if they disobeyed his ordinance. But on the whole the story shows a toleration verging on sympathy for the Christian religion—the same frame of mind which is displayed in the order restoring the Christian outcasts to Jerusalem and enabling them under Modestus to rebuild the churches. John of Nikiou relates [1] that Hormisdas' father, the great Anûshîrwân, after secretly professing Christianity, was baptized by a bishop. However that may be, the influence of Christian queens, physicians, and philosophers at the court clearly enlightened the King's mind and softened his disposition towards the Christian religion [2]. We have far more reason for astonishment

[1] p. 526.

[2] See also supra, p. 55, n. 3. I may add that, according to Ṭabarî (ed. De Goeje, vol. i. p. 1000), shortly after his accession Chosroes issued an edict allowing the Christians in his dominions to restore their churches *and to make converts of the Magians, if they could*, alleging that a similar edict had been issued by Anûshîrwân in consequence of a treaty with Caesar. Ya'ḳûbî relates (ed. Houtema, vol. i. p. 194) that when Chosroes announced his early victories to Maurice, the Emperor sent him a robe embroidered with crosses, which he wore to the scandal of his people. Moreover he 'issued

at the normal toleration which the Church enjoyed under Persian rule than for surprise at the occasional outbursts of ferocity from which it suffered.

But to resume. The contribution offered by John of Alexandria towards the reinstatement of the churches in Jerusalem is said to have been a thousand mules, a thousand sacks of corn and of vegetables, a thousand vessels of pickled fish, a thousand jars of wine, a thousand pounds of iron, and a thousand workmen[1]: and John wrote in a letter to Modestus—'Pardon me that I can send nothing worthy the temples of Christ. Would that I could come myself and work with my own hands at the church of the Resurrection[2].' He is also recorded to have sent a large convoy of gold, corn, clothing, and the like, under charge of one Chrysippus—though this, albeit separately related, may be the same story in another form—and to have commissioned Theodore bishop of Amathus in Cyprus, Gregory bishop of Rhinocolura[3], and Anastasius

a decree commanding that the Christians should be held in honour and publicly acknowledged and promoted to high places, and he announced that a treaty had been made between himself and the King of the Romans such as no king had made before him.'

[1] Eutychius, ap. Migne, *Patr. Gr.* t. 111, col. 1082 seq. Eutychius is of course wrong in saying that these events took place in the sixth year of Phocas: it should be Heraclius, as in Cedrenus and Theophanes. Leontius gives practically the same version of John's contribution, but he adds a thousand pieces of gold, and he writes 'strings of fish' instead of pickled fish in jars.

[2] Zacharias, who was Patriarch of Jerusalem from 609 to 628 or 629, and was carried off by the Persians, has left an account of the Persian conquest which may be read in Migne, t. 86, col. 3219 seq., and from which I have quoted.

[3] Rhinocolura was a town on the Egyptian frontier towards Palestine. Diodorus Siculus derives its name from a legend that

Abbot of the monastery of the Great Mountain of St. Anthony[1], with large sums of money to recover and redeem as many captives as they could. This was in the latter half of 615.

a King of Egypt called Artisanes used it as a place of exile for malefactors, who were marked by having their noses slit or cut off. The town was known in Arab times as Al ʿArîsh. See Quatremère, *Mém.* i. p. 53; *Rec. de l'Égypte*, ii. pp. x, xi, 20. Champollion rejects Diodorus' etymology, but cutting off the nose was a recognized and common form of punishment in Graeco-Roman law at this time: see Bury's Gibbon, vol. v. p. 529. Sebeos also relates that Heraclius inflicted this penalty on those who joined Athalaric's conspiracy after his return from Jerusalem.

[1] The monastery here spoken of may well be the well-known one on the Red Sea coast, as its description seems to imply; or it may be one of the same name on the mountain near Ḳifṭ on the Nile by Ḳanâh. See Abû Ṣâliḥ, *Churches and Monasteries of Egypt*, pp. 159–62 and 280. Sharpe in his *History of Egypt* (vol. ii. p. 368) speaks of a monastery of St. Anthony in the capital: but that seems to me a quite baseless conjecture.

CHAPTER VII

PERSIAN CONQUEST OF EGYPT

Union established between the Coptic and Syrian Churches. Advance of the Persians on Egypt. Capture of Babylon and Nikiou, and siege of Alexandria. Flight of Nicetas and John the Almoner. Death of the latter. The city betrayed by a student, Peter of Baḥrain. Death of Andronicus. The attitude of the Copts to the invaders: current fallacies refuted. Story of Pisentios and treatment of the Copts. Treatment of Alexandria. The Fort of the Persians.

About the same time that the caravans sent by John the Almoner were crossing the desert from Egypt to Jerusalem, in the early autumn of 615, the Coptic Patriarch Anastasius received a visit from Athanasius, the Patriarch of Antioch, who had been dispossessed by the Persian invasion. They met, as has been stated, in the celebrated Ennaton monastery on the sea-coast westward of Alexandria. One or two bishops from Syria probably accompanied their Patriarch; others, like Thomas of Harkel and Paul of Tella, were already settled at the monastery, working hard at their great task of revising the Syriac version of the Bible by collation of the Greek: and yet others were in Egypt as refugees. For 'while the Persians were ravaging Syria, all who could escape from their hands—laymen of all ranks, and clergy of all ranks with their bishops—fled for refuge to Alexandria[1].' It is therefore extremely probable that, as tradition avers, five Syrian bishops were present at the meeting of the two Patriarchs,

[1] Gelzer's *Leontius von Neapolis*, Anhang ii. p. 112.

which resulted in the establishment of union between the Syrian and the Coptic Church. Athanasius only remained a month in Egypt, after which he returned to Syria, where he witnessed the beginning of that curious toleration which seems almost everywhere to have followed not far behind the bloody steps of the Persian conquerors. Sword in hand the Persians showed a savage ferocity which passed all bounds of reason and necessity, and which seemed never to tire of mere slaughter: but when the reign of peace returned, they governed with unexpected mildness. So it was in Arabia, in Syria, and in Palestine: and so it was to prove in Egypt.

The subjugation of Syria had taken six years to accomplish. The capture of Jerusalem probably left little more work for the Persian armies to do in that region: and towards the autumn of the following year 616, their preparations were complete for a campaign in Egypt. Apparently it was not the same commander, Khorheam, the Shah-Waraz, who led the invading forces, but another general called Shahîn [1], and he followed the beaten track of

[1] The *Chronicon Orientale* and Maḳrîzî make Chosroes himself the invader of Egypt, but probably only by a loose manner of speech. Another account gives Saên or Sais, i. e. Shahîn, as the name of the general, and this is probably the truth, rather than that it was Khorheam, as Eutychius relates. There is no warrant for the statement that Chosroes abandoned his palace for the hardships of the field in either the Syrian or the Egyptian campaign. It was natural to suppose that Khorheam from Palestine pushed on to Egypt: but Ṭabarî's authority in such a matter is great, and he clearly states that Rumyûzân (Khorheam), was the general who captured Jerusalem; that another general, Shahîn, was ordered to Egypt and Nubia and sent home the keys of Alexandria to Chosroes; while a third, Ferruhân, was dispatched to Constantinople. That the general was Shahîn seems also proved by the Persian papyri in

war—the road taken by Cambyses, by Antiochus Epiphanes, by Alexander the Great, and destined not many years later to be taken by 'Amr at the head of his Arabs.

The route lay from Rhinocolura along the coast to Pelusium, from Pelusium to Memphis and round the apex of the Delta, from Memphis down the western Nile to Nikiou and to Alexandria. The people of the Nile valley had neither the means nor the spirit for any very serious resistance, nor is there record of any great battle fought or desperate effort made to save the country.

The Greek historians describe the whole campaign in a sentence: 'the Persians took all Egypt and Alexandria and Libya up to Ethiopia, and returned with a vast number of captives and a vast amount of spoil[1]'; and Egyptian authorities add less than could be desired to their barren narrative. We know, however, that Pelusium was captured without much difficulty, and that the Persians wrought havoc among its many churches and monasteries[2]. Not a word is written about the reduction of the great fortress of Babylon near Memphis: but although it is clear that the Persians were masters of the art of siege warfare, it is probable that Babylon was undefended. After the fall of Memphis the army marched by land, aided by a large flotilla on the Nile, and they followed the right bank of the main western branch, past Nikiou, to Alexandria[3].

the Rainer collection: see Karabacek's *Führer durch die Ausstellung*, p. 113.

[1] Theophanes and Cedrenus.

[2] Abû Ṣâliḥ, p. 168, and the British Museum MS. of Severus, p. 101, referred to in the note there.

[3] The occupation of Babylon and Nikiou before the capture of

Of the capture of Alexandria itself there remains an account which is interesting[1]. This great city, says the chronicle, was that 'which Alexander had built in accordance with the counsels of his master Aristotle, a city girt with walls, encircled with the waters of the Nile, and furnished with strong gates.' The siege lasted some time, and with all their skill the Persians were unable to force an entrance into the great fortress. Indeed its defences were so strong as to be virtually impregnable. It was now, i.e. in 617, some 117 years since a Persian army had overrun Egypt, and on that occasion the flood of conquest which had surged over the Delta beat in vain against the walls of Alexandria[2]. These same walls but eight years previously had flung back the desperate battalions of Bonôsus, like rock-shattered billows: and they were destined to prove their strength a quarter of a century later in prolonged defiance of the Saracen leaguer. Clearly then at this juncture the long lines of bulwarks and towers were as formidable as ever; and a united and resolute garrison, drawing endless resources from the sea, which the Empire still commanded, would have wearied out the besiegers, and either crushed

Alexandria is related by the Cyprian monk John, who was on a pilgrimage in Egypt. His words are—*παρεγενόμην ἐν Ἀλεξανδρείᾳ κατὰ τὸν καιρὸν ἐν ᾧ εἰσῆλθον οἱ Πέρσαι ἐν Αἰγύπτῳ, ἔτι ὄντων αὐτῶν ἐπὶ τὰ μέρη τῆς Νικίου καὶ Βαβυλῶνος τῆς κατ' Αἴγυπτον*; and he describes the *ταραχὴν καὶ θόρυβον τῆς Περσικῆς ἐπιδρομῆς* in Alexandria just as he was departing homewards. Quoted by Gelzer, *Leontios von Neapolis*, Anmerkungen, p. 152.

[1] The Syrian Chronicle (ed. Guidi and tr. Th. Nöldeke) cited by Gelzer, l. c.

[2] Circa 500 A.D. in the time of the Emperor Anastasius. The Persians set fire to the suburbs of Alexandria, but could do no more.

them when weakened or forced them to raise the siege.

But union had long been impossible to the motley and turbulent population of Copts, Romans, Syrians, Jews, and students and refugees from all parts of the Empire. The Copts and the Syrians hated the Romans, and the Jews hated the Christians, with an enmity on which no common peril could act as solvent: while all would have laughed to scorn the idea that between the different races, classes, and creeds there could be any bond of patriotism, which alone might have given them cohesion. It is therefore not surprising to learn that the city fell through treason.

During the period of investment the baffled Persians wreaked their fury on the country round, particularly upon the monasteries. Story tells of no less than six hundred monasteries in the neighbourhood of Alexandria, all built 'with keeps like the towers used for dovecotes[1].' Confident in the

[1] Severus of Ushmûnain, Brit. Mus. MS. p. 100; Paris MS. p. 87. Similar keeps still exist at the monasteries in the Wâdî 'n Naṭrûn. That there was a very large number of monasteries near Alexandria is undoubted. In an ancient Coptic document translated by Amélineau (*Histoire des Monastères de la Basse Égypte*, p. 34) Macarius says that he spent three years in the monasteries round about Alexandria, where he lived among remarkable men filled with every virtue to the number of 2,000. This was in the fourth century, and by the seventh the number of monks had largely grown. Even as early as 485 we read in the *Chronicle of Zachariah of Mitylene* that after the publication of Zeno's Henoticon 30,000 monks and ten bishops met at the 'Martyr Church of St. Euphemia' without the walls of Alexandria, where, after resolving not to enter the city for fear of creating a riot, they deputed Bishop Theodore with seven other bishops and 200 archimandrites to wait on the Patriarch Peter, and to confer with him in the cathedral. This record would show that there is a substantial basis of truth in Severus' statement.

security of these convent castles, the monks not only neglected all precautions for safety but ventured on acts of open defiance against the enemy. But a host of Persians, advancing from the west [1], where their camp lay, surrounded the walls and quickly battered down their rude defences. Nearly every man within them was put to the sword, only a very small remnant escaping by hiding in holes and corners. All the treasure and all the furniture in the monasteries was taken as plunder: churches and buildings were broken down or set on fire, and so fell into ruins, which remained visible till long after the invasion of the Arabs.

But among the precious spoil taken by the enemy, what became of those priceless literary treasures which filled the monastic libraries? No sure answer can be given: but while many libraries perished, some certainly escaped destruction. Most important of all, the great Ennaton monastery was left in security owing to its distance from Alexandria, and it is highly probable that its collection of books and manuscripts remained uninjured. The survival of the monastery is proved by the fact that the Patriarch Simon (A. D. 694) came from it and was buried in it [2]; and as Simon was born a Syrian and was renowned for his theological studies, it is clear that the monastery retained its Syrian connexion as well as its repute for learning.

[1] I have followed Severus, whose language implies either that most of the monasteries lay to the east of the city, which hardly agrees with what we know from other sources, or that the Persian forces had worked right round Alexandria, so as to attack it from the west or south-west.

[2] Von Gutschmidt's *Kleine Schriften*, ii. p. 501. The convent of Al Zûjâj named by Severus is of course the same as the Ennaton, as I have shown.

It is frequently mentioned in subsequent history. Another monastery which survived was Dair Ḳibrîûs, which lay to the north-east of Alexandria on the coast[1]. The range therefore of the devastation wrought by the Persians round the Great City was singularly limited: for during the siege they were either too busy or too indolent to send marauding parties a few miles across the desert sands to vex the sequestered shelters of the monks. The great group of convents which they sacked and ruined must have been almost or actually within view of the Persian encampment.

Here, however, we must part company with Severus. He alleges that, when tidings of the destruction of the monasteries and the slaughter of the monks reached Alexandria, the inhabitants in a mad panic opened the gates of the city. The Persian Salâr, or commander-in-chief, had had a dream in which some mighty personage appeared, promised to deliver the city into the hands of the Persians, and cautioned him not to treat the city leniently and not to let any of the inhabitants escape, as they were heretics and hypocrites. Thereupon the Salâr, or Shahîn as we may call him, made all the able-bodied men, from eighteen to fifty years of age, come out of the city on the pretence of

[1] Severus at the beginning of his *Life of Benjamin* expressly records the escape of this monastery from the Persians. The Abbot Theonas in the course of the story remarks that he had then, in 622, lived for fifty years in the monastery. This Theonas must be a different person from the Theonas, steward of the Ennaton, to whom Sophronius wrote an ode about 605, which ode is still extant (Migne, *Patr. Gr.* t. 87 (3)). The Cairo MS. of Severus gives the name of the monastery as قبريوس or Ḳibrîûs = Cyprius, while the London MS. seems to give قيرنوس or Ḳîranûs, which is not likely to be correct.

giving them two gold pieces a head; and when they were all gathered together and their names were written down, he ordered his soldiers to fall upon them and slay them, to the number of eighty thousand.

Such is the improbable story. We may dismiss the vision with its absurd denunciation of heretic Christians to a Persian, though the language reveals the Monophysite sympathies of Severus and the complacency which he felt at the thought of wholesale slaughter befalling the Melkite inhabitants of the Great City. But on the other hand the monks who perished were Monophysites or Copts, and the whole tone of Severus indicates hatred and abhorrence of the Persians; so that the story cannot be strained to countenance any sort of compact between the Copts and the Persians. Moreover, brutal as the Persians were, it was wholly against their laws of war to massacre the inhabitants of a city peaceably surrendered [1]. The promise of a money payment and the inscription of eighty thousand names as preliminaries to the slaughter are obviously ridiculous, even were it conceivable that the city gates would be thrown open without the conclusion of a treaty guaranteeing the lives of the citizens. Quitting Severus, therefore, we return to the Syrian Chronicle, which gives a much more credible version of the capture.

It will be remembered that the canal which supplied Alexandria at once with food and with water, after winding under the southern walls took a sharp turn to the north, and entering the city passed right across it till it reached the sea. Both entrances were closed by gateways strongly fortified

[1] This is quite clear from the history of Sebeos.

and defended by powerful engines of war. In time of siege the canal would be little if at all used for landward traffic, as it would be commanded and controlled by the enemy, at least where it lay out of the range of the garrison's artillery; and the besiegers would naturally have seized most of the corn-barges and shipping. But the seaward gate of the canal was constantly open, not merely for merchant vessels from the main, but for the many fishing boats which brought their daily burden to market. And as the gate abutted on the harbour, in which the Roman war-galleys rode unchallenged, it was doubtless somewhat laxly guarded.

In this fact the traitor saw his opportunity. He stole without the walls, and, making his way to the Persian general's tent, there unfolded a plan for the capture of the Great City. It promised well and was adopted. The Persians procured a number of fishing-boats, filled them with soldiers disguised as 'longshore fishermen, and sent them out to sea at dead of night. Well before daybreak the little craft stood in from the offing, and when they reached the northern gate they gave the password and moved unmolested on to the bridge, which carried the great main street of the city over the canal. Here, still in the dark, they seized their swords and disembarked. Trusting to their disguise, they passed quietly down the main avenue westward till they reached the Moon Gate, where they suddenly fell on the unsuspecting warders and killed them. It was the work of a moment. Ere the alarm could be given, they flung back the ponderous gates, and as day broke over the temples and palaces of Alexandria, the hordes of Shahîn rushed in and proclaimed the victory of Chosroes from the walls.

The Syrian Chronicle goes on to say that all who could then took flight; but that the ships on which the treasure of the churches and of the magnates had been placed as a measure of precaution were blown back by a storm and driven on to the shore by the Persian camp, i. e. westward of the city[1]. All the gold and silver and jewels thus captured by the Persian army were sent, together with the keys of the city, to Chosroes. It is curious that there is no mention of the great massacre recorded by Severus; but it is most improbable that in this the Egyptian writer, living in the midst of living traditions, could be wholly mistaken; and moreover such a massacre, where a town was not peaceably surrendered under treaty of protection, fully accords with Persian practice.

But it is clear that some kind of warning had prepared the city for its fate. It was doubtless the warning of despair. The garrison must have been dangerously weakened by the withdrawal of troops to other parts of the Empire or even to Byzantium, as province after province had been 'trampled under foot by the Persians as an ox tramples the threshing-floor[2].' Moreover all the corn supplies of Egypt had been cut off from Alexandria; and although the food of the citizens formed but a fraction of the enormous grain traffic which flowed through Alexandria to all parts of the Mediterranean, all the trade

[1] Called therefore 'the treasure of the wind.' But this story is told by the Arab writer Ibn Ḳutaibah (ninth century) of the ship in which Heraclius had placed his precious vessels and jewels when he resolved to quit Byzantium for Carthage. This ship was driven by storms, he says, to Alexandria, where it fell into the hands of the Persians. *Kitâb al Ma'ârif*, &c., ed. Wüstenfeld, p. 329.

[2] The words of Severus.

was outwards; and when it ceased, it was idle to think of reversing the machinery—of converting exports to imports. Hence, as time wore on and stores diminished, while no relief came from Heraclius, the pinch of want may well have been acute, and the people saw that they would ere long be forced to surrender from sheer starvation. This being the case, we are no longer puzzled by the flight of the governor Nicetas, whose valour, whose capacity for action, and whose loyalty to the Empire are alike unquestionable. It was 'when Alexandria was about to be delivered over to the godless Persians[1]' that Nicetas took ship for Byzantium in company with John the Almoner. They got as far as Rhodes, when the Patriarch was seized with illness, and foreboding his end, he sailed for Cyprus, where he landed and soon afterwards died at the place of his birth, Amathus, on November 11, 617[2].

That the Alexandrians had virtually abandoned all hope of deliverance must then be admitted; and

[1] ὡς ἔμελλεν Ἀλεξάνδρεια τοῖς ἀθέοις Πέρσαις παραδίδοσθαι are the significant words of Leontius.

[2] See Lebeau's *Histoire du Bas Empire*, vol. xi. p. 53: but it must be noticed that in this work the story of John is put long after the Persian conquest of Egypt, and therefore in wrong chronological order. The Copts seem to have made John the Almoner into a martyr as well as a saint in later days, if Breydenbach is to be believed. He visited Egypt in the fifteenth century, and had a spot in Alexandria pointed out to him as the place of John's martyrdom. See his *Descriptio Terrae Sanctae*, &c., p. 122 (fol. 1486). Of course this legend springs from some confusion. John's death is actually commemorated on Nov. 12 by the Eastern Church, the 11th being already assigned to St. Menas: see Von Gutschmidt's *Kleine Schriften*, ii. There is a slight sketch of the Patriarch by the Rev. H. T. F. Duckworth called *St. John the Almsgiver* (Blackwell, Oxford, 1901). He states that John's body now rests in the cathedral at Pressburg.

the action of Peter, the foreign student who betrayed them, probably hastened but little the inevitable doom of the city. All we know of the traitor is that he came from the region of Baḥrain towards the north-east of Arabia; and we cannot be sure whether he was Christian, Jew or Pagan, or whether he had any other motive for his action than the ignoble desire to save his own head at whatever cost to the great seat of learning which had welcomed him. We do know, however, that Baḥrain was a province of Persia, and that even at a later date the inhabitants were described as mostly Persians and Jews[1]. So that there is some presumption that he may have cloaked his treachery by patriotism. But the story is that he found in the city archives a book, at the end of which it was written—'When trouble arises over Alexandria from the western gate, which lies towards the sea, then will the city be taken.' This prophecy, doubtless manufactured after the event, though it would fit in with the capture by Nicetas in 609, discloses nothing of the traitor's motives or religious beliefs, though it does seem to mean that Peter knew the fate of the city to be sealed when he treated with the Persians for its betrayal.

It was probably at the beginning of 618 that the keys of Alexandria were sent to Chosroes. Great as was the slaughter at the fall of the city, a large number of the inhabitants were spared, of whom some were sent into captivity in Persia[2], while others remained unmolested. Among the latter was the Coptic Patriarch Andronicus, who seems

[1] See De Goeje's *Mémoire sur les Carmathes du Baḥrain*, p. 7.

[2] Prisoners from Alexandria are specially mentioned among those released after the capture of Dastagerd by Heraclius.

to have received the same measure of toleration as we know to have been bestowed on Modestus at Jerusalem by direct order of the Persian King; but the shock of the scenes he witnessed and the havoc wrought among his people throughout the land of Egypt seem to have weighed him down with sorrow to the ending of his days [1].

But, as we have seen, Andronicus was allowed to reside in Alexandria during his patriarchate owing to the fact that he possessed powerful relations, his cousin being Chairman of the Council of Alexandria at the time of his election. The fact is interesting, as proving that some of the Copts found their way to high office even under the rule of Heraclius; and it further indicates that the Persians, in settling the country after their conquest, availed themselves of the service of the principal officials of the government which they overthrew. Later we shall see that the Arabs acted in precisely the same manner; nor indeed could it be otherwise when an alien and less civilized army found itself responsible for a highly organized and complex administration. That the Copts fell in with this arrangement may be admitted; it would have been mere folly to refuse; but it is quite another thing to say, as the fashion is with modern writers, that the Persians were hailed as deliverers [2]. Such a charge is not only groundless; it is a complete reversal of the truth.

[1] Severus of Ushmûnain's *Life of Andronicus* is nothing but a record of the calamities due to the Persian conquest, and he concludes with the words, 'So when the Patriarch Andronicus had held his office for six years and had suffered from the barbarity of the Persians—when he had witnessed these terrible things, undergone and endured them—he went to his rest.'

[2] This statement seems to come from Sharpe, who says, 'The troops with which Chosroes conquered and held Egypt were no

For it must be remembered that the Persian army was flushed by a long career of plunder and slaughter, in which the victims were mainly Christians in formal union with the Coptic Church; and it is unlikely that the Persians would befriend in Egypt those whom they slew in Syria: while the long resistance of Alexandria and the presence there of escaped refugees from the Holy Land would serve to whet their anger. There can be little doubt that the massacre was indiscriminate. On the other hand, Maķrîzî alleges that there, as in Palestine, the Jews sided with the Persians. 'Chosroes and his soldiers,' he says, 'came into Egypt, where they killed a very great number of Christians and made of them count-

doubt in part Syrians and Arabs, people with whom the *fellahs*, or *labouring class* of Egyptians, were closely allied in blood and feelings. Hence arose the readiness with which the whole country yielded when the Romans were defeated. But hence arose also the weakness of the Persians and their speedy loss of this conquest when the Arabs rebelled' (*Hist. of Egypt*, ch. xxi. p. 37). Mr. Milne has closely followed Sharpe, accentuating both statements, with one difference. His words are: 'The new governors of Egypt entered into their inheritance quietly (!) and almost naturally, as the Persian army was largely drawn from Syria and Arabia. . . . Thus they had no great difficulty in ruling Egypt: the *wealthier classes* had probably a large intermixture of Arabs among them, who welcomed the rule of their kinsmen, while the fellahin at the worst only changed masters. . . . The revolt of the Arabs under the inspiration of the teaching of Mohammed deprived the king of Persia of his most effective soldiers and gave the Romans a chance of recovering Egypt' (*Hist. of Egypt under Roman Rule*, p. 114). Now these two statements, (1) that the people of Egypt welcomed the Persian invaders, (2) that the recovery of Egypt by Heraclius was due to a defection of the Arabs from Persia to Islâm, are, I believe, equally and totally baseless. At best the first is pure fiction, while the second is but one step removed from fiction. It is to be regretted that Mr. Milne in his admirable work should adopt Sharpe's vague surmises. Mrs. Butcher (*Story of the Church of Egypt*, vol. i. p. 347) does the same.

less captives: for the Jews helped them in their destruction of the Christians and their demolition of the churches[1].' The context of this passage is, as usual, somewhat confused; and inasmuch as it does not clearly distinguish between the Syrian and the Egyptian campaign, it may be argued that the action of the Jews refers only to the former. But there was always a large Jewish colony in Egypt and a Jewish quarter in Alexandria: and it is far more likely that the Jews welcomed another opportunity of aiding the enemies of the Cross than that the Copts showed any friendship for the idolaters whose hands were stained with the blood of their fellow believers in Antioch and in Jerusalem. Peter of Baḥrain may have been a Jew and the agent of a Jewish conspiracy: and were it so, his action would be at least less ignoble and more easily explicable.

But we are not dependent on deductions and surmises for a vindication of the Copts. It cannot be questioned that most of the monks who perished round about Alexandria were Copts: and if this fact stood alone it would serve to rebut the slanderous allegation that the Copts welcomed the Persians. But it does not. After the capture of Alexandria Chosroes' general marched his army southwards, ascending the Nile, for the subjugation of Upper Egypt. His treatment of the Copts was everywhere the same: everywhere his path was marked by death and devastation. When he reached the city of Pshati or Nikiou[2], as Severus relates, some enemy

[1] Malan's trans., p. 68.

[2] Quatremère (*Mém. Géog. et Hist.* t. i. pp. 420 seq.), in proving clearly the identity of Nikiou and Pshati, seems not to have known this passage of Severus, who says expressly, 'The city of Naḳyûs,

of the Copts filled his ears with tales of the wealth and wickedness of the monks who dwelt in the caves and mountains, and at the same time told him that a great number of them were then assembled in the fortress[1]. Moved by these malignant stories, he surrounded the place by troops at night, and at sunrise they rushed in, fell upon the Christians, and slew them to the last man.

It is not open to question that the monks here slain also were members of the Coptic Church. But what was done at Nikiou was repeated in Upper Egypt: and it so happens that here we possess a record even older and more authentic than Severus —a record in fact practically contemporary with the events it chronicles. For at the time of the Persian conquest there was at the town of Coptos in Upper Egypt a bishop of that diocese named Pisentios, whose biography fortunately remains and has been translated from the Coptic by M. Amélineau[2]. The story of Pisentios has so many points of interest that it may be given somewhat fully without apology.

It is known that it was customary every year for the Patriarch of Alexandria to write an encyclical announcing the date of the coming Easter. A frag-

which is also called Ibshâdî,' using of course the Arabic forms. But Quatremère's note is well worth reading. I have already shown that the site of Nikiou is to be found at the modern Shabshîr, and not at the village of Ibshâdî, which has no ancient remains.

[1] The fortress doubtless resembled that at Babylon in enclosing a number of Coptic churches. The town was the seat of a famous bishopric, and the gathering recorded by Severus was some kind of convocation on Church business or for a great festival.

[2] *Étude sur le Christianisme en Égypte au Septième Siècle* (Paris, 1887). The work is also called in the 'tirage à part' *Vie d'un Évêque de Keft au Septième Siècle.*

ment of such a letter, most beautifully written in uncials and dated about 577, is in the British Museum, and such letters or fragments are fairly common. The biography of Pisentios relates that about the time of the Persian invasion, on receipt of the Patriarch's letter, Pisentios wrote a pastoral to all his diocese, in which he said, 'Because of our sins God has abandoned us; he has delivered us to the nations without mercy[1].' He had heard of the arrival of the fire-worshippers, and was thoroughly alarmed by the stories of their barbarity. Having no mind to play the martyr, he resolved on flight; and when he had put all in order and distributed his goods to the poor, he went with his faithful disciple John to Mount Gêmi in the neighbourhood. This was done before the enemy appeared in Upper Egypt, and therefore not in a moment of sudden panic. It was the leisurely act of a man who knew that to remain at his post was to court death. The idea of seeking protection from the Persians by submission, or of claiming friendship from them, never entered the mind of the bishop: and his action is in ludicrous contrast with the theory that the Copts welcomed the Persians.

When Pisentios and John fled to the mountain, they laid in a good store of bread and Nile water. As soon as their water was gone, they suffered greatly, not venturing near the river: till at last Pisentios crept down by night to replenish. They stayed a long time in this retreat, 'praying night and day that God would save the people from bondage to those cruel nations.' This was before Coptos had been taken: but then, when it fell, Pisentios fled three miles further into the rocky desert. There

[1] Amélineau, op. cit., p. 30.

on a mountain-side the two friends found an open doorway, which they entered. Within was a chamber some 70 ft. square and high in proportion, hollowed out of the solid rock, and supported by six piers or columns. It was the burial-place of a vast number of mummies, which lay there undisturbed in their coffins or cases.

Here Pisentios resolved to live alone, directing John to depart and to return with a measure of meal and with water once a week. As John was about to leave the cave, he saw a roll of parchment which he gave to the bishop. The bishop on reading it found that it contained the names of all those whose bodies were laid to rest in that burial-place. It has been generally taken for granted [1] that the roll was written in hieroglyphics, and it is hence argued that the knowledge of hieroglyphic writing survived among the Copts till at least the seventh century. But this is not stated in the Coptic biography. The story goes on to tell how, when John returned, he heard his master talking in the cavern, and listening discovered that he was speaking with one of the mummies, which had come out of its case to demand the bishop's intercession: for the mummy declared that all its kith and kin had been Greeks and worshippers of the pagan gods. But this legend rather shows that the mummies were as late as the second or third century—as is indicated also by the fact that some were shrouded in the 'pure silk of kings' and by the separate embalming of the fingers: and it is at least a possible inference that the roll was written in Greek characters [2].

[1] By Amélineau and others. Dr. Wallis Budge seems of the same opinion.

[2] I cannot quite dismiss the idea that, even if we take the

When the mummy had done speaking, it went back to its coffin: but unfortunately we are told nothing more about the Persians—what they did after the taking of Coptos, or how long they remained in Upper Egypt. Pisentios ultimately got back to his flock, and when he died, was buried after a solemn vigil over his remains in the church at Psenti. On his deathbed he bequeathed all his books to his friend Moses, who succeeded him in the bishopric, and was the author of his biography. Both bishops were clearly men of some learning: but as usual with these Coptic writers, their whole mind is concentrated on childish fairy tales of wonders wrought by the saints. Their sole delight is in the miraculous and impossible: and it is only by some strange oversight or accident that they record any fact whatever relating to the great movements of history which they witnessed, and which they knew to involve the fate of their country.

But we learn two things clearly from this story—first that the Persians spread up the whole valley of the Nile to Syene; and next that, so far from being hailed as deliverers by the Copts, they were regarded, and justly regarded, with the utmost alarm and abhorrence.

The life of Pisentios was written in the seventh century. Of the same tenour is another document, dating from somewhat later in the same century, which shows in even stronger colours what the Copts suffered from the Persians. I refer to the life of the well-known Coptic saint, Anba Shanûdah[1],

hieroglyphics for granted, the ability of Pisentios to read them is recorded as another instance of his miraculous power.

[1] Amélineau, *Monuments pour servir à l'histoire de l'Égypte*

a work which has only recently been brought to light. These are the words in which the biographer records the Persian invasion—words uttered in the form of a prophecy, but written at a time when old men still living could remember the events recorded: 'The Persians shall come down into Egypt and shall make great slaughter: they shall plunder the goods of the Egyptians and shall sell their children for gold—so fierce is their oppression and their iniquity. Great calamities shall they cause to Egypt: for they shall take the holy vessels from the churches and drink wine before the altar without fear, and they shall dishonour women before their husbands. The evil and the suffering shall be very great: and of the remnant one-third shall perish in distress and affliction. Then after a while the Persians shall leave Egypt.'

No evidence could be clearer or more conclusive. It utterly destroys Sharpe's theory that the Copts welcomed the Persians, as well as his theory resting that imaginary fact on an imaginary kinship between the Egyptian people and the Persian forces. Severus too sums up his remarks about the Persian general by saying, 'this Salâr wrought many deeds of cruelty, for he did not know God: but time is too short to relate all his actions.' Before this passage was known, above all before these two almost contemporary documents came to light, history seemed singularly silent about the episode of the Persian invasion: but on the silence of history was founded

Chrétienne (Paris, 1888). The text in Arabic is taken from MSS. collated in Egypt: they are all from a Coptic original composed about 685 or 690. Shanûdah himself died July 2, 451: and the prophecies put in his mouth were of course written after the events, but while the memory of them was fairly fresh.

an airy fabric of conjecture most unjustly disparaging to the Copts. That now falls.

But the Persians remained ten or twelve years in possession of the conquered country. It seems to have taken them three years[1] to spread their dominion over the length and breadth of Egypt and Pentapolis, although there is no record of any serious or prolonged resistance except at Alexandria: and this lapse of time goes far to account for the discrepancy in the chronology of the period. But although during the work of conquest the Persians acted with a kind of frenzied barbarity, as soon as their rage was glutted and the work done, their rule was far from tyrannical. When therefore the Byzantine garrisons, or the remnant of them, were driven out of the Nile valley and escaped oversea, the Copts settled down in a measure of tranquillity under one more of those changes of masters which had constituted their political history from time immemorial.

So, when peace was established, the native Church, which had been harried and plundered and in places blotted out, was now left alone and enabled to recover in part from its wounds. Andronicus, how-

[1] See Abû 'l Faraj (ed. Pococke, p. 99), who mentions the term of three years. The great distances to be covered by the army of occupation postulate a corresponding time. Mistakes constantly arise in dealing with authors who summarize in a sentence and a date the results of a process which required months or even years for its accomplishment. Here, for example, it is extremely probable that the Persian conquest extended over the years 616–618 or 619. Some writers accordingly give the date of its commencement; others the date of its conclusion: and the discrepancy, though only apparent, serves to mislead critics who are a little wanting in thought or imagination. A like discrepancy concerning the duration of the occupation may be explained in like manner. It is given as ten and as twelve years, and probably both statements are in a measure right.

ever, did little or nothing towards the rebuilding of the ruined monasteries. It is more than likely that the Persians laid a tribute on the Church revenues, or at least confiscated the endowments of the banished Melkite establishment. But, as regards civil buildings, the behaviour of the Persians was less ruthless than elsewhere. In Syria, it must be repeated, all through the war with the Roman Empire, they spared all the towns and the people that surrendered peaceably: while, in case of resistance, the custom was not merely to sack the captured places of every movable treasure, but to demolish the very buildings for the sake of beautiful columns or friezes or precious marbles, which they sent to adorn some palace of the Great King. Egypt was at least protected from vandalism of this sort by its very remoteness. For the Byzantines were still in command of the sea; the Delta was covered with a network of unbridged waterways; and between Egypt and Syria lay long stretches of sandy desert: so that heavy transport was practically impossible from one country to another. Moreover there is explicit evidence that the splendid public buildings of Alexandria were for the most part left uninjured by the Persians, whatever may have happened to the monasteries without the walls. Indeed the invaders were probably remembered rather as builders than as destroyers in the capital, where a palace they erected was long known as the 'Palace of the Persians[1].' It would seem that their destructiveness

[1] *Chronicon Orientale.* Severus also says that the Salâr 'built at Alexandria the palace called Ṭarâwus, now named *Fort of the Persians.*' The fort is also mentioned by Barhebraeus (*Chron. Eccl.* t. i. ch. 362) in a passage which seems to indicate that it was at the landing-place for passengers coming in ships from the east.

in other places has been exaggerated. Gibbon, for example, alleges that Cyrene and Barca were finally extinguished at this time by the Persians: whereas a few years later the Arabs at least found those cities worth a fresh conquest, nor were they now even extinguished in the sense that they were finally sundered from the Roman Empire. There is no ground at all for the statement that their fate differed from that of Egypt, which for a while was annexed to the realms of Chosroes, but was destined to revert to the crown of Heraclius before passing for ever under the dominion of Islâm[1].

Few facts are known about the Persian occupation of Egypt. It is clear, however, that the conquerors were not fanatical enough to force the worship of fire on the conquered[2], and that here as in Palestine and in Arabia, when their rule was established, it was based on principles of religious toleration. Just as Modestus

Severus distinctly says the fort was at Alexandria, or one would be inclined to place it at some little distance. Indeed from Suyûṭî and others it is clear that it was not within the city walls.

[1] The Arab historians prove most clearly that Cyrene and Barca were held for the Empire and wrested from the Empire at the time of the Saracen invasion.

[2] In the Life of the Abbot Samuel there is an isolated story that the barbarians (i. e. obviously the Persians) tried to force him to worship the sun. When he refused, he was tied to a negress. But having cured the illness of his captor's son, he was released and returned to his monastery, where he died after predicting the arrival of the Arabs (which he may have seen) and their defeat by the Christians (which he did not see). See *Journal Asiatique*, 1888, pp. 384–5. But it is clear that the cult of Mithra was definitely established in Egypt during the Persian occupation, as is proved by many rude monuments, found at Memphis and other places, which are now in the Cairo Museum. The rays of the sun about the head, and the Phrygian cap, show that the figures sculptured are meant for Mithra.

was allowed by direct order of Chosroes to collect money and to rebuild the churches of Jerusalem, and the Coptic Patriarch was left in undisturbed possession of his see and allowed to reside in Alexandria till his death; so it seems that his successor Benjamin was peaceably elected, and passed the first years of his long and stormy pontificate in comparative tranquillity under the shelter of the Persian government. And as the stately splendour of the streets and public buildings in Alexandria suffered little at the hands of the Persians, so the fame of the Great City as the home of learning if dimmed was unextinguished.

CHAPTER VIII

ART AND LITERATURE

History, medicine, theology. The visit of John Moschus. Alexandrian libraries. Cosmas the Student. Astronomy. Architecture. Painting, mosaic, and *opus Alexandrinum*. Illumination of books. Sculpture. Ivory. Metal-work. Pottery. Paper and glass. Textiles. Trade. Ships and shipping.

THE literature of this period in Egypt is very scanty, although there was more writing than one is apt to imagine [1]. Some authorities aver that John Philoponus was still living at Alexandria: but, though this is erroneous [2], the influence of his theology or his heresy was still felt, and the Patriarch Sergius found it worth his while to denounce John's speculations in concert with George of Pisidia [3]. Though no original thinker, John had been a real student in many branches of learning, and some of his notes on Aristotle are still extant. It was at this time that a priest of Alexandria named Aaron wrote in Syriac the medical treatises which remained in great repute among the Arabs, as recorded by Abû 'l Faraj [4].

Indeed the physicians of Alexandria had long been famous, and the school of medicine there was

[1] A slight chapter on literature in the reign of Heraclius may be found in Prof. Bury's *History of the Later Roman Empire*, vol. ii. pp. 254–7. On the state of learning at Alexandria, see Matter, *École d'Alexandrie*, passim.

[2] Philoponus is shown to belong to the sixth century by A. Nauckius, *Encycl. Halensis*, sect. iii. t. xxiii. p. 465. See also my chapter below on the fate of the Alexandrian Library.

[3] Drapeyron, *L'Empereur Heraclius*, p. 293.

[4] Ed. Pococke, p. 99.

frequented by students from all parts of the Empire. Thus, speaking of the sixth century, Zachariah of Mitylene notes that the court physician to Basiliscus was an Alexandrian: and in another passage he tells of Sergius[1]—an arch-physician of Rhesaina—who was not only 'practised in reading many books of the Greeks,' but had 'studied divinity and medicine at Alexandria, for he was skilled in Syriac reading and speaking[2].' This seems to show a special connexion between the study of medicine and the Syriac language, and to render it probable that in the sixth as in the seventh century the principal works on medicine were in Syriac. And it is past question that the Syriac tongue was in constant use and Syriac literature under constant study in Alexandria, quite apart from the fact that at this period the Persian occupation of Syria had driven shoals of scholars from that country to Egypt.

It is curious that both Sergius and Aaron were, like the Patriarch Eutychius, learned in divinity as well as in medicine. But there is the clearest evidence that an independent school of theology flourished. Just before the Persian invasion we find Syrian scholars correcting the Syriac version of the New Testament and newly translating the Septuagint into Syriac. Thomas of Harkel and Paul of Tella are the two chief names mentioned in connexion with this work[3], which was mainly carried

[1] One Sergius is also mentioned by Abû 'l Faraj as having added two to the thirty treatises composed by Aaron. But he must be a different person.

[2] *Zachariah of Mitylene*, p. 266.

[3] See *Dict. Christ. Biog.*, s. v. Some information about these scholars is also given in Sharpe's *History of Egypt*, ch. xxi. p. 38. Sharpe makes them work at the monastery of St. Anthony and St. Zacchaeus near Alexandria, but he seems to have misunderstood

on at the celebrated Ennaton monastery. That there was great activity in Biblical studies needs no proof. But Agathias shows the amazing dishonesty to which theological controversy could condescend: for he mentions an Augustal prefect who employed fourteen scribes or copyists in the task of corrupting the writings of the Fathers, particularly Cyril, so that from published texts the highest authority could be quoted for the form of heresy which the prefect favoured. It is to be hoped that such frauds were rare: but this happened about the beginning of the seventh century, when sectarian religion was at the height of its strange ascendency over morality. Not only the Ennaton, however, but nearly every monastery had its library and its students. Probably the still surviving Dair Sûriânî—or the Syrian Convent[1]—in the Naṭrûn desert owes its foundation to this period, when so much of Syrian life and learning was removed to Egypt under stress of the Persian wars. And everywhere in the mountains and deserts, far from the intellectual life of the capital, monks and anchorites wrote in Coptic their controversial treatises, biographies of patriarchs, and but too rarely historical chronicles.

Of actual history written at this time but little remains. Theophylact Simocatta has left some useful records; but, though an Alexandrian, he scarcely mentions his native city: while the unknown writer of the *Chronicon Paschale* or *Alexandrinum* has left a contemporary document of the

his authority. I have spoken more fully on the visit of these Syrian students and of their work in the Appendix on the Chronology of the Persian Conquest; q. v.

[1] See *Ancient Coptic Churches*, vol. i. p. 316, for a description of this monastery.

greatest interest and value. The work of John of Nikiou, though written late in the seventh century, was certainly founded on earlier works, of which even the record has perished.

This list of names, though it implies the study of history, philosophy, theology and medicine, is nevertheless a poor one, and gives no idea of the manifold activities of intellectual society at Alexandria. Most of the writings of the time doubtless perished in the great hurricanes of conquest which swept over Egypt during the first half of the seventh century. But there is evidence enough to show that Alexandria might still claim to be the capital of the world of letters and the centre of culture. For although much of the learning of the place was theological, nevertheless the traditions of classical study still flourished. Essays in Christian idealism or Christian ethics were consciously based on Platonic or Aristotelian doctrine; and just as Paul the Silentiary had described the glories of St. Sophia in Homeric hexameters, so now Sophronius, writing from Alexandria, thought it no shame to pour out his passionate longing for the Holy Places in Anacreontic lyrics [1].

It so happens that some interesting details of life in Alexandria at this time are preserved in the writings of John Moschus. These details are not enough to fill a large canvas, and they are given more by accident than by design of the writer, yet the picture they form is curious. John Moschus was a Syrian by birth, though Greek was his native language. He travelled for some years in Egypt with his pupil and friend Sophronius, a native of Damascus, towards the close of the sixth century,

[1] Migne, *Patr. Gr.* t. 87.

and they spent a great deal of time together in the monasteries of the Thebaid or Upper Egypt. When they returned to their own country, John prevailed on Sophronius to take the order of monkhood. They are said to have been driven out of Syria in 605 during the wars of Phocas, and to have gone to Alexandria, where they spent a further period of eight or ten years, reading and writing and making frequent excursions to the monasteries about the city and in the desert and the great Oasis. Both scholars were friends of John the Almoner, though that prelate seems to have been far below them in intellectual stature, and like him they fled from Alexandria at the time of the Persian invasion. It is even related that they accompanied the Almoner to Cyprus, and that on his death Sophronius preached his funeral sermon, though the evidence is against this story. It is certain that they travelled among the Greek islands and ultimately found their way to Rome, where John Moschus put the finishing touches to his work, and upon his deathbed gave it to Sophronius to publish. About the year 620, when the peaceable practice of their religion had been restored to the Christians under Persian rule, Sophronius went back to Palestine, and in due course published the volume which still survives under the name of 'Spiritual Pastures[1].'

While much of this work with its stories of miraculous cures and visions is valueless to the historian, yet by dint of search one comes upon some really delightful pieces of information. There is too a kind of scholar-gipsy flavour about the

[1] Λειμὼν Πνευματικός, better known under its Latin title *Pratum Spirituale*. See Migne, *Patr. Gr.* t. 87 (3), and *Dict. Christ. Biog.*, s.v. Sophronius.

book which redeems even the more tedious parts from dullness. Some points in Alexandrian topography will be noticed in a later chapter: we may here remark on the intense intellectual curiosity which almost every page reveals. The two friends were restless in their quest after knowledge, as their travels show, even if some of their journeys were on Church business [1]. At one moment they are talking in Alexandria with the bishop of Darna (or Darnis) on the Libyan coast, at another with the Abbot Theodore the Philosopher, or again with Zoilus the Reader. Both Theodore and Zoilus were men of exceptional learning and character, and the Abbot as well as the Reader was very poor. Of both it is recorded that they possessed nothing but a mantle and a few books. While Theodore studied philosophy, Zoilus practised the art of illuminating manuscripts [2]. At the Ennaton monastery [3], near Alexandria, they found a venerable abbot who had spent eighty years in monastic life. He was a lover of men, but was further distinguished by a very rare quality—love of animals. Every day he fed the birds of the air, the ants great and small, and the very dogs that prowled about the monastery. But whereas Theodore and Zoilus clung to their books, when they parted with all besides, the animal-lover could never keep a coin or a garment or even a book: all he had was given away to the needy [4].

But the most keenly interesting and the most tantalizing passage in John Moschus is one that

[1] The phrase *ὠφελείας χάριν* is taken to mean 'on business,' but it may mean 'for our (intellectual) advancement,' i. e. 'for purposes of study.'

[2] John Moschus, cap. 171. [3] Id., cap. 184. [4] Id., ib.

describes the intimacy with Cosmas the Student[1] enjoyed by the two friends: for John most frequently writes in the plural, associating himself with Sophronius, his companion in travel and study alike. The passage is so remarkable that something like a transcription of it may be pardoned.

'Of Cosmas the Student,' says John, 'we shall write nothing from hearsay—only what we have seen with our own eyes. He was a simple-minded man, abstemious and clean-living: he was easy-tempered and sociable, given to hospitality, a friend of the poor. He rendered us the very greatest service not only by his speculation[2] and his teaching, but *because he possessed the finest private library in Alexandria and freely lent his books to all readers*[3]. He was very poor, and the whole of his house, which was full of books, contained no furniture but a bed and a table. His library was open to all comers. Every reader could ask for the book he wanted, and there read it. Day by day I visited Cosmas, and it is mere fact that I never once entered his house without finding him engaged either in reading, or in writing against the Jews. He was very reluctant to leave his library, so that he often sent me out to argue with some of the Jews from the manuscript he had written.

'Once I made bold to ask him a question and

[1] ὁ σχολαστικός. Id., cap. 172.

[2] The word is θεωρούμενος, which in Migne is rendered as a passive and so 'by his presence': but the term was still used of the philosophic θεωρία: e.g. John of Constantin 'became a gnostic and a theoretic,' says Zachariah of Mitylene, p. 211.

[3] διὰ τὸ εἶναι αὐτὸν πολύβιβλον ὑπὲρ πάντας τοὺς ἐν Ἀλεξανδρείᾳ ὄντας καὶ προθύμως παρασχεῖν τοῖς θέλουσιν. Unhappily the original contains no suggestion of contrasting private and public libraries in the city.

said, "Will you be so kind as to tell me how long you have lived in this retreat?" But he held his peace and made no answer. Then again I said, "In the Lord's name tell me"; and after some hesitation he replied, "For three and thirty years." When further pressed, Cosmas remarked that the three principal things he had learned in his studies were "not to laugh, not to swear, and not to lie."'

Such is the charming picture of a poor scholar in Alexandria keeping open house for book-lovers[1]. It is, as I have said, a tantalizing picture, and mainly for two reasons. First of all, not a word is said about the class or classes of books which the library contained, or about their number: and then, next, it is a grievous disappointment that John Moschus and Sophronius, with all their love of literature, with all their interest in books and book-collectors, tell us absolutely nothing about the great and famous public library of Alexandria. Was it, or was it not, still in existence? They stand on the very edge of the subject, and could, if they would, utter the word that would solve the still baffling mystery: but they turn away in silence and are gone.

Of course their very silence, coinciding as it does with the silence of so many other writers, has its own logic; but this is not the proper place for a discussion upon the date of the disappearance of the great library. Such a discussion will come later in this work. At present one can only deplore the fact that neither John Moschus in *Spiritual Pastures*, nor Sophronius in any of his fairly voluminous

[1] In the Cairo Museum is an interesting monument to a book-lover of this epoch. On the lid of a sarcophagus, sculptured in relief, is the figure of a student grasping in each hand a roll of MS.

writings which remain, gives a single hint with regard to the existence or non-existence in his lifetime of the library in the Serapeum.

But so valuable is every scrap and fragment of evidence about the books of Alexandria at or near this period that I may be pardoned for here recording another collection—that made by the Syrian bishop of Amida, Moro Bar Kustant, in the first half of the sixth century. He is described as 'fluent and practised in Greek,' but 'after remaining a short time in his see, he was banished first to Petra and thence to Alexandria. There he stayed for a time, and there formed a library containing many admirable books, in which is abundance of great profit for those who love knowledge, for men of understanding and students. These books were transferred to the treasury of the church of Amida after his death. He progressed more and more in reading in Alexandria, and there fell asleep.' From this interesting passage in Zachariah of Mitylene[1] we may draw at least two conclusions—that Alexandria was still a great place for the book-collector, and that the exportation of books was not forbidden.

But the intellectual interests of Alexandria were not limited to Greek literature or theology. The city of Ptolemy and Euclid was still famous for its devotion to astronomy, and for the skill of its students in mathematics and in mechanics. Astrology was still practised, and, postulating at least some knowledge of the stars, it was not without its use to science. When princes and rulers of the world sent to consult a monk in the desert about their future, they put their faith less in his saintliness than in his study of the planets. Nor were the

[1] p. 209.

astrologers wanting in political influence. The most famous astronomer of this time was Stephen of Alexandria, whose book on astronomy remains. He is also credited with the study of astrology: and if he forecast the coming empire of Islâm[1], it can scarcely be questioned that many of his credulous countrymen listened with an anxious sinking of the heart, and were weakened in their resistance in the hour of trial. But Stephen was a genius—universal philosopher and master, he is called,—and his astrology counts for little in his attainments. To the branches of learning which were studied at this time must be added geography. A great accession to the knowledge of the eastern seas had been made by the explorations of Cosmas, surnamed the Indian Navigator, a merchant adventurer of Alexandria, whom love of travel and discovery rather than love of gain had led to make long and scientific voyages round Arabia and India. Though he had died some years before this period, his works were in men's hands and were much valued: it is unfortunate for us that the greater and the most interesting part of them has perished[2].

But if literary traditions were still cherished in Alexandria, it is even more true that the arts flourished. The architecture of the city with its noble walls and towers, its shining palaces, its stately churches, and colonnaded streets was truly mag-

[1] H. Usener's monograph on Stephen of Alexandria leaves no doubt of his learning, but makes it pretty clear that this so-called prophecy is the invention of a much later period (*De Stephano Alexandrino*).

[2] On Cosmas Indicopleustes see Matter, *École d'Alexandrie* (t. ii. p. 381),—a work which contains a good deal of valuable information.

nificent: and the skill of the builders had in no way fallen off from the days of Justinian when the great Hall of the Thousand and One Columns at Constantinople, which still survives, was built by an Alexandrian. It was the capitals upon the columns in this hall which, according to Professor Freeman, completely broke with classical tradition and prepared the way for the magnificent construction of Anthemius at St. Sophia[1]. Moreover, the green and red porphyry used to adorn that building was quarried in Egypt and floated down the Nile[2]. From the days of the Pharaohs Egypt was renowned for its beautiful alabasters: and churches and palaces all over the world were decked with these costly marbles, the trade in which was centred in Alexandria, and there remained till the Arab conquest extinguished it.

Painting as a fine art was ancillary to architecture, and was employed together with mosaic of coloured glass[3], mosaic of marble, marble panelling, and

[1] See, however, Lethaby and Swainson's *S. Sophia, Constantinople*, p. 249.

[2] 'They loaded the boats on the bosom of the Nile' says Paul the Silentiary.

[3] On the subject of glass mosaics in Egypt see Abû Ṣâliḥ, p. 148, and my note. When I wrote the note, I was not aware that specimens of this work still survive in Egypt. But the head of the ḳiblah in the mosque of Ibn Ṭûlûn still preserves its tenth-century glass mosaics set round with a purely classical border. One other instance occurs at the mosque of Shajarah ad Durr, and two at Al Azhar, viz. in the ḳiblah of Aṭ Ṭabarsîah and of Al Akhbuḥaîah. These instances prove the rareness of the art, which was applied only on a very small scale to the adornment of the most splendidly decorated part of the Muslim building, but they prove also its survival to the fourteenth century. See the report of the *Comité de Conservation des Monuments de l'Art Arabe*, Exercise 1900 (Le Caire, 1900), by Max Hertz Bey.

marble pavements for the decoration of interiors. These arts—the art of building, the art of working in glass mosaic, and that form of marble work called characteristically *opus Alexandrinum*—were preserved by the Copts long after they had passed under the dominion of the Arabs: and both the walls of the new capital Cairo and its splendid mosques were built and embellished by Egyptian architects, whose genius and whose methods came by direct descent from ancient Alexandria.

Nor must the art of illuminating books be forgotten. We have already seen that Simocatta speaks of a friend who was an illuminator, and John Moschus describes Zoilus as practising the same craft. The fact is that all over the East at this time ornamental writing and miniature painting in books were carried to great perfection. The most sumptuous of these manuscripts were on vellum, which was stained purple and then overwritten in letters of gold. Books of this kind were generally destined for the Emperor's own library. There is an extremely interesting letter from an Archbishop of Alexandria, Theonas, to one Lucianus, the Emperor's chief chamberlain and librarian, which one may here fitly produce, though it was written about A.D. 290. It gives first of all advice as to keeping accounts, the custody of robes and ornaments, the making of inventories for gold and silver plate, for crystal and myrrhine vases, and for all the palace treasures. Then it proceeds to say that the library is the most important thing of all. No Christian should despise secular literature, and the librarian must know all about the books. He must arrange them in systematic order with a catalogue: he must take care that all copies are faithful and true: and he must restore MSS. or illuminations where they are decayed. Finally, says Theonas, it is not essential that *all* books should be written in letters of gold on purple vellum [1], unless the Emperor makes this a special requirement. This letter at least shows that the Archbishop was familiar with the work of a great and splendid library. In the three following centuries the art of illuminating spread rather than diminished, nor was there any great change of style up to the period of which we are treating. As in Europe in later days, so now in Egypt, much of this illuminating was done in the monasteries: and although the chief centres of production were Constantinople and Alexandria, yet at many places in Egypt, Asia Minor, Syria, and Persia might be found monks who spent their lives in writing precious books and adorning their pages with the richest splendour of design and colour [2].

Of the sculpture of this time little is known beyond the fact that it was still customary to set up statues of the reigning Emperor not only in the capital but also in the chief provincial towns; whence it is clear that the art was not wholly lost [3]. The Ptolemaic school of sculpture had been the first in the world at that time, and some of its works show a purely classical grace and refinement. Even in Christian times the tradition remained, as is shown for example by the magnificent colossal

[1] See Cozza Luzi's *Pergamene Purpuree.*

[2] See the late Prof. Middleton's *Illuminated Manuscripts* (Cambridge, 1892), ch. iv.

[3] It was, however, destined to a rapid decay in Egypt under the Arabs and in the Byzantine Empire under the ignorant iconoclast Leo the Isaurian in the early eighth century.

figure of an emperor sculptured in red porphyry now in the Cairo Museum[1].

There is no doubt, however, that by the sixth century the art of sculpture had fallen into decay. On the other hand, the peculiarly Byzantine art of ivory-carving attained its highest perfection, displaying marvellous taste and delicacy[2]. So too the goldsmith's art and the art of enamelling on metal flourished in the great school of Alexandria. And as these crafts traced back their origin to the workers of ancient Egypt, so they were preserved long after the fall of Alexandria. In the Middle Ages they had a brilliant renaissance, and to this day they have never been extinguished.

Among the industrial arts, which flourished in great vigour, may be mentioned paper-making, glass-blowing, weaving, and ship-building. Vast reed-beds of the tall and graceful papyrus plant grew in the thousand waterways of the Delta. Paper was formed of its pith, which was cut in slices, moulded

[1] The head is unfortunately missing, but the statue is thought to represent an emperor of the Later Empire, and Prof. Strzygowski regards it as Christian work. The drapery, pose, and finish are exceedingly good. As a specimen of earlier work, reference may be made to the admirable statue of Marcus Aurelius now in the Museum of Alexandria.

[2] See C. Diehl, *La Civilisation Byzantine au VIe Siècle*, pp. 651 seq. On p. 653 is an illustration from the 'chaire de Maximien,' on which work Diehl quotes Molinier's opinion: 'Aucun monument d'ivoire de la période antérieure ne nous montre une pareille entente de la décoration jointe à une habileté technique au-dessus de tout éloge': and he goes on to show that this work, as well as the small jewels and reliquaries, embroideries, &c., is Egyptian in origin or inspiration. The great 'Syro-Egyptian' school of art exercised an enormous influence at this time on Byzantine art in general. The remarks of Diehl on architecture (p. 642) and on miniature painting (p. 650) are well worth reading, as indeed is the whole book.

into sheets under pressure, and polished with an ivory burnisher: then the sheets were joined to form rolls of a manageable length. Enormous quantities of papyrus were exported from the busy quays of Alexandria: and it is not clear when the trade declined or what causes led ultimately to the total extinction of the plant in Egypt[1]. The glass-works of Alexandria and of the Nitrian desert were long famous. Strabo says that the glass-workers of Egypt had their own secrets, especially in the factories at Diospolis; that they counterfeited precious stones and made myrrhine vessels. Glass was part of the tribute imposed by Augustus[2], and beautiful products of the art may be seen in the Alexandria Museum. It cannot be doubted that the craft was handed down among the Copts to mediaeval times, and its last result was the manufacture of those sumptuous enamelled lamps, which once adorned churches and mosques and now are the glory of mediaeval museums. At what period the manufacture of porcelain arose is uncertain, but it was very early. A Persian traveller[3] who visited Fusṭâṭ in 1047 A. D. speaks not only of the fine glass but of the beautiful faience which he saw made there, 'so fine and diaphanous that through the vessel may be

[1] Some interesting information, however, may be found in *Mittheilungen a. d. Papyrus Erzherzog Rainer*, pp. 101 seq. We learn that in the ninth century a roll of papyrus called قرطاس (*χάρτης*) cost 6 kirâṭ, or the fourth of a dinâr=about *2s. 6d.*: while a tûmâr, which was about 8 ft. 6 in. long, cost one-sixth of this, or 5*d.*

[2] See *Notice historique de l'Art de la Verrerie* in the Napoleonic *Description de l'Égypte.* Also Abû Ṣâliḥ, pp. 149–50.

[3] *Relation du Voyage de Nāsiri Khusrau*, from C. Schefer, p. 151. The 'wastes' from the kilns often discovered among the rubbish mounds on the site of Fusṭâṭ fully bear out the existence of the native manufactures.

seen the hand that holds it': and he specially mentions iridescent lustre-ware, resembling the shot silk fabric called *bûkalimûn*, which changed its hue according as the light fell on the surface. This evidence is very remarkable, as proving beyond question the high development of the potter's and glass-worker's art in Cairo in the eleventh century. It is clear that the later and better-known Hispano-Mauresque ware traces its origin back to Cairo.

In textiles too there was a large trade and a great variety of fabrics. The finest linen was still woven, probably finer than anything wrought in the looms of ancient Egypt. Moreover, since the reign of Justinian silk had come into more common use[1],

[1] *Catalogue of Egyptian Textiles in S. K. M.*, by Alan Cole, 1887, p. x. Silk in the third century was worth its weight in gold. By the fourth century Gregory of Nazianzen and other Christian writers denounce the use of silk as a growing luxury. By the middle of the fifth century silk had become so common that not merely the Emperor but all courtiers and wealthy men dressed in it. The streets and houses of Constantinople were all aflutter with pure silk on the occasion of the baptism of the infant Theodosius II: see Bury's *Later Roman Empire*, vol. i. pp. 196, 204; ii. pp. 96–7: see also vol. i. p. 472. In Egypt, however, silk was more largely used at an earlier date than in Europe. By the end of the fourth century silk shrouds were employed for mummies. See an article 'On a Coptic Grave-Shirt' by Dr. Wallis Budge in *Archaeologia*, vol. 53, pt. 2, p. 442: and on the whole subject Yates' *Textrinum Antiquorum* there quoted. How general was the use of silk in the seventh century may be gathered from the pages of Ockley. Heraclius is said to have had 'above 300 loads of dyed silks and cloths of gold' at Damascus (pp. 150, 156). Vestures of silk are very frequent among the spoils, and all the generals seem to have worn silk even on the field of battle. See pp. 170, 172, 179, 185, 198, 211. Tapestry of scarlet silk flowered with gold is mentioned p. 226. Mas'ûdî says that awnings of green silk were hung over the streets of Alexandria as a protection against the glare from the marble buildings.

and both in silk and linen sumptuous fabrics were produced, embellished with splendid embroideries. Many textiles, dating from about this time, have recently been discovered at Akhmîm, the ancient Panopolis, in Upper Egypt, and are now in the South Kensington and other collections. These are nearly all linen or woven tapestry, and the style of ornamentation, which is in some cases quite classical, in others is distinctly Christian, while yet a third class shows clear evidence of Persian influence. The ten or twelve years of the Persian occupation may well have brought Persian designs into fashion with the Coptic weavers. Just as in the Theodore Graf papyri at Vienna, which range from 487 to 909 A. D., the Greek, Coptic, Sassanid-Persian, Hebrew, and Arabic languages are found, so in this collection of textiles, covering about the same period, the political changes which passed over Egypt are reflected as in a mirror [1]. It is exceedingly interesting to note further that the materials, as well as the designs and colours of specimens found at Saḳḳârah, in the Fayûm, and in Upper Egypt are virtually identical. The fact proves not so much the conservatism of the weavers as their community of

[1] Catalogue *S. K. M.* p. xiii. The whole of the introduction to this catalogue is well worth reading. See also Gerspach, *Les Tapisseries coptes*, and Forrer, *Römische und Byzantinische Seiden-Textilien.* In his book called *Le Costume en Égypte du IIIe au XIIe Siècle*, Mons. A. Gayet dwells on the extraordinary fineness of the linen, silk, tapestry and embroidery of Egypt: but he accounts for the variety of national styles by the variety of races employed in Egypt. This theory I think is mistaken. The workers were Egyptian, but their style was affected by the succession of conquests and the varying tastes of the conquerors. On p. 247 M. Gayet shows an Assyrian design of exceptional interest.

ideas. By the great highway of the Nile new processes and patterns passed quickly from guild to guild among the scattered towns of Egypt, and the produce of the looms was easily carried to the great markets of Memphis and Alexandria, or after a short caravan journey was shipped from the Red Sea port of Berenice. All these linens and tapestries, tissues interwoven with gold and needlework embroideries in fine colours, were the work of Coptic craftsmen: and the more the history of Egypt, both Byzantine and Saracen, is studied, the clearer becomes the truth that in all the handicrafts—in goldsmiths' work, in enamelling, in metal-work, in glass-work—and in every province of design and construction, it was the Copts who kept alive the artistic traditions of the country.

At the same time it would be wrong to imagine that in skill and taste the Copts far outshone the artistic workers of the Byzantine Empire or those of Armenia, Assyria, and Persia. All over the East woven fabrics and embroideries, vessels of gold and silver, and jewels of exceedingly fine workmanship were produced: and fine as were the carpets made in Egypt, it is doubtful whether they rivalled the magnificent products of Persia[1]. So too some of

[1] I may instance the well-known 'winter carpet' of the Persian kings captured by the Muslims at Ctesiphon. It was 300 cubits long by 60 broad, and was used in winter when flowers were over. It had a white ground with a border of emeralds richly designed: every beautiful and sweet-scented flower and plant was wrought upon it in precious stones of divers colours. It was sent to Omar at Medina, who had it cut up in pieces and distributed among his generals. 'Alî sold his portion for 8,000 dirhems (Ṭabarî, ed. Zotenberg, vol. iii. p. 416). Tinnîs, Ḳais, and other sea-coast towns in Egypt were the great centres for carpets and other textiles: see Quatremère, *Mém. Hist. et Géog.*

the finest illuminations were made not only in Byzantium, but in Persia and Mesopotamia. The most famous dye-works for the imperial purple were at Bostra in Syria, which was captured by the Persians and subsequently by the Arabs. We have seen that Chosroes was no semi-savage king, but a man of great culture: and the arts of the Sassanian Persians, while founded on the traditions of ancient Assyria and Babylon, not only vied with the arts of the Byzantine Empire in taste and refinement, but had perhaps a larger share in forming among the Arabs that school of design which in the Middle Ages rendered Damascus famous.

But of all the industrial arts practised at Alex-

t. i. pp. 141, 308, 335, 339. Cedrenus mentions linen, silk, and carpets among the spoil burnt by Heraclius at Chosroes' palace in Dastagerd. In the ninth century the Caliph Al Muntazar (who had slain his father Mutawakkal) was shown a carpet taken from the Persians, which bore the design of a crowned king on horseback, and on the border the legend, 'I am Shîrûyah, son of Khusrû: I slew my father and reigned only six months' (*Oriental Collections*, vol. i. no. iii. p. 224 n.). Damietta vied with Tinnîs at this time, and for three or four centuries later, in the fineness and splendour of its gauzes, brocades, and cloths of gold: see Abû Ṣâliḥ, pp. 62–3 and notes. Ya'ḳûbî writing circa 950 A. D. specifies various textiles then manufactured. In the Fayûm a coarse linen; at Ḳais garments called by the name of the town and excellent woollen materials; at Baḥnasâ veils or curtains called Baḥnasî; fine tissues at Aḥnâs; crimson carpets at Siûṭ; small carpets or rugs and leathern goods at Akhmîm; at Shaṭâ fine linen; at Tinnîs the celebrated tissues of Dabîḳî material, coarse and fine, besides gauzes and striped fabrics and velvet and damask and many other sorts of apparel; and at Damietta strong tissues of Dabîḳî, fine linen, and gauze were woven (*Bibl. Geog. Arab.*, part vii. pp. 330–332 and 337). These crafts were certainly not brought into the country by the Arabs, but survived from Roman times. On embroidered and woven stuffs actually found in Egypt see Strzygowski, *Orient oder Rom*, pp. 113 seq.; also 90 seq.

andria perhaps the most important was ship-building. Alexandria was the busiest port and the largest market in the world. Besides the enormous trade in corn, linen, paper, glass and other local products, and the traffic in gold and ivory from Nubia and Ethiopia, all the spices, silks, silver, precious stones, and other wares from the Indian and the Chinese seas came from the Red Sea by canal from Ḳulzum or Suez to Memphis and thence down the Nile to Alexandria, whence they were distributed over the Mediterranean. So vast a commerce required a very large amount of shipping: and though Egypt was always in historic times destitute of timber for ship-building, it was found more profitable to import balks from Syria and elsewhere, and to build the vessels where the trade which demanded them was centred. Egypt too was famous for a special kind of hemp, admirably adapted for cordage and ships' tackling[1].

We have already seen that one of the corn-ships owned by the Church at Alexandria carried a burthen of 20,000 bushels, nor is this recorded as in any way an exceptional cargo. The probability is that these merchant vessels were much larger than we are wont to imagine. The same is true of the war vessels. Not many years after this time, when Egypt was in possession of the Saracens, and when any purely Byzantine shipwrights must have been withdrawn from the docks at Alexandria, the Saracen leader in Syria, Mu'awîah, ordered a number of war-ships to be built in Alexandria and other

[1] Ibn al Faḳîḥ (tenth century) says, 'One of the wonders of Egypt is a kind of hemp called *duḳs*, of which ships' tackling is made, and such ropes are called *al ḳirḳis*' (*Bibl. Geog. Arab.* part v. p. 66).

seaports within his dominion. According to Sebeos the ships were of two classes, which one might almost call battleships and cruisers. The battleships each carried a thousand men, while the lighter vessels carried a complement of one hundred [1], and were specially designed for fast sailing and rapid manœuvring round the big ships. Very interesting details are given of the armament of the men-of-war. Not only were they equipped with formidable batteries—'catapults and stone-throwing engines'—but some of them had lofty towers built upon the deck, so that, when the vessels came alongside fortified walls, the assailants should be on a level with the defenders, and, by leaping or bridging the short space between tower and wall, should effect a lodgement on the ramparts.

But even more remarkable is the express testimony of Sebeos that these great ships were armed with 'fire-spouting engines,' i.e. machines for hurling the deadly flames known as Greek fire. This powerful compound of inflammable materials not merely burned with unquenchable fierceness, but seems also to have possessed an explosive or rending force, which wrought great destruction and caused great terror. But the special interest of this passage in Sebeos lies in this—that it makes ships built in

[1] These numbers are quite clear, as Mr. Conybeare tells me, in the MS. of Sebeos, and I see no reason to doubt them, although the text would give the number of large ships as 300, each carrying 1,000 men, and 5,000 cruisers each carrying 100, or a total of 800,000 men sent over sea to attack Byzantium, besides those that Mu'awîah took overland to Chalcedon. This is of course an impossible total; but even if the tale of ships should be reduced, the 'arms and engines' which Sebeos mentions, as well as tents, provisions, and perhaps horses, must have occupied a very large proportion of the space in the vessels.

Egypt after the Arab conquest to Arab orders armed with artillery for discharging the blazing chemicals, the composition of which is generally held to have been, in the seventh century at least, a Byzantine secret. The invention of Greek fire is usually ascribed to Callinicus, an engineer of Heliopolis, and the Heliopolis is too readily assumed to be the Syrian town of that name instead of the older and more famous city of Egypt. Gibbon clearly leans to Cedrenus' view, that Callinicus was an Egyptian, although he mistakenly speaks of Heliopolis as then in ruins[1]. It is scarcely conceivable that little more than twenty years after the Arab conquest of Egypt ships built at Alexandria should have been armed with these engines for shooting Greek fire, unless both the discovery of the composition and the construction of the engines had originated in the country.

Be that as it may, it is unquestionable that the art of ship-building greatly flourished at Alexandria during the first half of the seventh century in Egypt, and that it was not stricken with decline when the Byzantine overlordship of Egypt ended: a fact which proves that in this as in all the great branches of industry in the Nile valley the Copts were independent of Roman direction, if indeed they were not the master craftsmen.

This rapid review of the arts and of the literature of Alexandria about the time of the Persian conquest has of necessity in some points touched both

[1] *Decline and Fall*, ch. 52, note 2. 'Cedrenus brings this artist from the ruins of Heliopolis in Egypt, and chemistry was indeed the peculiar science of the Egyptians.' Lebeau too has an exhaustive note on the subject of Greek fire (vol. xi. p. 419). See also Prof. Bury's *Later Roman Empire*, vol. ii. pp. 311, 319.

on previous and on subsequent history. But it is designed both to serve as a rough sketch of the material civilization of the time, and to show that its continuity was not broken, at least by the Persians. The armies of Chosroes did little serious mischief either to the architectural or to the literary treasures of the capital. The great libraries, if they existed, did not find their destroyers in the Persian conquerors. The magnificent lighthouse called the Pharos—one of the world's seven wonders—still towered between the city and the sea, capped with clouds of smoke by day and with flaming fire by night: neither the ancient temples, nor the spacious colonnades, nor the countless palaces which made Alexandria famous, were overthrown. Even the churches within the walls were practically uninjured, and worshippers still thronged the great Cathedral of Caesarion and the church of St. Mark, where beneath the high altar still reposed the remains of the Apostle of Egypt[1].

[1] The safety of St. Mark's is known from the testimony of pilgrims at a later date. It survived the second Arab capture of Alexandria, in which the Caesarion seems to have perished.

CHAPTER IX

CRUSADE AGAINST PERSIA.

Heraclius sues for peace. His departure for Carthage arrested. War with Persia resolved upon. Futile embassy to Chosroes. Expedition to Cilicia. Command of the sea. Scene in St. Sophia. The campaign ends in the destruction of Persian power. Recovery of the Cross. Triumph of Heraclius.

THE fortunes of Heraclius had now fallen so low that his Empire was almost bounded by the walls of his capital. On the westward or landward side of Constantinople hordes of Tartars or Huns and other barbarian tribes had roamed for years unchecked, and were prowling round the very gates of the city. On the east the Persian armies, which had conquered Syria, Palestine, and Egypt, had advanced through Asia Minor sweeping all before them, and were in occupation of Chalcedon on the Asian shore of the Bosporus fronting Constantinople [1]. The hopes which had shone on the accession of Heraclius were extinguished or clouded, as the masterful vigour which had won him the throne gave way, or rather seemed to give way, to apathy or despair. The first act of his reign was to send a humble message to Chosroes asking for peace, which was disdainfully refused [2].

When the tidings came that Egypt was lost to

[1] The position of Chalcedon is accurately described by Theophylact, vii. 15, and again viii. 14 (Teubner Classics, ed. de Boor).

[2] Sebeos records that Chosroes answered, 'The Empire is mine. He has usurped it, and now sends us our own treasures as presents: but I will not rest till I have brought him into my power.' The ambassadors were put to death, and no reply was sent to Heraclius.

the Empire and the tribute of money and corn from that rich province cut off, with his exchequer and granaries empty and with ferocious enemies besieging or threatening his walls, which were guarded by an undisciplined and nerveless garrison, the Emperor seemed to resign all hope of deliverance. His meditated flight gives colour to the view that he felt unequal to the burden of the Empire; that all the heroic element in his character was overborne by the press of disasters; and that his moral strength was broken. It was certainly believed that he had resolved to fling off his crown and to return home to Africa: and his subjects might well recall the taunt of Phocas, 'Are you the man to govern the Empire better?' But there is some reason to think that Heraclius wished rather to shift the centre of government to Carthage, and there to prepare at leisure for the reconquest of his Asiatic dominions.

Whatever the truth may be, a vessel laden with treasures he wished to save had already sailed, bound for Carthage, and had reached the coast of Pentapolis, where it suffered shipwreck, when Sergius, the Patriarch of Constantinople, having discovered the design of Heraclius, stood angrily between him and his purpose. By what power of speech or magnetism of will he prevailed, can only be conjectured: it is certain that he breathed a new purpose into the Emperor, and led him to take a solemn oath at the high altar in the Cathedral that he would be true to his trust, and that he would fight for the deliverance of his Empire from the enemies of the Cross[1].

[1] Lebeau's *Histoire du Bas Empire*, ed. de Saint-Martin, vol. xi. pp. 19–21.

Whether it was the eloquence of Sergius in preaching what was really the first great crusade, or the stirring power of the scene beneath the great dome of St. Sophia, or some new gleam of hope from the altered disposition of his foes, or all combined with a reaction from deep discouragement natural in a man whose strong power of brain was governed by a highly nervous temperament, it is beyond question that from this moment a most remarkable change was wrought in the Emperor. To the outer world at least he seemed to cast off like a slough all his weakness and indolence, resuming the character of a strong leader, and to show a kingship worthy of men's allegiance. His whole mind was now given to collecting and organizing his resources for a war with Persia.

Nevertheless his counsels were guided by caution, and while he was preparing to fight, he resolved to ask terms of peace from the Persian general [1]

[1] Both the *Chronicon Paschale* and Theophanes give Σαὴν as the name, while Nicephorus gives Σάϊτος, i. e. Shahîn, to whom also is attributed the conquest of Egypt: see ante, p. 70 n. The *Chronicon Paschale* very clearly makes Saên the original captor of Chalcedon, and with equal clearness makes Khorheam (whom it calls Σαλβάρας, i. e. Shah-Waraz) commander of the Persian army of occupation at Chalcedon ten years later, dating his arrival there 626. Both statements can hardly be correct, but the confusion between Shahîn and Shah-Waraz is more perplexing than surprising. Gibbon calls this latter general 'Sarbaraza,' and two pages lower speaks of a general called 'Sarbar.' The two names refer to the one person, although Gibbon does not seem conscious of the fact. Gibbon places Saên in command at Chalcedon now, makes him accompany Heraclius' envoys, and says that he was flayed alive for his pains by Chosroes: but Theophanes makes Saên die of melancholy and disease some years later after a defeat, Chosroes insulting his dead body. Sebeos describes Shahîn as raiding Cappadocia in 610, and subsequently

at Chalcedon, whom he visited in person. The Emperor was advised to send ambassadors to Chosroes, who was represented as certain to grant a favourable reply. Accordingly three distinguished envoys were dispatched with a letter, which is still extant, and with costly presents. The ambassadors duly delivered their message to the Great King, who did not refuse the precious gifts they offered: but his reply was stern and uncompromising. 'Tell your master,' he said, 'that the Roman Empire belongs to me. Heraclius is a rebel and a slave: and I will grant no peace till he abandons the worship of the Crucified for the worship of the sun [1].'

The studied insolence of this answer gave the shock needed to rouse the deadened spirit of the Romans. It pointed afresh the religious aspect of the war, and fired at once the indignation and the enthusiasm of the people. The Emperor now found in them the material required for his new plans. While his ambassadors were on their way to the

co-operating with Khorheam. But Sebeos, who gives the speech made by Heraclius on this occasion at Chalcedon, alleges that Khorheam had now come to Chalcedon and was in command there. This is doubtless the truth, Shahîn being in Egypt.

[1] Part of this answer is given by Theophanes, part by Persian writers: see *Journal Asiatique*, 6e série, 1866, vol. vii. p. 201. Eutychius relates that Constantinople being hard pressed by Chosroes wished to surrender, but that Heraclius secured his retirement by agreeing to pay 1,000 talents of gold and of silver, 1,000 virgins, 1,000 horses, and 1,000 robes of silk. Gibbon adopts this story, but it does not seem worthy of credit. It is inconsistent with the ten years' occupation of Chalcedon, which is well attested, nor does Gibbon explain the inconsistency. The contemporary *Chronicon Paschale* knows nothing of any such arrangement: and the story is probably nothing but a late version of the embassy referred to in the text. Sebeos gives a somewhat different version of Chosroes' letter to the Emperor.

Persian court, Heraclius is said to have made peace for a while with his barbarian enemies [1], and so cleared the landward side of the capital. Later we are told that he made an alliance with a Turkish tribe to the north of Persia, and promised his daughter Eudocia in marriage to their chief in part payment for a force of 40,000 cavalry—a compact voided by the death of the chieftain. Yet the evidence of peace in the west is very difficult to establish [2]; because in 622 or 623 the Avars were still ravaging the country-side, and by an act of infamous treachery nearly succeeded in assassinating Heraclius and capturing Constantinople; and again in 626 an army of 30,000 Avars besieged the city acting in alliance with the Persians at Chalcedon, who were then commanded, as it seems, by the newly arrived Shah-Waraz. So that the peace with the Avars was neither real nor lasting. Heraclius probably estimated the treaty at its true value, and trusted rather to the strength of his walls and his galleys to secure Constantinople in his absence. But such was the warlike ardour of his people, that he soon enrolled and equipped a large army, which with allies ultimately numbered 120,000 men. His plan was first to find a training-ground where he could drill his levies into discipline and practise them in military movements and the use of arms, while vast supplies were being gathered and stored: and then,

[1] Cedrenus ascribes this peace to the eleventh year of Heraclius, i. e. 621 or 622.

[2] Theophanes' account of the matter is probably correct, but his dates are very hard to follow or to reconcile with other authorities, even allowing for the fixed error in his system of chronology. If the attack on Heraclius took place in 623, it would be in the winter when he returned for some weeks to Constantinople from the theatre of war.

when his forces were ready for the field, to strike at the heart of Persia. He resolved therefore to transport his army to the Bay of Issus at the north-east corner of the Mediterranean and to make Cilicia his base—a move of singular boldness which was rendered possible by the fact that his command of the sea was undisputed and his resources in shipping enormous.

This reveals at once the cardinal blunder of the Persians. Had they only followed up their early victories on land by learning to fight and conquer by sea, nothing could have saved the Empire[1]. Fortunately for the history of Christian civilization the Persians were not a seafaring people, and at this juncture they totally failed to realize the need of commanding the sea in order to complete and to secure their conquests. Sebeos indeed relates that Chosroes, in sending his insolent letter to Heraclius, sent orders to his own troops to cross over to Byzantium, whereupon they equipped a large squadron and made every preparation for battle by sea. But when the Persian flotilla advanced, the Roman galleys fell upon it with such fury that the Persians were shamefully defeated with a loss of 4,000 men[2] and all their ships, and were so dismayed that 'they never again ventured upon this kind of undertaking.' Consequently for not less than ten years they remained in idle occupation of their naval base at Chalcedon, and of the magnificent harbour of Alexandria, to say nothing of Syrian seaports and the

[1] Chosroes had actually endeavoured, after the Persian occupation of Chalcis, to build a fleet, but the material collected for the purpose was destroyed by fire and the attempt abandoned.

[2] So Thomas Ardzrouni, who mentions '4,000 mailed warriors' as slain. See Brosset's *Collection d'Historiens Arméniens*, t. i. p. 82.

more western ports in Libya and Pentapolis. At all these places they might have gathered and trained their fleets to sweep the Mediterranean: even at Alexandria alone such a navy might have been built and manned as would have given battle to the Roman armaments with every chance of victory. But the land-fighting Persians were blind to the value of sea-power: they failed to read the lesson which the Roman republic of old had been slow indeed to learn, but learned effectively in its wars with Carthage—the lesson which the Arabs were destined to grasp with rapid intelligence before the close of this seventh century. Consequently the Persian camps were chained to the coast: and so limited was their power of offence, that Heraclius before very long discovered his ability to disregard their presence. Even ten years after the capture of Chalcedon the Byzantine galleys rode the sea triumphant in the narrow strait between the Persian and the Hunnish armies[1].

Before starting on his expedition round Asia Minor, and in order to defray its cost, Heraclius borrowed all the immense treasures of gold and silver vessels which the churches could lend, to coin into money. It was a wasteful and deplorable method of replenishing the empty state exchequer, but perhaps no other was available. When all was ready, he made over the government to his son, with the Patriarch Sergius and the patrician Bonus as guardians. Then shod in black he entered the great Cathedral, and falling prostrate prayed for the divine blessing upon his undertaking[2]. George

[1] *Chronicon Paschale*, Migne, *Patr. Gr.* t. 92, col. 1014.

[2] Cedrenus tells this story, and gives the words of Heraclius' prayer.

of Pisidia, deacon and sacristan of the Cathedral, witnessed the Emperor's devotions and remarked, 'May you dye red in the blood of your enemies the sandals now black on your feet'—a pious wish which may more easily be pardoned in the poet laureate [1] than in the chaplain of the expedition: for George seems to have accompanied it in both characters. It was on Easter Monday, 622 [2], that Heraclius weighed anchor from the capital, and sailed southward. The armada, after weathering a storm in which Heraclius displayed at once the coolness of a commander and the hardihood of a common sailor, ploughed on its way and made a

[1] The tedious poems on the wars with Persia and with the Avars by George of Pisidia may be found in Migne's *Patr. Gr.* t. 92. A few lines from the *Heracliad* will bear translation, as showing the revival of spirit which Heraclius wrought:—

'When the army was filled with dread of the Persian,
When their manner of battle was flight from danger
And this had become second nature by use:
Who turned their hearts to war and clad them in the armour of his eloquence?
Who changed their craven souls,
And from their cowardice brought out courage?
Even thou, by thy wisdom and strength,
Which roused them to life, when they were like dull stones
Cumbering the earth with a profitless burden.'

[2] The year is fixed accurately by Theophanes, who expressly identifies it with the year in which Mohammed appeared, i.e. the year of the Hijrah, or 622. The *Chronicon Paschale* gives the same date: which may therefore be taken as a fixed point in the misty chronology of this period. George of Pisidia, who sailed with Heraclius, and after him Theophanes and Cedrenus, make the Emperor leave the capital on Easter Monday. Gibbon apparently follows them, but changes the day to Easter Tuesday, presumably from misunderstanding the *feria secunda* of the Latin version. *Feria prima* is of course Sunday. Theophanes confuses the first and the second expedition.

prosperous voyage to its destination. The force landed and camped at Issus, and seized the pass of Pylae on the frontier between Cilicia and Syria [1].

It is no part of the writer's purpose to follow in detail the six years' war which Heraclius now waged against the Persian Empire. From the first his arms were victorious. Out of the very unpromising material of which his army was composed he forged a weapon of the finest temper, which he wielded with consummate skill to break down the power of his enemies. His athletic strength and prowess in single combat, his enthusiasm, his burning faith in his mission as champion of the Cross, his readiness to share all hardships with his men, his personal ascendency and power of discipline, the rapidity and brilliancy of his tactics, and his coolness in meeting new combinations—all these qualities which he now revealed made him an ideal leader of men and secured him an unparalleled succession of triumphs.

The expedition to Cilicia drove a wedge into the very centre of the vast territory between the Nile and the Bosporus now controlled by the Persians. In the following year a second expedition to Trebizond drove in another wedge to meet it from the northern side of Asia Minor. The pressure thus exerted was enormous; and, as blow followed blow, the Persians were forced to recall their armies from

[1] George of Pisidia deals in tantalizing generalities: but Sebeos confirms and supplements his account. According to Sebeos there was a drawn battle close to Antioch city, with great slaughter on both sides. But the Romans retreated to Pylae, where they defeated the Persians, who however recovered and took Tarsus and all Cilicia. Does this mean that the expedition failed? George of Pisidia gives no hint of such a result, though he records the Emperor's return to Byzantium.

Alexandria and from Chalcedon. It is not clear in what year either event happened; but historians agree in making the occupation of both towns begin and end nearly simultaneously, and they differ little regarding the period of occupation, which in each case is estimated at ten and twelve years by different authorities. We shall not be far wrong in dating the withdrawal of the Persians from the Bosporus and the Nile early in the year 627 A. D.[1]

The crowning achievement of the war—the capture by Heraclius of Dastagerd, some eighty miles to the north of Madain or Ctesiphon—took place in February, 628. On the 24th of that month Chosroes fled ignominiously, but was caught and thrown into prison, where after suffering indignity and torture at the hands of his successor Siroes, he was put to death a few days later. Chosroes' palace was burnt to the ground, and all its magnificent and costly treasures[2] that could not be removed perished in

[1] The *Chronicon Paschale* assigns to June 29, 626, the arrival of the Avars and the Khakân before Byzantium, and makes it some days after the arrival of the Shah-Waraz to take over the command at Chalcedon. The siege failed owing to the fact that the Roman galleys retained their command of the sea and so prevented the designed co-operation between the Avars and the Persians. Thereupon the Khakân sullenly retired with his baffled and starving troops: and two years later the war was over.

[2] Theophanes deplores the destruction of 'most artistic and admirable buildings and astonishing palaces,' and gives an account of the aviaries and zoological gardens. He says too that vast quantities of aloes and spices, sugar, ginger, linen, silk, carpets and precious metals perished in the flames. Oriental authors have fabulous tales of the wealth and wonders of Chosroes' palace. Thus the *Tarîkh Regum Persiae* (p. 160) tells of an automaton with a sort of orrery which marked rain, thunder, &c.: the *Tarîkh Jahân Arâ* (translated by Sir W. Ouseley, p. 61) says that Chosroes had in his palace 15,000 female musicians, 8,000 household officers,

the flames. Multitudes of captives from Syria and from Egypt were released, the Patriarch Zacharias of Jerusalem among them; the reliquary enclosing the Holy Rood was brought uninjured and delivered into the hands of Heraclius[1]; and the war was

20,500 horses, 960 elephants: he also had a cup in which water never failed: an open ivory hand which he put in water when a child was born, when it closed and revealed the child's horoscope: a piece of gold soft as wax, and a kerchief which when soiled was thrown into the fire and so became clean again. See also Gibbon's *Decline and Fall*, vol. viii. p. 230 (Edin. 1848).

[1] It is not clear whether Heraclius recovered the Cross at once from Siroes. According to Brosset (*Collection d'Historiens Arméniens*, t. i. p. 86) Heraclius summoned Khorheam, the Shah-Waraz, and promised him the kingdom of Persia as ransom for the Cross. Brosset adds in a note that Khorheam was then at Chalcedon: but in this I think he is mistaken. For (1) Khorheam left Chalcedon before the fall of Chosroes (see Drapeyron, p. 258), and (2) even were it otherwise, the promise of the kingdom to Khorheam could only have been given after the death of Siroes. According to Drapeyron Heraclius returned to his palace near Chalcedon, leaving Theodore to recover the Cross from Khorheam: and Theodore, having succeeded in the quest, brought the Cross to the palace, whence Heraclius bore it in triumph over the water to Constantinople. This was four months later, viz. September 14, 628 (pp. 276–7), but the date, which is the date of the exaltation of the Cross at Jerusalem, may arise through confusion with that festival. Sebeos is somewhat at variance with this account, while agreeing that it was from Khorheam that Heraclius recovered the Cross, not from Siroes. Sebeos describes a personal meeting at which Heraclius promised Khorheam the sovereignty, on the death of Siroes in August, 628, asking in return for the Cross. Khorheam vowed assent, went to Ctesiphon, slew the child-king Ardashîr and many of the nobles, found the Cross, and delivered it to special envoys sent by Heraclius with all haste. If this story be true, the Cross cannot have reached the Emperor much, if at all, before Christmas, 628. But it is not clear why Heraclius failed, if he did fail, to get the Cross from Siroes, nor why Khorheam should have been more able and more willing to find and surrender it. It should be noted that Sebeos

ended by a formal treaty of peace between the Roman Empire and Persia. The great crusade was accomplished by one of the most romantic triumphs in history.

It was on Whit Sunday, May 15, in the same year, that the Emperor's dispatches announcing the victorious termination of the war were read from the great ambon in the Cathedral of St. Sophia[1]—an

represents Khorheam as being at 'Alexandria' when he received the letter of Heraclius which led to their meeting. That this is Alexandria of Syria is clear because (1) Sebeos does not say as usual when he so means 'Alexandria of the Egyptians': (2) geographically Khorheam must have been in proximity, because the story, which had left him in Cappadocia, speaks of him as still 'in the west' directly after the capture of Ctesiphon by Heraclius and as refusing to help Chosroes: and (3) while Ṭabarî, as we have seen, denies that the Shah-Waraz went to Egypt, Mas'ûdî says: فسار اليه من انطاكيه من بلاد الشام شهر بار, 'Shahr-bâr went against him (Siroes) from Antioch of Syria' (ed. Barbier de Maynard, vol. ii. p. 233).

[1] It is the *Chronicon Paschale* which, by incidentally mentioning that May 15, on which day the ceremony took place, was also Whit Sunday, renders us the great service of fixing another point in the chronology. The fact does not seem to have been adequately noticed, but it is very important. Now the only year about this time in which May 15 fell on a Sunday is 628, and the tables in the *Trésor de Chronologie* show that in the year 628 Easter Day was on March 27. And Easter Day being on March 27, it follows that Pentecost would fall on May 15, precisely in accordance with the explicit statement of the *Chronicon*. Just as, therefore, the beginning of Heraclius' crusade is fixed with certitude in 622 by its coincidence with the Hijrah of Mohammed, so its ending is fixed in 628 by the coincidence of the date and the festival given by the *Chronicon*; and the interval is six years, as all the authorities demand. So much then may be regarded as settled. Drapeyron (p. 267) agrees in the date: yet on the preceding page he makes the letter, which was read in St. Sophia on May 15, written from Armenia after May 8! On the other hand, Theophanes seems to close the war in 626, and to place the Emperor's visit to Jerusalem in the same year. The preface to the letter of Zacharias from his

incident which seems to have strongly impressed the imagination of contemporary writers, and which was doubtless accompanied by all the state and pomp of wonted use in that great building on a glorious occasion [1].

But the Emperor was still detained for some time in the east by the work of pacification. When, how-

captivity (Migne, *Patr. Gr.* t. 86, col. 3219 seq.) assigns the death of Chosroes to 627 and the restitution of Zacharias to the following spring, 628. But where was Zacharias in the interval? He certainly did not accompany the Emperor to Constantinople. The *Tarîkh Jahân Arâ* (see p. 125, n. 2) gives the tenth Jumâdâ al Awwal in A.H. 7, as the date of Chosroes' death. This is very precise: but as the date corresponds to September 15, 628, it must be rejected, the evidence for February being very strong. But with the month the year also would be wrong according to the Arab calendar, since February 628 falls in A.H. 6. The Arabic historian Makîn makes out that the deposition and death of Chosroes took place in A.H. 5. But the writer in the *Journal Asiatique* (6e série, vol. vii. 1866), following Sebeos and other Armenian authorities, gives the years of Chosroes' reign as extending from the summer of 590 to 628 A.D. These dates are in complete harmony with Ṭabarî, whose authority on Persian history is very high. For he states that the Hijrah of Mohammed took place in the thirty-second year of Chosroes' reign (622) and that Chosroes' death took place in the thirty-eighth year, which would be 628.

The agreement of these diverse writers with the *Chronicon Paschale* must be regarded as quite decisive in fixing February, 628, as the date for Chosroes' dethronement and death. Yet this date does not altogether square with the date I have given for the capture of Jerusalem by the Persians, viz. 615: unless one shortens the period of captivity, which is loosely said to have lasted fourteen years, a total which can only be made up by wrongly counting part of 615 and part of 628 as full years.

[1] No one interested in this splendid monument of Byzantine architecture should fail to read Messrs. Lethaby and Swainson's *S. Sophia, Constantinople*. The work is rich in historical as well as architectural details: in particular there is a good deal about the ambon.

ever, the remaining Persian garrisons in Syria and Asia Minor had been withdrawn under safe-conduct, and the Patriarch Zacharias had been restored to his seat in Jerusalem, then Heraclius turned homeward after six years of strife and entered Constantinople in triumph, bearing with him the Holy Rood which he had rescued from the heathen.

CHAPTER X

THE EXALTATION OF THE CROSS

Heraclius' pilgrimage to Jerusalem with the Cross. The Jews at Tiberias. The Cross exalted at the church of the Resurrection. Climax of the Emperor's career. He sanctions a massacre of the Jews. The Fast of Heraclius. Death of the Patriarch Zacharias, and of his successor Modestus. The Emperor's scheme of religious union. Cyrus, Bishop of Phasis, made Patriarch of Alexandria.

In the following year, 629, the Emperor set forth in the early spring on a pilgrimage to Jerusalem for the purpose of restoring to its place the Cross, which meanwhile had rested in St. Sophia. Two incidents are recorded of the journey.

According to some writers it was about this time that at Emesa[1] (or Edessa) envoys from Mohammed arrived, bearing letters which invited Heraclius to adopt the religion of Islâm. This episode, however, seems to belong to an earlier date, before the death of the Great King. The other event is as follows. When the Emperor reached Tiberias, the Jews sent a deputation with costly gifts to ask for a pledge of security. They remembered their own deeds against the Christians, and feared the Emperor's vengeance. But he generously gave them the promise of protection, and the Jews were prudent enough to obtain his bond in writing.

The journey was resumed, and at length the Holy

[1] Both places are named: but it is hardly likely that Heraclius went so far out of his way as to reach Edessa, though he stayed there a good deal later. The two places are constantly confused in the records of this time. But I think the whole story is out of place here, the letters having reached Heraclius before the end of 627. See below, p. 139 n. and p. 140, n. 2.

City was seen in the distance. It is easy to picture the glittering cavalcade—the flashing steel[1] and fluttering pennons of the horsemen, the bowmen and spearmen with shield and quiver and lance, and in the midst the Emperor and his staff[2], one blaze of gold and colour. As Heraclius drew near, he was met by a great procession of clergy and monks under Modestus, bearing gospels and tapers and censers—the customary ritual—and followed by a great multitude of the inhabitants. So accompanied he passed to the Golden Gate[3] on the eastern side of the city, where the Patriarch Zacharias was waiting. But after an act of homage the Patriarch rebuked his ruler for the splendour of his garb, and bade him lay

[1] The ordinary equipment of the Roman cavalry soldier at this time was a steel cap, a coat of mail, gauntlets, and steel shoes: see Mr. Oman's *Art of War in the Middle Ages*, pp. 184 seq. The writer remarks that the armour prescribed in Maurice's *Strategicon*, c. 578, is also prescribed with scarcely any change by Leo the Wise, in his *Tactica*, c. 900 A.D. Flags were also carried by military ordinance. They are often mentioned by Greek writers, and banners of silk were commonly carried by the Muslim as well as the Roman forces.

[2] Sebeos specially records that the Emperor had all his 'imperial attendants' with him on this journey. Some idea of the state in which he moved may be formed from Prof. Bury's description of what was customary even in the fifth century. 'A rich purple dress enveloped the whole body—wrought dragons shone on his silken robes . . . The caparisons of his horse were of gold, and as he rode, seated on a saddle white as snow, he was accompanied by the imperial guards, who carried spears with golden tips and shields with golden centres enriched by golden eyes' (? bosses). *Later Roman Empire*, vol. i. p. 196.

[3] In the twelfth century this Golden Gate was walled up and only used on Palm Sunday and on the feast of the Exaltation of the Cross—the latter because through that gate Heraclius passed on this occasion bringing back the Holy Rood from the Persian captivity. See Palestine Pilgrims Text Society, vol. vi, *City of Jerusalem*, p. 14.

aside his purple and gold, that he might approach the holy places with fitting humility: and the victorious Emperor marched on in the guise of a penitent pilgrim. On every side he saw signs of the ruin wrought fourteen years before by the Persians; but he thanked Modestus for the great work of restoration which he had done, especially at the churches of the Resurrection, of the Skull, and of Constantine. Then followed the grand ceremonial known as the Exaltation of the Cross, the memory of which is still celebrated by Eastern and Western Churches alike on September 14.

Legend has it that the Holy Rood, which was enshrined in a reliquary studded with jewels, had never been profaned by heathen eyes during the period of its captivity with the Persians: that even Chosroes had never dared to turn the key or to open the sacred treasure. It is extremely probable that the Rood was saved from destruction, partly owing to the superstitious reverence with which the heathen King regarded it, but partly also owing to the intrinsic value of the gold and precious stones enclosing it, Chosroes being a great collector of works of art. But however that may be, the relic was restored to the Cathedral church of the Resurrection, and there placed on the altar with solemn rites of great magnificence.

It is not fanciful to see in this triumphant restoration of the Cross the dramatic climax of the Emperor's career. He was now at the zenith of his power and his fame, and may well have felt that his mission was accomplished. During ten years of failure and shame he had sunk under that strange besetting weakness of will which had bowed his Empire to the dust, which had suffered province after province to crumble away at the touch of barbarian armies, till nothing was left but the walls of his capital and the narrow strip of sea that sundered the beleaguering hosts of his enemies. Then rising like a dreamer from sleep he had astonished the world by an exhibition of iron purpose and strength, of glowing enthusiasm, of consummate strategy, of swiftness in decision and commanding power over men—qualities which marked him as by far the greatest captain of his age. The armies created and led by his genius had conquered the conquering Persians and freed his empire of their yoke from the Bosporus to the Araxes, from the Araxes to the Jordan, and from the Jordan to the Nile. Above all he had saved Christendom from the imminent danger of being swamped by a heathen religion; he had rescued from a pagan king the most precious symbol of the Christian truth; and now the restitution of the Cross to its shrine in the Holy City sealed in him the union of imperial conqueror and victorious defender of the faith. He had delivered the Roman Empire and delivered Christendom from the very edge of destruction.

But from this moment both his fortune and his character wavered and began to decline. His first political act was one of fierce reprisal against the Jews. People and priests in Jerusalem vied with each other in denouncing that race to the Emperor, and in charging them with more guilt than the Persians for the slaughter of the Christians and the demolition and burning of the churches. The charge was probably true, or near the truth; it was not for nothing that the Jews had taken the Emperor's bond of indemnity, and it is clear that they felt at this time a far more bitter hostility against the Christians than against their heathen neighbours. Heraclius, however, was loth to depart from his plighted word. He was reminded that he had given the pledge in ignorance of the facts; that he was not bound by a promise cozened out of him by fraud; that, had he known how the Jews smote the Christians with fire and sword, he must have dealt very sternly with them; and so forth. The clamour or the casuistry, or both, prevailed. An edict was issued by which the Jews were driven out of Jerusalem and forbidden to come again within three miles of its walls. But banishment was the lightest punishment they suffered; for Heraclius seems to have sanctioned the full measure of vengeance which the Christians demanded, and something like a general massacre followed [1]. But in order to soothe the Emperor's conscience and their own, the Patriarch and bishops sent letters to every city ordering the institution of a week's fast for ever. That institution still remains, and to this day the first week of Lent with the Copts is called 'The Fast of Heraclius.' It may be taken that the Copts joined in the massacre, having their own scores to settle with the Jews from the time of the Persian capture of Alexandria.

The Emperor seems to have spent the winter in Jerusalem; indeed from the date at which the fast is kept, it may be argued that the massacre of the Jews took place early in the following year, 630. It was during this winter that the Patriarch Zacharias died [2], and Modestus, by the voice of King

[1] Maḳrîzî says that the Jews were 'massacred till none were left in the kingdoms of Rûm, Egypt, and Syria, save those who had fled and hidden themselves.' This would make the massacre extend all over the Empire (Malan's tr., p. 70). The story is found also in Eutychius.

[2] In the *Acta Martyris Anastasii* (ed. Usener, p. 12) it is stated

and people alike, was placed on the patriarchal throne.

It is not clear which of the two pontiffs was responsible for the massacre which sullied the fame of Heraclius; doubtless both men consented to it; but, when the Emperor turned northward again, he took Modestus with him to aid in the resettlement of Church matters consequent upon the recovery of Syria, and in the transfer to the orthodox party of those churches which Chosroes had made over to Monophysites or Nestorians[1]. The Patriarch was required too to aid in formulating that plan of reli-

that Heraclius reached Jerusalem in the third indiction, the twentieth year of his reign (which is equivalent to the year beginning September, 629), and that while he was there a bishop came from the Catholicus of Persia with letters for the Emperor and for Modestus, who had just been elected Patriarch. Here again is a statement and a date of great precision made by a contemporary writer—made in quite an incidental manner, but therefore all the more worthy of credit. Nor does the writer's belief in the miracles he records affect his trustworthiness on such a question of fact, where inaccuracy could have no motive. But if this date be accepted, it is clear that, inasmuch as Heraclius cannot have stayed very many months in Jerusalem, and Modestus was enthroned before he departed, Zacharias must have died not later than February or March, 630. The period of his primacy is given as twenty-two years: and this fairly agrees with the reputed date of his election in 609. Anastasius was martyred under Chosroes on January 22, 628, and his memoir was probably written a very short time after his death; so that it may at least be taken as confirming the chronology which makes the entry of Heraclius into Jerusalem take place on Sept. 14, 629.

[1] Makîn relates that in 625 Chosroes forced the people of Rûḥâ to embrace the Jacobite creed. One of the royal physicians named John was a Jacobite, and he persuaded Chosroes that so long as the people followed the orthodox party, so long would they favour the Romans; whereupon the King gave them the choice of changing their creed or death. Cedrenus too says that at Edessa the churches which Chosroes had given to the Nestorians were restored by Heraclius to the Melkites or orthodox.

gious union between the warring sects of the Empire which had long been among the Emperor's most cherished dreams, and which now seemed feasible to the victorious champion of Christendom.

But Modestus died in the winter of 630–1, after a reign of only nine months[1], and Heraclius failing to find a bishop whose mind would mirror his own Church policy left the patriarchal throne of Jerusalem vacant. But he was not to be shaken from his purpose of reconciling the Jacobite and Melkite, the dissentient and orthodox parties in the Church. Sergius of Constantinople brought to the cause the zeal and power for which his name was famous. He was a Syrian by birth, and with him originated the formula of compromise adopted by Heraclius, whereby it was settled to dismiss the question whether our Lord's nature was single or twofold, but to pronounce positively that there was but one will or operation. As long ago as 623, when the Emperor was in Armenia, he had come to terms with Paulus, so that the union of the State Church with the Armenian Church was accomplished: and four years later in a visit to the Lazians he gained over Cyrus, the Nestorian bishop of Phasis, to the new doctrine. He now offered the primacy of Antioch to Athanasius on condition of his recognizing the Council of Chalcedon with the Monothelite interpretation. The three prelates seem to have met in council with the Emperor at Hierapolis, and the result of their debates was complete agreement upon the terms of the compromise, which it

[1] Eutychius gives the term as nine months, Nicephorus one year. After the interval the next Patriarch was Sophronius, who in 633 was present as simple monk at the Synod of Alexandria. His appointment probably took place in 634, though Eutychius makes the vacancy last for six years.

was hoped would bring peace to the Church and heal her deep divisions.

This agreement was probably reached in the early part of the year 631 [1], and was immediately followed by the appointment of Cyrus to the primacy of Alexandria, with instructions to draw the Coptic and Melkite Churches together in the happy union devised by the wisdom of the imperial council. So far the plan of the Emperor had prospered almost beyond expectation. The dispatches which reached him from Egypt were at first encouraging. Cyrus gave glowing reports of his progress, and it seemed as if Heraclius, after recovering and reuniting the Empire which the Persians had torn from his grasp and shattered, was about to fulfil the dream of his life. In battle he had won glory enough, by conquering the heathen and saving Christendom; it would be a greater glory to bring peace and goodwill to the Church, to vanquish its dissensions [2], and join its members in a single brotherhood owning a single faith. The symbol of the recovered Cross was before his eyes; nor is it to be wondered at if above it he read that legend which had shone in the vision of his great predecessor, *ΤΟΥΤΩΙ ΝΙΚΑ*. By the Cross he had conquered in war, and the Cross was to be the inspiration of his statecraft in peace.

[1] Drapeyron (p. 303) is, as I have shown, clearly wrong in making the interview between Athanasius and the Emperor at Hierapolis take place in 629. Apart from the reasons already stated, Cedrenus says it was in the twentieth year of his reign that Heraclius at Hierapolis, after wavering between the Monophysite and the orthodox doctrine, finally forbade by an edict the recognition of either one or two natures. While the decision was no doubt taken in 631, the edict was not issued till a few years later.

[2] ὅπως ὁ πείσας ἠρεμεῖν τοὺς βαρβάρους
πείσῃ σὺν αὐτοῖς ἠρεμεῖν τὰς αἱρέσεις·
quoted by Drapeyron, p. 301.

CHAPTER XI

THE RISE OF MOHAMMED

Coincidences between Heraclius and Mohammed. The Prophet's letters to the rulers of the world, and the answers. Battle of Muta. Failure of Tabûk. Death of Mohammed and union of Arabia. The Cathedral at Ṣana'. Expedition against Syria. Causes of the success of Islâm: Christian opinion.

HISTORY is full of dramatic ironies: but in few periods are they more abounding or more striking than in the reign of Heraclius. Almost at the moment when Heraclius began his career as Emperor, the great rival of his life and work, Mohammed, began his career as Prophet, in the year 610[1]. Each of these two great men went through a period of discouragement and danger which lasted for twelve years, and each emerged from the fire of adversity with a spirit tempered to great purpose. It was in 622 that Heraclius started on his expedition to Cilicia, where he struck the first blow for the rescue of the Holy Rood and the recovery of his Empire from the Persians. In 622 Mohammed by his flight from Mecca to Medina virtually opened his war for the rescue of the great shrine of the Ka'bah and for the conquest of Arabia: so that from that point dates the Mohammedan era for all time.

Nor do the coincidences end here. From 622

[1] Mohammed was born in 570, and so was about forty years old at this time, as Arab writers agree. Heraclius was three or four years younger. I may add that this passage about coincidences was written before I had the opportunity of reading Drapeyron's most interesting work, *L'Empereur Héraclius et l'Empire Byzantin*: q. v., pp. 318–9.

onwards both King and Prophet advanced in a career of victory almost unchequered for the space of six years. With eager eyes Mohammed watched the long eventful combat between Rome and Persia. He had deplored the earlier success of the Persian arms in 614 and 615, as the success of an idolatrous over a believing nation: but when the tide of war so strangely changed, and Heraclius in six years of furious struggle overthrew the might of Persia, then Mohammed, fired with new dreams of dominion, rejoiced to see victor and vanquished both drained of strength, and read in the issue the finger of God preparing the way for the power of Islâm. So that the moment of Heraclius' greatest glory may well have been also the moment of Mohammed's greatest encouragement.

Even before that the Prophet had felt himself strong enough to challenge the submission of the rulers of the world to his new religion. In the course of 627 [1], Mohammed caused letters to be written, and

[1] There is as usual some doubt about the year. The Arab writers seem mostly (according to Mr. Evetts' note on Abû Ṣâliḥ, p. 100, n. 3) to place the dispatch of the letters in A. H. 6, which began May 23, 627 A. D. Sale and Ockley give the date 629, but quite inconsistently make the Persian monarch at that time Chosroes Parwîz, whose death occurred in March, 628. It is known that Mohammed started for Mecca in spring—the time of the yearly festival—and that the letters were sent out after his return from the expedition, which ended in the armistice with the Ḳuraish. Accordingly the expedition must have taken place in 627, in order that Mohammed's letter should reach Chosroes before his dethronement in March, 628, as the story requires. For Ṭabarî leaves no doubt that the Persian King who received the letter was Chosroes Parwîz, and that he received it several months before his death, and therefore well before the end of 627. Consequently we are driven to the conclusion that the letters were dispatched during that year. It follows that Heraclius must have

he sealed them in Eastern fashion with a seal on which was written 'Muḥammad the Apostle of God.' All contained the same claim of allegiance to Islâm and to the Arabian Prophet as Vicegerent of the Most High. These letters were sent to the princes of Yaman, of 'Umân [1], of Yamâmah, and of Baḥrain; to Al Ḥarith, prince of the Saracens on the borders of Syria; to George, wrongly called the Muḳauḳas, governor of Alexandria and Viceroy of Egypt [2]; to the Negus of Abyssinia; to Chosroes, King of Persia; and to Heraclius, Emperor of the Romans [3].

received his letter in the summer of 627. The alternative, which would place Mohammed's expedition in the spring of 628, requires the explicit rejection of Ṭabarî's evidence—a very strong measure. It raises other difficulties, because the letters cannot have gone out before May at the very earliest, and by that time Heraclius was in Armenia. This reasoning assumes the truth of Ibn Isḥâḳ's statement that the letters were all written together: on the other hand, it is just possible that the message to Persia was sent more than a year in advance of the message to Heraclius. This interval is unlikely, however, and the question is eminently one in which the Arab authorities may be trusted.

[1] Ibn Isḥâḳ (quoted by Dr. Koelle in *Mohammed and Mohammedanism*, pp. 194, 332–3) alleges that the bearer of the letter to 'Umân was 'Amr ibn al 'Aṣî, the future conqueror of Egypt. But he seems mistaken, since 'Amr was not converted to Islâm at the time.

[2] Ibn Isḥâḳ, from whom these details come, makes it quite clear that a person whom he calls (though wrongly, of course) Al Muḳauḳas was virtual ruler of Egypt at this time, and this ruler must either have been directly appointed by Heraclius upon the evacuation of the country by the Persians or else have been continued by the Emperor in an office which he held under the Persian government. But the whole chronology of the letters is full of difficulty, and the probability is that they were sent out at different times, as opportunity served. See a note in Hamaker's *Waḳidî*, p. 24, n. 5.

[3] In dealing with Arab authorities at least one must recognize the use of the term 'Romans,' in preference to 'Greeks' or 'Byzantines.' Indeed the importance of the first name is shown

Of the princes of Àrabia two sent fair answers, viz. the rulers of Yamâmah and Baḥrain, and they professed their conversion. From Yaman and 'Umân came rough replies, which Mohammed received with curses; while a polite but worthless acquiescence came from the King of Abyssinia: and it may be remarked that, of all the dominions whose allegiance Mohammed demanded, Abyssinia to-day remains the one power which has never bowed the knee to Islâm. The governor[1] of Egypt promised

by the fact that practically the only Arab name for people of the Empire was *Ar Rûm.* I am aware of Prof. Bury's condemnation of those historians who use any other epithet than 'Roman' for the Empire at this period (see the Preface to his *Later Roman Empire*), but I have not scrupled to speak of the 'Byzantine' government or the 'Greek' historians. Yet the people of the Empire called themselves 'Romans,' and to them 'Greek' was a term of reproach synonymous with 'heathen.'

[1] In the Appendix 'On Al Muḳauḳis' I have shown that the title is given to the governor at this time by an anachronism. I must of course entirely recant the views expressed in my note to Abû Ṣâliḥ, p. 81, n. 4. The office held by the receiver of Mohammed's letter must have been much higher than that of nomarch or pagarch; in fact it was none other than that of 'Praefectus Aegypti' or 'Augustalis,' or in other words Viceroy of Egypt. The very fact that Mohammed's letter was addressed to him is strong evidence of his position. The theory which makes the Roman official a mere pagarch reduces its advocates to something like absurdity. Thus Mr. Milne in his note on the subject (*Egypt under Roman Rule*, pp. 224–5) says, 'George was probably prefect of Augustamnica, as his province is not specified, and the names of the prefect of the province of Egypt and the prefects of Lower Egypt and Arcadia at this time are given elsewhere by John of Nikiou. His post on the eastern frontier of Egypt would make him the first person of high rank to whom the messengers of Mahomet came.' Now in the first place I think the three prefects mentioned are merely military prefects: and in the next it is utterly unreasonable to suppose that, while Mohammed knew all about the ruler of Persia, the ruler of the Roman

to consider the message, and treated the envoy, Ḥâtib, with all honour; he sent back with his reply some valuable presents, which included two Coptic maidens, Mary and Shîrîn, the mule Duldul—absurdly said to be the first mule seen in Arabia—the ass Nafûr, and a bag of money [1]. Mary adopted Islâm, and became a great favourite with Mohammed, but she died in 636, and so never saw the enslavement of her country.

The Persian King's answer was given in quite another temper. He tore the Prophet's letter to pieces in angry scorn, and wrote orders to Badhân [2], the Persian governor of the province of Hamyar,

Empire, and the various chiefs and princes of Arabia, he knew nothing of the ruler of Egypt, but sent a letter haphazard to be delivered to and answered by the first local official whom his envoy might encounter. The Arab writers correctly assign to the receiver of the letter the highest office in the country.

[1] Abû Ṣâliḥ, p. 101. Some writers add butter and honey.

[2] It may be useful briefly to recall the story of the Persian dominion in Arabia. Yaman, or Arabia Felix, though peopled mostly by a Jewish race, had been under Christian influence ever since the fourth century, and in the sixth the country was subject to Abyssinia. Wishing to throw off the yoke, the people had sent an envoy, Saif, to the Byzantine Emperor, who refused to aid a revolt which was directed against the Christian religion. Saif then went on to Persia in 574, and by a trick overcame the doubts of Anûshîrwân, who finally sent an army of gaol-birds, in number 3,600, under the general Horzâd of Dailân. This force was transported in eight vessels—each therefore carrying 450 men besides stores and equipments. On landing they were joined by vast hosts of the natives, and soon captured the capital Ṣana'. Some years later, on a rebellion of the Abyssinian party, Chosroes sent a fresh army under the same leader, who crushed all resistance, and drove the Abyssinians out of Arabia. The Hamyar dynasty was thus extinguished, and Yaman with Ḥadramaut, Maḥrâ, and 'Umân became a Persian province. It is clearly recorded that Persian rule was mild and hardly felt, while both the Jewish and

to send him the head of the impudent impostor. 'So shall God rend his kingdom,' said Mohammed when he heard how Chosroes had dealt with his letter—a forecast or a curse which had not long to tarry for fulfilment [1].

And what of Heraclius? While fresh from the ovations of the capital which had greeted the close of his conquests in Asia, as he was making his way in one long triumph through Syria and bearing the Holy Rood back to the Holy City, did any thought or remembrance cross his mind of the time when those wild horsemen dashed up to his encampment and their leader Daḥîah ibn Khalîfah delivered Mohammed's letter? The Emperor must have heard what manner of answer the Persian King had sent: perhaps also he had heard of the murder at Muta: but his own reply had been courteous enough —so courteous that the Arab writers embroider upon it the ridiculous story that Heraclius yielded

the Christian faith were freely tolerated. See Capt. R. L. Playfair's *History of Arabia Felix* (Bombay, 1859), pp. 72–7, and Wright's *Christianity in Arabia*, pp. 175–89. The Kingdom of Hirah was also subject to Persia. Its ruler, Nu'mân abû Kabûs, who reigned from 589 to 611 A.D., and who had been an idolater given to human sacrifice, became a convert to Christianity, and after his baptism melted down a statue of Venus in solid gold which his people had worshipped. This story is given in lib. vi. c. 22 of Evagrius, whom Wright alleges to be in remarkable agreement with the Arab writers.

[1] This remark, which is probably authentic, shows clearly that Chosroes and not Siroes received the letter. Siroes reigned only a few months—till August, 628. His successor, a feeble child, was put to death by the Shah-Waraz, whom Heraclius had nominated to the throne, seeing that a strong man was required. This was in the summer of 629. The Shah-Waraz, however, proved a tyrant of the worst description, and was assassinated early in 630. These dates seem well attested, but they are by no means undisputed.

obedience to Islâm. Nothing was further from his thoughts; nor was there the slightest reason why the master of so many war-hardened legions should take seriously the extravagant pretensions of an unknown Arabian chieftain.

So Heraclius passed on his way unheeding, or at least untroubled. But while the great procession was winding from the Golden Gate up to the church on Calvary for the festival of the Uplifting of the recovered Cross, while all Jerusalem was crying and sobbing with an emotion which broke down even the singers quiring their triumphal hymns[1], at that same time a band of 3,000 horsemen sent by Mohammed was crossing the desert to Muta, to avenge the murder of his messenger, and to begin that war with the Roman Empire which ended only in 1453, when Constantinople fell before Islâm, and the name of the Arabian dreamer was blazoned, where it still stands, on the walls of the great Cathedral of St. Sophia. It was not far from Muta that the Saracen army under Zaid was attacked by the imperial forces, and so severely handled that, after most of the officers had fallen, it was only saved from total destruction by the marvellous dexterity and prowess of Khâlid, called henceforth the 'Sword of God.' The remnant made their way back in dejection to Medina: but they found Mohammed undismayed. Before October closed, he put 'Amr ibn al 'Aṣī at the head of a small force to patrol the Syrian border, and deferred the more serious conflict till he had established his power over Arabia. The

[1] Sebeos, after saying that there was great gladness on that day, speaks of the 'weeping and sobbing and shedding of tears' on the part of the Emperor and princes, the troops, and all the inhabitants of the city, so that 'nobody could sing the songs of the Lord.'

conquest of Mecca soon followed and the victory of Ḥunain—events which made the name of Mohammed ring through the remotest deserts of Arabia.

Filled now with dreams of empire and blinded by his enthusiasm to every hindrance, he planned and openly proclaimed an expedition for the conquest of Palestine. But his project was received with a misgiving which showed that the faith of many of his converts was not proof against the fame of Heraclius. Instead of the 100,000 well-equipped men whom he wanted, he found that, without the hypocrites and malingerers, he could only muster a miscellaneous force of 30,000. With that number he advanced to Tabûk, about half-way to Muta. There he spent ten days doing nothing. Probably the reports of his scouts deterred him from advancing further north, or he was forced to return by want of food or water. Certain it is that he went back to Medina, and spent a year in organizing an army fit to take the field. From Tabûk, however, various treaties were made with local chieftains, and Khâlid with a band of 400 horse surprised and captured the Christian chief of Dûmah, who had to surrender his oasis, his town and castle, nearly three thousand camels, four hundred suits of mail armour, and finally his religion [1].

On the whole the failure of Tabûk scarcely retarded the progress of Islâm. With very few exceptions, the princes of Arabia now threw in their lot with Mohammed, and the 'year of deputations' practically saw the whole country united under a single man, whom all from motives of conviction or of policy agreed to regard as their sovereign king, their infallible general in war, and their God-sent prophet

[1] Dr. Koelle's *Mohammed and Mohammedanism*, pp. 207–10.

in religion. In the spring of 632[1] Mohammed accomplished his last pilgrimage to Mecca, where amidst countless throngs of believers he solemnly consecrated to Islâm the whilom idolatrous shrine of the Ka'bah, and established the ritual which still prevails. Two months later he sounded the trumpet for war against the Roman Empire, and gave the command of the expedition to Usâmah, the son of his slave Zaid, who had been killed in the battle of Muta. But three days after the appointment of Usâmah, the Prophet sickened of a fever, which carried him swiftly to his grave.

By the death of Mohammed the cause of Islâm was strengthened rather than weakened. For a moment it seemed to totter: but it was too firmly based to fall under any shock from within. Unlike the Emperor Heraclius, Mohammed died, if not at the summit of power, yet at a time when he had realized the dream of his life. He had no sense of failure to cloud his last moments, no feeling that he had outlived or tarnished his triumph. Indeed, had he possessed that gift of prophecy which he claimed, he might have known that the tremendous combination of political and religious forces which he was bequeathing would almost avail in after-time to achieve the conquest of the world.

Arabia was virtually united before the death of the Prophet. The fall of Chosroes had broken the last link of Persian dominion in Yaman and the south, while Heraclius made no effort to define or assert the somewhat shadowy authority of his Empire in the north of the peninsula. There seems no doubt too that the Arabian Christians were almost

[1] March 9 is the date given, and 'seems to be fixed beyond dispute.' See Mr. R. L. Michell's *Egyptian Calendar*, p. 35.

all Monophysite, and that consequently they profoundly distrusted the Emperor's statecraft, and were weak to resist the Empire's enemies[1].

What little remained to be done towards binding Arabia under a single sovereignty was done by Abû Bakr, now chosen Caliph, i.e. khalîfah, or successor to Mohammed. Within a single year he launched Usâmah on a victorious expedition into Syria, and, by the aid of the fiery Khâlid, crushed the rebellion of Musailima, the rival prophet who had sprung up in Yaman. The dying injunction of Mohammed was to drive every religion but Islâm out of Arabia; and this seems to have been accomplished almost at once. All the Christian communities were swamped and extinguished, and all the art and culture and the learning which flourished among them perished.

There is no complete picture of the arts in Arabia at this time: but some idea of the splendour they attained may be formed from the descriptions of the cathedral at Ṣana', which the Muslims defiled and ruined. It was built by Abraḥâ al Ashram, the viceroy of the King of Abyssinia, somewhat later than the middle of the sixth century. So intense, we are told, was the King's interest in the building and decoration of the fabric, that during the whole time he was living and sleeping in the church. In design the church was basilican. Lofty columns of precious marble divided the nave from the aisles. The spaces above the columns, the apse and the upper part of the walls, were adorned with magnificent mosaics in gold and colours, or embellished with paintings. The lower part of the walls was panelled, and the floor was paved with marble of many hues set

[1] Wright's *Early Christianity in Arabia*, p. 181.

in tasteful harmony. The choir was divided off by a screen of ebony inlaid with ivory most beautifully carved, and gold and silver ornament was lavished all over the interior. The doors were overlaid with plates of gold studded with silver nails, and plates of silver studded with massive nails of gold; while the doors leading to the three altars were wrought with large panels of gold set with precious stones. On every panel there stood in relief a jewelled cross of gold with a red jacinth in the centre, and round about the cross were flowers of open-work in gold with gems or enamel of many colours. Such was the glorious church which Justinian aided Abraḥâ to build[1]; St. Sophia itself was hardly a more richly embellished or a more glorious work of art.

Even a brief sketch like this may serve in some sort as a picture of the civilization which Mohammed found in Arabia. But the artistic spirit of Islâm was as yet undeveloped, and it saw in all this wealth and beauty mere matter for plunder or for iconoclasm. At what precise date this and other Christian buildings were demolished, is uncertain. Wright thinks that few, if any, Christians were left in 632[2], and the buildings would hardly have been saved or turned into temples for Islâm, as was done in other times and places. The Christian religion and Christian religious monuments were levelled by the first waves

[1] See Abû Ṣâliḥ, pp. 300–1, and the notes. Abû Ṣâliḥ's language might almost imply the existence of the cathedral when he wrote: but it is certain that he is merely following Ṭabarî, though probably an older MS. than we possess now.

[2] Op. cit., p. 187. Yet he quotes Asseman for a bishop of Ṣana' in the eighth century, and a priest of Yaman in the tenth. The titular bishop was probably an exile or a foreigner. Some very interesting information on Arabian Christianity before Islâm may be found in F. M. E. Pereira's *Historia dos Martyres de Nagran.*

of that Muslim fanaticism which was originally directed rather against Jews and idolaters. Doubtless the free use of pictures and frescoed figures in the Christian churches gave offence to the Muslims, and in some cases partially justified them in confounding Christian with heathen worship. However that may be, all Arabia now turned to the Ka'bah and obeyed the Ḳurân. Whether Christian, Jew, or idolater by religion, whether Abyssinian or Persian, Negro or Arab by race, the people were now brought under one form of faith and worship, and one form of government.

The Saracen Empire thus founded was really a federal republic under the hegemony of Mecca. Abû Bakr and the other leaders saw, as Mohammed had seen, that the one thing needed to weld the body politic—to give it complete solidity and cohesion—was foreign conquest. To the Arabs, as to the Jews of old, Palestine was the land of promise, flowing with milk and honey. The love of military adventure was in their blood; their brain was fired by the consciousness of a divine mission. Such a combination of motive has always proved formidable, and and was now to prove wellnigh irresistible.

'This is to acquaint you that I propose to send the true believers into Syria to take it out of the hands of the infidels. And I would have you know that fighting for religion is an act of obedience to God[1].' So ran Abû Bakr's letter summoning the princes and chiefs of Arabia to muster their forces at Medina. A large army was quickly formed, and after some delay went forward under the generalship of Yazîd ibn Abî Sufiyân, with 'Amr ibn al 'Aṣī in command of a division. It was a bold idea to

[1] Ockley, p. 93.

challenge the Roman and the Persian Empire at once to combat, but less daring than it seems. For just as it is a mistake to picture the people of Arabia as all idolaters before Mohammed, so it is a mistake to imagine them as a race apart, a race severed from the world by impassable deserts and living unknown, till the new force of Islâm enabled their hosts to leap across the wilderness and burst upon the nations of the world. Nothing could be further from the truth. The weakness of Byzantium and Persia, the quarrels and hatreds of Christendom, the flame of their own enthusiasm, their hopes of plunder in this life and dreams of delight in the next—all these were powerful factors in the success of the Saracen invaders; but perhaps even more powerful than all other causes was the fact that they had closest racial affinities with a large part of the population they invaded. From time immemorial the borders of Syria and Persia, and the country east of those borders, had been overrun by Beduin Arabs, sometimes settled, sometimes nomadic, and moving for trade or war freely within the heart of both Empires [1]. Some of the principal tribes were nominally subject to Heraclius, some to Chosroes; others were independent; and most of them were ready to throw their sword into either scale, as the interest of the moment demanded [2]. Saracen scouts accompanied the armies of Heraclius.

[1] Even in the fourth century we read of Saracens playing a striking part in the defence of Constantinople against the Goths. See Dr. Hodgkin's *Italy and Her Invaders*, vol. i. p. 284 (Oxford, 1892).

[2] Thus Zachariah of Mitylene speaks of Saracens raiding Roman territory by order of the Persian King; p. 206. Again, on pp. 222 and 233 they are described as acting against the Romans. Yet on p. 232 we read of 'Saracens of Arabia' fighting under Justinian's banners to quell the Samaritan revolt.

Yet almost the first of his victories in Asia Minor was, as George of Pisidia relates [1], won over a horde of 'long-haired Saracens' who were devastating the country. The Roman army at Muta is said to have been largely composed of Beduin troops; and on the other hand the conquest of Syria and of Egypt by Chosroes had been doubtless in some measure aided by troops of splendid irregular cavalry recruited from among the Saracens.

Here then was a vast amount of fighting material for the Muslim leaders akin to that of their own armies; to make it available they only required to set it ablaze with their own fanatical belief. At the very outset the task was not remarkably easy, since vast numbers of the Arabs professed Christianity [2]. Many of these Christian Arabs fought to the last for the Empire and the Cross [3]; others were not proof against the contagion of race; and while some threw off a faith which sat loosely upon them at best, some also observed a cautious neutrality, till they could safely range their forces on the winning side. Still the ties of race told largely in favour of the Muslims.

One more general remark may be pardoned. Among the causes of the Muslim success must be

[1] *De Exped. Pers. Acro.* ii. 209.

[2] St. Simeon Stylites was an Arab by birth, and furnishes an example of fanaticism on the Christian side, though one hesitates so to call an innocent, if mistaken, form of self-sacrifice.

[3] See for example Ockley's account of the battle of Yermouk, pp. 194 seq.: also for the reference to Christian Arabs, id. pp. 144–5, 172, 228–9, 232, &c. John Moschus gives an anecdote of a stranger meeting a Saracen woman and putting to her quite naturally the question 'Are you a Christian or a heathen?' (*Pr. Spir.* cap. 136). This of course was before Islâm. But communities of Christian Arabs survived the Muslim conquest of Palestine: for Abû 'l Faraj mentions a bishop of the Christian Arabs in the early eighth century (Barhebraeus, *Chron. Eccles.* t. i. col. 294).

mentioned the strange despondency which seized the Christians—a despondency as marked as the enthusiasm of the Muslims. 'While the Church was vexed by kings and godless priests,' says Cedrenus, 'there rose up Amalek of the desert to chastise us for our sins.' Such are the words in which he records the rise of Islâm; and brief as they are, they yet reveal a consciousness that Mohammed had a kind of divine mission—at least as the scourge of God—a consciousness which is betrayed very clearly by other Christian writers of this time, such as the Armenian Sebeos[1]. Of course it is a common reflection with a defeated people that they have suffered for their sins, nor is the reflection always ill-founded in fact or in philosophy; but there seems in these writers a touch of more tragic sorrow, a sense that Christianity in dealing with the Arabs had been weighed in the balance and found wanting, that it could no longer claim a monopoly of divine guidance. It is easy to see how powerfully the cause of Islâm was aided by sombre misgivings of this kind in the heart of Christian priests and warriors. Luke, the traitor of Aleppo, was taught by a priest that the Saracens were destined to conquer the country, and Basil, the traitor of Tyre, who owed his defection to the teaching of the monk Baḥirah, had himself preached the gospel

[1] His language is very curious: 'At that time a certain man of the sons of Ishmael whose name was Mohammed, a merchant, appeared to his people, as it were by the order of God, preaching the truth. . . . Inasmuch as the command was from on high, by his sole behest all came together in a union of law, and forsaking vain idols, returned to the living God, who had appeared to their father Abraham. Mohammed bid them not to eat of unslaughtered meat, or to drink wine, or to tell a lie, or to commit fornication.' Sebeos, it must be remembered, was not only a Christian, but a bishop.

of Islâm through the Empire[1]. Though these and the like stories come mainly from Arab sources, and may be classed as legends, yet they have at least this much historical foundation, that they record among some of the Christians a certain fearful foreboding of the truth and the triumph of Islâm.

[1] Ockley, pp. 230, 252.

CHAPTER XII

THE ARAB CONQUEST OF SYRIA

Heraclius' lost opportunity. Journey to Edessa. Persecution of dissentients. Sophronius made Patriarch of Jerusalem. Embassies of congratulation to Heraclius. Alliance between Jews and Arabs. Fall of Damascus. Theodore defeated by Khâlid. The Emperor's farewell to Syria. Rescue of the Holy Rood. Surrender of Jerusalem to Omar.

When Heraclius ended his sojourn in Jerusalem and bent his steps again northward through Palestine, he cannot have realized the danger from Islâm. The figure of Mohammed was already towering over Arabia, and its colossal shadow had actually fallen on the edge of the Roman Empire; but the Emperor saw in it nothing but the menace of one of those border wars with wild desert tribes which were a normal condition of the frontier. For if he had divined the real nature of the peril, he could hardly have delayed to grapple with it: and if he had taken in time those measures which his genius might have designed, and for which his resources, though weakened, were still equal, he would very probably have crushed the Saracen power in its beginnings and have wiped out the name of Mohammed from the book of history.

But it was not to be. Duty seemed to call the Emperor away from the south, and his thoughts were preoccupied with the work of settling the frontier towns under the treaty with Persia, and of reorganizing the finance and the whole administration of the eastern provinces, which had been thrown out of joint by six years of war. Above all he was now about to carry out those plans for the religious union of Christendom which, as we have seen, had so long been maturing in his mind. He aimed at a union of compromise, not of compulsion. The wisdom of the leaders of the Church could devise the magic formula required: and then, when all the elements of heresy, discord, and difference were cast into the crucible and molten, and there emerged one simple form of faith, refined and purified and annealed against all schism, what a tremendous force would the new Christianity possess against the enemies of the Empire and the Cross!

On quitting Jerusalem the Emperor made straight for Mesopotamia[1]. His route lay through Damascus, Emesa, Beroea, and Hierapolis to Edessa. Edessa was the home of his ancestors: it was the home of St. Ephrem, the father of the Syrian Church[2]: and as the see of Jacobus Barudaeus, it was the very shrine of the Jacobite or Monophysite confession, which prevailed in the three hundred monasteries in the neighbourhood and in most parts of Armenia, Syria, and Egypt. Edessa also, from its geographical position between the Euphrates and the Tigris, its proximity to Armenia, Persia, and Syria, was a political centre of enormous importance. There could be no more fitting place for the work which the Emperor had now to accomplish.

The tangle of events at this period is most difficult to unravel. A few threads are clear here in one chronicle; a few there in another; but so disconnected that hardly the most patient labour can bring them into order. It was, however, at Hierapolis, and in 631, that the Emperor launched his

[1] Sebeos.

[2] Drapeyron, p. 286: see also p. 299 for what follows.

project for the union of the Church, and made Athanasius Archbishop of Antioch and Cyrus Archbishop of Alexandria. The latter appointment was a ruinous miscalculation. We shall soon have to follow the journey of Cyrus to Egypt, and to see what shipwreck the Emperor's project there suffered, as it encountered not only the resistance of the Melkite Sophronius and his followers, but also the opposition of nearly the whole Coptic priesthood and people. We shall see also how Cyrus, baffled in his hopes of peaceably converting the Egyptians to Monothelitism, issued a declaration of war against their Church, and madly strove to goad the Copts into changing their creed by persecution.

It was a similar failure in Syria which led to a similar persecution of the Syrian Christians. While Cyrus was undoing the work of Heraclius' conquests and making smooth the way for Islâm in Egypt, much the same process went on in Syria; although on the one hand Athanasius seems to have shown a forbearance and a tact totally wanting in Cyrus, and on the other hand the presence of the Emperor may have tended both to reduce friction and to repress dissension[1]. But the evil results of the

[1] Abû 'l Faraj (Barhebraeus) gives a totally different account of the relations of Athanasius to the Emperor (*Chron. Eccles.* t. i. col. 271–4). He alleges that at Edessa the communion was refused to Heraclius: that at Mabûg Athanasius and twelve bishops presented to Heraclius their confession of faith, which he read and praised, but he urged them to accept the faith of Chalcedon. Upon their refusal Heraclius wrote an edict for all his Empire: 'Whosoever refuses obedience to the synod, let his nose and ears be cut off, and his house be thrown down.' Many conversions followed, while the people of Emesa and others showed great barbarity, and many churches and monasteries were destroyed. It is not easy to understand this: but it evidently comes from a writer who has no

Emperor's Church policy declared themselves unmistakably a little later. After a passionate but vain appeal to Cyrus at Alexandria, the able and learned Sophronius took ship to Constantinople for the purpose of pleading his cause before the Patriarch Sergius. Sergius, however—one of the most powerful prelates who ever swayed the destinies of the Eastern Church—was himself prime author of the Monothelite compromise: he could not disavow it, and all the astute and subtle refinement of his logic and the winning persuasiveness of his manner failed to move either the reason or the heart of Sophronius, who betook himself sadly back to Syria.

It seems probable that Sophronius made his way at once to Heraclius in order to strive with him as he had striven with Cyrus and with Sergius. There is no specific record of such an interview: but it consists with what is known, and without it one can hardly explain the undoubted fact that Sophronius was now appointed by Heraclius to the archbishopric of Jerusalem, which had been left vacant since Modestus died on his journey northward with the

sympathy with the Monothelite opinions with which Athanasius is credited, and which he doubtless professed, even if he abandoned them later. As regards the further difficulty that Athanasius was Patriarch of Antioch long before any arrangement with Heraclius—we have seen that his visit to Egypt in that capacity took place in 615—I think the explanation may well be as follows. On the Persian occupation of Syria in 614 Athanasius was *de facto* if not *de jure* driven from office. His formal reinstatement could only be made after the treaty of peace by authority of the Emperor. The Emperor offered to formally recognize Athanasius, Monophysite as he was, on the terms of the compromise. To this Athanasius agreed, but after his reinstatement he found that he could not carry his people with him: whereupon he frankly abandoned the compromise. The Emperor then retorted by an edict of persecution.

Emperor. It is certain that Sophronius never wavered in his hostility to the compromise. Almost his first act as Patriarch was to call a council of the Church, at which he denounced in unsparing language the Emperor's proposals and anathematized the Patriarchs who adopted them[1]. In accepting the office he had doubtless hoped that the Emperor would renounce the Monothelite heresy and return to the orthodox religion, while the Emperor thought that the gift of a patriarchate would convert Sophronius, as it had converted Athanasius. Next to the appointment of Cyrus, Heraclius could hardly have made a more disastrous blunder: it is scarcely too much to say that it went nearly as far to cost him the loss of Palestine as did the appointment of Cyrus to cost him the loss of Egypt.

It is easy to palliate these mistakes if one remembers the grandeur of the aim and the nobility of the motive which originally prompted them. But in Syria as in Egypt, the failure of the Emperor's Church policy turned to a gloomy intolerance of opposition. It was but a step from this to persecution, and his masterful but embittered spirit knew no hesitation. 'When our people complained to Heraclius,' says Abû 'l Faraj, 'he gave no answer. Therefore the God of vengeance delivered us out of the hands of the Romans by means of the Arabs. Then although our churches were not restored to us, since under Arab rule each Christian community retained its actual possessions, still it profited us not a little to be saved from the cruelty of the Romans and their bitter hatred against us[2].' It is

[1] See the *Epistola Synodica ad Sergium* written by Sophronius. It is given in Migne, *Patr. Gr.* t. 87 (3), col. 3193.

[2] Op. cit., 274. Abû 'l Faraj writes as a Monophysite Syrian.

melancholy reading, this welcome by Christians of Arab rule as a providential delivery from the rule of their fellow Christians; but it shows with fatal clearness how impossible was the Emperor's scheme for Church union, and how surely it led to his ruin.

There remains the third capital blunder, which has been already mentioned—the massacre of the Jews. It was the first in chronological order, and the first to bear baleful fruit. Shortly after the triumphal Exaltation of the Cross at Jerusalem, when the order went forth to banish or slay the Jews, all who had warning in time fled into the desert beyond Jordan, there to tarry a change of fortune. As they waited and watched, their hearts burning for revenge, at length they saw the advancing banners of Islâm, and they welcomed the hosts that came as enemies of the Roman Empire.

While clouds were thus gathering thickly on the horizon, the fame of Heraclius' achievements had

Precisely the same spirit is shown elsewhere by the writer (col. 266–7) where he says that Chosroes sided with the Monophysite Syrians, drove out the Chalcedonian bishops from all the land, and restored all the churches which Domitian, bishop of Melitina, had taken from the Monophysites in the days of Maurice. 'The memory of the Chalcedonians was wiped out from the Euphrates to the East: for God had visited on their heads their own crime, so that they received at the hands of the Persians retribution for all the evil they had wrought us.' It is the old story of Christians sacrificing country, race, and religion in order to triumph over a rival sect of Christians. So some fifteen years after the taking of Damascus we find a Nestorian bishop writing thus: 'These Arabs, to whom God has given in our time the dominion . . . fight not against the Christian religion; nay, rather they defend our faith, they revere our priests and saints, and they make gifts to our churches and monasteries.' The great church at Damascus was then used at the same time both by Christians and by Muslims (De Goeje's *Conquête de la Syrie*, p. 84).

spread over the known world, and princes from the farthest East and the farthest West—from India and from France[1]—sent envoys with costly jewels and tributes of admiration. But the Emperor was soon reminded of the mockery of his destiny. For almost at the very time when he was receiving these marks of world-wide homage, the Saracens were thundering at the gates of Assyria, and his own son Athalaric and his nephew Theodore were plotting with some Armenians to dethrone and murder him. The plot was denounced by one of the conspirators, and all the guilty had their noses and right hands cut off[2], except the *aspet*, who had refused to agree to the assassination and was rewarded by a merciful sentence of exile[3].

It seems to have been after this event, and after the sojourn of Heraclius at Edessa, that the Jews held a gathering in the town at which, according to Sebeos, all the twelve tribes were represented. Finding the place denuded of troops, as the Persian garrison had withdrawn and had not been replaced by the Romans, the Jews closed the gates, strengthened the defences, and defied the Emperor's forces. Heraclius laid siege to the town, which quickly capitulated: he granted easy terms, and told the Jews to return peaceably to their own places. Instead of obeying, they went into the desert and joined the armies of Islâm, to which they acted as guides through the country[4]. This must have been

[1] Drapeyron, p. 228.

[2] On the barbarity of some punishments still sanctioned by law see Prof. Bury's *History of the Later Roman Empire*, vol. ii. p. 390: also his edition of Gibbon, vol. v. p. 529, note on Graeco-Roman Law.

[3] The story is told with considerable detail by Sebeos.

[4] This incident is recorded by Sebeos. Another Armenian

about the year 634, when already the Saracens under Khâlid were overrunning Persia.

The result of this alliance between the Jews and the Arabs was a demand upon Heraclius to give back the promised land to the children of Abraham: else they would claim their inheritance with usury. There could be but one answer to such a summons, and war began. The defeat of the Romans under Theodore at Gabatha was followed by the more serious disaster of Yermouk, Sept. 1, 634. In the previous July Abû Bakr had died and was succeeded by Omar as Caliph. Bosrah had already fallen. Damascus, the ancient capital of Syria, was beleaguered by Khâlid, and was finally surrendered by the Prefect Manṣûr under a treaty which secured the life and property of the inhabitants, and their undisturbed possession of the churches in the city. This was in 635: and 'all the patriarchs and bishops in all the world smote Manṣûr with anathema, because he helped the Muslims[1].' Before the city fell, Heraclius sent a large army under his

historian, Ghevond, agrees that the Jews invited the Arabs to turn the Romans out of Palestine. Ghevond's date is the eighth century. A French translation by Shahnazarian was published in Paris, 1856. Drapeyron says (p. 327) that there was a renewed massacre of the Jews at Edessa, and gives Sebeos as his authority, but I can find no such statement. But this revolt of the Jews seems identical with the revolt of the Arabs described by Cedrenus as happening after the death of Mohammed. These Arabs had been in the pay of the Emperor and were employed to guard the desert passes. Their subsidy now being refused, λυπηθέντες ἀπῆλθον πρὸς τοὺς ὁμοφύλους καὶ ὡδήγησαν αὐτοὺς ἐπὶ τὴν χώραν τῆς Γάζης στόμιον οὖσαν τῆς ἐρήμου κατὰ τὸ Σίναιον ὄρος. In any case this revolt of the Arabs assisted the Muslim armies in much the same way as the defection of the Jews. For the fact that Heraclius made a systematic persecution of the Jews, see Prof. Bury's *Later Roman Empire*, vol. ii. p. 215.

[1] Eutychius.

brother Theodore, whose superior forces fought a desperate battle with Khâlid. The result long hung in doubt, but victory swayed at last to the Muslims, and the rout of the Byzantine legions was complete. Heraclius received the news at Antioch[1], and felt that all was over. God has abandoned the cause of the Empire: the victor of the Persian heathen was vanquished by the unbelieving Saracens. The thought was rendered the more bitter, because he was conscious of the guilt he had incurred by his marriage with his niece Martina. He was conscious too of already breaking health of body. On no other theory can his inaction be explained. The man who was foremost in every fight where his personal courage was needed, and master of every movement on the battlefield—the man who six years ago would have met Khâlid 'the Sword of God' on equal terms in duel, and whose genius as a tactician would have baffled and crushed the raw valour of the Arab chieftains, never once led an army in the field against them. His hand and his brain alike were paralysed. In the great assembly which he called in the Cathedral at Antioch, when he asked for counsel, there stood up a greybeard who said, 'The Romans now are suffering for their disobedience to the Gospel, for their quarrels and dissensions, their usury and violence: they must pay the price of their sins.' It was enough: the Emperor felt that with body, mind, and fortune failing his presence was useless, and in Sept. 636 he took ship for Constantinople[2].

[1] This seems the more probable account. Cedrenus, however, makes Theodore after his defeat return to the King at Edessa. Gibbon strangely says, 'In his palace of Constantinople or Antioch he was awakened by the invasion of Syria' (ch. 51).

[2] See De Goeje, *Conquête de la Syrie*, p. 102, where the date of

'Farewell, a long farewell to Syria!' There is infinite pathos in the well-known words of the Emperor: they are charged with the feeling that his career with all its splendour and triumph is closing in shame—that he is bidding farewell to his greatness. One thinks of the agony of Napoleon, as from the deck of the *Bellerophon* he gazed his last on France[1]. Indeed the decline of physical and military vigour in the two great generals has many points of resemblance. But Napoleon after all was king and commander at the very last of his battles; whereas Heraclius had spent his strength in the futile struggle to unite the Church. He was unable to rally or guide the remaining forces of the Empire in the hour of supreme danger. During three years of crisis his hopes had decayed and his activities had withered. He had suffered the power of Islâm to grow unchecked, till it overshadowed his dominion.

Most of the historians, following or misconstruing the Greek writers, represent Heraclius as suddenly bounding out of this torpor and making a frantic journey to Jerusalem to save the Holy Rood from the hands of the enemy[2]. There is no warrant for

Heraclius' departure is given as Sha'bân, A. H. 15. The evidence that he journeyed by land is by no means conclusive.

[1] Lord Rosebery's *Napoleon*, p. 112 (London, 1900).

[2] Drapeyron, p. 349, says, 'Toujours est-il que ce hardi fugitif courut au Calvaire, arracha la Sainte-Croix au patriarche Sophrone, son possesseur légitime, et traversa le Liban au milieu des populations stupéfaites!' He cites Nicephorus, Theophanes, Cedrenus, and Suidas. Lebeau takes the same view, and Prof. Bury (*Later Roman Empire*, vol. ii. p. 266) remarks, 'He was able, notwithstanding the proximity of the Saracens, to hurry to Jerusalem and seize the Cross, which he was resolved to prevent from falling again into the hands of unbelievers.' Now I venture to say that all this

this journey beyond the statement that Heraclius took the Cross with him to Constantinople. Unquestionably he did: but he did not travel to Jerusalem to fetch it. The loose and open phrases of Cedrenus and the like cannot stand for a moment against the precise and clear story of Sebeos. He tells how after the battle of Yermouk the Arabs crossed the Jordan, and the terror of them fell upon all the inhabitants of that country, so that they gave in their submission: and he adds, 'In that night,' i.e. the night after the news of the Saracen advance

story rests on a misconception. To begin with Nicephorus. His account of Heraclius' movements is a tissue of error. He represents Heraclius as taking the Cross to Jerusalem *before* his triumphal return to the capital, as going through the hurried ceremony of Exaltation, and then at once removing the Cross to Constantinople! Heraclius is recalled to the East when the Saracens are ravaging the country round Antioch; and, while he is still in the East, the Saracens are conquering Egypt! It is clear that Nicephorus, being hopelessly confused about this period, is of small value as an authority, and also that he does not make the particular statement attributed to him. The reference to Theophanes is equally unwarranted. Theophanes says that the Emperor, abandoning Syria in despair, *ἄρας καὶ τὰ τίμια ξύλα, ἐπὶ τὴν Κωνσταντινούπολιν ἀπῄει.* There is no word of any journey to Jerusalem. Cedrenus in copying the words of Theophanes inserts after *ξύλα* "*ἀπὸ Ἱεροσολύμων*," but the insertion rests on a mere inference from the fact that the Cross was known to have been left in Jerusalem. Suidas after speaking of the Exaltation of the Cross says in another sentence, 'And the Emperor sent it to Byzantium.' Thus not one of Drapeyron's four authorities proves his statement. I must add the remark that Theophanes is hardly less untrustworthy on these few years than Nicephorus. For example, he puts the flight of Heraclius before the battle of Yermouk and before the capture of Damascus by the Saracens. Directly after the capture comes the Saracen expedition to Egypt, and Theophanes' story of what happened there is as false as it is fragmentary. In dealing with the conquest of Egypt these Byzantine writers more often darken than illumine the page of history.

came, 'the people of Jerusalem saved the Cross of the Lord, and all the vessels of the churches, and bringing them to the sea-coast they sent them on board ship to the court at Constantinople.' Not a word about Heraclius in this: but the vessel with the sacred treasures doubtless coasted northward and joined the Emperor either at some port on his homeward journey, if he travelled home by sea, or at his palace at Hieria near Chalcedon, where he stayed for some time in a state of pitiful derangement[1]. Thence ultimately he bore the Rood once again to the Cathedral of St. Sophia. It had been hailed with triumph as the talisman of his prosperity: it was now received in gloom as the symbol and seal of his adversity. Surely of all the ironies that haunt the career of Heraclius none are more pointed or more bitter than this.

So far then from the Cross being torn from the hands of Sophronius, its lawful owner, it is clear that the Patriarch himself sent away all the treasures of the Church, and resigned them to the Emperor's keeping. It was the only way to save them. His enemy Cyrus was still at Alexandria: besides, it was not long since Egypt had fallen into the hands of the Persians, and there was at least risk of a Saracen conquest. But all the storms of the late wars had beaten in vain upon Constantinople: it was the inviolate city, as well as the metropolis of the Empire.

But this act of loyalty to Heraclius, if loyalty it were, proved the last in the life of Sophronius. Jerusalem was now beleaguered by Khâlid, who was joined in a few days by Abû 'Ubaidah. The place had been well provisioned, and the bulwarks had

[1] His so-called 'hydrophobia,' which came on at Hieria, was really the fear of wide open spaces, not of water.

been rebuilt and strengthened since the Persian occupation; so that the Arabs, who had no skill in siege warfare and no siege engines, prowled round the walls for months, exchanging volleys of arrows and repelling sallies of the garrison, but making no substantial progress. It had taken the Persian general but eighteen days to force an entrance: now even the fiery Khâlid chafed in helpless wrath under the cliffs and towers of Jerusalem. Authorities differ as regards the length of the siege. It seems to have lasted all through the winter of 636–7, and probably longer: but there is no doubt of the issue. The Saracens were quite unable to take the town by storm, while the defenders failed no less to break the leaguer. From the Roman armies there came no hope of help—only stories of ever fresh disaster—and the same despondency which had seized the Emperor now fell upon the inhabitants of the Holy City.

Under these circumstances, and probably under pressure of imminent famine, the aged [1] Patriarch Sophronius parleyed with the Arab leaders from the walls, and finally agreed to surrender, if Omar would come in person to settle the capitulation. It is needless here to repeat the well-known story of Omar's arrival on his camel; how by his uncouth mien, his coarse fare, and his shabby raiment the Caliph shocked Roman refinement; how he set his seal to the treaty, and forthwith visited the Holy Places in company with Sophronius; and how the Patriarch said aside to his attendants in Greek, 'Truly this is that abomination of desolation spoken of by Daniel the Prophet.' It is the last recorded remark

[1] Sophronius, as appears from John Moschus, must now have been well over seventy.

of the 'honey-tongued defender of the faith [1]': for the second time in his latter years he had witnessed the captivity of Zion, and the bitterness of this second captivity quickly ended his life.

[1] Sophronius was so called: see Mansi, *Conciliorum Nova Collectio*, t. x. col. 607.

CHAPTER XIII

THE GREAT PERSECUTION OF THE COPTS BY CYRUS

Benjamin called to the patriarchate of the Copts. George, the Melkite Patriarch, successor to Andronicus. Popularity of Benjamin, and his reforms. Evacuation of Egypt by the Persians. Cyrus appointed Patriarch of the Roman Church by Heraclius. Arrival of Cyrus in Alexandria and flight of Benjamin. Sophronius heads the Roman opposition to Cyrus—in vain. Resistance of the Copts. The Ecthesis of Heraclius never understood by the Copts. Complete restoration of Roman dominion in Egypt. The Ten Years' Persecution: various incidents. Its general effect in preparing the way for the Arab conquest.

WE have now followed the Emperor from the day of his triumph in Jerusalem, when he reached the summit of his victorious splendour, to the day of his farewell at Antioch, when the great conqueror sank, with brain and nerve past action, in the depths of failure and gloom: we have seen how from a little cloud on the southern borders of Palestine there slowly arose, like the form of a jinn in Arab romance, the giant figure of Mohammed, and how the ever-growing Muslim power grappled and wrestled with the Roman Empire in Syria, till it overthrew it and captured first Damascus and then the Holy City: and we have touched lightly on some of the causes which worked together to produce these world-astonishing changes.

Brief as the survey has been, and needful for the right understanding of the great drama in which Egypt played a large part, it has still taken us away too long from the Nile valley. It is therefore full time to return and to trace there the course of events from the beginning of the six years' war, which ended in the death of Chosroes. Unfortunately the records for this period are few and far from luminous: one has to grope through it as best one may by the feeble light they furnish.

One of the few monasteries in the neighbourhood of Alexandria which escaped destruction in the first storm of the Persian invasion was Dair Ḳibrîûs, which nestled amidst its palm-groves close to the shore north-eastward of the city and of the buildings which were plundered [1]. It was here that a young man called Benjamin, the scion of a wealthy Coptic family and a native of Farshûṭ in the province of Buḥairah, came and received the monastic habit from the aged superior Theonas. His education was aided by great natural talent, and in no long time he outstripped his teachers both in piety and in learning. It was his wont often to spend the night in prayer within the convent church; and legend tells that once, as he watched, there came to his ears a voice declaring that he was destined to be the Shepherd of the flock of Christ. Theonas, on hearing the story, told him to beware of the wiles of Satan, naively adding that such a thing had never happened either to himself or to any of the brethren during all the fifty years he had lived at Dair Ḳibrîûs. Nevertheless he went with Benjamin to Alexandria, and there brought him before the Coptic Patriarch, Andronicus, who was so struck with Benjamin's ability and strength of character, that he kept him in the city, while Theonas was sent back alone to his monastery. Benjamin was in due course ordained to the priesthood, and, remaining by the Patriarch,

[1] See above, p. 75 n. This story is from Severus' *Lives of the Patriarchs* (*Benjamin*); Brit. Mus. MS., pp. 102 seq.

won his fullest confidence, and 'aided him in the affairs of the Church and the administration of the whole patriarchate.'

It was about Christmastide, A.D. 621, that Benjamin first entered Dair Ḳibrîûs; and he had not been many months in the service of Andronicus, when the Patriarch died, after nominating Benjamin as his successor. Benjamin at this time is described as a young man, and was probably some thirty-five years old [1], but the pallium was duly placed on his shoulders in St. Mark's Cathedral.

We have already seen that, although Andronicus was not driven from office by the Persian conquest, the Melkite Patriarch, John the Almoner, fled before it to die in Cyprus. The successor of John in the Melkite chair was George: but the Byzantine power had been rooted out of Egypt, and there is little to show that even the nominal appointment of George took place before 621. Still less can it be shown at what date George's appointment was made effective by residence in Alexandria [2]. It is even questioned

[1] Benjamin died on 8 Tûbah, 662, after a pontificate of thirty-nine years. Severus gives the same date, 8 Tûbah (=3 January) for the death of Andronicus, and though the exact coincidence is improbable, Andronicus may well have died on some day in Tûbah. But taking Benjamin's reign as lasting from January 623 to January 662, and bearing in mind that he is described by Severus as suffering greatly 'from the infirmities of old age' in his latter years, I cannot think that Benjamin was less than seventy-five at his death: nor would the canons allow the consecration of a Patriarch at an age below thirty-five years, because he is required to be 'of middle age.'

[2] See note above, p. 53. Eutychius indeed says that George took ship and fled from Alexandria, when he heard that the Muslims had conquered the Romans, taken Palestine, and were advancing on Egypt (*Annales*, ed. Pococke, t. ii. p. 266). But this story falls to pieces on the chronology, and is probably a

whether he ever set foot in the country. From neither the Persians nor the Copts could he hope for any welcome, nor would his coming have served much purpose until the return of the Byzantine garrisons established again the Church and the Empire in Egypt. The Persians under the pressure of Heraclius' victories evacuated the country early in the year 627; and just as there is record of the existence of a civil ruler of Egypt in the interval between that date and the advent of Cyrus as governor, so it may be that George the Patriarch entered Alexandria in 627, and there remained until, as John of Nikiou seems to imply, he was superseded by the same Cyrus as Patriarch. But it is more probable that George's arrival took place rather later. The conclusion of peace with Persia in 628 gradually released some of the Roman forces, but only gradually: and the Roman military reoccupation of Egypt can hardly have been accomplished

reminiscence of the flight of John the Almoner. On the other hand, John of Nikiou mentions (Zotenberg, p. 571) Philiades, brother of George the Patriarch, and three pages lower (p. 574) occur these words: 'Avant l'arrivée du patriarche Cyrus, Georges, qui avait été nommé par Héraclius le Jeune, avait été traité avec déférence par le gouverneur Anastase. Lorsqu'il fut vieux, son autorité s'étendit sur toutes les affaires. Le patriarche lui-même lui laissait son autorité.' Zotenberg in his note says that 'Heraclius the Elder' should be written for 'Heraclius the Younger,' and with this view Dr. Charles agrees. It seems therefore that the George in question may be the Patriarch George. If so, it follows that (1) he did not die in 630 or 631, but was superseded by Cyrus; (2) he was living in Alexandria during the pontificate of Cyrus; (3) that he retained, notwithstanding his deposition, great personal influence; (4) that he was on friendly terms with Cyrus and acted as his Vicar-General during the latter's absence or exile from Egypt. All this is sufficiently novel and remarkable; but it seems difficult to resist this interpretation of John's language or to reject his testimony.

much before 629. If George did not arrive in Alexandria till that year, and his office determined, whether by death or by supersession, a year or two later, it is easy to understand why his position in the records of the Church is so vague and shadowy[1].

When Andronicus, the Coptic Archbishop, passed away at the end of 622 or the beginning of 623, the Persian dominion in Egypt was not even menaced by any revival of the Roman power under Heraclius. There is little question that before his death the Patriarch heard news of the Emperor's first expedition, which voyaged by Rhodes to Cilicia; very possibly too the gossip of Alexandria was enlivened by rumours brought by Arab caravans concerning the rising prophet of Mecca; but not the wildest dreamer could have imagined that within a period of twenty years to come the Persians would be driven out of Egypt again by the Romans, and that the restored Roman power would be extinguished and closed for ever by the rude legions of Mohammed.

Benjamin's election as Patriarch was a popular one: indeed, whatever doubt may be felt regarding the wisdom of Benjamin's after-policy, it cannot be denied that he won the love and veneration of his people, and retained them unimpaired through all the vicissitudes of the most eventful primacy in Coptic history. But he made no weak concessions to laxity of faith or morals. From the first he set himself sternly to rebuke the careless lives of many among his clergy, and to check the abuses which had

[1] Renaudot does not question the current story of George's death, although by a slip he writes *post Gregorii* for *post Georgii mortem. Hist. Pat. Alex.* p. 161; and Von Gutschmid thinks that George probably died in June of 631 (*Kleine Schriften*, t. ii. p. 475).

grown up in many places where the bishops had lost all control in the tumult of war. He had been on a visit to Babylon [1] before his consecration, and now wrote a pastoral letter to all the bishops, in which he said: 'During my stay at Ḥulwân and Babylon I saw a number of froward men, both priests and deacons; my soul abhors their works. I write this letter to all the bishops bidding them hold an inquiry once a month concerning every one of the clergy who had been ordained for less than ten years.' This letter made it clear that he was Archbishop, says the chronicle [2], and he made it clearer still by excommunicating several clergy in this diocese of Babylon. The letter was followed by a visitation, in the course of which it is recorded that from Babylon he went on foot, 'accompanied by Abba Mînâ, bishop of the Castle of Babylon, and Pilihîu, bishop of Ḥulwân, and a great crowd,' to bring to account a notorious offender, on whose house he called down fire from heaven. But wherever he passed, the people flocked to receive his benediction.

So chastening and chastising the Church, the Archbishop made his power felt all over Egypt. Unquestionably he did much to restore the unity of the Coptic Church and to bring it back to that settled and organized government which had been disturbed, if not shattered, by the political troubles of the time. For four or five years [3] Benjamin lived peaceably

[1] This is of course the Egyptian Babylon, in the region now misnamed 'Old Cairo.'

[2] See the Bodleian Library MS. Copt. Clar. Press b. 5, and Amélineau's translation entitled *Fragments Coptes pour servir à l'histoire de la Conquête de l'Égypte* in the *Journal Asiatique*, 1888. It is unfortunate that of this early Life of Benjamin in Coptic so small a fragment alone survives.

[3] Severus says definitely that the Persians remained in Egypt for

under Persian rule in Alexandria. There he first saw Shahîn recalled to retrieve, if possible, the falling fortunes of Chosroes; then, as Heraclius prevailed, he saw the departure of the Persian armies. With what eyes, we wonder, did the Patriarch watch the spearmen and bowmen of the unbelievers march out of the eastern gate of the Great City? And what were his thoughts as he pondered on the coming return of the Romans?

Most of the Persian garrisons in Egypt were probably withdrawn early in 627, while some few detached posts may have been held as late as 628 and evacuated under the terms of the treaty with Heraclius. Then at least it was that the Egyptian prisoners from Dastagerd and other cities of Asia came back to their country; and it was probably in the winter 628–9 that Heraclius, after his triumph at Constantinople, sent an army by sea to reoccupy Egypt and to restore the Roman Empire from Palestine to Pentapolis.

Admirable as were Heraclius' motives in raising Cyrus, bishop of Phasis in the Caucasus, to the archbishopric of Alexandria, his act was nevertheless a blunder, and that of the most tragic kind. The whole Christian world had been strangely drawn together as they watched with breathless interest the amazing developments of Heraclius' crusade against Persia. When the infidels were vanquished, when Jerusalem was delivered, and when the Cross was exalted, Copts and Melkites alike had gloried in a common triumph; they rejoiced together also in the

six years after Benjamin's election. That would bring us to the end of 628: but I think it impossible to accept this statement, as everything points to the withdrawal of the main Persian army early in 627.

vengeance wrought upon the Jews, and shared alike the penance enjoined in expiation of the sin. It was therefore the golden moment—the tide which taken at the flood might have led to a real and lasting union. This Heraclius saw: he knew too the blind devotion of the age to shibboleths and phrases: but he refused to see that his magic compromise of doctrine might fail to charm the Church in Egypt, or that, if it failed, the very worst way to bring about union was to thrust his message by sheer force down the gorge of those to whom its first savour was bitter. This, however, was the alternative which was offered in Egypt as in Syria. It was part of the philosophy of that age that religious belief could be and should be moulded by state decrees. In this the Emperor was not ahead of his time, and he resolved that by fair means or by foul the formula of his three Archbishops should be made to prevail against all other forms of belief with which it conflicted.

Still, even under that resolve, he courted disaster in making choice of Cyrus. For this was the evil genius who not only wrecked the Emperor's hopes of religious union in Egypt, but who after making himself a name of terror and loathing to the Copts for ten years, after stamping out to the best of his power the Coptic belief by persecution, made Coptic allegiance to Roman rule impossible; the tyrant who misgoverned the country into hatred of the Empire, and so prepared the way for the Arab conquest; and the traitor who at the critical moment delivered it over by surrender to the enemy. This was the man of evil fame, known afterwards in Egyptian history as Al Muḳauḳas—that mysterious ruler the riddle of whose name and nation have hitherto confused and baffled historians, but whose identity with Cyrus is now absolutely certain[1].

Benjamin seems never to have been consulted upon the feelings of the Copts and the prospects of the experiment in Egypt. It was a fatal omission; for from its very birth the Emperor's plan, so far as Egypt was concerned, was doomed to failure. The landing of Cyrus in Alexandria, which took place in the autumn of 631, was the signal for the flight of the Coptic Patriarch[2]. Legend avers that Benjamin was warned by an angel in a dream to fly from the wrath to come; and the story proves at least that whether he knew or did not know the precise nature of the overtures which Cyrus was bringing, he resolved in advance to reject them, and that he foresaw the consequences. The coming of Cyrus was in fact taken as a declaration of war against the Coptic faith. Ere leaving his post, Benjamin set the Church in order, and called an assembly of priests and laymen, at which he delivered an address 'charging them to hold fast the faith till death.' He also wrote an encyclical to all his bishops, bidding them flee into the mountains and the deserts and

[1] For the proof of this statement I must refer the reader to my essay on the subject in the Appendix.

[2] In Prof. Bury's *Later Roman Empire* (vol. ii. p. 215, n. 1), it is strangely stated that Benjamin fled from before the *Persians*, and hence it is inferred that 'the Monophysites *were not unanimously in favour of Persian rule*.' The statement is as erroneous as the inference. Benjamin fled some three or four years after the evacuation of Egypt by the Persians at the end of their long occupation: see *Chronicon Orientale*; Renaudot, *Hist. Pat. Alex.*, l. c.; Abû Ṣâliḥ, p. 230, n. 2; and Makîn, pp. 30 and 40, which make it quite clear that Benjamin's flight took place ten years before the death of Heraclius. As regards Prof. Bury's inference, see ante, pp. 81–9, where the idea of sympathy between Copts and Persians is proved to be mythical.

hide themselves till the anger of the Lord was overpast; for grievous troubles were coming upon the land, and for the space of ten years they must suffer persecution; then it would be over.

Such was the tenour of the letter. When he had sent it, the Patriarch took his departure from Alexandria by stealth under cover of night with only two companions. Leaving the city by the western gate he passed on foot to the town of Mareotis, and thence to Al Munā[1], an oasis city which lay at the intersection of the ways from Alexandria to Wâdî 'n Naṭrûn and from Ṭarrânah to Barca. It must have been at this time a town of great splendour; for even centuries later the traveller roaming across wastes of sand was amazed at the magnificent churches and buildings which broke upon his view[2]. Here the

[1] This is the form which Severus gives, but Quatremère seems to think the whole town was called Mînâ, from the saint who gave his name to the great church there (*Mém. Géog. et Hist.* vol. i. p. 488). In the Cairo MS. of Severus the word is quite clearly written مُنى (munā), not مينا (mînâ).

[2] There is at Paris the MS. of an unknown Arab geographer (quoted by Quatremère, l. c.) which gives some curious details of Al Munā or Mînâ worth citing: 'Leaving Ṭarrânah and following the road towards Barca, one comes to Mînâ, which consists of three abandoned towns in the midst of a sandy desert with their buildings still standing. The Arabs use it as a place for lying in wait against travellers. There may be seen lofty and well-built palaces with enclosure walls about them: they are mostly built over vaulted colonnades, and some few serve as dwellings for monks. There are some springs of fresh water, but somewhat scanty. Next one comes to the church of St. Mînâ, a huge building embellished with statues and paintings of the greatest beauty. There tapers burn day and night without ceasing. At one end of the building is a vast tomb with two camels in marble, and upon them the statue of a man carved in marble, who is standing, one foot upon each camel: one of his hands is open, the other closed. This figure is said to represent St. Mînâ. On the right

Patriarch doubtless worshipped at the great church of St. Menas, and after a short rest pushed on to the mountain called Barnûj [1]. He was now close to the Naṭrûn monasteries, but he found them nearly deserted: they had never recovered from the ravages which they had suffered some thirty years before [2], and the Beduin refused to allow any large resettlement or rebuilding of the churches. Here then was

as you enter the church is a great marble column, in which a shrine is carved containing figures of Jesus, John, and Zacharias; the door of the shrine is kept closed. There is also to be seen a figure of the Virgin Mary covered by two curtains, and figures of all the prophets. Outside the church are figures representing all kinds of animals and men of all occupations. Among the rest is a slave-merchant holding in his hand an open purse. Over the midst of the church rises a dome, beneath which are eight figures said to represent angels. Close to the church is a mosque where the Muslims pray, and all the land round about is planted with fruit-trees and vines. . . . The town of Fusṭâṭ sends every year 1000 dinârs for the maintenance of this church.'

Quatremère has in nearly all cases where I have used the word 'figure' given 'statue.' Graven images, however, always were and are still most strictly forbidden, and I feel certain that paintings are intended, at least in all those cases where saints or angels are mentioned. The colossal statue set upon the two camels is not to be explained away: it was probably, like the palaces and colonnades, a relic of Greek civilization, though the later Copts may have strangely identified it with St. Menas. But the whole account of this town is singularly interesting. Its position is now unknown, but it probably lay north-west of the Naṭrûn Lakes and nearly due south of Marîûṭ (which latter place is still marked by ruins), and it would thus be on what was called the 'Route of the Pilgrims' from North Africa.

[1] Amélineau, *Géog. Copte*, pp. 319–21. The author cites the Paris MS. Arab. 139, fol. 97, for the arrival of Benjamin at this place.

[2] In the time of the Patriarch Damianus. The monasteries were reinstated after the Arab conquest, and the church of St. Macarius was consecrated with great ceremony by Benjamin himself, as Severus records.

no place for the Patriarch; he was still too near the capital to feel secure, too remote from his people to help them. He therefore passed on towards the Pyramids, and by the edge of the desert, to Upper Egypt, till he reached the town of Ḳûṣ[1]; and not far from Ḳûṣ he took shelter in a little monastery in the desert, which for centuries later remained famous as his place of refuge.

This flight of Benjamin practically coincided with the arrival of Cyrus in Alexandria, and there is not a word in any record to suggest that Cyrus made the slightest effort to come to an understanding with the Coptic Patriarch. His very presence seems to have scattered the Coptic clergy in terror. Enthroned as imperial Patriarch of Alexandria, he was also armed with the civil power as Viceroy of Egypt[2]. It was doubtless this union of the two highest offices which made Benjamin's position untenable; it certainly clothed Cyrus with almost despotic authority. Professing, however, to have come on a mission of peace, Cyrus expounded the ingenious Monothelite formula, by which the Emperor hoped to heal the breach of Chalcedon. He had to win over both the Melkite and the Coptic communion; but from the first the proposed compromise seems to have been ill stated, ill understood, and ill received. To many of the Melkites it seemed sheer surrender of Chalcedon; while such of the Copts as heard the proposal

[1] On Ḳûṣ see Quatremère (*Mém. Géog. et Hist.* t. i. pp. 192–216), where an interesting note explains the position of the town, and also recounts some curious stories of magic and serpent-charming in connexion with it. Abû Ṣâliḥ mentions (p. 230) without naming the monastery in which Benjamin took refuge.

[2] The evidence for this union in Cyrus of civil and ecclesiastical power is partly given in the Appendix: there is no room for any doubt on the subject.

urged also that by admitting one will and one operation the doctrine admitted one nature—that in fact Cyrus had come over to the Monophysites.

To remove these misunderstandings, Cyrus held a formal synod or council at Alexandria, at which the matter was set forth for discussion and debate. It was here that our friend Sophronius, who was again in Egypt, led the Melkite opposition, and strove by the most earnest entreaty as well as the strongest argument to turn Cyrus aside from his purpose. Cyrus is said to have replied kindly [1], and to have referred Sophronius to the Primate Sergius at Constantinople for the settlement of his scruples: but he was quite unshaken, and the result of the council was to confirm the compromise and to smite with nine anathemas those who rejected it. In all this Cyrus seems to have shown very little of that tact and sympathy which were essential in the bearer of the Emperor's Eirenicon. He met resistance by sheer force of will and weight of authority, whereas only the most delicate adroitness could hope to deal successfully with the thorny problems of the Church in Egypt. Blame, however, may lie on both sides. If Cyrus was overbearing, the Copts might be held blind and intractable, if it were clear that the terms of the offer were ever fairly put before them. To the common lay intelligence there would seem to be little remaining difference

[1] The note by Dr. Murdock on Mosheim (eleventh edition, p. 256, n. 1) makes out that Sophronius was very humble, falling down and entreating Cyrus not to press matters, and that Cyrus was very conciliatory. I somewhat doubt this. Sophronius showed more passion than humility in his demeanour. 'With a loud and bitter cry he burst into tears and flung himself at Cyrus' feet imploring and beseeching him not to proclaim' the nine heads of anathema: but Cyrus disregarded the appeal. See Mansi, t. x. col. 691.

between Monophysite and Monothelite: and though it is right to remember that even now divisions between Christians are often equally bitter and equally baseless, yet it would be true that in scorning this offer of union the Coptic Church made a mistake which cost it untold suffering.

Others may hold that the compromise was unsound and impossible. But whatever judgement may be passed on the proposal made by the Emperor Heraclius and the three Eastern Patriarchs, and in whatever form it reached the Copts, rightly or wrongly they received it with the deepest hostility: they resented the thought of changing one iota in their shibboleth as treason to their faith and to their religious independence. It was this last point in which their passion centred. National independence they had never known, and such an ideal can scarcely have entered into their dreams; but for religious independence they had struggled and fought incessantly ever since the Council of Chalcedon. That ideal they cherished at all times in their hearts, and for it they were prepared to sacrifice all else whatsoever. In this lies the key to all their history.

When Cyrus found that neither cajolery nor malediction availed to win over the Copts, he used stronger measures, to which it cannot be denied that Heraclius was a party. But the Emperor at a later period made one more effort for union. As the doctrine of one will and one operation was rejected, Sergius suggested that while one will alone should be recognized, the question whether its operation were single or twofold should be waived and discussion forbidden: and he secured the assent of the Roman Pope Honorius to this solution, or rather evasion, of the problem. It was embodied in a formal edict or Ecthesis, and issued to the Eastern world as a binding ordinance. John, general of militia, was charged by Sergius to take a copy to Cyrus, and with it he took a rood or cross of great sanctity as a present[1]. But the effect of the famous Ecthesis was only to rouse further opposition. The Emperor, who had thought either to muzzle or to convert Sophronius by raising him to the see of Jerusalem, discovered in him an unrelenting foe to his policy[2]: while to the Copts the later edition of the new doctrine had, if anything, an even worse savour than the earlier.

It is, however, extremely doubtful whether the Ecthesis, or even the original Eirenicon, ever reached the Copts beyond the gates of Alexandria. For perhaps the most melancholy and pathetic feature of the whole story is this—that Coptic annals betray no gleam of consciousness that any Eirenicon was ever offered at all. All through the Great Persecution it is the doctrine of Chalcedon pure and simple—'the tome of Leo'—that is offered, with stripes or death as the alternative; and this is the conviction burnt into the mind of all Coptic historians and graven in all their records. It would seem therefore as if Cyrus, conscious at once of the failure of his mission, and resolved at all costs to drive the Copts within the pale of the established

[1] The Ecthesis is given in Harduin's *Concilia*, t. iii. p. 791. See also Mosheim's *Eccl. Hist.* p. 256 (eleventh edition). Cyrus' effusive acknowledgement of its receipt is given by Drapeyron (p. 389), who mentions the bearer. The cross is mentioned by John of Nikiou (p. 574). It may have held a portion of the so-called 'true cross.'

[2] Cedrenus in speaking of Sophronius' death says that the Patriarch died after having made great war against Heraclius and Sergius and the Monothelites.

Church, troubled little thereafter about the refinements of the Emperor's theology, and merely set out the plain alternatives—union or persecution.

For the whole country was now at the mercy of Cyrus, the Muḳauḳas. Not merely did the shining streets of Alexandria ring again to the tramp of legions from Byzantium, while its long line of walls and its towers were once more held by Roman guards and mounted with Roman engines of war: but Pelusium, commanding the route from Palestine to Egypt; the chief towns of the Delta, like Athrîb and Nikiou; and the great fortress of Babylon near Memphis, were garrisoned in the same manner. Thence the network of Roman dominion was woven again over the Fayûm and the valley of the Nile southward to the frontier town of Syene below the cataract. All the Roman forces were at the call of Cyrus to do his bidding. Against the reoccupation the Copts were of course quite passive; but little cause as they had to love the Persians, they soon found that their new rulers would leave them small reason to rejoice in the change. Chastisement with whips was to be followed by chastisement with scorpions. For under the Persians, as soon as the conquerors had established a settled government, the Copts had at least been allowed to practise their own form of religion: and this was the precious privilege which Cyrus, the Muḳauḳas, resolved to wrest from them.

So the Great Persecution began. All the authorities are agreed that it lasted for a period of ten years, in other words that it virtually coincided with the term of Cyrus' patriarchate. The synod at Alexandria probably was held in October, 631, and the persecution commenced a month or two later.

Of its fierceness there can be no question. 'These were the years,' says Severus, 'during which Heraclius and Al Muḳauḳas were ruling over Egypt: and through the severity of the persecution and the oppression and the chastisements which Heraclius inflicted on the orthodox, in order to force them to adopt the faith of Chalcedon, an innumerable multitude were led astray—some by tortures, some by promise of honours, some by persuasion and guile.' The biography of the Coptic Patriarch Isaac[1], which was written about 695, represents Isaac in his young days as meeting with a priest named Joseph, who had been haled before the tribunal of Cyrus, and had been beaten with many stripes for his confession of the faith. Benjamin's own brother, Menas, was tortured and drowned. First of all lighted torches were held against him and he was burnt 'till the fat dropped down from both his sides on the ground[2]': then as he still was unshaken in his confession, his teeth were pulled out: next he was placed in a sack filled with sand, and taken out to a distance of seven bowshots from the shore. Three times he was offered his life, if he would acknowledge the Council of Chalcedon: three times he refused: and then he was sunk in the sea. 'Yet it was not they who were victorious over Menas, that champion of the faith, but Menas who by Christian patience overcame them,' says the biographer of Benjamin.

[1] *Histoire du Patriarche Copte Isaac* (p. 12), by E. Amélineau. Amélineau's translation does not quite bring out the force of the pluperfect, as Mr. Crum tells me. The tense is important for the chronology: for when the meeting took place, the confession before Cyrus was clearly a thing of the past. Isaac died in 693, as I show in Appendix F.

[2] This account is from Severus (Brit. Mus. MS., p. 104, l. 10). The Cairo MS. agrees.

Another document—the life of Samuel of Ḳalamûn[1]—the original of which was certainly contemporary with Cyrus, shows so clearly the part which Cyrus himself took in the persecution, that one may be pardoned for quoting it at some length. The story tells how the Archbishop on coming to the monastery found it deserted except for the steward, who was scourged and questioned. The steward then said, 'Samuel the ascetic held much discourse with the monks, calling you a blasphemer, a Chalcedonian Jew, an atheist, a man unworthy to celebrate the liturgy, unworthy of all communion: and the monks hearing this fled before your visit.' At these words the impious blasphemer fell into a furious passion, and biting his lips he cursed the steward, the monastery, and the monks, and departed another way, 'nor has he returned to this day,' adds the chronicle[2]. Then the brethren came

[1] Published by Amélineau in *Mon. pour servir à l'Histoire de l'Égypte Chrétienne aux IVe–VIIe siècles* (*Mém. Miss. Arch. Franç. au Caire*, t. iv. 2, pp. 774 seq.). As to the date, see next note.

[2] This saying proves the original MS. to have been written before the death of Cyrus in 642. Samuel died at Ḳalamûn after foretelling the Muslim invasion and the final victory of the Christians (*Journal Asiatique*, 1888, p. 384): from which we may infer that his life was written at the beginning of the invasion and before the success of the Arabs was manifest—in other words early in the year 640. These biographies were written to be delivered as panegyrics directly after the death of a great saint or churchman: so that we may conclude that Samuel died in 639. Pereira points out that Samuel is said to have met at Ḳalamûn a certain Gregory, bishop of Ḳais; that Severus records a meeting between Gregory, bishop of Ḳais, and the Patriarch John of Samanûd (680–9); and that when the Patriarch Isaac, after his election had been confirmed by 'Abd al 'Azîz, entered Alexandria in 685, he was attended by a Gregory, bishop of Ḳais. This last date should be 690, not 685: but the correction only strengthens

back in peace to the convent. But as for the Kaukhios (Muḳauḳas), the Pseud-Archbishop, he came to the city of Piom (Fayûm), cherishing wrath in his heart. There he summoned his minions and ordered them to bring the holy Abba Samuel, his hands tied behind his back and an iron collar about his neck—pushing him on like a thief. So they came to the convent where he abode and took him.

Samuel went rejoicing in the Lord and saying, 'Please God, it will be given me this day to shed my blood for the name of Christ.' Therefore he reviled the name of the Muḳauḳas with boldness, and was led before him by the soldiers. When the Muḳauḳas saw the man of God, he ordered the soldiers to smite him, till his blood ran like water. Then he said to him, 'Samuel, you wicked ascetic, who is he that made you abbot of the monastery, and bade you teach the monks to curse me and my faith?' Holy Abba Samuel answered, 'It is good to obey God and His holy Archbishop Benjamin rather than obey you and your devilish doctrine, O son of Satan, Antichrist, Beguiler.' Cyrus bade the soldiers to smite him on the mouth, saying, 'Your spirit is kindled, Samuel, because the monks glorify you as an ascetic: but I will teach you what

Pereira's argument, which is that, if these three are one and the same Gregory, as the evidence seems to show, and if Samuel died in 639, then we must believe that the episcopate of Gregory covered a period of upwards of fifty years. That is not impossible, of course; but rather than place the date of Samuel's death later, I would prefer to suppose that, just as there were two towns called Ḳais, one on the north coast and one near Baḥnasâ, so there may well have been in that period two bishops called Gregory. See Quatremère, *Mém. Hist. et Géog.* t. i. pp. 141 and 337. Gregory, bishop of Ḳais, is named by Abû Ṣâliḥ as the founder of a church at Ḥulwân (p. 156).

it is to speak evil of dignities, since you render me not the honour which is my due as Archbishop and my due as Controller of the Revenues of the land of Egypt.' Samuel replied, 'Satan also was controller, having angels under him: but his pride and unbelief estranged him from the glory of God. So with you also, O Chalcedonian Deceiver, your faith is defiled and you are more accursed than the devil and his angels.' On hearing this, the Muḳauḳas was filled with fury against the saint, and signed to the soldiers to strike him dead. In a word the blasphemer essayed to slay the saint, but the ruler of the city of Piom delivered him out of his hands. When Cyrus saw that Samuel had escaped, he ordered him to be driven away from the mountain Neklône[1].

The Ethiopic version of the life of Abba Samuel is of much the same tenour. It recounts the visit of one Maximianus at the head of 200 soldiers to Samuel's monastery in the desert and the presentation

[1] Neklône, the Arabic An Naḳlûn, lay near Al Ḳalamûn, some two hours to the south-west of the city of Fayûm. The monastery called دير الخشب is described by Abû Ṣâliḥ, pp. 205–6, in close connexion with that of Al Ḳalamûn. It is also described by Maḳrîzî (id., ib., pp. 313–4), but seems to have long disappeared. See also Quatremère, *Mém. Hist. et Géog.* t. i. pp. 411, 473; and Amélineau, *Géog. Copte*, p. 273, *Journal Asiatique*, Nov. 1888, p. 398, and Pereira, *Vida do Abba Samuel*, pp. 36–40. Pereira is mistaken in placing Ḳalamûn at a distance of 15 miles or 29 kilometres from Alexandria on the authority of Rosweyde (*Vitae Patrum*, lib. x. c. 162). Either '115' must be read instead of '15,' or the Ḳalamûn referred to must be some other monastery and not that in the Fayûm. In the *Bulletin de l'Institut Français d'Archéologie Orientale*, t. i. p. 72, Dair Naḳalûn is described as being in the mountain east of Kûm Bashâ, and Dair al Ḳalamûn as lying at the foot of the mountain at the entrance of the Fayûm and as possessing twelve churches.

to him of a document for his subscription to the faith of Chalcedon [1]. Samuel tore it in pieces and flung it out of the door of the church, exclaiming, 'We have no Archbishop but Benjamin: cursed be the blasphemous document of the Roman Emperor; cursed be the Council of Chalcedon, and all who believe therein.' Samuel was beaten and left for dead, but he recovered and made his way to Ḳalamûn, where the same defiance of Cyrus is recorded and its result [2].

When these things were done in the desert, one may imagine the fate of the Copts in the Delta and the Nile valley. Stripes, torture, imprisonment and death were the portion of those who resisted Cyrus and refused to abandon their belief. Melkite bishops were appointed to every city in Egypt up to Anṣinâ [3], while the Coptic clergy were put to death or scattered abroad in various hiding-places. The search after Benjamin was keen and unrelenting; but he was never discovered. Severus says that he moved about from one fortified convent to another, while the life of Shanûdah [4] seems to

[1] Pereira, op. cit., p. 142.

[2] Id., ib., p. 146. Cyrus is not named, but is called the Governor: he claims both authority as Archbishop and supreme civil power over Egypt: so that there can be no question of his identity. I may note that in the Coptic Synaxarium, where this incident is recorded, the words are, 'When the news of Samuel's treatment to the tome of Leo came to *Al Muḳauḳas, the Patriarch,* he laid a snare till he caught him and smote him with heavy blows, saying, "Only confess that the Council of Chalcedon is orthodox, and go your way"' (*Journal Asiatique*, Nov. 1888, p. 397).

[3] Anṣinâ or Antinoe was at this time the capital of the Thebaid. It lay opposite Hermopolis Magna, some way north of Lycopolis or Sîûṭ. It would seem therefore that Cyrus' power was not effectively exercised south of Sîûṭ.

[4] The life is in Arabic and is published with a translation in the *Mém. Miss. Arch. Franç.* t. iv. 1, p. 340. The passage concerning

assign him a refuge in the great monastery of Anba Shanûdah, better known as the White Monastery; and this story again differs from the tradition which places his retreat near Ḳûṣ in the desert. Probably the White Monastery, in spite of the tremendous strength of its walls, was too near the Nile to shelter Benjamin for long, while in the mountains of the desert by Ḳûṣ, with their endless caves and rock-cut churches, he could rest safe and unmolested.

But of those who failed to escape, it is small wonder that a great multitude gave in their submission to Cyrus. It was a reign of terror, and though the spirit of the Copts was unbroken, a whole population could not turn martyrs. Some of the bishops too went over to the enemy, such as Cyrus, bishop of Nikiou [1], and Victor, bishop of the Fayûm

Cyrus and Benjamin is given in the form of a prophecy, and deserves to be quoted. 'The Persians shall leave Egypt. Then shall arise the Liar' (الدجال—the common name for Antichrist). 'He shall go before the Roman Emperor, and after receiving from him the two headships, that of the civil government and that of the episcopal, he shall enter into Egypt and shall take possession of Egypt and its dependencies. He shall make moats and strongholds and shall build the walls of towns in the desert, and he shall lay waste the East and the West. Then shall he fight against the pastor, the chief of the bishops at Alexandria, the Vicar of the Christians in the land of Egypt, who shall flee from him to the region of Tîman, until he come to thy monastery, in sorrow and affliction. After he has come there, I will restore him and will set him again upon his throne.'

For the White Monastery see my *Ancient Coptic Churches*, vol. i. p. 351, and the admirable work of the late W. de Bock, *Matériaux pour servir à l'Archéologie de l'Égypte Chrétienne*, pp. 39 seq. It may be, however, that the convent of Shanûdah referred to is that at Ḳûṣ, mentioned by Abû Ṣâliḥ, though it is clearly distinguished by that writer from Benjamin's place of retreat.

[1] The Brit. Mus. MS. of Severus gives Cyrus, Bishop of *Siknus*,

—examples which must have been contagious. Many of the people, however, who were unable to fly to the deserts and unwilling to renounce their faith, contrived to maintain secret observances. Even in Alexandria itself, during all the ten years of the persecution, there remained a remnant of the Coptic communion, though bereft of ministers. There was, however, one priest, a native of Mareotis named Agatho, who daily risked his life in the cause. Disguising himself as a carpenter, he used to go about the city by day carrying a bag of tools on his back; while at night he administered the rites of the Church to his Coptic brethren. It was this Agatho who subsequently became Benjamin's great friend and successor in the patriarchate.

The monastery of Matra, called As Suḳûnîah, is recorded to have resisted Cyrus successfully. It was either in or near Alexandria, and the reason given for its remaining scatheless is that all the monks were pure-bred Egyptians, with no single foreigner among them[1].

Boundless as was the patience of the Egyptians, they seem to have made one effort to throw off the yoke of Cyrus. Exasperated by his lawless plunder of their precious vessels, as well as by the stripes and imprisonments they suffered, the sect of Gaianites assembled in the church at Dafashîr near Mareotis, and formed a plot against the life of their oppressor. But a Roman officer named Eudocianus, brother of Domentianus and one of the most relentless enemies of the Copts, heard of the meeting and sent soldiers with instant orders to shoot down the conspirators.

but the Cairo MS. gives Nikiou correctly. Maḳrîzî for Cyrus reads Buṭrus or Peter.

[1] Severus, Brit. Mus. MS., p. 107, l. 11.

Some were killed outright, others wounded by the arrows, and others again had their hands cut off without the semblance of trial. So the conspiracy was crushed, and Cyrus was delivered from danger [1].

These various anecdotes show in the clearest light the severity of the persecution. It may seem incredible that it could have lasted for ten years, yet nothing is more certain. 'Even after the death of Heraclius,' says John of Nikiou, 'when Cyrus came back to Egypt' (i. e. in 641 after his exile or absence), 'far from abandoning his rage against the flock of God or ceasing to persecute it, he added violence to violence.' And similar language is used by Severus: 'Heraclius was like a ravening wolf, devouring the flock and yet never satiated, and that flock was the blessed community of the Theodosians [2].' But as usual persecution strengthened, in those who were strong enough to resist it, the form of belief it was meant to crush. The Coptic Church was smitten and torn asunder, but it never yielded. The great majority of the people stood fast and staunch in their faith. But the iron had entered into their soul. Through the sullen gloom of those ten years the canker worked in their wounds; and with the

[1] John of Nikiou, p. 566. Zotenberg justly remarks that the paragraph recording this incident is out of order. The incident is clearly prior to the Muslim invasion. On Dafashîr see Amélineau, *Géog. Copte*, p. 122. The place has been mentioned above (p. 25) in connexion with the revolt of Nicetas.

[2] This passage is curious as proving that in Severus' days the Copts still called themselves Theodosians—that in fact 'Copt' and 'Theodosian' were synonymous. The Gaianites must have been a very small body in the time of Cyrus: see p. 29 n. Yet Prof. Bury, speaking of Cyrus' appointment, says that 'his first act was to win over the important sect of the Theodosians or Phthartolatrai' (*Later Roman Empire*, vol. ii. p. 251).

final embitterment of their hatred for the Byzantine Church and Byzantine government all hope of peace and reconcilement passed away for ever.

In this frame of mind, what did the Egyptians feel with regard to that great movement which had sprung from Arabia and was already shaking the cities of Syria? To their honour, be it said, that there is not the slightest reason to think that they looked upon it with sympathy: yet when they heard that even the Muslims granted a measure of toleration to the Christians, the thought may have risen in their hearts that subjection to the Muslims would make life less unbearable, that the yoke of Mohammed would be lighter than the yoke of the most Christian Emperor Heraclius. That they abhorred the religion of Islâm is proved by every page of their history: but during those ten years of hopeless misery the sword of Cyrus had cut through wellnigh the last thread which bound their allegiance to the Roman Empire; and they regarded the advent of the Muslims as a plague sent by divine vengeance upon their persecutors.

To such a pass had misgovernment brought the finest province in the Emperor's dominions. How far in all this evil work the Muḳauḳas had obeyed, how far he had betrayed, the orders of his master, is hard to discover. It is clear that the original plan of Heraclius was shaped by a noble purpose. It was a grand ideal to give that peace and rest to the Church which he had given to the State: but he failed to realize the tenacious strength of religious opinion—that it beat through the remotest nerves and fibres of the body politic, and that to remove it by violence would be fatal. His choice of instruments, too, was most unhappy. His peace-maker in

Egypt changed at once into a tyrant, and his message of peace was either never delivered or never heard. That he sanctioned the persecution can hardly be doubted, though it may be questioned whether he sanctioned it save as a last resort; whereas with Cyrus it was the first and only resort. It was in any case the scheme of a visionary to root out sectarian hatred by an edict. The Emperor had hoped by his magic phrase to conjure to rest the angry billows of religious controversy: but then, when he found that he had only raised a furious storm, unable to brook failure, untaught to trust in time and toleration, he condescended, both in Syria and in Egypt, to strive for the end of peace by the method of religious war. In both countries he thus opened the way for the advancing armies of Islâm.

CHAPTER XIV

ARAB ADVANCE ON EGYPT

'Amr ibn al 'Aṣî unfolds to the Caliph his design for conquering Egypt. Omar's hesitation in giving leave. Letters of recall sent and opened at 'Arîsh. The Day of Sacrifice there celebrated. Character of the Arab leader. Stature and physique. Story of his stammering refuted. His history. Conversion to Islâm and appointment by Mohammed as captain. Various anecdotes illustrating his qualities.

After the surrender of Jerusalem by the aged Patriarch Sophronius, it seems that both the Caliph Omar and his general 'Amr ibn al 'Aṣī turned their steps northward. 'Amr at least was sent to take part in the siege of Caesarea [1], while Omar fixed his head quarters at Damascus. It was probably at Jerusalem that 'Amr unfolded his plan for the invasion of Egypt: but the time was not then judged propitious. When, however, fortune still shone on the Muslim arms, and the Syrian campaign was more nearly over, 'Amr renewed his proposal to Omar, pointing out the ease with which Egypt could be conquered and the vastness of the prize. There was no country in the world, he said, at once so wealthy and so defenceless [2]. He also reminded

[1] De Goeje, *Conquête de la Syrie*, p. 130. Ibn al Athîr and Ibn Khaldûn both say, 'When Omar had taken Jerusalem, 'Amr marched into Egypt'; but Balâdhurî—an earlier and far better authority—makes 'Amr's expedition start from the siege of Caesarea. Balâdhurî gives one account which represents 'Amr as acting without the knowledge of Omar, while he records also the contrary opinion that 'Amr acted under the Caliph's orders. Maḳrîzî too gives both versions.

[2] I have here followed Yâḳût's *Mu'jam al Buldân* (vol. iii. p. 893).

Omar that Aretion, the Roman governor of Jerusalem, who had escaped before the capitulation and fled to Egypt, was there rallying the imperial forces, and that no more time should be lost in striking[1]: moreover, the possession of Egypt would greatly strengthen the power of the Muslims. This conference between the two leaders took place at Al Jâbîah[2], near Damascus, in the autumn of the year 639 A.D., while the siege of Caesarea was still proceeding.

Omar saw that the conquest of Egypt was desirable, but thought that 'Amr underrated the difficulties of it, since he was unable to weaken the forces in Syria by detaching an army strong enough for the purpose. When 'Amr offered to start with a force of 3,500 or 4,000 men, the Commander of the Faithful in wavering mood could only promise to think it over; and 'Amr returned to Caesarea, where Constantine, son of Heraclius, was now in command of the city. There, however, a letter from Omar followed him, borne by Sharîkh ibn 'Aḥdâb. It sanctioned the plan for the invasion of Egypt, but ordered 'Amr to keep it secret and to lead his force southward by easy stages. 'Amr accordingly departed at dead of night, and marched his little army of horsemen without incident towards the borderland of Palestine and Egypt. He had already reached Rafaḥ[3], one stage from the Egyptian Al 'Arîsh,

[1] Ṭabarî, ed. Zotenberg, vol. iii. p. 411.

[2] Ibn 'Abd al Ḥakam, quoted by Maḳrîzî. This seems more probable than Eutychius' statement that Omar had returned to Medina and wrote the order for 'Amr to advance on Egypt from that city.

[3] On these places see the notes in Hamaker's edition of Waḳidî, p. 15; Quatremère, *Mém. Géog. et Hist.* t. i. p. 53;

when messengers spurred in hot haste into his camp bearing dispatches from the Caliph.

'Amr shrewdly guessed their tenour. Omar's doubts and hesitations had prevailed, and led him to repent his decision. The Caliph had spoken to Othman about the perils of the enterprise, and Othman not only thought the hazard very great, but reminded Omar that the rash and adventurous character of 'Amr was certain to hurry him into disaster. Omar therefore was seriously disquieted, and resolved if possible to recall the expedition: but he felt that if 'Amr's force were already in Egypt, it would be a confession of weakness and a dishonour to the Muslim name to retreat before the enemy. The dispatch accordingly ordered 'Amr to return, if he was still in Palestine, while if he were in Egypt, he must go forward. In that case Omar would pray for his victory, and would send reinforcements[1]. But 'Amr had put his hand

Champollion, *L'Égypte sous les Pharaons*, t. ii. p. 304; Amélineau, *Géog. Copte*, p. 404; Abû Ṣâliḥ, p. 70. The Arabic text of Waḳidî says that 'Amr 'left the desert and those fortresses which were upon the way to Egypt on his right hand, viz. Rafaḥ, Al 'Arîsh, Al 'Adâd, Al Bakârah and Al Faramâ' (p. 8). But the statement is not very probable in itself, nor borne out by other authorities. Ibn al Athîr indeed makes 'Amr send back from Heliopolis one of his commanders to besiege Faramâ and another to besiege Alexandria: but his account of the conquest is a mass of misstatement and confusion.

[1] This seems the natural version of an incident which some of the Arab historians have twisted into absurdity: I have chosen it from among the versions given by Maḳrîzî. Ibn 'Abd al Ḥakam and those who follow him represent Omar as giving his consent to 'Amr for the expedition and adding, 'I will shortly send a letter after you, and if it bids you return, you must do so, unless you have already crossed the frontier. In that case, go on and prosper.' It is hard to imagine a more fatuous proceeding: but Omar is not

to the plough, and was not the man to turn back. He knew that the letter boded no good to his project, and he refused to receive it until he had crossed the torrent-bed, which perhaps marked the frontier, and reached the little valley of 'Arîsh. There he read it, and asked 'Is this place in Syria or in Egypt?' and when the answer was 'In Egypt,' he read the dispatch aloud before his officers and said, 'The army will advance in accordance with the Caliph's orders.'

'Amr no doubt got the answer he wanted, but it is curious to remark that, although 'Arîsh or Rhinocolura was generally regarded as within the Egyptian frontier, the matter was not free from doubt[1]. It is clear, however, that the town, although fortified, was not held by a Roman garrison. Yet even as late as the thirteenth century might be seen the ruins of two splendid ancient churches and the remains of the city wall along the sea-front, while the finest marbles and the largest columns at that time found in Cairo were strangely said to have come from 'Arîsh[2]. From this point too, according to some authorities, started the

rightly charged with such folly. The truth of course is that he gave reluctant leave for the expedition, that he repented of it, and that he sent to recall 'Amr, if it still could be done with honour. Eutychius gives three versions of the story which may be compared with those of Makrîzî.

[1] Quatremère, l. c., shows that the frontier was sometimes regarded as ending at Wâridah, as he writes it. In the *Kitâb al Buldân*, by Ya'kûbî, c. 900 A. D. (*Bibl. Geog. Arab.*, ed. de Goeje, pt. viii. p. 330) the writer says: 'A traveller from Palestine to Egypt goes to Ash Shajaratân on the frontier of Egypt, then to Al 'Arîsh in the frontier district, then to the village of Al Bakkârah (*sic*), then to that of Al Warrâdah among the sand-hills, then to Al Faramâ—the first city of Egypt which he reaches: next to the village of Jurjîr, then to that of Fâkûs, then to that of Ghaifah, then to Fusṭâṭ.'

[2] Abû Ṣâliḥ, p. 167.

Great Wall of Egypt, which ran across to Ḳulzum or Suez, and thence up the eastern bank of the Nile as far as the First Cataract. This wall, attributed to Sesostris, but called by the Arabs the 'Wall of the Old Woman,' had long been broken down, so that it offered no hindrance to the movement of an army even in the seventh century, though fragments of its ruins may be seen at Jabal aṭ Ṭair and other places in Egypt to-day [1].

It was on the 10 Dhû 'l Ḥijjah, A.H. 18 [2], or 12 December, 639 A.D., that 'Amr's little force celebrated the Muslim Day of Sacrifice, or Feast of Offerings, or Feast of Pilgrims, as it was variously called. The rite was not without solemnity for this band of desert warriors, who were setting out to conquer the land of the Pharaohs, leagued as they were by ties of clanship and devotion to the great chieftain who led them. Most of 'Amr's following belonged to the tribe of 'Akk, although Al Kindî says that one third were of the tribe of Ghâfiḳ [3], and Ibn Duḳmâḳ gives a list of Roman converts to Islâm from Syria, who were in the Arab army. He also mentions Persian converts from the region of Yaman as taking part in the conquest, though these were more probably enrolled among the reinforcements which the Caliph sent later to Egypt [4].

[1] Abû Ṣâliḥ, p. 59, n. 4, where references are given to Diodorus, Eutychius, and some Arab writers.

[2] This date, given by Ibn 'Abd al Ḥakam, fits in so well with other known dates that it may be taken as settled. But to avoid needless repetition on matters of date, I must refer the reader to the essay 'On the Chronology of the Arab Conquest' at the end of this work.

[3] Yâḳût, l. c.

[4] Ibn Duḳmâḳ, part iv. pp. 4–5. These Persians are described

And what of 'Amr himself? The chronicles give many of his sayings, and a good deal of information about his character; and in a history of the conquest of Egypt it cannot be out of place to furnish some sketch of the conqueror. 'Amr ibn al 'Aṣī was somewhere about 45 years old at the time of the invasion of Egypt[1]. Short in stature, though strongly built, his athletic and hardy frame excelled in those feats of horsemanship and swordsmanship which Western chivalry has learned to link with the name of Saracen[2]. That he was broad-shouldered and broad-chested; that he had dark piercing eyes, quickly kindling to anger or humour, heavy eyebrows, and a large mouth; that his face, though powerful, was without sternness—wore indeed a pleasant and cheerful expression; that he used a black cosmetic for dyeing his beard: these are almost all the details of his outer appearance which have come down in history. The statement that he stammered is probably erroneous. It is true that Abû 'l Maḥâsin records this as 'Amr's one defect of body. On the other hand, it is known that 'Amr was remarkable for the quickness and wit of his repartees, as well as for his sustained eloquence; and the idea that he stammered seems founded on a misunderstanding.

as the remnants of the army sent by Chosroes to Yaman under the general Badhân (or Horzâd): see ante, p. 142, n. 2.

[1] This seems the most probable account of the matter, as I have endeavoured to show in Appendix E against some writers who would make him much older.

[2] Ibn Ḳutaibah, Ibn Khallikân, and Abû 'l Maḥâsin are the authorities, the works of the two former being a sort of biographical dictionaries. Ibn Khallikân's account of 'Amr has been translated by De Slane. Abû Ṣâliḥ (p. 78) adds one or two details to the description of 'Amr, which seems to come originally from Ibn 'Abd al Ḥakam.

For it is related[1] that Omar once hearing a man stammer remarked, 'I declare that the maker of this man and the maker of 'Amr are one'; which meant, not that 'Amr was given to stammering, but that God made the speechless and the most eloquent alike: just as 'Amr himself on one occasion, when provoked by a shallow fellow, smothered his scorn in the remark, 'He too is God's creature.' But the story has been misconstrued by some Arab writers, and taken to prove that 'Amr also stammered. Such a construction would make Omar's saying both rude and pointless, and it would seem to clash with the fact of 'Amr's eminence as well as that of his eloquence. For it is hardly conceivable that, if 'Amr had suffered from this defect, he would have been singled out from the beginning by Mohammed as a capable leader, or could ever have become a great commander. It may be added also that 'Amr acted as imâm, or leader of prayer, to the end of his days, and that Muslim law expressly forbids any one to take that office who stammers[2]. The story therefore that 'Amr had this defect is quite unworthy of belief.

For the rest, there are many sayings and stories which illustrate his life and character. He was of the tribe of the Ḳuraish, and his genealogy is known to tradition[3]. His conversion to Islâm took place in

[1] This story comes from Ibn al Ḥajar, though doubtless copied by him from earlier writers.

[2] Khârijah ibn Ḥudhâfah was assassinated while acting as leader of prayer in place of 'Amr, who was unwell; see below, p. 493. For the Muslim law see Míwardî, ***Kitâb al Aḥkâm as Sulṭaníah*** ch. ix; 'On the Superintendence of Prayers,' pp. 171 seq.

[3] Ibn Ḳutaibah gives it as follows: Ibn al 'Aṣî, ibn Wa'îl, ibn Hashim, ibn Saḥm, ibn Huṣaiṣ, ibn Ka'b, ibn Lu'aig, ibn Ghâlib, ibn Fiḥr, ibn Mâliḥ, ibn An Naḍr, ibn Kinânah: and Abû 'l

A. H. 7 or 8, and there are one or two anecdotes bearing upon it. He was once asked[1], 'What delayed your conversion so long, in spite of your intelligence?' and he answered that he was overawed by the authority of his betters, but that as he grew older and more independent, reflection taught him to slacken in his opposition to the Prophet. When the Ḳuraish sent one of their number to question him, 'Amr asked his questioner whether the Arabs held the true religion, or the Persians, or the Romans? On being told 'The Arabs,' he said 'Are we or they the wealthier?' 'They are.' 'Then,' he said, 'what advantage have we over Persians and Romans, if there is no life to come, since in this life they have all the advantage over us?' 'Amr went on to say that he became convinced of the truth of Mohammed's doctrine of a resurrection and of rewards and punishments after death, and so he resolved to give up what was false in the old Arab religion. Some say that 'Amr was in Abyssinia at the time of his conversion, which was brought about by Ja'far ibn Abî Ṭâlib.

Another story is that 'Amr said to Mohammed, 'O Apostle of God, I will acknowledge thee, if thou wilt forgive the sins of my past life,' and that Mohammed answered, 'Verily the profession of Islâm and the sharing of the Flight [2] cancel all the past.' 'Amr was so grateful for this free pardon that he could not take his eyes off the Prophet's face. ''Fore God,' he exclaimed, 'I could not take my fill

Maḥâsin calls him further Abû 'Abdallah, al Ḳuraishî aṣ Ṣaḥmî as Saḥâbî.

[1] Ibn al Ḥajar.

[2] This cannot mean that 'Amr accompanied the Flight: if it does, the story is apocryphal.

of gazing upon him, nor regard his countenance as long as I desired, without making him ashamed.'

Mohammed's opinion of 'Amr was a high one. He praised him as the best Muslim and the most trustworthy of men [1]. He called 'Amr 'one of the good men of the Ḳuraish,' and highly esteemed him 'for his knowledge and valour.' 'Amr had a half-brother named Hishâm, who was slain at the battle of Yermouk. When questioned about him, 'Amr said, 'Judge which was the better man. His mother was Umm Harmâlah, aunt of Omar ibn al Khaṭṭab, while my mother was an 'Anazîah. My father loved him more than me, and you know what a good eye a father has for his children. He became a Muslim before me, and has gone to God before me; for he died a martyr's death at Yermouk, while I was left behind.'

'Amr's great distinction is that he was made military commander direct by the Prophet. In appointing him Mohammed said, 'I am sending you forth as commander of a troop. May God keep you safe and give you much booty.' When 'Amr answered, 'I did not become a Muslim for the sake of wealth, but for the sake of submission to God,' the Prophet rejoined, 'Honest wealth is good for an honeṣt man'—a maxim which 'Amr doubtless remembered. He was placed at the head of the force which fought the battle of As Salâsil, or the Chains, but had to write for reinforcements. So Mohammed sent 200 more men, including Abû Bakr and Omar, under the orders of Abû 'Ubaidah ibn al Jarrâh. As they came up, 'Amr said quietly, 'I am your leader and you are my helpers.' 'No,' said Abû 'Ubaidah, 'I am chief of my men, you of yours';

[1] 'Uḳbah ibn 'Aâmir, quoted by Abû 'l Maḥâsin and An Nawawî in slightly different terms.

but when 'Amr declined this arrangement, he added, 'The Apostle of God enjoined that there should be no dissension; if therefore you refuse to obey me, I will obey you.' 'I refuse,' said 'Amr; whereupon Abû 'Ubaidah saluted 'Amr, and he stood behind him at public prayer.

After the battle of the Chains 'Amr was made governor of Umân, and there remained till the death of Mohammed; a year or two afterwards he was sent by Abû Bakr as one of the generals in the Syrian expedition. There his reputation both as a hard fighter and an able tactician was immensely strengthened, and he ill brooked the superior command which Omar on his accession gave to Abû 'Ubaidah. But perhaps the most striking passage about the conqueror of Egypt is that which records a speech made by 'Amr in self-defence, when Mu'awîah was charged with unduly favouring him[1]: 'I am the man who at the battle of Siffîn quoted the verse,

"When other eyes faltered, mine never quailed;
I half-closed my eyes to their failure, but not to danger."

Remember, how again and again I returned to the charge. I bear good and evil fortune alike; I am inexorable, like the serpent at the root of the tree. 'Fore God, I am no sluggard or weakling. I am the deaf adder, from whose bite none may recover, whose sting renders a man sleepless. I am a man who shatters what he strikes, who turns to cinders what he kindles. At the battle of Ḥarîr the foemen

[1] Hishâm ibn al Ḳalbî is the author from whom this is taken. Of course this incident belongs to a later period in 'Amr's career—after the conquest of Egypt.

knew me for the most dauntless of heart, the strongest of hand, the staunchest defender of the flag. To me in comparison with my traducer may be applied the words of the poet,

"If the tree of mine honour be made of gold,
Shall I not esteem it of higher worth
Than to be placed in competition with vile weeds?"'

Language like this seems to reveal the man in all his self-confidence and consciousness of power. In the dispute which followed the battle of Siffîn, 'Amr no doubt showed some unscrupulousness. Adh Dhahabî records how he clove through the false excuses and hypocrisy of Mu'awîah at the time of the battle, exclaiming, 'O Mu'awîah, my heart has burnt with wrath while I have listened to your pretences. Do you think that we are rebelling against 'Alî because our claims are more rightful than his? No, 'fore God; it is only that we fly like dogs upon the riches of this world; and by God, I swear that you shall give me a share in your wealth, or else I fight not upon your side.' In the matter of the arbitration his action reads like a breach of faith with Abû Mûsâ. The latter thereafter always mingled in his prayers curses against 'Amr, and he insulted his enemy, saying, ''Amr's likeness is the likeness of a dog; if you drive him away, he puts forth his tongue; and if you leave him alone, he puts forth his tongue!' 'And you,' retorted 'Amr, 'are the donkey laden with books, and none the wiser for them!'

Ibn al Ḥajar records that one of his friends said of 'Amr, 'I have never met a man who understood the Ḳurân better, or had a nobler character, or was more honest and open in his dealings.' One named

Jâbiz is quoted as saying, 'I never met a man more learned in the Book of God than Omar. When I was in Mu'awîah's company, I found none more gentle. When I was with 'Amr, I found a man of most intelligent conversation, a most excellent companion and counsellor.' One or two more brief anecdotes may be given, bringing out his goodheartedness, his candour of mind, and his love of musical measure. When he was reproached once for riding an old and ill-favoured mule, he replied, 'I do not grow tired of a beast that has carried me well, nor of a wife who makes my life happy by her society, nor of a friend who keeps my secrets.' On another occasion he had a dispute with Al Mughîrah ibn Sha'bah, who lost his temper and used some strong language. 'Will ye insult me, ye family of Huṣaiṣ?' cried 'Amr, blazing with fury. But 'Amr's son 'Abdallah was standing by, and when he called out 'Verily we belong to God! you have uttered the war-cry of the tribes, which is forbidden,' the father accepted the son's rebuke and freed thirty slaves as an act of repentance. But it was in his younger days at Medina that, after listening to Ziyâd's eloquent Khuṭbah, he exclaimed, 'How marvellous a talent hath God granted to that youth! Verily if he were a son of the tribe of the Ḳuraish, it were easy for him to drive the Arab nation before him with a switch [1].'

Such anecdotes might doubtless be multiplied. But enough has been said to show what manner of man 'Amr was. Putting together some of his characteristics, one may note that he combined great power of brain and body with great enthusiasm:

[1] This story is from 'Umârah's *Yaman* (ed. Kay), p. 219. That about the mule is from Abû 'l Maḥâsin.

he had an iron will and unfaltering courage, yet measured aright the advantage which coolness and skill possess over mere valour. In matters of religion and ceremonial he was devout, and, though fiercely swayed at times by worldly motives, yet in the main upright and high-principled. He was not unlearned, as the times went; indeed he was held to be the cleverest[1] of the Arabs, and one of the most accomplished; passionately fond of music and verse; gifted with imagination, a good talker. In 'Amr there mingled something at once of soldier, saint, adventurer, and poet. Frank and open in his bearing, heroic in aim and action, he possessed great charm of presence and manner—that talisman which so often avails great men to transmute admiration into personal devotion.

Such was the captain of the four thousand horsemen who were bent on wresting Egypt from the grasp of the Caesars.

[1] Makîn, p. 39. See also references to 'Amr in W. Nassau Lees' *Conquest of Syria* in *Bibliotheca Indica*, vol. i.

CHAPTER XV

OPENING OF THE CAMPAIGN

Action of Cyrus. Refutation of the story that the Arabs were bought off by payment of tribute. Siege and capture of Pelusium. Desert march to Bilbais. Capture of the town after much fighting. The Arabs arrive at Tendunias or Umm Dûnain. Indecisive engagements. Dangerous condition of the Muslim force. 'Amr's resolve to invade the Fayûm. Capture of Tendunias.

THE alarm was now sounded through Egypt, and Cyrus, the Muḳauḳas, heard that the dreaded Saracens were coming. Some measures of defence he had taken already: a moat had been dug round the great castle of Babylon near Memphis, other forts had been strengthened, and the walls of many cities which had suffered in the Persian invasion were repaired [1]. But it is false to say that Cyrus now bought off the Arabs by a promise of tribute. That is the statement which Theophanes makes, or seems to make [2]. But most unfortunately the Greek historians are quite in the dark both as to the facts and as to the order of events at this period. Nicephorus [3] is even worse than Theophanes, and the

[1] This is clear from the language of the prophecy in the *Vie de Shenoudi* (*Mém. Miss. Arch. Franç.* t. iv. i. p. 340).

[2] *Corp. Hist. Script. Byzant.* t. 44, p. 167: 'They march on Egypt. Cyrus, bishop of Alexandria, *hearing of the attack* bestirred himself, and under a convention promised, in fear of their avarice, that Egypt would pay 200,000 dinârs yearly as tribute. . . . So for three years he saved Egypt from ruin. Cyrus was then accused before the Emperor of paying Egyptian gold in tribute to the Arabs'—and there follows an account of Cyrus' supersession by Manuel! I shall further deal with this at the close of the book.

[3] He declares that 'while Heraclius was still in the East, he sent John, Duke of Barcaina, against the Saracens in Egypt,' and he

writer of the *Chronicon Orientale* worse than either[1]. They neither examined nor understood what they recorded, and their confusion of dates and perversion of truth are such that they have served only as false lights, luring into quagmires nearly every modern writer who has followed them[2]. But it must suffice

tells of some battles and some proposals for a treaty with 'Amr, who was to marry the Emperor's daughter and become a Christian! And all this is said to have happened before Heraclius quitted Syria, i.e. before September, 636, when the invasion of Egypt had not been even thought of.

[1] It alleges that when the Muslims appeared, Heraclius withdrew all the Roman troops from Egypt up to Syene, and paid tribute for ten years to the Muslims until all his treasure was exhausted. It would be difficult to say what period of ten years is intended: but the statement probably refers to events in Syria. If it means that Heraclius paid tribute for Egypt, it can only be described as utterly unfounded. It is curious to find the Cairo MS. of Severus giving almost the same story in the same words, with this exception, that it makes the period eight years instead of ten. In the British Museum MS. the passage has become childish nonsense. But it is clear that the Coptic writer of the *Chronicon Orientale* had Severus before him. Severus must have borrowed from Greek sources this story of tribute, but he never troubled to reconcile it with his narrative of the Arab invasion and the persecution of Cyrus. This legend about tribute is quite unknown to the Muslim historians.

[2] Perhaps the best example of this misleading is seen in Lebeau (*Histoire du Bas Empire*), who from p. 272 in vol. xi becomes totally unreliable. He actually places the incidents connected with Manuel before the invasion of 'Amr. Drapeyron is equally deceived (*L'Empereur Héraclius*, p. 396); and so are the English historians from Gibbon to Bury. The latter follows Lebeau about Manuel (*Later Roman Empire*, vol. ii. p. 269, n. 3). Mr. Milne also, in *Egypt under Roman Rule* (p. 115), alleges that the Arabs were at first bought off by subsidies, quoting Paulus Diaconus, xviii. 579. But Paul's authority is quite worthless. His story here is a mere transcript of Theophanes, who, as I have shown, is most inaccurate in all that concerns the Saracen conquest. What hitherto has passed for history on the subject of 'Amr's invasion may be seen summarized in an article in the *Asiatic Quarterly Review* by an

Map 2.

To face page 201

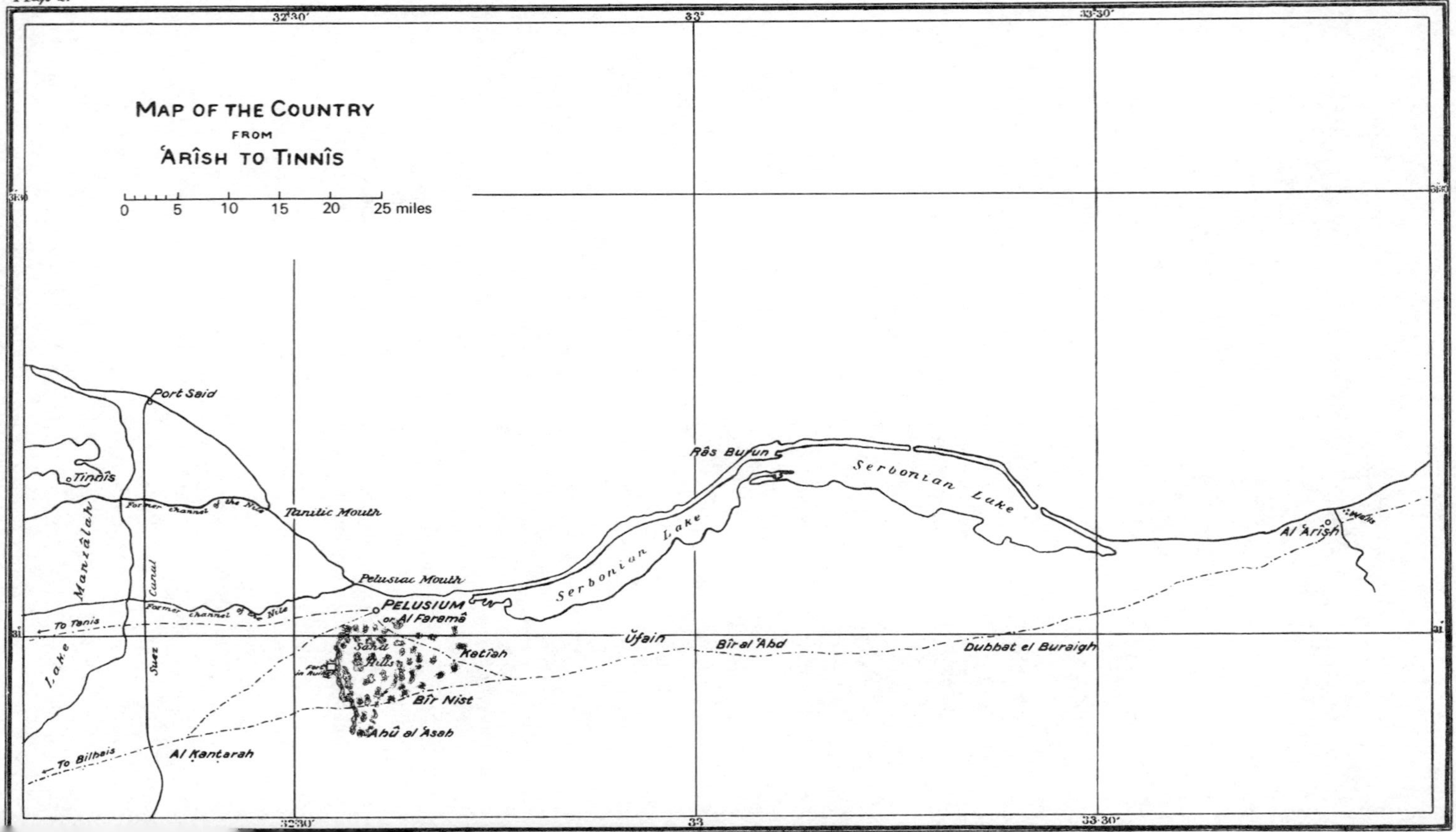

Oxford.

here to say that there is not a word of truth in the story of tribute paid to stave off the conquest of Egypt. There is no whisper or hint of any such arrangement in any single Oriental writer—Persian, Arabic, Syriac, or Coptic—with the exception of the passage in Severus copied by the *Chronicon Orientale*. The idea is a mere blunder of the Greek historians, a distorted image of a totally different and much later transaction, as will be set forth in due order. It was needful at the outset to sweep aside this misconception; but the way is now clear to follow 'Amr on his march through the desert.

From the valley of 'Arîsh with its groves of palm the road passed nearly due westward, but away from the coast, through a waste of desert, relieved by occasional watering-places and villages. It was the immemorial high-road to Egypt—the road which had witnessed the passage of the first prehistoric settlers in Egypt, the passage of Abraham, of Jacob and Joseph, of Cambyses, Alexander, and Cleopatra[1], of the Holy Family, and lately of the Persian

Oriental writer of some ability, S. Khuda Bukhsh (July, 1901). He writes thus: ''Amr was not received as an enemy but hailed as a deliverer. The Patriarch Cyrus, in concert with Muḳauḳas (!), fondly hoped to stave off the horror of war by paying an annual tribute to the Saracens, but Heraclius rejected the proposal and sent Manuel to defend the province,' &c. There is hardly a word of truth in all this. The same must be said of Ockley's account of the Saracen conquest, which is probably responsible for most of the erroneous versions current in modern histories. To what strange developments these false views about Cyrus and false stories about tribute can lead in the hands of an imaginative writer is shown by Drapeyron, who makes Cyrus a 'rusé Syrien,' who stopped the invasion at the Isthmus of Suez by a tribute of 200,000 gold pieces, part of which he raised on the credit of the Muḳauḳas! (*L'Empereur Héraclius*, p. 396).

[1] John of Nikiou, p. 407.

invaders. It was the road of merchants, travellers, and pilgrims at all times, and of the many caravans which here linked Asia to Africa. A few miles before reaching Pelusium the way trends north-westwards, plunging among dunes or moving sandhills; but no Roman soldiers were met by the Arabs till they came within sight of the city.

Pelusium, the Coptic Peremoun and the Arabic Al Faramâ, seems to have stood on an eminence about a mile and a half from the sea; it possessed a harbour, possibly connected with the town by a canal, and the Pelusiac arm of the Nile here joined the sea. The city was ancient and strongly fortified, full of old Egyptian monuments, as well as churches and monasteries[1]; and as the key of Egypt on the eastern side, it was a place of the greatest importance, commanding the desert approaches, the coast, and a waterway leading into the Delta. Yet it seems to have been poorly defended. The Persians, who were practised in the art of siege warfare, had captured it with very little fighting, and they probably had made havoc with its walls, wrecking them in parts, as they wrecked the churches. Still the Romans had warning enough, and might easily have repaired the damage.

But the Arabs under 'Amr had no engineering skill or resources, and they had to capture the city by storm or starvation. We do not know the

[1] See Abû Ṣâliḥ, p. 167, and my note there. It may be added that the tomb of Galen, the physician, was shown at Pelusium according to Iṣṭakhrî (*Bibl. Geog. Arab.*, ed. de Goeje, pt. i. p. 53). At present the site of Pelusium is marked by red mounds which may be seen in the distance from the Suez Canal. There are some remains of buildings said to be Roman, but it is greatly to be hoped that the site may be explored scientifically.

numbers of the garrison: but it is clear that the Saracen force was too weak to beleaguer the place, and there were frequent sallies. Desultory fighting lasted a month—or two months according to one authority[1]—till at last one of the gates was seized in the repulse of a sally, and the city was taken. The first Arab to force his way through the gate was called Asmaika' ibn Wa'lah as Sabâi'[2]. Maḳrîzî and Abû 'l Maḥâsin (who copied from him) mention a report that the Copts aided the Arabs at the siege, but it is certainly baseless. It seems a mere revival of the old falsehood which charged the Copts with aiding the Persians. It occurs, I believe, in no writer before the fourteenth century, and it seems refuted by the story of the capture which I have given. It is also inconsistent with the fact that the Arabs not only burnt the shipping and dismantled the fortress[3], but also, like the Persians, destroyed the remnant of the churches in Pelusium[4]. Finally, the charge is in direct antagonism to the statement of the nearly contemporary John of Nikiou[5], who says that the Copts did not lend any aid to the Muslim forces until after the enemy had taken possession of Fayûm and all its territory. What point of time this denotes is doubtful: it is certain that it was

[1] Yâḳût says two months; Eutychius, Maḳrîzî, and others one month.

[2] Al Kindî, quoted by Suyûṭî.

[3] Severus, Brit. Mus. MS., p. 105. It was rebuilt later, and was not finally demolished until Baldwin I utterly destroyed it before his retreat in A.D. 1118; Abû Ṣâliḥ, pp. 170–1.

[4] Abû Ṣâliḥ, p. 168.

[5] p. 559. Weil, who adopts and exaggerates this story against the Copts in his *Geschichte der Chalifen*, had not seen John's chronicle. He is in any case rather a compiler than a student or critic of this period.

subsequent to the capture of Babylon, and that the aid then given was very partial and limited.

By the reduction of Faramâ the Arab forces had now secured their only line of communication, and of retreat in case of disaster. They had also formed some measure of the gigantic task which lay before them, if they were ever to capture the far more powerful fortress of Babylon and the mighty city of Alexandria. 'Amr must have realized that without the promised reinforcements he was doomed to failure; and he knew that reinforcements could come by Faramâ alone[1]. He could spare no troops to hold the town, and he was therefore more than justified in razing its defences, and making it useless to the enemy, if recaptured. What the Romans were about meanwhile, it is difficult to conjecture. Cyrus must have known that it was merely a question of time, when the Muslim forces overrunning Syria

[1] This consideration quite refutes Ibn Khaldûn's extraordinary statement that 'The Arabs besieged 'Ain Shams (Heliopolis) and sent Abraḥah ibn aṣ Ṣaffâḥ to besiege Faramâ, and Anf ibn Mâlik to besiege Alexandria'! (*Kitâb al 'abar wa Dîwân al mubtadi' wal Khabar fî aiyam al 'Arab*, &c., supplement to pt. ii. p. 114). But Ibn Khaldûn's story is utterly discredited: for example, he makes Bab-al-Yûn the first point attacked, and from that 'Amr marches through the Delta to Miṣr! He thus confuses Pelusium with Babylon. Finally he makes 'Ain Shams the scene of a long siege, thus confusing that place also with Babylon. He has clearly copied or corrected various MSS. without the smallest understanding either of their history or of their geography. It is Ibn al Athîr who also says, 'The first place captured was Bab-al-Yûn, and the next march was to Miṣr' (ed. C. J. Tornberg, vol. ii. p. 440). I may add that Maḳrîzî quotes Saif ibn 'Umar as the authority for the dispatch of a force from 'Ain Shams to Alexandria: but such a march would have been almost a physical impossibility, and, from a military point of view, it would, even if possible, have been an act of sheer madness.

would turn their arms against Egypt. The event was bound to come. Common prudence would have established posts of observation along the desert, at least as far out as 'Arîsh, to give timely warning; and would have prepared an army to concentrate on Pelusium. Had the Romans sent only 10,000 men to harass 'Amr's line of march, or had they mustered such an army under the fortress, they could scarcely have failed to rout and crush the little force of Arabs, although even that result might not have deferred for long the fate of Egypt. Instead of that, they did nothing. They trusted to the normal garrison to defend the town; and though they were in a sense surprised by the sudden advance of the Arabs, yet during the month of siege they sent no troops to its relief or rescue. Their tame and needless loss of Pelusium was their first great blunder in the war; is it possible that one may call it the first act in the great betrayal of the Empire by Cyrus? Had he already formed in his mind the plan for rendering the patriarchate of Alexandria independent of Constantinople by an alliance with the Arabs against the Empire? On no other theory does it seem possible to explain his action, at least in its later developments.

It was now past the middle of January, 640 A. D., which year nearly coincided with the Muslim A.H. 19[1], when 'Amr resumed his march. His losses in the recent fighting were more than made good by a number of Beduins who, scenting war and plunder, had flocked to his standard[2]. From the

[1] A. H. 19 began on January 2, 640, and ended with December 20, 640.

[2] Maḳrîzî says that at Jabal al Jalâl the tribe of Râshidah and some of the tribes of Lakhm joined 'Amr. In the previous century,

salt-encrusted country round Pelusium he passed over a stretch of white shell-strewn sand, till he reached the ancient Migdol [1] to the south-west, thence to the point now known as Al Ḳanṭarah on the Suez Canal. Here the desert changes to a hard and pebbly surface, while its monotony is relieved by a few green patches of vegetation and reedy brackish lagoons. The Arabs kept to the desert, and probably made for Salaḥîah. Most ancient conquerors of Egypt, like Cambyses, took a different route, striking nearly due west from Pelusium to Synhûr and Tanis, and thence up through the Delta to Bubastis [2]: but by this time the swamps round Lake Manzâlah had spread so as to render that route more difficult. Besides, 'Amr's army were all mounted, and had no means of bridging canals or rivers. Moving then from Salaḥîah or Ḳassassîn nearly due south, 'Amr crossed the hills [3] of the Wâdî Tumilât near the

c. 565 A.D, Antoninus Martyr, who passed this way from his visit to the Holy Places, speaks of a great Saracen idol and festival as held on Mount Horeb, and of predatory Beduins as roaming the desert near 'Phara,' which may be the same as Faramâ or Pelusium (Palestine Pilgrims Text Society, vol. ii. pp. 30–33). The Lakhm, however, were not Arabs: see Ibn Duḳmâḳ, part iv. p. 5.

[1] Jacques de Vitry seems to mention Migdol when he says, 'Beyond Pharamia (Al Faramâ) comes another ancient city, which stands in the wilderness near the sea-shore': but he is very confused, for he continues, 'and next to it is the city of Belbeis, which is called Pelusium and is five stadia from the sea-shore' (Palestine Pilgrims Text Society, vol. xi. p. 14).

[2] John of Nikiou, p. 392. The present Arabic names of these towns are Sanhûr, Ṣân, and Tall Basṭah or Zagazig.

[3] This expression comes from Severus (Brit. Mus. MS., p. 105), and it is adopted by Abû Ṣâliḥ (p. 71). I do not see what other hills could be meant than those of the Wâdî Tumilât. The Cairo MS. says that they 'took the hills' (jabal), which may mean merely 'kept to the desert.'

place now known for the battle of Tall al Kabîr; and when once he was clear of the Wâdî, there remained but a short and easy march between him and Bilbais.

Here, however, the Roman forces began to show some resistance. Their scouts had watched the progress of the Arabs across the desert, but there had been no fighting beyond some trifling skirmishes. The story that two bishops, called Abû Maryam and Abû Maryâm (or Abû Martâm), were sent by the Muḳauḳas to parley with the Arabs, is somewhat legendary[1]. No bishops of such name ever existed, and the incident may be a myth which has arisen from the boundless confusion caused in the minds of Arab historians by the perusal of documents in which matters of legend and history are hopelessly intermingled, while the text has been corrupted at the hand of careless copyists. Yet there is reason to think that some sort of deputation headed by a bishop did parley with 'Amr at this time. Ṭabarî even relates that 'Amr urged the Copts to assist the Muslim forces on the ground of the kinship subsisting between Copts and Arabs through Hagar. The Copts, however, argued that this relationship was somewhat shadowy, whereupon 'Amr granted them four days to consider the matter. But the Roman general had no need to ponder arguments of this kind. Arṭabûn, as he is called by Arab writers, or Aretion as he should be called, was probably the same person as the Roman governor of Jerusalem[2],

[1] Ibn al Athîr seems responsible for this story, which I have examined and refuted in the Appendix, 'On the Identity of the Muḳauḳas.'

[2] See ante, p. 195. The corruption of اريطيون into ارطبون is obvious: Abû 'l Maḥâsin gives the correct form.

who, as we have seen, fled to Egypt when the city was about to surrender to Omar. As general of the Roman troops he decided to force a battle, and on the second day after the parley he surprised the Arab camp by a fierce onslaught at night. But the result was disastrous, and his force was cut to pieces [1]. Still the town of Bilbais was strong enough to detain 'Amr for a full month, during which frequent encounters took place, and its capture caused some loss to the invaders. On the other hand, the Romans are said to have lost 1,000 in killed and 3,000 prisoners [2].

'Amr was now but one day's march from the head of the Delta. He passed by Heliopolis, and still skirting the cultivated land, aimed for a point on the Nile called Umm Dûnain, which lay to the north of Babylon, in what is now the heart of

[1] Ibn Khaldûn.

[2] So much may be believed of the entertaining legend about Armanûsah, daughter of Al Muḳauḳas, told by Waḳidî. He relates that she was on her way to Caesarea to marry Constantine, son of Heraclius, when, learning that Caesarea was besieged by the Arabs, she returned to Egypt with all her servants and treasures, and reached Bilbais, only to be besieged by 'Amr's forces. 'Amr is said to have treated her with chivalrous regard, and to have restored her with all her jewels to her father. I need not waste time in dissecting this legend: the fact that Al Muḳauḳas was Patriarch of Alexandria would alone be decisive in disproving it. The story is given by Quatremère (*Mém. Hist. et Géog.* t. i. p. 53), and upon it is based the historical novel *Armenosa of Egypt* by the Very Rev. C. H. Butcher, D.D. It is worth adding that 'Armanûsah' is given as the old name of Armant by Abû Ṣâliḥ (p. 279). Ibn 'Abd al Ḥakam with similar unreality speaks of the *wife* of Al Muḳauḳas, and tells a story about a vineyard which she owned and flooded, so that Lake Mareotis was formed. It is a pity that these myths, which are often inspired by the fancy of the Arabian Nights, must be banished from the domain of history.

Cairo[1]. But the Roman troops were at length more alert, and were not prepared to allow the seizure of this fortified position, with its harbour and shipping, which were both of great strategical value. The commander-in-chief of all the Roman forces in Egypt at this time was Theodore, a dilatory and incompetent general, who had only just discovered that he had something more than a raid of Beduins to deal with. Cyrus, the Muḳauḳas, the Viceroy of Egypt and imperial Patriarch of Alexandria, seems now to have hurried up with Theodore to the fortress of Babylon, where enough troops were assembled to put in the field against the Arabs. Umm Dûnain itself was strongly held, and the main force of the Romans,

[1] There is, I think, no doubt that this place, called by the Arabs *Umm Dûnain*, is the same as that called by John of Nikiou *Tendunias*. If the initial letter, which doubtless represents the Coptic feminine article, is removed, the resemblance between the two names is close enough. Zotenberg (p. 557, n. 2) is mistaken in putting Tendunias to the *south* of the fortress of Babylon. The course of the narrative makes this improbable: but further Umm Dûnain is expressly identified by Yâḳût and Maḳrîzî with a place which they call Al Maḳs, situated on the west bank of the canal (i.e. Trajan's canal) and on the river Nile. Maḳrîzî adds that at the time of the conquest it formed the harbour for Miṣr. Now it is well known that the original Al Maḳs occupied what is now the Esbekîah Garden of Cairo. The Nile, which passed under the walls of Babylon and Dair Abû 's Saifain, ran considerably to the east of the present channel, and after rounding Al Kabsh the stream passed north to the position indicated. Here then, near the Esbekîah, must be placed the Roman fort of Tendunias, with the harbour and docks of Miṣr, and this is the scene of the fighting. The name Tendunias probably is derived from the Coptic ⲧⲁⲛⲧⲱⲛⲓⲁⲥ, as M. Casanova suggests, and the Arabic is a mere echo of the sound without meaning. That the Nile should have so far shifted its course in twelve centuries is not surprising; and Ibn Duḳmâḳ leaves no doubt on the subject. See also Prof. Lane-Poole's *Cairo*, plan on p. 256.

secure behind the massive walls of their fortress, could choose their own moment for attack and for retreat. Several weeks accordingly passed in a series of indecisive engagements, which hurt the Romans little, but wore down slowly the numbers of the Muslims, already perilously weak for the enterprise on which they had ventured.

Indeed 'Amr was now in a somewhat serious predicament. He had reconnoitred the country round, and found that he could not hope with his present forces either to invest or to storm the castle of Babylon, nor even to seize the city of Miṣr, which adjoined and nearly surrounded it. The recent battles had not been so uniformly in favour of the Muslims as their enthusiasm and their fighting powers had led them to anticipate. It was known that Omar had promised to forward reinforcements, and 'Amr now sent urgent dispatches to press for their arrival. But there was no sign of their coming. Every day's delay was now a gain to the enemy, and it seemed that the issue of the war hung in the balance: either scale might prove the scale of victory[1]. But though the position was critical, it was not in the nature of the Saracen general to despair or to think of retreat. Recognizing, however, the fact that his main objective, the capture of Babylon, was for the moment out of reach, 'Amr resolved on a diversion of singular boldness. His project was nothing less than to make a dash for the Fayûm, a rich province some fifty miles further south, but on the opposite or western bank of the Nile. For this purpose the

[1] The Arab writers admit this. Maḳrîzî says that at Umm Dûnain 'there was much fighting, and victory delayed,' while Abû 'l Maḥâsin's words are even stronger—'there was much fighting, and it was now doubtful which side would have the victory.'

undisputed possession of Umm Dûnain was essential, at least for a time; and he resolved to achieve it at all costs. How the place was carried is not known, but the demand which 'Amr made on the endurance of his men is shown by an anecdote of this period. He was speaking sternly to some of them, in whom he had noticed a failure of strength or of heart, when a trooper murmured, 'We are not made of iron!' 'Silence, you dog!' roared the commander. 'If I am a dog,' rejoined the trooper, 'you are a leader of dogs'—a remark which turned the laugh against 'Amr, and which seems to have gone unpunished. But the task was accomplished, and the capture of Umm Dûnain established 'Amr's force on the Nile banks, and enabled him to seize boats enough to transport his diminished army across the river[1].

[1] The Chronicle of John of Nikiou, our most important authority, which is a total blank as regards the earlier part of the invasion, now begins to deal with the movements of the Arabs. The blank most unfortunately covers the whole reign of Heraclius from his accession to this point. It is most lamentable that all the leaves with John's account of the Persian wars, of the Persian occupation of Egypt, and of the ten years' persecution, have been entirely lost, while those that remain are in the most puzzling disorder. It is certain that some chapters are entirely out of place in the text: it is equally certain that whole sentences are out of place in some chapters: while repetitions and omissions make confusion worse confounded. But there seems no doubt that this raid into the Fayûm took place at the time and in the order I have given. It is not mentioned, I believe, by any Arab historian. Indeed Suyûṭî, who appears to be quoting Ibn 'Abd al Ḥakam, says that though 'Amr after the capture of Miṣr sent troops of horsemen to the towns and villages round about, yet the Fayûm remained unknown to the Arabs for a year (*Ḥusn al Muḥâḍarah*, p. 85). This is in direct contradiction to John's story, but there can be no hesitation in preferring the seventh-century native historian. Balâdhurî, who wrote in the ninth century (about 150 years after John), puts the

capture of the town of Heliopolis, of the Fayûm, of Ushmûnain, and Upper Egypt generally after the fall of Babylon (*Futûḥ al Buldân*, p. 217): but as regards Heliopolis the mistake is so indisputable that it may be safely presumed with regard to the other places. Ibn ʿAbd al Ḥakam's account of the occupation of the Fayûm, as cited by Maḳrîzî, is given by Quatremère, *Mém. Géog. et Hist.* t. i. pp. 407 seq.

CHAPTER XVI

BATTLE OF HELIOPOLIS

Amr's raid on the Fayûm. The Roman position. Capture of Baḥnasâ. John, general of militia, slain. Roman movement from Nikiou to Babylon. Partial failure of the raid and retreat of 'Amr. Arrival of Muslim reinforcements. Arab armies unite at Heliopolis. Roman forces advance from Babylon to give battle. 'Amr's tactics. Defeat of the Romans. Second capture of Tendunias and occupation of the Fayûm. Treatment of Roman officials.

As soon as the passage of the river was safely accomplished, 'Amr's force marched southward by the cultivated land to Memphis. This ancient city (which has now completely disappeared) had been falling into decay ever since the foundation of Alexandria: but vast ruins and remains still marked the site of the capital of the Pharaohs at this time, and there were still a good many inhabited houses, although the town of Miṣr, which lay mostly south of Babylon on the opposite side of the Nile, had become far more populous and important and had even usurped the name of Memphis[1]. It was here,

[1] The remains of Memphis are recorded in the tenth century by Ibn al Faḳîh, who heard from an old man of a great palace which was in one block of stone. He himself oddly remarks, 'Memphis, the city of Pharaoh, has seventy gates and walls of iron and copper' (*Bibl. Geog. Arab.* part vi. pp. 58 and 73). Ya'ḳûbî, rather earlier, says, 'The city of Memphis is falling into ruin.' The town in the region round Ḳaṣr ash Shama' was undoubtedly a Pharaonic settlement. Pharaonic monuments have been found there: one well-known statue stood near the southern gate of the fortress, and stones with hieroglyphic inscriptions have been found in the fortress walls. This town was called Miṣr, but Miṣr and Menf seem sometimes interchanged. Thus 'Abd al Laṭîf says, 'Then there are the monuments which are in Miṣr al Ḳadîmah:

perhaps, from the western bank that the Saracen army first had a clear view of the city of Miṣr and the great towers of Babylon rising from the water's edge across the isle of Rauḍah. A nature like 'Amr's may have been stirred as he surveyed the Pyramids on his right, the Nile and Babylon on his left, and the ruins of Memphis about him, though his troop of desert warriors, as they threaded among the palm-groves, recked but little of the ancient civilization or of the Roman or Byzantine buildings that met their gaze.

The course of their journey is far from clear. The city of Piom or Fayûm was held by the governor Domentianus, while Theodosius the Prefect of the province was with Anastasius, Prefect of Alexandria, in the Delta not far from Nikiou. The defence of the province was entrusted to John[1], general of the militia or local levies, with John of Mârôs under his orders. The points of entrance to the Fayûm were strongly guarded, and in particular a post of observation was established by the Romans

and this city is by Al Jîzah beyond Fusṭâṭ, and it is the city which the Pharaohs dwelt in, and which was the seat of the kingly government' (ed. J. White, p. 117). The term Miṣr seems to have had almost a generic force: thus Al Miṣrain (the two cities) is used of Kûfah and Bosrah by Ibn Khallikân (ed. de Slane, vol. iv. p. 204): but in Egypt as a rule it meant the town on the eastern bank of the Nile by Babylon.

[1] Zotenberg (p. 554, n. 1) identifies this John with the John, Duke of Barca or Barcaina, mentioned by Nicephorus. I have shown that Nicephorus' story of the invasion is totally untrustworthy (p. 207 supra); still this John was a person of importance, and there is every reason to think that he was directly commissioned by Heraclius. For it was doubtless the same 'general of the militia' who had brought the famous Ecthesis from Sergius to Cyrus, and who with the Ecthesis brought the cross referred to by John of Nikiou. See supra, p. 182, and note.

at Ḥajar al Lâḥûn[1] to keep watch over the enemy and report his movements to John, who was stationed on the bank of the river. A force of cavalry and archers was also sent against the Arabs to arrest their march. The Saracen army seem to have found it impossible to break through the Roman cordon, and edged off to the desert hills, capturing a large quantity of cattle on the way. They advanced in this way to a town called Baḥnasâ, which they took by storm, and slaughtered all before them—men, women, and children[2]. 'Amr now faced about suddenly, as he heard that John with a small force of fifty men had been following him and spying his movements, and was at some distance from his supports. John, realizing his danger, endeavoured by a rapid retreat to regain his camp at Abûîṭ[3] at no great distance on the bank of the Nile. His troop marched by night,

[1] For information on this place reference may be made to Drs. Grenfell and Hunt's *Fayûm Towns and their Papyri*, p. 13 and pl. xviii. Al Lâḥûn was on the Baḥr Yûsuf, about ten miles from the city of Fayûm, and it blocked the mouth of the valley dividing the mountain ranges which encircled the Arsinoite nome. It was a place of great strategic importance for the defence of the province. See also Mas'ûdî, op. cit., pp. 385–6.

[2] John of Nikiou, p. 555. The story of the massacre must be believed: it was not against the laws of war at that time, and we shall find other instances of the same thing. The Baḥnasâ here meant was of course in the Fayûm district, and not the well-known Baḥnasâ, which marks the site of the ancient Oxyrhynchus: this was fifty miles further south. See Amélineau, *Géog. Copte*, p. 92.

[3] The position of Abûîṭ is uncertain. Zotenberg identifies it with the place of that name in the province of Lycopolis or Siûṭ, but this is absolutely impossible, as that place is considerably further south than Baḥnasâ. Amélineau (*Géog. Copte*, p. 3) shows that there were two places called Abûîṭ, and the one here in question must be that now in the mûdîrîah of Banisuaif. It lies near Bûsîr Kûridus, nearly due east of Ḥajar al Lâḥûn.

taking cover by day in palm-groves and thickets. But their hiding-place was betrayed to ʻAmr by a Beduin chief[1]. They were surrounded and slain to the last man. The general John and his lieutenant both perished, for the Arabs took no prisoners.

When the commander-in-chief Theodore heard of this disaster, he broke into loud lamentations. Too late as usual, he now hurried all available troops up the river to the island of Lokyôn, while Anastasius and Theodosius hastened from Nikiou to the castle of Babylon to strengthen the garrison. From Babylon, however, a further force was sent under a general named Leontius to the Roman camp at Abûîṭ. On reaching the camp, Leontius, who was obese and indolent and knew nothing of war, found that the Egyptian forces were already in touch with the Arabs, and that Theodore, who had thrown his troops into the city of Fayûm, was making frequent sorties against the Arab head quarters at Baḥnasâ. Judging that ʻAmr would soon be repulsed from that region, he left only half of his men with Theodore, and returned with the other half to report what he had seen to the commanders at Babylon.

There is no doubt that the Saracens failed to capture the city of Fayûm, and that they now began to retire down the river northward again. Theodore gave orders to search for the body of John the general, which had been thrown into the Nile. It was recovered at last with a net, and embalmed; then it was placed on a bier with every sign of mourning, and carried down the river to Babylon,

[1] Zotenberg translates 'le chef des partisans,' but Dr. Charles renders 'the chief of the brigands,' by whom are doubtless meant the marauding dwellers in the desert.

whence it was sent on to Heraclius[1]. The defeat and death of John made a deep impression on the Emperor, who lost no time in signifying his displeasure to Theodore; and the commander-in-chief, knowing that he must have been judged guilty of John's death upon reports from Theodosius and Anastasius, conceived a bitter enmity against those officers.

But it was not mere failure which brought about the retirement of the Arabs from the Fayûm. Indeed 'Amr had probably done more than he had expected. He had extricated his army from a dangerous position at Tendunias, and had removed it to a place of comparative safety: he had kept it employed and had won several successes, if no very great victory: and above all he had gained time. The long-delayed reinforcements were now coming, and it was the news of their arrival which caused the Muslim chief to retrace his steps for the purpose of meeting them. Theodore, likewise, came down the river again with his troops to the fortress of Babylon, where a large army had assembled from different quarters of Egypt.

The expedition to the Fayûm had started about the beginning of May, and it had taken some weeks—weeks which had been worse than wasted for the Romans, while they greatly advantaged the Arabs. It was probably on June 6[2] that the second Muslim

[1] This fact is a further proof that John had a direct commission from the Emperor. Theodore evidently relied on John's military skill, and was deeply concerned by his death. The direct evidence that John was the bearer of the famous Ecthesis to Egypt, and that he brought with him a cross of great sanctity from the Emperor, has already been given above (p. 182, n. 1).

[2] I have shown in the essay on 'The Chronology of the Arab

army dispatched by Omar arrived in the neighbourhood of Heliopolis. This contingent was under the command of a noted leader named Az Zubair ibn al 'Awwâm, a kinsman and Companion of the Prophet and one of the six counsellors. The legion under him numbered 4,000 men, but was being followed at a short distance by two other columns of equal strength, so that the total reinforcements amounted to 12,000 men[1]. The Nile begins to rise in its deep channel about midsummer, and the Romans were anxious to give battle with their now united forces before the waters overflowed. But they seem to have failed entirely to prevent the junction of the divided Saracen army. They

Conquest,' that the Coptic tradition associates this date with the appearance of the Arabs in Egypt, and that it cannot possibly apply to 'Amr's first arrival. It may, however, mark the arrival of the reinforcing army.

[1] Authorities differ about the numbers. Ibn 'Abd al Ḥakam says 4,000; Balâdhurî says 10,000 or 12,000; Yâḳût 12,000; Maḳrîzî quotes from Al Kindî a statement of Yazîd's that 'Amr's fighting force amounted to 15,500—i. e. an original force of 3,500 augmented by 12,000; while Suyûṭî definitely says that the 12,000 came in detachments—a view also noticed by Maḳrîzî—and he mentions one detachment, viz. that under Zubair, as consisting of 4,000 men. This explains why some Arab writers allege that the total of reinforcements was only 4,000 men. John of Nikiou, curiously enough, gives the same number 4,000, and adds that their commander, named Walwâryâ, was a barbarian, or negro. The name is unrecognizable, but there was a black commander named 'Ubâdah in one of the contingents: and, as Zotenberg remarks, 'Walwâryâ' is an obvious corruption. Yâḳût makes 'Ubâdah ibn aṣ Ṣâmit, Al Miḳdâd ibn al Aswad, and Maslamah ibn Mukhallad leaders each of 1,000 men, and Zubair the same.

There is no sort of confusion not found among Arab historians, so that it is not surprising to find Maḳrîzî deferring the arrival of the reinforcements—12,000 men under Zubair—until the time when the investment of Babylon was proceeding.

possessed Babylon; they held the command of the river; and they had reoccupied the fortified outpost of Umm Dûnain: so that with common skill and prudence they might have foiled all 'Amr's efforts to recross to the eastern bank, and might have crushed him while he was thus isolated.

Yet with every advantage in their favour they did not prevent 'Amr from stealing or forcing the passage. It seems likely that he crossed somewhat lower down, to the north of Umm Dûnain; for Trajan's Canal had silted up from neglect, and would have presented no obstacle, even had the Nile already risen. 'Amr had been aware that the Muslim reinforcements were marching in two columns on 'Ain Shams or Heliopolis, and his position on the western bank had been decidedly dangerous[1]: indeed, he had been seriously alarmed lest the Romans should, by barring his passage, render it impossible to join forces with Zubair. But as usual Theodore lost his opportunity of striking home, and 'Amr's army, elated with their adventures, marched into the Muslim camp at Heliopolis.

In ancient times Heliopolis had been one of the most famous cities of Egypt. Its name of Ôn[2], familiar in the Mosaic narrative, was still preserved as the name in common use among the Copts in the

[1] John's text in chapter cxii (p. 556) is hopelessly dislocated. The sentence (l. 2, 'Laissant de côté les villes fortifiées ils s'étaient dirigés vers une localité nommée Tendounyas et s'étaient embarqués sur le fleuve,' refers to the start of the expedition to the Fayûm; the next sentence speaks of the capture of Miṣr; and the next of the return from the Fayûm! A critical reconstruction of the text is much wanted. But 'Amr's disquiet at his position comes out clearly.

[2] Champollion le Jeune has an interesting note on this place, *L'Egypte sous les Pharaons*, t. ii. pp. 36–41.

seventh century, and that it connoted the idea of 'sun-city,' expressed in the Greek form Heliopolis, is not questioned: even the Arabs retained this idea when they changed the name of the place to 'Ain Shams, i.e. Fountain or Well of the Sun [1]. Ôn had been no less famous for the splendour of its monuments than for its renown as a religious centre and seat of learning. When Strabo visited it six hundred years before this period, although wars and sieges and the changes of time had overthrown and ruined most of the temples and statues, yet people still pointed out the halls in which Plato had studied. But when the Arabs came, little of the ancient grandeur remained beycnd some broken walls and half-buried sphinxes, and the solitary obelisk, which stands to this day as a memorial of a vanished world.

Heliopolis was on a slight eminence and had been surrounded by a rampart of great thickness, some traces of which are still visible [2]. Though it had no great military importance at this time, yet it was capable of defence; it was well supplied with water; and it was convenient for provisioning the army. For these reasons 'Amr retained it as his head

[1] The modern name Maṭarîah seems to have prevailed over 'Ain Shams. The place is well known to travellers for the Virgin's Tree, and the fountain by which the Holy Family rested.

[2] Although Heliopolis and Ôn are usually identified, the recent War Office map identifies Ôn with Tall al Yahûdîah and Heliopolis with Tall al Ḥassan. The ruins at Tall al Yahûdîah are on an eminence girt with a crude brick wall, while at Tall al Ḥassan there still remains on the south side a rampart twenty feet high. It must have been at the latter place that 'Amr camped, as Tall al Yahûdîah is some twelve miles further north. The entire level of the country has risen several feet since the seventh century, as is proved both by the depth to which the obelisk is now sunken and the depth at which other remains now lie beneath the desert plain.

quarters, while preparing for the conflict which was impending. We have already seen that Theodore at Babylon had been drawing troops from the Delta towns: but by the time he had massed an army capable of driving the Muslims out of Heliopolis, it is probable that the whole of the reinforcements sent by Omar had arrived, and 'Amr now found himself at the head of about 15,000 men, including some of the most renowned soldiers of Islâm[1]. What numbers the Romans mustered can only be conjectured. They had a sound estimate of the enemy's valour. Earlier in the war a Copt was overheard expressing astonishment that the Arabs had dared to enter Egypt and array their handful of men against the immense forces of the Emperor's army; to which another Copt answered that the Arabs were incapable of yielding—they must either prove victorious or die to the last man[2]. Another story is that the Romans were reluctant to fight, saying, 'We have small chance against the men

[1] Ibn 'Abd al Ḥakam, according to Abû 'l Maḥâsin, gives the following list of the chief companions and helpers of the Prophet with the army. (1) The *Companions* were 'Amr and his son 'Abdallah; Az Zubair; 'Abdallah, son of the Caliph Omar; Sa'd ibn Abî Waḳḳâs (whose presence is disputed); Khârijah ibn Ḥudhâfah; Ḳais ibn Abî 'l 'Âṣ as Saḥmî; Al Miḳdâd ibn al Aswad; 'Abdallah ibn Sa'd ibn Abî Sarḥ; Nâfi' ibn 'Abd Ḳais al Faḥrî; Abû Râfi', the freedman of the Apostle of God; Ibn 'Ibdah; 'Abdarraḥman and Rabî'ah, sons of Shuraḥbîl ibn Ḥasanah; and Wardân, the freedman of 'Amr. (2) The *Helpers* were 'Ubâdah ibn aṣ Ṣâmit; Muḥammad ibn Maslamah; Abû Aiyûb Khâlid ibn Yazîd; Abû Dardâ 'Uwaimir ibn 'Aâmir, also called 'Uwaimir ibn Yazîd. The same writer also gives some other names of less illustrious Arabs: see *An Nujûm az Zâhirah fî Mulûk Miṣr wal Ḳâhirah*, ed. Juynboll et Matthes (Lugd. Bat. 1885–61), vol. i. p. 22.

[2] Abû 'l Maḥâsin, p. 8.

who have conquered Chosroes and Caesar in Syria.' But these stories are from Arab sources, and the latter is certainly doubtful. It is incontestable, however, that the Romans had a vast superiority in numbers, and their forces now available for battle—apart from fortress garrisons—were not less than 20,000.

It was evidently 'Amr's policy to draw the Roman army into the open plain away from Babylon; and when Theodore felt himself strong enough to take the offensive, his force moved out towards Heliopolis —a distance of six or seven miles from his camp. Theodosius and Anastasius were in command of the cavalry, but the bulk of the Roman army were foot soldiers—spearmen and archers. 'Amr's spies had given him warning in good time of the enemy's intentions, and he had disposed his forces in position. He himself with the main body of the Arabs would advance from Heliopolis to meet the Romans: but under cover of night he detached two other bodies of troops, placing one not far from Umm Dûnain and the other under Khârijah at a point further east—probably in the fold of the hills[1], close to what is now the citadel of Cairo. The line of the Roman advance thus lay between the two detached corps of Arabs, which had orders to fall on the flank and rear of the enemy when the right opportunity offered[2]. It was early morning when the

[1] This is probably the incident mentioned in a wrong connexion by Maḳrîzî, where he says that 'Amr sent 500 horsemen under command of Khârijah that they might hide and fall on the enemy as they came out from among the monasteries. 'They went off by night and entered the caves of Banû Wâil before morning.' Early after dawn when the battle began, they surprised the Romans by falling on their rear and completed their discomfiture.

[2] Zotenberg finds it difficult to understand the battle in view of

Roman forces emerged from the gardens and monasteries which covered the ground north-eastward of the fortress, and deployed in the open[1].

the distances between the places mentioned. He errs in putting Tendunias (Umm Dûnain) to the *south* of Babylon instead of to the north. John of Nikiou doubtless regarded it as more *north-west*, and so he calls the other point in contrast *north* of Babylon: but apart from other objections, 'Amr's plan of battle is reduced to absurdity by placing one of his detachments south of Babylon, one north, and the main army at Heliopolis. Besides, the way to the south was entirely blocked by the Roman fortress and camp. By supposing that 'Amr advanced to meet the Roman army, instead of waiting at his base, one gets rid of the difficulty about distance. Moreover, Zotenberg forgets that the Nile flowed much further east than at present. Place one Arab detachment near the Esbekîah (Umm Dûnain) and the other near the Citadel or the Red Mountain, and the course of the battle is clear enough. One more remark. The ancient Heliopolis covered a far larger area than can now be easily imagined. This is clear not merely from remains discovered, but from the express testimony of Ibn Duḳmâḳ, who says: 'The city of 'Ain Shams in ancient times was of great width and length and *contiguous to* ancient Miṣr on the site of the present Al Fusṭâṭ' (pt. v. p. 43). This must mean, I think, that there was very little interval between the outskirts of the two towns, though these outskirts consisted only of scattered houses and churches.

[1] My account of the battle of 'Ain Shams will appear to be totally at variance with that given by Ṭabarî (ed. Zotenberg, vol. iii. p. 463). For Ṭabarî alleges that (1) the battle took place after the capture of Babylon: (2) Al Muḳauḳas with the Coptic army was in possession of 'Ain Shams intending to march on Miṣr: (3) 'Amr's army advanced up to the very gates of 'Ain Shams: (4) The Coptic army was broken at the first shock, losing a great number of killed and prisoners: (5) much booty was taken, and the prisoners were sent to Medina. It may seem presumptuous to reject so circumstantial an account; but quite apart from the necessity of preferring John of Nikiou's nearly contemporary evidence, it is quite clear that Ṭabarî is making a geographical blunder. His story of the battle is doubtless true, but it was not the battle of 'Ain Shams. This is proved (1) by the order of events; this battle cannot conceivably come after the capture of Miṣr, while other battles can and did: and (2) by the fact that

They were in complete ignorance of 'Amr's stratagem, but they knew that his main army was marching from Heliopolis to meet them. The encounter probably took place about half way between the two camps, somewhere in the region now called 'Abbasîah. Both sides knew that on that field the fate of Egypt would be decided; and both fought with obstinate courage. But while the struggle was at its fiercest, the Arab detachment

Ṭabarî himself virtually admits the blunder in describing 'Ain Shams as 'a considerable town in the country of the Copts and *situated towards the west*.' This could only mean either west of the Nile, or west of the Delta: but 'Ain Shams cannot possibly be described as either. The reference, however, is perhaps to one of the battles fought between Babylon and Alexandria, of which more anon: for these were fought in the west.

This mistake of Ṭabarî (who as a foreigner was ill acquainted with Egyptian geography) has been a fruitful source of error to Arab writers like Ibn al Athîr, Ibn Khaldûn, &c. It is one more example of those confusions and perplexities which every historian of this period finds even in the best authorities, and has to unravel by the slow labour of criticism and comparison. But I think that there is a simple and certain explanation of this confusion, which reappears in other Arab writers. When Ibn al Athîr says the Arab leaders besieged 'Ain Shams, and makes Zubair mount the walls of 'Ain Shams (as we shall see that he mounted the walls of Ḳaṣr ash Shama'), we have the same confusion. Its origin lies in the name Babylon. This the Arabs, or some of them, took to mean *Bâb-al-Ôn*, i. e. gate of Ôn, or gate of Heliopolis, and '*Ain Shams is the Arabic name for Heliopolis*. Hence the two places are confounded: for while Balâdhurî clearly says that Fusṭâṭ at the time of the conquest was called Ayûn, later writers read this as *Al Yûn* and then took it to mean *Ôn*, i. e. 'Ain Shams. Naturally, then, a siege of 'Ain Shams is constructed upon the error, and incidents are transferred to it from Babylon.

This solution has not, I think, been given before, but it explains many difficulties in the Arab writers. The forms Bâb-al-Yûn, City of Liûn, Ḳaṣr-al-Yûn, Bâb-al-Lûḳ, Lunîah, and Ayûn all express in various ways the one misunderstanding of the Roman word Babylon.

under Khârijah issued from the hills, and fell like a whirlwind on the rear of the Romans. Caught thus between two forces they fell into disorder, and moving somewhat to their left towards Umm Dûnain were met and charged by what seemed a third Arab army. Disorder now turned into disaster, and in headlong flight they strove to escape the flashing scimitars of the Arabs. Some few got back to the fortress by land: many others, pressing towards the river, seized boats and sailed back to Babylon: but great numbers perished. The victorious Arabs took possession of Umm Dûnain a second time. Of its Roman garrison all but 300 men had perished in the fight. These survivors retreated to the fortress of Babylon and shut the gates: but when they heard of the terrible slaughter which the Romans had suffered, they lost heart and fled down the river by boat to Nikiou.

Even tradition is silent as regards the losses on either side. But it is known that the commander-in-chief, Theodore, and the two governors, Theodosius and Anastasius, were not among the slain. Enough Roman troops too were left to form, with those who had held the fortress during the battle, an effective garrison. But the advantages of the victory to the Arabs were enormous. The town of Miṣr, which had been hitherto protected by the Roman army at Babylon, was now at their mercy, and it was captured without further fighting [1]. They were now masters of the whole river-bank, above

[1] The heading of c. cxv in John's Chronicle reads, 'Comment les Musulmans s'emparèrent de Miṣr dans la quatorzième année du cycle lunaire,' but there is nothing about the capture in the text. It is but one proof among a hundred of the utterly defective and dislocated state of the text.

and below the fortress, and moving up their camp from Heliopolis, they pitched it north and east of the fortress in the region of the gardens and churches—the region known in subsequent history as Fusṭâṭ. Their forces too were now both sufficient to beleaguer Babylon and free to concert measures for its investment. The Roman army was swept away as a fighting force, and any remnant which escaped was either shut up within the fortress walls or scattered through the Delta in panic. Moreover the news of the Arab victory at once cleared the city of Fayûm of its defenders. For Domentianus, on learning the result of the battle, evacuated the city by night, and marched the garrison to Abûîṭ: there they hastily embarked and fled down the river to Nikiou, without even telling the people of Abûîṭ that they were abandoning the Fayûm to the enemy. As soon, however, as the flight of Domentianus was reported to 'Amr, he flung a body of troops across the Nile; the towns of Fayûm and Abûîṭ were captured amid scenes of ruthless massacre; and the whole province was brought under Muslim dominion.

When the last sparks of resistance had thus been quenched in the Fayûm, 'Amr directed the troops there to concentrate at the town of Dalâṣ[1] as the most convenient place of embarkation. The command of the river had for the moment passed to the victors—not the least result of the battle. The Romans still held the fortified island of Rauḍah in close connexion with Babylon, maintaining communication by boat between the two strongholds:

[1] Dalâṣ, the Coptic Tiloj, the Greek Nilopolis, was on the western bank of the river, south of Memphis, and east of Fayûm city. See Amélineau, *Géog. Copte*, p. 136.

and for a while longer the navigation of the river remained more or less open, because the Arabs were as yet no sailors, and they were busy with further conquest by land. For 'Amr now recalled the various troops of horsemen [1], which had scoured the country after the battle of Heliopolis; and he ordered Apa Cyrus [2] of Dalâṣ to supply Nile boats for the transport of the force in the Fayûm from the western to the eastern bank. His intention was to subjugate the whole province of Miṣr, which extended over the apex of the Delta.

The battle of Heliopolis was probably fought about the middle of July, 640 A.D. Not less than a fortnight was spent in taking possession of the Fayûm, so that we are brought to the beginning of August for the expedition to the Delta. 'Amr wished to strike a blow there before the rise of the Nile made it impossible. George, the Prefect of the province of Miṣr, had either been captured when the town was taken or had sent in his sub-

[1] Ibn 'Abd al Ḥakam (quoted by Suyûṭî) says that 'after the completion of the conquest of Miṣr (i.e. the town), 'Amr sent troops of horsemen to the towns and villages round about.' John of Nikiou says of the same time, 'Il réunissait auprès de lui toutes ses troupes pour exécuter de nombreuses expéditions'—a clear agreement.

[2] This is the *Abâkîrî* in John of Nikiou, p. 559. Zotenberg, puzzled by the word, remarks, 'Il n'est pas certain que ce mot soit un nom propre.' But all shadow of doubt is removed by documents in Karabacek's *Papyrus Erzherzog Rainer: Führer durch die Ausstellung*. No. 551 is a letter from the well-known Khârijah (p. 230 supra) to Apa Cyrus, pagarch of Heracleopolis Magna, and no. 558, written in Greek and Arabic and dated April 25, 643, is from 'Abdallah ibn Jâbir to Christophorus and Theodorakius, sons of the same Apa Cyrus. This latter is the earliest document of Islâm in Egypt, if not in the world. No. 554 gives the same name again.

mission. Indeed the terror of the Arabs' name now secured all the country within reach of their sword, save only the fortified places.

But the Delta was covered with waterways, some of which were unfordable: and George was ordered at once to have a bridge built over the canal at Ḳaliûb. 'And,' says John of Nikiou, 'people began to help the Muslims[1].' It is unfortunate that the bishop's language is not more explicit; but, taken in connexion with the context and with subsequent passages, this remark seems to prove nothing except that service was requisitioned from the country folk. It was, in other words, forced, not voluntary. Indeed this very passage makes that meaning clear. For after recording that the Arabs captured the important towns of Athrîb and Manûf with all their territory, and subjugated the whole province of Miṣr, the writer continues, 'Not content with that, 'Amr had the Roman magistrates arrested and their hands and feet fettered with chains or logs of wood: he extorted great sums of money, laid a double tax on the peasants, whom he forced to bring forage for his horses, and he committed innumerable acts of violence.' That measures of this kind crushed resistance, and disposed the people to obey the will of their conqueror, is not surprising: but so far there is not a word to show that any section of the Egyptian nation viewed the advent of the Muslims with any other feeling than terror.

Although Athrîb and Manûf had fallen, the town of Nikiou, which lay on the western branch of the

[1] c. cxiii. p. 559. Zotenberg's rendering, 'C'est alors que l'on commença à prêter aide aux Musulmans,' goes beyond the original, which merely says 'And they began to help the Muslims.' I think that the help was for a specific purpose, not general.

Nile, was too strongly fortified to be taken without a regular siege, for which neither time nor means were available. It remained therefore as a link between Babylon and Alexandria. But the mere report of the Muslim victories determined the Roman chiefs who were there to retire on the capital. They left, however, Domentianus with a small garrison, and sent to Dâres at Samanûd the order to defend the country between the two branches of the Nile. But the alarm now became a panic, which spread through every town of Egypt. From all parts the inhabitants streamed towards Alexandria, abandoning lands and houses, goods and chattels, cattle and crops. A new reign of terror had begun for the people who had been scourged by ten years of persecution under Cyrus, Al Muḳauḳas.

But 'Amr was not prepared to follow the flying crowds northwards. The Nile, now rising fast as August waned, was making the country impassable: besides he had no wish to leave in his rear the powerful fortress of Babylon unmasked, while to mask it such a number of troops were needed as would leave him no army capable of conquering Alexandria. His next step therefore must be the reduction of Babylon.

CHAPTER XVII

THE FORTRESS OF BABYLON

Present state of the fortress. Its position and description. Towers and gates. The Iron Gate. Island of Rauḍah. Origin of the fortress and of its name. Churches within it.

Up to nearly the beginning of the twentieth century enough of the ancient fortress still stood to give a clear idea of its structure and its importance. These remains owed their preservation entirely to the Copts, whose churches had clustered within the walls from the very beginnings of Christianity, and had found in them a sure bulwark in times of persecution. The walls were Coptic property, save where the Melkite church of St. George or the Jewish synagogue claimed a small section of them; and the Muslims seem never to have shown any care to preserve a monument which played so large a part in the conquest, and about which so much is written in the pages of their own historians.

But with the British occupation came a sense of security which has led to the most deplorable destruction. The need of a fortified enclosure having vanished, Copts, Greeks, and Jews vied together in demolishing the walls, wherever their fancy suggested a new entrance or a new building. It is the simple truth that in the last eighteen years more havoc has been wrought upon the Roman fortress than in the previous eighteen centuries.

At last, when nearly all the mischief was done, the government interfered, and all that now remains is placed under government protection. But that is little enough.

The ruined castle lies in the region now miscalled Old Cairo. Three sides of the enclosure were almost uninjured a few years ago; but now of two sides only some fragments remain, while the third is sadly mutilated. The walls were about eight feet in thickness, built of brick and stone courses alternating, and they seem to have formed an irregular quadrilateral, the full extent of which cannot be known until the foundations of the fourth or vanished side are rediscovered. On the south and on the eastern side of the fortress the line of walls was broken out by four projecting bastions at somewhat uneven intervals. Three of the four bastions on the south were recently visible: now one has been completely destroyed, but between the other two may be seen the magnificent ancient gateway, which has been excavated from the encumbering rubbish mounds to a depth of some thirty feet[1]. On the western side of the fort there was no bastion—a fact which one may explain by remembering that when the fort was built, and even at the time of the conquest, the Nile flowed under the wall, so that boats moored beneath it. Another gate, opening on to the river, probably lay between the two enormous round towers, which were little injured before the recent changes. Now one of them is all but demolished, the other has been entirely obliterated from view by being enclosed and encased in a rectangular block of modern Arab construction. Each tower was circular on plan, upwards of 100 feet in diameter, and contained an inner circle of wall: radiating walls divided the

[1] Historians and antiquarians alike owe a great debt of gratitude to Max Hertz Bey for his able work in saving this gateway and showing it to the light.

space between the two concentric circles into eight compartments, one of which was occupied by a stone staircase leading to the top of the building. The ordinary walls of the fortress were some sixty feet high, as is proved by recent excavations, although the whole fortress is now buried to a depth of thirty feet by the accumulations of ages. But the towers rose higher still, and from their top opened an immense view embracing the Muḳaṭṭam Hills on the east, long reaches of the Nile to north and south, Jîzah, the Pyramids, and the Libyan desert on the west. And at the time of the conquest, before Cairo was built, the field of vision must have reached as far as Heliopolis [1].

The two towers were joined by a curtain wall, which was pierced by the gate above mentioned. But it was not this gate, all trace of which is destroyed or buried, but the southern gate now opened out to view, which the Arab writers dwell upon and associate with the Muḳauḳas. This is no longer doubtful. For the recent excavations have disclosed one very curious result: they show that either the Nile itself or a short inlet from it came right up to the main southern gate of the fortress (the 'western' gate of the Arab writers [2]), and to the quay at which the Roman boats moored. The quay is graduated with steps to suit the changing level of the Nile: but its existence is a

[1] The present writer has verified this. A full account of the towers is given in *Ancient Coptic Churches*. The plan showing such part of the enclosure as existed just before the British occupation of Egypt is here reproduced with slight changes.

[2] Neither 'southern' nor 'western' is strictly accurate according to the points of the compass; but the side of the fortress towards Cairo is more naturally called the northern, and that towards Ḥulwân the southern side.

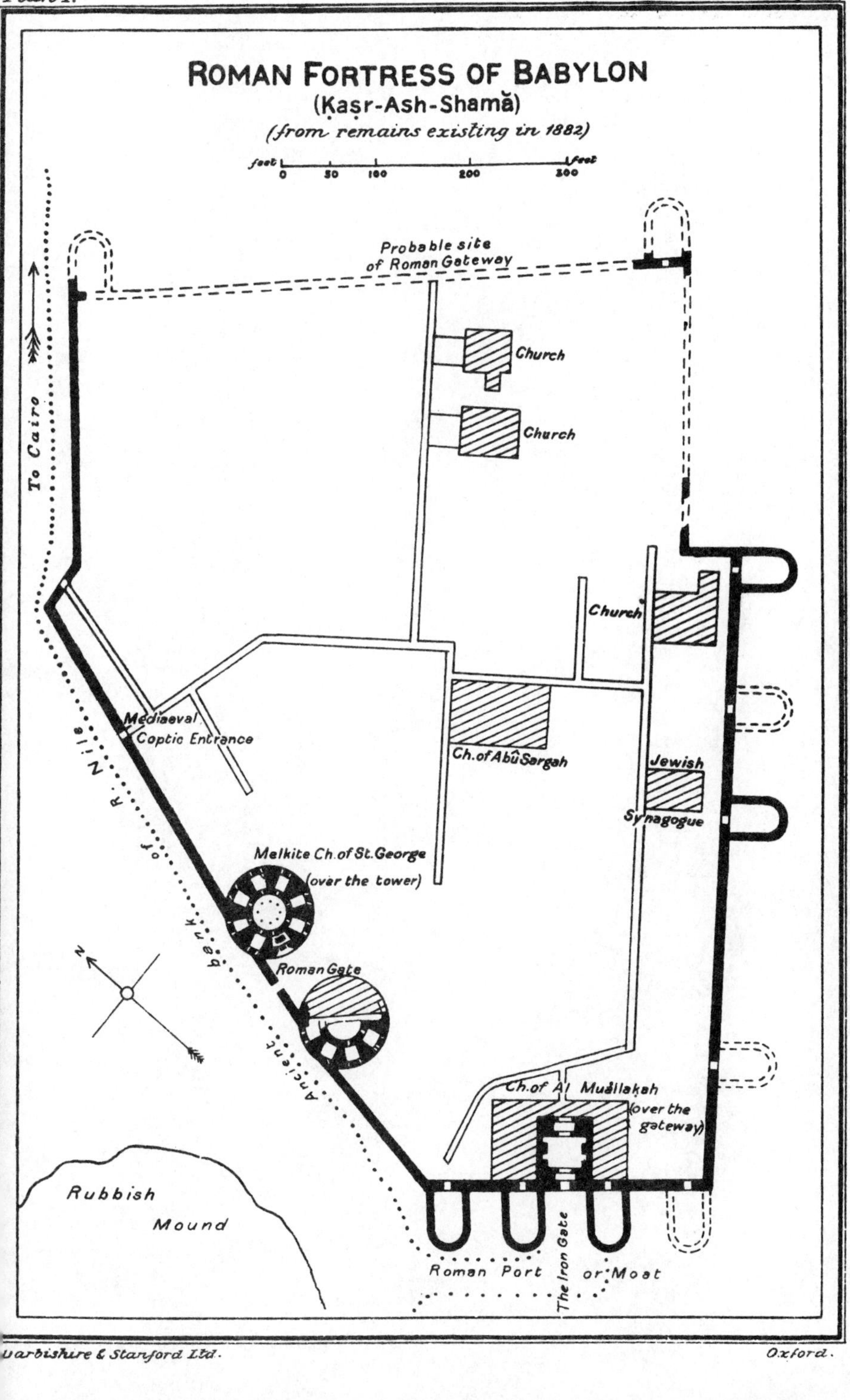
ROMAN FORTRESS OF BABYLON
(Ḳaṣr-Ash-Shamă)
(from remains existing in 1882)
feet 0 50 100 200 300 feet
Probable site of Roman Gateway
Church
Church
To Cairo
Church
Mediaeval Coptic Entrance
Ch. of Abû Sargah
Jewish Synagogue
R. Nile
Ancient bank of
Melkite Ch. of St. George (over the tower)
N
Roman Gate
Ch. of Al Muâllakah (over the gateway)
Rubbish Mound
Roman Port or Moat
The Iron Gate

Darbishire & Stanford Ltd.

Oxford.

singular confirmation of the minute accuracy with which facts are sometimes recorded by the Arab historians. Possibly the same arrangement existed at the gate between the round towers towards the Isle of Rauḍah. But unquestionably it was this southern gate—the gate of Al Mu'allaḳah—which was the Iron Gate of Arab story. This is proved first by the discovery of the quay: next by the fact that the gateway now standing still shows deep chases cut in the masonry for the portcullis or drop-gate, which was either made of iron or plated with iron: and lastly by the fact that Maḳrîzî[1] expressly identifies the Iron Gate with the 'western' gate (which I call the southern), while his contemporary Ibn Duḳmâḳ[2] identifies the 'western' gate with the gate which is under the church of Al Mu'allaḳah.

It is curious in this connexion to note that even as late as the year 1400 A.D. this Iron Gate, marked by the ancient quay, was used as the ordinary entrance to the fortress. Just outside stood the

[1] *Khiṭaṭ*, i. p. 286.

[2] Pt. iv. pp. 25–6. The writer gives no description of the fortress, but names the gates, streets, mosques, and churches in it. I give an extract from this important passage: '*Road of Al Mu'allaḳah.* This is the road which passes underneath the church of that name. It is the gate of the fortress, by which the whole of the Castle of the Romans called Ḳaṣr ash Shama' is entered from the Great Market. *Road of the Stone.* This is entered from the guard-house of Al Binânah, and by that you pass into the fortress, of which it forms the (north-)eastern gate, the last named being the (south-)western gate. The other gates will be mentioned below, if God will. *Road of Maḥaṭṭ al Ḳarb.* This is entered from the Fish-Market and the Meat-Market. This is the north(-western) gate of the fortress . . . and it is the last of the well-known gates of the castle.' What I have called the southern gate under Al Mu'allaḳah is called by Ibn Duḳmâḳ, with equal correctness but less convenience, the western gate: see p. 240, n. 2 supra. See also Ibn Duḳmâḳ, pp. 15, 16, 30, 33, 49, 81, 103–4, 107–8.

Great Market, as it was called, and from this the main road passed through the gateway under the church of Al Mu'allaḳah, and crossing the enclosure issued out of the walls again by a gate on the northern side towards the mosque of 'Amr. On this side also was the 'guard-house of Binânah,' possibly the detached Roman building of which a fragment still remains. Although Ibn Duḳmâḳ's language implies the existence of several other gates, only one more is mentioned—that upon the western side—which may be the gate between the towers. The western walls, then, were washed by the Nile, and boats came up also to the Iron Gate. At the present day the Nile has retreated far from the ramparts, and the level of the soil has risen so high all round the fortress that the walls lie buried to half their original height. This underground portion at least of the ancient circuit has escaped the hand of the destroyer, and it is to be hoped that some day it may see the light again.

The island of Rauḍah itself was strongly fortified at this epoch; and by its commanding position in mid channel of the Nile it added immensely to the military value of Babylon. Ibn Duḳmâḳ[1] seems to say that the Arabs attacked the island during the investment of Babylon, and that when the Romans retreated, 'Amr threw down part of the island walls and towers, which remained in a dismantled state till Ibn Tûlûn rebuilt them in the year 876, for the purpose of guarding there his treasure and his seraglio. The island from another

[1] Pt. iv. p. 109. See also *Cairo Fifty Years Ago* (E. W. Lane, p. 132: London, 1896), where the writer mentions remains of a massive wall with round towers of Roman work as visible in his day on the island.

use was called also Arsenal Island by the Arabs in later ages. The Nilometer at the south end of the island was built in the year 716 A.D. in replacement of an earlier monument of the kind, which was inside the fortress of Babylon.

At the time of the conquest the whole region eastward of the fortress was an open cultivated plain. Northward spread gardens and vineyards, while all the region between the vineyards and the mountains as far as the present mosque of Ṭûlûn and Al Kabsh was dotted over with churches and convents, some few of which remain to this day, both within and without the walls of Cairo, though the greater number were destroyed in the fourteenth century by Al Malik an Nâṣir ibn Ḳala'ûn [1].

As regards the origin of the fortress, the conjecture which I ventured to make [2], that it was built by Trajan c. 100 A. D., has been amply confirmed by the since-published work of John of Nikiou. He relates that, in consequence of a Jewish rebellion at Alexandria, Trajan first sent Marcius Turbo with a large army, and then 'himself came to Egypt and there built a fortress with a powerful and impregnable citadel, and he brought there abundance of water [3].' This last expression may refer to the wells sunk below the round towers and in other parts of the fortress. John goes on to say that the original

[1] The whole of this paragraph is taken from Maḳrîzî, *Khiṭaṭ*, vol. i. p. 286. He also says, 'The fort overlooked the Nile and boats came up to the western gate, called the Iron Gate. . . . The waters of the Nile have retreated westward since that time.' Abû Ṣâliḥ mentions many churches in this region which long survived the conquest. Yet he alleges that 'Amr destroyed a large number of churches here (p. 133).

[2] *Ancient Coptic Churches*, vol. i. p. 178.

[3] p. 413.

foundations of the fortress were laid by Nebuchadnezzar, who gave it the name of Babylon, his own capital, at the time of his invasion of Egypt, and that upon these Trajan raised the circuit walls and otherwise enlarged the buildings[1]. All, however, that stands above ground now is undoubtedly Roman, nor is it likely that Trajan followed the lines of any previous construction upon that spot.

On the other hand, the existence of an earlier fortress in the vicinity is certain. Strabo[2], who visited Egypt about 130 years before Trajan, mentions a strong fort standing on a rocky ridge, and traces the name to some Babylonian exiles who settled there. Diodorus[3] recounts that some captives brought by Sesostris from Babylon established themselves in a castle which they called after their mother city. Josephus[4] thinks the castle was built during the Persian conquest under Cambyses. Finally, Eutychius[5] gives Akhûs, i. e. Artaxerxes Ochus, as the builder of the fortress. It may then be taken for granted that near the present site there was a stronghold called Babylon for many centuries

[1] Curiously enough, Maḳrîzî gives much the same tradition; but he says that the fortress was '*destroyed* by Nebuchadnezzar and afterwards rebuilt by a Roman governor, Arjâlîs, son of Maḳrâṭîs, on its original foundations' (*Khiṭaṭ*, vol. i. p. 287). Archelaus, son of Mercatus (for this seems the Roman name denoted by the Arabic), may possibly be the name of Trajan's prefect or of the architect.

[2] *Geog.* lib. xvii. c. 1, § 35.

[3] Diodorus Siculus, *Hist.* lib. i. c. 56. 3.

[4] *Ant. Jud.* ii. 15.

[5] See Abû Ṣâliḥ, p. 177, n. 3, where Eutychius' words are quoted. Vansleb in 1672 saw the ruins of a once magnificent Persian fire-temple, said by tradition to have been built by Artaxerxes Ochus (*Nouvelle Relation d'un Voyage fait en Égypte*, p. 240). The ruins were apparently inside Ḳaṣr ash Shama'.

before the days of Trajan: but I have shown elsewhere[1] that the original castle stood rather to the south on the rocky ridge (which is still clearly visible), as required by Strabo's description. At the time of 'Amr's invasion this ridge and the adjacent locality were probably occupied by the town of Miṣr, which spread as far as the Roman fortress, if not further, to the north. The fortress, however, was surrounded by a moat, which Al Muḳauḳas, or Cyrus, had lately cleared out and furnished with drawbridges[2]. It is probable too that in the town of Miṣr many ancient Egyptian buildings were still standing, as excavations are constantly yielding large stones covered with hieroglyphic inscriptions.

The name Babylon has caused much confusion among Arab writers. It lingers on to-day not as the name of the fortress, which is called Ḳaṣr ash Shama', Castle of the Torch or Beacon, but in connexion with a little convent a short distance to the south, which is still called Dair Bablûn. At the time of the conquest the fortress was called in Coptic 'Babylon an Khemi' or 'Babylon of Egypt[3].' The name lent itself easily to misconstruction in Arabic, as the first syllable means 'gate' in that

[1] *Ancient Coptic Churches*, vol. i. pp. 172–5.

[2] Severus mentions moats as amongst the works of Cyrus, and Abû 'l Maḥâsin says, 'The Romans had dug a moat round the fortress, with gates,' i. e. drawbridges crossing to the gates. Abû Ṣâliḥ (p. 73) also says, 'The people of Fusṭâṭ dug a moat against the Arabs.'

[3] ⲃⲁⲃⲩⲗⲟⲛ or ⲃⲁⲃⲩⲗⲱⲛ ⲛϫⲏⲙⲓ or ⲛⲕⲏⲙⲏ: see Champollion, *L'Égypte sous les Pharaons*, t. ii. p. 34. There is no evidence at all to support his conjecture that the form ⲃⲁⲃⲏⲗ was ever in use in Egypt; neither Coptic nor Arabic writers recognize such a form. But ϫⲏⲙⲓ is identified with ⲕⲉϣⲣⲱⲙⲓ in a MS. given by Zoega, *Cat. Codd. Copt.* p. 88.

language, and the remainder suggests a genitive case, as we have already seen[1]. How the name Ḳaṣr ash Shamaʿ arose is not so easy to discover. It may well be that 'Shamaʿ' is a mere echo of the Coptic 'Khemi.' On the other hand, there is a very distinct tradition that a fire-temple was built in connexion with the old Babylonian castle, and also that a similar temple was erected on one of the Roman towers, at least during the Persian occupation, in the seventh century. We find even mention of a Ḳubbat ad Dukhân—Dome or Temple of Smoke—in the Arabic writer Yâḳût[2]. But considering the importance of the towers as signal-stations in time of war, it is easy to imagine that upon one or both of them arrangements were made to light beacon-fires, and that from this fact arose the name Ḳaṣr ash Shamaʿ[3]. It is, however, curious to remark that, however ill the Arabs understood the name of the fortress, yet among European writers in the Middle Ages it was 'Babylon' and not 'Miṣr' which survived as the name of the place; and the title was even transferred after the building of Cairo to that city, so that its ruler was spoken of as Soldan of Babylon[4].

[1] See above, p. 232 n.

[2] On the other hand, the same Yâḳût seems to have ill understood the name, for he speaks of a 'fortress named Ḳaṣr al Yûn or *Ḳaṣr ash Shâm* or Ḳaṣr ash Shamaʿ' (vol. iv. p. 551).

[3] Waḳidî is quoted by Maḳrîzî as saying that a torch was lighted on the fort upon the first day of every month, when the sun entered a new constellation of the Zodiac; and that the fortress was founded by one of the Pharaohs called Ar Riyân. This is in Waḳidî's usual romantic vein.

[4] See for example Marino Sanuto and the other authors bound together in vol. 29 of the Palestine Pilgrims Text Society's publications.

One word more. Though little is told of the buildings which stood in the interior of the fortress when 'Amr pitched his camp against it, we know that it contained a Nilometer, of which traces remained in the days of Maḳrîzî[1]. We know also that some at least of the churches which were frequented by the Roman garrison, such as the cathedral church of Abû Sargah and possibly Al Mu'allaḳah, may be seen at the present day after the lapse of nearly thirteen centuries[2].

[1] Of the Dair al Banât in Ḳaṣr ash Shama' he says, 'Here before Islâm was the Nilometer, of which there are traces to this day' (*Khiṭaṭ*, quoted in Abû Ṣâliḥ, App., p. 325).

[2] There seems no reason for doubt in the case of Abû Sargah, although when I wrote *Coptic Churches* I did not venture to assign so high an antiquity to any of these buildings. Abû Sargah is mentioned c. 690, in Amélineau's *Vie du Patriarche Isaac*, p. 46. We know also from the fragment of the Life of Benjamin that there was at the conquest a bishop of the castle of Babylon as well as a bishop of Ḥulwân—a singular proof of the number of churches in this region. On the whole subject of the fortress, see Amélineau, *Géog. Copte*, pp. 75 seq.; Quatremère, *Mém. Géog. et Hist.* t. i. pp. 45 seq. and 71 seq.; Hamaker's *Futûḥ Miṣr* by Waḳidî, n. pp. 90 seq., and text p. 41; also n. p. 110 and text p. 60, where Al Mu'allaḳah is stated to have been redeemed by the Copts by purchase from 'Amr, and to have borne a tablet commemorating the fact. On the other hand, though the church existed, one may question whether it occupied its present position across and over the Roman gateway. The exterior walls are certainly non-Roman, and the church rests partly on walls so constructed as to render the use of the gate impossible, and therefore later than the conquest. Waḳidî is mistaken in saying that Dair Bulîs is the same as Ḳaṣr ash Shama' and contains Al Mu'allaḳah. Dair Bulîs, as he calls it, must be that little convent outside the fortress called Dair Bulus, or the Convent of St. Paul, standing in a hollow among the rubbish-mounds south of the fortress. A good illustration of the southern gateway, as it was, may be found in R. Hay's *Illustrations of Cairo* (London, 1840, fol.), but I know of no plan of the building as it originally stood save Pococke's, which is

most inaccurate. The plans under preparation by the Committee for the Conservation of Arab Monuments will furnish a most valuable record at least of the Roman gateway.

The very interesting Jewish synagogue, which was a Christian church dating from before the conquest, has recently been demolished by the Jews to make room for a new place of worship. The Jews have also thrown down a large section of the wall.

PLAN 2.

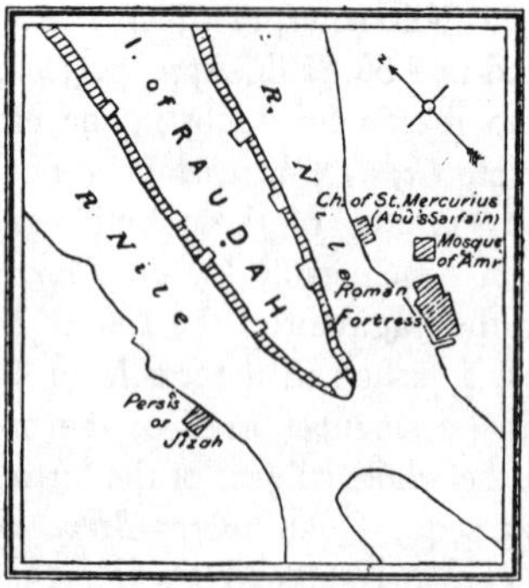

ISLAND OF RAUḌAH AT THE CONQUEST.

CHAPTER XVIII

SIEGE AND SURRENDER OF BABYLON

Position of the Copts. Cyrus the Muḳauḳas beleaguered in the fortress. Weakness or treachery of Cyrus. He crosses to Rauḍah and makes overtures to 'Amr. Roman impressions of the Arabs. 'Ubâdah, 'Amr's envoy, comes to Rauḍah to negotiate. The Arab terms, and their refusal by the Romans. More fighting, followed by a treaty, which Cyrus refers to the Emperor. Recall, disgrace, and exile of Cyrus. Treaty rejected by Heraclius and siege resumed. Fall of the Nile. Campaign in the Delta. Death of Heraclius. The fortress scaled by Zubair. Surrender of the garrison under treaty. Roman barbarity upon the Copts.

WITH the beginning of September 'Amr had not only returned to Babylon, but had made all his dispositions for a regular blockade of the fortress. Its massive walls and lofty towers encircled by the Nile—for the moat was now full of water—promised a long defiance to enemies ignorant of engineering and unprovided with siege equipment. Some few engines of war had been captured in the Fayûm and in Trajan's citadel at Manûf, but the Arabs had no skill to work them or to keep them in repair, and they did but little damage to the garrison [1], though the ridge some 200 yards south of the fortress offered an admirable vantage-ground for the besiegers' batteries.

The fortress stood, as we have seen, on the edge of the river, its long line of western wall awash with the flood, while the Iron Gate opened on the moat or dock on the south side. Opposite lay the island

[1] One or two Arab writers speak of 'Amr setting up his *manganika* against the fortress, but there is no word to suggest that they proved of any advantage to the besiegers.

of Rauḍah, the southern end of which in times of peace at any rate was connected with the fortress by a bridge of boats. Whether the bridge was left standing in war is doubtful; but it is certain that pontoons were kept moored by the Iron Gate in a position of security, and that boats readily passed from the fort to the island. In spite of his victory 'Amr was not yet able to dominate the river. Its swelling tide would have baffled more skilful navigators than the Arabs; and if he had risked an attack from that side, his boats would have been swept away by the flood or sunk by the defenders' catapults.

All the Arab writers are agreed that when the siege began, the Muḳauḳas himself (or the Patriarch Cyrus) was within the walls of Babylon[1]. Theodore too had been there before the battle of Heliopolis, though his actual presence at that battle is not recorded: but when the Roman forces were defeated, he seems to have joined the fugitives and hastened to Alexandria. Cyrus therefore, as Heraclius' Viceroy, was the real commander in Babylon, although the general in charge of the garrison bore another name which the Arabs give as Al 'Araj[2], and which

[1] Ibn 'Abd al Ḥakam, Eutychius, Yâḳût, Maḳrîzî, Abû 'l Maḥâsin, &c. are in harmony on the presence, though of course they differ on the personality, of the Muḳauḳas.

[2] See the Appendix C on Al Muḳauḳas. The confusion on the subject of the commander is very great. Ṭabarî, for example, who actually puts the capitulation of Alexandria before the siege of Miṣr or Babylon, alleges that 'Al Muḳauḳas, prince of the Copts, had named Ibn Maryam as commander of the fortress.' This is very curious, for Al Muḳauḳas, we know, was Cyrus, the bitter enemy and persecutor of the Copts, while Ibn Maryam represents, as I have shown, the Coptic Patriarch who was hiding in Upper Egypt. All that Ṭabarî's sentence can mean is this—that

is probably a corruption of 'George,' though this George must be a different person from his namesake the Prefect, whom 'Amr forced to bridge the canal at Ḳaliûb. Another general who remained through the siege was Eudocianus, elder brother of Domentianus [1]. The forces under George may have amounted to 5,000 or 6,000 men—hardly more—but the garrison was amply provided with food and warlike stores of all kinds. The civil population had been swollen by a number of refugees from the adjacent city of Miṣr and the convents round, but it is probable that most of these were sent away by river, so as to leave the garrison more freedom. All the churches within the walls were now, it must be remembered, in possession of clergy professing Chalcedonian or Melkite opinions, and no other opinion was tolerated. Cyrus had not changed his character as arch-enemy of the Coptic faith—a character which he maintained to the end; and his

a Patriarch was virtual commander. That Patriarch is unquestionably Cyrus. This fact disposes of Eutychius' statement that Al Muḳauḳas 'had kept back the revenues of Egypt ever since Chosroes had been beleaguering Constantinople.' Cyrus did not even come to Egypt until three years after the final defeat of the Persians and death of Chosroes. I should hardly notice this particular misstatement of Eutychius but that it has been accepted as true by modern historians. Thus Gibbon (c. li) makes Al Muḳauḳas 'a rich and noble Egyptian' who 'during the Persian wars had aspired to independence,' and adds that 'the abuse of his trust exposed him to the resentment of Heraclius.' So Prof. Bury makes Al Muḳauḳas 'a Copt who administered Egypt for the Persian king' (*Later Roman Empire*, vol. ii. p. 214), and who subsequently came to terms with 'Amr. See also p. 208, n. 2 supra, where I have quoted a recent writer as speaking of 'the Patriarch Cyrus, in concert with Muḳauḳas.' The fact is that the discovery of the true identity of Al Muḳauḳas profoundly modifies the history of this period.

[1] John of Nikiou, p. 570.

presence in the fort is the strongest proof, if proof were needed, that the only Copts there remaining were those who had been driven by persecution to renounce their creed. Indeed even of those, some, whose sincerity was doubted, were thrown into prison, where, as we shall see, they were treated with great barbarity.

It is therefore a mere perversion of history to speak, as many Arab writers do, of the Copts as the defenders or the dominant party within the fortress. The Copts had simply no existence as a belligerent body. Even their religious unity had been shattered by the ten years' persecution. In the mountains and caves and deserts and in fortified monasteries of Upper Egypt there were still Copts and Coptic communities; but at Babylon, in the Delta, and at Alexandria, all the Copts had been forced within the pale of the established Church, where their secret disloyalty was powerless. Arab historians, writing some centuries after the conquest, naturally speak of Egyptian armies and Egyptian leaders without distinction of Roman or Copt, and the consequent mistakes and misunderstandings are legion: but it cannot be too clearly understood that at this time there was no such thing as a Coptic party in the field. The Copts were wholly out of action—crushed by Cyrus; and it is untrue to represent them as capable of combining among themselves or of fighting or treating with the Arabs.

But while the heart of Cyrus was still hardened against the Copts, he must have felt how ill he had prepared the country to resist a powerful enemy. His reign of violence had brought about a false semblance of religious unity, but it had torn asunder every shred of sympathy between governors and governed. At the best he could only expect that the Copts should watch in sullen aloofness the struggle between two alien and equally detested powers. All hope of saving Egypt by force of arms was ebbing away: was this the result on which he had calculated?

For the moment Al Muḳauḳas was secure in an almost impregnable castle, girdled by the waters of the Nile. The Roman catapults were more than a match for the Muslim bolts and arrows that volleyed across the moat. But as time wore on, the water in the moat was certain to sink, and already the fierce pertinacity of the assailants was causing some misgiving in the fortress and some division of opinion. It was about a month after the siege had begun, i. e. at the beginning of October, 640, that Cyrus summoned those officers of the garrison whom he trusted, together with the Melkite bishop of Babylon, to a secret council of war, and set before them his views. The war had gone against them. Their main army had been destroyed, and they were now beleaguered by a superior force of men, whose fighting capacity was most formidable. For some months at any rate there was no chance of any relieving army taking the field. The fortress might hold out, no doubt; but even so, were the chances of war in their favour? If not, would it not be better to buy off the enemy—to pay him a certain sum to clear out of the country? If such a peace could be purchased—if payment of an indemnity would secure the retirement of the Arabs—would not Egypt be saved for the Empire? Arguments like these, expanded and fired by the eloquence of which Cyrus undoubtedly was master, prevailed with the council, and it was resolved if possible to carry out the plan. But it was essential not to alarm the garrison and the advocates of war to the death: so it was decided that Cyrus and his confederates should take boats by night and steal across to the island of Rauḍah, whence they could open negotiations with the Arab leader in complete tranquillity[1].

The plan was carried out with the utmost secrecy. The Iron Gate on the Nile was opened; and taking the boats there moored, the party crossed to the island, landing at the spot where afterwards the arsenal was erected. George, the commander of the fortress, was probably in the plot, but he remained within the walls to silence any rumours of treachery that might arise when the departure of Cyrus was discovered[2]. Cyrus removed all the pontoons, so

[1] It is needless to dwell on the reasons for rejecting the absurd story of Eutychius that Al Muḳauḳas, being a Copt in sympathies, beguiled the Roman garrison out of the fortress in order to betray it to 'Amr in the Coptic interest. It would be an endless task to criticize here the various versions of the incident in the text; but two facts seem to stand out in most of the versions. These are, (1) that a Patriarch or bishop opened negotiations, and (2) that the Muḳauḳas retired to Rauḍah at the time of high Nile. The intervention of the bishop is put by different authorities at different times, and the retirement to Rauḍah is variously given as occurring one month after the commencement of the siege and as following the capture of the fortress. But even those authorities, like Yâḳût and Suyûṭî, who take the latter view, make the capture occur at high Nile. This of course is wrong; the date of the capture is fixed irrevocably to the beginning of April—the time when the Nile is at its lowest; but the fact that negotiations took place at flood-time is just one of those undesigned coincidences of tradition which may be safely trusted. Its accuracy is further strengthened by the independent tradition which places the time one month after the beginning of the siege. Now the siege began about the end of August, and a month later—about the end of September—the Nile is in fact at its highest. Thus the chronology of the incident is somewhat strongly established.

[2] Maḳrîzî says that opinions differ whether George accompanied

that, in case a panic seized the garrison, they would be unable to leave the fortress; and as soon as he had secured his position on the island[1], he sent envoys to 'Amr, among them being the bishop of Babylon. They were courteously received, and delivered their message. 'You and your army,' they said, 'have invaded our country, and seem bent on fighting us. Your stay in the land is long, no doubt: but you are a small force, far outnumbered by the Romans, who are well-equipped and well-armed. Now too you are surrounded by the waters of the Nile, and are in fact captives in our hand. It would be well for you therefore to send envoys with any proposals you wish to make for an agreement, before the Romans overwhelm you. Then it will be too late, and you will regret your error[2].'

the Muḳauḳas or not. Suyûṭî says that at first he stayed behind, but soon joined the Muḳauḳas.

[1] It must be remembered that at this time the channel on the eastern side of the island, i. e. between the island and the fortress, was as wide as that on the western side. This is clear from the Sefer Nameh, which expressly states that such was the case even 400 years later (1047 A. D.), though it adds that the current on the eastern side was sluggish, showing that the channel had silted up. Now the eastern channel is extremely narrow, and the Nile flows almost entirely on the west. The head of the island or south end remains in its original position, as it has always been strongly walled and fortified against the action of the river. For the Sefer Nameh, see *Relation du Voyage de Nâsiri Khusrau*, p. 153.

[2] This account is from Maḳrîzî, whose detail I shall on the whole follow. He, together with Abû 'l Maḥâsin and Suyûṭî, gives two separate traditions of the conference. The first is that 'Amr entered the fortress to parley, and that a plot was laid to treacherously assassinate him as he was leaving. This story I unhesitatingly reject as pure fiction, noting, however, that the same story is told by Eutychius with reference to Gazah in Palestine (Hamaker's *Futûḥ Miṣr*, p. 84 of notes). The second tradition is that which I have embodied in the text. It may, how-

No immediate answer was given, but the envoys were detained in the Arab camp for two days, during which time they were allowed to go about freely and make their own observations on the life and character of the Muslims. 'Amr then dismissed them with the usual offer of terms. 'Only one of three courses is open to you; (1) Islâm with brotherhood and equality; (2) payment of tribute, and protection with an inferior status; (3) war till God decides between us.'

Cyrus was relieved by the return of the envoys. He had been anxiously asking whether it was lawful under the Muslim religion to kill ambassadors. But the simplicity and the enthusiasm of the Arabs had deeply impressed the Roman messengers. 'We have seen,' they reported, 'a people who prefer death to life and humility to pride. They sit in the dust, and they take their meals on horseback. Their commander is one of themselves: there is no distinction of rank among them. They have fixed hours of prayer at which all pray, first washing their hands and feet, and they pray with reverence.' And despite the harsh precision of the terms offered, Cyrus thought it better to treat now, while the Arab forces were hemmed in by the floods, rather than await the time when they could move freely through the country. He therefore sent back to 'Amr the request that special envoys might be empowered to discuss terms for agreement. 'Amr accordingly deputed ten of his officers, headed by a powerful

ever, be remarked that even according to the first tradition the negotiations with 'Amr, which are alleged to have taken place within the fortress, came to nothing. The two traditions therefore agree in this, that the first overtures for peace made by the Romans proved abortive.

negro called 'Ubâdah ibn aṣ Ṣâmit: but their orders were to accept no terms incompatible with one of the three defined courses.

The Arabs were ferried across to Rauḍah; but when 'Ubâdah was ushered into the presence of Al Muḳauḳas, the latter was shocked and exclaimed, 'Take away that black man: I can have no discussion with him.' But the Arabs explained that 'Ubâdah was one of their most trusted and capable leaders, and that 'Amr had commissioned him personally to treat with the Romans. To the Archbishop's further astonishment, they added that they held negroes and white men in equal respect—that they judged a man by his character, not his colour. And 'Ubâdah, when bidden to speak gently, so as not to frighten the delicate prelate, replied, 'There are a thousand blacks, as black as myself, among our companions. I and they would be ready each to meet and fight a hundred enemies together. We live only to fight for God, and to follow His will. We care nought for wealth, so long as we have wherewithal to stay our hunger and to clothe our bodies. This world is nought to us, the next world is all.' This profession of piety moved the Archbishop. 'Do you hear this?' he said to his companions; 'I much fear that God has sent these men to devastate the world.' Then, turning to 'Ubâdah, he remarked, 'I have listened, good sir, to your account of yourself and your comrades, and I understand why your arms so far have prevailed. I know too that the Romans have failed by caring overmuch for earthly things. But now they are preparing to send against you immense numbers of well-armed battalions. Resistance will be hopeless. But for the sake of peace, we will agree to pay a sum of money at the rate of two dinârs a head for every man in the Arab army, a hundred dinârs for your commander, and a thousand for your Caliph, on condition that you return to your own country.'

To this 'Ubâdah answered, 'Do not deceive yourselves. We are not afraid of your numbers. Our greatest desire is to meet the Romans in battle. If we conquer them, it is well; if not, then we receive the good things of the world to come. Our prayer is for martyrdom in the cause of Islâm, not for safe return to wife and children. Our small numbers cause us no fear; for it is written in the Book, "Many a time hath a small company overcome a great host, by the will of God." Understand, therefore, that we can accept no terms save one of the three conditions which we are ordered by the Caliph to offer you.' Cyrus in vain endeavoured to obtain terms more in accordance with his proposal; his arguments fell on deaf ears; till at last in answer to his final inquiry, 'Ubâdah, losing patience, raised both his hands above his head and exclaimed vehemently, 'No, by the Lord of heaven and earth and all things, you shall have no other terms from us. So make your choice.'

Thereupon Cyrus and his companions held a consultation. To the first alternative they answered uncompromisingly, 'We cannot abandon the religion of Christ for a religion of which we know nothing.' Thus ruling out the adoption of Islâm, there remained only submission, with payment of tribute, or war. They argued that submission to the Muslims and payment of tribute would be tantamount to slavery: death would be easier. But 'Ubâdah explained that both their persons and their property would be respected; that they would retain full control over their possessions and all existing rights of inheritance; that their churches would be left uninjured, and the practice of their religion unmolested. So interpreted, the terms seemed reasonable and even generous to the Muḳauḳas, Cyrus, whose courage was sapped by the secret conviction that the Muslims were destined to conquer. But the Christians were not all prepared to surrender their country so tamely as the foreign Archbishop of Alexandria. George, the commander of the fortress, seems by this time to have joined the conference, and it is certain that violent opposition was offered to Cyrus' proposal to capitulate: but here, as so often in this history, a veil falls on the scene, and one can only conjecture what lies behind[1].

[1] The invincible confusion of the Arab writers (on whom we are just now totally dependent in the silence of John of Nikiou) is nowhere better illustrated than in the close of this incident of the conference. Maḳrîzî says that 'Amr's terms were all refused; that the siege was pressed on; and that the fort was taken, while the Nile was still high. Then, however, the Muḳauḳas 'persuaded his companions to agree to the terms of the Arabs, and wrote to 'Amr that *the Romans and Copts* had prevented acceptance of the conditions before, but now they were desirous of paying tribute.' But the order of events is plainly wrong here, as the fort held out till April. Abû 'l Maḥâsin has much the same story, but he says that Al Muḳauḳas had promised submission *on behalf of the Copts but against their will*, and they refused to ratify the compact. Then the siege was resumed and the fort taken with great slaughter—still at high Nile. The treaty followed. Yâḳût is a little clearer. Referring to the conference with 'Ubâdah, he says that 'the Muḳauḳas made a compact with 'Amr on behalf of the Romans and Copts, subject for the former to the approval of the Emperor, who was at once to be communicated with.' He adds that 'the most learned of the Egyptians' in his day 'took the view that the matter was not settled before the interview between the Muḳauḳas and 'Ubâdah.' Yet even Yâḳût represents the fortress as captured by storm at

It seems, however, that failing agreement upon the Muslim proposals, the Roman chiefs asked for a month to consider the matter. 'Amr answered decisively that he would grant only a three days' armistice. By this time Cyrus' secret action was known to the Roman garrison. His party probably returned from Rauḍah to within the walls of Babylon, where the popular feeling set strongly against Cyrus. Accordingly the advocates of resistance had an easy triumph: the soldiers of the Emperor absolutely refused to surrender. Indeed, this decision was reached so quickly, that by the time the armistice had expired, measures were taken to prepare a sudden onslaught upon the besiegers. No answer

high Nile, and the interview as taking place directly after the capture. These stories therefore are all inconsistent with known fact in some detail or other. But from them we may gather that (1) the interview did take place at high Nile, early in October; (2) it resulted in disagreement and a fresh appeal to arms; (3) the fight was disastrous to the Romans, who now changed their mind; (4) a treaty was concluded subject to the Emperor's approval, which was to be at once demanded. We know that Heraclius repudiated the agreement. This comes out in the Muslim writers, though usually in connexion with Alexandria—an entirely wrong place, because (1) Heraclius was dead when the treaty of Alexandria was made; and (2) the treaty of Alexandria was made by direct authority of the then reigning Emperor. Balâdhurî, in his confused summary of various traditions, gives one which is correct: for he says that the compact made by Al Muḳauḳas with 'Amr was repudiated by Heraclius, who sent an army to Alexandria: the gates were shut, and the city prepared for siege. So also through the strange distortions of Eutychius' narrative the fact that a treaty between 'Amr and the Muḳauḳas was made at Babylon emerges. The treaty accordingly must be regarded as historical, though the precise circumstances attending its conclusion are lost. The incident of the attack after the three days' armistice comes from Ṭabarî, who, however, errs in company with the Arab writers in making no appreciable interval between the armistice and the final surrender of the fortress.

was sent to 'Amr; but on the fourth day, when the armistice was over, while the Arab commander was considering what action to take, the Romans sallied out over their drawbridges and fell upon the camp of their unsuspecting enemy. The Arabs, though completely surprised, flew to arms, and a desperate battle ensued. But bravely as the Romans fought, their army, which was ere long outnumbered, was slowly driven back, and after severe losses made good its retreat within the walls.

Al Muḳauḳas, whose dark and tortuous mind was still haunted by thoughts of surrender, now found his opportunity. The army, which had scorned his counsel, had trusted to the sword: in the battle they had demeaned themselves as Roman soldiers should: yet though they had taken the foe at a disadvantage, by the sword they had fallen. As Viceroy of Egypt, Cyrus could see no prospect of driving the invaders out of the country, and this fresh failure only confirmed his evil forebodings. He found the party of resistance weakened and disheartened, and he had little difficulty now in securing a gloomy assent to his proposal for re-opening negotiations with 'Amr. It is somewhat surprising to find that the terms offered by 'Amr remained the same, but there is no reason to think that they varied either now or at any later period in the war. The alternative chosen by the Romans was, of course, subjection and tribute; and this arrangement was embodied in a treaty, which was concluded on the express condition that it was subject to the approval of the Emperor. Cyrus undertook to submit the treaty to Heraclius immediately, and it was agreed that pending ratification there should be no change in the military situation, or at least that the fortress should not be surrendered.

It was at this juncture that Cyrus, Al Muḳauḳas, took his departure from Babylon and hastened down the Nile to Alexandria, whence he sent urgent dispatches to the Emperor, regretting the action which he had been forced to take, and explaining the absolute necessity of coming to terms with the Arabs. He therefore prayed the Emperor to confirm the agreement for a treaty and so deliver Egypt from the miseries of war. Heraclius may well have been puzzled by this communication. Did the proposed treaty relate to Babylon alone, or did it cover the surrender of all Egypt, including Alexandria? Were the Arabs merely to receive a tribute of money and to retire, or were they to remain masters of the country? Was Egypt, in a word, to be torn from the Empire and delivered to the enemies of Christendom? For months past the Emperor had been reproaching his generals and Cyrus, his Viceroy, with their shameful mismanagement, which had suffered a handful of Saracens to plant their standards in Egypt and to defy the imperial forces. Now it was proposed either to bribe the barbarians to retire, or to yield them possession of the whole province, with all its corn and gold. What was the meaning of this surrender? Cyrus must come and give an account of his viceroyalty.

It was probably about the middle of November when a peremptory message of recall reached Cyrus. Its tone was not reassuring, and his conscience may well have quailed as he prepared the account of his stewardship for his master. He alone knew how far he had betrayed and how far he had followed either the letter or the spirit of the Emperor's instructions during the ten years of the Great Persecution: but he could not disguise the fact that his religious mission had been a disastrous failure, while the ruin of his schemes was bringing about the political ruin of Egypt. Withal he must have been conscious, that however honest his motives might be as shaped to himself, yet his easy despair of the Roman cause, and his readiness—even anxiety—to parley with the enemy, clouded his conduct with the suspicion of treachery. Thoughts like these must have weighed down his spirit, as he reached the Emperor's presence in Constantinople. He met with an angry reception. He could only admit the truth of the charge that he had agreed to pay the gold of Egypt to the Arabs[1]: but apparently he thought, or feigned to think, that they could still be prevailed upon to quit the country, and he urged that the tribute might be met by a special tax upon merchandise at Alexandria, so that the imperial revenues would be in no way diminished. For the rest, he saw no hope. The Arabs were not as other men: they had, as they said, no earthly wants but bread for sustenance and a garment to cover their bodies. They were 'a people of death,' holding it gain to be killed and sent to paradise, whereas the Romans loved the things of this life and clung to them. If the Emperor saw the Arabs and knew their fighting powers, he would be forced to acknowledge that they were

[1] It is this fact which, taken out of its proper setting and misconstrued by Theophanes, has given rise to the story of tribute paid by Cyrus prior to the Arab conquest in order to purchase immunity from invasion. The commission of Manuel to carry on the war, which Theophanes assigns to this period, comes in reality much later, long after the death of Heraclius, as will be shown towards the close of this volume.

invincible. It was therefore better to come to terms with 'Amr, before the capture of Babylon placed Egypt at his mercy.

Such was the defence of the Viceroy. Nicephorus adds that before the recall of Cyrus the Emperor had dispatched Marinus to take council with him, and to devise with him measures for dealing with the Saracen crisis: and that, concurrently with the proposal to pay tribute, Cyrus had suggested that Eudocia, or another daughter of the Emperor, should be given in marriage to 'Amr, who would then receive baptism and become a Christian. This story seems to me extremely improbable—a mere wild echo of the arrangement by which Eudocia was promised in marriage many years previously to the chief of the Khazars. Cyrus can have been under no illusion with regard to the uncompromising quality of the Muslim religion, and such a conversion of 'Amr passes all romance. Nor is there the slightest warrant for the story in any other chronicle. But it needed not this to fire the wrath of Heraclius. He asked angrily if 100,000 Romans were not a match for 12,000 Saracens. Al Muḳauḳas—as we may still call Cyrus even in the Byzantine capital—was arraigned on a charge of betraying the Empire to the Saracens, and being adjudged guilty was threatened with death. Heraclius taunted him with behaviour worthy of an Egyptian peasant, called him an abject coward and a heathen, and delivered him over to the city Prefect, at whose hands he suffered great indignities[1]; then he was sent into exile.

Meanwhile the rejection of the treaty by the Roman Emperor must have become known in the

[1] The word used by Nicephorus, αἰκισομένῳ, seems to mean this rather than torture, as interpreted by Le Quien.

Arab camp at Babylon before the end of the year 640. All truce or half-measures were now over, and both sides braced themselves afresh for the struggle. The Nile was fast falling, and, as it fell, the waters in the moat sank lower and lower: with it sank the hope, if not the courage, of the defenders. But as the receding flood emptied the moat, the Romans sought to make good the loss by sprinkling the bottom of the ditch with spiked caltrops, which they sowed more thickly in front of the gates. These tactics the Muslims doubtless met by throwing down the embankment and endeavouring to level an approach. But generally few details of the siege operations remain. We read of missiles and battering-rams, of sallies and assaults; but it is abundantly clear that the Arabs, owing to their want of engineering science, made very slow progress towards the reduction of the fortress. It may even be doubted whether the blockade, though closely set on the landward side, was ever effective on the side of the river. But here the Muslims seemed to have derived some help from a local combination of the Green and Blue factions, probably those of the conquered Fayûm[1]. Bands of adventurers under Menas, chief of the Greens, and Cosmas, son of Samuel, chief of the Blues, were in the habit of crossing the river in boats by night and raiding the island of Rauḍah, or falling on any Roman vessels passing to the fortress or moored at the Iron Gate. These tactics harassed the defenders, and partly cancelled their advantage in the freedom of the river.

But even on land the watch was not always well kept by the Muslims. One day a small patrol went

[1] John of Nikiou, p. 568.

out of the fortress and fell upon Zubair and 'Ubâdah at the time of their devotions. The Arab chiefs at once leapt on their horses, charged, and chased the Romans, who, as the enemy were gaining upon them, threw off their girdles and ornaments. The proffered spoil was neglected, but the Romans managed to secure their retreat within the fortress, 'Ubâdah being slightly wounded by a stone slung from the battlements [1]. Scorning to lift the Roman trappings the two Arabs returned to their place and finished their prayers, while the Roman soldiers came out again and recovered what they had thrown away.

Waḳidî gives particulars of another battle. One Friday, as the Muslim host were gathering together for prayer, 'Amr moved among the crowd exhorting his men to fight valiantly. A Roman spy watched the proceedings and reported them at Babylon. After the usual sermon 'Amr came down from the rude platform on which he had spoken, and while he was leading the solemn recital of prayer, a Roman force, which had crept up unobserved, suddenly swooped on the defenceless Muslims, and caused them some loss [2].

But as the winter waned, sallies and combats without the walls grew rarer, assaults upon them fiercer and more frequent. The Romans, worn out by watching and fighting, found their defences harder to guard. Although the ramparts were little

[1] This account, taken from Abû 'l Maḥâsin, is much more probable than that of Maḳrîzî, who says that when the Roman soldiers re-entered the fort, 'Ubâdah threw stones over the walls and went away!

[2] Ed. Hamaker, p. 104, notes. On p. 55 of text are the names of several Muslims slain in the siege.

weakened, if at all, the numbers within were thinned by the plague[1] which now was making havoc in the garrison: while the sentinels upon the round towers scanned the horizon in vain for the flash of Roman spear and cuirass beyond the white domes of the convents which dotted the plain northwards. For now was the time, when the floods were down, if ever a relieving army was to save Babylon.

Indeed it was probably at this period of the war that news reached 'Amr of an army assembling under Theodore in the country between the two branches of the Nile. 'Amr did not wait to be attacked; but leaving a strong enough force to maintain the investment of Babylon, he moved up the Damietta branch, crossed the river at Athrîb, and struck northwards in the direction of Samanûd. Theodore dispatched two of his generals to hold that city, and their column effected a junction with a body of local militia. These, however, refused to follow the Roman standards or to fight the Arabs. Nevertheless battle was given in the region of Samanûd, with somewhat disastrous results for the Muslim force and for some renegade Christians who had adopted Islâm and enrolled under its banners. Great numbers of Muslims and their allies perished, and 'Amr found that he could inflict no serious mischief on the northern towns, which were protected against cavalry by moats and canals. He therefore fell back to Bûṣîr and fortified it: the defences of Manûf and Athrîb were also repaired, and garrisons were left within them. But if Theodore won some

[1] It is Yâḳût who mentions the plague, and the fact may be accepted, although coupled with the absurd statement that 12,300 persons within the fortress were slain by the arrows of the Muslims.

advantage in this brief campaign, he was unable to follow it up, and he never succeeded in placing a relieving force anywhere near beleaguered Babylon[1], to which place ʻAmr now returned.

The inaction of Theodore may have been partly due to treachery and desertion on the Roman side. How far the local militia was composed of Copts and how far of Roman troops is not known: but during the centuries of Roman occupation there must have been a mingling of blood and of sentiment which is too often forgotten by historians. The Copts had good reason to hate the Empire; and on some of the Romans, even apart from religious motives, their loyalty sat so lightly that it was shaken off by the passion or self-interest of the moment. Two cases of the kind are recorded in connexion with this episode. A general named Kalâdjî had gone over to the Muslims, but Theodore contrived to see him, and used the strongest arguments to secure his return. Kalâdjî had left hostages in the shape of his wife and his mother in Alexandria, and he agreed to purchase their safety and his own pardon from Theodore for a large sum of money. Accordingly he stole away

[1] This episode is not free from doubt. It is given in John of Nikiou, chapter cxiv, which, however, is full of perplexity. The text says on the one hand that ʻAmr started upon this expedition ʻ leaving a strong force *in* the citadel of Babylon,' and on the other hand it leaves the Romans in possession of Nikiou. Zotenberg suggests altering the text in a way that would read *at* (or *before*) Babylon instead of *in* Babylon: and this is the best solution. If this emendation is rejected, the alternative is to place the expedition between the fall of Babylon and the fall of Nikiou: but the interval of time is too short, and this alternative is practically impossible. The fact is that the events in this and the following chapters of John's Chronicle are tumbled topsy-turvy, and the task of resetting them in order is almost hopeless.

with his troops from the Muslim camp at dead of night, and rejoined Theodore, who sent him on to strengthen the garrison of Nikiou under Domentianus. The other traitor who repented was called Sabendîs[1]. Like Kalâdjî he made his escape from the Muslims by night, but he fled down the river to Damietta, which was held by a general named John. By John he was sent on to Alexandria with a letter to the acting governor. He confessed his crime with tears, but said, 'I acted as I did because I had been put to open shame by John, who regardless of my age, had struck me in the face. Thereupon I, who had been a devoted servant of the Empire, went over to the Arabs.' So weak were the bonds of patriotism and religion even among the Romans.

So at Babylon day followed day without any sign or message of hope to cheer the defenders. It was only ill news that reached them. They had heard of Heraclius' indignation against Cyrus and his policy of surrender, and of the sentence of exile pronounced on the Archbishop: but the legions of which the Emperor boasted still tarried, and the imperative orders which he sent to his generals seemed resultless, so far as concerned the fate of Babylon. Yet hope was not quite abandoned, until at last one day early in the month of March, 641, a great shout went up in the Muslim camp, and the garrison heard that news had come of Heraclius' death. Then indeed their courage failed. They can but have dimly conjectured the turmoil into which this event was destined to plunge the Empire; but the end of the old warrior king was enough to cause profound discouragement and depression. 'God broke down

[1] These names are certainly corrupt; but I give them as they stand in John of Nikiou.

the power of the Romans by his death,' says the Arab historian[1], and his words well express the effect of the change upon the armies in Egypt. It gave corresponding elation to the Arabs, who redoubled their efforts to carry the fortress.

But for more than another month Babylon defied capture. Then as victory still delayed, Zubair is said to have solemnly devoted himself as the leader of a storming party, for which preparations were ready. The moat had been filled in at the place destined for the assault, despite all resistance of the sickly and enfeebled garrison. But the actual moment of the attack was skilfully concealed, and the assault was delivered with such swiftness under cover of night[2] that Zubair's scaling-ladder was set against the wall unnoticed[3]. The Arab hero sprang

[1] Suyûṭî, who however gives the wrong date, A. H. 19, while quoting Al Laith for the true date, A. H. 20, or 641 A. D. Makîn has the same remark with the same error of date, and, like Suyûṭî, he makes the news of Heraclius' death arrive during the siege of Alexandria instead of Babylon. Heraclius died Feb. 11, 641, months before the siege of Alexandria commenced. Maḳrîzî makes the same blunder, but he adds that 'the Muslims were encouraged by the Emperor's death, and continued the siege with renewed vigour.'

[2] Ya'ḳûbî is the only writer who mentions the fact that the assault was made at night: see *Ibn Wâdhih qui dicitur Al Ja'cûbî Historiae*, ed. M. T. Houtsma, vol. ii. p. 168.

[3] It is not easy to decide at what point the Arab scaling-ladders were applied. Both Maḳrîzî and Abû 'l Maḥâsin say that it was near what was called in their day the Market-place of Al Ḥammâm, and Yâḳût says it was 'near the site of the subsequent house of Abû Ṣâliḥ al Ḥarrânî, adjoining the Baths of Abû Naṣr as Sarrâj, by the aforesaid Market-place.' Eutychius agrees that it was by the Sûḳ al Ḥammâm, and adds that it was on the south side of the fortress—a detail which seems curiously confirmed by Balâdhurî. For this writer, after speaking of Zubair's arrival, which of course was from the north, says that he planted the ladder on the

from it, sword in hand, upon the battlements, shouting the Muslim war-cry 'Allahû Akbar,' while, as the defenders rallied, a fierce rain of arrows swept the walls from without, and gave Zubair's companions time to swarm up the ladder and make good their footing upon the parapet within. It seems that, in expectation of an assault upon this section of the wall, the Romans had blocked the ramparts by a cross-wall at either end, so that the scaling-party, after overpowering the guard upon that section and winning possession of the top of the wall, found their passage barred, and were unable to reach the stairs that led down within the fortress. They had effected a lodgement on the ramparts, but could go no further. Now was the opportunity for the defenders: if they had only retained strength and spirit enough, they might in turn have poured such a fire of arrows into the band of Muslims as would have cleared them off. But the limit of their endurance was reached. After a hurried consultation among the leaders of the

opposite side, i.e. the south. But the place named as Sûḳ al Ḥammâm was probably part of the subsequent city of Fusṭâṭ, which has now entirely disappeared. It would seem, however, that the assault was delivered somewhere near the south-east angle of the fortress, where the walls are still standing.

The authenticity of the incident cannot, I think, be doubted. Balâdhurî says that when Fusṭâṭ was built, Zubair built a house for himself, 'which his son inherited, and in which the ladder wherewith the wall of Babylon was first mounted *is still kept*'; i.e. ninth century. Yâḳût also says, 'Zubair's ladder is said to have been preserved in a house in the Market-place of Wardân until the house was burnt down after A.H. 390' (circa 1000 A.D.).

Yâḳût speaks of a second ladder as having been mounted by Shuraḥbîl ibn Ḥajîah al Marâdî 'near the Street of the Flute-Players'; but this indication also has perished with the city of Fusṭâṭ.

defence in the dawning light, a parley was sounded, and George, the commander of the fortress, offered to capitulate, provided the lives of his soldiers were spared. 'Amr at once approved the terms, much to the indignation of Zubair, who urged that he had been on the point of taking the fortress by storm. 'If you had only waited a little,' he said, 'I should have got down from the wall inside the fortress, and then it would have been all over.' But 'Amr paid no heed to his remonstrance: a treaty of surrender was drawn up, under which it was agreed that in three days' time the garrison should evacuate the fortress, retiring by river, and carrying only what was necessary for a few days' subsistence; that the fortress itself, with all treasure and war material, should be delivered over to the Arabs[1]; and that the town should become tributary.

[1] It has been very difficult to construct an intelligible story of the fall of Babylon. The story of Zubair's escalade seems to come originally from Ibn 'Abd al Ḥakam, but generally is twisted by the Arab chroniclers into a shape of absurdity. As Maḳrîzî gives it, the garrison fled on hearing the Muslim cry: Zubair opened the gates, and the Arabs rushed in: whereupon 'the Muḳauḳas, in fear of his life, proposed submission and tribute.' The Muḳauḳas was no longer there, and such proposals would be ridiculous *after* a complete capture by storm. Abû 'l Maḥâsin gives precisely the same version. Suyûṭî is nearly as bad; for he says that when the Muslims had entered the fort, the Muḳauḳas began to negotiate with 'Amr. But the version in the text above comes from Ṭabarî, and is at once so clear and so rational that I have no hesitation in believing it, much as that author has in other respects confused the incidents of the conquest. I should add that there is a general agreement fixing the duration of the investment at seven months, although the date of surrender is confused with that of the unratified treaty of Cyrus, and so is made to coincide with high Nile. Weil in his *Geschichte der Chalifen* has been completely misled on this point, affirming the capture at high Nile, and rejecting the seven months' siege: but his whole scheme of chronology is wrong, e. g.

The final assault of the Muslims took place on Good Friday, April 6, 641, and the evacuation on the following Easter Monday[1]. In the interval the fleet of boats was collected from Rauḍah and provisioned, and all preparations were made for the retreat of the garrison down the Nile. It was a mournful coincidence for the Christian army that their last day within the fortress should be the day of the Resurrection; and one would fain picture them as thronging the churches in sorrow and self-abasement for their defeat by the followers of Mohammed. It must, however, be recorded that neither the solemnity of the crisis in the history of Christian rule in Egypt, nor the solemnity of the day, availed to abate the fury of religious passion in the hearts of the Roman leaders. We have already seen that early in the siege a number of Copts in Babylon had been thrown into prison, either from their refusal to abandon their creed or

he makes 'Amr arrive at Babylon in January. The account of Ṭabarî is supplemented by that of John of Nikiou, who in chap. cxvii (which is obviously out of order) gives the actual surrender of Babylon, though the story of the siege is missing.

[1] Easter Monday is given with absolute clearness by John of Nikiou. He does not mention Good Friday: but (1) Friday is the Muslim *dies faustus*, and is the most probable day for Zubair's act of self-devotion; and (2) John of Nikiou makes it clear that the garrison were allowed an interval of a day or two before the evacuation, because they had leisure on Easter Day to commit the acts of barbarity, which he records, upon the Coptic prisoners. I may add that Ibn 'Abd al Ḥakam gives a letter from Omar to 'Amr complaining of the delay in the capture of Alexandria (the context shows, I think, that Babylon is intended), and in the letter are the words 'Let the attack be made on Friday evening, for that is the time when mercy descends and prayer is answered.' This is recorded by Suyûṭî (p. 72): and we know that Zubair's assault was at night.

on suspicion of disloyalty. Easter Day was made a day of vengeance upon these unfortunate prisoners, who, after being dragged out of their cells and scourged, had their hands cut off by soldiers acting under the orders of Eudocianus. It is small wonder that the wrath of the Egyptian bishop is launched upon 'those enemies of Christ, who have defiled the Church by an unclean faith, and who have wrought apostasies and deeds of violence such as neither pagan nor barbarian hath wrought: they have despised Christ and His servants, and we have not found such evil-doers even among the worshippers of false idols[1].' He describes the groans and tears of the mutilated captives, as they were driven out of the fort in scorn; and, however illogical, it is not unnatural for him to think that the fall of Babylon was a divine chastisement upon the Romans for their savage maltreatment of the Copts. Truly the incident shows what implacable hatred divided the two religious parties among the Christians even at the moment when the fruits of disunion were fatally visible in the triumph of Islâm.

[1] John of Nikiou, p. 567.

CHAPTER XIX

MARCH ON ALEXANDRIA

The Treaty of Babylon: its nature and limits. Arab lesson to the natives. Renegade Christians. Restoration of Nile bridges. Advance of the Arab army northwards. Nikiou their objective. Battle at Ṭarrânah. Cowardly retreat of Domentianus, and capture of Nikiou by the Arabs. Massacre there. Advance continued. Fighting at Kûm Sharîk, Sunṭais, and Kariûn. Defeat of the Romans and retreat of Theodore. The Muslims reach Alexandria. Their view of the city, and their powerlessness against it. 'Amr's Delta campaign. Failure at Sakhâ. His march to Tûkh and Damsîs, and return to Babylon. Historical fallacies refuted.

THE siege of Babylon, which ended on April 9, 641, had lasted for seven months. That fact is clearly preserved in Arab tradition, although the abortive treaty made by Al Muḳauḳas at high Nile, a few weeks after the siege began, is confounded by practically all the Arab writers with the final treaty of surrender, made when Al Muḳauḳas was banished from Egypt. In the light of the true story one sees how the confusion arose, and with it another confusion scarcely less remarkable. No question is more keenly debated by these writers than the question whether Miṣr—by which they sometimes mean Babylon and sometimes Egypt—was taken by treaty or by force. As regards Babylon we now know that there is a real foundation for a difference of opinion; for on the one hand it was an act of force—the storming of Zubair—which put an end to the resistance of the Romans, and on the other hand that act of force was not a full capture by storm, though it caused the fortress forthwith to capitulate. Still the truth remains that Babylon was surrendered under treaty, and that the treaty provided for the retirement of the garrison. Hence we must reject the story of great slaughter wrought within the walls as a mere growth of legend upon the version of capture by force[1].

But the compact made at Babylon was a military convention and not a political treaty. 'Amr was content to purchase possession of the fortress at the price of the withdrawal of the Romans, who neither accepted Islâm nor agreed to pay tribute. But tribute was laid on all the inhabitants of the city who remained behind. As this arrangement was of purely local significance, so the tribute imposed was but slight and temporary. One authority gives it as a dinâr for each of the Arabs, together with a change of raiment[2], which latter they greatly needed. This squares very well with a story told by another writer[3], who says that after the sur-

[1] Eutychius says that while the garrison retreated by boat to Rauḍah, the Muslims slew, took captive, and plundered. Maḳrîzî agrees that 'many of the inhabitants were slain, many made prisoners.' Possibly some bloodshed did occur; but Suyûṭî says, 'The Muslims took the fort and *slaughtered the garrison*'—a very different story, in which he improves on Abû 'l Maḥâsin, who alleges that 'when the fort was taken, there was great slaughter.' No credence whatever can be given to the report noticed by Maḳrîzî and Suyûṭî that 12,300 Romans were slain by arrows within the fortress after the siege was over.

[2] Maḳrîzî cites the Ḥadîth of Ibn Wahb, quoting from 'Abdarraḥman ibn Shuraib for this highly probable statement. The raiment consisted of *jubbah*, *burnus*, turban, and pair of shoes. If the Arab forces were by this time reduced to 12,000 men, this would account for the 12,000 dinârs recorded, of course mistakenly, by some writers as the total tribute imposed on Egypt, the name *Miṣr* being wrongly extended, as often happens, from the town to the country.

[3] Ṭabarî. When he speaks of *Coptic* soldiers, he may mean Egyptians who had been enrolled in the Roman army as local

render there remained at Miṣr a great number of Coptic soldiers. These seeing the Muslims in rags and tatters remarked, 'Alas! why did we not know that the Arabs were in such an evil plight? For we would have continued the struggle, and not delivered the city.' When 'Amr heard of this, he invited some of the leaders among them to dinner. He had a camel slaughtered, and the flesh boiled in salt water and set before a mixed company of Copts and Arabs. The Arabs ate of the meat, but the Copts only turned away in disgust, and went home dinnerless. Next day 'Amr ordered his cooks to search the town of Miṣr for every dainty and delicate dish it could provide to dress a banquet. This was done, and the same company sat down to a sumptuous repast. When dinner was over, 'Amr spoke to the Copts as follows: 'I must have for you all the regard which our kinship imposes. But I understand that you are plotting to take up arms once more against me. Now aforetime the Arabs ate camel's meat, as you saw yesterday; but now when they have discovered all this dainty fare that you see before you, do you think that they will surrender this city? I tell you they will give their lives first; they will fight to the death. Do not therefore hurl yourselves to destruction. Either embrace the religion of Islâm, or pay your tribute, and go your ways to your villages[1].'

militia—a force which certainly existed, as is clear from John of Nikiou. The remark about kinship would be meaningless applied to Roman soldiers. Yet it is fair to observe that Ṭabarî often speaks of Copts where he can only mean Romans. In any case the story is not of serious importance, though it illustrates 'Amr's character.

[1] Ibn al Athîr gives a rather different version of this tradition. 'Amr, he says, learned that the Copts spoke disparagingly of the

This anecdote is at least curious as showing the other side to those lofty professions of indifference to the good things of this world which we have seen uttered by 'Ubâdah and quoted by Cyrus. It is perhaps memorable for another reason, because it cannot be questioned that now the alternative of Islâm was chosen by some of the Copts rather than payment of tribute. The temptation of equality and honour and brotherhood with the conquerors, together with the prospect of plunder in lieu of taxation, proved too strong for many of those Egyptians whose own creed had been crushed out by the millstones of Cyrus' persecution; and some of the Roman soldiers and settlers similarly abandoned their religion. These are the men who, in the words of the Coptic bishop of Nikiou, 'apostatized from the Christian faith and embraced the faith of the beast'; renegades who now, under the cloak of zeal for the Muslim cause, aided in seizing the possessions of those Christians whom the war had driven from their homes and in blaspheming them as 'enemies of God[1].' But these apostates were few

Arabs for their poverty and rough way of life; whereupon, fearing that this frame of mind might lead to rebellion, he resolved to overawe the Copts by illustrating the difference between the luxury of Egypt and the coarse diet of the Arabs, and by pointing out that on this hard fare the Muslims had conquered the far more numerous armies of their enemies. The lesson made a deep impression on the Egyptians, who remarked, 'The Arabs are invincible: they have cast us down beneath their feet.' When this story was reported to Omar, he is said to have remarked that 'Amr made war by argument, as other warriors by force.

[1] John of Nikiou, p. 560. Abû Ṣâliḥ has a curious tradition that the district adjoining Cairo on the south, long called Al Ḥamrâ, derived its name from the fact that there 'the Red Standard (Ar Râyat al Ḥamrâ) stood at the time of the conquest of Miṣr by the Arabs, and around it were gathered those who

in number; the bulk of the Coptic people scorned them and their new-found religion alike, as is proved by the bishop's language. Once more, however, it must be repeated that the Copts at this period had neither leader nor organic unity. They were therefore incapable of corporate action. Isolated persons and isolated communities among them determined their own course of conduct from time to time, but always in isolation, since there were no means either for the formation or for the execution of any collective purpose. Accordingly it is quite erroneous to speak of the Copts in general as party to the treaty of Babylon, which concerned only the people of that locality. But the terms of the convention were offered to people in the vicinity; thus 'Abdallah ibn Ḥudhâfah as Saḥmî went by 'Amr's orders to Heliopolis and received the submission of the town and the country round it[1], a fact which

asked protection of the Muslims and marched in their rear-guard' (p. 102). On the other hand, Ibn Duḳmâḳ, in describing the several quarters of Fusṭâṭ, writes: 'Then the three Ḥamrâs, which were so-called because the Romans settled in them: for they were the quarters of Bilî ibn 'Amr ibn al Hâf ibn Kuḍâ'ah, and of the Banû Baḥr, and of the Banû Salâmât, and of Yashkur of the tribe of Lakhm, and of Ḥudhail ibn Madrakah, and of the Banû Naid, and of the Banû 'l Azraḳ, who were Romans' (part iv. p. 5). I do not know what is the connexion between 'Ḥamrâ' and 'Roman,' but it is stated in the context that these Romans and one Rûbîl, a Jew, 'had marched from Syria to Egypt, and were among the non-Arab inhabitants of Syria, who accepted Islâm before the battle of Yermouk.'

[1] This comes from Balâdhurî. The statement is doubtless correct, and to it we may trace that confusion between the first capture and the final subjection of Heliopolis which vitiates the narrative of Ṭabarî and others. That the number who came under this treaty was small is indicated by Abû 'l Maḥâsin, who gives 6,000 souls as the total, while he quotes 'Abdallah ibn Lahî'ah as giving 8,000, who by it were rendered liable to poll-tax (p. 19).

seems to show that at the previous occupation of the place no Muslim administration was established.

But though the treaty was local, its results were felt all over the Roman Empire. Babylon or Memphis had long ceased to be the capital of Egypt: it had been eclipsed by the power and splendour of Alexander's city: but it was the gate between Upper and Lower Egypt, and a strong enemy planted in the wellnigh impregnable fortress had all Upper Egypt at his mercy, and dominated the Delta far northwards. What the Roman generals were doing all the winter through, and why they allowed the Muslim army to slowly wear down the resistance of Babylon, are questions that perhaps will never be answered; but it is certain that by the capture of the fortress their own power, both moral and material, was greatly shaken, and that of the Arabs immensely strengthened. By Pelusium, Bilbais, Athrîb, and Heliopolis 'Amr now held all the east side of the Delta: at Babylon he held its apex and gripped the whole valley of the Nile in the middle. The conquest of Egypt was half accomplished.

It must have been after the fall of the fortress, and not before as the chronicles imply, that 'Amr ordered a bridge of boats to be built—or rather restored—from Babylon to Rauḍah, and Rauḍah to Jîzah, thus spanning the whole width of the Nile and controlling all traffic and transport upon it. But the Arab commander was anxious to launch his army, too long chained to their camp at Miṣr, on the way towards Alexandria. In less than three months the Nile would begin to rise again, and therefore time was precious. While dispatches were sent to Omar reporting progress and requesting more troops, arrangements were rapidly made for the administration of the conquered town and territory: the fortress walls were repaired, and a strong garrison was left under the command of Khârijah ibn Ḥudhâfah[1]. Then, with his army remounted, 'Amr turned his back on Babylon, rejoicing to take the field again, and pushed northwards, following the western main of the Nile. The general's tent was left in position; for just as it was ordered to be struck, it was discovered that a dove had nested in the top part and there laid her eggs; whereupon 'Amr remarked, 'She has taken refuge under our protection. Let the tent stand, till she has hatched her brood and they are flown away.' It is even said that a sentinel was left to prevent the dove from being molested[2].

It is not very easy to trace the movements of the Arab forces in the campaign which now opened, because the Chronicle of John of Nikiou in these last chapters often seems a mere collection of fragments of history flung together at haphazard, and such narrative as can be founded upon it is often at total variance with Arab records. Yet a certain amount of reconcilement is possible, and there are points on which the coincidence is striking.

There can be no doubt that the first point at which 'Amr aimed on his march to Alexandria was Nikiou. This was a city of great importance and

[1] I have already noted that this statement, which comes from Arab sources, is supported by a contemporary document, No. 553 in Karabacek's *Papyrus Erzherzog Rainer: Führer durch die Ausstellung*.

[2] I have given Yâḳût's version of this familiar story. It fits very well with the time of year when 'Amr left Babylon—the end of April—and it has the ring of truth. The appeal for protection, even on the part of an enemy, was sacred in the eyes of the Muslims.

a fortress of great strength[1]. It lay on the river bank—on the east side of the western or Rosetta branch of the Nile—a long day's journey from Babylon, but only about two hours distant from Manûf, which was already in the Arabs' possession. Nikiou was not merely a flourishing town, marking its antiquity by colossal remains from the days of the Pharaohs; it was also the seat of one of the chief bishoprics of Christian Egypt, and a place of the highest strategical value in the defence of the military route between Babylon and Alexandria. It was here therefore that the Roman resistance should have centred for a fresh stand against the Arabs.

Moreover it seems that 'Amr began his northward march on the western[2] or desert side of the Nile, where his cavalry could move with freedom, unhampered by the network of canals in the Delta. The Romans were prepared in a fashion for this movement, and the first encounter took place at the

[1] I have shown in the note on p. 16 that the site of the ancient Nikiou is to be found at the modern village of Shabshîr towards the north-east of Manûf on the Nile.

[2] The name Wardân preserved in a village on the western side, coupled with the tradition given by Maḳrîzî, clearly suggests that 'Amr at first followed the western bank on his march to Nikiou. Indeed, provided that he was sure of crossing the Nile at Aṭrîs or Banî Salâmah, that route offered fewer obstacles than the canal-seamed country between the two branches of the river. Maḳrîzî's words are as follows: 'On his way to Alexandria 'Amr laid waste the village called Kharbat Wardân. There is a dispute as to the cause of this devastation. Sa'îd ibn 'Ufair says that when 'Amr marched to Naḳyûs to fight the Romans, he left Wardân behind in this village to settle affairs, but the people seized and carried him off. When at last he was found hidden in a house, 'Amr ordered that the village should be destroyed. Another account is that some of 'Amr's rearguard were slain here.'

ancient and important city of Terenouti, or Ṭarnûṭ, or Ṭarrânah, as the Arabs learned to call it. Ṭarrânah was a regular crossing-place on the Nile, on the way to Alexandria[1]: it was also the point of departure for the great Coptic monasteries in the Libyan desert: and it was natural that the Roman armies should not yield it without resistance. They gave battle[2] to 'Amr, and at least saved their honour, though they suffered defeat, and the Arabs were able to continue their advance towards Nikiou.

Nikiou lay, as we have seen, on the right bank of the river, near the place where the Pharaonic canal from Athrîb and Manûf joined the Nile. It was too strong a fortress to leave on his flank: so the Arab leader was compelled to cross the river for its reduction, and to recross subsequently. The Roman commander therefore had a fine opportunity for aggressive tactics. But instead of taking the command here in person with the bulk of his forces, Theodore relied on the weak and cowardly Domentianus to hold Nikiou with an inadequate garrison. Domentianus had a considerable fleet of boats, which he meant to employ merely

[1] See Amélineau, *Géog. Copte*, p. 493, 'C'est là qu' Apatîr va passer le Nil, venant d'Alexandrie, pour se rendre à Babylone d'Égypte,' and the other references given.

[2] This battle is recorded by Yâḳût, who says, 'At Ṭarnûṭ there was a battle between 'Amr and the Romans.' Maḳrîzî makes a strange blunder in this connexion. For in his account of 'Amr's march from Babylon against Alexandria, he says (vol. i. p. 163, Bûlâḳ ed.) that 'Amr encountered none of the Roman forces till he reached Mareotis, and a few lines lower he places 'Amr behind at Mareotis, while his advance columns are at Kûm Sharîk! The absurdity of this vanishes if instead of Marîûṭ مريوط we read طرنوط Ṭarnûṭ, which is certainly correct: but the slip illustrates the manner in which history is perverted by writers or copyists ignorant of geography.

for the defence of the town or to contest the subsequent passage of the Nile, which 'Amr here must make, and which possibly he might even essay if he failed to capture the fortress. But when the Roman general found that the Muslim army was in close proximity, his heart failed, and abandoning army and fleet he took flight in a boat to Alexandria. Finding themselves thus betrayed by their leader, the garrison flung away their arms and rushed down into the canal [1] in a mad endeavour to cross it or to reach the boats. But the panic spread to the boatmen, who, thinking of their own safety, unmoored with all speed and fled in disorder down the Nile, each man making for his own village. Meanwhile the Arabs came up, and falling on the defenceless Roman soldiers in the water put every man to the sword, with the single exception of Zachariah, a man who showed extraordinary valour, and was perhaps spared for that reason. The entry of the Arabs into the town was unopposed: there was not a soldier left to offer resistance. Nevertheless they signalized their victory by a cruel massacre. 'They slew every one whom they encountered in the streets, and those who had taken refuge in the churches, sparing neither men nor women nor little children. From Nikiou they went to other places round about, plundering and killing all before them. In the town of Ṣaûnâ they found Scutaeus and his people (who were related to Theodore) hiding in a vineyard, and they put them to the sword. But it is time to cease: for it is impossible to recount the iniquities committed by the Muslims after their capture of the island of

[1] This description proves the canal to have lain northward of the town of Nikiou, and confirms the identification of the site with Shabshîr.

Nikiou on Sunday, the eighteenth day of the month Genbôt, in the fifteenth year of the cycle,' which date corresponds to May 13, 641 [1].

This passage of the Coptic bishop I have given in full, because it shows how little reason the Copts as a body had to sympathize, and how little they did in fact sympathize, with their Saracen conquerors. For Nikiou was a stronghold of the Coptic faith; and though Cyrus had scourged the people till they renounced its open profession, yet it cannot be questioned that in their hearts the victims of the persecution retained their old allegiance. But Copts and Romans alike were now overwhelmed in indiscriminate slaughter, the record of which contains no word to suggest that Copts were entitled to look for different treatment. At the same time it is clear that division and disorder were spreading like a plague through the country, and it was not long before civil war was added to the calamities of the time. Lower Egypt was split into two camps, one party siding with the Romans, while the other wished to join the invaders. Whether the dividing lines were those of race or creed, or, as seems probable, of faction, is a question left unanswered. But battle and pillage and burning of towns were common incidents in the conflict of the two parties, while the Arabs looked with contempt and distrust on these uncovenanted partisans.

[1] John of Nikiou, p. 568. For the date see my Appendix D. Zotenberg gives the name of the town as Ṣâ. But Ṣâ, the ancient Sais, lies nearly as far north as Damanhûr, quite beyond the range of the Arabs at this moment. The heading to the chapter gives Ṣaûnâ as the name of the town, and this I have adopted. For Zotenberg's *Esqoûṭâos* I have ventured to conjecture *Scutaeus*, for a vowel would necessarily be prefixed to render such a name in Arabic, through which language the story passed into the Ethiopic.

The capture of Nikiou[1] and the dispersal of the Roman fleet on the Nile opened the way for the advance on Alexandria, towards which the main body of the Roman army under Theodore was slowly retiring.

'Amr took up his quarters at Nikiou for a few days; but, ere resuming his march after crossing the river, he sent his lieutenant, Sharîk, to pursue the retreating enemy. The way now lay along the left bank of the Nile, skirting the edge of the desert, and the country was favourable for cavalry. The Muslim advance forces overtook the Romans at a place about sixteen miles due north of Ṭarrânah, but they found the enemy in greater strength than they had expected. Indeed, so far from routing the Romans at the first onset, they are said to have fought for three days; and at one period of the contest the Arabs were repulsed and driven up some rising ground, where they stood at bay under fierce assaults from the Romans, who surrounded them. In this dangerous plight Sharîk ordered Mâlik ibn Nâi'mah, who possessed a bay horse of unrivalled swiftness, to make his way through or round the enemy and carry a message to 'Amr. This Mâlik succeeded in doing: for though some of the Romans gave chase, they were unable to overtake him. On hearing of the danger in which Sharîk stood, 'Amr hurried troops forward at the utmost speed. It is said that the mere news of their coming turned the army of Theodore to flight: it is certain that Sharîk was relieved, and the Romans lost the opportunity of overwhelming this detachment of the Saracens, as

[1] The Arab historians know nothing of this event and pass it over in absolute silence. The battle of Nikiou mentioned by Yâḳût is that which took place in Manuel's rebellion.

they had lost every opportunity which fortune offered. The scene of the battle was called after the Arab leader, Kûm Sharîk[1], or the Mound of Sharîk, which name remains to this day.

Steadily pushing the enemy before him, 'Amr now probably marched north-east, still following the canal which borders the desert, till he reached Dalingât, and from that point struck due northwards in the direction of Damanhûr. Once more he found a Roman army barring his passage at a place called Sunṭais[2], about six miles south of Damanhûr, and once more an obstinate engagement resulted in the retreat of the Romans. They made no effort to rally at Damanhûr or to hold the town; but streaming north from the battlefield they struck the high road to Alexandria, crossed the canal, which now was nearly empty, and took refuge under the fort of Kariûn after a march of some twenty miles. Kariûn was the last in the chain of fortresses between Babylon and Alexandria, and it was a place of great importance for the corn traffic. Strategically too it controlled the canal on which Alexandria mainly depended both for food and for water: but although

[1] The details of this incident come from Maḳrîzî, who seems to be copying Ibn 'Abd al Ḥakam. Ockley gives the odd form Keram 'l Shoraik to the place: but his whole account of the conquest is a tangle of misstatement and misplacement which fairly rivals that of the Arab writers. Eutychius calls the place the Vineyard of Shurîk, but it is very unlikely than any vineyard was there.

[2] Maḳrîzî gives the form *Sulṭais*. In the translation of Eutychius the name appears as *Salstan*—an obvious corruption. Weil in giving the form *Siltis* suggests that it should be *Samiatis*, or, as Ewald conjectures, *Sunṭais*. There can be no question that the last is the right form. Sunṭais is a considerable village, almost equidistant from Kûm Sharîk and Kariûn.

the defences had been strengthened by the Romans, they in no wise compared with strongholds like Babylon or even Nikiou [1]. Here, however, Theodore resolved to make his last stand, nor could he have chosen a better position than this, where the advantage of numbers was aided by the works of the fortress and the canal, while his retreat on Alexandria was easy to secure.

Although the Roman army had been greatly dejected by the fall of Babylon and Nikiou, and by the treason and cowardice displayed by some of its leaders, yet even the Muslim writers admit that during this phase of the struggle it fought with obstinate valour. It was strong in numbers, large reinforcements having come over-sea from Constantinople. Theodore himself, though totally incompetent as general, was not wanting in courage or fighting spirit. Not merely the Alexandrian

[1] As regards the name Kariûn see Amélineau, *Géog. Copte*, p. 217, who gives the Coptic form ϫⲉⲣⲉⲩ and the Greek χαιρεου (*sic*), but does not give the more familiar *Chaereum*. John of Nikiou in chap. lxvii says that the sweet-water canal (which the heading calls the canal of Kariûn) was made by Cleopatra. Procopius in *The Buildings of Justinian* avers that 'the Nile does not flow as far as Alexandria, but, after reaching the city of Chaereum, proceeds to the left. The ancients dug a deep channel from Chaereum and turned part of the Nile stream into it to flow into Lake Marea. This channel is nowhere navigable for large ships, but at Chaereum the corn is transferred from the large vessels into barges and so brought to Alexandria' (Palestine Pilgrims Text Soc., vol. ii. p. 152). John specially says that Cleopatra's canal was navigable for large vessels, but of course the navigation depended on the state of the waterway. Ibn Ḥauḳal describes Kariûn in his day as 'a large and beautiful town on both banks of the Alexandrian canal. In summer when the Nile rises, merchants take boat there for the journey up to Fusṭâṭ. . . . The town is the seat of a governor, who has under his orders the garrison composed of cavalry and infantry' (Quatremère, *Mém. Géog. et Hist.* t. i. p. 419).

army, but all the country round, realized the critical nature of the coming conflict at Kariûn, and contingents flocked to the Roman standard, not only from Sunṭais, but from more distant towns like Khais, Sakhâ, and Balḥîb[1]. It was no single engagement that decided the fate of Kariûn. The fighting was not only severe, but it lasted over a period of ten days. In one of the battles, Wardân, the well-known freedman of 'Amr, was carrying the Muslim colours, and 'Amr's son 'Abdallah was badly wounded by his side. Half fainting in the heat of the combat, 'Abdallah asked his comrade to retreat a little that

[1] This is from Balâdhurî (p. 220), who directly associates the Copts with the Romans in the struggle at Kariûn. Sakhâ is between the two branches of the Nile, about twenty miles north-west of Samanûd. I cannot find any name in modern Egyptian charts corresponding to Balḥît, or Balḥîb as Yâḳût more correctly writes it, in accord with the Coptic πελϩιπ; but the place was well known and was the scene of a revolt by the Copts in A.H. 156 (Quatremère, *Recherches*, &c., p. 198). Its position is discussed by Quatremère (*Observations sur quelques Points de la Géographie de l'Égypte*, pp. 45 seq.), who shows that Ibn Ḥauḳal places it six *saks* north of Sandiûn on the Nile, at the junction of a small western branch with the Rosetta main. This, taking the *sak* at about one and a quarter miles, would place Balḥîb, as Quatremère shows, somewhere near what he writes *Mentoubes*, but what is given in the Domains map of the Delta as *Metoubes*. But clearly Balḥîb was on the left, not on the right, bank of the river. The small branch has long disappeared in a morass, but there is a hamlet called Dîbî in the place required, and the name *Dîbî* may even be an echo of the lost Balḥîb. It lies in the bend of the river some ten or twelve miles south of Rosetta. Amélineau (*Géog. Copte*, p. 314) is wrong in saying that the junction spoken of by Ibn Ḥauḳal was formerly at the village of 'Dirouet.' Dairûṭ is close to Sandiûn, though across the river, and Amélineau cannot have read Quatremère very carefully.

Khais was in the region of Damietta: see Quatremère, *Mém. Géog. et Hist.* t. i. p. 337. Yâḳût gives Farṭasâ (or Ḳarṭasâ) among the towns that resisted 'Amr, while he adds that 'Amr made terms with Balḥîb.

they might have more air to breathe in. 'Air?' replied Wardân: 'you want air in front of you and not behind you': and they pressed forward together. 'Amr, hearing of his son's mishap, sent a messenger to inquire of his welfare, whereupon 'Abdallah quoted some verses of reassuring tenour. This answer was brought to the chief, who exclaimed, 'He is my son indeed[1].' Fiercely, however, as the Muslims charged time after time, the issue hung in doubt, and 'Amr prayed the 'prayer of fear.' It looks as if this was a drawn battle, although the Arab writers make it a crowning victory. However that may be, there can be no doubt that at the end of the ten days the Muslims were so far victorious that they captured the town and fortress of Kariûn, driving back the Roman army. Whether the Romans were chased in headlong flight to the gates of Alexandria, or whether Theodore retreated in good order, cannot be determined, although the impartial record of John of Nikiou seems in favour of the latter alternative.

These various engagements from Ṭarrânah to Kariûn must have caused serious losses on both sides. The Romans were better able to bear them; but if allowance is made for the garrisons left by the Muslims at Babylon and various points in the Delta, it becomes clear that 'Amr's further advance would have been impossible, if he had not received heavy reinforcements during the preceding winter or spring.

[1] Maḳrîzî gives this story, and is the authority for the ten days' fighting. Balâdhurî merely speaks of an engagement at Kariûn. John of Nikiou is unhappily very brief. He remarks that 'Amr launched a great force of Muslims towards Alexandria, and they took possession of Kariûn, its garrison under Theodore retiring to Alexandria.

He could not have ventured to appear before Alexandria with less than 15,000 men: it would probably be nearer the truth to place his effective force now at 20,000. The capture of Kariûn had completely cleared the way to the capital; and as soon as his troops had recovered from the strain of the recent fighting, 'Amr moved on, and covered unopposed the last stage of the march to Alexandria.

Many of the soldiers in that army must have seen beautiful cities in Palestine, like Edessa, Damascus, and Jerusalem; some may even have gazed on the far-famed splendours of Antioch or the wonders of Palmyra; but nothing can have prepared them for the extraordinary magnificence of the city which now rose before them, as they passed among the gardens and vineyards and convents abounding in its environs. Alexandria was, even in the seventh century, the finest city in the world: with the possible exception of ancient Carthage and Rome, the art of the builder has never produced anything like it before or since. Far as the eye could reach ran that matchless line of walls and towers which for centuries later excited the enthusiasm of travellers. Beyond and above them gleamed domes and pediments, columns and obelisks, statues, temples, and palaces. To the left [1] the view was bounded by the lofty Serapeum with its gilded roofs, and by the citadel on which Diocletian's Column stood conspicuous [2]: to the right the great cathedral of St. Mark was seen, and further west those obelisks, called Cleopatra's Needles [3],

[1] The Arabs approached the city from the south-east.

[2] That the so-called Pompey's Pillar was on the citadel is proved by the recent researches of M. Botti, Director of the Alexandrian Museum.

[3] These obelisks it was reserved for British and American

which even then were over 2,000 years old, or twice as old as the city's foundation. The space between was filled with outlines of brilliant architecture: and in the background, towering from the sea, stood that stupendous monument known as the Pharos, which rightly ranked as one of the wonders of the world. Even these half-barbarian warriors from the desert must have been strangely moved by the stateliness and grandeur, as well as by the size and strength, of the city they had come to conquer [1].

The garrison amounted at this time to not less than 50,000 men: the place was amply provisioned,

vandalism to remove from Egypt: one is now on the Thames Embankment, one in New York. They were originally brought from Heliopolis in the reign of Augustus. Their height, about 68 feet, would enable at least their tops to be seen from some little distance without the walls.

[1] There is a legend that 'Amr had seen Alexandria before. The story is that in his younger days he twice saved the life of a Greek deacon—once by giving him water when he was dying of thirst, and again by killing a snake which was about to attack him in his sleep. The deacon in gratitude promised him 2,000 gold pieces (£1,000) if he would come to Alexandria. 'Amr therefore accompanied him, and while in the city took part in a game played with a crown-embroidered ball in the Hippodrome. 'Amr succeeded in catching the ball in his sleeve. 'Such a thing never happened to any one,' say the Arab writers, 'without his becoming ruler of Egypt.' The reward named in this legend is not the least romantic part of it. Still 'Amr may well have visited Alexandria in the course of trade, and he may have played a game in which a player who caught the ball was called 'king.' The story can be read in Ockley and Weil, but it comes from Ibn 'Abd al Ḥakam, and is quoted at length by Maḳrîzî. One version makes the encounter with the deacon take place near Jerusalem, another near Alexandria. Abû Ṣâliḥ (p. 75) says, ''Amr had visited Egypt during the days of ignorance, and knew the roads leading thither, through trading there together with one of the tribe of the Ḳuraish'; and this is very likely the truth. Maḳrîzî's account is in *Khiṭaṭ*, vol. i. p. 158.

resting on the sea, where the Muslims had not a single vessel to contest the Emperor's supremacy: and the walls were armed with that powerful artillery which, as we have seen, in the time of Nicetas had availed to crush and sink the river-fleets of an enemy. On the other hand the Arabs were totally destitute of siege equipment, being unable to transport the engines of war they had captured, and totally untrained in the art of siege warfare. The Romans therefore had every material reason for confidence in defying the rude methods of the Saracen horsemen; while they in turn, reviewing their extraordinary successes against the fenced cities of Palestine and of Egypt, found moral causes enough to give them assurance of ultimate victory. But such moral causes were destined to operate slowly: and when 'Amr launched his troops in a mad tilt against the walls, the Roman catapults on the battlements hurled such a rain of heavy stones upon them that they were driven back out of range, nor could they again face the fire delivered by that artillery. All that the Muslims could do was to maintain their camp at a respectful distance in the hope that the enemy might be unwise enough to sally out and give battle.

There is no trustworthy record of any such engagement. This incident of the ill-judged attack and its easy repulse under the pounding of the catapults sums up all that John of Nikiou[1] has to say about the use of force against Alexandria; and his silence must be taken to mean that siege in the proper sense there was none. On the north the city was defended by the sea, on the south by the canal and Lake Mareotis, and on the west again by the Dragon

[1] p. 570.

Canal: on the east side and south-east alone the approach was open, and here the besiegers were unable to come even within bowshot of the walls. They were accordingly reduced to the necessity of proceeding by blockade, and that could only be of the most partial and ineffective kind: the idea of surrounding the city even on the landward side was quite chimerical. At the same time the maintenance of an army encamped outside Alexandria was a permanent challenge to the Romans, and cut them off from the rest of Egypt. Precisely where the camp was pitched is hard to determine. Suyûṭî says that it was 'between Ḥulwah and Ḳaṣr Fâris, and beyond the latter.' Ḳaṣr Fâris, or the Fort of the Persians, was on the east side [1], and it may have been built by them as a necessary part of their siege operations, just as we know that Diocletian had been totally unable to make any impression on the strength of Alexandria until he had built a fortress to the east of the city [2]. But even then it required a vast army, a siege of long duration, and treason within the walls, to enable Diocletian to break through the almost impregnable defences. But we may take it for granted that the Muslims were at once reduced to passive measures, and that their camp, wherever situated, was merely

[1] See note, p. 90 supra, and the passage in Barhebraeus there referred to. Abû 'l Fidâ agrees with Suyûṭî; while Ibn 'Abd al Ḥakam says that after remaining two months at Ḥulwah, the Arabs advanced to Al Maḳs on the west side.

[2] John of Nikiou, p. 417. The passage deserves quoting: 'He succeeded in capturing Alexandria only after he had raised a fortress to the east of the city, and there spent a long time. At last some of the inhabitants came and showed him a place where he could effect an entrance; but it was only with an immense army that he vanquished the resistance of the city with the utmost difficulty.'

a camp of observation. Indeed there is reason to doubt whether any encampment was maintained within sight of Alexandria, or nearer than Kariûn.

It was now about the end of June. The Arab leader was not the man to cherish illusions with regard to the chances of storming the city. He realized that for offensive warfare he was completely powerless against it. On the other hand, he could trust his followers to hold their own against superior numbers, if the enemy dared come out to battle. Therefore, as the Nile was now about to rise, he resolved to leave an adequate army in the camp, and to take such troops as could be spared across the Delta before the country became impassable[1].

[1] One ought not perhaps to pass over in silence the statements of the Arab historians with regard to the Copts at this period. Ibn 'Abd al Ḥakam says that the Copts helped the Arabs in every way they required, and that the Coptic chiefs kept the roads and bridges and markets open for them on the march to Alexandria; and other writers have copied this report. Unfortunately Ibn 'Abd al Ḥakam completely disarranges the order of events, and no reliance whatever can be placed on this assertion as indicating any general action on the part of the Copts at the moment in question. At the same time it is true, as we have seen, that assistance was rendered by the renegades who had turned Muslim and by those Egyptians whose services were requisitioned. But I have no doubt that the whole statement refers to the period of Manuel's revolt. Even less worthy of credence is Balâdhurî, who says that when the Arabs appeared before Alexandria, the Copts in the city wished to come to terms, and Al Muḳauḳas asked for an armistice, which was refused. The story goes on to tell that Al Muḳauḳas then, in order to give the Arabs an impression of the great numbers of the garrison, put women and children on the walls with their faces turned inwards, while the men stood facing the enemy. 'Amr thereon sent a message saying, 'Our conquests have not been made by force of numbers. We have encountered your Emperor Heraclius, and you know the result.' The truth of this remark so struck Al Muḳauḳas, that he again counselled submission; but the people reproached him with cowardice and treachery, and insisted

But as the Romans had abandoned the country round Alexandria, all the pleasant houses and wealthy villas outside the walls fell a prey to the Saracens. They secured an immense booty, and pulled most of the dwellings to pieces, merely for the sake of the wood and the iron, which they sent by barges on the Nile to Babylon for use in bridging operations there against some hitherto inaccessible city[1].

The column which 'Amr now led across the Delta cannot have been a large one. Little resistance was likely to be encountered, except at the fortified places, and these it was now too late in the season to besiege, even had he any such intention. But as he had to return to Babylon, 'Amr purposed at any rate to

on fighting. All this is pure romance. Al Muḳauḳas had long been in exile, and the story is a mere echo from the siege of Babylon. Both Copts and Romans in isolated cases went over to the Muslim side; neither as a body welcomed or sided with the invaders.

[1] This is from John of Nikiou's ch. cxv, which is needlessly misunderstood, and wrongly corrected, in Zotenberg's note (n. 1, p. 562). Upon the text, which runs as follows, 'Alors il alla rejoindre ses troupes établies dans la citadelle de Babylone d'Égypte et leur remit tout le butin qu'il avait fait à Alexandrie. Il fit détruire les maisons des habitants d'Alexandrie qui avaient pris la fuite,' Zotenberg remarks 'il faut lire "Babylone" au lieu de "la citadelle de Babylone"'; but the latter is quite correct, as the Arabs were in possession of the citadel. He adds, '"Le butin fait à Alexandrie" et "les habitants d'Alexandrie" sont deux autres erreurs de traduction'; but surely the plunder of the suburbs is rightly described as 'taken at Alexandria,' and it is no stretch of language to call the dwellers in the suburbs 'inhabitants of Alexandria.'

I agree with Zotenberg in finding it impossible to understand the passage describing the purpose for which the wood and iron were employed. The 'city of the two rivers' cannot mean Rauḍah, but must be some city in the Delta. The road to it from Babylon must have necessitated bridges of some sort.

make his presence felt in Lower Egypt. Accordingly he marched back to Kariûn and Damanhûr, and thence struck eastward through the province now called Gharbîah till he came to Sakhâ. This place, which lies about twenty-two miles nearly due north of the modern Ṭanṭah, was then and for long after the conquest regarded as the capital of the province, and it was strongly fortified[1]. Any hopes of surprising the town were disappointed: once again the Arabs had to acknowledge their weakness and failure against strong walls encompassed by water: and they pushed on southward, probably following the Baḥr al Nuzam, till they came to Ṭûkh, which lies about six miles north-east of Ṭanṭah, and from Ṭûkh to Damsîs[2]. At both places they were easily

[1] Yâḳût says, 'Sakhâ is the fortress of the province of Al Gharbîah and the residence of the wâlî. It was taken by Khârijah ibn Ḥudhâfah, when 'Amr invaded Egypt' (vol. iii. p. 51). But Khârijah was left in command at Babylon, and John of Nikiou (p. 561) distinctly says that on this occasion 'Amr could do nothing against Sakhâ. The capture was made at a later stage in the war. Sakhâ is one of the few places in the Delta mentioned both by John and by the Arab writers.

[2] In John of Nikiou's account of this matter the words are 'Il marcha sur Sakhâ et sur Ṭûkhô-Damsîs,' as rendered by Zotenberg. Amélineau ingeniously conjectures that in the latter name the Ethiopic has run together the two Arabic names Ṭûkh and Damsîs, mistaking the copulative for a termination (*Géog. Copte*, p. 525). This is quite convincing. As regards Ṭûkh, there are at least six places of that name in the Delta—Ṭûkh al Aklâm in Dakhalîah; Ṭûkh Dalakah, Ṭûkh al Balâghtah, and Ṭûkh Ṭanbîshâ in Manûfîah; Ṭûkh al Malik in Ḳaliûbîah; and Ṭûkh Mazîd in Gharbîah. The last of these is probably, from its position, the one in question here.

Damsîs, now called Mît Damsîs, lies about nine miles due east of Ṭûkh Mazîd on the right bank of the Damietta branch. In the Domains map of Lower Egypt (Cairo, 1888) the name is wrongly given as 'Mit Ramses'—a curious error. Niebuhr gives it correctly as 'Miet Demsîs' (*Voyage en Arabie*, &c., t. i. map, p. 71).

repulsed. A raid down the eastern branch of the river to Damietta is mentioned in the same connexion, and may have been made by 'Amr's column at this time. Its object was to burn the crops now ripening for harvest, and it achieved no other result. No progress was made in the task of reducing the Delta to subjection, a task in which the Muslims had now been occupied for twelve months[1], and 'Amr, after many futile acts of violence and pillage, brought his column back to the fortress of Babylon. The number of points at which 'Amr encountered resistance throughout the Delta, and his almost total failure against the more northern provinces, add one more to the many proofs destructive of the two current fallacies—that 'Egypt surrendered almost without striking a blow,' and that 'the Egyptians hailed the invaders as deliverers.'

[1] John says that 'Amr 'spent twelve years in warring against the Christians of northern Egypt, but failed nevertheless in reducing their cities' (Dr. Charles' version). Zotenberg conjectures *two* years instead of twelve; but this would be wrong in point of chronology. If we read twelve *months* instead of years, the chronology is right, because it was now about the end of July, 641, and the first operations against the Delta towns began after the battle of Heliopolis in July, 640.

CHAPTER XX

EVENTS AT CONSTANTINOPLE

Last days of Heraclius. Constantine and Heraclius II left partners with the Empress. Recall of Cyrus from exile. Death of Constantine. Rebellion of Valentine. Plan for restoration of Cyrus to Alexandria. Cyrus' motives for yielding to the Arabs. Accession of Constans. Martina in favour of peace with the Muslims. Theodore and Cyrus sent back to Egypt. Theodore's plan for escape to Pentapolis, and its miscarriage. They land at Alexandria.

WHILE the events thus chronicled were passing in Egypt, great changes had also taken place at Constantinople. The death of Heraclius has been briefly recorded as happening towards the end of the siege of Babylon. After his melancholy farewell to Syria in 636, his mind, which had suffered some derangement, slowly recovered its balance in the seclusion of Chalcedon: and in dealing with the crisis on the European side of his Empire he displayed something of his old alertness and skill in diplomacy. But his health was broken: and the ravages of a painful disease were quickened by the monotonous recurrence of disasters, first in Syria, then in Egypt. The fall of Jerusalem had been followed by the fall of Antioch and of Caesarea and by the practical abandonment of Syria to the enemy: yet Heraclius was keenly alive to the importance of saving Egypt for the Empire. The drain of men and money caused by years of war had been enormous, but his diminished armies and exchequer could still furnish large reinforcements for the defence of the Nile. When Arab historians assert that he intended to command an expedition in person[1], they forget that the invasion of Egypt began little more than a year before his death, and by that time the mortal disease which was upon him had robbed him of all physical activity, if not of the very power of motion. The Emperor died on Sunday, February 11, 641[2], in the thirty-first year of his reign, aged sixty-six, two months before the surrender of Babylon.

[1] E.g. Suyûṭî, who writes: 'Reinforcements kept arriving by sea from the Emperor for the Romans in Alexandria; for he said, "If the Arabs take Alexandria, there will be an end of Roman sovereignty." Now the Romans had no more important churches than those of Alexandria; and when the Arabs had conquered Syria, their festival (i. e. Easter) was kept at Alexandria. The Emperor commanded that the city should be well provisioned and its walls put into good repair, intending himself to take part in its defence, because of its great importance; but as the Emperor was finishing his preparations, God destroyed him' (p. 70). The date which the writer gives for the Emperor's death, and the context generally, make it clear that Heraclius the elder is referred to.

[2] This date may be taken as fixed, but there are the usual discrepancies on the subject. Theophanes and Cedrenus give March 11, Indict. 14, after a reign of thirty years and ten months: which is impossible, as the reign began in October. The *Chronicon Orientale* says that the Emperor died on Feb. 9 or 15 Meshîr, after a reign of thirty-one years and five months. Though Feb. 9 does correspond to 15 Meshîr, this term properly reckoned would bring us to March, 642. But Nicephorus put the duration of the reign very precisely at thirty years, four months, and six days. Heraclius was proclaimed on Oct. 5, 610 (*Later Roman Empire*, vol. ii. p. 206), and counting from that date the term given by Nicephorus we come to Feb. 11, 641. This day was Sunday, as the *Chronicon Orientale* requires, whereas Feb. 9, which it gives, was Friday. Lebeau has the date correct; but his editor, de Saint-Martin (*Histoire du Bas Empire*, t. xi. p. 283), in a note prefers the mistaken date of Theophanes and Cedrenus, remarking, 'As no other author gives the precise date of Heraclius' death, there must be an error in Lebeau's text'! I may add that John of Nikiou gives 'the month of Yakâtit, which is February of the Romans, in

So ended the strange vicissitudes of a great career. The work of his life had been to rebuild the shattered fabric of the Eastern Empire. It was a hopeless task when he essayed it: yet he accomplished it, or seemed to accomplish it, in an almost miraculous manner. But his downfall began with his triumph. The fabric he had raised lacked all cohesion, since his own unwisdom loosened or destroyed those bonds of common citizenship and common Christianity which might have held the people together under a system of religious toleration. That this fatal policy of the Emperor synchronized with the rise of the Muslim power from unknown Arabia is one of the most strange and most inscrutable coincidences of history. So fell, however, the destined order of the world: and Heraclius lived long enough to realize the mistakes he had committed, or at least to deplore the fatality which destroyed all the fruits of his labours. In matters relating to the Church he had followed the maxims of his time: his misfortune was that he had not risen above them, nor devised new principles of Church statesmanship to meet the new requirements of the age. For that failure he deserves rather pity than blame, though some remorse must have been added to the physical sufferings which closed his life. Before he died, he made all arrangements for the succession, and he made his son Constantine swear to show mercy to all prisoners and exiles, and to recall those whom he had banished[1]. The Emperor was buried in the church of the Holy Apostles, and his tomb was left open for three days: with his body was placed the

the fourteenth year of the cycle, and the year 357 of the Martyrs,' which is right in every particular.

[1] Sebeos.

crown of gold. This Constantine removed, but it was subsequently restored by Heraclius II, and dedicated to the church [1].

By the will of Heraclius, Constantine, the son of his first wife Eudocia, and Heraclius, the son of his second wife Martina, were left co-heirs of the Empire with the Empress. It was an impossible compromise; and the strong-willed Martina, who had virtually ruled alone during the close of her husband's life, was not a woman to brook such a division of authority. Constantine, the elder of the two half-brothers, was given the pre-eminence by the people, and the treasurer, Philagrius, sided with him as well as Valentine, who was now created general and sent in command to Asia Minor [2]: so that Martina's designs in favour of her own son, Heraclius (or Heraclonas, as he was called for distinction), met with strong resistance. Sergius, the Patriarch, had passed away before his sovereign, and a monk named Pyrrhus had been elected in his place. Pyrrhus seems for awhile at first to have sided against Martina with Constantine, and to have proclaimed Constantine Emperor to the exclusion of Martina and her children [3]. But David and Marinus had

[1] Nicephorus, who says the crown was valued at 70 lb. of gold.

[2] This comes from Sebeos. Prof. Bury justly remarks that 'the history of the successors of Heraclius is veiled in the most profound obscurity,' and regrets that there are no contemporary historians (*Later Roman Empire*, vol. ii. p. 281). But Sebeos and John of Nikiou are both practically contemporary, and both contribute a fair amount to the history of this period. Sebeos, no doubt, is chiefly concerned with Armenia; John has a wider scope, though naturally his main interest is in Egypt. Both, however, are hard to understand.

[3] John of Nikiou, p. 564. The statement is very clear, although quite against the received story. Thus Prof. Bury makes Martina 'in close league with the monothelitic Patriarch Pyrrhus' (Id., ib.,

Pyrrhus kidnapped and secretly conveyed to an island in the west of Africa[1].

In fulfilment of his father's behest, Constantine now sent a large fleet to bring Cyrus back from exile[2]. He wished to confer with the Archbishop on the state of Egypt, and Martina also pressed for his recall, as she was sure of his sympathy with her ambitions. Both the date and the result of this conference are quite uncertain, because it is not known where Cyrus was exiled, or how long it took for him to return to the capital. But Theodore was also summoned from Egypt to advise the Emperor, while Anastasius[3] was left in command of Alexandria and the towns on the littoral, which had not yet

p. 282). Pyrrhus must have changed sides: for John himself (p. 579) quotes a letter, said to have been addressed in the joint name of Martina and Pyrrhus to David, the Matarguem, urging him to make war against the elder branch of Heraclius' family.

[1] Possibly Malta or Gozo is intended.

[2] Mr. Brooks, in his article in the *Byzantinische Zeitschrift* (1895, p. 441) discussing this passage of John of Nikiou, says that the fleet was merely sent to bring Cyrus from Constantinople to Chalcedon. But John's words are: 'Constantine assembled a great number of vessels, and sent them under Kiriûs and Salâkriûs to bring the Patriarch Cyrus to him.' Surely no large fleet was necessary for such a short journey. It is clear that Cyrus was still in exile, and though the place is unknown, the fact of his exile is not doubtful. John ascribes the recall of Cyrus to Martina, who doubtless urged it upon Constantine (p. 582).

[3] I have here taken a slight liberty with the text of John of Nikiou, transposing the two names. The text runs, 'he sent orders to Anastasius to come to him, leaving Theodore to guard the city of Alexandria and the cities of the coast' (p. 564). But I think that these names must have been interchanged, because (1) Theodore was the commander-in-chief, and Anastasius' superior; (2) on p. 574 we find that Anastasius was actually governor of Alexandria prior to the return of Cyrus; and (3) on p. 573 Theodore is with Cyrus at Rhodes on his way back to Egypt.

fallen to the Muslims. Theodore was not in favour of any peace policy: and, whatever Cyrus may have said, he prevailed on the Emperor to promise that he would send large reinforcements to Egypt during the summer. Orders were actually given and vessels were made ready for the embarkation of troops, when Constantine, whose health had been failing ever since his accession to the throne, was seized by a fatal illness. He died on May 25, 641, after a reign of about a hundred days. Whether he died a natural death, or whether he suffered from foul play at the hands of Martina, is uncertain: but the charge of murder was openly made by Constans against the Empress, and the suspicion of it haunts the records of the time [1].

Martina profited by the death of Constantine to proclaim Heraclonas sovereign of the Roman Empire. As a concession to popular feeling, Pyrrhus was recalled from exile; but the renewed ascendency of Martina kindled a resentment which soon flamed into rebellion. When Valentine heard of the death of Constantine and of Philagrius' disgrace which followed, he came with his army to Chalcedon, where Martina was, and demanded Philagrius' reinstatement. This was agreed to by the troops of the Empress, and confirmed in a set speech by

[1] John shows that Constantine's sickness began with his accession, but that his end came from a vomit of blood—possibly the rupture of a blood-vessel. Nicephorus agrees that the illness was of long duration. Theophanes seems to accuse Pyrrhus of contriving the murder with Martina, but Pyrrhus was in exile, and not a partisan of Martina's. Cyrus may be meant, as the two names are often confused (see Zotenberg's note 1, p. 564 of John of Nikiou): but the charge is probably groundless. Sebeos uses a curious expression in saying that Constantine 'died, deceived by his mother.'

Heraclonas; but, not content with this measure of success, Valentine crossed with Domentianus and other patricians to the capital, and there crowned the son of Constantine, known as Constans II, in association with Heraclonas [1].

It seems certain that before this revolt of Valentine broke out, Heraclonas had already arranged for the restoration of Cyrus to his charge in Alexandria. The coronation of Constans must have taken place early in September, 641 [2], after the departure of Cyrus on his journey to Egypt. Cyrus was accompanied by a large number of priests; but so far from being shorn of his civil power, he was expressly authorized by the Emperor to conclude peace with the Arabs, to put an end to all further resistance in the country, and to arrange for the proper administration of Egypt. The terms of the authority given him suggest that Cyrus still cherished some hope of retaining the suzerainty of Egypt for the Empire: but there can be no doubt that he had impressed his conviction—honest or dishonest—of the necessity for

[1] According to Sebeos, Valentine on his arrival at Constantinople seized Martina, and, after having her tongue cut out, put her and her sons to death, and crowned the younger Constantine. John of Nikiou (p. 580) speaks of a revolt of the army at Byzantium led by Theodore, who seized Martina and her three sons, tore off their diadems, slit their noses, and sent them to Rhodes. The two versions differ, but both refer to the second revolt of Valentine, which occurred at a later period. Sebeos seems to indicate that Valentinian and Valentine are the same person; for he speaks of Valentianus and Valentin indifferently in c. xxxii. Prof. Bury (*Later Roman Empire*, vol. ii. p. 287) doubts the identity, but perhaps without sufficient reason.

[2] Mr. Brooks shows (l. c., p. 440, n. 2) that the Synod of Rome, held on Oct. 5, 649, is described as being in the ninth year of Constans: but he was not crowned as *sole* ruler till some time in November.

surrender upon the childish Emperor, the feeble senate, and the incapable courtiers of the capital. It is clear too that he had won over Martina to his pusillanimous counsels, that the party of Martina was the party of peace at any price with the Muslims, and that her policy was the policy of surrender incessantly preached by Cyrus.

What tangle of motives crossed in the recesses of the Patriarch's mind, almost passes conjecture. He had been a craven, if not a traitor to the Empire, for months before the question of the imperial succession had divided men to the point of civil war. Why was he so ready to abandon the field of his work, or at least the fruits of his labours? For ten years he had scourged and smitten the Copts into some semblance of subjection, but he knew that upon the removal of his heavy pressure they would spring back to their old faith. Had he come to see that his whole plan of persecution was a blunder and a failure? Nothing is further from the fact. It is far more probable that, with the lessons of Syria before his eyes, he despaired of the fortunes of the Empire in Egypt, and counted not merely on tolerance for his own form of religion in Egypt, but on such a reward for his aid to the Muslims as would enable him to maintain his ascendency over the Coptic Church in Egypt, while securing at the same time absolute independence of Constantinople.

Upon the ruins of the Empire Cyrus was building new schemes for the aggrandizement of the patriarchate of Alexandria. Such at least seems the most probable theory of his action, the theory which best explains his mysterious relations with 'Amr and his betrayal of the Roman cause. He was a traitor to the State in the imagined interest of the Church.

Meanwhile he was content to follow or to guide the Empress, and to set at nought the strongly-expressed opinion of his Church against the scandal of allowing the issue of an incestuous marriage to sit upon the throne. There is clear evidence that Cyrus on his return journey to Egypt was furnished with a military force, destined presumably to strengthen the garrison, in case his peace proposals were rejected, or it may be to strengthen the faction of the Empress among them. Moreover, a new general of militia, named Constantine, was sent with him to replace the fallen John; and Theodore either sailed at the same time, or was already at Rhodes when Cyrus arrived, waiting to join the expedition. Martina was also there, though it is doubtful whether her journey was caused by the progress of Valentine's rebellion, or by alarm at the specific act of the coronation of Constans. Probably she wished to consult with Theodore and Cyrus on this new development: but there was matter enough for anxiety in the troubled state of the court and the capital.

For the plots of Valentine were as unscrupulous and as far-reaching as those of Cyrus. He had already sounded the depth of the army's affection for the Empress, and found it, at least in places, very shallow. All the treasure of Philagrius he squandered in bribing the soldiers in Egypt, and he so divided the forces there, that they ceased fighting the Muslims and turned their arms against each other. Civil war therefore had already broken out, and that not between Copts and Romans [1], but be-

[1] See p. 285 supra.

tween different portions of the imperial army. It was, however, important to secure the adherence of Theodore, and to detach him from the cause of the Empress. Nothing was impossible in that atmosphere of conspiracy and cabal; and Theodore had his own unavowed ambitions. When therefore Theodore received at Rhodes a secret missive from Valentine urging him to renounce allegiance to Martina, and when he learned that a similar message had been sent to Pentapolis and in fact to every province of the Empire, while treason was at work among the very troops ordered to Egypt with Cyrus, he made up his mind to abandon the cause of the Empress and to sail clandestinely for Pentapolis. His motive in this is by no means clear. He may have desired merely retirement and shelter from the coming storms; or he may have resolved, like Heraclius, to stake his fortune on a throw for the crown, and to found a new empire at Carthage; or he may have wished to gather resources and watch events, detesting the policy of surrender and hoping to strike a blow at the Muslims from Carthage. His scheme was to part company in the darkness with the fleet convoying Cyrus, and the captain of the vessel on which he sailed was the only soul made privy to it. Apparently the captain promised acquiescence, but repented of his promise, and alleged that the wind was contrary for the voyage to Pentapolis. So it befell that Theodore's design miscarried, and he found himself in Cyrus' company [1],

[1] The question of the date of Cyrus' arrival at Alexandria is dealt with in the Appendix on the Chronology of the Arab Conquest. Since writing it I have only found fresh reason to strengthen the conviction that he landed with Theodore upon the day given above. It is probable that Theodore was in a different vessel, and it seems

with the rest of the convoy, in the harbour of Alexandria before daylight on the morning of Holy Cross Day, September 14, 641.

as if he stole away from Rhodes without informing Cyrus of his plan. If so, he must have been overtaken by the ship carrying Cyrus.

CHAPTER XXI

SURRENDER OF ALEXANDRIA

Civil war in Egypt. Factions in the capital. Arrival of Cyrus. Triumphant procession to the Caesarion. His sermon there. Persecution of the Copts resumed. Cyrus' secret journey to Babylon. Affairs in Upper Egypt. Conferences between Cyrus and ʿAmr. Cyrus agrees to surrender. Treaty of Alexandria. Its provisions as variously related. John of Nikiou's version. The Arab text, and Arab commentaries.

During the absence of Cyrus in exile, there had been frequent outbreaks of civil strife in Egypt. For a time the people of the province of Miṣr were at open war with those of the more northernly provinces. Peace was restored after many acts of hostility; but no sooner had this quarrel ceased than fierce feuds arose within the walls of the capital. The Roman commanders were divided by jealousy and hatred, while the Green and Blue factions were more ready to fly at each other's throats than to face the enemy at their gates. Domentianus, the betrayer of the Fayûm and of Nikiou, was at odds with Menas, his rival for the reversion of the commandership-in-chief. Menas had a bitter grudge against Eudocianus (brother to Domentianus) for the barbarities he had committed that Easter Day on the Copts in Babylon[1]; while Theodore

[1] This shows, no doubt, that Menas was a Copt or had Coptic sympathies. The Menas here named by John (p. 570) must be a different person from the Menas who was Prefect of Lower Egypt under Heraclius (p. 577), and who is described as loathing the Copts. But the difference in the sentiments is a clear proof that no argument as to sympathy can be founded on the Coptic or non-Coptic character of a name.

had not forgiven Domentianus for his cowardly desertion of his post and his army at Nikiou. The wonder is that Domentianus was not cashiered or put to death; the resentment of his superior officer was a small punishment. But he probably escaped the fate he deserved by the favour of Martina and by reason of his kinship to Cyrus, whose sister he had married. Still in spite of kinship and friendship and claims of gratitude, Domentianus showed towards Cyrus disrespect and unreasoning hatred. The Blue Faction were with Domentianus, and he enlisted a large force of the Blues in his quarrel—a move which Menas met by enrolling a body of the Greens. In this dangerous state of tension there came to Alexandria one Philiades, Prefect of the province of Fayûm, and brother to George, the predecessor of Cyrus in the office of Melkite Patriarch. Philiades had been befriended by Menas, but ill requited his friendship. Moreover, he had been guilty of corruption or embezzlement of public money, and had made himself as unpopular with the army as Menas was popular.

Matters soon came to a head. One day while Menas was at service in the great church called Caesarion with his Coptic fellow worshippers, the townsfolk rose in revolt against Philiades, and meant to kill him. He escaped, however, and hid in a friend's house, whereupon the rioters went to his own dwelling, plundered it, and set it on fire. The rioters were of the Green Faction, and Domentianus at once sent his Blue company against them. A fierce encounter took place in the streets; six men were killed and many wounded; and Theodore had the greatest difficulty in repressing the disorder. In the end Philiades had his property restored, and

Domentianus was deprived of his military rank, though he seems to have been reinstated later when Theodore was summoned to Constantinople. The fact is that Domentianus, in spite of his personal hostility to Cyrus, was in close agreement with him on political questions; both were high in the favour of the Empress Martina; and both pressed upon her the policy of surrender to the Arabs.

In relating the story of the faction fight in Alexandria, John of Nikiou seems to confess that he is unable to explain its causes. For while his language suggests that the riot arose both from private enmities and from political partisanship, he is careful to add that by some its ferocious character was attributed to religious dissension: and yet he throws no ray of light on the nature of that dissension. Was it between Monophysite and Melkite? or between orthodox Melkite and Monothelite? or between Jew and Christian? The matter is too complex for conjecture: but when one remembers that a vast number of refugees from the Delta and Upper Egypt had flocked to Alexandria for protection, and that John here speaks of the Caesarion as the scene of a Coptic service[1], it might be argued both that the number of Copts in Alexandria had greatly increased, and that during the absence of their persecutor, Al Muḳauḳas, in exile, they had recovered some of their confidence and freedom. The Copts therefore may have been strong enough to fling their sympathies and antipathies into the seething cauldron of Alexandrian party warfare. Yet one is astounded to read that when Cyrus, Al Muḳauḳas, landed on that September morning,

[1] He would not speak of any other than a Coptic congregation as an 'assembly of the faithful' (p. 571).

the whole city went wild with delight, 'rejoicing and giving thanks for the arrival of the Patriarch of Alexandria[1]'; and all the people, men and women, young and old, flocked to greet him and do him honour. Not a note of discord is sounded or a whisper of fear. Yet the Copts can have felt no joy or even hope at the return of Al Muḳauḳas, and the conclusion is irresistible that after all they were but a very small body, lost in the great population of the capital.

But ere the news of his arrival spread through the waking city, Cyrus betook himself in secret with Theodore to the convent of the monks of Tabennesi, which probably lay near the landing-place[2].

[1] These words are Dr. Charles' rendering of the Ethiopic version. Nothing to my mind more clearly proves the impartiality and conscientiousness of John of Nikiou than this account of Cyrus' return. It would have been easy to represent his reception as cold, or to say nothing about it. John writes that it was very warm, and that it was the return not so much of the man as of the 'Patriarch of Alexandria' which caused the rejoicing (p. 574). Amélineau in his strange critique upon John actually makes this truthfulness a cause of reproach: 'Je suis en outre bien étonné que Jean de Nikiou, évêque Jacobite, reconnaisse à Cyrus, qu'il devait exécrer et anathématiser, la dignité de Patriarche d'Alexandrie, alors que le Patriarche Jacobite Benjamin, le seul légitime à ses yeux, vivait en exil dans la Haute-Égypte' (*Vie du Patriarche Copte Isaac*, p. xxvi). Surely John's candour vastly increases our confidence in him as a historian.

[2] Tabennesi was a place about ten miles north of Tentyris or Ḍanḍarah in Upper Egypt. It was the centre of the brotherhood of the order of St. Pachomius: see Quatremère, *Mém. Géog. et Hist.* t. i. p. 281, and Amélineau, *Géog. Copte*, p. 469, and the authorities there quoted. It was a strictly Coptic order, but the convent in Alexandria had clearly been appropriated by Cyrus for the Melkites, or else the monks there were among the many thousands whom the persecution had detached from the Coptic profession of faith.

The door of the church was closed, and a message was sent summoning Menas to the monastery. Theodore at once gave Menas the office of military commander of the garrison, deposing Domentianus, whom the populace forthwith hounded out of the city. The coincidence of Cyrus' arrival with the festival of the Exaltation of the Cross was well calculated to revive the drooping spirits of the Romans, and Cyrus made the most of it. It will be remembered that when John, general of militia, was dispatched to Egypt by Heraclius as bearer of the famous Ecthesis to Cyrus, he brought also with him for the Patriarch a cross of special sanctity—possibly enclosing a portion of the Holy Rood itself[1]. This treasured relic had been deposited in the convent of the monks of Tabennesi, and nothing was more natural than that it should be carried in procession with Cyrus to the great church of Caesarion, at which the festival service was to be holden. All the way from the convent to the cathedral Cyrus' path was strewn with carpets, while streamers and banners of silk fluttered, the smoke of incense rose, and hymns resounded in his honour. Yet broad as were the streets of the Great City, they were so thronged that people trod one upon another, and the Archbishop had the utmost difficulty in making his passage through the crowds to reach the cathedral. The procession, however, moved slowly onward, and at length, after passing between the two ancient Egyptian obelisks and through the cloistered court, entered the door of the Caesarion.

There, as was fitting, the Archbishop in his sermon dwelt upon the Invention of the Cross[2] and its

[1] See above, p. 182, n. 1, and p. 222, n. 1.

[2] This passage in John of Nikiou (p. 574) is obviously corrupt,

Exaltation, which the Eastern Church, then as now, celebrated together. It was a theme which might have fired a less eloquent tongue than that of Cyrus, as he recalled the strange eventful history of Heraclius' crusade, the recovery of the Holy Rood from captivity with the Persians, and its uplifting on that day of triumph in Jerusalem. Yet what lesson did Cyrus draw, or wish to draw, from the story? Jerusalem itself was now in captivity to the Muslims, and the Muslims were at the very gates of Alexandria. The position was almost as bad as when Chosroes held all Palestine, Syria, and Egypt: but did Cyrus dare to point the moral of hope and faith to his hearers, to encourage them in resistance in the name of the Cross, when in his own heart he had forsaken the cause of the Cross and resolved to bow it down before the standards of Mohammed? Perhaps he avoided politics altogether: but it is certain that he did not unburden 'the secrets of his overcharged soul' that day in the ambon.

and has been misconstrued by Zotenberg, who renders thus: 'Il fit ouvrir (?) la citerne dans laquelle se trouvait la Sainte-Croix qu'il avait reçue avant son exil du Général Jean. Il avait pris aussi la vénérable croix du couvent des Tabennésiotes.' Zotenberg himself puts the query after the words which he translates 'Il fit ouvrir'; for he sees that the whole sentence makes no sense. Dr. Charles renders: 'He highly extolled the well in which the Holy Cross had been found' and this gives a clear allusion to the Invention by Helena. The words which follow have, I feel sure, slipped from their proper order. It was not the Holy Cross itself which Cyrus had received through John before his exile: Heraclius never would have sent and never did send that most precious of all relics to Egypt. The cross which came to Cyrus was the cross kept by the Tabennesi monks, and the passage should run: 'He had taken also (to the Caesarion) from the convent of the Tabennesi monks the cross which he had received at the hands of the general John.' This makes complete sense out of absurdity.

But the service ended unhappily. When they came after the sermon to the mass, the deacon instead of reading the verses proper to the day gave out another psalm with direct reference to the return of the Archbishop, whom he desired to praise and congratulate. The people who heard it said at once that the change was against the canons and was of very evil omen for the Archbishop, and, as the story runs, that he would never look upon another Easter[1]. No doubt they thought him looking worn and ill. His exile had told upon him physically: his rough passage through the crowds and the exertion of preaching had tried his strength: and above all he must have carried on his face tokens of that inner conflict which was tearing him to pieces. These people trusted him; hailed him as their champion and deliverer; their hearts were lifted up and their faith in the Cross exalted; they would fight and conquer in that sign. But while their hopes were kindled, the Archbishop was depressed by the gnawing consciousness that he was about to betray them all, to betray the cause of the Cross and the cause of the Roman Empire. It was a dramatic situation, and it is small wonder that haggard looks told of the strain even on that haughty temper, and that in them men read the omen of death.

For some little time after his arrival Cyrus was busied in dealing with matters of Church and State which demanded urgent attention in Alexandria. Anastasius seems to have acted as civil governor

[1] The question of the coincidence of Cyrus' return with that of Theodore, and the question of the day upon which the wrong chant was used, are discussed in the Appendix upon the Chronology of the Arab Conquest.

of the city during the absence of Cyrus, and it is just possible that the George to whom Cyrus had delegated his episcopal authority upon his departure was none other than his predecessor in the office of Patriarch [1]. George was now an old man but very influential, and he was treated with great deference by all from the governor downwards. He had no part in the persecution of the Copts; indeed the absence of Cyrus on the one hand, and the severance of whole districts from imperial control on the other, had given the Copts a breathing-space. But Cyrus had not forgotten his hatred against the native Church of Egypt. He was ready to hand over the country to the enemy, and to make peace with the unbeliever; but for the Copts there was no peace and no forgiveness. The sword was again drawn: and so far from being softened by his own adversity, Cyrus hardened his heart and renewed his reign of violence and oppression against those who were not beyond his reach [2].

It is indeed strange that the Muḳauḳas should have thought it worth while to revive his persecution. Possibly, however, his action may have served to blind the people of Alexandria to his real design, which was to deliver all Egypt over to the Arabs. For that he had no doubt the Emperor's warrant; but it was a warrant wrung from a puppet ruler by

[1] This is only a bare possibility. John of Nikiou says that he had been nominated by Heraclius, but the office is not stated. It must, however, have been either the patriarchate or the governorship of the city, and John's language implies the former: see p. 170, n. 2 supra. On the other hand if this George were governor, could he be the George said by Arab writers to have been governor in 627 at the time of Mohammed's mission to Egypt—the George son of Mînâ wrongly called Al Muḳauḳas?

[2] John of Nikiou, p. 566.

cowardice and chicanery, and a warrant which he dared not avow either, as it seems, to the highest officers of state in Alexandria or to the people. Alone, or accompanied only by some of his priests, who may have shared his secret, the Muḳauḳas made his way to Babylon. It was now the season of high Nile again [1]—towards the end of October—and just about a year had passed since he had made his abortive treaty of Babylon, which the old Emperor tore up in indignation.

'Amr himself had only just returned to Babylon; but whether up to this time he had been engaged against those Delta towns which foiled him, or whether he had in person led an expedition which was sent to Upper Egypt, is uncertain [2]. The fact of the expedition is not doubtful, and a small column of Muslims got as far as Antinoe, the modern Anṣinâ, then the capital of the Thebaid. As the Roman troops were not yet all withdrawn from this region, the townsfolk took counsel with their Prefect, named John, and desired to offer resistance to the Arabs. John, however, absolutely refused to fight: he seized all the public money which had been collected, and carried it off with his troops, making his way across the desert westward to Alexandria. He had no wish to meet the fate which had befallen the garrison of the Fayûm, and was besides quite unable to cope with the Muslims. So the conquest of Upper Egypt was comparatively easy. 'When

[1] The fact that Al Muḳauḳas twice negotiated at the time of the inundation explains and excuses much of the confusion in the Arab writers between the siege of Babylon and that of Alexandria.

[2] Ibn Ḳutaibah says that 'Amr's return from the Delta was in Dhû 'l Ḳa'dah, A. H. 20 (Oct. 12–Nov. 10, 641), but John of Nikiou makes out that he returned earlier and went himself to Upper Egypt (p. 562).

the Muslims saw the weakness of the Romans and the hostility of the people to the Emperor Heraclius because of the persecution, wherewith he had visited all the land of Egypt, against the orthodox faith at the instigation of Cyrus, the Chalcedonian Patriarch, they became bolder and stronger in the war[1]': for little as the Copts loved the Saracens, here in Upper Egypt the feeling against their persecutors was most bitter. In the Fayûm, which was already settling down under Arab rule as a tributary province, matters had gone so far that the inhabitants killed any Roman soldier they chanced to encounter, and further south the Copts had even less motive to fight for the Empire.

But, after the subjugation of Upper or at least Middle Egypt, the Arab commander had come back to Babylon to rest there during the flood-time: and it was in the great fortress that he received Cyrus, when he came on his mission of surrender. 'Amr gave him a kindly welcome, and, on hearing that his purpose was to sue for peace, he remarked 'You have done well to come to us.' The Patriarch said that in order to put an end to the war, the people would be willing to pay tribute, adding, 'God has given this country to you: let there be no more enmity between you and the Romans[2].' One may well believe that negotiations and consultations were spun out over several days in oriental fashion; but in the end an agreement was reached on all points, and a treaty was signed on November 8, 641.

[1] John of Nikiou, l. c.

[2] 'Heretofore there has been no strife with you' are the concluding words of Cyrus in the text. Zotenberg inserts the word *prolongées* before *hostilités*, but that scarcely redeems the curious inaccuracy of the statement. There is clearly some error in the MS.

This treaty—which may be called the Treaty of Alexandria, both to distinguish it from the former Treaty of Babylon and because it turned mainly on the surrender of Alexandria—sealed the Arab conquest of Egypt. Its terms are somewhat variously reported, but the principal covenants are given by John of Nikiou as follows:—

(1) Payment of a fixed tribute by all who came under the treaty.

(2) An armistice of about eleven months, to expire the first day of the Coptic month Paophi, i. e. September 28, 642 [1].

(3) During the armistice the Arab forces to maintain their positions, but to keep apart and undertake no military operations against Alexandria; the Roman forces to cease all acts of hostility.

(4) The garrison of Alexandria and all troops there to embark and depart by sea, carrying all their possessions and treasure with them: but any Roman soldiers quitting Egypt by land to be subject to a monthly tribute on their journey.

(5) No Roman army to return or attempt the recovery of Egypt.

(6) The Muslims to desist from all seizure of churches, and not to interfere in any way with the Christians.

(7) The Jews to be suffered to remain at Alexandria.

(8) Hostages to be given by the Romans, viz.

[1] This would be just eleven months by Arab reckoning, rather less by Roman. See Appendix on the Chronology. The armistice is clearly recorded by Ibn al Athîr, though it is made to cover only such time as was required to obtain Omar's answer about the disposal of the prisoners.

150 military and 50 civilian, for the due execution of the treaty.

These articles are not set out by the Coptic historian quite in the order in which, for the sake of convenience, I have ventured here to place them. Under the first article a general security was given for the life, property, and churches of the Egyptians, who were also to be allowed the free exercise of their religion. For the payment of tribute and taxes constituted them a protected people (*ahl adh dhimmah*) with a status implying these privileges. The tribute was fixed at two dinârs per head for all except very old men and children, and the total capitation-tax was found to amount to 12,000,000 dinârs, or about £6,000,000[1]: but in addition to the capitation-tax, a land-tax or property-tax was imposed. The third article must, I think, be limited by reference to Alexandria alone, because, although Cyrus made the treaty on behalf of the Egyptians in general, he could not guarantee that every city and community would consent to be bound by it; and it would be unreasonable that the Arabs should be debarred from fighting in case of further resistance. It is, moreover, clear that in fact such

[1] The number of the able-bodied male population is very variously given by the Arab authorities, who make the capitation-tax vary between 12,000 and 300,000,000 dinârs: but 12,000,000 is the most probable estimate. The land-tax was at first made payable in kind—a fact which seems to be the foundation for the statement that the Copts supplied the Arabs with provisions after the surrender of Babylon. Abû Ṣâliḥ says that 'Amr imposed a yearly tax of 26⅔ dirhems, but from the well-to-do he exacted two dinârs and three ardebs of wheat. 'In this way the country produced 12,000,000 dinârs without reckoning the tribute of the Jews in Egypt' (p. 75): but on p. 74 is a rather different account, clearly from another source.

resistance was offered in places, and was conquered, during the term of the armistice.

It will be noticed that John of Nikiou's version of the treaty says nothing about the date of the first payment of tribute or of subsequent payments, but he implies clearly that an instalment was demanded very shortly, and this is explicitly confirmed by the Arab writer Ibn Khaldûn [1].

We are now in a position to appreciate the perplexity of the Arab writers and the divergence of their answers to the question they are so fond of debating—whether Egypt was taken by treaty or by force. One must, however, so far anticipate the later history of Alexandria as to remark that, three or four years after its surrender by Cyrus, it was recovered by the Romans, and retaken by the Arabs: but the second capture was by force of arms, and not by capitulation. Here, then, we have some curious coincidences. First of all Babylon was surrendered by Al Muḳauḳas at the time of high Nile under a convention, which the Emperor refused to ratify. Subsequently the fortress was stormed; but, before the storming party made good their entry, the garrison offered to surrender, and did actually capitulate under treaty. Next, Alexandria surrendered at the time of high Nile under a treaty and almost without pressure; but after the city had been for some time in possession of the Arabs, it was recovered by the Romans, who were only

[1] John makes the Arabs come shortly after the treaty to take the tribute from Alexandria: Ibn Khaldûn, quoting the terms of the treaty, says, 'The people of Egypt are bound to pay the poll-tax as soon as they have come to an agreement upon this treaty, and the overflow of the river has ceased.' The extract is further important as showing that the treaty was made at high Nile.

driven out after a siege which ended in capture by force.

Looking at these strange results, when one remembers that the earliest Arab authorities wrote some two hundred years after the conquest, and when one reflects on the immense difficulty of preserving these bewildering coincidences in their original shape through two centuries of tradition mainly oral, then one may feel astonished, not that the story has passed through endless confusions and contortions, but that the Arab mind, so wanting in historic sense, so blind to historic proportion, should have stored up so many fragments of truth, however out of order and relation. It is quite intelligible now that some writers should represent Babylon as taken by treaty, others by force; and the same in regard to Alexandria. The fact is, that while both versions are in a sense true in each case, neither is true in either case without qualification.

It is worth while briefly to examine some of these authorities, who add some interesting details. Thus Balâdhurî, who wrote in the ninth century, quotes 'Abdallah, the son of 'Amr, as saying, that after the capture of Babylon by force, 'Amr took counsel with his chiefs and resolved to come to terms with the Egyptians. He made a treaty imposing a tribute of two dinârs a head on all able-bodied males, and a tax on all landowners[1]: moreover, every Muslim was to be provided with a complete change of raiment every year. By request of the governor, Al Muḳauḳas, this treaty was to apply to the whole of Egypt, but all Romans who wished were permitted

[1] This tax is given as three ardebs of wheat, two ḳists of olives, two of honey, two of vinegar, to be collected and stored in the public storehouse (p. 215).

to quit the country. Balâdhurî wrongly represents the Emperor as rejecting this treaty, for it is quite clear that he is describing the Treaty of Alexandria. On the other hand, in proof of the statement that Egypt was taken by force, he records a story that 'Amr, speaking once from the pulpit, said, 'I have taken my seat in this country without a compact with one of the Copts. If I please, I can kill them or sell them as slaves.' These words, if rightly reported, could only mean that the Copts had no voice in the matter—that the only parties to the treaty were the Arabs and the Romans. This, of course, was true; but the Copts were covered by the treaty; and Balâdhurî goes on to prove this. For he relates that when Mu'awîah wrote to Wardân pressing him to increase the tribute of the Copts, Wardân pointed out that he could not do so without violating the treaty of peace. So too he quotes a son of Zubair as saying, 'I lived seven years in Egypt and married there. The people were taxed above their means and were in distress, *although 'Amr had made a treaty with them with fixed conditions.*' He adds that there is other evidence for the existence of the treaty. But he cannot get rid of the idea that Alexandria was taken by force, although he admits 'that 'Amr did not kill or enslave the inhabitants, only making them protected allies.' The two things are quite inconsistent, and his admission is proof that, in speaking of capture by force, Balâdhurî is thinking of the second capture of Alexandria.

But the text of the treaty is actually given by Ṭabarî, who by a strange confusion calls it the Treaty of 'Ain Shams, instead of the Treaty of Alexandria. Here are the words:—

'This is the security which 'Amr ibn al 'Aṣî gave

to the people of Egypt for themselves, their bodies, and their possessions, for the whole and the part and all their numbers. Nothing shall be added to this treaty or taken away from it. The Nubians shall not be allowed to invade the country. The people of Egypt are bound to pay the poll-tax as soon as they have come to an agreement on this treaty of peace, and when the overflow of the river has ceased—fifty millions[1] in amount. 'Amr is bound to protect those whom he taxes. But if any of the Egyptians refuse to accept the treaty, the tribute shall be reduced in proportion; nevertheless we decline to give protection to those who refuse payment. If the Nile fails to rise to its full height in any year, the tax shall be abated in proportion to the level it reaches. All Romans and Nubians who come under this treaty of peace shall retain their possessions and shall be bound to pay the same taxes; but those who refuse and prefer to depart shall have a safe-conduct, until they leave our dominions and reach a place of security. The tribute is to be paid in three instalments, each instalment being a third of the total[2]. Upon all within this document is the covenant of God and His protection, and the protection of His Apostle, and the protection of the Khalîfah and Prince of the Faithful, and the protection of all the faithful. Nubians who come under this treaty are bound to help the Muslims with so many slaves and so many horses; not to make raids into Egypt; and not to hinder the passage of merchandise, going or coming.

[1] This of course is incorrect.

[2] This seems to be the meaning of the obscure passage—
و عليهم ما عليهم اثلاثاً فى كل ثلث جباية ثلث ما عليهم

'Witnessed by Zubair and his two sons, 'Abdallah and Muḥammad. Written by Wardân[1].'

This form of treaty, though by no means inconsistent with the terms given by John of Nikiou, is not coextensive with them: one account in fact supplements the other. Yâḳût quotes Ibn 'Abd al Ḥakam as saying, 'All Egypt was occupied by treaty, a tribute of two dinârs a head being imposed on every man, with the understanding that it was not to be increased, while landowners also had to give a proportion of their produce. The Alexandrians, however, had to pay poll-tax and land-tax, the amount to be determined at the will of the governor, because they were conquered by force of arms without treaty or compact.' Here again the second capture is confused with the first surrender of Alexandria. But the best discussion on the subject is to be found in Maḳrîzî, who states the various views with great clearness, and cites the various authorities[2]. The

[1] This treaty is preserved by Ibn Khaldûn, who quotes it from Ṭabarî; but it does not seem to occur in Ṭabarî's extant account of the conquest of Egypt; see Zotenberg's edition, vol. iii. pp. 461 seq. Nevertheless it is clear that Ṭabarî makes Alexandria taken under capitulation.

[2] *Khiṭaṭ*, vol. i. p. 294. Certain local treaties are named, but the Copts are said to have made in the general treaty six conditions: (1) that they should not be driven from their homes, (2) or parted from their wives, (3) or removed from their villages, (4) or deprived of their lands, (5) that the tribute should not be increased, and (6) that they should be protected from their enemies. These headings do not seem very accurate or logical, and nothing is said about religious freedom, which certainly came within the covenants. Zaid ibn Aslâm is quoted as saying that Omar possessed a box containing all the treaties, but there was none with Egypt; and Ibn Shiḥâh avers that, although Egypt was taken partly by treaty and partly by force, yet Omar made the people in every part of the country a protected people. For example,

evidence for the occupation by treaty is overwhelming, and one may sum up the matter in the words of the old man who, on hearing it remarked that there was no treaty with the Egyptians, retorted, 'He who says there was no treaty will forget to say his prayers.'

when 'Abdallah ibn Sa'd wanted some land in Egypt, he paid purchase-money for it, on the ground that the country was occupied by treaty. Mâlik ibn 'Anas, 'Abdallah ibn Lahî'ah, and Nafi' ibn Yazîd assert that Egypt was taken by force of arms. Al Laith, 'Abdallah ibn Abî Ja'far, Yaḥîa ibn Aiyûb, and others rightly maintain the occupation by treaty.

CHAPTER XXII

REDUCTION OF THE COAST TOWNS

'Amr sends news of the surrender to Omar. Its date. Cyrus breaks the news to the chief men in Alexandria. The arrival of Arab envoys makes it known to the populace. Their fury, and its appeasement. Criticism of Cyrus' treachery. The military position of Alexandria. Effect of Heraclius' death. Treaty ratified by Heraclonas. Building of the Muslim city of Fusṭâṭ, and of the Mosque of 'Amr. Restoration of Trajan's Canal. Campaign in the northern Delta. Capture of Ikhnâ, Balhîb, Baralus, Damietta, Tinnîs, Shaṭâ, &c. Story of Shaṭâ, and importance of the date. Historical fallacies once more refuted.

WHEN the treaty was duly completed, 'Amr called Mu'awîah ibn Ḥudaij al Kindî, and told him to carry the news of the surrender to Omar[1]. Mu'awîah asked for a letter, but 'Amr retorted, 'What have I to do with a letter? Are you not an Arab who can give a report of what you have witnessed?' So Mu'awîah departed on his long desert journey, and, arriving at Medina at noonday, he made his camel kneel down at the door of the mosque and entered. While he was there, a maid came out of Omar's house, and, seeing a stranger with the marks of travel upon him, asked his name. He gave it, adding that he brought a message from 'Amr ibn

[1] The messenger's name is thus more correctly given by Balâdhurî, but as Ibn Khadîj by Maḳrîzî, who tells the story apparently in connexion with the *second* capture of Alexandria. But Maḳrîzî (or his authority Ibn Lahî'ah) says that Mu'awîah's errand preceded 'Amr's letter descriptive of Alexandria. That letter was written upon the first entry of the Arabs into the city. Moreover, Omar was dead before the second capture. He was buried on 1st Muḥarram, A. H. 24 = Nov. 7, 644 (Ibn al Athîr, vol. iii. p. 38). The story therefore rightly falls where I have placed it.

al 'Aṣî. The maid went back to the house, but returned so hastily that Mu'awîah 'heard the veil flapping against her feet' as she ran. She bade Mu'awîah follow to the house, where Omar demanded his news. 'Good news, O Commander of the Faithful,' was the answer; 'God has opened Alexandria to us.' They went back at once to the mosque, where the muezzin called the people together, and a service was held in thanksgiving. On returning to his house with Mu'awîah, Omar said a further prayer, and then ordered bread and oil to be set before his guest, who was somewhat embarrassed and ate shyly. Dates were added to the repast, but there the Caliph's luxuries ended. When Mu'awîah excused himself for the rather tardy delivery of his message on the ground that he thought Omar would be taking his noontide rest, the Caliph answered, 'Bad is what you said, and bad is what you thought. If I slept by day, I should lose my subjects: if I slept by night, I should lose myself. How can I sleep with these two reasons against it?'

So simply was the news delivered and received at Medina: very different was its reception in Alexandria.

The Treaty of Alexandria was signed at Babylon on Thursday, November 8, 641[1]. It of course

[1] I have given the reasons for this date in the Appendix. Prof. Lane-Poole quotes from Ṭabarî the statement of Ziyâd that peace proposals reached 'Amr at Balhîb; that they were referred to the Caliph; and that the Muslims waited for his reply at the same place, Balhîb. This story is most improbable as it stands; it conflicts equally with Ibn Ḳutaibah and with John of Nikiou, who both bring 'Amr to Babylon at this time; and it is hardly credible that 'Amr's army remained so long in that one position. The truth doubtless is that while the treaty was made at Babylon, its ratification was received from Omar at Balhîb.

required ratification by the Roman Emperor as well as by the Caliph Omar; but the armistice of eleven months allowed ample time for all formalities. Cyrus now hastened back to the capital, bearing the treaty with him.

His first care was to communicate the terms of the compact to the general Theodore, commander-in-chief, and to Constantine, general of militia. It is curious to find that, although Theodore bore the title of Augustal Prefect, he had no lot or part in the negotiations, and was not even present at Babylon. But Theodore's position altogether is puzzling. One cannot even say whether he was made privy to Cyrus' design of surrendering the city. If he was, he must have changed his mind and come over to the peace party: if he was not, it is strange that he should acquiesce so readily in what can only be called a shameful capitulation.

Meanwhile news of the secret treaty passed in confidential whispers among the heads of departments and the leading men in the capital. The populace were kept in ignorance; but dispatches were sent to the Emperor Heraclonas, announcing the terms of surrender and recommending them for ratification. It seems that both the generals concurred in this recommendation, and their concurrence must be held in some measure to exonerate Cyrus from responsibility, although Theodore's proved incompetence as military commander deprives his judgement upon the military situation of all real value. However, when Cyrus had prepared the ground in Alexandria, he summoned the chiefs of the army and of the civil government to a council. Headed by Theodore and Constantine, they came and presented their homage to the Patriarch, whom we must imagine seated and robed in full pontificals. With his wonted skill he explained the terms of the treaty, enlarging upon its necessity and its advantages, till he saw with melancholy triumph conviction carried to the minds of his hearers.

Thus one more step was gained by Cyrus in his plans for the betrayal of Egypt. But the veil of mystery in which he had shrouded them could not last much longer. The disclosure to the people was made not by open avowal of Cyrus, or by the voice of rumour, but by the sudden appearance of an Arab force advancing towards the city. The alarm rang out, and from every quarter the people hastened to man the walls and towers. The Arabs rode forward unconcerned, while the Roman generals, who had now destroyed all fighting spirit in the army, tried to calm the people by arguing that further resistance was hopeless and impossible. Ere the Saracens came within range of the Roman artillery, they were seen to be bearing flags of truce. Answering signals were made: but when the Saracens stood within speaking distance, what was the amazement of the Romans to hear that the enemy had come, not to attack the city, but to receive the tribute agreed upon by Cyrus, Al Muḳauḳas, in the treaty which he had proposed and had signed for the capitulation of Alexandria. Furious and incredulous the mob tore through the streets towards the Archbishop's palace; and when at last Cyrus appeared, for a moment his life was in danger, as the people ran upon him to stone him.

His age and dignity saved the Archbishop. Staying the rage of the people with a gesture, he found his tongue, and summoned all his eloquence to soften the public confession of his treason, and to justify his conduct. The action he had taken, he said, was forced upon him: no other course was possible in the interests of his hearers and of their children. The Arabs were irresistible: God had willed to bring the land of Egypt under their dominion. Either the Romans must come to terms, or they must see their streets deluged with blood, and after pillage and massacre the survivors must forfeit the remnant of their possessions. The capitulation secured life and property and religion. Besides, all who preferred to live under a Christian government were free to quit Alexandria. The alternatives of exile from Egypt and submission to Muslim rule were indeed bitter; and the Patriarch was moved to tears, as he besought the people to believe that he had done his best and to accept the treaty which he had made for their deliverance.

Once more the sinister counsel of Cyrus prevailed. Popular opinion swung round into agreement with the army, and consented to surrender the Great City to the Arabs on the terms of the treaty. The rioters felt ashamed of their outburst of anger against His Holiness the Archbishop, who had used his powerful intercession to save them from destruction at the hands of their conquerors. So the citizens not only furnished the instalment of tribute now demanded, but added to it a large sum of gold. The money was placed on board a vessel, which passed out of the southern water-gate of the city, and was delivered by Cyrus himself to the Muslim commander[1].

[1] This is not stated in the text (p. 576), but it is given in the heading to ch. cxx on p. 358 of John of Nikiou's Chronicle.

Thus was sealed the surrender of Alexandria. A computation of dates makes it possible that this first payment of tribute took place on the first day of Muḥarram, A.H. 21 (December 10, 641). Although there is no specific authority for such a statement, Arab tradition fixes that day as the day of the conquest; and the tradition may well have arisen from the impression made upon those present when the act of submission was performed by the first payment of tribute. It is true, nevertheless, that the Arabic authorities one and all make the 1st Muḥarram fall on a Friday, whereas no 1st Muḥarram fell on a Friday at this time, or nearer than 645. It follows that the tradition cannot be true in its entirety, and it may therefore be altogether false: but it is so firmly rooted in the Arab lore of the conquest that it probably possesses some historical basis[1]. In any case it is interesting to remark one more of those singular coincidences which emerge from, and partly explain, the confusion in the chronology of this period. It is this; that, although some of the Arab historians insist that the fall of Alexandria took place three years after the entry of 'Amr's army into Egypt, while others aver that both Babylon and Alexandria fell in the same year, viz. A.H. 20; yet, in spite of the apparent discrepancy, both sets of historians are right. Babylon surrendered in April, 641, and Alexandria in November, 641, which dates both fall within A.H. 20: and on the other hand, while 'Amr's invasion began in December, 639, his army did not actually occupy

[1] Mr. E. W. Brooks thinks that the date really applies to the second capture of Alexandria, which he would place on Friday, 1st Muḥarram, A.H. 25, or October 28, 645. But I shall show reason against this theory in a later chapter.

Alexandria till three years later, in October, 642, at the end of the eleven months' armistice. It is pleasant to find truth behind such a veil of contradictions.

But what is to be said of this amazing treaty of surrender? Of the dark and subtle part played by Al Muḳauḳas or Cyrus, the Patriarch, of his strange intimacy with the leader of the Arabs, and of his strange anxiety all through the war to hasten the submission of Egypt, it is difficult to speak in measured language. The guilt of deliberate treason to the Roman Empire must remain an indelible stain on his memory, stained already by the folly and the brutality of the ten years' persecution. If from the moment of his appointment the Archbishop had bent all his powers to the single end of destroying the Roman dominion over Egypt, he need not have swerved for a moment from the course he actually followed. But one is filled with wonder to see with what avidity he seized that opportunity of betraying Egypt which was mainly the result of his own scandalous misgovernment. It is no palliation of his conduct to say that he had the formal authority of Heraclonas, the Emperor, for the capitulation. It was easy to talk over a weakling prince who knew nothing of Egypt, and whose policy answered every touch of the helm in his mother's hand.

Moreover the treachery of Cyrus began months before at Babylon. This fact alone disposes of any defence on the ground of military necessity. True, the greater part of Egypt was now conquered; but that was not true at the time of the abortive treaty of Babylon. Besides, Alexandria had not even been seriously menaced, nor had any of the coast towns fallen. When the Muslim army had first ventured to assault the capital, it was beaten off ignominiously, nor, as was hinted above, is there any reason to believe that it remained permanently encamped within sight of the city. This is clear both from the silence of John of Nikiou with regard to any such encampment, and from his statement that when a Muslim force was seen advancing—the force sent to receive the tribute—its appearance caused a stir of alarm in the city. No such commotion could have arisen if the Muslim army had been in daily view from the walls for some months, as the Arab writers allege. It is clear that here again they are confounding the first surrender of Alexandria with the second capture, when there really was some kind of siege; but this first surrender did not result from any military necessity [1].

[1] One is sorry to dismiss all the romantic stories woven by Arab fancy into the siege of Alexandria, but there really is no alternative. The truth seems to come out in Suyûṭî's account of 'Amr's letter to Omar, which states that only twenty-two Muslims fell during the siege, although this letter is given as written after the second capture of the city. The well-known story of 'Amr and Wardân being taken prisoners, during the repulse of a storming-party which had broken into the town, is a mere fable. Virtually the same story is told of the same warriors in reference to the siege of Damascus, and both anecdotes may be found in Eutychius, who winds up the siege of Alexandria by making the Arabs drive the Romans out of Alexandria by sea and by land. Another version of the story gives the same details, but sets them in the siege of Gazah in Palestine. The legend seems to come originally from the fairy tales of Ibn 'Abd al Ḥakam. The Grand Mufti of Egypt remarks, in a note on Ṭabarî with which he furnished the present writer, 'In this account also no mention is made of any battle of Alexandria, which, according to tradition, took place only after an uprising in the year 25,' and this is doubtless the truth.

But it is interesting to note Abû Ṣâliḥ's remark (p. 76) that the number of Muslims slain in the conquest of Egypt, without reckoning those killed in the siege (what siege is uncertain), was

It must be repeated that Alexandria was practically impregnable to any force which 'Amr could bring against it. The total circuit of the walls was some nine or ten miles, of which about three rested on the sea, while lake, morass, and canal protected the greater part of the remainder. Since, then, only a very small section of the walls was open to attack, it was easy for the defenders to concentrate all their force in repelling an assault: and even if the Arabs could have put out of action the formidable engines on the ramparts, their rude methods would never have breached the walls. In fact there appears no instance in all the history of Alexandria in which the city was captured by storm without betrayal from within.

Consequently, as long as the fleets of the Empire ruled the sea—and the Muslims had not yet dreamed of sea-power—there can have been no military reason for the treaty made by Cyrus. The army no doubt was disheartened by the fall of Babylon and by the remembrance that they had been beaten in every pitched battle during the campaign; they knew also that their leaders were either cowardly or incapable. But all that might have been changed by fresh troops with fresh leaders and fresh spirit. The fact, however, is that since the death of Heraclius there was no longer a ruler able to weld or to wield the forces of the Empire. At Alexandria itself the population was split into groups so divided in sentiment and interest that a state of feud and riot was the normal state of society; but the death of Heraclius rent in two the central government, leaving nothing but a war of factions. 'It broke

12,300—a fair estimate for the various battles of that long campaign.

the strength of the Romans' in more ways than the Arab writer meant: for the great issue of the moment—the defence of the Empire—fell into abeyance. In the chaos wrought by the intrigues of Martina and the plots of Valentine Egypt was cast adrift; and Alexandria, on which the fate of Egypt now depended, lost hope of any such help from without as would not merely save the city but clear the enemy out of the country.

That at the time of the surrender there was no apparent prospect of the Romans taking the offensive and rolling back the invasion, may be granted. But Alexandria might have defied capture for two or three years at least; and when once the sceptre was in firm hands again, the hope of recovering all Egypt would not be chimerical, though the blunders of the past had given the Muslims a grip on the country difficult to loosen. The military position was by no means past retrieval; and though Cyrus could plead the moral weakness of the army and the political disunion of the people, nothing can acquit him of the charge of losing Egypt to the Empire. Alexandria should have been held at all costs: Cyrus delivered it to the enemy by a clandestine and gratuitous surrender.

It remains a problem why the people of Alexandria, who were ready to stone Cyrus for his treason, were so quickly prevailed upon to pardon him and to accept the treaty. Fickle and frivolous as the people were, it was no mere whim which decided them to abandon their allegiance to the Empire and to bow under the dominion of Islâm. There can, I think, be but one explanation beyond those already suggested, and that is that the Alexandrians were wearied out both by the vicissitudes and by the misgovernment which they had suffered during the past forty years, and that they hoped to find under Muslim rule a period of settled peace, of religious tolerance, and of lighter taxation. It may have been this relief from taxation which turned the scale: for while it is difficult to estimate the fiscal burdens borne under the Romans, there can be no doubt that the taxes were manifold and heavy, as well as vexatious, whereas the poll-tax and land-tax demanded by 'Amr had at least the charm of simplicity, directness, and fixity, and amounted, or seemed to amount, to less than the sums exacted for the imperial exchequer. In proportion as patriotism in Egypt was weak, the appeal to the purse was strong: and this promise of reduced taxation may count for a great deal in all the Muslim conquests. In the case of Alexandria it may have been the determining factor [1], although it is known that the hope of financial relief was bitterly disappointed.

The treaty was ratified—possibly by the last act of Heraclonas, whose reign ended that November. It seems that the terms were rehearsed in a proclamation now issued by 'Amr to the people of Egypt. The proclamation offered protection to the 'person, property, religion, churches, and crosses' of the Egyptians, and promised to defend the people against Nubians and all other enemies on condition of payment of tribute [2]. But neither the

[1] Mr. Milne in his *Egypt under Roman Rule* gives a good deal of information about the taxes, but does not make it clear what was the total of taxation payable by the Alexandrians or Egyptians at this time, nor whether Alexandria was still exempt from the Roman poll-tax as in the days of Josephus (p. 122).

[2] This proclamation is from Ibn Kathîr (quoted by Abû 'l Maḥâsin). Ibn Kathîr says that it was made after the capture of

news of the surrender of the Great City, nor the liberal nature of the terms offered, availed to paralyse all further resistance. The cause of the Empire was now quite hopeless, with Alexandria under captivity, and it was the plainest unwisdom to reject the treaty: yet although the country as a whole came under it, some few towns in the north of the Delta stood loyal to their colours. These towns therefore had to be conquered before the campaign was over; but 'Amr was free to move against them at a time of his own choosing.

Meanwhile he had other work in hand at Babylon. He had resolved to build a new Muslim city in the plain which stretched from the Roman fortress to the Muḳaṭṭam Hills, and which had been the scene of his encampment. This city is said by Balâdhurî to have been planned by Zubair, who built himself a house, in which the ladder used in scaling the fortress was kept till it perished in a fire. Yâḳût, however, mentions four different persons[1] as directly appointed by 'Amr to superintend the laying-out of the streets and quarters, which were assigned to different tribes of the Arabs. In any case it may be taken for granted that both the architect and the builders of the new town were Copts, no Arab as yet possessing the requisite art and knowledge. The name Fusṭâṭ, by which the town became known, is clearly a foreign word, and it is a source of

'Ain Shams: but this is a mere blunder. The terms he gives are exactly those of the Treaty of Alexandria, and he adds that all the people of Egypt accepted the conditions. Broadly speaking, this is true of the Treaty of Alexandria, but it is certainly untrue with regard to any other treaty, nor indeed was any treaty made at Heliopolis.

[1] Mu'awîah ibn Ḥudaij, Sharîk ibn Summayyî, 'Amr ibn Ḳaḥzam, and Jibrîl ibn Nâshirah.

perplexity to the Arab writers. They say generally that it means either a tent[1] of leather or skin, such as 'Amr is said to have used, or else an assembling-place: one tradition even avers that every city is a fusṭâṭ. But Yâḳût gives six ways of pronouncing the word[2], and its connexion with the tent of 'Amr and the story of the dove's nest has at least an element of truth. For the form *Fussâṭ* takes us back at once to the Byzantine φοσσᾶτον (the Roman *fossatum*) which was in common use at the time of the conquest in the sense of *camp*. The Romans at Babylon naturally spoke of the place where 'Amr's army encamped as the φοσσᾶτον, and the Arabs learned the word from them. It is strange that this explanation should appear novel[3].

[1] Abû Ṣâliḥ casts doubt on this interpretation. He says, 'It was called Fusṭâṭ, or the meeting-place of the people, and the Arabs did not put up a tent, not being acquainted with the use of tents' (p. 74).

[2] Fusṭâṭ, Fisṭâṭ, Fussâṭ, Fissâṭ, Fustâṭ, and Fasṭâṭ. In support of the theory that the name comes from the Roman 'fossatum,' see Sophocles' *Byzantine Lexicon*, s.v. φοσσᾶτον. The term might have been heard by the Arabs in Syria as well as at the fortress of Babylon. It would be used mainly in connexion with a fortified city, and this association may account for the fact that some Arab writers actually say that 'fusṭâṭ' means a city. See Maḳrîzî, *Khiṭaṭ*, vol. i. p. 296. The tradition referred to in the text is given by Yâḳût, who writes: 'A tradition says, "You are bound to assemble together, for the hand of God is upon the fusṭâṭ," meaning the town in which men assemble: so every town is a fusṭâṭ.' Ibn al Faḳîh says that Bosrah was called Fusṭâṭ.

[3] Dr. Wallis Budge in his little book called *The Nile*, p. 112 (T. Cook & Son, London, 1890), gets near the truth. But although in a note he remarks, 'Arab. فُسْطَاط, another form of فسّاط = Byzantine Greek φοσσᾶτον,' yet in the text he says, 'Fosṭâṭ means a tent.' It is questionable whether the Arabs used tents for military purposes at this time: but apart from that doubt, the meaning of *camp* is so strongly founded on both historical and philological reason as to be virtually incontestable.

It is very unlikely that at first the town of Fusṭâṭ was laid out on any large scale or with any idea of making it the Muslim capital [1]. The troops in the fortress were too cramped for either health or pleasure, and it was not lawful or not desirable to dispossess the people of Miṣr of their houses. Consequently, as all fear of further war in this part of the country was removed, the Arabs could build outside the walls of Babylon quite unmolested. From small beginnings the town had a rapid growth when, a year later, Omar refused ʿAmr permission to retain the seat of government at Alexandria. Fusṭâṭ Miṣr—for it was called by the double name—soon spread over the whole area now occupied by the rubbish mounds south of Cairo, and became the recognized capital of Egypt. Outside the city of Fusṭâṭ to the northward later arose the suburb of Al ʿAskar, to which the central power was attracted. Further north again Al Ḳaṭâiʿ was founded by Aḥmad ibn Ṭûlûn, and all the rulers of the Tulunide dynasty had their palaces in that quarter [2]. After

[1] The date of the foundation of Fusṭâṭ is of course disputed. Balâdhurî seems to place it after the capture of Babylon, while most of the other Arab writers place it after the occupation of Alexandria and the Caliph's refusal to allow ʿAmr to reside in Alexandria. It seems probable that the town was begun after the *surrender* of Alexandria at the time given in the text, and that later it assumed the dimensions and importance of a capital city, when Omar had pronounced against Alexandria. Weil, I think, is mistaken in putting the first building of Fusṭâṭ after the Muslim *entry into* Alexandria, as he certainly is in the statement that Alexandria 'fell by the sword.' Abû 'l Maḥâsin says very clearly, ''Amr founded Fusṭâṭ in A.H. 21 after the taking of Alexandria,' and the winter of 641–2 after Dec. 10 falls in A. H. 21.

[2] The name Ḳaṭâiʿ means 'landed estates' or 'fiefs.' Quatremère translates from Maḳrîzî a very interesting description of the quarter called by this name and of the fine buildings it contained

the Tulunides, Al 'Askar regained for a while its preëminence, until it was finally discrowned towards the end of the tenth century, in the time of the Fatimides, by the building of Miṣr al Ḳâhirah—Miṣr the Victorious, or Cairo as it was called by the Venetians, who passed on the epithet instead of the name to Europe.

A little to the north of the ruined Roman fortress there stands to this day the venerable mosque of 'Amr—the oldest mosque in Egypt. It is a familiar object to travellers, and no description of it is here necessary. But it seems probable that the first foundation of the original mosque took place in this same winter of 641–2[1]. The spot chosen was that on which 'Amr had set up his standard and which came to be called the Place of the Standard[2]. It lay among orchards and vineyards[3] close to the bank of the river[4], and it had been occupied by one Abû 'Abdarraḥman Ḳaisabah ibn Kulthûm, but at the request of 'Amr he surrendered it as a free gift for all the Muslims. A common place of worship was their first necessity; but the original mosque of 'Amr was a very simple building. Its dimensions were only fifty cubits by thirty: the roof was very

(*Mém. Géog. et Hist.* t. ii. pp. 458 seq.); and a description of Al 'Askar precedes it (p. 452).

[1] Both Yâḳût and Abû 'l Maḥâsin give this date (A. H. 21).

[2] This is from Yâḳût. The account which makes it the place of 'Amr's standard and not of his tent is the more probable, and renders the derivation of Fusṭâṭ from φοσσᾶτον even more certain.

[3] Ibn 'Abd al Ḥakam, quoted by Suyûṭî.

[4] See Quatremère, *Mém. Géog. et Hist.* t. i. pp. 71 seq. Hamaker (*Expugnatio Memphidis*, p. 132 of notes) refutes Waḳidî's statement that the mosque was founded on the site of a Christian church. The error doubtless arose from the fact that in the later structure some columns were employed obviously taken from Christian buildings.

low: there was an open space in front of the mosque, but no courtyard, and a roadway round it: six doors gave access to the building. It soon proved too small for the congregation, who had to sit in rows in the open space. The ḳiblah is said to have been built by eight[1] of the Prophet's companions, chief among them being Zubair, Al Ḳaddâd ibn al Aswad, and 'Ubâdah ibn aṣ Ṣâmit. It had a more direct orientation than the present ḳiblah. When the building was finished, a *minbar* or pulpit was placed in it, and from this 'Amr used to hold forth[2], until Omar rebuked him for exalting himself above the heads of his fellow believers, and ordered its destruction. The first additions to the mosque were made c. 673 A.D.[3] by Maṣlamah ibn Mukhallad, who made an extension on the north side, substituted mats for the pebble pavement, built a turret at each angle, added minarets, on which his own name was inscribed, and increased the number of muezzins, ordering them also to chant the call to prayer at daybreak instead of beating the wooden gong[4] as heretofore. About

[1] Suyûṭî. Other writers say thirty or even eighty.

[2] Abû 'l Maḥâsin quotes from Ibn 'Abd al Ḥakam a long report of a sermon preached by 'Amr. It is at least an interesting composition.

[3] Yâḳût and Suyûṭî give A.H. 53, while Abû 'l Maḥâsin writes A.H. 63—by a slip, doubtless.

[4] The nâḳûs or wooden gong was in use by the Christians prior to the use of bells, and remains in use to this day in many Muslim countries, where bells are disliked or forbidden. Its discontinuance by the Egyptian Muslims is recorded by Abû 'l Maḥâsin. The nâḳûs was sometimes made of metal—a plate of iron or copper suspended by strings. See Vansleb, *Histoire de l'Église d'Alexandrie*, p. 59; Butler, *Ancient Coptic Churches*, vol. ii. pp. 79–80; Pereira, *Vida do Abba Daniel*, p. 50, n. 1; and Hamaker, *Expugnatio Memphidis*, pp. 166 seq., where the matter is treated at great length.

the year 696 [1] 'Abd al 'Azîz pulled down a portion of 'Amr's mosque—or possibly only the extension—and rebuilt it: and somewhat later in 711 [2] the Caliph Walîd ibn 'Abd al Malik wrote to Ḳurrah ibn Sharîk, the governor of Egypt, ordering him to pull down the whole of the mosque and rebuild it. It was then that the mosque took in the main the form which it still preserves [3], although several subsequent alterations are recorded [4].

Of the domestic architecture at Fusṭâṭ some few details are known. The houses were chiefly of brick, and soon rose to a height of four or five stories. We must picture large irregular piles of building, with Roman columns used freely as supports, but possessing no merit of design and little ornament—precisely such buildings as may be seen, or might be seen twenty years ago, still standing in Rosetta. Some of these blocks at Fusṭâṭ are said to have

[1] A. H. 77.

[2] A. H. 92.

[3] So says Suyûṭî, writing circa 1500 A. D. There has certainly been no material alteration since that date.

[4] It was enlarged in 750 when Ṣâliḥ ibn 'Alî was governor of Egypt, and again in the days of Hârûn ar Rashîd, c. 791. Further additions were made in 826 by 'Abdallah ibn Tâhir, and in 871 by Abû Ayûb Aḥmad ibn Muḥammad: but the additions of 'Abdallah ibn Tâhir were destroyed in 884 by a fire and replaced by the magnificent Sultan Khamârawaih. Various improvements were made in the tenth century, but the mad Caliph Al Ḥâkim disfigured the mosque by removing the mosaics and replacing them with whitewash. The reader is referred for further details to a very full history and description of the mosque of 'Amr given in an admirable paper by Mr. E. K. Corbett in the *Journal of the Royal Asiatic Society* for Oct. 1890, vol. xxii. N. S. The article is accompanied by plans and illustrations. There is also an extremely close and interesting account of the mosque in Ibn Duḳmâḳ (pt. iv. pp. 59–67), whose MS. was discovered and published subsequently to the appearance of Mr. Corbett's article.

contained as many as two hundred people, and the ground floor was seldom inhabited. Khârijah ibn Ḥudhâfah, the well-known lieutenant of 'Amr, is said to have been the first to have a balcony or loggia built: but Omar on hearing of it wrote to 'Amr that it could only be for the purpose of spying out the secrets of the neighbours, and that it must be taken down. Baths also were built at Fusṭâṭ, but they were called at once Ḥammâm al Fâr, or the Mouse Baths, owing to their ridiculous smallness in comparison with the splendid baths of the Romans.

Besides houses and baths and a mosque, a graveyard was necessary. A curious legend is told that Cyrus, the Muḳauḳas, offered 'Amr 70,000 dinârs for a plot of ground by the ravine at the foot of the Muḳaṭṭam hills; and when he was pressed to give his reason for offering so large a sum, he replied that, according to the ancient writings, this was the Plantation of Paradise. Omar settled the matter by remarking that he knew of no Plantation of Paradise save the ground in which believers are buried. The request of Cyrus was refused: the ground was marked out as the Muslim burial-place: and in after years 'Amr himself and four other of the Prophet's companions were there laid to rest.

The other great work which 'Amr seems now to have undertaken was the excavation of Trajan's Canal[1]. This ancient waterway, which had left the

[1] In placing the excavation of Trajan's Canal in this winter 641–2 I am running counter to Al Kindî, who says it took place in A. H. 23, which year begins in Nov. 643. But it is known that, before the death of Omar in Dhû 'l Ḥijjah, A. H. 23, Egyptian vessels were landing their cargoes in Arabia, and it is scarcely conceivable that the whole length of the canal could have been cleared out and rendered serviceable in less than a year. Of course it is possible

Nile a little to the north of Babylon, and, passing by Heliopolis and the Wâdî Tumilât to Al Ḳanṭarah, had joined the Red Sea at Ḳulzum [1], had silted up through long neglect under the Romans. It was of far more ancient date than the time of Trajan, who merely restored it to utility, as 'Amr proposed doing. Indeed, as Weil shows [2], part of it at least

that the work was done in the previous winter 642–3; but that date is unlikely, because 'Amr was then engaged in the expedition to Pentapolis. Moreover it can scarcely be doubted that John of Nikiou means to place this work in the winter 641–2. At least he seems to speak of it as begun during the life of Cyrus and before the expedition to Pentapolis; and although it is true that he makes it come after the Muslims had taken full possession of the country, it is clear that John regards that possession as effective before the death of Cyrus, and therefore at this period. The argument from order in John's disordered narrative may be worth little (pp. 577–8) in itself, and it might be argued that the Arabs were not placed in full possession of the country by the Treaty of Alexandria. This is true to the letter, but for all practical purposes possession was complete, save in the extreme north of the Delta. Moreover, Balâdhurî's authority is in favour of the earlier date. For he says (p. 216) that in the year of famine, A.H. 21, Omar wrote ordering 'Amr to send the tribute paid in kind, i.e. corn and other produce, to Medina *by sea*, and it so continued to be sent with some intermission until the reign of Abû Ja'far al Manṣûr. This does not prove that the canal was open in A.H. 21 (ends Nov. 29, 642), but it does prove that 'Amr felt in that year the advantage of a continuous waterway to the sea. On the whole therefore, in spite of Weil, the evidence seems in favour of the commencement of the work being made early in 642. Possibly it was not finished before 643: but, as Weil points out, Ibn 'Abd al Ḥakam's very detailed account of Omar's journey to Jâr, the port of Medina, to see the arrival of the ships from Egypt, proves that the canal was in full working order some time before his death in Nov. 644. Possibly the canal was *finished* in the winter 643–4, and used at the following flood of the Nile for the first time.

[1] See Quatremère, *Mém. Géog. et Hist.* t. i. pp. 176 seq.

[2] *Geschichte der Chalifen*, i. pp. 130 seq. Weil refers to Hdt. ii. 158, Mannert's *Geographie der Gr. und Römer*, x. 1 S., pp. 503 seq.,

was laid out by Pharaoh Necho, who also pierced the Isthmus of Suez from sea to sea. In the time of Ptolemy Philadelphus II the canal was repaired and reinstated, but it was made to branch off the Nile at Phacusa instead of Bubastis. The date at which the waterway was cut from near Babylon to Bubastis is uncertain: but this channel was not wholly successful, being available for use only at high Nile; and for want of proper care it became unnavigable some time after the second century of our era. The mere drift of the sand would soon choke up the bed, when once it was neglected: and it is alleged that the line of the waterway was so lost, that it had to be pointed out to 'Amr by a Copt, whose services were rewarded by exemption from tribute. On the other hand, the rapidity with which the excavation was accomplished must be taken to show that some sections of the course of ninety miles were still in fair order, although it is true that rapid results were accomplished by the vast gangs of natives, who were driven like slaves to the work and kept at it by taskmasters, according to the custom in vogue from time immemorial. The Arabs indeed seem to have applied this system of forced labour with exceptional rigour: insomuch that the Egyptian bishop is betrayed into very strong language: 'The yoke they laid on the Egyptians was heavier than the yoke which had been laid on Israel by Pharaoh. Him God judged by a righteous judgement by drowning him in the

and Letronne in *Revue des Deux Mondes*, xxvii. 215. There is also some information to be found in Abû Ṣâliḥ, pp. 172–3 and notes, and p. 88 n. The bed of the canal where it passed through what is now Cairo has recently been filled up, and is occupied by an electric tramway.

Red Sea after He had sent many plagues both on men and cattle. When God's judgement lights upon these Muslims, may He do unto them as He did aforetime unto Pharaoh[1]!' Yet it would seem that this great severity was rather incidental to the period of conquest than a permanent characteristic of 'Amr's government.

It is related that 'Amr contemplated excavating a branch canal from Lake Timsah northward to join the Mediterranean, so that the whole isthmus would be pierced as now by a waterway: but Omar forbade the design on the ground that the Romans would then be able to sail through into the Red Sea and stop the pilgrimages. This story deserves all credence.

But these works of peace did not altogether divert the Arab commander's attention from military matters. Although the Treaty of Alexandria had practically completed the subjugation of the country, there were still a few towns in the north of the Delta, particularly on the sea-coast, which refused to be bound by it. Against these 'Amr was entitled to proceed even during the armistice; and there seems no doubt that he sent an expedition to reduce them in the spring of 642. The movements of the Arab army are, however, difficult to follow. On this phase of the conquest John of Nikiou sheds no light whatever; while the details given by the Arab writers, who are our only authorities, are hard to correlate or to understand.

It may, however, be conjectured that the army set out from Kariûn and moved along the coast eastward. In what was known as the western Ḥauf there was a town called Ikhnâ, not far from

[1] John of Nikiou, p. 578.

Alexandria [1]. Ṭalamâ, the governor of Ikhnâ, had received from 'Amr a dispatch communicating the terms of peace agreed upon with Cyrus; but being dissatisfied, he is said to have sought an interview with 'Amr and inquired about the amount of the poll-tax. The Arab chief, irritated by the discussion, pointed to a neighbouring church and exclaimed, 'If you filled that building with gold to the roof, I would not define the amount of the poll-tax. You are our treasury, and if you give us abundant supplies, we shall treat you liberally, but if we are in want, we shall make heavy demands upon you [2].' Ṭalamâ naturally resented this language and decided not to surrender; and it was against Ikhnâ accordingly that the Muslims now marched. But the town was soon forced to capitulate: and, although it yielded under a written treaty, many prisoners were taken and sent to Omar at Medina. A like fate befell Balhîb [3], which was a strong place a few miles south of Rosetta: and it was here apparently that 'Amr received Omar's ratification of the Treaty of Alexandria [4]. In the Caliph's letter, which was read out

[1] Yâḳût, vol. i. p. 166. I am unable to identify Ikhnâ on modern maps or lists of villages.

[2] This language is so totally at variance with the solemn agreement fixing the poll-tax and making it unalterable, that if it was used at all at this stage, it can only have been uttered as an ill-humoured jest. But it is far more reasonable to suppose that the words were spoken later, when Ikhnâ was reduced to the last extremity and had to capitulate. In that case the words were better justified, as 'Amr was not bound by the Treaty of Alexandria, which the conquered town had rejected.

[3] See n. 1, p. 289 supra. Balâdhurî calls this place Balḥît—a mistake reproduced by Abû 'l Maḥâsin and Suyûṭî—but Yâḳût gives it correctly.

[4] I have already shown reasons for disagreeing with the story of Balḥîb as given on p. 10 of Prof. Lane-Poole's *Egypt in the Middle*

before the troops, instructions were given that all prisoners who chose to adopt Islâm should be set at liberty and received as brothers. The story is that a great number of the captives went over to the Muslim religion, their decision being hailed with shouts of triumph by the Arabs. But a sudden and wholesale conversion of this kind was certainly an unusual, if not an unparalleled event. If made, it was clearly made under the strongest pressure of worldly motive by men of easy convictions: probably, however, the story is greatly exaggerated.

In close connexion with Ikhnâ, treaties of peace are recorded as made with Ḳuzman (perhaps Cosmas), governor of Rosetta, and with John, governor of Baralus [1]. From Baralus it would seem as if the Arab forces still followed the coast line till they came to Damietta [2]. John, the governor, offered no further resistance to the Arabs, who now controlled all the outlets of the Nile. Khais, in the region called the Ḥauf near Damietta, was also

Ages. Both on geographical and on historical grounds it is quite impossible that 'Amr can have spent the time of the armistice here.

[1] Rosetta of course commanded the entrance to the western branch of the Nile, and Balḥîb commanded the waterway from the Rosetta branch towards Alexandria. Baralus (Πάραλος) was a town at the Sebennytic mouth of the Nile, and both town and district retain the name to this day, although the Sebennytic channel has long since been choked, forming a lake which is only parted from the sea by a narrow strip of sand. Ikhnâ, Rosetta, and Baralus are mentioned together by Maḳrîzî.

[2] The submission of Damietta is mentioned by Balâdhurî, who says, nevertheless, that the expedition to Tinnîs, Damietta, Tûnah, Damîrah, Shaṭâ, Daḳahlah, Banâ, and Busîr was under 'Umair ibn Wahb al Jumaḥî. It seems more probable that the command was entrusted to a lieutenant. Balâdhurî does not record any fighting, but says that 'Umair made terms with the people of these places on the same conditions as those of the general treaty.

reduced to submission [1] : and it is probable that the whole country of the Delta was now subjugated with the exception of some towns which stood on islands in the vast but shallow waters of Lake Manzâlah.

A century before the Arab conquest [2] this region, now covered by flood, had been unrivalled in Egypt, save perhaps by the Fayûm, for its climate, its fertility, and its wealth. Gardens, palm-groves, vineyards, and cornlands were watered by never-failing streams from the Nile, and flourished in great luxuriance. But the sea broke through the line of sandhills, which served as a rampart, and year by year encroached further, till it swamped all the low-lying land, leaving only a number of islands lifted above the flood. Tilth and villages were swept away, though a number of towns stood high enough to escape the devastation. Of these the most famous was Tinnîs—a town of some magnitude and archi-

---

[1] The Arab authorities differ considerably about the names of the resisting towns. Balâdhurî gives Balḥît (Balḥîb), Khais, and Sulṭais in one place, and in another, as we have seen, he names Sakhâ, Balḥît, Khais, and Sulṭais as assisting the Roman army at the battle of Sunṭais. To this list Yâḳût adds Fartaṣâ, and he remarks that ' when 'Amr had taken Alexandria he made captives of the people of those towns, and sent them to Medina.' Yâḳût gives the position of Khais. Maḳrîzî records written treaties with Ikhnâ, Rosetta, Baralus, Sulṭais, Masîl, and Balḥîb; so does Suyûṭî. As to Khais, this must be the town which Yâḳût (vol. ii. p. 507) describes as in the western Ḥauf and as being taken by Khârijah ibn Ḥudhâfah, and the western Ḥauf is described as being towards Damietta, the eastern towards Syria. The Khais in the description quoted by Quatremère (*Mém. Géog. et Hist.* t. i. p. 337) would seem to lie east of Pelusium, and to be therefore a different place.

[2] In the year 251 of the Coptic era. For all this information about the lake towns see Quatremère, *Mém. Géog. et Hist.* t. i. pp. 287 seq. Quatremère translates at some length from Maḳrîzî and Mas'ûdî.

tectural beauty, with an enormous manufacture of the finest textiles. Other towns on the lake, like Tûnah, Damîrah and Dabîḳ, boasted the skill of their weavers, but they could not compare with Tinnîs, which ranked with Damietta and Shaṭâ for the richness and delicacy of its fabrics. Only at Tinnîs and Damietta could the weavers produce a robe of pure linen worth 100 dinârs (50 guineas): while Mas'ûdî records a garment made for the Caliph in a single seamless piece costing 1,000 dinârs. This was woven of gold thread with an extremely small admixture of fine linen. It is also on record that the trade of Tinnîs with Irak alone amounted to between 20,000 and 30,000 dinârs yearly before it was crushed by vexatious tariffs.

Tinnîs stood on an island[1] of considerable size, and was reached from the south by a channel called Baḥr ar Rûm, which may have been identical with the Tanitic branch of the river and ran to Salaḥîah. There was also easy and direct communication by water with Pelusium, or at least with Tînah its harbour. Even as late as the tenth century Tinnîs is said to have possessed many ancient monuments, besides 160 mosques, each adorned with a lofty minaret, 72 churches, and 36 baths; and its fortified walls had 19 gates, all heavily plated with iron[2]. From other islands the dead are said to

[1] Quatremère thinks the name of the town is derived from νῆσος—with the Coptic feminine article prefixed. If so, this part of the country must have been flooded long before the sixth century. Indeed Cassian, who was in Egypt in 390–7 A. D., says definitely that 'Thinnesus' is so beset on all sides with sea or salt marshes, that the people were wholly dependent on sea traffic, and they had to bring soil in barges when they wanted to make more building-ground.

[2] Quatremère, l. c., p. 329. Yet the dimensions of the town are

have been ferried across the lake for burial at Tinnîs, where they seem to have been embalmed. A century later the Persian traveller, Nâsiri Khusrau[1], who visited Tinnîs in 1047 A.D., is amazed at its prosperity. He speaks of 10,000 shops and 50,000 male inhabitants. A thousand vessels were moored at the island, which grew nothing, and depended on trade for all provisions. The rise of the Nile swept away the girdling flood of salt water, and filled the vast underground cisterns and reservoirs with sweet water enough to last for a year. The splendid coloured stuffs woven by the Copts were of more value than ever. In the Sultan's looms fabrics were woven for him alone; a single turban cost 4,000 dinârs; but these fabrics were never put on the market. The Roman Emperor offered a hundred cities in exchange for Tinnîs, but was refused. Besides these royal textiles, a fabric was woven called *bûkalimûn*—a shot silk of lustre so fine that it was said to change colour every hour of the day. But the steel cutlery of Tinnîs was almost as famous as the products of its looms; and altogether it was a place of curious interest and great importance.

There is a legend that the governor of Tinnîs at the time of the conquest was a Christian Arab named Abû Ṭûr, who went out at the head of an army of 20,000 Copts, Romans, and Arabs to fight the Muslims on their advance against Tinnîs after the capture of Damietta[2]. Several engagements

given as about a square mile only—an obvious error. Tinnîs was destroyed in A.H. 624, nothing but ruins remaining. The island is still called by the same name, and there are ancient remains upon it.

[1] See *Sefer Nameh,* ed. C. Schefer, pp. 110 seq.

[2] Quatremère, l.c., p. 307, quoted from Mas'ûdî. The Arab

were fought before the Muslims were able to rout the Christian army and to capture its commander. The surrender of Tinnîs followed: and after the division of the spoil the Muslim army moved on to Faramâ. Whatever proportion of truth and error this story may contain, two things are fairly certain—that Tinnîs came under the Muslim dominion at this time, and that its industrial activities were not directly impaired by the conquest. Neither here indeed nor at Tûnah, Bûrâ, Dabîḳ, or the other islands lost in the blue expanses of Lake Manzâlah, was there anything to attract Muslim settlers, and it may safely be said that this region remained almost exclusively Christian for a long time subsequently[1]. Its disappearance from history can be dated.

force must have come by water, and it is absurd to suppose that the governor of Tinnîs could muster 20,000 men or transport them over the lake. But numbers in Arabic documents are seldom to be taken literally, and one should doubtless read 2,000. Of course Abû Ṭûr may be a mere invention of legend. There is no other record of any Christian Arab leader in Egypt. This story, however, appears in an early Arab writer, and though it is dated 300 years after the alleged event, yet Mas'ûdî himself appears to be quoting from a lost History of Damietta.

[1] About the year 824 A. D. Dionysius, Patriarch of Antioch, was driven by stress of weather into the harbour of Tanis, where 30,000 Christians are said to have met him with great rejoicing. He was welcomed by the Patriarch of Alexandria and a number of bishops, who remarked that no Patriarch of Antioch had visited Egypt since the days of Severus. Dionysius, with a better historical memory, reminded them of Athanasius' visit, which took place early in the seventh century, and of the formal union then effected between the two Churches. See Barhebraeus, *Chron. Eccl.* t. i. c. 360.

By the harbour of Tanis must be meant the harbour at the mouth of the Tanitic branch of the Nile. It would of course be nearer to Tinnîs than to the city of Tanis, which is much further inland.

The island of Tinnîs was much exposed to raids from the sea, though it was always strongly garrisoned, and in the year 1192 Saladin ordered its evacuation. A few years later, in 1227, Malik al Kâmil had its forts and walls razed to the ground, and it became a mere heap of ruins[1].

There is another anecdote relating to the conquest of this region, which claims at least some notice. Maḳrîzî in speaking of Shaṭâ describes it as a town which lies between Tinnîs and Damietta, and which legend avers to be named from one Shaṭâ, son of Al Hamûk, the uncle of the Muḳauḳas[2]. This derivation is pure romance: but the story goes on to say that when the Arabs laid siege to Damietta and captured it, Shaṭâ, who was governor of the town, went out at the head of 2,000 men and declared his adherence to Islâm—a religion which he had long studied with interest. When he saw that the Arabs encountered prolonged resistance at Tinnîs, Shaṭâ collected and armed a force from the towns of Baralus, Damîrah, and Ashmûn-Tanah;

The modern Arab name of Tanis is Ṣân or Ṣân al Ḥajar. The position of the harbour is still marked on the coast about half way between Port Said and Pelusium.

[1] A good description of the ruins is given in Ghillebert de Lannoy's *Œuvres Recueillies et Publiées*, par Ch. Potvin, Louvain, 1878, pp. 138–9, quoted by Schefer, l. c.

[2] Waḳidî gives the name (p. 130) as الهامرك (Al Hâmirak), perhaps more correctly. It is of course impossible to credit for a moment these details about the relations of Al Muḳauḳas. The myths about his so-called daughter and wife have already been rejected as wholly unfounded, and his uncle and cousin must be dismissed with as little ceremony. Cyrus cannot have had any relations in Egypt, unless he brought them with him.

As a matter of fact Shaṭâ lies near to Damietta on the east, but is a long way from Tinnîs. But the ancient Tamiatis, here intended, was some distance further north.

then, joining his levies to the Arab reinforcements sent by 'Amr, he marched against the enemy. In a battle which followed Shaṭâ displayed brilliant valour, slaying with his own hand twelve of the foremost captains of Tinnîs: but he fell in the thick of the combat and was buried outside the town, where, says Maḳrîzî, 'his tomb is still shown, and is still frequented on the day of his death, 15th Sha'bân, by pilgrims from all the country round[1].'

Now it would be easy to destroy nearly the whole of this story. The town of Shaṭâ was so named long before the Arab conquest, when it was already famed for the fineness and splendour of its textiles. Moreover we know from John of Nikiou that the governor of Damietta at this time was not called Shaṭâ at all, but John[2]. And lastly, the relationship of Shaṭâ to Al Muḳauḳas is clearly apocryphal. But though the personality of Shaṭâ is legendary, there is one circumstance which redeems the story from fiction, and that is the date. For the Arab historian gives the day of the hero's death as Friday, 15th Sha'bân, A.H. 21. This corresponds to July 19, 642, and the date is one that cannot be shaken. For in the first place, the year 642 is the year postulated by the whole course of this history; and in the next place July 19 in that year did in fact fall on a Friday. Such a double coincidence is very rare, but where it occurs the date must be absolutely

[1] Quatremère, l. c., p. 339. It is not quite clear whether Maḳrîzî means that the warrior was buried at Tinnîs or at Shaṭâ. It would seem, however, that the place where he fell would be the place of his burial, and this is the more likely because the battle took place in the heat of summer. I may add that the story of Shaṭâ is also given by Waḳidî in very similar terms, text pp. 130 seq., 147–8, and notes 179, 190).

[2] John of Nikiou, pp. 561 and 584.

authentic: and it is further confirmed by the fact of the yearly pilgrimage, lasting even to the time of Maḳrîzî. It may therefore be taken as proved that a battle took place on the date in question close to Tinnîs on the island, and that a Roman or Coptic general from Shaṭâ was slain after greatly distinguishing himself while fighting on the side of the Muslims.

This date is both interesting and important, because it shows to what a length of time resistance to the Saracens was protracted in the Delta, even after the surrender of Alexandria. And when it is remembered how intensely Coptic in sentiment were the people of Tinnîs and all this region of the lake, it will not be denied that the record of the battle at this date gives one more shock to those twin time-honoured fallacies—that 'Egypt fell almost without striking a blow' and that 'the Copts welcomed the Arabs as deliverers.' The betrayal of Alexandria by Cyrus must have extinguished the last hope of triumph for the Christian cause in Egypt; and it is astonishing that nevertheless these isolated communities in the Delta should have held out for nearly a year longer. It argues in them a stubborn courage and a devotion to their religion, for which history has too long refused them the due meed of honour.

CHAPTER XXIII

END OF THE ROMAN DOMINION

Roman withdrawal from Upper Egypt. Refugees in Alexandria. Action of Cyrus. His loss of influence and fears for his safety. His depression and death. Story of the poisoned ring. Roman officials retained in office. Appointment of Cyrus' successor in the patriarchate. Gloom in the capital. Evacuation of Alexandria by the Roman army under Theodore.

LONG before the last embers of hostility were thus smothered in the Delta, the reduction of Upper Egypt, at least as far as the Thebaid, seems to have been completed by a separate Arab column under Khârijah ibn Ḥudhâfah. The Nile valley had been denuded of Roman troops, with very few exceptions, during the previous year, 641; and the scanty remnant of the imperial garrisons had neither spirit nor numbers left to dispute the Muslim claim to dominion. Hence there is no record of further fighting in that region, and it may be taken that the surrender of Upper Egypt followed peaceably on the surrender of Alexandria.

Upon what passed in the capital itself during the remainder of the armistice, history is not altogether silent. The city, as we have seen, was crowded with refugees swept in from all parts of the country before the advancing tide of invasion. By the terms of the treaty Roman soldiers and settlers within the walls were free to leave by land or by sea; while no provision was made for the Egyptians. But as the refugees witnessed the constant departure of vessels bound for Cyprus, Rhodes, and Byzantium, they became restless, and pined to return to their villages. Consequently they approached Cyrus, whose influence with 'Amr was known to be potent, and begged of him to sue for the requisite permission. Apparently leave was refused. Nor is the failure of the Patriarch's mission surprising, when one remembers that it must have taken place before March, and therefore some time before the actual cessation of hostilities in the Delta. As most of the refugees belonged to Lower Egypt, clearly there was danger of their carrying arms or aid to some of the still unconquered cities.

But Cyrus took the refusal deeply to heart. It was a direct check to that policy of winning favour with the Copts by which, it seemed, he now hoped to cancel something from the heavy reckoning of their resentment. He appears already to have despaired of retaining the ascendency over them which he had hoped to found on his alliance with the Muslim power. Gloomy presentiments overcast the mind of the Muḳauḳas, as he saw the end of the Roman sovereignty drawing nearer. All the news from Constantinople was against him. Martina and her sons had been put aside, or put to death, and Constans had been proclaimed sole Emperor by the end of November (641). Pyrrhus, who was on friendly terms with Cyrus, and had apparently been converted by Cyrus to the interests of Martina, had been banished, and Philagrius, the enemy of Cyrus, had been recalled. A second revolt by Valentine[1] had failed owing to the hostility of the

[1] John of Nikiou, p. 582. Zotenberg makes out that this second rebellion took place in 644: but his date can hardly be correct. Sebeos says that the revolt occurred in the second year of Constantine (Constans), which would be 642–3, unless the second year were regarded as beginning on Jan. 1, 642, as is possible. In any

populace: but when Valentine was seized and brought before Constans on a charge of usurping the purple, the rebel swore the most solemn oath that he was guiltless of any such design, and that his only purpose in gathering an army was to fight the Muslims. Thereupon the Emperor, accepting these professions of loyalty, reinstated Valentine, and agreed to marry his daughter: and Valentine gave proof of his sincerity by striking wildly at all who could be imagined to favour Martina and Pyrrhus. Among the rest, he charged Arcadius, Archbishop of Cyprus, with treason, and sent a troop of soldiers to arrest him. Death, however, intervened, and released Arcadius from the summons.

But the incident revealed to Cyrus his own imminent danger. Arcadius was a man of the most blameless and saintly repute; yet he was to have been haled like a malefactor to Constantinople to take his trial. How then could Cyrus hope to stand, if arraigned on the same charge of treason? His friendship for Martina and for Pyrrhus was notorious, as well as his guilt for the loss of Egypt. Moreover the court party had now realized what the loss of Egypt meant, and were furious with the man who had brought this evil and dishonour upon the Empire.

It is no wonder that, as message followed message telling of these events at Constantinople, the Archbishop sank into profound depression. Menaced by fear of exile or death at the Emperor's bidding, which was still law in Alexandria; baffled in his

case John of Nikiou is perfectly clear in making 'the triumph and power of Valentine' after this revolt one of the things which depressed Cyrus. As Cyrus died in March, 642, Valentine's rebellion must have taken place about January of that year.

plans for conjuring away the memory of the persecution and making friends of the Copts; his Church policy for ever discredited; and his statecraft rendered for ever infamous by its very triumph —Cyrus was now a broken man in mind and body. All his dreams of ambition had dissolved: his very hopes of personal safety were gone. As he felt the shadows closing round his life, his conscience awoke to a sense of his crimes as well as his failures. Torn by unavailing remorse, he deplored his betrayal of Egypt with ceaseless tears [1]. So plunged in gloom and despondency he fell an easy victim to a dysentery, which seized him on Palm Sunday, and on the following Thursday, March 21, 642, he died.

It is quite clear that Cyrus died a natural death, and that his end was hastened by the misery and ignominy into which he had fallen. Of the two passages in which his death is recorded by John of Nikiou, the first says that 'overwhelmed with sorrows, he was taken ill of a dysentery and died,' the other says that 'he wept unceasingly, fearing lest he should suffer the same fate that had befallen him previously, i. e. exile: and in the midst of this grief he died according to the law of nature [2].' But in the one case it is stated that he was afflicted by the calamities which had come upon Egypt and the brutal treatment of the Egyptians by the Arabs,

[1] In the text John of Nikiou is made to say (pp. 582–3), 'His greatest sorrow had been to see the refusal by the Muslims of his requests in favour of the Egyptians': but the title of the chapter runs, with far more reason, 'Of the death of Cyrus, the Chalcedonian, with the remorse of having delivered Alexandria into the hands of the Muslims.' This doubtless points to the need for correcting the reading of the text.

[2] pp. 578 and 582.

while in the other we are told that his chief sorrow was the refusal of his intercession on behalf of the Egyptians. There is no reason to doubt this account of his end, although a Coptic tradition as old as Severus[1] gives a somewhat different version. 'When 'Amr took Alexandria,' it runs, 'and settled the affairs of the city, the misbelieving governor, who was both Prefect and Patriarch of Alexandria, feared that 'Amr would put him to death. Accordingly the misbeliever touched a poisoned signet-ring with his tongue, and so perished on the spot.' It was not so much 'Amr as the Roman Emperor whom Al Muḳauḳas feared: but the fact of his terror, and the fact that it hastened his death, are both curiously preserved in this dramatic legend.

One other point in connexion with the story of Cyrus' death calls for notice. We have already seen that 'Amr treated the Egyptians during the conquest with great harshness[2], and that the Coptic historian's wrath is roused against him for the severity of the tasks laid on his countrymen. So here, in speaking of the Patriarch's last days, John says, "'Amr had no mercy upon the Egyptians, and he failed to observe the treaty they had made with him: for he was of barbarian race[3].' In another passage[4] he enters into more detail, and records that a man named Menas, who had been nominated Prefect of Lower Egypt by Heraclius, was continued in office by the Arabs. Menas was a presumptuous man, unlettered, and a deep hater of the Egyptians. Similarly one Sinôdâ, or Sanutius, was continued as

[1] Brit. Mus. MS., p. 106. See also Pereira's *Vida do Abba Samuel*, p. 48, where the Synaxarium is quoted.

[2] p. 347 supra.

[3] p. 578.

[4] p. 577.

Prefect of the Rîf, and one Philoxenus[1] as Prefect of Arcadia, or the Fayûm. All three of these men are described as loving the heathen and hating the Christians, upon whom they laid grievous burdens. The Copts were forced to carry fodder for the cattle of the Arabs, and to provide them with milk, honey, fruit, vegetables, and other things in great abundance over and above the ordinary rations, i. e. the taxes in kind: and these orders the Copts executed under the stroke of incessant terror.

This account is highly interesting for two reasons. The three Prefects named—the most important in Egypt save the Prefect of Alexandria—were not only Roman officials, but Roman officials under the governorship of Cyrus, and therefore Melkites, without any religious or political sympathy with the Copts: and this is a proof that, so far from the converts to Islâm coming exclusively from the Copts, some at least of the most influential of the renegades were from among the Romans. One almost begins to wonder whether the conduct of Al Muḳauḳas himself could not be explained on the theory that he was a secret convert to the religion of Mohammed. The second point is this. It is now established that 'Amr treated the Copts, both before and after the surrender of Alexandria, with the sternest rigour. But if so, how is it possible to maintain that, in the hackneyed phrase, the Copts welcomed the Arabs with open arms? Such a theory might be demolished from this passage alone

[1] Among the papyri of the Archduke Rainer Collection is a letter from this same Philoxenus, Prefect of Arcadia, naming the contribution to be paid to Khârijah at Babylon (Karabacek's *Führer durch die Ausstellung*, p. 138, No. 553). This is one more confirmation of John of Nikiou's remarkable accuracy.

in John of Nikiou: and those Arab writers, of much later date, who seem to countenance it, must be held either to convict themselves of error or to convict their hero 'Amr of the blackest ingratitude. But the closer one examines the history of this period the clearer it becomes that Cyrus was not alone in his treason to the Empire. The ease with which these three great Roman officials ransomed their office by the transfer of their political and their religious allegiance to Islâm, and the manner in which they used their new lease of power to strike at the faith and the fortunes of the Copts—these things prove beyond cavil that there was a wider conspiracy against the Empire among the Romans, and that the conspirators were as hostile to the Copts as they were benevolent to the Arabs.

Little remains to be told of the six months in Alexandria between the death of Cyrus and the entry of the Arab forces. Indeed, the only event of which we have any certain knowledge is the appointment of the successor of Cyrus in the Melkite patriarchate. This did not take place till some three months later, when, on July 14[1], the festival of St. Theodore, the deacon Peter was duly clothed with the pallium and seated on the throne left vacant by the last of the imperial Patriarchs of Alexandria. The delay may have been caused by reference to Constantinople, or by the difficulty of finding a candidate for an office which was henceforth to be sundered from the hierarchy of the Empire, and therefore to be held on a most precarious tenure. For all hope of aid from Byzantium had now finally vanished. The boasted army of Valentine proved utterly powerless to attempt the recovery of Egypt,

[1] Mr. Brooks rightly corrects Zotenberg's date, July 26.

although the people there were already beginning to discover how idle were their dreams of a settled government with fixed taxation. The whole country is described as suffering oppression at the hands of the Muslims; but the burden fell most heavily upon the city of Alexandria. There the interruption of the traffic which had enriched the people, and also the departure of those wealthy nobles and merchants who had resolved to abandon their home in Egypt, made the incidence of the new taxation very severe upon those that remained. In spite of the smooth phrases of Cyrus, they were feeling now the bitterness of subjection to the enemies of their country and their religion.

Depression and melancholy hung over the city during the last few weeks of the armistice. Already many of the houses were left empty, and the bustle of departure from the quays grew less, as vessel after vessel, laden with retiring Romans and their goods and chattels, sailed northwards to return no more. But a great fleet was gathering in the harbour to remove the remaining legions of the imperial army. Theodore, who was appointed governor of Egypt on the death of Cyrus, and Constantine, who succeeded him as commander-in-chief, seem to have personally undertaken the mission of arranging for the withdrawal of the Roman forces throughout the Delta, acting in concert with the Arabs [1]. The Nile was now rising high, and all the waterways

[1] Zotenberg (p. 583, n. 2) is right in his view that the presence of Theodore and Constantine in the interior was in consequence of the armistice, and that there is no suggestion of any resumption of hostilities at this time. Zotenberg offers no opinion on the reason of their absence from Alexandria; but the reason I have given above seems adequate.

were available for transport. This accordingly was the season agreed upon for the evacuation, and with its arrival the remnant of the Roman garrisons embarked in boats under Theodore and Constantine, and passed down to Alexandria. At the same time the hostages held at Babylon by the Arabs were released, or at least escorted down the river to join their comrades in the capital[1].

Once more the Feast of the Cross had come round. By a strange irony that festival of September 14, which a year ago was marked by the arrival of the traitor Archbishop, Al Muḳauḳas, was now marked by the final act in the downfall of the Christian dominion in Egypt. Even as the Exaltation Service was sounding in the Cathedral, the last touches were being given to the vessels in harbour and the last orders for embarkation were issued. And three days later[2], on September 17, Theodore's fleet, bearing the mournful residue of the imperial army, cast off its moorings and set sail for Cyprus[3].

[1] The release of the hostages before the entry into Alexandria is curious, but it shows the strength of the Muslim position and the weakness of the Romans by this time. Most of the Romans must already have cleared out of the country.

[2] Mr. Brooks shows that the words 'Après la fête de la Croix' in Zotenberg's version (p. 582) of John of Nikiou are displaced. I agree in the main with his contention, but I think rather that the following two lines 'le 20 du mois de ḥamlê . . . siège pontifical' are wrongly here inserted and should be put back at the beginning of the paragraph before the words 'Ensuite Théodore.' Then 'après la fête de la Croix' need not be moved, but runs on naturally with 'le 20 du mois de maskaram.'

[3] Suyûṭî says, 'There were 200,000 men of the Romans in the city, of whom 30,000 fighting-men fled in 100 large ships with all the property they could take, while those who remained had to pay tribute.' The context lends some colour to the idea that the

Only a few days now remained for the wretched inhabitants to set their house in order. On September 29 the eleven months of the armistice expired: the great gates were flung open: and 'Amr at the head of his rude desert warriors marched in past the long lines of gleaming colonnade and the stately palaces of the great city of Alexandria. So the Roman Empire in Egypt ended.

reference is to the second capture of Alexandria; but the balance of evidence is against it, and the language used seems clearly to point to the evacuation under the treaty. It will be remembered that the treaty expressly provided that the Romans should take their property with them, whereas at the second capture there certainly was no leisure for such a proceeding. In any case it is not likely that an army of 30,000 men all embarked and set sail together, though the proportion of ships to men is not unreasonable. By the date of the evacuation the garrison had doubtless dwindled to a much lower number. Suyûṭî's account of the evacuation seems to come from Maḳrîzî, who quotes Abû Ḳabîl as his authority. The 100 large ships carried away 30,000 Roman soldiers *with money and goods*; and it is added that 600,000 inhabitants were left to pay the poll-tax, besides women and children—which must be an exaggeration.

CHAPTER XXIV

ALEXANDRIA AT THE CONQUEST

'Amr's letter to the Caliph. Dazzling brightness of the city. Colonnades. Reservoirs. The Bruchion. The Cathedral church of Caesarion: its description and history. Cleopatra's Needles: confusion of obelisks with the Pharos. Crabs of bronze and glass: Arab testimony vindicated. The Serapeum described: original plan and structure. Position of the Library. Diocletian's Column. Arab legends. Amphitheatre. The Pharos: classical and Arab authorities. Structure of the tower. The marvellous mirror: story of its destruction. Ruin of the Pharos. The Cairo minaret modelled upon it.

'I HAVE taken a city of which I can but say that it contains 4,000 palaces, 4,000 baths, 400 theatres, 12,000 sellers of green vegetables, and 40,000 tributary Jews.' Such is the current form of the well-known letter[1] of 'Amr reporting his capture to the Caliph. While these round numbers contain an obvious overstatement, which was probably not in the original letter but has arisen from copyists' errors[1], they show clearly enough what an impression the city made upon its conquerors. But amazed as they were at the size and splendour of Alexandria, they were even more struck by its extraordinary brilliancy. 'Alexandria is a city containing much

[1] If we read 400 palaces and baths, 40 theatres, 1,200 sellers of vegetables, and 40,000 Jews, there is nothing improbable in the estimate. Zachariah of Mitylene, who gives careful statistics of Rome, says there were 1,797 houses of magnates or palaces, and 926 baths there (pp. 317–8). 'Amr's letter comes in Ibn 'Abd al Ḥakam, also in Eutychius, in Maḳrîzî, and in Makîn. Maḳrîzî gives a typical exaggeration from Abû Ḳabîl: 'Among the baths were 12,000 vaulted buildings, the smallest of which contained 1,000 sitting-rooms'!

marble in pavements, buildings, and columns,' says one writer[1]. 'The city was all white and bright by night as well as by day,' says another[2]: and again, 'By reason of the walls and pavements of white marble, the people used all to wear black or red garments: it was the glare of the marble which made the monks wear black. So too it was painful to go out by night: for the moonlight reflected from the white marble made the city so bright that a tailor could see to thread his needle without a lamp. No one entered the city without a covering over his eyes to veil him from the glare of the plaster and marble.' Yet a third Arab writer[3], of the tenth century, alleges that awnings of green silk were hung over the streets to relieve the dazzling glare of the marble[4].

All the streets were colonnaded, according to the same author. This certainly was true of the two great avenues which, as we have seen, intersected the city. One of these ran from east to west, joining the Sun Gate to the Moon Gate[5], while the other

[1] Iṣṭakhrî (*Bibl. Geog. Arab.*, ed. de Goeje, part i. p. 51).

[2] Suyûṭî (*Ḥusn al Muḥâḍarah*). The monks of Serapis used to wear black, but it may be doubted whether this was the reason: see Dr. Botti's *Fouilles à la Colonne Théodosienne*, p. 37, n. 2.

[3] Mas'ûdî (p. 429).

[4] The general impression made on the Muslim mind by Alexandria is well illustrated by Ibn Duḳmâḳ (part v. p. 117), who writes: ''Abd al Malik ibn Juraij said, "I have made the pilgrimage sixty times; but if God had suffered me to stay a month at Alexandria and pray on its shores, that month would be dearer to me than the sixty prescribed pilgrimages which I have undertaken."' And again (p. 118): 'According to the law of Moses, if a man make a pilgrimage round Alexandria in the morning, God will make for him a golden crown set with pearls, perfumed with musk and camphor, and shining from the east to the west.'

[5] Some authorities put these gates in the wrong place, viz. north

ran from north to south: they met and crossed in a large open space enclosing gardens and surrounded by fine buildings. Beautiful gardens too belonged to many of the palaces in the middle of the city[1]. Suyûṭî, apparently quoting from Ibn 'Abd al Ḥakam, writes that 'Alexandria was composed of three cities side by side, each with its own wall, and the whole encircled by another wall.' This must refer to the Egyptian quarter, the Roman quarter, and the Jews' quarter: but its accuracy is perhaps doubtful. 'Abdallah ibn Ẓarîf alleges that there were seven forts and seven moats, and the Fort of the Persians was certainly regarded as one of the wonders of Alexandria.

Nor were the Arabs less amazed at the buildings than at the substructure of the city—that marvellous subterranean labyrinth of cisterns, many descending to a depth of four or five stories, and each story showing a forest of columns and chambers. 'Alexandria is a city upon a city: there is nothing like it on earth,' exclaims Suyûṭî, 'so full is it of columns loftier and larger than any to be seen elsewhere.' These underground chambers were for the storage of fresh water. They were fed by conduits running

and south of the city. If there were any doubt, it would be removed by John of Nikiou's plain statement (p. 415) that Antoninus Pius built the Sun Gate at the east and the Moon Gate at the west. Amélineau is among those who appear mistaken: 'La Porte du Soleil se trouvait au sud de la ville, près du canal amenant l'eau du Nil' (*Géog. Copte*, p. 32). The Gate of the Sun was no doubt also the Gate of Heliopolis (Id., ib., p. 42), but the road to Heliopolis ran through the East Gate: there was no great highway out on the south except for boats. Amélineau's article on Alexandria is meagre and disappointing.

[1] John Moschus says, εἰσὶ γὰρ παράδεισοι μέσον τῆς πόλεως ἐν τοῖς οἴκοις τῶν μεγιστάνων (*Pratum Spirituale*, cap. 207).

from the Nile canal, which passed through the city in the Egyptian quarter; and being filled at flood-time they held enough water to last the whole year through[1].

In former times the most splendid part of the city was that called the Bruchion, which was bounded on the north by the harbour and on the south by the great avenue running from the Sun Gate to the central garden. The destruction wrought in this quarter by Aurelian was no doubt great, but probably it has been exaggerated[2]: and it is unlikely that the ruin would have been left unrepaired. Here in any case had stood the palaces of the Ptolemies: here also had been the Mausoleum, where Alexander's body rested in its golden shell, and the Museum with its marvellous libraries, the centre of the learning of the world. In the same quarter towards the east was still to be seen the Tetrapylus, an open temple or pavilion with four rows of columns about it. Here Alexander was said to have laid the bones of Jeremiah the Prophet, and the place was held

* [1] Some of these reservoirs remain to the present day. See an article entitled *Les Citernes d'Alexandrie* by Dr. Botti in the *Bulletin de la Société Archéologique d'Alexandrie*, No. 2, 1899, pp. 15 seq., where some interesting plans are given. Caesar, *De Bell. Civ.* iv, mentions these cisterns and the canal which supplied them.

* [2] Ammianus Marcellinus (xxii. 16) seems to say that the city lost the greater part of the area called Bruchion owing to the ruin caused by civil broils in the time of Aurelian. But John of Nikiou proves conclusively that the area of the city had not shrunk in the manner alleged, and that the old line of wall on the eastern side was standing as strongly as ever. Antoninus Martyr, who visited the place in the century before the conquest (c. 565 A.D.), says 'Alexandria is a magnificent city,' which he could hardly say if its finest quarter was in ruins (Palestine Pilgrims Text Society, vol. ii. p. 35).

in great veneration[1]. Close by the Tetrapylus was the church of St. Mary Dorothea, built by Eulogius, and further east, near the walls and near the shore, * the great church of St. Mark[2] was still standing and within it the marble shrine containing the bones of the Apostle himself. 'Coming from Egypt as one enters the city,' says Arculfus[3], 'one meets on the north side a large church, in which Mark the Evangelist is buried. His sepulchre is shown before the altar in the east end . . . and a monument to him has been built of marble above it.' In the same part of the town were the churches of St. Theodore and St. Athanasius[4].

But more renowned in the seventh century even than St. Mark's was the church called the Caesarion, which stood in the same quarter toward the middle of the bend of the great harbour. This church had almost usurped the place of the Cathedral. Its vast fabric, with the two ancient Egyptian obelisks

[1] John Moschus, *Pratum Spirituale*, cap. 77. Amélineau (*Géog. Copte*, p. 29) cites a Coptic MS. which places the Tetrapylus in the middle of the town and concludes that it was on the 'Grande Place.' The expression is too vague to warrant such an inference.

[2] John of Nikiou says (p. 524) that it was close to the sea, and (p. 548) that it was near a gate of the city. There seems, however, to have been a second church of the name; see Amélineau, *Géog. Copte*, pp. 37–8.

[3] Arculfus was in Egypt c. 670 A.D.; see Palestine Pilgrims Text Society, vol. iii. p. 52. Two hundred years later the city had so shrunk that Bernard the Wise, c. 870, says: 'Beyond the east gate is the monastery of St. Mark: there are monks here at the church where he formerly lay. But the Venetians coming by sea bore away his body to their own island' (id., ib., p. 5). By 1350 the church where St. Mark was martyred was 'about two miles east of Alexandria' (id., vol. vi. p. 33). So clearly is the dwindling of the city shown.

[4] John of Nikiou, p. 543.

standing in its fore-court, towered above the city walls, and was the most conspicuous object in the near foreground of the view [1], just as the acropolis with the Serapeum and Diocletian's Column was in the background, as the traveller entered the harbour by the Pharos. The Caesarion had originally been a heathen temple. It was begun by Cleopatra in honour of Caesar, and was finished by Augustus. The description given by Philo is worth quoting [2]:—

'That temple of Caesar's in Alexandria under the name of Sebastian (Augustus) is a piece incomparably above all others. It stands situate over against a most commodious harbour; wonderful, high, and large in proportion; an eminent sea-mark; full of choice paintings and statues, with donatives and oblations in abundance; and then it is beautiful all over with gold and silver; the model curious and regular in the disposition of the parts, as galleries, libraries, porches, courts, halls, walks and consecrated groves, as glorious as expense and art could make them, and everything in the proper place; beside that the hope and comfort of seafaring men, either coming in or going out.'

This 'superb palace,' as John of Nikiou [3] terms it,

[1] This is confirmed by Strabo, Philo, and Pliny. See an interesting article by Monsignor Kyrillos II entitled *Le Temple du Césareum* in the *Bulletin de la Soc. Khédiviale de Géographie*, Ve Série, No. 6, Fév. 1900 (Le Caire, 1900). I am indebted to this article for much information. Amélineau, forgetful alike of classical and of Arab authorities, strangely says: 'Je ne sais pas trop où placer le Césarion, car les détails manquent absolument' (*Géog. Copte*, p. 32). The site of the obelisks being well known, that of the Caesarion cannot, as we shall see, be doubtful.

[2] Philo's Embassy from the Jews of Alexandria to Caligula in Josephus, ed. Sir R. L'Estrange, London, 1702, fol., p. 1087.

[3] p. 405.

was changed by Constantine the Great into a Christian church and dedicated to St. Michael[1], but at the date of the conquest it still retained its old name, Caesarion. It was about 350 A.D. that it became the patriarchal church or Cathedral. But in 366, in the days of Athanasius, a furious crowd of pagans and Arians met in the great open space before the church, and rushing in they burned the altar, the throne, carpets, veils, and all they could lay hands upon. If any books remained from the libraries mentioned by Philo, they must then have perished; but the church was restored in 368. Readers of *Hypatia* will remember that it was in the Caesarion, some fifty years later, that the maiden philosopher was torn to pieces by a mob of Christian

[1] The Coptic Synaxarium for 12 Ba'ûnah (Festival of the Archangel Michael) is curious. It runs thus: 'The reason why we keep the feast of St. Michael to-day is that there was in the city of Alexandria a great temple built by Cleopatra, daughter of Ptolemy, in honour of Saturn; and his feast was kept there on this same 12 Ba'ûnah. In the temple was an idol of brass (or bronze) called Saturn, to which upon this day many sacrifices were offered. This custom was kept up by the people until the time of the Patriarch Alexander in the reign of the Emperor Constantine.' The Synaxarium goes on to say that Alexander wished to destroy the idol, but the people refused to renounce their ancient custom and the rejoicings of the day. Finally, the Patriarch offered to retain the festival and holiday, to make the sacrifices to the true God for the benefit of the poor instead of to the idol, and to change the dedication to St. Michael. This offer was accepted, and the idol was broken in pieces; but the name Caesarion remained. The church stood until the Muslims came, and then was destroyed. So the record closes. Eutychius says that a cross was made out of the bronze statue: he adds that the church 'Igne periit cum Occidentales Alexandriam ingressi eam vastarunt'—which is somewhat obscure—and that the Copts in his day continued the feast, at which they slew many victims in sacrifice (Migne, *Patr. Gr.* t. 111, col. 1005).

fanatics[1] in an orgie truly worthy of the ancient temple of Saturn. It was in the baptistery of the Caesarion that Timothy Aelurus took refuge nearly half a century later, only to be dragged out and sent into exile; and when after twenty years of banishment Timothy landed again at Alexandria 'he was received with great state, with torches and songs of praise, by the various people and languages there,' and escorted in triumph to the same Caesarion[2].

There is no description of the interior of the Caesarion remaining; but it may be taken for granted that it was of the basilican type, and retained its splendid embellishment. The last great scene of pomp under the Caesars was the service of rejoicing for the return of Cyrus, whose sermon must have rung strangely in the memories of those who now watched the entry of 'Amr's army. But the church did not long outlast the conquest. Yet its name in the Arab form, Ḳaiṣarîah, given first to some kind of palace or public building, survives to-day, though with a changed meaning[3].

[1] The authority for this is Socrates, who wrote soon after the event (*Hist. Eccl.* vii. 13–15). John of Nikiou (pp. 464–6) gives an account which, accusing Hypatia of magic arts, approves her death, but makes it appear that after being stripped in the Caesarion she was dragged through the streets till she died, and was burned at the place called Cinaron.

[2] Zachariah of Mitylene's *Chronicle*, p. 110. Zachariah speaks of the 'Great Church' here and also p. 76: but on p. 64 he expressly says 'The Great Church is called Caesarion,' which establishes the identity. The welcome given to Timothy is curiously like that given to Cyrus on his return from banishment.

[3] The principal street, or High Street, in an Arab town is now called the Ḳaiṣarîah. A passage in Shams ad Dîn al Maḳdasî almost looks as if in early days the term were applied by the Muslims to their larger mosques (*Bibl. Geog. Arab.* part iii.

The two obelisks of red Aswân granite, which stood before the Caesarion, excited the curiosity and wonder of the Arabs, and their historians have many particulars about them, Thus Ya'ḳûbî (ninth century) says, 'There are two obelisks of variegated stone standing on two brazen crabs with ancient inscriptions[1]'; and Ibn Rustah (early tenth century) in much the same manner speaks of 'two monuments like lighthouses (manârah), square, and standing on two figures of scorpions, made of copper or brass, on which are inscriptions. It is also reported that the figure of the scorpion was melted by a fire kindled beneath it, and that the monuments fell[2].' His contemporary, Ibn al Faḳîḥ, discloses already the beginnings of a strange confusion between these obelisks and the great lighthouse or Pharos, which the Arabs called *Al Manârah.* For he says, 'The manârah of Alexandria stands on a crab of glass in the sea'; and again, 'it has two pillars standing on two images, one of brass and one of glass, the brazen image in the form of a scorpion and the glass image in the form of a crab[3].' By Mas'ûdî's time the legend had crystallized into one of those fairy tales in which the imagination of the Arabs delighted. He says: 'The lighthouse was built on a foundation of glass in the form of a crab, on a tongue of land

p. 197). It was certainly used to denote a quadrangle surrounded by colonnades, which might serve as mosque or as market-place; and it is from this latter use that the modern acceptation of the term is derived: see Abû Ṣâliḥ, p. 116, n. 1. The high street is the natural place for sale and barter in an eastern town.

[1] *Bibl. Geog. Arab.* part vii. p. 339.

[2] Id., ib., p. 117. See also *Athenæum*, July, 1887, and de Goeje's note on this passage.

[3] Id., part v. pp. 70, 71.

projecting into the sea. On the top of the lighthouse were images of brass. One figure pointed with its right hand to the sun, wherever it might be in the heavens, and lowered its hand as the sun sank; another pointed to the sea in the direction from which an enemy was approaching, and as the enemy drew near, it cried out in a terrible voice, which could be heard two or three miles away, and so alarmed the inhabitants[1].'

Of course the Pharos was an entirely distinct monument—a solid structure of stone towering an immense height into the air—and it is ludicrous to imagine that its wide and vast foundations could rest on a crab of crystal. Nevertheless it is exceedingly interesting to trace the origin of this seemingly idle legend. For it comes from a mere misunderstanding of historical fact most accurately reported by the earliest Arab chroniclers. There is no doubt whatever that, at the time of 'Amr's entry into Alexandria, the two obelisks in front of the Caesarion stood on crabs as described. This was proved at the time of the removal of the obelisk which is now at New York. It was found that the monolith rested on four gigantic crabs of metal, which held it clear of the pedestal. The pedestal was formed of a single block of granite, which rested in turn on three graduated courses of stone. At the time of the excavation—for the base had been buried for centuries

[1] Quoted by Maḳrîzî, *Khiṭaṭ*, vol. i. p. 255. Suyûṭî, giving his authority as the writer of *Mubâhij al Fikr*, goes a step further in saying that 'the lighthouse was built of hewn stone fixed with lead over vaults of glass, which again stood on a crab of glass'! (*Ḥusn al Muḥâḍarah*, vol. i. p. 53). Ibn Rustah marks the confusion when he says that 'the manârah was built on *four* crabs of glass.'

—only one of the four crabs was discovered, and that in a mutilated condition; but the design and purpose of the crab were unmistakable, an inscription in Greek and in Latin upon the metal was still legible, and the truth of the Arab historians was vindicated[1]. This is a striking example of the way in which archaeology sometimes comes to the rescue of history.

But, it will be said, what becomes of the crabs or scorpions of glass under the other monolith? Is this a mere romantic fancy? No answer could be more illogical. Given two closely related statements, one of which is proved to be pure truth—to be indeed a statement of singular exactitude—to argue that the other is pure invention would be something like a wanton defiance of history. Nor is one forced to choose between defying the laws of history and defying the laws of natural science. Of course it may be the case that no monolith the size of Cleopatra's Needle could rest on crabs of glass of modern make, nor could crystal have been found in blocks of size adequate for the purpose. But there is a mineral of extreme hardness and polish, viz. black obsidian, which so resembles glass that it is defined as natural glass. The crabs under the second

* [1] A photograph of the crab may be seen on pl. v of Lt.-Col. H. H. Gorringe's *Egyptian Obelisks* (London, 1885), and other plates show the substructure. Néroutsos Bey in his *L'Ancienne Alexandrie*, pp. 16, 17, gives a full description of the original setting of the obelisk. Of the four supports in the form of crabs only one remained: this was of ancient copper—'cuivre reputé aurifère.' 'Ce support représentait un crabe marin couché à plat ventre sur le bloc de granit et portant sur le dos une broche qui entrait au dessous de la carne du monolithe.' The three other supports were of the same design, and kept the obelisk up clear of the substructure.

obelisk—that now in London—may have been formed of black obsidian; or, if this be impossible, then some other hard and highly polished stone was employed. Or finally, rather than discredit the Arab writers in a matter wherein their truth shines out clearly, one may accept their statement quite literally. That the Egyptians had not merely great skill but great secrets in the making of glass is undoubted; and it may well be that they were able to produce a material so toughened as to withstand the pressure of the monolith. One may note at the same time that the obelisk of London did actually fall long before its fellow.

We now see the two great monuments reared above their storied bases before the Caesarion, one held up on four crabs of copper or bronze, the other on four scorpions of toughened glass or obsidian. And, when we dispel the confusion between these obelisks and the Pharos, it is clear that the brazen images recorded by Maḳrîzî stood not on the top of the Pharos, where they would have been almost invisible, but on the top of the obelisks. The figure 'pointing to the sun' was undoubtedly a winged Hermes or Nike, probably standing on one foot upon the cap of the column [1], and stretching forth its right hand in an attitude familiar enough in Greek sculpture; while the other figure, 'pointing to the sea,' was designed with a view to symmetry. Exceedingly splendid must have been the appearance of these ancient monoliths in the setting devised by the taste and skill of the Augustan age, and very impressive the view of their lofty summits, as seen from the ships passing in and out of the harbour.

Of the Museum itself there is practically no record

* [1] It is proved that there was a metal cap on the obelisks.

remaining at this time, and it must be taken to have perished long before—possibly in the conflagration caused by Julius Caesar when he was besieged in this quarter by the Egyptians under Achillas [1], possibly in later wars or in the convulsions of dying paganism [2].

But it is time to pass on to the Serapeum—a group of buildings of great beauty, and one which greatly struck the Arabs. It stood of course in a different part of the city, in a position now marked by Diocletian's Pillar. This quarter was known as the Egyptian quarter, and never lost its original name of *Rakoti*: indeed to the Copts Alexandria was always known less by the name of its great founder than by that of the fishing-village which existed for ages before Alexander—a curious instance of their time-defying conservatism. The site of the Serapeum is fixed precisely both by ancient written documents and by recent antiquarian researches. It is usually named in close connexion with Diocletian's Pillar, which the Arabs called *'Amûd as Sawârî*—Pillar of Columns—and this was near the southern gate of the city called by the Arabs the Gate of the Tree [3]. It is not generally understood, and the present levels of Alexandria make it very difficult to realize, that the Serapeum was built on a veritable acropolis, rivalling

[1] See below, pp. 407 seq., where this question is discussed.

* [2] Matter says the Museum is not named after the fifth century (*École d'Alexandrie*, t. i. p. 331). Dr. Botti assigns the disappearance of the Museum to an earlier date: 'après Caracalla l'ancien Musée n'existe plus' (*Fouilles à la Colonne Théodosienne*, p. 138). This study of Dr. Botti's is exceedingly valuable for the history and topography of ancient Alexandria. By the *Colonne Théodosienne* he means what is generally called Diocletian's Pillar: the name *Pompey's Pillar* comes from a mistaken reading of the inscription beneath it.

[3] Both Yâḳût and Kazwînî give this name.

that of Athens. This citadel, however, while it towered above the city, was mainly artificial. For although there was a core of natural rock in the middle of the site, the vast mass of the acropolis had been reared by the hand of man, the lofty outer walls enclosing vaulted substructures which rose story above story [1]. Thus a huge quadrangular fortress was formed, with a broad level summit, adorned with magnificent buildings. There seem to have been two ways of access; one by a carriage road, the other by a long flight of one hundred steps, though it is not easy to see the use of the latter [2]. The

[1] The core of rock is visible to this day, while the description of Rufinus leaves no manner of doubt that the citadel was in the main a huge pile of masonry. He says: 'Locus est non natura sed manu et constructione per centum aut eo amplius gradus in sublime suspensus, quadratis et ingentibus spatiis omni ex parte distentus: cuncta vero, quo ad summum evadatur, opere forniceo constructa. . . . Extrema totius ambitus spatia occupant exedrae et pastophoria et domus in excelsum porrectae, in quibus vel aeditui vel hi quos ἁγνεύοντας vocant, id est qui se castificant, commanere soliti erant. Porticus quoque post haec omnem ambitum quadratis ordinibus distinctae intrinsecus circumibant. In medio totius spatii aedes erat pretiosis edita columnis et marmoris saxo extrinsecus ample magnificeque constructa. In hac simulacrum Serapis ita erat vastum ut dextra unum parietem, alterum laeva perstringeret: quod monstrum ex omnibus generibus metallorum lignorumque compositum ferebatur' (*Hist. Eccl.* ii. c. 23). Rufinus does not mention the library, but he witnessed the destruction of the idol and presumably the temple. Eunapius speaks of the destruction of the building as very thorough: τῷ τε Σαραπείῳ κατελυμήναντο καὶ τοῖς ἀναθήμασιν ἐπολέμησαν . . . τοῦ δὲ Σαραπείου μόνον τὸ ἔδαφος οὐχ ὑφείλοντο διὰ βάρος τῶν λίθων· οὐ γὰρ ἦσαν εὐμετακίνητοι. συγχέαντες δὲ ἅπαντα καὶ συνταράξαντες, κ.τ.λ. (*Vita Aedesii*, cc. 77–8). This was in the reign of Theodosius, while Theophilus was Patriarch of Alexandria and Romanus commander of the garrison.

[2] Dr. Botti in his first study of the subject (*L'Acropole d'Alexandrie*, p. 7) seems to overlook the carriage road, not having the

staircase lay on the eastern side of the acropolis. At the top of the long flight of stairs one entered the propylaeum, which was upheld by four enormous columns, two on each side of the passage; the passage was closed by gates or grills of bronze[1].

The general arrangement of the buildings on the summit is not easy to understand from the descriptions which remain: but it seems to have been as follows. The space was oblong—some 500 cubits in length and 250 in breadth[2]. On the edge of the

whole passage of Aphthonius before him: 'Donc pas de routes d'accès, mais seulement un escalier monumental de cent degrés; pas de route carrossable.' But in his *Colonne Théodosienne* (p. 24) the passage set out in full proves that there was a way open for carriages on one side. Dr. Botti in the latter work (p. 82) gives a somewhat curious translation of Aphthonius' words—*εἰσιόντι δὲ παρ' αὐτὴν τὴν ἀκρόπολιν τέτταρσι πλευραῖς εἷς χῶρος ἴσαις διῄρεται (? διῄρηται) καὶ τὸ σχῆμα πλαίσιον τυγχάνει τοῦ μηχανήματος.* He renders 'quand on entre dans l'acropole (on ne trouve qu') un seul plateau, lequel est divisé en quatre ailes semblables, et son ordonnance quadrilatère tient de la figure d'un moule à briques.' Surely *τὸ σχῆμα τοῦ μηχανήματος* goes together, and the sentence means 'the general plan of the arrangement is quadrilateral.' The preceding words mean that the space occupied by the quadrangle is divided into four by 'ribs' of equal length, i. e. by cross colonnades, as I show in the text.

[1] This citadel and its entrance are mentioned by Polybius in reference to the revolt of Cleomenes: 'the commander of the citadel secured the entrance gate' (v. 39). Had Matter recollected this passage, he would not have questioned Aphthonius' use of the term acropolis (*École d'Alexandrie,* t. i. p. 325).

[2] The measure is from Mas'ûdî. The description of the buildings is the result of a careful comparison of the statements of Rufinus and Aphthonius: but the latter is very far from clear even where he means to be precise. Aphthonius visited Alexandria c. 315 A.D. His *Progymnasmata* gives a comparison between the acropolis of Athens and that of Alexandria, which is full of interest, if obscure: see Dr. Botti's *Colonne Théodosienne*, pp. 24 seq. But the whole work should be read together with the same writer's *L'Acropole*

plateau on every side stood a range of handsome and lofty buildings, connected in various ways with the service of the temple. All round the great quadrangle enclosed by these buildings ran a broad colonnade; while four other colonnades were built out at right angles, one from the centre of each side. Thus the outer colonnade with the others formed roughly the design of a cross set in an oblong. But the centre of the whole quadrangle and of the whole acropolis had been occupied by the temple of Serapis. This temple unfortunately had long been overthrown when the Arabs entered Alexandria: but there is no doubt that it was a building of surpassing beauty and grandeur. The main fabric was oblong: it enclosed a central hall upheld by great columns of most precious marble, and its walls were of marble, within and without. In the midst of the hall stood a colossal chryselephantine statue of Serapis, whose outspread arms nearly touched the wall on either side, the left hand bearing a sceptre, while under the right hand of the deity was a monstrous image of Cerberus, round whose triple head of lion, dog and wolf coiled the folds of a huge python[1]. The whole chamber was embellished with priceless works of sculpture in marble and bronze, among which a series representing the combats of Perseus was conspicuous. Adjoining the temple walls, and running round them, was a magnificent colonnade, which thus stood parallel with the outer colonnade, and was joined on

d'Alexandrie et le Sérapeum, to both of which I am much indebted.

[1] Macrobius, lib. i. c. 20. So Pseudo-Callisthenes (Βίος Ἀλεξάνδρου, c. 33), describes the image as *τῇ δεξιᾷ χειρὶ κομίζοντα θηρίον πολύμορφον τῇ δὲ εὐωνύμῳ σκῆπτρον κατέχοντα.*

to it by the four cross colonnades above mentioned. But those porticoes which girt the temple were of exceptional splendour. The capitals of the columns were made of bronze overlaid with gold; the ceilings were covered with gold or brilliant colours; and walls and floors were of costliest marble [1].

But, above all, it was from these temple cloisters that doors opened into those bays or chambers of the main fabric, some of which contained the great library of Alexandria [2], while others had served as shrines for the ancient divinities of Egypt. Somewhere in the temple precincts had stood two antique obelisks; there had also been a marble fountain of great size and beauty; and at whatever time the

[1] The description of Ammianus Marcellinus is worth quoting (xxii. 16): 'His accedunt altis sublata fastigiis templa, inter quae eminet Serapeum: quod licet minuatur exilitate verborum, atriis tamen columnariis amplissimis et spirantibus signorum figmentis et reliqua operum multitudine ita est exornatum ut post Capitolium, quo se venerabilis Roma in aeternum tollit, nihil orbis terrarum ambitiosius cernat.' Possibly the plan given of the temple of Isis and Serapis at Rome, conjecturally restored, may furnish some idea of the arrangement at Alexandria: see Lafaye, *Histoire du Culte des Divinités d'Alexandrie* (Paris, 1883), plan facing p. 224. The language of Tacitus is very restrained (*Hist.* iv. 84); he merely notes that the temple was of grandeur proportioned to the size of the city ('pro magnitudine urbis extructum')—a phrase which Matter strangely misunderstands, alleging that Tacitus compares the whole group of buildings to a town—'cet ensemble que Tacite compare à une ville' (*École d'Alexandrie,* t. i. p. 323). The same mistake occurs in de Saint-Martin, who says, 'Sa grandeur, dit Tacite, égalait celle d'une ville' (*Histoire du Bas Empire* par Lebeau, t. iv. p. 406 n.).

[2] This seems the undoubted meaning of Aphthonius' language: *παρῳκοδομῆνται δὲ σηκοὶ τῶν στοῶν ἔνδοθεν, οἱ μὲν ταμεῖα γεγενημένοι ταῖς βίβλοις, τοῖς φιλοπονοῦσιν ἀνεῳγμένοι φιλοσοφεῖν καὶ πόλιν ἅπασαν εἰς ἐξουσίαν τῆς σοφίας ἐπαίροντες· οἱ δὲ τοὺς πάλαι τιμᾶν ἱδρύμενοι θεούς.*

great column, familiarly known as Diocletian's Pillar, was erected, it is certain that at the time of the Arab conquest it towered above the citadel[1]. One part of the Serapeum was occupied by a church dedicated to St. John the Baptist. Among other churches, which were also standing in the citadel, are named that of SS. Cosmas and Damian, and the Angelion[2]. The latter survived the conquest, and

[1] Dr. Botti (op. cit.) thinks that it was erected after the destruction of the Serapeum which took place in 391, and calls it the Theodosian Column.

[2] According to Dr. Botti, the Angelion was originally called the Arcadion, and the Arcadion was originally called Claudion. He further identifies the Arcadion with the Hadrianon (op. cit., pp. 135, 138, 139). These identifications seem to me scarcely established. The Hadrianon was a temple which had been turned into a sort of Record Office, where registers and archives were kept: see some remarks in *Oxyrhynchus Papyri*, vol. i. pp. 68–72, and ii. p. 182. It seems doubtful whether this building was on the Serapeum plateau at all; nor is there any reason why it should have been turned into a church, when it served so useful a purpose. Gregorovius, however, for the conversion into a church refers to Epiphanius, *Haeres.* xix. 2 (*The Emperor Hadrian*, p. 358). Eutychius (Migne, t. 111, col. 1025–6 and col. 1030) records that Theophilus *built* a large church in the name of the Emperor Theodosius, covering it all over with gold, besides many other churches, such as that of St. Mary and that of St. John: while as to the Arcadion, he says 'ecclesiam magnam Alexandriae *struxit* Arcadii nomine dicatam,' and this was certainly not prior to 398. This quite agrees with the much earlier record of John of Nikiou, who expressly states (p. 450) that the Patriarch Theophilus *built* a magnificent church to which he gave the name of the Emperor Theodosius, and another which he called after his son Arcadius: he also *converted* a temple of the Serapeum into a church which he called after *Honorius*. This church of Honorius, he adds, was also called the church of SS. Cosmas and Damian, and it lay opposite the church of St. Peter. Unless John is wrong, the Arcadion was a new structure at the end of the fourth century. But the question is one of some perplexity, because Sozomen's language (*Hist. Eccl.* v. 15) almost makes it appear that it was the temple of

being in danger of falling was splendidly reinstated towards the end of the seventh century by the Patriarch Isaac[1].

One other building remains to be noticed. Adjoining the propylaeum, and forming part of it, was the Oecus or House, distinguished from the other buildings of the acropolis by a lofty golden dome, which rested on a double ring of columns. Its purpose is not clear, and it may have been merely ornamental; but it seems to have survived the destruction of the temple, and is noticed in Arab chronicles with the 'Amûd as Sawârî[2]. Strange stories are told of the latter. It was part of a temple built by Solomon, according to the general opinion. Ibn al Faḳîḥ says that if a man threw a bit of pottery or glass against it with the words 'By Solomon, son of David, break in pieces,' then it broke; but without the talisman it broke not. Another legend was that if a man closed his eyes and walked towards the pillar, he always failed to reach it: and Suyûṭî naively records that he proved the truth of this himself by several trials. The same writer quotes 'the learned men of Alexandria' as saying that upon the pillar was a cupola under which Aristotle sat to study astronomy—a reminiscence of

Serapis which was turned into the Arcadion: *τὸ μὲν οὖν Σεράπιον* (*sic*) *ὧδε ἥλω καὶ μετ' οὐ πολὺ εἰς ἐκκλησίαν μετεσκευάσθη* Ἀρκαδίου *τοῦ βασιλέως ἐπώνυμον*. Yet *Σεράπιον* must mean here the acropolis, not the temple merely, and *μετεσκευάσθη* must mean 'rebuilt,' not converted, because Sozomen makes it clear that the temple was pulled down.

[1] Amélineau, *Vie du Patriarche Copte Isaac*, pp. 57–8.

[2] This seems to be the 'dome overlaid with brass which shone like gold,' which is spoken of by Suyûṭî: but Maḳrîzî speaks of 'a dome formed of one block of white marble of the finest workmanship.' They may be the same.

the dome and the library. Makrîzî's account of the Serapeum, quoted from Mas'ûdî, is truthful enough: 'There was in Alexandria a great palace without equal on earth, standing on a large mound opposite the gate of the city. It was 500 cubits long and 250 broad, with a huge massive gateway, each pier of which was a monolith and the lintel a monolith. In the palace were about 100 pillars, and in front of it a great pillar, of unheard-of size, surmounted by a capital.' Yet the same writer alleges that the pillar rocks in a wind. All these extraordinary buildings were supposed to have been raised by genii or giants of old. 'The jinn built an assembly hall for Solomon at Alexandria with 300 columns, each 30 cubits high, of variegated marble polished like mirrors, so that a man could see in them who was walking behind him. In the midst of the hall was a pillar 111 cubits high. The roof was a single block of green marble, square, hewn by the jinn[1].' These jinn were men whose heads resembled great domes, and whose eye would rend a lion. Another explanation, however, is that in ancient days the stones were as soft as clay, or, as another writer puts it, 'In the marble quarries it was easy to work before mid-day, for the marble was as soft as paste; but in the afternoon it became hard and intractable.'

These tales record the astonishment of the Arabs at the buildings which now passed into their possession. It is melancholy to trace the record of their destruction, though only fair to say that much of it was due to earthquakes. By the eleventh century the city was all in ruins, though strangely enough the many columns, which some writers make 500 in

[1] Suyûṭî, *Ḥusn al Muḥâḍarah*, p. 55.

number, are all described as standing[1]. A hundred years later Idrîsî saw them still: round the great pillar was a court with sixteen columns on each of the shorter sides and sixty-seven on each of the longer[2]. Benjamin of Tudela[3] in 1160 saw 'a large and beautiful building with columns of marble dividing the various halls' in what he calls the 'school of Aristotle,' just as the Muslim writers call it the 'porch of Aristotle' or the 'house of wisdom.' But in 1167 a wretched governor of Alexandria, named Ḳarâjâ, the vizier of Saladin, had all these columns broken down and most of them taken to the seashore, where they were thrown into the sea to render an enemy's landing more difficult[4]. And from that day to this Diocletian's Pillar has risen in solitary grandeur as the one remnant of that matchless group of buildings which stood on the acropolis of Alexandria[5].

Reserving for the moment the question of the fate which befell the great library, one may pass on to notice one or two other monuments. The amphitheatre, which the Arabs mention, seems to have been one which lay to the west of the citadel,

[1] Dr. Botti, *Colonne Théodosienne*, pp. 1, 2. [2] Id., ib., p. 12.

[3] Id., ib. But these columns probably belonged to the exterior colonnades: those of the temple had disappeared, or at least been overthrown, in the time of Theodosius.

[4] Maḳrîzî, *Khiṭaṭ*, vol. i. p. 159. 'Abd al Laṭîf, however, who says that he saw about 400 large columns broken into pieces and lying on the edge of the shore, thinks that Ḳarâjâ's intention was either to deaden the force of the waves which were undermining the city walls, or to keep off the enemy's fleet—in any case a childish piece of mischief, he adds (p. 113).

[5] Yâḳût's impression is thus given: 'When I visited Alexandria, I went round the city and saw nothing admirable or wonderful except one column called the 'Amûd as Sawârî by the gate called Bâb ash Shajarah.'

although there certainly was a hippodrome also outside the eastern gate of the city. This amphitheatre, they say[1], held a million spectators, so arranged that one and all, from the highest tier of seats to the lowest, could see all that went on and hear every word uttered without any crushing or inconvenience. The theatre, which stood somewhere in the Bruchion, was a distinct and a magnificent building.

But it was on the Pharos that the Arabs lavished their greatest wonder and admiration. This colossal lighthouse-tower stood, as is well known, at the north-east corner of the island of Pharos, which was linked to the mainland city by a long causeway on arches called the Heptastadium. At the time of the conquest the island was fringed by quays and occupied by various buildings, conspicuous among which stood the two churches of St. Sophia and St. Faustus and the guest-house which lay between them[2]. In Caesar's time the island had been occupied by a large village, the people of which were lawless freebooters. The lighthouse itself he calls a marvellous piece of architecture[3]. Strabo describes it as a tower wonderfully constructed of white stone in several stories[4]. It was built by Sostratus of Cnidus in the reign of Ptolemy Philadelphus as a guide for mariners, and though it had suffered from the action of the sea and other causes, yet it had always been strengthened as need

[1] Maḳrîzî, op. cit., p. 158.

[2] These details are from John Moschus, *Prat. Spir.* cap. 105 and 106.

[3] Pharus est in insula turris magna altitudine, mirificis operibus exstructa, quae nomen ab insula accepit (*Bell. Civ.* iii. sub fin.).

[4] *Geog.* xvii. i. 6.

arose[1], and at the time of the Arab conquest it was in full working order and flashed the sun by day and its own fire by night for many leagues over the sea. The coast was low and harbourless: moreover vessels coming to Alexandria had to cross a wide space of open sea out of sight of all land: so that it was an enormous advantage to have this conspicuous landmark visible by day and by night at a distance of sixty or seventy miles.

Many remarks on the Pharos may be found in the Arab writers. Iṣṭakhrî[2] says, 'The manârah, founded on a rock in the sea, contains more than 300 rooms, among which the visitor cannot find his way without a guide.' Ibn Ḥauḳal[3] adds that it 'was built of hewn stones fitted together and fastened with lead: there is nothing like it on earth,' and the same style of construction is recorded by Idrîsî[4] more fully. 'The lighthouse,' he says, 'is unparaleled in all the world for its architecture and strength of structure. It is built of the hardest Tiburtine stone, bedded in molten lead, and so firmly set that the joints cannot be loosened. On the north side the sea washes against it. Its height is 300 cubits, taking three palms to the cubit, and so its length is 100 statures of man. From

[1] The Greek Anthology records such a case of repair (674 Epid.): I have rendered the lines thus in *Amaranth and Asphodel*:—

'A tower of help for mariners on the main
Flashing my safety-beacon through the night,
I tottered in the thundering hurricane
Until Ammonius' toil renewed my might.
The wild waves past, to him upon the land,
As to the great Earth-shaker, sailors lift the hand.'

[2] *Bibl. Geog. Arab.* part i. p. 51.

[3] Id., ib., part ii. p. 99.

[4] *Geographia Nubiensis*, pp. 94–5.

the ground to the middle story are 70 statures, from the middle to the top 26, and the lantern on top is 4 statures[1].' There is no doubt about the general design of the tower. It was built in four stories, each less in diameter than the one below. The lowest, or ground story, was square on plan; the next was octagonal; the third circular; and the topmost was an open lantern containing fireplaces for the beacons and a wonderful mirror. On the top of the square and at the foot of the octagonal section was a broad terrace commanding a wide view of city and sea, and a smaller terrace of the same kind marked the division between the octagonal and the circular section[2]. The ascent was by a wide stair-

[1] What precise measure is intended I do not know, but even if a stature were put at only 5 feet, the height of the tower would be 500 feet. Most of the Muslim writers give 300 cubits as the measurement, and one will not be far wrong in taking this as 500 feet English. It is curious that Idrîsî does not distinguish between the first and the second stages of the tower. Ya'ḳûbî gives the height as 175 cubits, and Mas'ûdî says 'it is now (tenth century) 230 cubits, but was formerly 400, it having been ruined by time, earthquakes, and weather.' Kazwînî says that the first and second stories were equal in height (he makes each 90 cubits); and if this were so, Idrîsî's measurements would give 105 cubits for each of the first and second stories, 78 for the third, and 12 for the lantern. This sounds probable enough. Maḳrîzî mentions a different measurement, viz. 121 cubits for the square story, 81½ for the octagonal, and 31½ for the circular. Ibn al Faḳîḥ says that, according to some, the cubits were 'royal' cubits, so that 300 would equal 450 'cubits of the hand.' 'Abd al Laṭîf says that he read the MS. of a traveller who measured the Pharos and gives 121, 81½ and 31½ for the three stories, but he adds 10 cubits for the lantern or shrine (masjid) on the top. Holm in his *History of Greece* (tr. F. Clarke, vol. iv. p. 304) gives the height as 650 feet: but for merely mechanical reasons this is scarcely credible.

[2] Mas'ûdî in *Bibl. Geog. Arab.* part viii. p. 46, and other writers.

case roofed over with slabs spanning the space between the walls[1]; and under the stairs were chambers. After the second story the staircase narrowed so as to fill the whole of the interior, save for a shaft like a well in the centre: it was lighted by small windows from top to bottom[2].

The number of the rooms and the intricacy of the interior made a great impression on the Arabs. 'It is said that whoever entered this lighthouse became distracted and lost his way, by reason of the number of chambers and stories and corridors which it contained.... So it is reported that when the Moors arrived at Alexandria in the caliphate of Al Muḳtadir with an army, a body of them entered the lighthouse on horseback and lost their way, till they came upon a crevice in the crab of glass[3] upon which the structure was founded; and many of them fell

[1] Yâḳût, vol. i. pp. 256 seq.

[2] It does not seem quite clear whether there were actual steps or an inclined plane for mounting the tower. Some writers speak of steps, while Mas'ûdî says 'it was ascended by an inclined passage without steps,' and others say that a loaded horse could ascend to all the rooms. It would be interesting to know how the fuel for the beacon-fire was raised to the top of the tower; but it was probably hoisted up the shaft in the centre by a windlass.

[3] I have explained the origin of this above, p. 376. No writer better illustrates the confusion between the Pharos and the pair of obelisks than Ibn al Faḳîḥ, who after saying (*Bibl. Geog. Arab.* part v. p. 70), 'the manârah of Alexandria stands on a crab of glass in the sea,' remarks on the next page, 'the manârah of Alexandria has two pillars standing on two images, one of brass and one of glass: the brazen image is in the form of a scorpion, the glass in the form of a crab. The observatory is beside them, and it is called the *manârah*.' Suyûṭî quotes a statement that the lighthouse was built on vaults of glass, which again rested on a crab of brass! Yâḳût explains the glass foundation by the legend that when Alexander (*sic*) wished to build the tower, he threw stone, brick, granite, gold, silver, copper, lead, iron, glass and

through it and perished[1].' But even more marvellous stories are told about the mirror, which all the Arab writers agree in regarding, quite apart from the lighthouse on which it stood, as one of the wonders of the world. In the ancient Egyptian city of Rakoti there is said to have been a dome on pillars of brass, all gilded, and above this dome rose a lighthouse, on which was a mirror of composite metal, five spans in diameter[2]. This mirror was used as a burning-glass to destroy the ships of an enemy. It was in imitation of this that in Alexander's city the mirror was erected on the summit of the Pharos: but its purpose was rather to reveal a distant enemy 'coming from the land of the Romans.' This was soon exaggerated: and 'Abdallah, son of 'Amr, is quoted as saying, 'One of the wonders of the world is the mirror hanging in the manârah at Alexandria, which shows what is passing at Constantinople[3].' But Mas'ûdî describes it as 'a large mirror of transparent stone, in which ships could be seen coming from Rûm at too great a distance for the eye to detect them': while another

all kinds of minerals and metals into the sea to test them; and when they were taken out and examined, the glass alone was found of full weight and unimpaired. Accordingly glass was chosen for the substructure.

[1] Maḳrîzî. The account of the manârah begins vol. i. p. 155 of the *Khiṭaṭ*.

[2] Here Maḳrîzî quotes Ibn Wasîf Shâh's *History of Miṣrâîm*. Murtadi agrees: 'They made in the midst of that city a little turret on pillars of copper gilt, and set upon it a mirror consisting of divers materials, in length and breadth five spans, the turret 100 cubits high. . . . It was used as a burning-glass against the enemy. The Pharos also had not been made but for a mirror that was upon it' (*Egyptian History*, p. 102).

[3] Ibn al Faḳîḥ in *Bibl. Geog. Arab.* part v. p. 71.

writer, in substantial agreement, alleges that the mirror was made of 'finely wrought glass[1],' and a third gives the material as 'Chinese iron' or polished steel[2]. All say that it showed vessels at sea far beyond the range of common vision: a man sitting under the mirror could see all the way to Constantinople.

What was the purpose of this mirror? Was it a mere reflector to flash the sun-rays by day and the beacon-light by night? and was it an ordinary mirror, or had it a complex refracting surface, so that it might really serve as a burning-glass under the intense heat of the sun in Egypt? These are questions for men of science: but it is at least curious that, as early as the tenth century of our era, the Arab writers in their account of this mirror should anticipate the use of the telescope. It is also curious that different writers should describe the mirror as made of some transparent material—'finely wrought glass' and 'transparent stone': for these terms suggest a lens rather than a mirror. Is it conceivable that the great Alexandrian school of mathematics and mechanics discovered and constructed the lens, and that their discovery was lost and forgotten in the destruction of the Pharos?

That the Pharos was used as a signal-station as well as lighthouse is certain: but it is not quite clear whether the fire was kept up day and night. Idrîsî speaks of a fire by night and 'a cloud of smoke by day': but another account represents the

[1] *Zajâj mudabbar* is the term used by Maḳrîzî.

[2] Suyûṭî, who says that the mirror was seven cubits wide; that it showed all ships coming from Europe; and that it was used as a burning-glass. 'They turned the mirror towards the westering sun, and the rays being reflected burned up the enemy's ships.'

lighthouse keepers as living in the building and ready always to light the beacon by night[1]. Unfortunately no evidence of the original practice is obtainable: for the Pharos suffered serious injury within a century of the conquest. The story is that in the caliphate of Al Walîd ibn 'Abd al Malik, i.e. early eighth century, the Romans were so annoyed at the advantage which the Pharos gave to the Muslims as a watch-tower against sea-raids and surprises, that they resolved to destroy it by stratagem. Accordingly one of the courtiers[2] of the Emperor went with rich presents to the Caliph, and feigning to have incurred the Emperor's mortal enmity, professed his desire to become a Muslim. He was believed and welcomed to Islâm, and to the friendship of Al Walîd, whose imagination he fired with stories of buried treasure in Syria. This was duly discovered; and the Caliph, becoming greedy of wealth, listened eagerly to the report of the wily Roman, that a vast store of gold and jewels, which had belonged to the ancient kings of Egypt, was buried in vaults and chambers beneath the Pharos. So the Caliph sent troops to conduct the search, and they pulled down half of the lighthouse tower, removing the mirror, before the plot was suspected.

[1] Arculfus (c. 670 A.D.) speaking of this 'very high tower' says, 'Men are employed there by whom torches and other masses of wood, which have been collected, are set on fire to serve as a guide to the land, showing the narrow entrance to the straits. . . . Round the island also,' he adds, 'beams of immense size have been regularly laid down to prevent the foundations from yielding to the constant collision of the sea' (Pal. Pil. Text Soc., vol. iii. p. 50).

[2] Another account says that it was some Christian priests, who showed an ancient book containing the secret of the buried treasure.

Then the people resolved to stop the work of destruction, and to send a report to the Caliph: whereupon the traitor fled by night to his own country. But of course the mischief was done: one half, or at least a third part, of the tower had been thrown down: and the traitor had accomplished his purpose by destroying the magic mirror. Too late the Arabs saw that they had been duped: 'they rebuilt the manârah of brick, but could not raise it to its former height; and so, when they replaced the mirror, it was useless [1].'

There is no reason to question the substantial truth of this story: nor is it surprising that the damage proved irreparable. The Pharos must indeed have been a miracle of construction to stand secure for centuries, while towering in the air to that astonishing height; and the builders under the Arab dominion could not hope to rival the architecture of the Ptolemies. Indeed Mas'ûdî seems to deny that there was any attempt at restoration, though in this he is probably mistaken. Little is known of the subsequent history of the Pharos. Aḥmad ibn Ṭulûn [2] built a wooden cupola on its summit c. 875 A.D.—a statement which seems to show that the building was no longer used as a lighthouse, but merely as a watch-tower. This cupola did not last very long; and when it was swept away by the winds, a small mosque was built in place of it under Al Malik al Kâmil. A few years after Ibn Ṭulûn one of the piers on the western side, where the sea washed the walls, was found to be ruined, and was rebuilt by Kha-

[1] Suyûṭî, op. cit., p. 53: but the Arab writers generally think that the mirror was broken in pieces, as is far more probable.

[2] The author of *Mabâhij al Fikr*, quoted by As Suyûṭî.

mârawaih[1]. In the next century, on the 10th day of Ramaḍân, A.H. 344 (December 28, 955 A.D.), about thirty cubits of the top were thrown down by a severe earthquake, which was felt all over Egypt, Syria, and North Africa, in a series of fierce shocks lasting half an hour[2]. In 1182 another mosque on the summit is recorded by Ibn Jubair[3], who gives the height of the tower as 'above 150 cubits,' showing how it had diminished from its original stature: and Yâḳût, writing perhaps forty years later, actually gives a diagram showing 'a square building like a fort,' with a shortened second story, and a small cupola above it. Upon this he rather hastily argues that all accounts of the vast size of the Pharos are 'shameless lies.' But he hardly seems aware of the great changes which time had wrought. 'I sought the place of the mirror and found no trace of it,' he remarks; as if he expected to find it on the reduced and mutilated building, which was all that remained at the date of his visit[4]. But even greater destruction followed. In the time of Ḳala'ûn the Pharos is already described by an Arab writer as a 'shapeless ruin[5],' in spite of some repairs carried out by the Sultan Baibars: and though there was some subsequent attempt at restoration, the earthquake of 1375 seems to have demolished all but the lowest story of the tower[6].

[1] Al Mas'ûdî.

[2] 'While I was at Fusṭâṭ,' says Mas'ûdî.

[3] Quoted by Maḳrîzî.

[4] Yâḳût's account of the manârah may be read in Wüstenfeld's *Geographisches Wörterbuch*, vol. i. pp. 286 seq.

[5] Ibn Faḍl Allah, quoted by Suyûṭî.

[6] There can be little doubt that the Fort Pharos which was battered in the bombardment of Alexandria is on the site of the old lighthouse. Some part of it appears to be ancient, but apparently

But if the Pharos has long vanished, the tradition of its grace, and even of its use, has been preserved in the Egyptian minaret, to which it gave the name and to which it served as model[1]. Though the mediaeval minarets of Cairo vary in combination of design, in many of them one may see an exact reproduction of the design of Sostratus, which was a tower springing four-square from the ground, then changing to a smaller octagonal and from the octagonal to a still smaller circular shaft, and crowned on the top with a lantern.

No antiquarian history of Alexandria has yet been written; and much research, of a kind now in many places impossible, would be needed to provide materials for it and to settle points at issue. But even a rough sketch like the present, wanting as it is, may serve to give some idea of what met the eyes of the Arabs as they entered the city. Nor was the view from without less imposing. The northern walls followed the curving shore, as we have seen, while the southern walls rested on the canal, till it entered and flowed through the city; and all round on every side they were built with such strength and skill, and so varied by towers and

archaeologists have not seriously examined the site with a view to planning and preserving what may be worth preserving An American writer, Mr. Kay, thinks that he discovered traces of the original foundations under the walls of the existing fortress, which was built by Ḳait Bey circa 1480: see the *American Architect and Building News*, vol. xi. no. 348, pp. 101–2, Aug. 26, 1882. Others, however, place the site to the east of the fort on a spot now covered by the sea.

[1] This theory I broached in the *Athenæum* of Nov. 20, 1880, and I still hold by it. As to the name, *manârah* is not now used in Egypt for minaret, but it was so used originally, as the Shaikh Muḥammad 'Abduh, the Grand Mufti, informs me.

bastions, that their architecture roused the enthusiasm of travellers far into the Middle Ages[1].

[1] Nearly all plans of ancient Alexandria err in leaving a considerable space between the walls and the canal. That this is wrong is conclusively proved first by the testimony of John of Nikiou in the story of the fighting between Nicetas and Bonôsus given in the opening chapters of this book, and next by the explicit evidence of Arculfus, who remarks, 'The city is surrounded by a long circuit of walls fortified by frequent towers constructed along the margin of the river and the curving shore of the sea' (op. cit., p. 52). Again the same writer says: 'On the south it is surrounded by the mouths of the Nile, on the north by the sea; so that on this side and on that it is surrounded by water' (id., ib., p. 49). Of course I am aware that the city shrunk and the walls with it, so that the line standing in the Middle Ages differed considerably from the original walls: see H. de Vaujany's *Recherches sur les anciens Monuments situés sur le Grand Port d'Alexandrie*, pp. 74–84 (Alex. 1888). But the general style of the walls was probably preserved. Certainly they made a great impression on travellers even seven or eight centuries after the conquest. Thus in 1350 Ludolph von Suchem writes: 'Now Alexandria is the first seaside city of Egypt, one of the best of the Soldan's cities. On one side it stands on the Nile, the river of Paradise, which falls into the sea, and its other side is on the sea. This city is exceedingly beauteous and strong, and is fenced about with lofty towers and walls, which seem impregnable. . . . In this city still stands entire to this day a great and exceeding beauteous church, adorned in divers fashions with mosaic work and marble. . . . Indeed many other churches are still standing in Alexandria at this day, and in them rest the bodies of many saints' (*Description of the Holy Land*, tr. by Aubrey Stewart, pp. 45–6, London, 1895). So Breydenbach, c. 1486, speaks of viewing the 'gloriosam civitatem Alexandriam, mari magno pro parte una cinctam, pro alia amoenissimis et fertilissimis ortis circumseptam'; and he goes on to say that several of his fellow travellers mounting the outer wall took a view of the circuit of fortresses and moats, and agreed 'that they had never seen a more lovely or better fortified city, with beautiful ramparts and strong and lofty walls and towers.' Yet within they found ruin and desolation, save for a few churches (*Descriptio Terrae Sanctae*, p. 120). A plan of ancient Alexandria may be found in the Khedivial Library at Cairo, dated c. 1600: it shows a complete

circuit of walls, double in places, but is poorly drawn without scale or perspective. Much better is D'Anville's plan at p. 52 of his *Mémoires sur l'Égypte*, showing the ancient and modern walls together. A rude sketch is given in Janssonius' *Theatrum Urbium*, t. 4 (Amstelodami, n. d.). In J. White's *Aegyptiaca* (Oxon. 1801), there is a plan and a good deal of information: so in Parthey's *Alexandrinisches Museum* (Berlin, 1838). Most of the encyclopaedias give some kind of plan, as does Tozer's *Selections from Strabo*. All these plans are small, and most of them take for granted debateable points. The plan in Matter's *École d'Alexandrie* is somewhat larger, though wanting in detail and in accuracy. Néroutsos Bey in *L'Ancienne Alexandrie* also gives a plan on a larger scale, which is perhaps the best, although it seems in places not to distinguish Byzantine from Arab walls, and it is clearly wrong in placing the church of St. Mark and the Tetrapylus south of the Caesarion: but the Phiale and canal ports are well shown. The new Museum at Alexandria contains a plan of the ancient and modern town on a very large scale. Present researches will doubtless in time recover most of the old lines of the city, though the subsidence of the soil over the whole area of ancient Alexandria, as well as the encroachment of the sea, renders the reconstruction of the plan very difficult. See Dr. Hogarth's article on his excavations in *Egypt Exploration Fund Report*, 1894–5.

CHAPTER XXV

THE LIBRARY OF ALEXANDRIA

Question of its destruction by the Arabs. Abû 'l Faraj's story. Internal evidence against it. John Philoponus not alive at the invasion. Did the Library exist then? The original Museum Library. Probably burned in time of Julius Caesar. Library from Pergamus. The Daughter Library in the Serapeum. Destruction of the Temple of Serapis. Extent of the destruction: various authorities. The Library annexes perished: what became of the books? Silence of two centuries of writers. Bearing of the Treaty of Alexandria on the question. Silence of writers after the conquest. Summary and conclusion of the argument.

WHETHER the Arabs upon the capture of the city burned or did not burn the great Library of Alexandria is a question which has long been keenly debated: but inasmuch as learned opinions still differ, and the problem remains unsolved, it cannot be left unexamined in a work professing to deal with the conquest.

The story as it stands in Abû 'l Faraj[1] is well known, and runs as follows. There was at this time a man, who won high renown among the Muslims,

[1] Ed. Pococke, p. 114 tr. and 180 text. Renaudot thinks the story has an element of untrustworthiness: Gibbon discusses it rather briefly and disbelieves it. Pococke translates only the Arabic abridgement of Abû 'l Faraj. In the *Nineteenth Century* for October, 1894, there is an article on the question by Vasudeva Rau, who alleges (p. 560) that the story is not in the original Syriac, and probably was a later interpolation. The abridgement, however, was written by Abû 'l Faraj himself, and the suggestion of interpolation is a mere conjecture. Nor would the fact, if established, be material. The article generally is based rather on *a priori* argument than research, and consequently is not of much value.

named John the Grammarian. He was an Alexandrian, and apparently had been a Coptic priest, but was deprived of his office owing to some heresy by a council of bishops held at Babylon. He lived to see the capture of Alexandria by the Arabs, and made the acquaintance of 'Amr, whose clear and active mind was no less astonished than delighted with John's intellectual acuteness and great learning. Emboldened by 'Amr's favour, John one day remarked, 'You have examined the whole city, and have set your seal on every kind of valuable: I make no claim for aught that is useful to you, but things useless to you may be of service to us.' 'What are you thinking of?' said 'Amr. 'The books of wisdom,' said John, 'which are in the imperial treasuries.' 'That,' replied 'Amr, 'is a matter on which I can give no order without the authority of the Caliph.' A letter accordingly was written, putting the question to Omar, who answered: 'Touching the books you mention, if what is written in them agrees with the Book of God, they are not required: if it disagrees, they are not desired. Destroy them therefore.' On receipt of this judgement, 'Amr accordingly ordered the books to be distributed among the baths of Alexandria and used as fuel for heating: it took six months to consume them. 'Listen and wonder,' adds the writer.

Such is the story as it makes its appearance in Arabic literature. Abû 'l Faraj wrote in the latter half of the thirteenth century, and he says nothing about the source from which he derived the story: but he is followed by Abû 'l Fidâ in the early fourteenth century, and later by Maḳrîzî [1]. It is true

[1] This author, like 'Abd al Laṭîf, reports the story by way of allusion, taking it for granted. Thus speaking of the Serapeum

that 'Abd al Laṭîf, who wrote about 1200, mentions incidentally the burning of the Library by Omar's order, and, giving no details, seems to take the fact for granted. This allusion seems to show that in his day the tradition was current. Nevertheless the story is not to be found in any written document until five and a half centuries after the capture of Alexandria, and it is challenged by the silence of every writer from John of Nikiou to Abû Ṣâliḥ. It may of course be argued that it survived for several hundred years as an unwritten tradition; and this view may be held to receive confirmation from the undoubted fact that the tradition lives to this day among the Copts, although they give seventy days, instead of six months, as the period of burning. There is, however, nothing to show that this Coptic tradition is older than Abû 'l Faraj: in other words, though current as a popular story, it may have been derived from mediaeval writers. This one can neither prove nor disprove: but the doubt deprives the tradition of independent value.

Let us, however, examine the story as it stands. It is undeniably picturesque, and the reply of Omar has the true Oriental flavour. This really is the strongest point about it. But unfortunately precisely the same reply of Omar is recorded in connexion with the destruction of books in Persia [1]; and just

he says, 'Some think that these columns upheld the Porch of Aristotle, who taught philosophy here: that it was a school of learning: and that it contained the library which was burnt by 'Amr on the advice of the Caliph Omar' (*Khiṭaṭ*, vol. i. p. 159).

[1] See Prof. Bury's ed. of Gibbon, vol. v. p. 454 n., where Ibn Khaldûn, quoted by Ḥajî Khalfah, is given as the authority. I may add that the feelings of the Muslims towards the books of the idolatrous Persians would be very different from their feelings towards

as the story of 'Amr's captivity and his escape from detection and death owing to the timely cuff administered by Wardân, has been taken out of its proper setting and put into the siege of Alexandria by Muslim writers, so may this anecdote be wrongly told of the Alexandrian Library, although it may rest on a foundation of fact, such as the evil wit of Omar's words seems to postulate. But there are other points in the story which will not bear the strain of criticism. Granting for a moment that the destruction of the Library took place as related, we have to believe that, instead of being made into a bonfire on the acropolis, the books were laboriously put into baskets and taken down to the city; that they were then laboriously distributed among the countless baths; and that they served as fuel for the space of six months. This is a tissue of absurdities. Had the books been doomed, they would have been burnt on the spot. Had 'Amr refused them to his friend Philoponus, he would not have placed them at the mercy of every bath-keeper in the city. If he had so placed them, John Philoponus or any other person might have rescued a vast number of them at a trifling cost during the six months they are alleged to have lasted. Further, it cannot be questioned that in the seventh century a very large proportion of the books in Egypt were written on vellum [1]. Now vellum is a material which will not burn as fuel,

the books of the Christians. In their early history at least the Muslims disliked the destruction of the written name of God.

[1] Drs. Grenfell and Hunt have shown, against the received opinion, that the use of papyrus in book-form remained as long as Greek was written in Egypt, although vellum was preferred by the Copts in particular: see *Oxyrhynchus Papyri*, vol. ii. pp. 2–3. Still even the more ancient books in the Serapeum Library would have been mostly on vellum.

and all the Caliph's orders could not make it burn: what then became of all these manuscripts? And when one has deducted all the writings on vellum, how can it be seriously imagined that the remainder of the books would have kept the 4,000[1] bath-furnaces of Alexandria alive for 180 days? The tale, as it stands, is ridiculous; one may indeed listen and wonder.

But, it may be said, these small points are unfairly pressed; a minute dissection of details will not get rid of the broad fact of the destruction by burning. Let us then relinquish mere internal criticism, and pass on to consider how far external evidence is for or against the main facts of the story. There are two points presumably vital—the existence of John Philoponus[2] at the time of the conquest, and the existence of the Library. Now there can be very little doubt about the former point; John was not alive in 642. I need not recapitulate the whole proof of this statement. It is known that John was writing as early as 540[3],

[1] I have already shown, p. 384 n., that this figure, given by the Muslim writers, is doubtless exaggerated: but however the figure be reduced, Abû 'l Faraj's statement will not stand the test of simple arithmetic.

[2] The Arab story calls John 'Grammaticus,' the word being transliterated by Abû 'l Faraj. There is no doubt that Philoponus is meant: see e.g. Nicephorus Callistus, who says, τὸν γραμματικὸν Ἰωάννην ὃς ἐπεκλήθη Φιλόπονος (xviii. 45).

[3] I have already referred to Nauck in this connexion. But the facts are set out more clearly and accessibly in the *Dict. Christ. Biog.*, s.v. Johannes Philoponus. The evidence that John's life lay in the sixth century, if not actually bounded by it, is conclusive, despite the doubtful document quoted by Gibbon from Fabricius as dated 618, and the statement attributed to Nicephorus which makes John a contemporary of George of Pisidia in the reign of Heraclius. The Nicephorus in question is Callistus, who wrote in

if not before the accession of Justinian in 527; and though he may have survived for a few years at the beginning of the seventh century, if he had been alive in the year 642 he would not have been less than 120 years old. It is therefore clear that Philoponus had been dead for some thirty or forty years when 'Amr entered Alexandria.

The question whether the Library itself was in existence at that time is at once more interesting and more difficult of solution. The earliest and the most famous Library was, as is well known, in the Bruchion quarter. If the idea of founding this vast collection of the world's literature came from Ptolemy Soter, and if he actually formed the Library, it was completely equipped and organized by Philadelphus his successor. It seems to have been part of the splendid group of buildings known as the Museum [1].

the fourteenth century, and is of no great authority: but I confess that he appears to be wrongly quoted. His evidence seems to me to tell wholly against the theory that Philoponus was alive in 642. For John is associated with Dioscorus, Gaius, and Severus of Antioch, as writing against the Council of Chalcedon and prevailing 'until Justinian ascended the throne (527 A.D.), when these champions of heresy carried their studies into holes and corners' (Hist. xviii. 45 in Migne, *Patr. Gr.* t. 147, p. 422). Moreover John is described as ἀκμάσαντα ἐπὶ τῆς παρούσης ἡγεμονίας, and the context shows that this refers to Justinian and not to Heraclius. Nor is John declared to be contemporary with George of Pisidia. As I read it, George is called contemporary, though much younger, *with Leontius Monachus*. Now Leontius Monachus seems to have died early in the seventh century—his list of Alexandrian Patriarchs closes with Eulogius, ob. 607; and Leontius Monachus uses language implying that John Philoponus was dead when he wrote (Migne, t. 86, col. 1187). Matter deals with this question of the date of Philoponus very inadequately (*École d'Alexandrie*, t. i. p. 339).

[1] Prof. Mahaffy questions this point, for whatever reason: *Empire of the Ptolemies*, p. 98.

The Museum, as Strabo says, adjoined the royal palaces, which were of vast extent, occupying quite one fourth of the whole area of the city. It consisted of a great central hall with a colonnade about it, and cloistered courts. These communicated with other buildings, such as the Schools of Medicine, Anatomy and Surgery, Mathematics and Astronomy, Law and Philosophy: a park was also attached, with a botanical garden and an observatory[1]—all the apparatus of a great University. What was the precise structural arrangement of the Museum buildings, and where precisely the Library was situated, cannot be determined: nor indeed is there any agreement even about the site of the Museum. Strabo is provokingly silent concerning the Library, when his evidence would settle the question whether, as some ancient writers allege, it perished in the conflagration of 48 B. C., a few years before his visit. Caesar was then besieged in the Bruchion quarter by the Egyptians under Achillas, and he set fire to the harbour shipping: it is alleged that the fire

[1] See an interesting pamphlet entitled *La Bibliothèque des Ptolémées*, by V. Nourisson Bey. The particular statement in the text is on p. 8: but I have to acknowledge my debt to the writer on several points. Other authorities beside Parthey's *Alexandrinisches Museum* and Ritschl's *Alexandrinische Bibliotheken* in *Opuscula* (1866) are Weniger, *Alexandrinisches Museum* (1875), Holm's *History of Greece*, vol. 4, and Susemihl's *Geschichte der griechischen Litteratur in der Alexandrinerzeit* (1891–2). Gustave le Bon in *La Civilisation des Arabes* (Paris, 1884) rejects the story of the burning of the Library; but his work is rather a popular book than a serious study. Sédillot's *Histoire Générale des Arabes* (2nd ed., Paris, 1877) casts doubt on the story: but he does not discuss it closely. He refers, however, to the *Revue Scientifique de la France*, 19 Juin, 1875, no. 51, pp. 1200 seq., for an essay on the subject, which I have been unable to see.

spread and utterly destroyed the Library. Caesar himself—if he wrote the account[1]—gives no hint of any such catastrophe; on the contrary, he remarks that Alexandria is practically fire-proof, as the architects used no timber, but raised their buildings on vaulted substructures, and roofed them with stone or concrete[2]. Such a remark would be deliberately misleading, if the writer were suppressing the fact that he witnessed and caused the burning of the Library. It is difficult either to convict or to clear Caesar of the charge. Plutarch has no doubt of the fact: 'As his fleet was falling into the hands of the enemy, he was forced to repel the danger by fire: this spread from the dockyards and destroyed the great Library[3].' Seneca clearly believed the story: 'Four hundred thousand books were burned at

[1] If *De Bello Alexandrino* was written, as modern critics think, by Asinius Pollio, it is easy to understand the writer's silence on this incident.

[2] *De Bello Civili* iv. ad init. Yet somewhat later, when the Egyptians had suffered a great naval defeat, they are described as refitting all the old vessels they could muster and bringing up the Nile guard-ships. Oars were wanting to equip these vessels; so the Egyptians *stripped colonnades, gymnasia, and public buildings of their roofs to provide wood for the making of oars*. This inconsistency in the narrative deserves attention. Moreover John of Nikiou says that Diocletian burned the city—'la livra aux flammes entièrement' (p. 417). Orosius speaking of Diocletian's victory says 'urbem direptioni dedit'—an equally strong expression though fire is not mentioned (*Hist.* vii. 25. 8). Eulogius, brother of the martyred Macarius of Antioch, was sent by Constantine with an army to Alexandria and 'burned all the temples of Alexandria, destroyed them, and seized their possessions' (Hyvernat, *Actes des Martyrs*, p. 74). These instances seem to show that Caesar's view is mistaken or exaggerated.

[3] Plut. *Caes.* 49 περικοπτόμενος τὸν στόλον ἠναγκάσθη διὰ πυρὸς ἀπώσασθαι τὸν κίνδυνον· ὃ καὶ τὴν μεγάλην βιβλιοθήκην ἐκ τῶν νεωρίων ἐπινεμόμενον διέφθειρεν.

Alexandria[1].' The language of Dio Cassius[2] is rather odd: 'The conflagration was widespread; besides the dockyard and much else, the stores of corn perished, and the stores of books; and these books, it is said, in vast numbers and of great value.' But there can be no doubt what the tradition was in the fourth century. The words of Ammianus Marcellinus[3] are plain enough; he speaks of Alexandria's 'priceless libraries, about which ancient writers agree that the 700,000 volumes got together by the unremitting care of the Ptolemies were destroyed by fire

[1] Prof. Mahaffy, in quoting Seneca's sneer against Livy, seems inclined to accept his opinion that these books were valued rather as ornamenting the dining-hall than as aiding the advancement of learning (*Empire of the Ptolemies*, p. 99). One may perhaps prefer Gibbon's view: 'Livy had styled the library *elegantiae regum curaeque egregium opus*—a liberal encomium, for which he is pertly criticized by the narrow stoicism of Seneca' (chap. li).

[2] xlii. 38. 1 *τάς τε ἀποθήκας καὶ τοῦ σίτου καὶ τῶν βίβλων—πλείστων δὴ καὶ ἀρίστων, ὥς φασι, γενομένων—καυθῆναι.* The 'storehouses for corn' one can easily understand, but what are the 'storehouses for books'? One cannot imagine, however, a vast collection of valuable books as piled in warehouses ready for exportation, nor book-warehouses as a part of the ordinary trade equipment of the docks. After all there is far less difference between *ἀποθήκη τῶν βίβλων* and *βιβλιοθήκη* in the Greek than between book-warehouse and library in the English.

[3] xxii. 16. Aulus Gellius gives the same number of books, but the estimates vary. Epiphanius, who also wrote in the fourth century, gives 54,800. See Parthey, *Alexandrinisches Museum*, p. 77. The truth is that there was not one library but several: Ammianus even speaks of 'bibliothecae innumerabiles': and this fact may account for the difference in the estimates. Susemihl gives the number of books in the time of Callimachus as 42,800 in the Outer Library (which is doubtfully, I think, identified with the Serapeum), while in the Royal Library were 400,000 composite volumes or rolls and 90,000 simple (*Geschichte der griechischen Litteratur in der Alexandrinerzeit*, i. 342). Susemihl's account of the general arrangements (pp. 336 seq.) is interesting.

in the Alexandrian war, when Caesar devastated the city.' Orosius closely agrees with this account: 'During the combat orders were given to fire the royal fleet, which happened to be drawn on shore. The conflagration spread to part of the city, and burned 400,000 books, which were stored in a building which happened to be contiguous. So perished that marvellous record of the literary activity of our forefathers, who had made this vast and splendid collection of works of genius[1].' On the whole it seems more natural to believe than to disbelieve that the Library perished in Caesar's conflagration.

But seven or eight years after this adventure of Caesar's, the library of the Kings of Pergamum was sent by Mark Antony to Alexandria[2]. Whether the Museum was still able to house such a collection, or whether these volumes formed the foundation of the later Serapeum Library, is a question which has

[1] 'In ipso praelio regia classis forte subducta iubetur incendi. Ea flamma cum partim quoque urbis invasisset quadringenta milia librorum proximis forte aedibus condita exussit, singulare profecto monumentum studii curaeque maiorum, qui tot tantaque inlustrium ingeniorum opera congesserant' (*Hist.* vi. 15. 31). Orosius seems to have had before him either the passage of Livy or that of Seneca. The words 'proximis forte aedibus condita' might appear at first sight to bear out the singular theory of some critics that the books *happened to be stored in a warehouse* close to the shore. The improbability of such an arrangement is almost enough to refute the theory, nor would the word *condita* be chosen to express a temporary deposit of the kind. All difficulty vanishes if *forte* is taken as qualifying *proximis*, as I have done in my translation. At the same time it looks as if both Orosius and Dio Cassius were following a common original not very clear in expression.

[2] Plutarch in his Life of Antony says that Antony gave to Cleopatra the libraries from Pergamum, which contained 200,000 simple rolls.

exercised scholars[1]. I think it very possible that neither alternative is true. We have already seen that the great temple of the Caesarion was begun by Cleopatra in honour of Julius Caesar and finished by Augustus; and that its libraries are mentioned among its most splendid embellishments[2]. Nothing would be more natural than to suppose that, if the Museum Library had perished, room was provided for the Pergamum collection, or some part of it, in the Caesarion, while the remainder perhaps went to the Serapeum.

However that may be, two things are fairly certain; that some of the Museum buildings remained in use till the time of Caracalla, who drenched the city with blood, closed the theatres, and suppressed the *syssitia* or Common Hall at the Museum in the year 216 A.D.; and that at some date early in the Christian era, in place of the vanished Museum Library, another great Library was founded in the Serapeum on the acropolis. The Museum buildings are said to have been razed to the ground by Aurelian[3] in 273, when he wrought havoc in the Bruchion quarter to punish the Alexandrians for the revolt of Firmus; and the members or Fellows of the Museum then either fled over sea or took refuge in the Serapeum. The Serapeum Library was called the Smaller or 'Daughter Library[4],' but it is not

[1] Susemihl thinks that the Pergamum collection was probably stored in the colonnades of the temple of Athene Polias (op. cit., ii. 666): but where was this?

[2] By Philo Judaeus: see supra, p. 373.

[3] Eusebius, however, attributes the destruction of the Bruchion quarter to Claudian; and he may be right: see the note on p. 415 of vol. ii of Heinechen's *Eusebius*.

[4] Epiphanius, *De Pond. et Mens.* xii. Epiphanius was a bishop, for whose date see p. 409, n. 3.

possible to fix a date either for the end of the Mother Library[1] or for the beginning of the Daughter, though the latter is said to have been founded by Ptolemy Philadelphus. Nor is the question very material. We know that in the fourth century the elder Library had perished, and the younger had been some time established.

Here then in the Serapeum all the traditions of the earlier learning were maintained; the University, with its great collection of books, was established; and that association of Aristotle's name with Alexandrian study which began at the Museum, was continued at the Serapeum unbroken[2]. In other words, those courses of philosophic and scientific study which had made Alexandria the centre of the

[1] One is bound, however, to give the opinion of Dr. Botti: 'Après Septime Sévère il n'est plus question de la grande bibliothèque. Après Caracalla l'ancien Musée n'existe plus: le Claudium tient ferme jusqu'à Aurélien,' *Colonne Théodosienne*, p. 138. The Claudium was a sort of School of History opened by Claudius and attached to the Museum: it was not very successful. Dr. Botti seems to attribute the origin of the Daughter Library to Trajan or Hadrian: but see Prof. Mahaffy's *Empire of the Ptolemies*, p. 167.

[2] This explains the frequent connexion of Aristotle's name with the Serapeum buildings by Muslim writers: see above, p. 388. Matter is mistaken in thinking that this association first occurs in Benjamin of Tudela—'tradition que jusque-là aucun écrivain n'avait constatée non plus' (*École d'Alexandrie*, t. i. pp. 327–8). The fact is that it is a commonplace of Coptic and Arabic tradition alike: see e.g. the Paris Coptic MS. 129[14], f. 92 seq., translated in part by Mr. W. E. Crum, and shown to be founded on Eusebius (*Proceedings of Soc. Bibl. Arch.*, Feb. 12, 1902). The reference to Alexandrian learning and the school of Aristotle is on the twelfth page of Mr. Crum's paper. It is an easy transition from school in the sense of *system* of learning to school in the sense of *place* of learning; and the traditional study of Aristotle's system gave rise to the belief that he had taught in person both at the Museum and at the Serapeum.

culture of the world were still in being; only the seat of learning had been moved from the Museum to the Serapeum.

But towards the end of the fourth century the Serapeum was doomed to destruction by the Christians under Theophilus. We have already seen that in 366 the Caesarion was wrecked and plundered in a fierce religious contest, in which there is too much reason to think that the Caesarion library perished. As Christianity gathered strength, the war with paganism became fiercer. The Serapeum naturally served as the camp and fortress of the pagans; and for a while they used the advantage which the position gave them to raid the city and slaughter the most zealous of the Christians. Siege was laid to the acropolis; but before matters were forced to the last arbitrament it was agreed to take the Emperor's decision. The edict of Theodosius pronounced wholly in favour of the Christians. It was read aloud between the contending parties in the court of the Serapeum; and as the worshippers of the old Egyptian idols fled, the Christians, under their bishop Theophilus, dismantled and demolished the great temple of Serapis. This happened in the year 391, and the fact is uncontroverted.

The case is changed when we come to the question, Did the Library perish in the ruin? To that question no positive answer can be given[1]; it is matter

[1] Yet positive opinions are ventured upon by some writers. Thus Nourisson Bey (*La Bibl. des Ptolémees*, p. 21) says that when the Serapeum was taken by the Christian force, which he puts in the year 389, the library was methodically plundered, and the books were sent to Rome and Constantinople, where Theodosius was forming a great collection. I do not know on what authority this assertion rests. Prof. Bury takes quite a different view in his edition of Gibbon (vol. iii. p. 495, App.): 'I conclude that there is no evidence

of debate: one can only examine and test certain fragments of evidence, in the hope that they may justify a conclusion. Now there can be no manner of doubt that the temple itself was destroyed in 391, and that the destruction was thorough. It was razed to the foundations, as Eunapius alleges, perhaps with some exaggeration; and one or more Christian churches were built upon the site. Since, however, there is no specific evidence that the Library perished in the destruction of the temple, one must show one of two things in order to prove the ruin of the Library—either (1) that the Library was housed in the temple, or (2) that the whole of the buildings on the acropolis were wrecked by the Christians under Theophilus[1]. Of these alternatives the second is easily refuted. I have already shown that as late as the twelfth century there were remains of considerable magnificence still standing. The exact position of

that the Library of the Serapeum did not survive till the Saracen conquest.' Gibbon himself, of course, believes in the destruction of the Library by the Christians under Theophilus, and not by the Arabs under ʿAmr. Dr. Botti agrees with Nourisson Bey in affirming at least the removal of the Library before 391: 'La *bibliothèque fille* tombée au pouvoir de George de Cappadoce est saisie par le gouvernement central de Constantinople en 362: on peut se demander si elle ne fut pas brûlée d'ordre de Jovien' (*Colonne Théodosienne*, p. 138).

[1] Matter justly says: 'To make the destruction complete, not only must the sanctuary of Serapis have been destroyed, but also its vast annexes—the courts, porticoes, dwelling-rooms, and the library, which had been established *there* over six centuries' (*École d'Alexandrie*, t. i. p. 321): but the word 'there' rather begs the question. He thinks the damage to these buildings was slight and soon repaired; and his conclusion is that, as the remembrance of the older Museum faded, the Serapeum took its place in tradition as well as in fact, and that 'the new establishment so prospered, that at the time of the Arab conquest the Serapeum still possessed a considerable library.'

these remains is as unknown as their original purpose[1]. Accordingly their survival proves nothing except that, if the Library was in these buildings, it may have survived with them. There is, however, some fairly explicit evidence to show both the position of the Library and the amount of the destruction wrought by the Christians. For on the one hand we have the testimony of Aphthonius, who visited the Serapeum in the fourth century some time before its destruction[2]; and on the other that of Rufinus, who

[1] I must, however, protest against Matter's inference from the passage in Benjamin of Tudela which he quotes (op. cit., pp. 327–8). Benjamin's words are: 'Outside the city is the School of Aristotle, tutor to Alexander. It is a great and beautiful building adorned with marble columns between every school. There are about twenty of these schools, to which people used to come from all parts of the world to hear the wisdom of Aristotle.' This passage proves unquestionably that in the twelfth century, among the fine buildings which remained, there were some twenty halls or rooms adjoining a colonnade: but it does not and cannot prove that these particular rooms were those used by students of philosophy. Tradition associated Aristotle with the Serapeum buildings in general, and therefore with those surviving when Benjamin wrote: but it cannot be taken to prove that any particular surviving buildings were those devoted to purposes of study, still less that they were those in which the Library had been housed. I may further remark that Benjamin's account does not agree with that of an earlier writer, who says of the Serapeum that it is a ruin, and 'nothing now remains of it except the columns or pillars, which are all standing, not one of them having fallen' (Arabic MS. of 1067 A.D. at Paris, quoted by Dr. Botti, *Colonne Théodosienne*, p. 1). Now given the fact that in the fourth century the central temple was completely demolished, and also the fact that in the eleventh century certain columns are all described as still standing *in situ*, it is quite clear that the columns referred to are those of the exterior colonnade of the acropolis and not those of the temple.

[2] Matter (op. cit., p. 324) tries to place Aphthonius' visit after 391, but cannot escape the difficulty in which the language of Aphthonius places him. For the Syrian writer says distinctly that the annexes

was present at the destruction, and wrote after it. The two accounts help each other out: yet it is very curious that while Aphthonius does not directly mention the temple, Rufinus is totally silent about the Library. It is nevertheless quite clear that Aphthonius associates the Library with the temple building as opposed to the other buildings upon the acropolis[1]; and that at the date of his visit the Library was there, open as usual to readers.

of the temple are built adjoining the colonnades on the inner sides, some used for the library and open for students, others devoted to the service of the ancient gods. Either therefore Aphthonius wrote before the destruction of the pagan shrines, or else the Christians, having wrecked the sanctuary of Serapis, spared and tolerated the other pagan sanctuaries. Matter is forced to choose the latter alternative, but it will not commend itself to many candid minds, nor is there any evidence to support it. Sozomen on the contrary says that the Serapeum remained in the occupation of the Christians from its capture to his own time.

[1] In describing the four colonnades which were built one from the middle point of each side of the temple at right angles to meet the exterior colonnade, he says *αὐλὴ δὲ κατὰ μέσον περίστυλος*. A comparison both with the context and with the language of Rufinus proves that this *αὐλή* must mean the temple itself: for Rufinus is unmistakable—*In medio totius spatii aedes erat.* The *αὐλή* therefore corresponds to the temple, which had a peristyle about it and on each side a colonnade at right angles. Then follows the passage already quoted (supra, p. 384, n. 2), *παρῳκοδόμηνται δὲ σηκοὶ τῶν στοῶν ἔνδοθεν, κ.τ.λ.*; which passage makes it quite clear that both the chambers set apart for the Library, and the chapels of the ancient gods, were built within the peristyle of the temple, or opened out of the surrounding cloister, as we might say. If there were any doubt on the point, it would be removed by the inscription found by Dr. Botti on the site: Σαράπιδι καὶ τοῖς συννάοις θεοῖς ὑπὲρ σωτηρίας αὐτοκράτορος Καίσαρος Τραιάνου Ἀδριανοῦ Σεβαστοῦ, which expressly places the other deities *in the same temple* (*L'Acropole d'Alexandrie*, p. 22). Moreover, either these shrines were in the temple, or they were in the great exterior range of buildings. But of the latter Rufinus says that they comprised lecture-rooms, or abodes for the priests, or for the staff of custodians, or for the

But if the Library was part of the temple building, and if the temple building was utterly destroyed, how can it be argued that the Library did not perish? The destruction of the temple was complete: it was thrown down to the foundations. Eunapius[1] says that 'they wrought havoc with the Serapeum and made war on its statues. . . . The foundations alone were not removed owing to the difficulty of moving such huge blocks of stone.' Theodoret, speaking of the same events, says, 'The sanctuaries of the idols were uprooted from their foundations[2].' Socrates says that the Emperor's order was for the demolition of all the heathen temples in Alexandria, and that 'Theophilus threw down the temple of Serapis': and again, 'The temples were overthrown, and the bronze statues melted down to make domestic vessels[3].' The same writer records

monks or ascetics or the like. I have no hesitation, therefore, in concluding that the books were actually stored in the temple building, and this agrees with all we know of such arrangements. There may be a question about the Museum; but I have already shown that the Hadrianon and the Caesarion had their libraries, and I may clinch matters by giving the words of Orosius—*hodie in templis extent, quae et nos vidimus, armaria librorum* (*Hist.* vi. 15. 31).

[1] l. c. supra, p. 381, n. 1.

[2] *Hist. Eccl.* v. 22 *ἐκ βάθρων ἀνέσπασε τὰ τῶν εἰδώλων τεμένη*: and he speaks of the temple of Serapis in a tone of regret: *τῶν πανταχοῦ γῆς, καθὰ φασί τινες, μέγιστός τε οὗτος καὶ κάλλιστος.*

[3] *Hist. Eccl.* v. 16 *λύεσθαι τοὺς ἐν Ἀλεξανδρείᾳ ναούς . . . ἀνακαθαίρει μὲν τὸ Μιθραῖον καταστρέφει δὲ τὸ Σαραπεῖον.* The Mithraeum was a temple in which the bloody rites of Persia were celebrated. There is nothing to prove that it was on the acropolis; but the Emperor made a special grant of the site, and the building was turned into a church. So Sozomen speaking of a temple of Dionysus says, *τὸ Διονύσου ἱερὸν εἰς ἐκκλησίαν μετεσκεύαζε*='rebuilt in the form of a church': a different expression from *ἀνακαθαίρει* ='purified and consecrated.'

the discovery of stones with hieroglyphic inscriptions during the demolition of the temple of Serapis : and similar language is used by Sozomen [1], who describes the Christians as having uninterruptedly occupied the Serapeum from its capture by Theophilus to his own time. All these writers, be it noted, belong to the first half of the fifth century, and so are almost contemporary. It is to be regretted that they are not explicit about the fate of the Library, nor do they mention the destruction of other buildings on the acropolis. Rufinus, however, throws some light on the subject, because he speaks of the exterior range of buildings round the edge of the plateau as practically uninjured, though void of its former pagan occupiers : but he makes it clear, that while this outer range remained, with its lecture-rooms and dwelling-rooms, not only the great temple of Serapis, but the colonnades about it, had been levelled to the ground [2].

[1] V. 15 *τοῦ ναοῦ τούτου καθαιρουμένου.* See preceding note, and also supra, p. 385, n. 2.

[2] I have already given the passage from Rufinus (supra, p. 381, n. 1). Dr. Botti not having the Latin text before him, gives La Faye's translation, which is correct ; and he justly shows that, as Rufinus was a witness of the destruction of the temple, his tenses, past and present, must be taken as distinguishing what survived and what did not survive at the time his record was written. Accordingly Rufinus proves, in Dr. Botti's opinion, that not only the statue and the temple were demolished, but also 'le portique carré de la cour centrale.' The words of Rufinus here are, 'Porticus quoque post haec omnem ambitum quadratis ordinibus distinctae intrinsecus circumibant.' The language is rather obscure perhaps, but I translate: 'Next (to this outer range) came colonnades, which used to run round the whole space of the interior, dividing it into quadrangles.' This agrees with the design as disclosed by Aphthonius ; but if I am right in this interpretation, the destruction extended further than the peristyle round the temple, to which Dr. Botti seems to confine it (*Colonne Théodosienne*, p. 35).

The argument now stands as follows: the Library is proved to have been stored in rooms which, like the shrines of the old Egyptian gods, formed part and parcel of the temple building. The temple building is proved to have been utterly demolished and destroyed. Therefore the Library suffered the same destruction [1].

Of course it may be urged that the books, as opposed to the chambers which contained them, may possibly have been rescued. It is indeed alleged that the books had been removed bodily by George of Cappadocia some thirty years before the capture of the Serapeum by the Christians under Theophilus: and it is asserted also that now, upon the capture, they were packed off to Constantinople [2]. It may well be doubted whether the mob which hacked the statue of Serapis to pieces, burning the fragments on the spot [3], and which left not a stone standing of the grandest and most glorious temple in the world, was in any mood to care tenderly for those literary treasures, which after all were pagan, and were under the guardianship of the great idol. Strange as the silence is of contemporary writers,

[1] I may here remark that John Philoponus is made by Abû 'l Faraj to speak of the books as stored 'in the imperial treasuries.' This description is at once false and instructive. It is false, because the rooms in the Serapeum could by no stretch of language be called 'the imperial treasuries': and it is instructive, because the phrase seems to carry an echo of the *fiscus Caesaris* associated with the old Museum.

[2] See supra, p. 413 n.

[3] Theodoret, *Hist. Eccl.* v. 22, distinctly says that the statue, which was mainly of wood, was thus treated, only the head being dragged round the city. This agrees with Michael the Syrian, who says, 'L'idole fut brisée; on la jeta au feu, et on promena sa tête par les rues' (ed. Chabot, tom. i. fasc. ii. p. 318).

it is far easier to believe that the books perished in the flames[1] which consumed the image of Serapis, than that they were plucked from the ruin of the temple and sent oversea. Orosius indeed is quoted as having seen the empty shelves or cases in the Serapeum. If the quotation were accurate, it would prove both that the books had disappeared by 416, when Orosius wrote, and that the Library building remained: but it is not accurate; the words do not justify the construction put upon them[2]. For Orosius makes no mention of the Serapeum. He is speaking of the destruction by fire of the original Museum Library, and he argues roughly as follows:—Granted that *in certain temples* empty bookshelves may be

[1] Dr. Botti seems rather to lean to the view that the Library of the Trajanum mentioned by Suidas (s. v. Ἰοβίανος) as burned by Jovian may have been that at Alexandria, although the context seems to associate the event with Antioch (*Colonne Théodosienne*, pp. 139–41).

[2] *Hist.* vi. 15. 31. After describing the destruction of the original Library in Caesar's conflagration (see passage quoted supra, p. 410, n. 1), Orosius continues: 'Unde quamlibet hodieque in templis extent, quae et nos vidimus, armaria librorum, quibus direptis exinanita ea a nostris hominibus nostris temporibus memorent—quod quidem verum est—; tamen honestius creditur alios libros fuisse quaesitos qui pristinas studiorum curas aemularentur, quam aliam ullam tunc fuisse bibliothecam, quae extra quadringenta milia librorum fuisse ac per hoc evasisse credatur.' The language is rather obscure: but its sense may be closely rendered as follows: 'On this point, however true it may be that at the present day there are empty bookshelves in some of the temples (I myself have seen them), and that these shelves were emptied and the books destroyed by our own people in our own time (which is the fact): still the fairer opinion is that, subsequently to the conflagration, other collections had been formed to vie with the ancient love of literature, and not that there originally existed any second library, which was separate from the 400,000 volumes and owed its preservation to the fact of its separateness.'

seen to this day; and granted that they were emptied by acts of violence done in our own time; these facts prove that libraries existed in recent years, but they do not prove that a library survived which had formed a section of the old Museum Library and had escaped the fire through being housed in a separate building: they prove rather that other books were collected, in emulation of the old Library, at a date subsequent to the conflagration.

Such is Orosius' argument: it is directed to show that no part of the great Ptolemaic Library was rescued from the burning; and, as Matter and others contend, it contains no reference to the Serapeum[1]. Precisely; but that fact has a double bearing. For if there is one inference which the language of Orosius warrants beyond doubt, it is this—that at the time when he wrote there was no great and ancient library in existence in Alexandria. Had such a library

[1] Matter's discussion of this question is singularly unconvincing: see *L'École d'Alexandrie*, t. i. pp. 336 seq. He quotes John Philoponus, *Ad Arist. Analyt.* pr. I, fol. 2 B, as saying that ἐν παλαιαῖς βιβλιοθήκαις there were reported to have been forty books of Analytics: and Matter from this expression infers the existence of *new* collections. But when he quotes Ammianus (*Comment. in Arist. Categ.*, ap. *Ald.*, fol. 3 A) as saying that forty books of Analytics and two of Categories must have existed ἐν τῇ μεγάλῃ βιβλιοθήκῃ, he rightly urges that this statement merely proves the disappearance of the Museum Library by the fifth century and not the non-existence of any other library. Matter is also justified in insisting that Orosius says nothing about the Serapeum; but he hardly appreciates the consequences of that argument. Prof. Bury, in his Appendix to Gibbon already cited, urges that Gibbon's statement of the destruction of the Alexandrian Library rests only on Orosius. I have shown that there is a good deal of evidence independent of Orosius. When Prof. Bury adds, 'It is highly improbable that Orosius was thinking either of the Alexandrian Library or the Serapeum' in regard to the empty shelves, I agree with him.

existed in the Serapeum in 416 A.D., it is simply inconceivable that Orosius, in following the train of thought which I have set out, should have passed it over in silence. Orosius therefore is really a witness not to the destruction of the Serapeum Library in 391, but to its non-existence in 416.

The case, however, against the existence of the Library in the seventh century, which is the point at issue, is not yet complete. Of course no one supposes that even in the great wars upon books—such as the war made by Diocletian upon Christian books and the war made by Theophilus upon pagan books—all the books in Alexandria perished. Even after the destruction of the great public libraries, there must have been many volumes in private collections, and many in the remoter monastic libraries. The very fact that Alexandrian learning was not extinguished proves the use of books. But if the great Serapeum Library had continued in existence into the seventh century, how comes it that not a single writer in the fifth or sixth century can be cited to establish the fact in clear and unmistakable language? Take one particular instance. I have already related the visit of John Moschus and his friend Sophronius to Egypt not many years before the Arab conquest; and I have shown the keen intellectual interest of the two scholars and their fondness for anything in the shape of a book[1]: but though they were both fairly voluminous writers, and though they travelled and resided a great deal in Egypt, their pages will be searched in vain for any allusion to other than private libraries in the country. Two centuries of silence, ending in the silence of John Moschus and Sophronius, seem to

[1] Supra, pp. 96 seq.

render it impossible that any great public library can have existed when the Arabs entered Alexandria.

One or two other points remain to be noticed. Let it be granted for a moment that all the foregoing reasoning has not seriously shaken the theory of the survival of the Serapeum Library; and suppose also that the Library was intact when the Arabs captured Alexandria; I would still say that its destruction by the Arabs is extremely improbable. For this reason: that the Arabs did not enter Alexandria for eleven months after its capture, and in the treaty of surrender it was expressly stipulated that during the interval, not only might the Romans themselves depart, but that they might carry off all their movable possessions and valuables [1]. During all this period the sea was open, and the passage to Constantinople and other ports was absolutely unhindered. The mere market value of the books in the Serapeum Library, if it existed, must have been enormous: their literary value must have been keenly appreciated by a large number of persons with intellectual interests: and these students would surely have forestalled the fabled zeal of John Philoponus by securing the removal of such priceless treasures while it was still time, instead of leaving them to the ignorant mercy of the desert warriors to whom the city was to be delivered.

Finally, the silence that prevails among fifth and sixth century writers reigns also after the conquest. There are no Arab historians of Egypt in the seventh or eighth century; and it might be said that later writers were anxious to suppress the story of the

[1] See supra, p. 320, clause 4 in the Treaty of Alexandri , and John of Nikiou, p. 575.

burning of the Library. But this cannot apply to the Coptic bishop, John of Nikiou, who was a man of learning, and who wrote before the end of the seventh century. The range and the detail of his work prove that he had access to plentiful sources of information fifty years after the conquest. Abû 'l Faraj himself—the author of the charge against the Arabs—proves that Alexandria continued to be frequented by students about the year 680 A. D.: for he represents James of Edessa as going to Alexandria to complete his education after receiving a thorough instruction in the Greek language and in the Scriptures at a Syrian convent[1]. This evidence warrants the assertion that some private and monastic libraries continued after, as before, the conquest. But if there had been a great public library before the conquest, and if it had been burned by the Arabs at the conquest, is it possible that John of Nikiou—an almost contemporary writer, who deals minutely with the capture of Alexandria—should have consigned to oblivion an event which not merely impoverished his history of its best materials, but robbed the literary world of its great storehouse of treasure for all time?

It may not be amiss to briefly recapitulate the argument. The problem being to discover the truth or falsehood of the story which charges the Arabs with burning the Alexandrian Library, I have shown—

(1) that the story makes its first appearance more than five hundred years after the event to which it relates;

(2) that on analysis the details of the story resolve into absurdities;

(3) that the principal actor in the story, viz. John

[1] Barhebraeus, *Chron. Eccl.* t. i. c. 290.

Philoponus, was dead long before the Saracens invaded Egypt;

(4) that of the two great public Libraries to which the story could refer, (*a*) the Museum Library perished in the conflagration caused by Julius Caesar, or, if not, then at a date not less than four hundred years anterior to the Arab conquest; while (*b*) the Serapeum Library either was removed prior to the year 391, or was then dispersed or destroyed, so that in any case it disappeared two and a half centuries before the conquest;

(5) that fifth, sixth, and early seventh century literature contains no mention of the existence of any such Library;

(6) that if, nevertheless, it had existed when Cyrus set his hand to the treaty surrendering Alexandria, yet the books would almost certainly have been removed—under the clause permitting the removal of valuables—during the eleven months' armistice which intervened between the signature of the convention and the actual entry of the Arabs into the city;

and (7) that if the Library had been removed, or if it had been destroyed, the almost contemporary historian and man of letters, John of Nikiou, could not have passed over its disappearance in total silence.

The conclusion of the whole matter can be no longer doubtful. The suspicion of Renaudot and the scepticism of Gibbon are more than justified. One must pronounce that Abû 'l Faraj's story is a mere fable, totally destitute of historical foundation [1].

[1] My only concern in this matter has been to establish the truth, not to defend the Arabs. No defence is necessary: were it needful,

it would not be difficult to find something in the nature of an apology. For the Arabs in later times certainly set great store by all the classical and other books which fell into their hands, and had them carefully preserved and in many cases translated. Indeed they set an example which modern conquerors might well have followed. Thus Sédillot relates (*Hist. Gén. des Arabes*, t. i. p. 185) that when the French captured the town of Constantine in North Africa they burned all the books and MSS. which they captured, 'comme de vrais barbares.' The English on the capture of Magdala found a large library of Abyssinian books, which they carried off: but before long they abandoned the greater part at some wayside church, because it was too much trouble to transport them. The selection of books for keeping seems to have been made at random: but the value of the books saved is some measure of the loss to the world of learning of the books abandoned. The British Museum MS. of John of Nikiou was among the treasures rescued in this haphazard manner.

CHAPTER XXVI

CONQUEST OF PENTAPOLIS

Expedition to the West. Small opposition. Surrender of Barca under treaty. Capture of Tripolis and of Ṣabrah by storm. Return of 'Amr to Alexandria, and to Babylon. Fortress built at Jîzah. Expedition to Nubia forced to retreat. 'Amr's description of Egypt, and his sermon. Story of the virgin and the Nile.

THOUGH the fall of Alexandria extinguished the Roman Empire in Egypt, 'Amr ibn al 'Aṣî did not regard it as marking the accomplishment of his mission. The main of the Roman armies had left the country—under a compact never to return. Such resistance as still lingered clung to remote places in the Delta, relying on natural defences of river or lake, but powerless to reverse the broad result of the war: thus the cities of Manzâlah, as we have seen, kept alive hostilities for several months after the occupation of Alexandria. But since the time when the Arab horsemen under Zubair had first saved the imperilled fortunes of 'Amr, a steady stream of reinforcements had been poured into Egypt, not merely repairing the waste of war, but swelling the strength of the Arab army. Consequently 'Amr now had at his disposal a large body of troops, apart from those required to garrison the chief towns and to capture the last remaining strongholds of the enemy.

The spirit of conquest was as much in the genius of 'Amr as the spirit of expansion was in the genius of Islâm. As soon, therefore, as Egypt was secured, and before the fighting there was all over, the Arab chief decided upon an expedition to Pentapolis, the next province of the Roman Empire westward of Egypt. The establishment of settled government for the Nile valley must have been nearly completed during the eleven months of the armistice; so that, when the Arabs entered Alexandria, they had to provide merely for the administration of the city. Had it been otherwise it would have been impossible for the expedition to follow so closely upon the occupation of the capital as it did follow; for the date cannot be much later than the beginning of the year 643[1].

It has been shown in connexion with the revolt of Heraclius against Phocas that, in the seventh century, stations or towns were dotted along the whole

[1] Ibn al Athîr (vol. iii. p. 19) says that the invasion of Barca was in A. H. 22, i. e. Nov. 30, 642—Nov. 20, 643. The same writer (p. 38) gives correctly the date of Omar's death, and he must be preferred to Yâḳût and Ibn Khaldûn who give A. H. 21 for this invasion. I have elsewhere suggested that the discrepancy may be due to the fact that 'Amr must have started soon after the beginning of the Muslim year. There was of course a second expedition to Pentapolis in A. H. 25; but the two are clearly distinguished at least in Ibn al Athîr. Severus, as might be expected, confuses them; and, in speaking of an expedition which followed the restoration of Benjamin to the patriarchal throne, he fails to make it clear that he is not referring to the first, but to the second invasion of Pentapolis. Yet there is no manner of doubt on the subject: as the second invasion exactly fits with the known chronology, while if the first were understood, other events of well-ascertained date would be thrown into hopeless disorder. Moreover Eutychius here is of service: for he says, ''Amr took Tripolis in the west in A. H. 22, in the twenty-second year of Heraclius and the tenth of Omar's caliphate.' The date of Heraclius must be ruled out, because Eutychius chooses always to give it wrongly. But A. H. 22 does coincide for about half the year with the tenth year of Omar, since Omar began to reign July 24, 634, and his tenth year would begin in the early summer of 643, while A. H. 22 ended in November, 643. Tripolis was probably captured in May or June of that year.

route between Alexandria and Cyrene, and that much of the way lay through fertile country [1]. The march, which was an easy one for Roman troops, was a mere promenade for Arab horsemen [2]. Nor was much opposition encountered. There is no record of any fighting at all at Barca, which seems at once to have capitulated under treaty, agreeing to pay 13,000 dinârs as yearly tribute [3]. Two curious stipulations were made, (1) that the people of Barca might sell their children to raise the tribute-money, and (2) that the tribute should be delivered in Egypt, no tax-collector being allowed to enter the country. According to Yâkût, most of the people here became Muslims. From Barca 'Amr swept on to Tripolis, which was better fortified and had a larger Roman garrison. The city shut its gates, and for some weeks withstood the blockade which the Arabs established [4]. The sea was open, but no relief came by the sea; and when the garrison was nearly worn out with fighting or hunger, the Arabs

[1] See ch. i. supra.

[2] Suyûṭî implies that only cavalry were taken: *Ḥusn al Muḥâḍarah*, p. 86.

[3] Ibn al Athîr, Yâḳût, and Ibn Khaldûn all agree that 'Amr 'made peace' on these terms, but there is no mention of fighting.

[4] Yâḳût gives three months, Ibn Khaldûn one month, as the duration of the siege. Yet Ibn Khaldûn, whose whole account is better written and truer-looking than that of Yâḳût, speaks of the inhabitants as 'worn out by the siege.' Ibn 'Abd al Ḥakam dates the capture of Tripolis A. H. 23, according to Weil (*Geschichte der Chalifen*, vol. i. p. 124 n.), but this would make an impossibly long interval after the surrender of Barca. John of Nikiou speaks of the wealthy men of the province taking refuge with Abuliânos, the Prefect, and his troops in a strongly fortified city, which he calls Dûshera (p. 578). But apparently John means to say that the Arabs failed to capture Dûshera: they certainly can have had little or no equipment for siege warfare.

discovered that the city was undefended on the harbour side, and that an entrance was practicable. A few men managed to force a passage round between the city wall and the sea, and rushed on the enemy. As their war-cry, 'Allahû Akbar,' rang through the streets and the flash of the scimitars was seen, a panic seized the defenders, who caught up what goods they could carry, ran to the ships, and hoisted sail. Meanwhile the gates were abandoned, and 'Amr entered with the bulk of his army.

Moving with characteristic swiftness, 'Amr next surprised the city of Ṣabrah [1], dashing upon it early in the morning. The inhabitants were entirely off their guard, as they fancied that the Arabs were still occupied in beleaguering Tripolis, and the city fell at the first onset. It was taken by force of arms and plundered. This marked the end of the rapid campaign. 'Amr returned to Barca, where he received the formal submission of the Berber tribe of Lawâtah [2], which occupied most of the country; and thence he led his victorious forces back to Egypt [3],

[1] Mr. Alex. Graham in his *Roman Africa* (London, 1902) gives at the end of his work a list of correspondences between ancient and modern names. In this Sabrata (presumably the same as the Arab Ṣabrah) is represented as the modern Zurârah, and Barca as the modern Tolometa. On p. 156 will be found an account of Roman remains at Tripoli, and the whole book is full of illustrations of Roman architecture, which dates from an earlier period no doubt, but was not very materially altered before the Arab conquest.

[2] The Arab historians say that this tribe of Lawâtah came originally from Palestine in the time of Goliath. The tradition is worth recording, and it goes as far back as Ibn 'Abd al Ḥakam.

[3] According to Weil, who is presumably quoting Ibn 'Abd al Ḥakam, 'Amr wished to pursue his career of conquest further westward, but was recalled by Omar, who saw more danger than advantage in such a compaign. Moreover 'the Muḳauḳas wrote to 'Amr that the Romans would make an effort to recover Egypt.'

with a long train of captives and with abundance of spoil.

It is said that 'Amr wished to take up his abode in Alexandria, particularly as he found so many of the splendid palaces deserted. But Omar had already determined that Fusṭâṭ was to be the future capital of Egypt, and he did not choose to have his Viceroy established in a great city resting on the sea and sundered from the Arabian desert by all the network of the Nile. It was probably in the summer of 643 that 'Amr returned to Babylon, where the two bridges over the Nile—joining the island of Rauḍah with Babylon on the eastern bank and with Jîzah on the western—as we have seen, had been reinstated[1]. But the western bank with the town of Memphis was exposed to sudden raids from the wild desert tribes beyond the Pyramids, and to meet this danger, as well as to plant the Arab power firmly astride the Nile, 'Amr ordered a fortress to be built at Jîzah. The work was finished before November of that year[2].

This latter statement is certainly erroneous. Al Muḳauḳas was dead, if Cyrus was meant: while if the title were given to Benjamin (as Ibn 'Abd al Ḥakam seems to give it), he was still hiding in Upper Egypt.

[1] These bridges were made of boats or barges, moored with their heads up stream, and joined by planks. They existed before the conquest, and it was part of the contract made on the surrender of Babylon that the Copts should keep in repair 'the two bridges' صلاح الجسرين. See n. 19 on p. 129 of Hamaker's *Expugnatio Memphidis*.

[2] Abû Ṣâliḥ, p. 173, says that the fortress was built in A. H. 22, which ended Nov. 20, 643. Yâḳût says that the Arab colony established at Jîzah consisted of Himyarites, Abyssinians, and members of the tribes of Hamdân, Rua'in, and Al 'Azd ibn al Ḥajar (vol. ii. p. 177). As far as I know, this is the only mention of Abyssinians as forming part of the conquering army. Abû Ṣâliḥ

Peace now reigned throughout the whole of the Delta and the Nile valley as far as the southern border of Egypt at Aswân. But the Sudân now, as ever, was a thorn in the side of the government. Its untameable tribes, secure in their mountains and deserts, had no notion of changing their Christian faith to Islâm, nor of abandoning their ancestral right of raiding the wealthy cities of Egypt. An expedition which 'Amr sent against the Nubians not merely failed to vanquish them, but was forced to retreat[1], having suffered much loss from the exceptional skill of the Nubian archers, whom the Arabs henceforth distinguished as the 'eye-wounders.' Desultory fighting lasted for some years; till in the reign of Othman a treaty of peace was made, under which the Nubians engaged to deliver an annual tribute of slaves to the ruler of Egypt, while the Arabs undertook to deliver convoys of provisions and a robe of honour. It was clearly a peace on equal terms: the time had not yet come for the conquest of the Sudân[2].

mentions only the Hamdân: and I think Yâḳût must be mistaken, because Balâdhurî speaks of the Abyssinians as enemies. 'When the Muslims occupied Egypt, an army of Abyssinians marched from Al Biyamâ and attacked the Arabs, continuing to fight with them for seven years,' he says: and he adds the curious remark, 'They made themselves invincible for the time by flooding the country' (ed. de Goeje, p. 223). Of course in both cases the term may be loosely used to denote either Sudânis of some sort or else men from Yaman in South Arabia.

[1] These are the very words of Ibn al Athîr. The campaign may be the same as that mentioned in the preceding note as recorded by Balâdhurî, but Ibn al Athîr says nothing about the country being flooded. According to Ya'ḳûbî the invasion of Nubia under 'Uḳbah ibn Nâfi' took place before the foundation of Jîzah, but he agrees that the Arabs met with a stout resistance.

[2] The final subjection of Nubia was accomplished in 652. The

Meanwhile the country was settling down under the mild and just government of 'Amr ibn al 'Aṣî; for that was the character it assumed when the long struggle of the conquest was over. The description of Egypt, which he now wrote on the demand of the Caliph Omar, gives an interesting glimpse of 'Amr both as poet and as statesman. It was in rhymed prose, and ran as follows[1]: 'Know, O Commander of the Faithful, that Egypt is a dusty city and green tree. Its length is a month, and its breadth ten days. It is enclosed by a barren mountain range and yellow sands. The Nile traces a line through its midst: blessed are its early morning voyages and its travels at eventide! It has its season for rising and for falling, according to the course of the sun and the moon. It causes milk to flow, and brings cattle in abundance. When the springs and fountains of the land are loosened, it rolls its swelling and sounding waters till the fields are flooded on both sides. Then there is no escaping from village to village save in little boats, and frail skiffs, and shallops light as fancy or the evening mist. After the river has risen to its full measure, it sinks back again to its former level. Moreover the people, who are devout in worship, and are our protected allies[2], have learnt to plough the earth well and truly and to hasten the seed-time, trusting that the Most High will give the increase and will grant the fruit of their

treaty of peace is given by Maḳrîzî, and may be found translated in Prof. Lane-Poole's *Egypt in the Middle Ages*, pp. 21–3.

[1] I have followed the version given by Abû 'l Maḥâsin. It differs somewhat from that given by Gibbon in his fifty-first chapter from Vatier's rendering of Murtadi.

[2] The use of this expression by 'Amr of course confirms the fact that relations of protection and alliance between the Arabs and the Egyptians were established by treaty.

labour, though the labour is light. So the crop is grown, and streams of water bring on the harvest, as moisture from beneath gives nourishment. At one time Egypt is a white pearl; then golden amber; then a green emerald; then an embroidery of many colours.

'Blessed be God, because it has pleased Him to bestow benefits upon this land, to give it increase, and so to establish the inhabitants in their country, that no sound of complaint is heard from the people to their ruler; that the land-tax is not demanded before its due season; and that a third of the revenue is spent on bridges and sluice-gates. If the governors continue to act thus, the revenue will be doubled, and God will reconcile the different religions and the variety of worldly interests.'

The same genial wisdom shines through the sermon which the conqueror of Egypt delivered at the mosque of 'Amr, as it is still called, on the Friday in Easter week of 644[1]. It is recorded from the lips of one of his hearers, who went to the mosque with his father. He saw the crowd driven

[1] This date is the result of a series of inferences. Ibn 'Abd al Ḥakam, from whom the sermon comes, gives it as related by Yaḥyâ ibn Dâḥir al Ma'âfirî, who says, 'I went with my father to the Friday prayers, at the end of winter, a few days after the Great Thursday of the Christians.' If the Great Thursday means Maundy Thursday, as I presume, this fixes the day. The year is less certain; but 644 seems the only year about this time in which 'Amr was at Fusṭâṭ and was in a position to exhort his hearers to a quiet enjoyment of the country at pasture-time. The sermon is given also by Suyûṭî, who calls the narrator Baḥîr ibn Dâjir al Maghârî —a good illustration of copyist corruption. Mr. Corbett in his article on the mosque of 'Amr (*Royal Asiat. Soc. Journal* for Oct. 1890, p. 768) thinks that Epiphany is meant: but the Egyptian winter cannot be described as over in the middle of January.

back with whips, as they pressed too closely; heard the muezzin call to prayer; and watched 'Amr as he mounted the pulpit. 'Amr's strong build, his capacious head, dark eyes, and cheerful countenance made a deep impression on the young Muslim, who notes also that he wore a striped garment in the texture of which were threads of gold.

'Amr briefly gave praise and glory to God, and prayed for the Prophet [1]. He urged his hearers to give alms, and to render dutiful obedience to their parents. He recommended moderation and forbade excess. He warned the Muslims against those things which cause fatigue in place of repose, narrow means in place of abundance, and weakness in place of strength: and those things are mainly the enlargement of the household, avarice in heaping up money, and vain and purposeless chatter. Idleness and frivolity are the chief sources of vice, and crush out the nobler desires of the soul. Then 'Amr changed his subject and said: 'O ye congregation, the Twins are hanging in the sky and Sirius is still covered; the heavens have begun their yearly course, the sky is clear and there is no plague; the flood is diminished, the pasture is good; milk abounds for kids and lambs, and the shepherd must watch well over his flock. Therefore go forth with the blessing of God to your cultivated land, and enjoy its benefits—milk and flocks and herds and game: feed your horses and fatten them, guard them and better them, for they are your defence against the enemy, and through them you gain booty and wealth.

'And take good care of your neighbours the

[1] What follows is little more than a transcript of Abû 'l Maḥâsin's story of the sermon taken from Ibn 'Abd al Ḥakam.

Copts. Omar, the Commander of the Faithful, told me that he heard the Apostle of God say: *God will open Egypt to you after my death. So take good care of the Copts in that country; for they are your kinsmen and under your protection.* Cast down your eyes therefore, and keep your hands off them [1].

'Know that you are an army of defence up to the Day of Resurrection, because of the many enemies who surround you, and the desire of their hearts towards you and your country, which is a storehouse of corn and money and wealth and blessings of every kind. Omar told me that he heard the Apostle of God say: *When God opens Egypt to you, gather a large army there, and it will be the best army in the world.* So Abû Bakr asked: *Why, O Apostle of God?* And he said: *Because they and their wives form an army of defence until the Day of Resurrection* [2].

'Therefore praise God, O ye congregation, because He has made you rulers of this country; and enjoy

[1] Ibn 'Abd al Ḥakam in his *Futûḥ Miṣr* proves by Muslim tradition how strong was the claim of the Copts to good treatment, and how strong was the injunction laid by Mohammed upon his followers to accord it. The passage is extracted from Ibn 'Abd al Ḥakam by Abû Ṣâliḥ: see pp. 97–100, with Mr. Evetts' notes. It would be well if the Muslims had remembered more often in their history the dying command of their Prophet.

[2] The story as here given is not very clear. It usually takes another form, viz. that Mohammed on his death-bed said three times, 'Take charge of the men with curly hair'; then swooned away. When he recovered they asked his meaning, and he said, 'The Copts of Egypt are our uncles and our brothers-in-law. They shall be your allies against your enemy and your helpers in your religion.' When asked, 'How shall they be our helpers in religion?' Mohammed answered, 'They shall relieve you of the cares of this world, so that you shall be at leisure for religious worship.'

your green fields, so long as they remain pleasant to you. But when the weather grows oppressive, and the posts grow hot; when flies multiply and the milk turns sour; when the herbage withers, and the roses are gathered from the trees; then come back to your Fusṭâṭ with God's blessing.

'I have said my say, and may God preserve you.'

The Muslims have a curious tradition that one of the first acts of 'Amr's administration was to abolish the annual custom of sacrificing a virgin to ensure the rise of the Nile. The story is that the river, deprived of its immemorial tribute by 'Amr's ordinance, refused to lift its flood, until a letter of the Caliph's was thrown in the stream and secured its obedience [1]. This of course is mere legend: there is no more reason to believe in the toleration of human sacrifice in Christian Egypt than in the miraculous power of the Caliph's letter. Yet this legend, like most others, seems to have some foundation in history, inasmuch as among the savage tribes in the far south of the Sudân the custom did prevail of throwing into the Nile a virgin apparelled as a bride [2]; and it is possible that a

[1] The story may be found in Ibn al Faḳîḥ (*Bibl. Geog. Arab.* part v. p. 65). It gives the date for the sacrifice as 12 Ba'ûnah (6 June): the refusal of the Nile continued till 'the day before the festival of the Cross,' i.e. till 13 September, when the Caliph's letter was flung into the river. The date shows the absurdity of the story. An English version occurs in H. S. Jarrett's *History of the Caliphs* in *Bibliotheca Indica*, vol. xviii. series iii. p. 130.

[2] That the custom lingered in Bornu down to modern times is clear from the travels of Harnemann (vol. i. p. 143) and Burckhardt (*Travels in Nubia*, App. ii. p. 444), quoted by Hamaker in *Expugnatio Memphidis*, p. 133. Hamaker also refers to Rich's diary in *Quarterly Review*, 1820, p. 232, and his whole note is well worth reading.

similar custom was found in some barbarous region of Nubia which was conquered in the early days of Islâm. It is possible also that in Egypt itself the practice of sacrificing a maiden to the Nile subsisted under the Pharaohs, as it is certain that a good deal of more innocent superstition of ancient origin was preserved in ceremonies attending the invocation of the river, which lasted down to the fourteenth century[1]. But it is quite false to charge the Christians with keeping up inhuman rites totally repugnant to their religion.

The utterances of 'Amr already quoted indicate clearly enough his methods of government and the relations he sought to establish between victor and vanquished. Even more decisive evidence of the same spirit was shown in the order, which he now issued, for the recall and reinstatement of the Patriarch Benjamin. It was a recognition of the fact that the political and the religious settlement of the country were bound up together.

[1] Hamaker, ib., p. 134, records in particular the use of certain relics of St. George for the purpose of raising the flood. The church of St. George to which they belonged was pulled down, and the relics were burned and the ashes scattered in the river, in A. H. 755, or 1354 A. D.

CHAPTER XXVII

RESTORATION OF BENJAMIN

State of the Coptic Church at Cyrus' death. Recovery of freedom. 'Amr's invitation to Benjamin. Return of the Patriarch from exile. His interview with 'Amr. Revival of the Church. Repair of desert monasteries. Exultation of the Copts. Their verdict on the expulsion of the Romans.

By the death of the Roman Patriarch, Cyrus, and by the departure of the Roman armies on which his power had rested, a tremendous change had been wrought in the position of religious parties. The long ordeal of the Great Persecution was over. Though a new Melkite Patriarch had been appointed in Alexandria, he had little or no jurisdiction beyond the city walls: his power was gone, and his following greatly minished. But the Coptic Patriarch was still in hiding—an exile and a wanderer in Upper Egypt. His Church lay weakened and almost lifeless, it seemed, from the blows rained upon it during the space of ten years by the relentless hand of Cyrus. Now, however, Christianity had ceased to be the state religion; over both parties was thrown the shield of Islâm, and between them its sword. This state of things allowed free play to religious sentiment. The Muslims had no interest in the truth or falsehood of the pronouncement of Chalcedon; while the Copts were no longer under the dominion of a terror which forced them to renounce or to conceal their true belief. In the novel atmosphere of religious freedom the Coptic Church revived, and soon proved its claim to be considered the Church of the nation. 'Amr's admission of this claim was sealed by his decree for the recall of Benjamin.

The decree is said to have been prompted by information given to 'Amr by one Sanutius (or Shanûdah), who, though a Copt by creed, had held the position of *dux* or general in the Roman army [1]. But even Sanutius was ignorant of Benjamin's hiding-place [2], so that the decree had to be published in general terms. It ran as follows: 'In whatsoever place Benjamin, the Patriarch of the Egyptian Christians, is living, to that place we grant protection and security, and peace from God. Wherefore let the Patriarch come hither in security and tranquillity, to administer the affairs of his Church and to govern his nation [3].' It is not improbable that the action of Sanutius coincided with a general act of submission to Muslim authority made by the monks of Wâdî 'n Naṭrûn. For Maḳrîzî quotes Christian historians as relating that 70,000 monks from these monasteries went to meet 'Amr ibn al 'Aṣî, each carrying a staff, and that when they declared their allegiance, he gave them a letter—doubtless a 'writing of security,' and perhaps the very decree in question [4]. As usual in Arab documents, cyphers

[1] Severus, Brit. Mus. MS., p. 106, l. 10. Most of the facts here given come from the same source.

[2] This is one more proof, if proof were wanted, of the absurdity of making Benjamin play the part of Al Muḳauḳas at the conquest.

[3] Abû Ṣâliḥ says that in the decree it was written: 'Let the Shaikh and Patriarch come forth in confidence with regard to his own person and to all the Copts who are in the land of Egypt or elsewhere: for they shall be safe from all violence and treachery,' and so on (p. 231). This is much the same in substance, though not so precise as the earlier Severus.

[4] Maḳrîzî speaks of this letter as still existing at the Wâdî 'n

have grown upon the original number and swollen it to absurdity; but that a deputation of 70, or even 700, monks waited upon the conqueror and was very well received may be regarded as historical.

The bill of immunity was not long in reaching Benjamin, who now came forth from his retreat, and went in triumph to Alexandria. Great were the rejoicings of the people upon his return. It was now full thirteen years since he had abandoned his seat on the arrival of Cyrus, and had stolen away by the western desert. Ten years of this period corresponded to the ten years' persecution, and three years had been spent under the rule of the Muslims[1]. During the whole of this time Benjamin

Naṭrûn. He speaks also of another letter from 'Amr 'about the treasurership of the northern districts' as preserved at Dair Macarius: see Abû Ṣâliḥ, App., p. 320. Severus says nothing about the deputation, but writes that it was 'Sanutius, the believing duke, who had secured the return of the Patriarch, and obtained his safe-conduct from the Muslim commander.' The existence of the letter at Dair Macarius is also mentioned in Amélineau's *Histoire des Monastères de la Basse Égypte*, p. xxxii.

[1] There is a general agreement upon Benjamin's period of exile and its division. Severus says that he came back 'after an absence of thirteen years, of which ten were in the reign of Heraclius and three under the Muslims,' though he adds erroneously 'before they conquered Alexandria.' John of Nikiou (c. cxxi. p. 584) says that he came back 'thirteen years after he had taken flight to escape from the hands of the Romans,' although the rubric of the chapter makes the period of exile fourteen years, viz. ten under the Roman Emperors and four under Muslim rule. Makîn gives thirteen years. I think there can be little doubt that the return of Benjamin fell towards the autumn of 644, i. e. the end of A. H. 24. Makîn absurdly puts it in A. H. 20, while Severus with equal error connects it with 'Amr's expedition to Pentapolis. One might produce a sort of agreement between Severus and John of Nikiou by taking the period of exile as fourteen years, which would date Benjamin's

had been moving about among his people in secret, or lurking in desert monasteries; and it is worth remarking that neither the decisive conquest of Egypt by the Muslims nor the expulsion of the Roman armies furnished the exiled Patriarch with any reason for emerging from concealment. No fact could more clearly show how history has maligned the Copts in charging them with aiding the Arabs or hailing their country's enemies as deliverers. If the Copts had welcomed the Arabs, it could only have been by command or consent of their Patriarch: and if Benjamin had sanctioned any such alliance, he would not have waited for three years after the complete victory of the Arabs, and then have been lured from his retreat only by an uncovenanted promise of protection. Such an argument, if it stood alone, would be strong, if not conclusive: it is, however, but a link added to a chain of evidence which has become wellnigh irresistible.

When Sanutius reported Benjamin's arrival in Alexandria, 'Amr commanded the Patriarch's presence, giving orders at the same time that he should be received with all due honour and ceremony. Benjamin's handsome and dignified bearing and his grave eloquence are represented as having made a deep impression on 'Amr, who remarked to his companions, 'In all the countries I have conquered up to this day, I have never seen a man of God like this.' Of the 'noble oration,' which Benjamin is said to have delivered, 'Amr can have understood nothing;

return A. H. 25: which was the date of the second expedition to Pentapolis. But this is to do violence to Severus' story, which seems to refer, however wrongly, to the first expedition; and the fact is, that it is not worth while trying to reconcile all of these desperate discrepancies.

but the practical suggestions of the Patriarch were well entertained, and he was given full authority to bear rule over his people and to administer the affairs of the Church.

The restitution of Benjamin saved the Coptic Church from a perilous crisis, if not from destruction. Never was the guidance of a strong character more needed. Under the persecution of Cyrus, as we have seen, thousands had been forced out of their allegiance, and had professed adherence to Chalcedon. Of course conversions wrought by threat or violence could not at first be real. But the process had been working for ten years; habit had been growing; and the result could not be undone in a moment. Even more formidable, however, was the defection of the Copts to Islâm. Nor would it be right to attribute this defection solely to motives of worldly advantage. The offer of brotherhood with the conquerors and of freedom from tribute was potent enough to sweep down the tide all those whose religion was not strongly anchored; but it must be sorrowfully granted also that many men of thoughtful mind may have sickened of a Christianity which so belied its Founder—a Christianity out of which all love and all hope had vanished in the war of sects—and hence may have sought refuge and repose in the calm simplicity of Islâm.

There was little or no prospect of bringing back to the fold those who had renounced the Christian faith altogether; but it was otherwise with regard to many of those who had been driven by force or fear into the Melkite communion. The news of Benjamin's reappearance and return to the throne of Alexandria roused the greatest enthusiasm throughout Egypt. Most of the common people returned with joy to their old pastor, 'and received the crown of confession [1].' The apostate bishops, who had joined the Church of the Empire, were also invited to resume their old allegiance. Some of them were received back with bitter tears of penitence; but one bishop in particular is mentioned as refusing to return for very shame and for fear of being known as an apostate. His case was probably typical of many. Still the cause of the Coptic Church progressed. While at first Benjamin 'turned all his thoughts by day and by night to bringing back the scattered members of his flock that had gone astray in the days of Heraclius,' later, as he succeeded in reuniting and reorganizing the body of his people, he gave his mind to rebuilding the ruined monasteries, particularly those of the Wâdî 'n Naṭrûn, which had never recovered from the devastation wrought early in the seventh century.

The money was found and the work was done. Severus gives a long and interesting account of events in this connexion. He shows how a deputation of monks came to Alexandria and entered the 'Porch of the Angels [2],' as Benjamin was celebrating on Christmas Day; how they begged him to come and consecrate the newly built church of St. Macarius in the desert; how Benjamin granted their request, and travelling by Al Munā and Mount Barnûj arrived at the monastery of Baramûs, whence he went to visit other monasteries. So on the 2nd January he came to the Dair Macarius, whence he

[1] Severus, l. c., p. 107.

[2] The term is 'Stoa Angelon,' a mere transcription of the Greek. It clearly refers to the church called the Angelion, and would seem to prove that *Angelion* is more correct than *Euangelion*.

was welcomed by the 'great teacher' Basil, bishop of Nikiou, and a procession with palm-branches and censers. On the following day, 8th Tûbah, the church was solemnly consecrated—with attendant miracles which need not here be recorded. One may, however, notice the words of Basil, who 'gave thanks to the Lord who had made the Patriarch worthy to see that glorious desert once more, and those holy fathers and brethren, and the proclamation of the orthodox faith; who had saved him from the heretics, and had delivered his soul from the great and cruel dragon which drove him away, and had granted him to behold his children once more around him [1].'

This is not the language of people suffering under oppression, but the language of people rejoicing in deliverance. Its tenour is fully confirmed by other passages of the same writer. 'I was in my city of Alexandria, and *found a time of peace and safety* after the troubles and persecutions caused by the heretics [2],' are the words put into the mouth of Benjamin; and his people are described as 'rejoicing like young calves when their bonds are loosened, and they are set free to suck their mother's milk.' John of Nikiou wrote fifty years after the conquest, and he is unsparing in his denunciation of the Muslim religion and the renegades who adopted it; but of 'Amr he remarks that 'while he exacted the taxes which had been determined upon, he took none of the property of the churches, and committed no act of spoliation or plunder; nay, he preserved the churches to the end of his days [3].' The relief,

[1] Severus, l. c., p. 111, ll. 15–20.

[2] Id., p. 110, l. 5, and p. 108, l. 18.

[3] p. 584. Vansleb alleges that he saw on the walls of Al

therefore, of the Copts was very great. They had passed out of the long reign of terror, under which the folly of the Byzantine government had placed them, into a state of peace and security. Before they had been under a double bondage, civil and religious; now their civil bondage was lightened and their religious bondage removed. True, their new rulers brought a strange and unchristian creed into the land, but even in this result they could read the divine judgement. For all agreed in saying, 'This expulsion of the Romans and victory of the Muslims is due to the wickedness of the Emperor Heraclius and his persecution of the orthodox by means of the Patriarch Cyrus; this was the cause of the ruin of the Romans and the subjugation of Egypt by the Muslims[1].' Such was the popular verdict. The verdict of history will not take quite so sectarian a colour; but it will most surely confirm the reasoning which links together the misgovernment and the downfall of the Roman Empire.

Mu'allaḳah in Ḳaṣr ash Shama' or Babylon a contract given by 'Amr ibn al 'Aṣî in his own hand for the protection of the church: it cursed all Muslims who should wish to deprive the Copts of it. He alleges that the Copts ransomed the church from 'Amr (*Nouvelle Relation d'un Voyage fait en Égypte*, p. 237).

[1] Id., ib.

CHAPTER XXVIII

MUSLIM GOVERNMENT

Equality of Christians before the law. Status of a protected people. Religious conditions. Political settlement. Roman officials retained. Land-tax and poll-tax: nature and amount. 'Amr's just government and the Caliph's displeasure: their correspondence. Omar's avarice imitated by Othman. Story of Peter the Copt. Exemption of converts from the poll-tax and its consequences. Decline of state revenue. Pressure on the Christians.

AFTER all that the Copts had suffered at the hands of the Romans and the Patriarch Cyrus, it would not have been unnatural if they had desired to retaliate upon the Melkites. But any such design, if they cherished it, was sternly discountenanced by 'Amr, whose government was wisely tolerant but perfectly impartial between the two forms of religion. Many facts might be cited in proof of this contention: for example, the admission of Severus that a Melkite bishop remained a Melkite to his death; his evidence that Benjamin worked on the perverts only by persuasion and remonstrance; the continued mention of Melkite churches in later history[1]; and the fact that the Melkites are spoken of in considerable numbers fifty years after the conquest[2]. So

[1] One such church on the top of the tower in Ḳaṣr ash Shama' has remained to this day in the very centre and stronghold of the Copts.

[2] The contemporary document *Vie du Patriarche Isaac* (tr. Amélineau, p. 52) records that the Patriarch 'convertit un grand nombre de leur hérésie; il les amena à la foi orthodoxe: à quelques-uns il donna le baptême, il reçut les autres en les faisant anathématiser eux-mêmes leurs hérésies,' &c. The heresy must

that the two forms of Christianity must be imagined as subsisting side by side under the equal protection of the conquerors.

Nor does this protection seem at that early date to have been trammelled with conditions which the law of Islâm carried in its later developments. The status of a protected people was created by the treaty of peace, by which the Christians engaged to pay tribute in return for security at home and protection against foreign enemies. But as early as the tenth century the law declares that the obligation to pay tribute is governed by two classes of conditions—the first absolutely binding in all cases, the second depending in each case on the terms of the treaty. The binding conditions are these: (1) the Ḳurân is not to be reviled, nor copies of it burned; (2) the Prophet must not be called a liar nor spoken of contemptuously; (3) the religion of Islâm is not to be condemned, nor must any attempt be made to refute it; (4) no Christian may marry a Muslim woman; (5) no attempt may be made to seduce a Muslim from his religion, nor to injure him in purse or person; (6) the enemies of Islâm must not be assisted, nor the rich men among them entertained. The contingent conditions are as follows: (1) subjects must wear a distinctive garment with a girdle fastened round the waist; (2) their houses must not be built higher than those of the Muslims; (3) the sound of their bells[1] must not be forced on the ears of Muslims, nor their reading or chanting, nor their opinions on their peculiar tenets, whether Jewish or

be mainly if not exclusively that of the Byzantine Church—the following of Chalcedon.

[1] The nâḳûs is more strictly a wooden gong than a bell. See supra, p. 343, n. 4.

Christian; (4) crosses must not be displayed nor wine drunk in public, nor must swine be seen; (5) the dead are to be mourned in private and to be buried in private; (6) subjects must ride only common horses or mules, not thoroughbreds [1]. There is nothing very unreasonable in any of these conditions, but it may be doubted whether they were attached to the payment of tribute so early as the conquest of Egypt. Many regulations, which grew out of usage into law, came in the days of law to be regarded as part of the original constitution of Islâm. For example, Ma'wardî says, 'It is not lawful for subject people to build a new church or synagogue in the territory of Islâm, and any such building must be demolished; but they may restore old churches or synagogues which have fallen into ruin.' But this distinction cannot be traced in the beginnings of Muslim rule in Egypt, because not only is Benjamin described as receiving a large sum of money from the duke Sanutius for the purpose of building a church to St. Mark in Alexandria [2], but the Patriarch John of Samanûd did actually build a church with the same dedication [3], and under his successor, Isaac, the ruler of Egypt 'Abd al

[1] These details are from Míwardî, who wrote in the first half of the eleventh century; died A. H. 450 = 1058 A. D. His work, *Kitâb al Aḥkâm as Sulṭânîah*, is the chief authority for early taxation, and is freely used in the present chapter. The long passage about the taxes begins on p. 245 for the tribute, and 253 for the land-tax.

[2] Severus, l. c., p. 108, l. 10. It is not quite clear whether Benjamin succeeded in raising enough money. The text does not support the idea that there was any question of rebuilding the original church of St. Mark.

[3] *Vie du Patriarche Copte Isaac* (ed. Amélineau), p. 44. John's date was 680–9 A. D.: see Appendix F.

'Azîz himself is represented as giving orders for the erection of a church at his newly settled town of Ḥulwân [1]. It would seem, therefore, that in matters ecclesiastical the Copts were granted every reasonable freedom.

It is less easy to define the political settlement of the country. Broadly speaking, however, the civil administration was maintained unaltered. The Arabs were good fighters, but they had received no tradition and no training in the arts of government, nor did they possess any system which they could substitute for or graft upon the ancient and highly organized civil service of Egypt. But they had a quick and receptive intelligence, and were perfectly capable of taking over and directing machinery which they found in working order. It has been shown above that some of the highest Roman officials not merely retained their posts, but adopted the religion of Islâm, and probably a number of Roman people followed their example. On the other hand, a great number of vacancies must have been created by the departure of those Romans who declined to remain as Muslim subjects. These places were filled with Coptic Christians, and in no long time practically the whole business of the state was managed by Christians. This was not merely a result logically flowing from the conquest of a highly civilized by an uncivilized people, but it was prudently foreseen and expressly sanctioned by Mohammed himself. In this way, unfettered by worldly cares, the Muslims could better devote themselves to religion. It is, however, curious to find with what vitality the old Roman titles persisted

[1] *Vie du Patriarche Copte Isaac*, p. 78. The date would doubtless be 693.

under Arab rule: for quite at the end of the seventh century the Copts continued to speak of a registrar or secretary as *chartularius*, of his superior as *eparchos of the land of Egypt* or *archon*, of the governor's residence as the *praetorium*, while the governor of Alexandria is actually called *the augustal*[1]: moreover, the term *dux* is found in several eighth-century documents[2], mostly legal, and is used by the tenth-century writer Severus[3].

But while the Roman system of registration and of collection was continued, it seems probable that the taxation fixed under treaty by the Arabs was at once somewhat less vexatious and less burdensome than the Roman. It is hard to get at the truth in such matters. One is dependent upon Arab writers, whose proneness to differ on points of history reaches its climax on questions of statistics. Thus Ibn 'Abd al Ḥakam[4] alleges that when 'Amr was firmly established, he made the Copts pay a similar tribute to that exacted by the Romans, but it was to fluctuate in proportion to their wealth and prosperity. This, I think, can only mean that he continued the Roman system of land-tax: for the poll-tax imposed by the Arabs was a fixed payment, while undoubtedly the land-tax varied in accordance with the rise of the Nile and the general conditions of agriculture. Ibn 'Abd al Ḥakam goes on to say that it was the duty of the village headmen to meet and examine into the state of agriculture, and to distribute the burden

[1] *Vie du Patriarche Copte Isaac*, pp. 5, 7, 73.

[2] See Mr. W. E. Crum's *Coptic Ostraka*, no. 356.

[3] Mr. Milne shows how the framework of the Roman system of local government is preserved under Muslim arrangements even to this day; see his *Egypt under Roman Rule*, p. 216.

[4] Quoted by Suyûṭî, p. 87.

of taxation accordingly. They were in fact a sort of local commissioners for the assessment of the land-tax. Any surplus above the prescribed amount was to be expended on local improvements, and a portion of land in every township was set aside to provide a fund for the maintenance of public buildings, such as churches and baths. Any hospitality which the Muslims claimed of right from the Copts was to be taken into account, as well as the stated expenses for the entertainment of the governor upon his visit.

Such no doubt is a fair description of the incidence of the land-tax. But it is not clear whether this land-tax was specially imposed by treaty at the conquest, or was merely continued and regarded as the ordinary incident of land tenure; nor is it always clear whether Arab writers in speaking of the revenue of Egypt refer to the total of taxation, or to the amount of the poll-tax, or tribute, alone. On the whole it would seem that they are dealing with the tribute. For on the one hand we are told that the population paying the capitation-tax of two dinârs under the capitulation was 6,000,000; and on the other the revenue raised by 'Amr after the settlement is given as 12,000,000 dinârs[1]. This

[1] Suyûṭî, l. c., quotes 'Abdallah ibn Ṣâliḥ for these figures, and Abû Ṣâliḥ (p. 82) makes the very interesting statement that in A. H. 20 'Amr raised 1,000,000 dinârs, while in A. H. 22 he raised 12,000,000. In other words, in the year coincident with the capture of Babylon the poll-tax amounted to one million, which increased to twelve on the completion of the conquest. This sounds extremely probable. The same figure of 12,000,000 is given by Ibn Ḥauḳal on the authority of Abû Hâzim al Ḳâḍî (*Bibl. Geog. Arab.* part ii. p. 87), who expressly states that the amount in question represented the poll-tax alone. When Balâdhurî states that the revenue raised by 'Amr in Egypt was 2,000,000 (p. 216), one must regard

sum is contrasted by Muslim historians with the 20,000,000 said to have been levied by Al Mukaukas[1]. If these figures could be taken as accurate, and as calculated upon the same basis, so as to furnish a fair comparison, they would of course prove that Arab rule brought to the Egyptians a great relief of taxation. But while the Arab figures denote the revenue raised by the poll-tax alone, it is hardly likely that the Roman figures refer to that one heading, although a poll-tax was one among the many items in the Roman schedule of taxation[2]. Still there can be no doubt either that the Roman taxes were excessive in amount and unjust in their incidence, owing to the exemption of privileged persons or communities[3], or that Heraclius was very hard pressed for money in the years preceding the Arab conquest: and there is no reason for discrediting the plain statement of

the discrepancy as due to a copyist's blunder, which blunder is repeated in the figure 4,000,000 given instead of 14,000,000 as the revenue raised by 'Abdallah ibn Sa'd. Ya'kûbî says (id., part vii. p. 339) that 'Amr raised 14,000,000 in his first year and 10,000,000 in the next. Here the difference is not easily explained; but 12,000,000 seems settled by a concurrence of testimony, in spite of the fact that Maḳrîzî, *Khiṭaṭ*, i. p. 76, makes the population on which the tribute was levied 8,000,000.

[1] Abû Ṣâliḥ is not very consistent. He seems to say (p. 81) that the Romans levied 20,000,000, and at the same time that the tribute which Heraclius required of Cyrus was 18,000,000. He may mean that the balance was retained by Cyrus.

[2] See Mr. Milne's *Egypt under Roman Rule*, pp. 121–2. The whole of this chapter is worth reading, for it shows at once how arbitrary and complex the taxation was, and how closely in many details the Arab system followed the Roman: see, for example, pp. 119 and 125.

[3] Mr. Milne, l. c., quotes Josephus as showing that the Alexandrians were exempt from the poll-tax; but how long that exemption continued is not stated.

the Muslim historians that upon the conquest the burden of taxation was lightened. On the other hand, exemptions were abolished. Some obscurity hangs over the position in Alexandria. It is certain that the people sorely fretted under the new system. This result might be due to the loss of a privileged immunity from poll-tax, if such immunity existed; or it might be due to the fact that the city suffered out of all proportion both by the interruption and the loss of its lucrative commerce during the long war, and by the departure of many wealthy merchants and burghers upon the capitulation. But the capitulation itself is harder to understand, if under it the city had to sacrifice an ancient immunity from direct tribute. On the whole it seems more probable that Alexandria had been robbed of its privilege at some time before the conquest.

The tribute, which the Arabs call *jizîah*, was fixed, as has been shown, at two dinârs a head, and was not levied on old men or children, or women or slaves, or madmen or beggars. But although every man was liable for his share of tribute, so that the total amount of the poll-tax depended on the count of polls, it seems that the incidence of the tax varied, and consequently shares were not equal. The two gold pieces would be nothing to a rich man, but a heavy burden to the fellâḥ. Hence the governor seems to have had the right to divide the tributaries into three classes—the poor, the middle-class, and the wealthy—and to assign to each a different proportion of the tribute[1]. This arrange-

[1] Maḳrîzî quotes Yazîd ibn Aslam for the statement that Omar wrote to the military commanders, ordering the tribute to be so apportioned that the rich man's poll-tax should be four dinârs, the poor man's forty dirhems. This seems too sharp a division. On

ment, however just in theory, was obviously liable to abuse; and it did in fact lead to arbitrary increase of taxation in defiance of the treaty. Nothing could be more equitable in the abstract than that the tax on each poll should vary with a man's means of payment, while the total remained unchanged; or that, while the total of land-tax varied with the season, the charge on any particular holding should vary with the productiveness of the soil: but it was not in human nature that such a system should continue to be honestly administered. It demanded ideal justice, but opened the door to every form of avarice and corruption: and it is no wonder that it broke down in practice.

In this connexion it is interesting to notice Ibn 'Abd al Ḥakam's story that 'Amr, upon the request of the Caliph Omar, asked the Patriarch Benjamin[1]

the other hand, Mîwardî says, 'There is a dispute among lawyers as to the amount of the jizîah. According to Abû Ḥanîfah there are three different amounts: (1) from the rich are due forty-eight dirhems; (2) from the middle-class twenty-four; (3) from the poor twelve. These sums he gives as the maximum and the minimum, and he forbids governors to exercise their own discretion as to the amount.' It is impossible to read Mîwardî without being struck by admiration for the extraordinary sense of justice and fairness which animates the theory and system of taxation he is describing. I give one example: 'Even when a protected people breaks its treaty by refusing payment of tribute, it is not lawful to kill or to rob them or to take their children, so long as they abstain from violence. Such rebels, however, must be given a safe-conduct and quit the territory of Islâm; and if they refuse to depart submissively, they must be ejected by force.' Nothing could better show how permanent was the idea of a contract subsisting between protectors and protected.

[1] Ibn 'Abd al Ḥakam says it was Al Muḳauḳas who was consulted: but he clearly identifies the Muḳauḳas with Benjamin in many passages. Of course 'Amr might have asked the same questions of Cyrus: but Ibn 'Abd al Ḥakam represents the Muḳauḳas

what was the best way of keeping the country in order and raising the revenue. The conditions laid down by the Patriarch were these: (1) that the taxes should be collected at the right time, viz. the end of the agricultural season; (2) that no taxes should be demanded after the vintage; (3) that the canals should be dug out yearly; (4) that the dykes and sluice-gates should be kept in repair; and (5) that no unjust or tyrannical official should be appointed. This fifth condition was the hardest of all to secure; for the very nature of the appointment tended to develop just those qualities which would render it fatal.

That the early government of 'Amr was animated by a spirit of justice and even sympathy for the subject population, can hardly be questioned. He received, however, little encouragement from the Caliph. 'Amr had filled the Caliph's granaries with corn from Egypt, had poured gold into his coffers, and had extended his dominion: in return he received little but abuse and ingratitude from Omar. The relations of the two men at this time are shown in a vivid light by some correspondence which has been preserved, and which must be regarded as quite authentic[1]. 'I have been thinking,' writes

as alive at the time of Manuel's rebellion. Moreover the incident of the consultation seems the same as that quoted above from Severus, although Severus makes Benjamin's advice quite general. Maḳrîzî gives the terms of the reply rather differently: for he places among the conditions of good government (1) that the land-tax be levied only in kind, (2) that no delay be allowed, and (3) that the officials be paid punctually.

[1] See Weil, *Geschichte der Chalifen*, t. i. p. 125 n. Ibn 'Abd al Ḥakam, who gives the letters, had actually seen them, and De Sacy is quoted as fully admitting their authenticity, basing his opinion partly on the archaic character of the language used. I have followed Weil's translation closely.

Omar, 'upon you and your condition. You find yourself in a great and splendid country, whose inhabitants God has blessed in number and power, by land and by water. It is a land which even the Pharaohs, in spite of their unbelief, brought by useful works to a state of prosperity. I am therefore greatly astonished that it does not bring in the half of its former revenue, although this falling-off cannot be excused by reason of famine or failure of crops. Moreover you have written ere this of many taxes which you have laid upon the country. I hoped now that they would come to me, instead of which you bring excuses which have no meaning. I shall surely not take less than was formerly paid. . . . Even in the past year[1] I might have demanded this of you, but I hoped that you would yourself fulfil your duty. Now, however, I see that it is your bad administration which hinders you. But, by the help of God, I have means to compel you to render me what I demand'; and so forth.

'Amr answers by admitting that under the Pharaohs, who gave great attention to agriculture, Egypt was more productive than now under the rule of the Muslims[2]: but he goes on to complain of the hard words used by the Caliph. 'I have served

[1] This seems to date the correspondence to about the beginning of 644.

[2] Ibn Rustah (*Bibl. Geog. Arab.* part vii. p. 118) says that the revenue of Egypt under the Pharaohs was 96,000,000 dinârs. Abû Ṣâliḥ says that the Pharaoh of Moses' time raised 90,000,000, and Maḳrîzî gives 90,000,000, adding that, according to Ibn Daḥîah, the dinâr then was worth three of Muslim date. 'Ash Sharîf al Ḥarrânî says that from a Sahidic list translated into Arabic he found that the revenues of Egypt in the time of Joseph amounted to 24,400,000 dinars,' i. e. 73,200,000 Muslim dinârs: see Mr. Evetts' note on p. 80 of Abû Ṣâliḥ.

the Apostle of God,' he proceeds, 'and his successor, Abû Bakr; I have (praise be to God) answered to the trust reposed in me, and I have rendered towards my prince the duty which God laid upon me. . . . Now take back the governorship which you have given me: for God has kept me free from the avarice and meanness wherewith you have charged me in your letters. . . . You could not have said more of a Jew of Khaibar. God forgive you and me.'

This simple and dignified language produced no effect upon Omar, who replied bluntly: 'I did not send you to Egypt in order to sate your lusts and those of your people, but because I hoped you would by good administration increase our revenue. Therefore upon receipt of this letter send me the taxes; for I have here people in great need.'

'Amr begged for a respite till the time of harvest —precisely in accordance with Benjamin's maxim. He urged that he could not raise a large revenue without injustice to the natives, and that it was better to be merciful to them than to oppress them, or to force them to provide the money by selling their necessaries[1]. It is needless to credit him, as Weil does, with insincerity and with sordid motives: for even if the love of money was growing upon the conqueror, it had not at this time filled his mind to the dispossession of his sense of justice and sense of duty to the Egyptians. But Omar set his face like flint against mercy in money matters. He dispatched Muḥammad ibn Maslamah to Egypt with orders to raise what he could beyond the tribute

[1] This sentence is translated from Maḳrîzî, *Khiṭaṭ*, i. p. 78. An account of the correspondence is also given by Balâdhurî (p. 219).

which 'Amr had already remitted, or, according to another account, to demand from 'Amr one half of his private possessions. It is true that Ibn Maslamah charged 'Amr with protecting the Egyptians for his own profit, just as Omar charged him with neglect of duty and fraud. But the admission that 'Amr did protect the Egyptians, together with the language of his own apology, outweighs the evidence against him. And in truth the charge of greed recoils on Omar, who, as Balâdhurî says, 'was in the habit of fixing and writing down the total of the revenues of each province, when he appointed a governor for it; and whatever was raised beyond this amount he used to share with the governor, *or in some cases take entirely for himself*.' Thus even the heroic Khâlid had been called upon in Syria to give an account of all his possessions, and had been ordered to surrender one half of them, even it is said to the abandonment of one of the sandals on his feet. When counselled to restore what he had taken, Omar replied, 'Before God, I restore nothing: I am a merchant for the benefit of the Muslims.' By the Muslims he meant either himself or the narrow clique at Mecca: and this purblind view of his duty to Islâm, this policy of filling his exchequer at the expense of his newly won dominions, was destined to cost him his life.

But the disastrous lesson had been too well learnt by his successor. When 'Abdallah ibn Sa'd, who was made governor of Upper Egypt and the Fayûm by Omar, replaced the conqueror as Viceroy of Egypt, he contrived to wring another 2,000,000 dinârs from the natives, raising the sum to 14,000,000. 'The milch-camel gives more milk than in your time,' said Othman to 'Amr. 'Yes,' was the reply;

'and the reason is that you are starving her young ones.' Not merely that, but to raise the tribute was clearly unlawful. I have already shown that when Wardân was ordered by the Caliph Mu'awîah to increase the tribute levied on the Copts, he answered that it was impossible owing to the terms of the treaty[1]: and I have quoted 'Urwah son of Zubair as saying that 'the people were taxed above their means and were in distress, notwithstanding the fact that 'Amr had made with them a treaty on fixed conditions.'

All this contrasts with and vindicates the justice of 'Amr. One anecdote told by Ibn 'Abd al Ḥakam, if it deserved credence, would give rather a different impression. 'Amr, he says, threatened death to any Copt who concealed treasure. A Christian of Upper Egypt, named Peter, was charged with such concealment, but when brought before 'Amr, he stoutly denied it, 'and *so* was imprisoned.' Shortly afterwards 'Amr inquired if Peter had mentioned any name, and was told that he had only spoken of a monk of Mount Sinai. Thereupon 'Amr had Peter's signet-ring removed, wrote a letter to the monk saying, 'Send me what you have,' and sealed it in Peter's name. In due time there came a messenger bearing in answer a small jar closed with a leaden seal. This was opened by 'Amr, who found inside a paper with the words, 'Your property is under the cistern.' So 'Amr had the water drawn off from the cistern, and when the stone slabs of the floor

[1] Balâdhurî, p. 217. Maķrîzî agrees. He gives Wardân's answer as follows, 'How can the tribute be increased, when it was expressly stipulated that it should not be increased?' but he adds the information that Mu'awîah's order was merely to increase the tribute by one ķîrâţ, i. e. by $\frac{1}{48}$, or say two per cent.

were taken up, a chamber was found containing thirty-two [1] bushels of gold coin. Thereupon Peter was beheaded in front of the mosque of 'Amr at Babylon. One ought not perhaps to pass over such a story in silence; but it would not stand and is hardly worth serious criticism. It is just one of those romances with which the writer loves to embellish his history. It is certain that the Copts had bitter reason to regret the removal of 'Amr from the government.

Little more need be said here about the incidence of the taxation: there is, however, one point of great importance to notice. The Muslims were at first forbidden to acquire land, and the land grants made were very few [2]. The idea was that they should remain as soldiers, and not engage in agriculture as settlers. As the permanency of the occupation was realized, this restriction was withdrawn or abandoned, and the Muslims became landowners. But in all cases the land which they acquired remained subject to land-tax, of which the equitable apportionment in no wise varied when possession was transferred from a Copt to a Muslim. Consequently if a Copt changed his religion for Islâm, he gained no remission of the land-tax. It was otherwise, however, with the poll-tax. The payment of poll-tax or tribute was the sign of subjection and the token of unbelief. The adoption of Islâm cancelled at once the unbelief and the subjection. On this point the Arab writers are agreed. The Caliph Omar ibn 'Abd al 'Azîz (who died in January,

[1] Ibn Duḳmâḳ says fifty-two.

[2] Ibn 'Abd al Ḥakam says that the only grant made by Omar was that of 1,000 feddâns at Munyat al Aṣbagh to Ibn Sindar—a very excellent estate.

720 A. D.) is condemned by Maḳrîzî for his rule that if a tributary dies, the poll-tax is due from his representatives: because 'it seems,' he says, 'that Egypt capitulated, and the terms of the capitulation are still in force: so if a man dies, the tribute, which is a tax on polls, cannot be levied from his survivors.' But the same Omar II 'released all converts to Islâm from payment of the poll-tax, although it had been exacted in such cases. The first to exact tribute from members of the protected peoples who were converted to Islâm was Al Hajjâj ibn Yûsuf. Then the Caliph 'Abd al Malik wrote to 'Abd al 'Azîz ibn Marwân bidding him do the same in Egypt: but Ibn Ḥujaîrah persuaded the latter *not to introduce this unjust innovation*, saying, 'Let us exact the poll-tax from Christian monks, but how can we take it from converts to Islâm?'

It is related that Ibn Sharîk, who received this ruling of the Caliph's, made a remonstrance showing that conversions had largely reduced the total of the poll-tax, causing a deficit of 20,000 dinârs in the sum apportioned for official salaries in the government service. The answer of the Caliph was in sharp, decisive language: 'I have received your letter. I made you commander-in-chief of the army in Egypt, but I recognize your weakness: therefore I have bidden my messenger to give you twenty blows on the head, after which I order you to relieve converts from payment of the poll-tax. Your opinion is hateful to God, who sent Mohammed as a guide, not as a tax-collector.' On this the Arab historian comments very justly: 'Upon my life, Omar's great desire was to convert all men to Islâm [1].'

[1] Maḳrîzî, *Khiṭaṭ*, vol. i. p. 78: see also the two preceding pages.

There was therefore a direct premium placed on a change of religion; and although religious freedom was in theory secured for the Copts under the capitulation, it soon proved in fact to be shadowy and illusory. For a religious freedom which became identified with social bondage and with financial bondage could have neither substance nor vitality. As Islâm spread, the social pressure upon the Copts became enormous, while the financial pressure at least seemed harder to resist, as the number of Christians or Jews who were liable for the poll-tax diminished year by year, and their isolation became more conspicuous. This vicious system of bribing the Christians into conversion had also the obvious effect of crippling the state revenues. The fall in the income from tribute was rapid. For while 'Amr, as we have seen, raised 12,000,000 dinârs, and the tyrannical 'Abdallah ibn Sa'd raised 14,000,000; in the caliphate of Mu'awîah, when many had been converted, the total was reduced to 5,000,000. Under the great Hârûn ar Rashîd it fell to 4,000,000; and after that it remained at 3,000,000, till towards the end of the ninth century[1]. As the public

[1] Ya'ḳûbî (died A. H. 260) gives this information (*Bibl. Geog. Arab.* part vii. p. 339). He does not quite agree with Abû Ṣâliḥ, who makes out that the tribute stood at 5,000,000 dinârs in the time of Aḥmad ibn Ṭûlûn; at 4,000,000 under Ya'ḳûb ibn Yûsuf; and that from this it dropped to 3,000,000 (p. 82). But the earlier writer here must clearly be preferred. Indeed Ibn Rustah says that under 'Abdallah ibn al Habhâb the revenue was 2,700,337, but under Mûsâ ibn 'Isâ it had fallen to 2,180,000. This was circa A. H. 180, or about the end of the *eighth* century (*Bibl. Geog. Arab.*, ib., p. 118). Yet it is difficult to believe that so vast a change had taken place in 150 years. Indeed according to Prof. S. Lane-Poole (*The Story of Cairo*, p. 60), conversions came slowly: 'About ninety years after the conquest a governor, despairing of any con-

exchequer thus became impoverished, new methods of taxation had to be devised to counterbalance the loss on the tribute; and it can scarcely be doubted that in fixing fresh taxes some discrimination was made in favour of the Muslims as against the Christians. It is thus probable that in fact, as well as in seeming, the burdens of the Christians grew heavier in proportion as their numbers lessened. The wonder, therefore, is not that so many Copts yielded to the current which bore them with sweeping force over to Islâm, but that so great a multitude of Christians stood firmly against the stream, nor have all the storms of thirteen centuries moved their faith from the rock of its foundation.

Nevertheless, few things are more remarkable in history than the manner in which a handful of victorious Arabs from the desert absorbed and destroyed in Egypt, broadly speaking, both the Christian religion and that older Byzantine culture, which owed at once its refinement and its frailty to the blending of the three great and ancient civilizations of Rome, Greece, and Egypt.

siderable accession to the Muslim ranks, was driven to import 5,000 Arabs into the Delta. It was only by slow degrees, after much intermarriage and many partial immigrations, that Egypt became Muslim.' This would seem rather to under-estimate the pressure put upon the Copts and its results.

CHAPTER XXIX

REVOLT OF ALEXANDRIA UNDER MANUEL

Death of Omar. Othman deposes 'Amr from the governorship. Character of 'Abdallah ibn Sa'd. Alexandrians intrigue with Constantinople. Manuel sent to recover Egypt, and welcomed at Alexandria. Gibbon's misstatement traced and corrected. 'Amr reinstated as commander-in-chief. The Copts side with the Arabs. The Roman army advances to Nikiou. Hotly contested engagement there. Romans driven back to Alexandria. The Arabs recapture the city by force of arms. Benjamin's demands from 'Amr. Importance of the incident. Origin of some current historical errors explained.

BUT the conquest of Egypt was not quite ended. The war, which seemed to have closed, was reopened by a fierce attempt on the part of the Romans to recover their dominion, and the story of this adventure has yet to be briefly recounted.

Omar's evil policy of keeping all his Viceroys under suspicion and displeasure, and of wringing the last farthing from his dominions, hastened his end. He was assassinated a few days before the close of A. H. 23, and buried on 1 Muḥarram, A. H. 24[1], on which day Othman was proclaimed his successor in the caliphate. But bad as the rule of Omar had been, the change of rulers was a doubtful gain to the Muslim Empire. If Omar worried and abused his best agents, Othman deposed them. One of Omar's last acts had been to diminish the authority of 'Amr ibn al 'Aṣî by giving the government of Upper Egypt and the Fayûm to 'Abdallah ibn Sa'd ibn Abî Sarḥ, whom he also made controller of the

[1] November 7, 644.

land-tax. Othman completed 'Amr's discomfiture by removing him altogether from the government of Egypt in favour of this same 'Abdallah, who was summoned from Shadmûḥ [1] in the Fayûm where he happened to be residing.

Estimates of the new governor vary somewhat unaccountably. According to Nawawî, 'he was one of the most intelligent and noblest of the Ḳuraish' [2]: while 'Amr unsparingly condemned his incompetence both as governor and as military commander, and Ṭabarî brands him with the strongest possible censure: 'Of all the wakîls of Othman the worst was 'Abdallah, governor of Egypt' [3]; and this at a time when the whole Muslim Empire was in a ferment of revolt against the iniquitous rule of the Caliph and his Viceroys. The more favourable opinion of 'Abdallah seems merely a pleasant platitude, void of historical value. His oppression of the Egyptians is not a text which admits of two readings. The Caliph's purpose in appointing 'Abdallah was to get a larger return from the tribute, and there is reason to think that

[1] Yâḳût, ed. Wüstenfeld, vol. iii. p. 265.

[2] Ed. Wüstenfeld, p. 345.

[3] Ed. Zotenberg, vol. iii. pp. 583 seq. When Othman called a council of his Viceroys in view of the disaffection, this 'Abdallah thus spoke his mind with cynical frankness: 'Prince of the Faithful, men are all greedy: divide the public treasure among the discontented, and you will secure them all.' But this was not the language of 'Amr, whose stern but fearless rectitude comes out in his speech: 'Othman! or Prince of the Faithful, I should say: there is not one of the Prophet's companions whom you have not wounded. The people groan under your tyranny and that of your wakîls. Recall your wakîls, or else renounce your authority and your responsibility. But if you think to essay violence—then, in the name of God!' Othman called 'Amr a lousy fellow for his pains, yet acted upon his advice for the moment.

'Abdallah's first measure was to increase the proportion borne by the Alexandrians. Unquestionably the burden of taxation now lay very heavily upon them; and it was their distress under its weight which prompted some of their leading men to write letters to the Emperor Constans at Byzantium, praying to be delivered from the tyranny of the Muslims. At the same time they pointed out that Alexandria was held by a very weak garrison, quite incapable of resisting a Roman army.

These arguments prevailed with Constans, who had never forgotten the wound to the pride and to the prosperity of the Empire caused by the loss of Egypt. He ordered a large armament to be prepared with the utmost secrecy. The Romans were still masters of the sea: their naval supremacy was as yet uncontested and unchallenged. Omar had heard vague rumours of ocean warfare, and had written to ask 'Amr's opinion about it, saying, 'Describe to me the sea and its rider.' To this 'Amr had quaintly answered: 'Verily I saw a huge construction, upon which diminutive creatures mounted. If the vessel lie still, it rends the heart; if it move, it terrifies the imagination. Upon it a man's power ever diminishes and calamity increases. Those within the ship are like worms in a log. If it rolls over, they are drowned; if it escapes peril, they are confounded.' And this description had sufficed to daunt Omar, who was remarkable for his fierce courage, and to deter him from ordering Mu'awîah to adventure upon the sea[1]. It was not till Mu'awîah himself became Caliph that the Arabs learned the meaning and the value of sea-power.

[1] Suyûṭî's *History of the Caliphs*, tr. by H. S. Jarrett, p. 160.

There was therefore no Arab vessel afloat now to bring news of the expedition which the Emperor had dispatched under the command of Manuel for the recovery of Alexandria. A great fleet of three hundred sail bore into the harbour without warning, and anchored without resistance [1]. There were only a thousand Arab soldiers to defend the city: these were quickly overpowered and slain, very few making good their escape: and Alexandria came once more under the dominion of the Caesars.

It is this incident which has given rise to the curious statement, found in Gibbon and other writers, that three or four days after the original capture of Alexandria the Romans, who had departed by sea, returned and surprised the scattered forces of the Arabs, and regained for a brief space possession of the city. There is no foundation for such a story, which rests on a mere misunderstanding. It springs in fact out of that confusion between the first and the second capture of Alexandria which blends the details of the two events. For example, the story postulates a capture by storm in the first instance, and has nothing to rest on if there was no capture by storm. But it has been proved beyond question that Alexandria was taken in the first instance under capitulation; that an armistice of eleven months was granted to the inhabitants; and that on the expiry of that term the Arabs made

[1] There is one of the usual contradictions on this point among the authorities. Ibn Khaldûn says that the fleet remained off the coast because Al Muḳauḳas forbade the Romans to land. Al Muḳauḳas was of course dead. Ibn 'Abd al Ḥakam's account is that the fleet anchored at Alexandria, and the Romans in the city joined the imperial forces: and all the other Arab writers make it clear that the Romans took possession of the city and slaughtered the garrison.

a peaceable entry. Their occupation of the city was undisturbed from that moment until the arrival of Manuel[1].

Upon the date of this seizure of Alexandria by the Romans there is unusual agreement among the Arab writers, who place it at the beginning of A. H. 25, i.e. towards the end of 645 of our era[2]. With regard to the position of 'Amr ibn al 'Aṣī at that moment, the same consent is not to be found. If Ṭabarî is to be believed—and his authority is very high—'Amr had actually been recalled to Mecca[3],

[1] The story is justified by the language of Suyûṭî, who says: 'After the capture of the city and the flight of the Romans by land and sea, 'Amr left 1,000 of his companions within the walls, and went in pursuit of the fugitives by land. But those who had escaped by sea returned to Alexandria, killed all the Muslims who were unable to flee, and took possession of the city' (p. 73). But the confusion is that of a compiler selecting events in ignorance of their true historical order. The incident is a mere gleam reflected back from the later story of Manuel's raid. It may be said that the same double account of a descent on Alexandria occurs almost textually in Eutychius (ap. Migne, *Patr. Gr.* t. 111, col. 1112). This points no doubt to a common origin; but the original source is vicious; and when once it is proved, as it has been, that the first capture of Alexandria was by peaceable surrender, the whole fabric of the romance falls to pieces. Briefly then the story has no genuine warrant; it clashes with facts ascertained beyond dispute; John of Nikiou knows nothing about it; and it must be banished from history.

[2] Balâdhurî (p. 221) gives this date with a possible alternative of A. H. 23. Ibn al Athîr (p. 62) says A. H. 25. Yâḳût and Abû 'l Maḥâsin agree. Maḳrîzî says that the seizure of Alexandria by the Romans took place in A. H. 24, and its reconquest A. H. 25; which account is also given by Abû 'l Maḥâsin, who places the defeat of the Romans in the month Rabi' I, a month nearly coinciding with January, 646. This, however, seems hardly to allow time enough for the events of the campaign.

[3] Ed. Zotenberg, vol. iii. p. 559. He says that in the beginning of A. H. 25 Othman began to depose Omar's Viceroys: but when

and, when the news of the revolt arrived, he there received orders to resume the command in Egypt. In any case it seems certain that he had been removed from office prior to the landing of the Romans, and that his incapable successor had let the defences of the country fall into a state of dangerous weakness. Manuel's army not only held Alexandria unchallenged, but they roamed over the adjacent country of the Delta, plundering the towns and villages and levying supplies of corn and wine and money with impunity. Nor do they seem to have paid much regard to professions of friendship[1]: wherever the army moved, or detachments were scattered in idle occupation, the people were for the most part treated as conquered enemies.

Yet there must have been marked exceptions.

he heard of the revolt of Alexandria, he made 'Amr *start for Egypt*. This clearly would throw the reconquest considerably later into the year 646. Balâdhurî agrees that 'Amr was deprived of his government in A. H. 25 in favour of 'Abdallah ibn Sa'd (p. 222); whose appointment is dated in the same year by Nawawî (p. 345), but in A. H. 26 by Ibn al Athîr (p. 67). Ibn 'Abd al Ḥakam in speaking of the revolt says, 'By this time Othman had removed 'Amr from the government,' as quoted by Maḳrîzî (*Khiṭaṭ*, vol. i. p. 167); and in another passage on the governors of Fusṭâṭ, Maḳrîzî speaking of 'Abdallah says: 'When Manuel the Eunuch attacked Alexandria, the people begged the Caliph to reinstate 'Amr, so that he might fight the Romans.' On the whole it seems established that 'Amr was removed before the revolt: but it is not clear whether he had actually left Egypt. Eutychius says distinctly that he was then in Egypt, while Abû 'l Maḥâsin says that 'Othman relieved him of the cares of government, that he might give all his energy to fighting Manuel' (p. 73).

[1] Ibn al Athîr says that the Romans 'extorted money and supplies from people in the neighbourhood of the capital, whether friendly to their cause or not' (p. 62). Al Maḳrîzî says that they 'began to occupy the villages and drink their wines and eat their food and lay waste all the country.'

For this revival of Roman power was due of course to the Roman element, which was strong in Alexandria, and which counted on a certain amount of sympathy among the people of the Delta: and whole villages are mentioned as having sided with the Romans. On the other hand, the Copts had little enough to hope from a renewal of Roman ascendency. The record of Cyrus' persecution was graven too deep upon their memories: and even now, though the shadow of another tyranny was coming over them, they had a measure of civil and religious freedom greater than they could dream of retaining under the rule of Byzantium. The Copts, therefore, not only sided with the Arabs at this crisis, but they would have been guilty of supreme folly if they had again courted the stripes and fetters of the imperial government. Whether the Patriarch Benjamin remained in Alexandria, or whether he fled before the returning Roman army, is not quite certain, although the evidence points strongly to his flight or absence at the moment: but there is no question that both in act and in sympathy he stood with his people loyal to the cause of the Arabs, as bound by the Treaty of Alexandria.

While the Roman army were amusing themselves in tasting the delights of Egypt again, and were proving again their skill in throwing away golden opportunities, 'Amr had, on the urgent petition of the Arabs, been reinstated in the military command at Babylon. It was felt at once that his unrivalled prestige and unrivalled ability were demanded to cope with a situation as dangerous as any in the history of the conquest. For if the Roman army, instead of wasting their time in the Delta, had marched straight for Fusṭâṭ, it is quite possible that they might have defeated 'Abdallah and have recaptured Babylon. As it was, they allowed 'Amr ample time to take up his post and to organize his army. He was in no way hurried. Indeed Khârijah ibn Ḥudhâfah, the commander of the fortress of Babylon, thinking that delay was all in favour of the Romans, urged 'Amr to strike at once before the enemy were reinforced, or the whole of Egypt would be in insurrection. 'Amr took a different view. 'Nay,' he said, 'I will challenge them to come out and attack me. So they will do damage to the people of the country through which they pass, and God will confound one part of our enemies by the other.' It is worth remarking that the Arab generals at this stage made no distinction between Copts and Romans: they clearly thought that both parties alike were in armed rebellion. This proves that they had no ground of presumption that the Copts were friendly or even neutral: yet they would have had very strong ground if it had been true that the Copts on the original invasion hailed the Arabs as deliverers.

Accordingly the Romans, moving leisurely, were drawn on southwards as far as Nikiou[1] before they

[1] Weil (*Geschichte der Chalifen*, vol. i. p. 158 n.) cannot settle the name of the town, which is given by Ibn 'Abd al Ḥakam in many forms—Nafyûs, Taḳyûs, Tayûs, Nafuîs, &c. These are simple and easy transformations of the original نقيوس—mere variations of the points. Maḳrîzî gives the form correctly, and the words 'Then a battle took place on land and on the river' would almost alone remove any doubt. Moreover Yâḳut (vol. iv. p. 810) says, 'At Naḳyûs there was a battle between 'Amr and the Romans, when they rebelled against him,' clearly pointing to the revolt of Manuel. Weil of course had not seen John of Nikiou's Chronicle, and he had no very clear idea of the topography of the conquest.

encountered the advance of the Arabs, who numbered perhaps 15,000 men [1]. We are not told whether Nikiou itself was taken: but a desperate battle took place between the two armies under the walls of the fortress and on the canal or river which ran by the town. The Roman army fought with signal valour. 'Amr himself was in the thick of the combat, and having his horse wounded by an arrow was obliged to dismount and fight on foot. In one part of the field the Arabs were routed and put to flight. Conspicuous on the Roman side, both for his prowess and for the magnificence of his armour chased and inlaid with gold, was a mounted officer, who, as the battle hung in doubt, shouted a challenge to the Arabs to single combat. One Ḥaumal of Zabîd took up the challenge, and the two champions tilted with spears without decisive result. Then the Roman flung away his lance and a long duel followed, sword against scimitar. Meanwhile the two armies paused and watched the encounter, standing in serried ranks beside the lists and shouting encouragement to the combatants. At last a fierce lunge made by the Roman was parried and returned with a blow of the Arab's scimitar, which clove deep through the collar-bone of his adversary and killed him. Ḥaumal himself was covered with wounds, which shortly proved fatal; and 'Amr had his body sent on a litter to Fusṭâṭ, where it was buried at the foot of the Muḳaṭṭam Hills.

On the fall of the Roman champion the battle was renewed with fresh fury; but it ended at last in the defeat of Manuel's forces, which were driven

[1] Balâdhurî puts 'Amr's army at 1,500, but this is probably a mistake for 15,000. The Roman army was doubtless superior in numbers.

in headlong rout towards Alexandria. The broken army reached the capital in great disorder, hotly pursued by the Arabs, but they closed the gates and prepared to stand a siege [1]. As 'Amr marched through the Delta he was everywhere assisted by the Coptic villages, which provided bridge-builders and such supplies as they could furnish after being plundered by the Romans. When the Saracen army came once more before the walls of Alexandria, and 'Amr surveyed the almost impregnable defences of the city, he was keenly mortified, as he reflected on the folly which had left them standing, and yet unarmed by a proper garrison; and he swore that if he captured the city a second time, he would level its walls and make it as easy to enter as the house of a harlot. The Arab camp was pitched on the eastern side of the city—the only side open to siege operations—and he is said to have set up his engines of war, and battered the walls till a breach was effected. This story, however, runs counter to all that is known of the vast strength of the ramparts; and it is much easier to credit another account which in this siege, as in the siege of Diocletian, makes the capture due largely to treason from within. For it is said that one of the warders of the gate, named Ibn Bassâmah, entered

[1] Balâdhurî makes no mention of Nikiou: but he gives an engagement near Alexandria. ''Amr encamped near Alexandria, where he was attacked by the Roman forces, who were ravaging the country. After enduring the attack for an hour behind their trenches, the Arabs charged and put the Romans to flight, so that they retreated in haste without stopping or turning till they had re-entered the gates of Alexandria' (p. 221). Of course there may have been a second battle near the city. In any case the extract is interesting as showing that the Arabs had adopted the Roman system of entrenched camps.

into communication with 'Amr, and undertook to throw open the gate, if his own safety and that of his family and property was guaranteed[1].

In whatever manner an entrance was made, the city was taken by storm in act of resistance, and the Arabs rushed in plundering, burning, and slaying all before them. Nearly all that remained in the eastern quarter by the gate, including the church of St. Mark, perished in the fire; and the work of slaughter went on till somewhere in the middle of the city 'Amr himself put an end to it. The spot on which he had bidden his followers to sheath the sword was afterwards marked by a mosque called the Mosque of Mercy. Some part of the Roman soldiers managed to reach their ships and put out to sea: but great numbers perished in the city, and Manuel himself was among the fallen. The women and children were taken as the prize of war.

This was the second capture of Alexandria; it took place in the summer of 646, and it was a capture by force. The two events are very clearly distinguished in time and in circumstance: but unfortunately they have not been kept apart by Arab writers, and it is past the power of criticism to bring back to their right order the two series of incidents, which are found in almost every possible permutation. This, however, is beyond question the place for recording one incident which has caused much perplexity, having been taken out of its proper setting and thrust into the story of the first capture, viz. the visit said to have been paid by Al Muḳauḳas to 'Amr for

[1] This account is preserved by Suyûṭî, who seems to connect it with the first capture. In this he is wrong, but the story may well be true of the second capture. The confusion between the two events is invincible.

the purpose of making some very strange proposals. Of course Al Muḳauḳas was dead long ago: but just as the title is mistakenly carried back by Arab writers to the governor before the conquest who received Mohammed's mission, so it is mistakenly preserved after the conquest, and applied to Benjamin, the Coptic Patriarch [1]. Accordingly, when one reads that during the siege of Alexandria Al Muḳauḳas came to 'Amr and offered to help him on three conditions, the episode must be construed as referring to Benjamin's action in connexion with the revolt of Alexandria, when Manuel's army had seized the city.

The dislocation of this incident is of extreme importance for the history of the conquest: it is in fact the main cause of the misunderstanding upon which the most erroneous versions are founded. There is no such thing as a critical history of the conquest. All the Arab historians give a selection of passages from various writers recording different events; but in their process of selection they often fail to distinguish what ought to be distinguished, and they group together incidents which are out of true chronology and order. When once the story

[1] See Appendix on the Muḳauḳas. The fact of Cyrus' death is truly recorded in the story of the poisoned signet-ring, though the story itself is, as I have shown, quite apocryphal. Balâdhurî is conscious of the difficulty of representing Al Muḳauḳas as alive at this time. His words are (p. 222): 'It is said by some that Al Muḳauḳas deserted the Alexandrians when they rebelled, and that consequently 'Amr retained him and his friends in their offices. Others say that Al Muḳauḳas was dead before the rebellion broke out.' The fact is that Benjamin was now Patriarch and leader of the native Egyptian community, as Cyrus had been Patriarch and leader of the Roman-Egyptian community: and it is not surprising that some Arab historians transferred the title from the one personality to the other. But this confusion of persons naturally led to confusion of events and dates.

gets out of place and out of relation to its true context, it becomes insensibly modified to suit its new surroundings, and in many cases degenerates into falsehood or absurdity. So it is here. For Maḳrîzî [1] gives the three stipulations named by Al Muḳauḳas to ʿAmr as follows: (1) that the Arabs should never break their treaty with the Copts, *and should reckon him* (Al Muḳauḳas) *among them*; (2) that they should make no treaty with the Romans; (3) that they should bury him by the bridge at Alexandria [2]. Now this statement of the terms is not only wholly improbable in itself, but it is a gross perversion of the original account from which it was taken. It represents Al Muḳauḳas as, by inference, a Roman begging the Arabs to observe their compact with the Copts and to make no compact with the Romans; and from this springs the story that the Copts, as opposed to the Romans, made a treaty with the Arabs on their arrival in Egypt; and from this again springs the legend that the Copts welcomed the Arabs as deliverers. But the same authority gives another version of the terms, as follows, from Ibn ʿAbd al Ḥakam [3]: (1) that the Romans should not be treated as generously as the Copts, because they had suspected Al Muḳauḳas on account of the advice he had given them; (2) that the treaty made with the Copts, to which they assuredly would adhere, should not be broken; (3) that Al Muḳauḳas himself should be buried at St. John's church. Here we get back to an earlier version and so nearer the truth; and it is specially to be noted that there is not

[1] *Khiṭaṭ*, vol. i. p. 293.

[2] بجسر الاسكندريه. In Suyûṭî it is given فى ابى حنش, a corruption of يوحنس or St. John.

[3] *Khiṭaṭ*, vol. i. p. 163.

a word corresponding to the sentence I have put in italics. The supposed request of Al Muḳauḳas to be reckoned as a Copt is a wholly unauthorized insertion of a writer who sought by it to clear up a position which quite naturally passed his understanding. The insertion was made to support the erroneous theory that Al Muḳauḳas was with the Copts in sympathy, and had negotiated a treaty in their favour.

But fortunately there survives in Balâdhurî a version of the demands of Al Muḳauḳas, which proves clearly that the incident belongs not to the first capture of Alexandria but to the revolt of Manuel, and that by Al Muḳauḳas only Benjamin can originally have been intended. In that version what Benjamin asked of 'Amr was as follows: '(1) not to grant as favourable terms to the Romans as to me, and (2) not to ill-treat the Copts, *because it is not they who have broken the treaty*; and (3) if I die, have me buried in such a church [1].' Now this phrase

[1] The Arabic فان النقض لم يات من قبلهم for the words in italics is very clear: نقض can only mean the 'breaking of the treaty.' These words I have taken from an extract made for me by the Grand Mufti of Egypt from some Cairo MS. De Goeje's version (p. 215) puts the terms rather differently: (1) that the Romans, who had suspected and rejected Al Muḳauḳas' pacific proposals, should receive less favourable terms than the Copts; (2) that the treaty made with the Copts should not be broken, while the Copts on their part would remain faithful to the Arabs; (3) as before. Amélineau in referring to this incident (though he associates it with the first capture) cites the third demand, viz. that for burial in a church, as proof that Al Muḳauḳas referred to must have been a Patriarch. He says: 'Il était patriarche parce que *les seuls patriarches* avaient la prérogative de se faire enterrer dans une église. Je n'ai jamais rencontré dans un document Copte la plus petite mention qu'un évêque, un saint moine, un martyr aient été enterrés dans l'église de leur paroisse épiscopale, de leur monastère,

in italics illuminates the whole matter. The Copts were no party to the rebellion of Alexandria, which was a breach of the treaty made by Cyrus, Al Muḳauḳas. They had no sympathy with this conspiracy to restore the Roman Empire. Accordingly their chief—Benjamin as he now was—approached 'Amr, and promised the aid of his people, provided that they, who had been loyal, should be honourably treated and not confounded with the rebels. Thus replaced in its proper context the incident becomes as intelligible and interesting as before it was obscure and puzzling. I venture to dwell upon it at some length, because it really is of great historical moment, and because it gives a good illustration of the difficulties which criticism has to encounter, and may hope to remove.

Such then were the Patriarch's proposals. On hearing them 'Amr had remarked, 'The last is the easiest of the three.' It was easy to promise Benjamin burial in the church of St. John, but it was not easy to distinguish in all cases between the action of the Copts and that of the Romans,

de leur village: au contraire, rien n'est plus fréquent dans l'histoire des patriarches' (*Journal Asiatique*, Nov.–Dec. 1888, p. 401). But Amélineau's argument does not hold good of the Melkites, because Abû Ṣâliḥ expressly states that the Melkites, as well as the Armenians and Nestorians, '*bury in their churches*' (p. 136). Assuming that Amélineau is correct as regards the Copts, though there may be some doubt about it, his argument could then only prove that it was a Coptic Patriarch, and not a Roman, who approached 'Amr; that it was in fact Benjamin and not Cyrus. This only corroborates my view that the episode belongs to the period of Manuel's revolt, when Cyrus was dead and Benjamin was in power again. Among the Copts at the present day bishops also have the privilege of being buried in the churches; but I cannot say how far back such a privilege was recognized.

or to decide how far the Copts were responsible for the insurrection. The point at which the interview between 'Amr and Benjamin took place is doubtful, but it may be conjectured that it was at Babylon before 'Amr set out on his march to meet the Romans, and before he felt sure what part the Copts had been playing. From the first they had probably shown a passive hostility to Manuel; they certainly aided the march of the Arabs through the Delta; and this attitude must have been determined by Benjamin in virtue of his arrangement with the Arab leader.

Here, then, at last we find the Copts in willing co-operation, under regular agreement, with the Arabs, and their co-operation continued until the Roman army was destroyed and Alexandria recaptured. And this discovery reveals the true foundation on which rests the story of an alliance made between the Copts and the Arabs upon the first entry of the Arabs into Egypt—a story which is false in itself and has been refuted over and over again in these pages, but which has been built on a basis of mingled fact and misunderstanding. Briefly the story is true of the campaign ending with the *second* capture of Alexandria, and not of any earlier campaign; it is true of the rebellion, and not true of the conquest; it is a historical picture, but set in the wrong framing[1].

[1] Since writing the above I have found a passage in Ibn Duḳmâḳ which completely corroborates the fact that the three conditions demanded of 'Amr must be referred to the time of Manuel's revolt. I give it in full: 'Ibn Waḥb says that, according to Al Laith ibn Sa'd, Al Muḳauḳas the Roman, who was Viceroy (ملك) of Egypt, made terms of peace with 'Amr. The terms were, that those of the Romans who pleased should be allowed to depart, and that a tribute of two dinârs a head should be paid by the Copts.

But there is one other legend which has perplexed and misled historians, and which may now be once for all banished. I have already mentioned the story—found in the pages of Severus and Theophanes—that Cyrus paid tribute to the Arabs for three or more years *before the invasion of Egypt* and in order to buy off the Arabs; and this story I have denounced as wholly unworthy of credence [1] without finally demonstrating its falsity. Now, however, the clearest light is thrown upon its genesis, and it is seen to be a fallacious inference from a misunderstood passage in a compressed and garbled narrative. I have no doubt that the story came originally from a Greek authority, such as Theophanes, who had run the events of several years together in a confused summary which has little or no regard for chronology. Theophanes alleges that when the Arabs attacked Egypt, Cyrus promised under a convention that Egypt should pay a yearly tribute of 200,000 dinârs; and he goes on to say [2]: 'So

Heraclius, however, repudiated these terms, *and in his anger sent Manuel to fight the Arabs.* When 'Amr was besieging Alexandria, Al Muḳauḳas came out to him and said, "I ask three things of you." "What are they?" (1) "That you will not grant the same terms to the Romans as you have to me; for I advised them to submit and they were deaf to my counsels; (2) that you will not break your treaty with the Copts, for they have not broken their treaty with you; and (3) that I may be buried in Abû Yuḥannis when I die."' Of course this passage has its own confusions: e.g. it seems to make Manuel's expedition follow closely upon Heraclius' rejection of the first treaty, and it confuses Cyrus, Heraclius' Viceroy, who died long before Manuel's arrival, with Benjamin: but it clearly shows the connexion of the three demands with the campaign of Manuel. See Dr. Vollers' ed. of Ibn Duḳmâḳ, part v. p. 118.

[1] Supra, pp. 207–9.

[2] *Corp. Hist. Script. Byzant.* t. 44, p. 167. This convention

Cyrus *for three years saved Egypt from extermination.* Cyrus then was accused before the Emperor of paying Egyptian gold in tribute to the Arabs, and the Emperor in wrath summoned Cyrus and appointed Manuel, an Armenian, as Augustal. When the year was out, the Arabs sent to receive their money; but Manuel answered, "I am no defenceless Cyrus to pay you tribute, but am well armed," and so sent them empty away. Then the Arabs armed against Egypt, and, making war, drove Manuel before them; but he got safely with a few followers to Alexandria. Then the Arabs again put Egypt under tribute. When the Emperor heard of all this, he sent Cyrus to persuade the Arabs to retire from Egypt under the former convention. Cyrus came to their camp, and said he was innocent of the treachery, and would confirm on oath the former agreement. The Arabs wholly refused this arrangement.' It is really impossible to characterize the blunders and the confusions of this narrative: it is a tissue of misstatement. Yet any one reading it would be bound to infer that the Arabs were met by Cyrus on their first advance, and bribed to retire from the country; that Manuel was sent by Heraclius directly he heard of the arrangement; and that after the defeat of Manuel, the Arabs

can only be the Treaty of Alexandria, which is confused with the Treaty of Babylon. The 'three years' are a reminiscence of the period between the actual occupation of Alexandria, 642, and the mission of Manuel, 645. What 'the year' may mean cannot be known. The demand for tribute could only have reached Manuel in Alexandria, yet just below Manuel is driven back to that place. Theophanes makes Cyrus alive after this event, just as some of the Arab writers make Al Muḳauḳas alive, of course quite wrongly: Cyrus is confused with Benjamin. But the whole account is as uncritical and unhistorical as possible.

refused to renew the original convention, which bound them to evacuate the country. Such is the perversion of history upon which this legend of the tribute is founded: it needs no further refutation[1]: and yet serious works of the present day regard the legend as truth[2].

[1] Theophanes appears to make these events happen in the twenty-fifth year of Heraclius. Von Ranke quotes Michael the Syrian (ed. Langlois from the Armenian) as confirming the story of tribute. Of course Michael followed Theophanes, or the same source as Theophanes, down to 746 at least: but if Von Ranke had quoted another sentence or two, he would have had to acknowledge the absurdity of Michael's narrative. For Michael makes Omar invade and conquer Egypt previous to the conquest of Jerusalem, or rather its surrender by the Patriarch Sophronius. The mistake of Omar for 'Amr is pardonable: but the historian who makes payment of tribute by Cyrus anterior to the Arab invasion of Egypt must be judged by the fact that on the same page he makes the Arab conquest of Egypt anterior to the fall of Jerusalem.

[2] E.g. Prof. Bury's *Later Roman Empire*, vol. ii. p. 269, n. 3.

CHAPTER XXX

CONCLUSION

Treatment of Alexandria. Story of Ṭalamâ. Restoration of captives. Remonstrance of the loyal Copts, and award of compensation. Reinstatement of ʿAbdallah and departure of ʿAmr. Final effort of the Romans baffled. Close of this history. Questions of interest which might be followed. Death of Benjamin. Death of ʿAmr, and the place of his burial.

ALEXANDRIA met and deserved the fate of a conquered town. The city had been guilty of rebellion in taking up arms against the Arabs and in calling upon the Romans for aid. The revolt might have been justified, if it had been successful: but the rebels now were doubly in the wrong—they had broken the treaty of capitulation, and they had failed to reconquer the country. It is not easy to decide whether they had any moral ground for the breach of treaty. Such ground could only be furnished if the treaty had been broken by the Arabs. There are hints that this was the case—that tribute had been exacted in excess of the covenanted amount; but clear proof is wanting. In any case the action taken by the Emperor would seem quite indefensible. He had put his hand and seal to a solemn compact, in which he had promised that the withdrawal of his forces from Egypt should be final, that no Roman army should again land in the country. If he considered that the Arabs had not kept the terms of the treaty, he might have denounced it as no longer binding: but it was against all the laws of war to equip a vast armament in secret, and to seize the capital of Egypt in direct defiance of treaty[1]. The Arabs therefore were entitled to treat the rebels with some sternness. And in their entry, when the city was given over to fire and sword, no discrimination could well be made between friend and foe, Copt and Roman. It was otherwise with regard to the country places. As soon as the revolt had been stamped out in Alexandria, 'Amr in fulfilment of his vow ordered the walls on the eastern side of the city to be razed to the ground. He then turned his arms against those towns in the Delta which had overtly aided the rebellion. It seems that Ṭalamâ[2], the governor, or ex-governor, of Ikhnâ, a coast-town between Alexandria and Rosetta, had been one of the prime movers in the rebellion, having himself journeyed to Constantinople and returned in company with the Roman armament. The defeat of the Romans left him in a forlorn position. He was taken prisoner, and brought before 'Amr, who was advised to put him to death. The Arab commander, however, treated the matter lightly. He ordered golden armlets to be put on Ṭalamâ, a crown on his head, and a purple robe on his

[1] The Arabs had a great regard for the point of honour in such matters. When a little later than this the Caliph Othman was besieged in his own house by a force from Egypt, the cutting off of his water-supply aroused great indignation in Islâm. Ṭabarî says, 'This is a thing which is disallowed against the besieged even among the Romans.' The statement is at least curious.

[2] See above, p. 349. Weil has no warrant whatever for his assertion that Ṭalamâ was a Copt: on the contrary, he was distinctly a Roman governor. The whole movement of the revolt came from the Byzantine party, or Melkite party, in Egypt. The Copts had neither sympathy with it nor share in it. To speak of the Copts as desiring the return of the Romans at this juncture and as promising their whole force in aid of it, is an extraordinary perversion of history.

shoulders: then mockingly told him to depart and bring another of his imperial armies against Egypt. In the end Ṭalamâ was thankful to be allowed to stay in Egypt and pay the poll-tax[1]. The other towns which fought on the side of the Romans in the revolt of Manuel were in the main the same as those which offered strongest resistance to the Arabs in the original conquest of Egypt, viz. Balḥîb, Khais, Sunṭais, Farṭasâ, and Sakhâ[2]. From all these places,

[1] The Arab writers associate Ṭalamâ's demand concerning the tribute (see above, l. c.) with this incident. It is exceedingly difficult to say which of the incidents told in connexion with Manuel's revolt belong properly to the first, and which to the second, capture of Alexandria. But there is very strong evidence that a separate special treaty was concluded with Ṭalamâ, and this can only have been on his first capitulation. I have little doubt that he was continued in office by the Arabs, and abused the trust reposed in him to foment the rebellion. But in the second instance, when he was absolutely at 'Amr's mercy as a captured rebel, there could be no question of a special treaty. The account of his treatment by 'Amr is given by Maḳrîzî and others.

[2] Here again there is some difficulty in getting at the truth. Thus when Yâḳût says (vol. i. p. 733) that with Balḥîb 'Amr made peace on the terms of the poll-tax and land-tax on his way to Alexandria, he can only refer to 'Amr's first march on Alexandria. Yet he goes on to say, 'The people of Egypt helped 'Amr in his struggle with the Alexandrians, except Balḥîb, Khais, Sunṭais, Farṭasâ, and Sakhâ, which all assisted the Romans. Therefore when 'Amr had taken Alexandria, he made captives of the people of those towns, and sent them to Medina and other places; but Omar restored them to their homes, and included them in the general protection granted to the Egyptians': and this passage can relate only to the time of the rebellion. It is true that Omar's name is wrongly used instead of Othman's, but that mistake is easily accounted for and easily corrected; whereas the opposition between the statement that Balḥîb made a treaty of peace, and that Balḥîb continued hostile and was conquered by force, is irreconcilable. The truth seems that this place, having originally come under treaty, joined in Manuel's rebellion. So of Khais, Yâḳût

as from Alexandria itself, captives were taken and were sent to Medina: but when the Caliph Othman was formally consulted with regard to the treatment of the rebel towns, he had the good sense to return the captives and to grant an indemnity to the inhabitants concerned in the revolt, restoring their status as protected people, subject to payment of the fixed poll-tax[1]. In other words, the Caliph renounced his right to treat Alexandria and the other places as the lawful prize of war and their inhabitants as slaves at the mercy of their conquerors. There seems to have been a strong desire on the part of some of 'Amr's forces both to divide the city of Alexandria and to remain there: it is

says (vol. ii. p. 507) that 'it was conquered by Khârijah ibn Ḥudhâfah,' and that 'its inhabitants helped the Romans against 'Amr': where the first statement relates to the conquest, the second to the rebellion. Maḳrîzî cites earlier writers for the fact that 'Sunṭais, Mâsil, and Bilḥait (Balḥîb) fought for the Romans against the Arabs,' which tells one nothing; but Suyûṭî's language removes all doubt: 'The villages of Bilḥait, Al Khais, Sunṭais, and Ḳarṭasâ *rebelled*, and the captives taken thence were sent to Medina and elsewhere: but Omar (Othman) sent them back and made all the Copts a protected people, including *Alexandria and the rebel villages*.' These words could have no meaning except in relation to Manuel's revolt, although it is certain that the Arab historians transposed the record which they found, and mistakenly inserted it in the narrative of the first capture of Alexandria. The whole story that Alexandria was taken *in the first instance* by force arises from similar confusion. A certain amount of this confusion may be reduced to order by criticism, but some of it is past all remedy.

[1] One now sees the true meaning of Yahyâ ibn Aîyûb and Khâlid ibn Ḥamîd when they say that all Egypt except Alexandria was occupied by treaty, and though the three villages named fought for the Romans, 'yet Omar (Othman) decreed that they and Alexandria were to be treated like the rest of the country.' The reference is to the rebellion of Manuel, and not to the first invasion of Egypt by the Arabs.

even said that 'Amr himself wished to fix his abode in the sea-side capital. But any such intention, now as before, was repressed by the Caliph. Moreover, 'Amr was only allowed to stay for one month in Alexandria, after which he handed it over to 'Abdallah ibn Sa'd.

One characteristic anecdote must not be passed over in silence. After the recapture of Alexandria, the Copts of the various Delta villages which had been ruthlessly plundered by the Roman army, came to 'Amr and complained that while they had stood loyal to the Arabs as bound under treaty, they had not received the protection to which under the same treaty they were entitled, and in consequence they had suffered severely. The justice of this remonstrance is obvious: but it is not every victorious general whose conscience would be troubled by such a protest. Of 'Amr, however, it is recorded that he was struck with remorse, and exclaimed: 'Would that I had encountered the Romans as soon as they issued forth from Alexandria!' What is more, he at once ordered full compensation to be paid to the Copts for all their losses. This frank admission of responsibility and frank restitution prove at once the excellence of 'Amr's principles of government and the nobility of his nature.

But these very virtues were regarded as vices by the jaundiced eye of the Caliph. He was not blind to the supreme military talent of the conqueror, and so offered to reward his service by giving him the post of commander-in-chief of the army, while the unscrupulous 'Abdallah was to be retained as controller of the taxes and governor-general. Such an offer could only meet with contemptuous rejection; and 'Amr's resentment of the mockery is well preserved in his caustic remark, 'I should be like a man holding a cow by the horns while another milked her.' But he had served the Caliph's turn in crushing the rebellion, and was no longer wanted. What the Caliph required was a man to wring money out of the Egyptians, and the man for that purpose was 'Abdallah [1]. 'Amr accordingly quitted the country.

Here then the story of the Arab conquest may fitly close. The suppression of Manuel's revolt and the recapture of Alexandria by the Arabs mark the definitive establishment of Muslim dominion upon the Nile valley. It is true that nine years later the Emperor Constans fitted out a second armada, which he destined for the recovery of Egypt. But it was too late. By this time the Arabs had learned something of seamanship; and their fleet, though inferior in numbers and fighting capacity, so baffled the Roman force that the expedition never effected a landing in Egypt. Its failure in battle was turned to disaster by storm: the broken remnant of the great fleet was scattered and driven over the seas. From that moment the Muslim power was not again seriously menaced, although the coast towns long continued subject to isolated and fruitless raids on the part of Byzantine sailors or pirates.

It might perhaps be interesting to follow out the social and other changes which resulted from the conquest; to trace the rapid decay of Graeco-

[1] Severus says of him: 'He loved money and collected treasure for himself in Egypt. He was the first to build the divan at Miṣr, and he ordered that all the taxes should be collected there' (Brit. Mus. MS., p. 108, l. 20). He associates with his government also a terrible famine—the worst since the days of Claudius.

Roman culture and the slow growth of a new Saracenic civilization; and to distinguish those unyielding elements of old Egyptian life and thought which no transmutation of society could alter. One might show how the old classical learning strove in vain to maintain its position in the fallen city of Alexandria, but was dispossessed by slow degrees and finally banished to the cells and convents of the desert; where it lingered in inanition till the Coptic language itself dwindled and disappeared. One might study the process by which the use of Arabic spread over the country, finding its first expression in the coinage late in the seventh century and then adopted in the public offices and public documents [1], gaining upon the Coptic and driving out the use of Greek in common speech, save for some few words which took Arabic shape or those terms and phrases which remain as fossils to this day embedded in Coptic literature. One might also sketch the decline of those great and splendid cities which the Romans had left in Egypt: for Alexandria, though first among the cities of the East, if not of the world, was only one among many which reached from Syene to the Mediterranean [2]. One would find

[1] Suyûṭî seems to say that Arabic coins were first struck in A.H. 75 and that Arabic was first introduced into the divans between A.H. 86 and 90 (*Ḥusn al Muḥâḍarah*, vol. ii. p. 226 and p. 8).

[2] For example, Antinoe (Anṣinâ) was built on a scale of great splendour. It was on plan a long quadrilateral divided by a great main street, which was intersected by three principal cross-streets. These streets were all colonnaded, as at Alexandria, and statues adorned the cross-ways. At the harbour on the Nile a triumphal arch with three gateways was reared on Corinthian pillars, with equestrian statues on each side. Outside the town were baths, circus, and gymnasium. See Gregorovius' *The Emperor Hadrian*, p. 357.

that temples and palaces were suffered to fall into ruins; that precious marbles were quarried for building or burned for lime; that bronze statues were melted down and turned into coin or domestic vessels; and yet that, through all the melancholy history of decadence and destruction, certain forms and traditions of classical art were kept alive by Coptic craftsmen, and that from these traditions, moulded afresh by the Arab spirit, there sprang a new school of art and architecture, with schemes of decoration from which all suggestion of the human form was banished, but which achieved results as remarkable for originality as for grace and beauty and splendour. But a great deal has already been done towards tracing the descent of Saracenic from Byzantine art[1]; and in any case researches of this kind lie beyond the limits of the present work.

So too of the Coptic race and religion. It has already been shown how powerful were the forces tending to drive the Copts into complete social and religious union with Islâm: and few things are stranger in history than the absolute absorption of the one part of the Copts and the stubborn refusal of the other part to renounce their ancestral customs and their religion—a refusal which has stood the test not only of the severest persecution, under which sufferers may be sustained by fire of enthusiasm, but also of that long dull wearing pressure of a daily life in which a sense of subjection, a consciousness of inferiority, was ever present. Of course the survival of Christianity was largely due to the influence of the monasteries, and their security was due in some degree to their re-

[1]See Prof. Lane-Poole's *Art of the Saracens in Egypt*, and M. Gayet's *L'Art Copte.*

moteness in desert or mountain fastness. Yet few passages in the annals of Egypt are more agreeable reading than those which tell of the extremely friendly relations which prevailed between some of the Coptic abbots and the Caliphs, and the delight which the latter took in visiting picturesque and pleasant convents[1]. But studies of this kind belong to a later period, and here must be left alone.

It might be thought perhaps that one ought at least to follow out the fortunes of the conqueror of Egypt. This would be an easy task: for in coming to the time of settled Arab government one emerges from the dark labyrinth of controversy and contradiction into the open light of history. But the part which 'Amr played in the troubled politics of Islâm after his dismissal from Egypt; the story of Othman's murder; the contest between 'Alî and Mu'awîah; 'Amr's victorious march into Egypt and his reinstatement as governor—all this is written in the chronicles of the caliphate, which have been long accessible to the reader.

It was in Rabi' I of A.H. 38 (Aug.–Sept. 658) that 'Amr entered upon his second governorship. He soon pacified the country, and after rewarding his army entered on the enjoyment of the revenues, in the disposal of which Mu'awîah left him unfettered discretion. The curious episode of the arbitration between the rival claims of 'Alî and Mu'awîah

[1] See e.g. Abû Ṣâliḥ, pp. 149–50, 312–3. A somewhat curious glimpse of the friendly relations subsisting between Copts and Arabs is given in a MS. catalogued by Zoega (*Cat. Codd. Copt.* p. 89). There a Copt of the Thebaid is mentioned, one John, son of Mark, a deacon, 'who lived with the Ishmaelites and Elamites; for he was a trader in wares relating to women's apparel or adornment.' This was soon after the conquest, in the caliphate of Othman.

recalled him for a short space from Egypt, and upon his return he had a narrow escape of being assassinated. A conspiracy having been formed to put to death the three great leaders of Islâm—'Alî, Mu'awîah, and 'Amr—one Yazîd was told off to murder 'Amr while he was leading the Friday prayers at the mosque. On the day destined for the deed it so happened that 'Amr was somewhat unwell, and he deputed the well-known general Khârijah ibn Ḥudhâfah to take his place. Unaware of the change, the assassin plunged his dagger into Khârijah. When confronted with the governor Yazîd said boldly, 'By God, it was you I wanted.' 'But God wanted Khârijah,' said 'Amr.

On January 3, 662, the Patriarch Benjamin passed away after a long period of illness and infirmity. He had been Archbishop of Alexandria for the space of thirty-nine years—a strange and stormy epoch, rich in great events, stirred with the adventure of nations, as race met race and creed encountered creed in combat for the dominion of souls and for the empire of the East. Benjamin, elected under Roman rule, had seen the Persians under Chosroes take possession of Egypt and of almost the whole realm of the Caesars. He had seen the grandly victorious campaigns of Heraclius ending in the recall of the Persians from the Nile valley; and with the return of the Roman armies he had seen the arrival of Cyrus, before whose persecution he fled into the desert, there to remain for thirteen years till the era of Roman dominion was closed for ever. Above all he had seen a new power and a new religion issue from the wastes of Arabia, challenging Magian and Christian alike, sweeping in conquest over Syria, Persia, and Egypt. After all the wars and revolutions he had witnessed, he was able to leave his Church in comparative peace under the rule of the conquering Muslims and their great chieftain 'Amr ibn al 'Aṣî.

'Amr survived him almost exactly two years. The Berbers of Pentapolis had been causing continual trouble, and from 661 to 663 'Amr had sent more than one expedition against them. When at the end of 663 his lieutenants returned in triumph, they found 'Amr at Fusṭâṭ in his last illness. It is related that when he lay dying, Ibn 'Abbâs went to 'Amr and said: 'You have often remarked that you would like to find an intelligent man at the point of death, and to ask what his feelings were. Now I ask you that question.' 'Amr replied: 'I feel as if the heaven lay close upon the earth, and I between the two, breathing as through the eye of a needle.' When his son 'Abdallah entered the room, 'Amr pointed to a chest and said, 'That is for you.' 'I have no need,' said 'Abdallah. 'Take it,' said 'Amr; 'it is full of money': but 'Abdallah still refused[1]. The last words of 'Amr are recorded as follows: 'Almighty God, thou hast commanded, and I have disobeyed; thou hast forbidden, and I have transgressed. I am not innocent enough to deserve thy pardon, nor have I strength to prevail against thy will.' He died on Yûm al Fiṭr A.H. 43, or January 6, 664, at the age of about seventy[2]. 'Abdallah carried his body to the place

[1] The Muslim writers make 'Abdallah's refusal prompted by the fear that 'Amr's wealth was ill-gotten. This is a most dishonouring accusation against both. There is no evidence that 'Amr got wealth by ill means, or that his son had any such thought. Surely in his natural grief, at his father's death-bed, the last thing 'Abdallah would care about is his money.

[2] See Appendix E, 'On the age of 'Amr.'

of prayer and prayed over it, his prayer being followed by all who werẹ present.

'Amr was buried at the foot of the Muḳaṭṭam Hills, 'near the entrance to the ravine.' But the place of his grave has been clean forgotten. For centuries the mountains have been scarped and quarried, till even the landmark of the ravine has so long disappeared that tradition itself has sunk into silence. The new capital of Fusṭâṭ which 'Amr founded, and which rose later to great magnificence, has long since been levelled with the dust, leaving no vestige but the mosque which bears 'Amr's name, and which still marks at least the site of his original building. Close by in Dair Abû 's Saifain and in Ḳaṣr ash Shama' churches are still standing which date their foundation, if not their structure, back to the Roman Empire. The very walls of Babylon, which were nearly complete some twenty years ago, still remain in places, and probably the whole circuit could be revealed to a great depth, like the gateway, by excavation. But one may search the desolate plain and the fringe of the mountains in vain for any stone to mark the grave of 'Amr: for the Muslims have neither memorial nor remembrance of the place where the conqueror of Egypt is buried.

APPENDIX A

ON THE RELIC CALLED THE HOLY ROOD

THE story of the finding of the cross in May, 328, is well known, and it is certain that the wood found by the Empress Helena was preserved for some centuries. Socrates (*Eccl. Hist.* lib. i. xvii) says that Helena put one portion in a silver chest and left it at Jerusalem, sending the other portion to the Emperor. The evidence for the subsequent history of the cross is fairly complete and continuous.

To begin with the fourth century. In the paper on the *Churches of Constantine at Jerusalem*, in vol. i of the Palestine Pilgrims Text Society's publications (pp. 23–5), there is a quotation from the Breviary showing that in the basilica of Constantine was an altar of silver and gold supported on nine columns, and that the cross was adorned with gold and gems. Theodosius (*De Terra Sancta*) speaks also of 'the chamber wherein is the Cross of the Lord Jesus Christ. The Cross itself is adorned with gold and gems, the open sky being above and a latticed railing of gold round it.' So too St. Silvia of Aquitania (circa 385 A.D.)—who, by the way, mentions the use of incense at the church of the Resurrection—records the Good Friday ceremony, which she witnessed, as follows: 'Then is brought a silver-gilt casket, in which is the holy wood of the Cross: it is opened, and, its contents being taken out, the wood of the Cross and also its inscription are placed on the Table.' Then all the people come and kiss the cross (id., ib., p. 63).

Antoninus Martyr visited the Holy Places circa 565 A.D., and there saw the relic still in the atrium of the basilica of Constantine, where it was kept in a shrine or chamber. He says nothing about the case, but he mentions the sponge and the reed, which Nicetas is said to have rescued later—in the seventh century.

We have seen that in 615 the rood was taken by the Persians, when they captured Jerusalem, and sent with other spoil to Chosroes; that it was recovered by Heraclius in 628, taken to Constantinople that winter, restored to its place in the church of Constantine with great pomp in 629, and again sent to Constantinople a few years later, c. 636, to save it from falling into the hands of the conquering Muslims.

It was seen at Constantinople about the year 670 by the pilgrim Arculfus, who had been to Jerusalem and had beheld the great churches just as they were left after their reinstatement by Modestus,—an interesting piece of evidence, because it shows how tolerantly the Christian churches were treated by the Muslims towards the end of the seventh century. But of the cross Arculfus says that it was kept at St. Sophia's in a wooden case, which rested in a large and very beautiful aumbry or shrine. On three consecutive days in the year, i.e. Maundy Thursday, Good Friday, and Easter Eve, the reliquary was placed on a golden altar. On the first day the Emperor and the army entered and kissed the cross—all in order of rank. On the next day the Queen with her ladies and other noble women kissed the cross. On the third day the Patriarch and clergy went through the same ceremony, with the same regard to precedence. The reliquary was then closed and carried back to its aumbry (id., vol. ii. pp. 55–6).

In the tenth century Porphyrogenitus gives a similar account of the cross, though apparently the chest containing it was then kept in a different part of the cathedral. There is some obscurity regarding the ultimate fate of this and of other relics kept at St. Sophia; but the subject is exhaustively treated in Messrs. Lethaby and Swainson's admirable work, *S. Sophia, Constantinople,* pp. 92, 93, 97 seq., &c.

APPENDIX B

ON THE CHRONOLOGY OF THE PERSIAN CONQUEST

It may be doubted whether it is possible at present to establish with finality the dates connected with the Persian conquest of Egypt. Some recent writers tend to put the event later than 616 A.D., and Gelzer, who has written a learned note on the subject (*Leontios von Neapolis*, p. 151), argues that Alexandria cannot have fallen before 619. In this he dissents from Von Gutschmid, who places it a year or two earlier.

The evidence cited by Gelzer is as follows. Theophanes makes the conquest take place in 616. Barhebraeus gives the seventh year of Heraclius, following the Patriarch Michael, who says (Jerusalem edition, p. 293) that the Shah-Waraz invaded Egypt in the seventh year of Heraclius. The conquest of Egypt is put by Isidore (Roncalli, *Chron. Min.* ii. 461) in 616, while Ṭabarî records that the keys of Alexandria were delivered to Chosroes in the twenty-eighth year of his reign, i.e. 617–8; 'thus giving the date handed down by Michael.'

I may here remark that the seventh year of Heraclius = October, 616—October, 617, whereas the twenty-eighth of Chosroes falls about evenly between 617 and 618, and no part of it can fall in 616: so that the agreement between Michael and Ṭabarî is not very obvious. Further, Barhebraeus (or Abû 'l Faraj) elsewhere (*Hist. Dyn.*, ed. Pococke, p. 99) clearly assigns the capture of Jerusalem by the Persians to the fifth year of Heraclius, and so, in this as in many points, is inconsistent.

Gelzer goes on to say that Von Gutschmid has shown with great acuteness (*Kleine Schriften*, iii. 473 seq.) that the Persian invasion cannot have taken place before 617, because *Syrian authorities prove that the visit of Athanasius of Antioch to the Monophysite Patriarch Anastasius of*

Alexandria took place in 616, whereas the Patriarch in office when the Persians entered Alexandria was Andronicus. Moreover, as Barhebraeus shows, the real promoter and author of the union was Nicetas, who fled with John the Almoner at the approach of the Persians. Von Gutschmid puts the death of Anastasius on December 18, 616. Andronicus, his immediate successor, stayed on and was able to reside (as I have shown in the text) within the city. 'From this,' says Gelzer, 'it clearly follows that at least at the beginning of the patriarchate of Andronicus (end of 616) Alexandria was still in the possession of the Greeks. Accordingly the earliest date for the Persian conquest must be the summer of 617, as Von Gutschmid supposes.'

On the whole I think Von Gutschmid's dates are correct, though not free from difficulty. To begin with, it is by no means certain that the year given by the Syrian authorities is rightly identified as 616; because, while they generally reckon by the Greek or Seleucid era, they often differ by a year from the ordinary calculation of that era, inasmuch as they start from 311 B.C. instead of 312 (*Trésor de Chronologie*, col. 36). It is therefore possible that Syrian evidence is rather in favour of 615 than 616, in which case it would be in agreement with the *Chronicon Orientale*, which alleges that the visit of Athanasius to Egypt took place in the same year in which Jerusalem was stormed by the Persians. Then, again, the Egyptian writer Severus of Ushmûnain dates the death of the Coptic Patriarch Anastasius on 22 Khoiak (December 18) in the year 330 of Diocletian. This Renaudot wrongly identifies with 614, because Khoiak falls in 613. These statements are hopelessly incompatible: but it is impossible at least to place the capture of Jerusalem in 613.

There are, however, some other Syrian authorities whose evidence must be cited. For it is well known, though not mentioned by Gelzer, that there exist Syriac biblical MSS. which are dated in the seventh century, and which were writen at the Ennaton monastery near Alexandria by Thomas of Harkel and Paul of Tella, under the direct orders of the Patriarch Anastasius, and in direct connexion with his visit to Egypt. These MSS. were part of a systematic revision of the Syriac text by collation of the Greek version of Philoxenus; the dates they bear are of capital importance.

'Thomas of Harkel is known to have completed his version of the New Testament into Syriac in 927 of the Greek era[1].' Now this 927, unless equivalent to the ordinary 926, would run from October, 615, to October, 616. There is also another Syro-Hexaplar MS. in the British Museum (Add. MSS. 144,376), which is subscribed as completed in the same year 615–6.

The MS. of the Third Book of Kings is dated Shabat, 927, which = February, 616. That of the Fourth Book of Kings has a subscription which represents *both Paul and Athanasius as dwelling at Alexandria in 928*, which runs from October, 616, to October, 617, thus fixing the visit of the Syrian Patriarch to the autumn of 616. In another Syro-Hexaplar MS. at Milan we find the date of completion given as 928 or 616–7.

In these MSS., then, there is a record of peaceable study at the Ennaton Monastery extending over the two years 615–7 and incidentally fixing the visit of the Syrian Patriarch in October, 616, because his host the Coptic Patriarch died in December of the same year. The dates here are reckoned according to the ordinary calculation of the Greek era. But if we are to regard them as based on the special Syrian computation of that era, the result will be to place the visit in 615–6, and the record of work from 614–6. In this latter case we fall into agreement with Barhebraeus, who states (*Chron. Eccles.* t. i. 267–9) that 'Athanasius went to Alexandria, where Anastasius was Patriarch, and entered into union with him. This union between our (Syrian) Church and the Church of Egypt was in the year of the Greeks 927,' i.e. October, 615—October, 616, as Barhebraeus does not follow the Syrian variation of the era. There is no way of reconciling these discrepancies

[1] See *Dict. Christ. Biog.*, s. v. Thomas of Harkel and Paul of Tella.

otherwise than by reference to a different method of calculating the era: and as it was especially the Syrians of Babylonia who advanced the Greek era by a year, there is nothing improbable in ascribing that method to Thomas of Harkel and Paul of Tella. In that case we have an agreement between the *Chronicon Orientale*, the biblical MSS., and Abû 'l Faraj, which practically dates the union of the two Churches in October, 615. This seems a fair and a reasonable solution.

I think it would be still necessary to assign the death of the Coptic Patriarch to Dec. 18, 616, not to 615; and for this reason, that there is no other way of making the reign of Andronicus, his successor, fit in with the known dates for its duration and for its termination. For the duration is fixed to a few days over six years ending 8 Tûbah, or 3 January. But given some 3 January as the date for the death of Andronicus and for the beginning of Benjamin's patriarchate, no other year but 623 will fulfil the necessary conditions. For on the one hand it is clear that Andronicus saw the beginning of the Persian invasion, which I put late in 616; and on the other hand it is clear that the same Patriarch saw the beginning of Islâm. For the *Chronicon Orientale*, while giving Andronicus' date as 611 to 617, yet adds, 'In his time the power of the Muslims had its rise,' i.e. July, 622, and this is corroborated by Makîn, who places the election of Benjamin in the first year of the Hijra, 622–3. Abû Ṣâliḥ's testimony is equally explicit; for he records that Andronicus was Patriarch 'at the first appearance of the Muslims in the twelfth year of Heraclius' (ed. Evetts and Butler, p. 231). This concurrence of evidence for dating the enthronement of Benjamin in January, 623, is very strong—indeed, almost irresistible. Le Quien follows the dates of Severus, who makes Andronicus' term of office from 614 to 620; while Echellensis claims greater accuracy for his scheme, in which Andronicus reigns from 619 to 622.

Now if, as seems proved, Andronicus died about Jan. 3, 623, and reigned for just over six years, starting Dec. 18, it follows that his reign began in 616, and that Anastasius died on Dec. 18, 616. This date agrees with that fixed by Von Gutschmid (*Kleine Schriften*, ii. pp. 471–4).

The discussion has taken us somewhat far from the biblical MSS. written at the Ennaton Monastery, but it is necessary to go back to them for a moment.

These MSS. show that (1) Thomas of Harkel was working at the translation for at least two years before the visit of the Syrian Patriarch.

(2) The visit itself may well be assigned to October, 615.

(3) Paul of Tella continued at work at least three months after the visit, till January, 616.

A difficulty is raised by the fact that Athanasius is loosely stated to have gone with five other Syrian bishops, whereas the language of Barhebraeus shows most decisively that Thomas of Harkel was driven from his diocese of Mabûg, and fled to Egypt for refuge. That Thomas and Paul were present during the visit need not be doubted, nor that three other bishops either travelled with Athanasius, or were driven to Egypt by the Persian occupation of Palestine. We have the express statement of John Moschus that many bishops were so driven to Egypt. But it is far more likely that the very residence of these Syrian scholars at Alexandria, and their consequent intimacy with the Coptic Patriarch prior to the Patriarch of Antioch's visit, settled all the preliminaries for that formal union which was so quickly ratified after the actual meeting of the two Patriarchs.

There is one further piece of evidence furnished by these MSS. It is highly significant that of the other books of the Bible attributed to Paul of Tella, not one is dated, the last date being, as I have shown, the very beginning of 616. It does not seem reasonable to argue that the work must nevertheless have been done in the same monastery 'of the Antonians[1]' under the same conditions, and that therefore the Persian invasion must be put later than 616.

[1] Strangely called 'Of the Antonines' by the *Dict. Christ. Biog.* Of course it means that the monks followed the rule of St. Anthony.

On the contrary, these Syrian scholars, who had seen or heard of the great havoc wrought in their own country by the Persians, would naturally take alarm at the first news of the Persian advance into Egypt; and it is highly probable that in the summer of 616 they fled oversea accompanied by the monks of the Ennaton and their more precious possessions, including the Greek MSS. of the Scriptures. But without recourse to this hypothesis, there is another possible explanation, consistent with the continuance of the work in Egypt.

This brings us to a point which has been singularly overlooked, and which therefore requires some emphasis. It is the almost invariable custom of writers upon this period to speak of the Persian conquest as a single incident to be dated in a single year; in other words, *they fail to distinguish between the invasion of Egypt and the fall of Alexandria.* These two events must be at least a year apart, and there is not the smallest doubt that ancient writers sometimes fasten their date upon the one event and sometimes upon the other; and this fact accounts for much of the prevalent confusion.

That the Persians were not advancing on Egypt early in 616 may be regarded as proved. Moreover, even were they ready for a fresh campaign so soon after the fall of Jerusalem, it is more probable that they would not cross the desert in the summer. We may therefore conclude that the advance began in the autumn of 616, and that the army took Pelusium, where they sacked the monasteries, before the end of that year. They had then to march to Memphis, to capture the formidable fortress of Babylon, and to fight their way down the western branch of the Nile past Nikiou (as we know they did) to Alexandria. We know also that they spent a long time besieging the city before it was delivered over to them by treachery. All this must have taken at least a year. Consequently it is impossible on any theory of dates to place *the capture of Alexandria* before the end of the year 617 or the beginning of 618.

It is thus easy to suppose that the Syrian scholars continued their work at the Ennaton Monastery till the Persian forces were approaching, and then took refuge in the city, whence escape by sea was always open. They would thus have gained another two years, which would probably have sufficed to finish their labours.

So much then for the Syrian authorities. But it will be noticed that the argument which has brought us to the winter of 617–8 as the earliest date for the fall of Alexandria brings us into precise agreement with the date given by Ṭabarî. It also, though proceeding on different and partly discordant data, brings us into near agreement with Von Gutschmid's conclusions, viz. that in December, 616, 'Alexandria was still in the possession of the Greeks, and that the earliest date of the *Persian conquest*' (if by that he means the capture of Alexandria) 'must be the summer of 617.' Ṭabarî in saying that the keys of Alexandria were not sent to Chosroes before the winter, goes a little beyond this statement, and I agree with him.

Briefly then the dates may be set out thus:—

(1) Capture of Jerusalem	End of May, 615.
(2) Visit of Athanasius to Alexandria	October, 615.
(3) Persian advance into Egypt . .	Autumn, 616.
(4) Death of Coptic Patriarch . . .	Dec. 18, 616.
(5) Capture of Babylon	Spring, 617.
(6) Capture of Alexandria	End of 617.
(7) Subjugation of the whole of Egypt	618.

I may add that the conquest of Upper Egypt cannot have been completed much before the winter of 618, because we know from a dated Coptic papyrus that Arsinoe, or Fayûm, was still under Roman rule on June 9, 618 (*Corpus Papyrorum Raineri*, vol. ii, *Koptische Texte*, ed. J. Krall, 1 bd. p. 22). But, broadly speaking, this table shows that from the capture of Jerusalem to the complete occupation of Egypt there is a period of three years, exactly as recorded by Abû 'l Faraj (ed. Pococke, l.c.).

This scheme now enables one to place John the Almoner's mission of relief to Jerusalem in the winter of

615–6; for the envoys clearly went by land, and they certainly could not have gone while the Persian armies were on their way to Egypt. The flight of John with Nicetas will naturally fall in the autumn of 616, if they fled at the news of the Persian invasion, though Leontius' words rather suggest that they escaped only a short time before the surrender of Alexandria, i. e. a year later. Above all, this scheme will fit in with the chronology of the Arab writers both for the lives of the Patriarchs and for the period of the Persian occupation. This period, as Gelzer rightly remarks, is ten years.

For the Coptic Patriarchs I give the following dates:—

(1) Anastasius . from June, 604, to Dec. 18, 616.
(2) Andronicus . " Dec. 616, " Jan. 3, 623.
(3) Benjamin . " Jan. 623, " Jan. 3, 662.

And for the Melkite Patriarchs:—

(1) Theodore, killed in 609.
(2) John the Almoner from 609 to 616 or 617.
(3) George . . . " 621 " 630 or 631.
(4) Cyrus . . . . " 631 " 642.

Now if with Gelzer, on the single authority of Thomas Presbyter, the union of the Syrian and Egyptian Churches be put in 618, we have to dislocate the whole scheme of the succession of the Coptic Patriarchs, and above all to put Benjamin's enthronement at least as late as 625; whereas the Egyptian writers insist that his pontificate began in 622–3, the year of the rise of Mohammed. For me that correspondence is decisive, even if it stood alone, to determine the date of Benjamin; but it would be easy to multiply evidence from Egyptian sources to refute 625.

Then as to the ten years' occupation. Gelzer would make this end in 629, i. e. at least a year after the conclusion of peace between Heraclius and Siroes. Now there are three strong reasons against this: (1) the whole aim of Heraclius' strategy in 622 and the following years was to relieve the Persian pressure on his capital and on Egypt; and it is, if not proved, yet highly probable, that Egypt was evacuated by reason of this pressure even as early as the spring of 627—a little over ten years from the invasion, as I contend; (2) even if this were not so, Sebeos distinctly records that Siroes, in the treaty of February, 628, agreed at once to evacuate all the Roman possessions, and did evacuate them; (3) Mohammed's envoys were sent out to the different rulers in the summer or autumn of 627 at latest, as Ṭabarî shows, because he represents Chosroes' messengers to Yaman as detained there for some months before the news came of the king's death, which occurred in February, 628; and it is beyond question that when Mohammed sent to Egypt, that country was recovered to the Empire and ruled by Heraclius' viceroy, 'Al Muḳauḳas,' as he is wrongly styled.

Gelzer's appeal to Nicephorus will not support his date of 629. Nicephorus' words are: 'Sarbaros after hearing of the death of Chosroes, Siroes, Kaboes, and Hormisdas, returned from the country of the Romans'; and 'when peace was ratified, Sarbaros gave back Egypt and all the East to the Romans, removing the Persian garrisons, and he sent the life-giving cross to the Emperor.' But the Shah-Waraz did not become king by agreement with Heraclius till at least the end of 629 (*Journal Asiatique*, 1866, p. 220), whereas it is certain that Heraclius recovered the cross in 628. Moreover, Nicephorus himself, after recording certain other events, goes on to say that subsequently the cross was taken by Heraclius to Jerusalem, then again returned to Constantinople, where the Patriarch Sergius received it; 'and it was in the 2nd Indiction that these things happened,' i.e. 629! If this incoherent story proved anything, it would be that Egypt was evacuated before the recovery of the cross, and therefore before September, 628; but it proves nothing except that Nicephorus is an incompetent witness.

The fact is that the ten years of the occupation may count from the entry of the Persians into Egypt, or from the capture of Alexandria, or from the completion of the conquest of Egypt up to Syene; and the length of the period must of course depend on the starting-point.

I have endeavoured in this note to show that much of the confusion arises from the failure to distinguish between the invasion of Egypt and the conquest of Egypt, which are neither synonymous nor synchronous. One other source of confusion is the failure to distinguish between the year Anno Domini (beginning January 1) and the Greek year of Alexander's era (beginning September 1), which spreads over part of two years of our reckoning. Further, there is the failure to take into account the Syrian reckoning of the Greek era, which sometimes differs from the ordinary reckoning by one year, and which begins the year in October instead of September. A final source of error may be mentioned—the attempt to found the chronology on too narrow a basis. This may be done in two ways, by unduly narrowing either the period or the sources of evidence. It will not answer to discuss the dates of a period of ten or twelve years and to settle them without regard to the consequences, i.e. without facing the bearing of those dates on previous or subsequent chronology, and ascertaining whether the inevitable deductions will stand criticism. But it should also be remembered that, in dealing with these events of the seventh century, the sources of history are many and various. There are Greek, Armenian, Syrian, Arab, and Egyptian writers who have something to say; and it is not legitimate to base any system of chronology upon the evidence of one or two sets of writers without due regard to the others.

In making these remarks I am profoundly conscious of the difficulties besetting any attempt to reconcile authorities which are often really, as well as apparently, irreconcilable. But it may not be presumptuous to indicate some of the pitfalls which research must encounter. I would only add that in differing with Gelzer, I do so with all admiration for his learned and scholarly work. But while I am far from claiming that the scheme of chronology I have put forward is free from all difficulty, I may perhaps claim that it is broadly based, and reconciles a large number of very different and wholly independent authorities.

APPENDIX C

ON THE IDENTITY OF 'AL MUḲAUḲAS'

(*Revised and amended from a paper in the 'Proceedings of the Society of Biblical Archaeology.'*)

THERE is in the history of Egypt no figure at once so familiar and so mysterious as that denoted by the Arabic title Al Muḳauḳas, or Al Muḳauḳis. That the person in question played the leading part on the Roman side at the crisis of the Saracen conquest—that he was chiefly responsible for the surrender of Egypt—is agreed: but here all agreement ends. His personal identity, his name and nationality, the office he held, and the action he took, the very meaning of the title by which he is known—all these are questions debated, disputed, and answered in a fashion, but in such a fashion as to reveal the most hopeless discord of opinion. Nor is this discord to be wondered at; for it is clear that from the earliest times the Arabic authorities themselves are completely bewildered on the subject.

Among modern historians, Von Ranke (*Weltgeschichte*, V. i. 142 seq.) calls Al Muḳauḳas governor of Egypt and a Copt, but seems to doubt his historical character. De Goeje ('De Moḳauḳis van Egypte' in the *Études dédiées à Leemans*) remarks that the Arabic historians seem to have confused the Muḳauḳas in some points with Cyrus, the imperial Patriarch of Alexandria, although he was a different person and held a different office. Prof. Karabacek, in his article 'Der Moḳauḳis von Aegypten' (*Mittheilungen aus der Sammlung der Papyrus Erzherzog Rainer*, vol. i. pp. 1–11), concludes that the proper name of the Muḳauḳas was George, son of Mînâ Parkabios, thus explaining the name فرقب or rather قرقب given to his father by some of the authorities. Karabacek assigns to the Muḳauḳas the office of pagarch, and explains the title as the Arabic form of the Greek μεγαυχής, which he *assumes* to have been an honorary designation, analogous to *ἐνδοξότατος* and the like commonly found in seventh-century papyri. Mr. Milne in his note on 'George the Muḳauḳis' (*Egypt under Roman Rule*, p. 224) identifies the man with a George the Prefect mentioned by John of Nikiou, who is assumed to have been Prefect of Augustamnica (i.e. Athrîb: see Hyvernat's *Actes des Martyrs de l'Égypte*, vol. i. p. 296), though Athrîb is hardly 'on the eastern frontier of Egypt,' as Mr. Milne's argument requires. Prof. Stanley Lane-Poole (*Egypt in the Middle Ages*, p. 6, note 2) leans to the *μεγαυχής* theory of the name, and adopts Mr. Milne's identification of the man with George the Prefect, in spite of the Arab traditions which make the Muḳauḳas 'governor of all Egypt, ruling from Alexandria.' He further accepts the conventional story which makes the Muḳauḳas a Copt. So Professor Bury speaks of him as 'the Coptic governor' of Egypt (*Later Roman Empire*, vol. ii. p. 270). The varying accounts of these writers are at best but partial and incomplete, because they have not grappled closely with the problem in its bearings on the history of the conquest, and so tested their theory against the various difficulties which its application must encounter. Moreover, Al Muḳauḳas is not the only person whose identity is disputed. Almost all the chief actors on the Roman or the Egyptian side in the war are equally shadowy personalities, and they are often confounded together. Hence to identify the Muḳauḳas is only half the problem. Other figures have at the same time to be examined, and their identity determined. But this is a necessity which, I believe, no writer has yet fully appreciated: so that one may say that the problem in its entirety has never yet been adequately stated. The fact is that confusion of names and persons permeates the whole history of the conquest to such a degree that only in writing, or attempting to write, that history does one realize the magnitude or the intricacy of the problem.

I propose first of all to cite the evidence of the principal Arabic writers, and to see what material they furnish for stating or solving the questions at issue.

Balâdhurî (born 806 A.D.) mentions the Muḳauḳas as having made peace with 'Amr, and as siding with the Copts after Heraclius' disapproval of the treaty. In Manuel's rebellion some say that he sided with the Arabs, others that he was dead. Balâdhurî gives no name to the Muḳauḳas.

Ṭabarî (839–923 A.D.) distinguishes the prince of Alexandria from the prince of Memphis: the latter was the Muḳauḳas, who was also prince of the Copts. The Muḳauḳas sent to Memphis an army under command of *the Catholicus, who was chief of all the bishops of the Christians, and whose name was Ibn Maryam.*

Eutychius (born 876 A.D.) was a Melkite. He avers that Al Muḳauḳas was controller of the finances of Egypt in the name of Heraclius, a Jacobite at heart, though by profession a Melkite, and that he had kept back the tribute due to the Emperor ever since the Persians had beleaguered Constantinople. No name is given to the Muḳauḳas, who is made to live till after the revolt of Manuel.

The MS. of *Severus of Ushmûnain* (? flor. early tenth century) is very important. His words are: 'When Heraclius had recovered his territories, he appointed governors in every place. To us in the land of Egypt Cyrus was sent *to be governor and Patriarch together*.' Of the ten years' persecution, the time of Benjamin's flight, he says: 'These were the years during which Heraclius and Al Muḳauḳas were ruling Egypt.' Again he says: 'When the ten years of the reign of Heraclius and the government of Al Muḳauḳas were over.' He further describes 'the misbelieving governor, who was both Prefect and Patriarch of Alexandria.' Finally, Benjamin is made to speak of 'the time of the persecution which befell me when Al Muḳauḳas drove me away'; and it is Severus who represents Benjamin as driven from his seat by the arrival of Cyrus. To Severus then Cyrus is the Mukauḳas.

There is now a gap of nearly two centuries till we come to *Ibn al Athîr* (born 1160 A.D.), who mentions both Abû Maryam and Abû Maryâm, the former *Catholicus of*

Memphis (notice the absurdity of this title), the latter a bishop. Both were sent by Al Muḳauḳas to attack 'Amr, but parleyed with him, and brought terms which the Muḳauḳas rejected. The Muḳauḳas himself was in command at the battle of Heliopolis, and later appears as governor of Alexandria during the siege. He made peace with 'Amr, and was alive during Manuel's rebellion.

Ibn al Athîr is very confused as to the order of events in the early part of the conquest.

Abû Ṣâliḥ wrote circa 1200 A.D. He testifies that 'Mohammed sent Ḥâṭib ibn Abî Balta'ah to Al Muḳauḳas, *governor of Alexandria*,' i.e. in A.H. 6, which began May 23, 627. After the recovery of Egypt, 'The country was placed by Heraclius under the government of George, son of Mînâ, the Muḳauḳas, جريج ابن مينا المقوقس. Again, of a monastery in Upper Egypt he says, 'It was here that Benjamin lived in concealment in the reign of the Roman Emperor Heraclius, who was a Chalcedonian, and while George, son of Mînâ, the Muḳauḳas, was ruling in Egypt, until the completion of the ten years, through fear of both of them, according to the warning of the angel.' The writer goes on to say that these were the ten years of the persecution suffered by the orthodox (i.e. Copts). But Abû Ṣâliḥ also quotes from the Book of Al Janâḥ the statement that 'the bishop of the Romans at Miṣr and Alexandria was named Cyrus' (p. 73).

Yâḳût (born circa 1178 A.D.) further complicates matters. He says that the fortress of Babylon 'was commanded by Al Mandafûr called Al 'Uairij on behalf of Al Muḳauḳas *ibn Ḳarḳab al Yûnânî*' (بن قرقب اليونانى), son of Ḳarḳab, the Greek, 'whose usual residence was at Alexandria.'

Makîn (born circa 1205 A.D.) says that 'the governor of Egypt in the name of Heraclius was Al Muḳauḳas, who together with the chief men of the Copts made peace with 'Amr.'

Ibn Khaldûn (born 1332 A.D., flor. late fourteenth century) follows Ibn al Athîr, but has his own confusions. He makes the Muḳauḳas a Copt.

Ibn Duḳmâḳ (wrote circa 1400) speaks of 'Al Muḳauḳas, the Roman, the Viceroy of Heraclius.'

Maḳrîzî (born 1365 A.D.) quotes Yazîd ibn Abî Ḥabîb for the statement that 'the Muḳauḳas the Roman, being governor of Egypt, made peace with 'Amr.' Ibn 'Abd al Ḥakam is quoted as the authority for the survival of Al Muḳauḳas to the time of Manuel's rebellion. Ibn 'Abd al Ḥakam was an early writer (died 870 A.D.), whose work survives in MS., but he is a romancer as well as an historian, though often of value. Weil has quoted largely from him.

Maḳrîzî follows Yâḳût about Al 'Uairij, and in making the Muḳauḳas son of Ḳarḳab (or Ḳarḳat) the Greek. He says that the Copts had a bishop at Alexandria called Abû Mayâmîn; that the Muḳauḳas made terms with the Arabs; but that Heraclius repudiated the agreement, reproaching him with imitating the meanness and cowardice of the Copts. Of Cyrus he says that Heraclius, اقام فيرش بطرك الاسكندرية, 'made Fîrush (*sic*) Patriarch of Alexandria'—a mistake for قيرس. Waḳidî (so called, romance of uncertain date) says that 'the king of the Copts at that time was the Muḳauḳas, son of Ra'îl.'

'*Abû 'l Maḥâsin* (born 1409) makes Benjamin the Coptic bishop of Alexandria, and states that 'the commander of Ḳaṣr ash Shama' was Al 'Ughairij, who was subordinate to the authority of Al Muḳauḳas'; and two MSS. give the name of the Muḳauḳas as Juraiḥ ibn Mînâ, جريْح ابن مينا, obviously a mistake for جُرَيْج ابن مينا, or George, son of Mînâ. Elsewhere, however, the same writer says that the fortress was 'commanded by Al Mandafûr, called Al 'Ughairij, on behalf of Al Muḳauḳas, son of Ḳarḳab al Yûnânî.'

This author also cites Ibn Kathîr's story (compiled from Ibn Isḥâḳ and others), that the Muslims on their entry into Egypt were met by Abû Maryam, the Catholicus of Egypt, and Abû Martâm, the bishop; and these two prelates are introduced at the building of Fusṭâṭ.

Suyûṭî (born 1445 A.D.) nearly agrees with the last writer. He states that the fortress was commanded by Al

Mandaḳûl, called Al 'Araj, for the Muḳauḳas ibn Ḳarḳab al Yûnânî: that the Muḳauḳas' usual residence was at Alexandria: that he made terms with 'Amr, which Heraclius repudiated: and that 'the name of the Coptic bishop is Abû Mayâmîn.'

This review of the chief Arabic authorities brings out their many discrepancies: but it is clear that there are three persons to be identified, viz. Al Muḳauḳas, Abû Maryam, and Al 'Araj. I will take them in reverse order.

(1) *Al 'Araj*, *Al 'Uairij*, or *Al 'Ughairij*. This name seems first to occur in Yâḳût (early thirteenth century) as the name of the commander of the fortress of Babylon, whose title was Al Mandafûr, which may be a mistake for Al Mandaṭûr, and so a transcription of the Byzantine *μανδάτωρ*, though the word does not seem to be elsewhere used as commander. Yâḳût is followed by Abû 'l Maḥâsin and by Suyûṭî, though the latter changes the title to Mandaḳûl by a mistake in copying (منْدفور becomes منْدقول). Prof. Lane-Poole asserts that this Al 'Araj or Al Ara'ij is identical with Arṭabûn, one of the Roman generals, and that he was also called 'Ibn Ḳurḳub' (*Egypt in the Middle Ages*, p. 5, note 2). But there is no real authority for the identification, nor for transferring the name 'Ibn Ḳarḳab' from the Muḳauḳas to Al 'Araj.

I think, however, that *Al 'Araj* is merely a perversion through much copying of an original *Jurij* or *Jurîj*, and that in fact the name of the commander of the fortress was George, probably a different person from the 'George the Prefect' who is mentioned by John of Nikiou.

(2) *Abû Maryam*. This person is described by Prof. Lane-Poole as a 'Catholic' of Miṣr, who 'joined 'Amr's army.' The term *Catholicus* means nothing more nor less than Patriarch. It occurs among our authorities first in Ṭabarî, whose Persian associations made him familiar with it, as the common designation of the chief bishop of the Nestorian and Armenian Churches: it is of very frequent use in Sebeos and other writers, and is perfectly well known to Du Cange. Indeed Ṭabarî himself defines the term as

meaning 'chief of the bishops of the Christians,' but he adds the perplexing statement that his name was *Abû Maryam.* Now, it may be taken that there were only two Chief Bishops or Patriarchs at the time of the conquest, viz. Cyrus and Benjamin, with the possible but immaterial exception of a Gaianite Patriarch unknown. 'Ibn Maryam' cannot possibly stand for 'Cyrus,' but it can very well stand for 'Benjamin'; and I hope to show that the two are identical. By Ibn al Athîr's time the name had been corrupted to *Abû Maryam*, who is 'Catholicus of Memphis.' Maḳrîzî says that the Coptic bishop of Alexandria was called Abû Mayâmîn: while Abû 'l Maḥâsin says, rightly of course, that the Coptic bishop of Alexandria was called Binyâmîn or Benjamin. Finally, Suyûṭî avers that the Coptic bishop is *Abû Mayâmîn.* One has only to put these facts side by side to see at a glance how easily 'Abba Binyâmîn' became twisted into 'Abû Mayâmîn,' and then into 'Abû Maryam,' while 'Ibn Maryam' probably is a corruption of the simple 'Binyâmîn.' The Arab writers of course knew the name Maryam (Mary) as one held in high reverence by the Christians, and they mistook the unfamiliar 'Abba' for the familiar 'Abû,' while the first syllable of Binyâmîn بن was detached and mistaken for ابن. From these confusions, aided by copyists' errors, sprang the extraordinary names 'Father of Mary' and 'Son of Mary,' as applied to a bishop. But we may now confidently dismiss 'Abû Maryâm' and 'Abû Martam' and 'Ibn Maryam' and 'Abû Mayâmîn,' and substitute in place of these fantastic figures in every case the name of Benjamin, the Coptic Archbishop of Alexandria.

But it is not enough to drive away these phantoms. Admitting that the historical person intended is Benjamin, it is quite impossible to accept the statement that he had any part or lot in the dealings with 'Amr, whether by parley or by battle. The rôle assigned to Benjamin by Ṭabarî and those who follow him, like Ibn al Athîr, is ridiculous. He is made into a military chieftain under the orders of Al Muḳauḳas, and Ṭabarî, to achieve consistency, has to make Al Muḳauḳas prince of the Copts. But the whole weight of the Egyptian authorities (Ṭabarî was a foreigner, who travelled in Egypt) is against both suppositions. They agree clearly in recording that for ten years before the conquest, and also for the three years of its duration, Benjamin was in hiding in Upper Egypt. Even if it stood alone, Severus' *Life of Benjamin* would be quite decisive on this point: but all the authorities, from John of Nikiou onwards, on this point are in harmony.

What, then, is the explanation of the Arab writers assigning an active part in the conquest to Benjamin? It is this: they found in early records, or traditions, that the leader of the defenders and the foremost person in arranging terms with the invaders was an Archbishop of Alexandria; and they found that after the conquest and in all Coptic story the only recognized Archbishop of Alexandria was called Benjamin. Moreover, at the *second* capture of Alexandria, at the time of Manuel's rebellion, it *was* Benjamin who approached 'Amr and treated with him; and this episode has been confused with the treaty made by Cyrus. Hence the two persons were confounded, and Benjamin has been given the part played by Cyrus *at the conquest.* But, lest this explanation be regarded as *obscurum per obscurius*, we now come to the crucial question, who was Al Muḳauḳas?

(3) *Al Muḳauḳas.* While practically all the Arabic authorities speak of a person called by this title, it is very noticeable that in the list I have given no name, as distinguished from the title, occurs in Balâdhurî, Ṭabarî, Eutychius, Severus, or even Ibn al Athîr. Waḳidî, it is true, calls him 'son of Ra'îl'; but that is merely one of those fanciful names given to kings, magicians, &c. of prehistoric times by Arab romance. It is not till we get to the year 1200 A.D. that we find Al Muḳauḳas named as *George, son of Mînâ*, by Abû Ṣâliḥ, while his contemporary Yâḳût gives the name as *George, son of Ḳarḳab the Greek.* This difference points to two separate traditions, or two separate sources of information—an inference which is curiously

confirmed by the fact that we find a little later *both paternities* given for the same George in different passages by one and the same writer, Abû 'l Maḥâsin.

For the moment I will only note that these names are irreconcilable, and that they are of quite late authority. In themselves they can throw no light on the personality of Al Muḳauḳas. We must therefore leave them, to see if the identity of the Muḳauḳas can be established on an independent basis, and, if so, whether the solution of the problem of identity will enable us to understand the names. Now if Balâdhurî gives little help to our inquiry, Ṭabarî is decidedly misleading. He not only makes the Muḳauḳas 'prince of the Copts,' but he makes him head the surrender to the Arabs from inside the fortress of Babylon. In this he is doubly mistaken; for the Muḳauḳas was not a Copt, and he was not in the fortress when it was taken. But whereas Balâdhurî represents the Muḳauḳas as governor of Alexandria, Eutychius represents him as controller of finance, acting for Heraclius. Eutychius, it must be remembered, was a Melkite, and while admitting that the Muḳauḳas professed the same faith, declares that he was in heart an adherent of the Coptic communion—an absurd statement fabricated to explain the Muḳauḳas' action.

It is not till we come to Severus that the riddle of the Muḳauḳas' identity is solved; and there the solution is clear and unmistakable. Severus was a Copt; he had no motive to disguise the action of the Muḳauḳas; and above all he wrote his history upon a collation of Coptic and other documents, which were preserved in the library at Dair Macarius, at the monastery of Nahîyâ, and in private collections. He is sometimes, no doubt, inaccurate and impossible. Yet he gives a good deal of information not to be found in the early writers I have cited. This is what he says:—

'*Cyrus was appointed by Heraclius after the recovery of Egypt from the Persians, to be both Patriarch and governor of Alexandria.*' We know that he held office for ten years, during which he fiercely persecuted the Coptic Church.

This time Benjamin describes as '*the ten years during which Heraclius and Al Muḳauḳas were ruling over Egypt*'; yet he names Cyrus as '*the misbelieving governor who was both Prefect and Patriarch of Alexandria under the Romans.*' Further, whereas Severus represents Benjamin as fleeing before the arrival of Cyrus on the warning of an angel, he also represents Benjamin as saying '*Al Muḳauḳas drove me away.*' There remains, then, not the smallest doubt that Severus identifies Al Muḳauḳas with Cyrus, and distinguishes him from Benjamin.

That Severus is right, and all the other Arabic authorities wrong where they differ from him, I shall endeavour to prove.

Of the few undisputed facts about this period, one is that Cyrus was armed with both civil and ecclesiastical power, and another that as Patriarch and Viceroy of Heraclius he persecuted the Copts for a period of ten years. John of Nikiou speaks of 'the persecution which Heraclius made through all Egypt against the orthodox (Coptic) faith, at the instigation of the Chalcedonian Patriarch Cyrus'; and Coptic history is full of it. So John's whole story of the conquest assumes the Viceroyalty of Cyrus, which is incontestable. But Abû Ṣâliḥ says that the country was placed by Heraclius under the government of *Al Muḳauḳas*; and that Benjamin's flight lasted for ten years, according to the warning of the angel, while Al Muḳauḳas was ruling in Egypt. True, Abû Ṣâliḥ calls Al Muḳauḳas George, son of Mînâ: but of that anon. Ibn Duḳmâḳ and Makîn agree that Heraclius' Viceroy was Al Muḳauḳas. Maḳrîzî represents the Muḳauḳas as making terms with the Arabs, and his master Heraclius as repudiating the bargain; and Abû 'l Maḥâsin follows him in this, as does Suyûṭî. There is, therefore, fair agreement among the Arab writers as to the position occupied by the Muḳauḳas, but none as to the name he bore. And if they were the only authorities, the case would not be so strong as it is, though it might well rest on the single evidence of Severus.

There are, however, a few Coptic documents, as well as

Arabic, which bear on the question. The Arabic life of Shanûdah, published by Amélineau, is from a Coptic original written in the seventh century. It contains by way of prophecy these words: 'Then shall Antichrist arise and shall go before the Roman Emperor, and be made governor with the double office of ruler and of bishop. He shall come down to Egypt . . . and he shall make war on the chief of the bishops at Alexandria . . . who shall fly to the region of Tîman.' This, of course, is a description of Cyrus and his treatment of Benjamin. More important is a fragment in the Bodleian Library (MSS. Copt. Clar. Press, b. 5), which has also been published by Amélineau under the title of the 'Life of Samuel of Ḳalamûn.'

This fragment recounts the visit to a monastery of a person who is called ⲡⲕⲁⲩⲭⲓⲟⲥ ⲡⲉⲡⲥⲉⲩⲧⲟⲁⲣⲭⲏⲉⲡⲓⲥⲕⲟⲡⲟⲥ or 'the ⲕⲁⲩⲭⲓⲟⲥ, the false Archbishop.' The story is told in my text (ch. xiii), and need not be repeated. But the ⲕⲁⲩⲭⲓⲟⲥ is there clearly called not only Patriarch but also 'controller of the revenues of the land of Egypt' (ⲧⲁⲝⲓⲁⲣⲭⲏⲥ ⲉϫⲛ ⲇⲏⲙⲱϭⲓⲟⲛ ⲛⲧⲉⲭⲱⲣⲁ ⲛⲕⲏⲙⲉ). Hence in a contemporary[1] document we have a 'Chalcedonian' (or Melkite) Archbishop, whose authority is disowned by the Copts in favour of their own Archbishop Benjamin, yet who claims in his person the union of civil and ecclesiastical sway over Egypt; further this person is called ⲡⲕⲁⲩⲭⲓⲟⲥ.

How exactly this description tallies with the description given by Severus of the office and function of Cyrus, the Chalcedonian Patriarch and Viceroy of Heraclius, needs no pointing out; it agrees also in part with Eutychius, Makîn, Ibn Duḳmâḳ, and Maḳrîzî; but the most interesting thing about this fragment is that here we have the name Muḳauḳas in its original Coptic form, and it is assigned to a person whose identity with Cyrus is no longer open to question.

Yet Amélineau misses the true solution. Forced to the conclusion that the Muḳauḳas was a Melkite Patriarch, he

[1] The actual MS. in the Bodleian is dated by Hyvernat about the tenth century.

has no thought of identifying him with Cyrus ; he says, in fact, that it is difficult to place him ; that Cyrus must have left Alexandria in 639, 'and perhaps it was at this time that the Muḳauḳas was chosen to replace Cyrus: perhaps even he was the enemy of Cyrus!'

But among the brilliant services which the French savant has rendered to the cause of Egyptian literature, he does not pretend to have made a special study of the Arab conquest. Hence, although his article on the Muḳauḳas ('Fragments Coptes' in *Journal Asiatique*, October–November, 1888, pp. 389–409) has a real importance, it does not range over a wide enough field; it does not set out the authorities it cites with due regard to their chronology or their value; and it adopts some theories of previous writers without critical examination. For example, having settled that Al Muḳauḳas was a Melkite Patriarch, the objection is raised, 'If this is so, how comes it that the Coptic historians who have written in Arabic—Eutychius, Makîn, Abû 'l Faraj, &c.—have said nothing about it?' This objection looks formidable, but vanishes at a touch of criticism. Amélineau's own reply is as follows: 'Je dois répondre naïvement que je n'en sais rien. Des deux derniers, Al Makîn ne consacre que deux lignes au Muḳauḳas, Abû 'l Faraj n'en parle pas. Eutychius lui est favorable, et, s'il savait la chose, peut-être la lui a-t-il pardonnée en faveur de sa conduite postérieure; s'il ne savait pas, c'est une raison péremptoire pour qu'il n'en parlât pas. D'ailleurs, ... il écrivait longtemps après les évènements, au moins 600 ans.'

Eutychius a Copt, and writing at least 600 years after the conquest! It is a curious statement. For of the three historians named by Amélineau, Abû 'l Faraj was not a Copt at all, nor even an Egyptian, but a Syrian. A second, Eutychius, was not a Copt, but actually Melkite Patriarch, though he does not identify Cyrus with the Muḳauḳas: and Eutychius wrote, not 'at least 600 years,' but less than 300 years, after the conquest. Moreover, Eutychius expressly states that the Muḳauḳas was controller of the revenue in the name of Heraclius: and in this he agrees almost textually with Amélineau's document. Makîn was a Christian, and may have been a Copt; but he is a late authority, and of no great value. It thus appears how utterly baseless is Amélineau's objection concerning his so-called Coptic writers. There is, however, one Coptic historian of early date and of capital importance, who wrote in Arabic, and whose evidence, as I have shown, would, even if unsupported, establish the identity of the Muḳauḳas beyond discussion. I mean Severus, whom Amélineau does not quote. Briefly, however, I may now give Amélineau's conclusions as follows:—

1. The story of Mohammed's mission to the Muḳauḳas in 627 is a myth.
2. The Muḳauḳas was named George, son of Mînâ, and the 'Ibn Ḳarḳab,' which should be written, as Karabacek shows, 'Ibn Farḳab,' denotes a second name = Παρκάβιος.
3. The Muḳauḳas was of Coptic race on one side, if not on both. He was in the Emperor's service, and was originally a Melkite by faith.
4. He was a Melkite Patriarch, but his date can only be conjectured.
5. The name Muḳauḳas was a nickname derived from καύχον or καύχιον, a small bronze coin used from the time of the Justins.

We now come to an extremely interesting contribution to the subject made by the learned Portuguese scholar, F. M. E. Pereira (*Vida do Abba Samuel do Mosteiro do Kalamon*). This translation of the Ethiopic 'Life of Samuel' is enriched with valuable notes and essays, among which is a short treatise on the Muḳauḳas (pp. 41–53). Like Amélineau, whom he largely follows, the writer does not cite the MS. of Severus, and he does not accurately classify or appraise his authorities: but he shows how closely the Ethiopic tallies with the Coptic story, though very singularly—like nearly all our authorities—it refrains from naming the chief actor in the episode, whom it calls 'the governor,' and whom the Coptic fragment calls ⲡⲕⲁⲩⲭⲓⲟⲥ, and Archbishop. Pereira's conclusions differ somewhat from Amélineau's and are as follows:—

1. The author of the persecution was a person known by the title of ⲡⲕⲁⲩⲭⲓⲟⲥ or Al Muḳauḳas.
2. He was a Greek by origin.
3. He was Patriarch of Alexandria, governor of Egypt, and controller of the finance.
4. His proper name was Cyrus.
5. The name Muḳauḳas is derived from *καύχον* or *καύχιον*.

As to the identity of Al Muḳauḳas with Cyrus only one more word need be said. Amélineau quotes the Coptic Synaxarium under 8 Tûbah—the day of Benjamin's death—as follows: 'Benjamin suffered great evil at the hands of Al Muḳauḳas; he fled to Upper Egypt during ten full years . . . *The Muḳauḳas was the head of the faith of Chalcedon, and had been made ruler and Patriarch over Egypt.*' The Ethiopic Synaxarium is in complete accord with this. It is given in full by Pereira, and contains these words (text p. 173, tr. p. 180), 'The Muḳauḳas, that is to say the *governor and Archbishop of the city of Alexandria and all the land of Egypt.*' It is true that the MS. of this version of the Synaxarium seems to be dated fifteenth century (*Catalogue des MSS. Éthiopiens de la Bibl. Nat.*, 1877, p. 152). But it nevertheless goes back to a very ancient original. In any case it is remarkable to find with what extraordinary accuracy the true tradition is preserved in these office-books of the two Churches (which were, of course, in very close relation), while the secular writers for the most part confused and darkened the story, and finally lost the truth.

But that Cyrus was Al Muḳauḳas and that Al Muḳauḳas was Cyrus, appointed Viceroy and Archbishop of Alexandria by Heraclius, may now be regarded as finally settled. It is curious that John of Nikiou never uses any title corresponding to Al Muḳauḳas or ⲡⲕⲁⲩⲭⲓⲟⲥ, but his whole history of the period teems with evidence that Cyrus the Patriarch was the author of the ten years' persecution and the governor of Egypt. To the objection that the Muḳauḳas is spoken of as governor of Egypt in 627, when Mohammed sent his letter claiming submission to Islâm, the answer is easy. It is the plainest of truth that not a single Arab writer who uses the term Al Muḳauḳas has any conception of its meaning or origin; and the use of the term, as applied to the governor of Egypt in 627, is a mere anachronism. The Arab chroniclers had two facts before them: (1) that Mohammed sent a mission to the governor of Egypt in 627, and (2) that the governor of Egypt at the time of the conquest—the man who occupies the most prominent position in its annals—was called Al Muḳauḳas. They wrongly inferred that the earlier governor was called by the same title, and this confusion between the two was so easy as to be almost inevitable to minds naturally uncritical. There is no ground, therefore, for rejecting, as Amélineau does, the whole incident of the mission, an incident as well attested as any in the history of Islâm. A similar confusion explains the application of the title Al Muḳauḳas to Benjamin at the time of Manuel's rebellion.

To sum up. The term Al Muḳauḳas is applied to three persons: (1) to a governor who received Mohammed's mission some years before the conquest; (2) to the governor at the time of the conquest; (3) to the Head of the Copts at the time of Manuel's rebellion. This shows that the Arabs had no clear idea about him, but the whole evidence proves that the title belongs properly to the governor *at* the time of the conquest. For all the Arabic authorities show that the action of the Muḳauḳas centres in the surrender of Egypt; and John of Nikiou proves conclusively that the betrayer of Egypt was Cyrus.

It remains now to explain how Cyrus comes to be called 'George son of Mînâ,' or 'George son of Ḳarḳab.' John of Nikiou, as we have seen, mentions one George the Prefect, whom 'Amr ordered to construct a bridge over the canal at Ḳaliûb. George, therefore, was an historical person who occupied a prominent position at the time of the Saracen invasion; and he may be the same person whom we have encountered under the guise of Al 'Ughairij. It is easy to believe that Arab writers have confounded him with Cyrus. Whether this George were 'son of Mînâ' or 'son of Ḳarḳab,' in my judgement cannot be settled, and matters next to nothing; but I am unable to think with Karabacek that George's father bore both names, though it may be that 'Ḳarḳab' should be written 'Farḳab,' and 'Farḳab' stands for Παρκάβιος. The word قرقب occurs far too late in Arabic literature to represent anything but a blunder or a series of blunders in copying. Abû Ṣâliḥ (p. 156) says that قرقر is derived from 'Gregorius.' Now if we suppose that قرقر was corrupted into قرقب—an extremely probable supposition—we have the simple explanation that Ibn Ḳarḳab is a mistake for Ibn Ḳarḳar and that it means 'son of Gregory.' Note also that Gregory appears as 'Grigor' in Armenian, and that the name was a very favourite one in that part of the world. The form 'Karkûr' is the common equivalent of 'Gregory' among Copts and Armenians to-day. Hence it is perfectly possible that Cyrus was son of Gregory, and George son of Mînâ. M. Casanova, however, suggests to me that ابن قرقب is a mere corruption of ابو قرص Abû Ḳiruṣ, so that we get in fact the name Cyrus concealed in the 'Ibn Ḳarḳab.' This is both ingenious and plausible.

The meaning and origin of the title Al Muḳauḳas are more difficult. Late authorities like Damîrî's *Zoological Dictionary* (c. 1400), and the *Kamûs*, of about that date (fourteenth century), are cited to show that the term القوقس means a ringdove, and various legends are told in explanation of the title: but it can hardly be questioned that this derivation is a mere inversion of the fact that in more modern times the name Al Muḳauḳas has been given to the ringdove as a playful nickname. Nor can Karabacek's conjecture, that the term is derived from μεγαυχής, be accepted. Apart from the fact that there seems no evidence for the existence of any such title, the very closeness of the correspondence between the Greek and the Arabic form is really fatal to the theory. It is hardly conceivable that the Arabs should have reproduced such a Greek form so nearly.

We have seen that the title Al Muḳauḳas occurs in the early Coptic form ⲡⲕⲁⲩⲭⲓⲟⲥ, and that Amélineau and Pereira agree in deriving the term from a Byzantine word said to signify a small hollow piece of bronze money, and in thinking that the name was given to Cyrus in derision of his rôle as controller of the finance, or taxes, or tribute. This explanation, though very far-fetched, might be more convincing if there were any clear evidence for the use of *καύχον* or *καύχιον* in Egypt or elsewhere at this time or any other. As far as I know, there is none. Where does Amélineau find these forms at all? He refers to Du Cange, who gives *καυκίον* as = a little bowl or cup, and one instance of its use in the sense of a hollow coin, where the reference is cited as 'Nov. 105 Justin.' Du Cange is careful to add that the reading *καυκίον* in that passage is doubtful, and may stand for *κοκκίον*. This seems Amélineau's warrant for the existence of the supposed 'piece of Byzantine money in use since the time of the Justins'! Pereira adopts this etymology without question: 'Esta palavra, que tambem se escreve *καύχον* e *καύχιον*, é o nome de uma moeda cavada, em uso no imperio Byzantino, desde o tempo do imperador Justino' (p. 53); but it rests on very slender evidence if any, and must be rejected.

So far, then, there seems no satisfactory explanation of the title Al Muḳauḳas; and perhaps the problem is hopeless. But I venture to offer two possible solutions for what they are worth.

(1) The Arabic writers who give the vocalization of Al Muḳauḳas write المُقَوْقِس, which is also the vocalization for the late word in the sense of ringdove, and it may have been so written to produce identity. On the other hand, the Ethiopic is very clear in writing 'Muḳauḳăs,' and there can be no doubt that the term passed into Ethiopic at a very early date. Now, not a single author who has dealt with this problem has asked the question, Where did Cyrus

come from? what was his origin? Remember he was not an Egyptian, nor even a Constantinopolitan; and surely there is no question that would have been heard more often among the eager and curious crowds of Alexandria. And the answer would have been, ἐκ τοῦ Καυκάσου—Καυκάσιος: for Cyrus was translated by Heraclius from the see of Phasis in the Caucasus. It is, therefore, extremely probable that he was at once called ὁ καυκάσιος in Greek, and this Greek form may have taken shape in Coptic either as πκαⲩⲭασιος or πκαⲩⲭιος, giving origin in its less corrupted form in the seventh or eighth century to the Arabic 'Muḳauḳas,' and surviving in the tenth century in the more corrupted πκαⲩⲭιος of the MS. in the Bodleian Library. The Coptic π would easily go into the Arabic *mu-*, the process aided by the analogy which would result with the participial form in Arabic.

Though not free from objection, this explanation is at least based on historical fact: and if the change of καⲩκασιος into καⲩⲭιος be thought too violent even for two centuries of Coptic speech and script, I may urge that Phasis was in Colchis, and that Cyrus might also with equal propriety have been called πκολⲭιος (the Colchian), from which to πκαⲩⲭιος the transference is very easy.

(2) The other explanation is as follows:—

In Du Cange's *Glossary* will be found the word καῦχος, in the sense *amatus, amasius* (with the corresponding feminine καύχα, *concubina*), connoting a form of vice. From this word it would be quite simple and natural to coin, if it did not exist, the adjective ὁ καύχιος, denoting a person addicted to that form of vice. This term ὁ καύχιος would go straight into the Coptic as πκαⲩⲭιος, the adjective unaltered and the article changing, exactly on the analogy of πασεβηс for ὁ ἀσεβής, which is found more than once in the very document in which πκαⲩⲭιος occurs, and is there applied to the same person, Cyrus. But, it will be said, this imputation on Cyrus is quite without warrant in history. Granted; but that is no proof that the Copts did not make it. On the contrary, it is extremely probable that they did. The ten years' persecution of Cyrus planted in their hearts the bitterest hatred, which found vent in savage denunciation of the enemy. In this very document Cyrus is called 'The Impious One,' 'Jew,' 'Atheist,' 'Son of Satan,' 'Antichrist'; his doctrine is 'devilish,' his faith is 'defiled,' and he is 'more accursed than the devil and his demons.' Is it likely that, when the religion of Cyrus was assailed in terms like these, his moral character would escape censure? If then his private life was the mark of the same unmeasured abuse, nothing is more likely than that he was charged with the vice which is suggested by the term ὁ καύχιος, however ill-founded the charge may have been.

These two solutions which I have given seem independent and incompatible; but I would suggest that they may really be closely connected. For it is easy to imagine both that Cyrus was originally called ὁ Καυχάσιος or ὁ Κολχικός (or Κόλχιος), and that the quick wit of the Egyptians caught up the name and transformed it into the abusive epithet ὁ καύχιος. Thus a term, purely geographical in origin, was transformed into a foul invective; and the name has lasted for centuries after its real significance was totally forgotten.

APPENDIX D

ON THE CHRONOLOGY OF THE ARAB CONQUEST

So great are the difficulties of dealing with the dates of this period that the task of finding the truth seems almost impossible. It is not one problem that a writer has to face, but a number of problems so entangled and interlaced that a solution in one direction seems always to bring fresh complications in another. But a great deal has been done to simplify matters by Mr. E. W. Brooks, whose learned article on this subject in the *Byzantinische Zeitschrift* (1895, pp. 436–45) may be said to have rescued the chronology from the domain of conjecture, and to have set it on a scientific basis. His article must be the foundation of any study either of the dates or of the order of events of this epoch, and I most readily acknowledge my great obligations to it.

The Greek authorities, as Mr. Brooks shows, are of no value. Neither Theophanes nor Nicephorus mentions the fall of Alexandria, although the latter does say that Heraclonas, after the death of his half-brother Constantine in May, 641, restored Cyrus to the patriarchate of Alexandria, implying that the city was not then captured or near capture. Nicephorus' history breaks off in 641, and the story is resumed only in 668. But both Nicephorus and Theophanes are totally untrustworthy with regard to the earlier part of the invasion; their stories are full of discrepancies, and they confound the order of events in a way that must prove, and has proved, seriously misleading to historians who rely upon them.

Syrian and Armenian authorities seem equally useless. Elijah of Nisibis (Brit. Mus. Add. MS. 7. 197, fol. 29, cited by Mr. Brooks) puts the conquest of Alexandria in A. H. 20 (Dec. 640—Dec. 641). Abû 'l Faraj is silent, save for the well-known story of the destruction of the library. Sebeos also is silent.

The Arabic writers rival the Greek in omissions, confusions, and discrepancies; but a study of them is not fruitless.

Ibn 'Abd al Ḥakam (quoted by Weil, *Geschichte der Chalifen*) says that 'Amr was at Al 'Arîsh on the Day of Sacrifice, 10 Dhû 'l Ḥijjah, A. H. 18 = Dec. 12, 639; and also that the siege of Alexandria lasted for nine months after the death of Heraclius. Suyûṭî cites the same writer as saying that, while after the conquest of Miṣr 'Amr sent troops of horsemen to the towns and villages round about, the Fayûm remained unknown to the Arabs for a year.

Balâdhurî puts the invasion of Egypt in A. H. 19 (begins Jan. 2, 640), and makes both the battle of Heliopolis and the expedition to the Fayûm subsequent to the fall of the fortress of Babylon. He says that 'Amr marched northwards, i.e. to Alexandria, in A.H. 21 (Dec. 10, 641—Nov. 29,

642), after having stayed some time at Babylon; and that in the same year—the Year of Famine—Omar wrote bidding 'Amr send the tribute by sea. He also quotes the statement that Miṣr was conquered A. H. 20. *Miṣr* is generally translated here and elsewhere as 'Egypt,' whereas in this case it means unquestionably the town of Miṣr (or Memphis), the predecessor of Fusṭâṭ.

Ibn Ḳutaibah says that 'the battle of Bâb al Yûn was won by 'Amr in A. H. 20.'

Ṭabarî alleges that the order to invade Egypt came to 'Amr at the beginning of A. H. 20 = end of December, 640; and he gives the precise date of Rabi' II in the same year (March 20—April 17, 641) for the fall of Babylon. The two statements are inconsistent, since it is impossible that Babylon could have been taken within three months of 'Amr receiving in Palestine the order to march. But the second date is corroborated from independent sources, so that the first must be erroneous; and if we put the invasion in the beginning of A. H. 19 instead of 20, we find Ibn 'Abd al Ḥakam, Balâdhurî, and Ṭabarî in practical agreement as to the opening of the campaign. Indeed it is certain that Ṭabarî *must have written* 19; because in his account of the death of 'Amr he places exactly four years of his government under Omar, whose death took place in Dhû 'l Ḥijjah, A. H. 23: consequently 'Amr's rule began Dhû 'l Ḥijjah, A. H. 19; and it would be absurd to date his rule of Egypt from a time anterior to the invasion.

Ṭabarî further says that Alexandria capitulated after five months of siege; and that the revolt (which I call Manuel's revolt) occurred early in A. H. 25.

Eutychius' statements are as follows. Faramâ, i. e. Pelusium, was taken after one month's siege, and the fortress of Babylon after seven months' siege. Al Muḳauḳas escaped from the fortress at the time of high Nile. There were three battles between Babylon and Alexandria, and the Great City was taken 'on Friday of Muḥarram in the new moon in A. H. 20, the twentieth year of Heraclius and eighth of Omar's caliphate.' The conquest of Barca followed, and Tripolis was subdued in A. H. 22. If by Friday of Muḥarram is meant the first day of the month, 1 Muḥarram in A.H. 20 = Dec. 21, 640: but 1 Muḥarram in the eighth year of Omar = Dec. 10, 641. Neither day fell on a Friday. The former date would be in the thirty-first of Heraclius, and at the latter Heraclius was no longer alive. So much for Eutychius.

Severus of Ushmûnain says that 'the prince of the Muslims sent an expedition . . . under 'Amr in the year 357 of the Martyrs,' and 'the army of Islâm marched down into Egypt in great force on 12 Ba'ûnah, i.e. the Roman month of December.' Here again is an error: for the 12 Ba'ûnah or Payni = June 6: while if December, 357 A. M. is right, that must be December, 640, not 641. The *Chronicon Orientale* says that 'on 12 Payni, 357 A. M. 'Amr came to Egypt and took it.' But 12 Payni, 357 A. M. = June 6, 641; and Maḳrîzî specially says that 'the Coptic date for the capture of the *fortress* is 12 Payni.' Severus adds that 'in 360 A. M. the Muslims took the city of Alexandria and threw down its walls'—a touch which shows that he is thinking of the second capture after Manuel's revolt. Clearly the chronology of Severus is not helpful.

Abû Ṣâliḥ adds little to our knowledge. He quotes from the Book of Al Janâḥ that 'Amr conquered Egypt (or Miṣr) in A. H. 19 (Jan. 2—Dec. 20, 640): that he encamped outside a place called Janân ar Rîḥân (p. 73). He also says that 'Amr conquered Egypt (or Miṣr) on Friday, 1 Muḥarram, A. H. 20: he quotes or misquotes the date given by Severus.

Yâḳût is important. He says that 'Amr begged Omar's leave to invade Egypt in A.H. 18 (Jan. 12, 639—Jan. 2, 640). The Roman forces first met the Arabs at Faramâ, and fighting continued about two months. After that little resistance till Bilbais was reached, where there was constant fighting for a month: then came an easy march to Umm Dûnain or Al Maḳs, where the Arabs were delayed fighting about two months.

This gives a total of nearly six months from the invasion, making allowance for the time spent in marching, and would bring us from Dec. 12 with great nicety to June 6.

It was at this point, says Yâḳût, that 'Amr sent for reinforcements; and the fortress was taken at the time of high Nile, i. e. September or a little later. Yet the same writer a page or so lower says, ' The conquest of Babylon took place on Friday, 1 Muḥarram, A. H. 20' (= Dec. 21, 640), the date usually assigned for the capture of Alexandria. This is bewildering enough. Yâḳût adds that 'Amr set out towards Alexandria in Rabi' I, A. H. 20 (Feb. 20— March 20, 641)—probably an error for Rabi' II—and on reaching the city 'Amr besieged it for six months. Elsewhere he says that Alexandria was taken after a siege in A.H. 20 (ends Dec. 9, 641), and that 'Amr made peace with Barca in A.H. 21 (Dec. 10, 641—Nov. 29, 642).

According to *Ibn Khaldûn*, after the capture of Jerusalem 'Amr asked leave to invade Egypt, and this was in A. H. 21: 'Amr also marched into Africa (Barca) in A.H. 21!

Maḳrîzî is rather voluminous. He repeats that 'Amr was at 'Arîsh on the Day of Sacrifice: that he spent a month at Faramâ: that Al Muḳauḳas evacuated the fortress at high Nile, and that it was still high Nile when the fortress was taken. But he quotes Al Kindî as saying that after the capture of Babylon 'Amr set out for Alexandria, and this was in Rabi' I, A. H. 20—or Jumâdā II, according to another writer (Rabi' I begins on Feb. 20, Rabi' II on March 20, Jumâdā I on April 17, 641, and Jumâdā II on May 18: the true date lies in Jumâdā I, as we shall see). Heraclius' death is wrongly given as A. H. 19, and the writer says that it encouraged the Muslims, who continued the siege with increased vigour: but he quotes Al Laith for the alternative date A. H. 20, which is correct. The capture of Alexandria took place nine months and five days after the death of Heraclius, and that was on Friday, 1 Muḥarram, A. H. 21 (Dec. 10, 641, but Monday). Al Laith says the first capture of Alexandria was in A. H. 22 (begins Nov. 30, 642). Maḳrîzî gives a list of authorities for dates in relation to the conquest, varying from A. H. 16 to 26, but adds that 'A. H. 20 is the most probable and the most generally accepted.'

Abû 'l Maḥâsin cites Adh Dhahabî for the statement that Omar wrote the order for the invasion in A. H. 20 (begins Dec. 21, 640): and Ibn 'Abd al Ḥakam for the statement that the siege of Babylon lasted seven months. He himself puts the 'conquest of Egypt,' or perhaps of Miṣr, 1 Muḥarram, A. H. 20; he quotes Ibn Kathîr, Waḳidî, and Abû Ma'shar for the same date for the capture of Miṣr. Waḳidî puts the capture of Alexandria in the same year, while Abû Ma'shar puts it in A. H. 25. Saif says that both Miṣr and Alexandria were taken in A. H. 16. The first year of 'Amr's government was A. H. 20.

Suyûṭî, after quoting Al Laith for A. H. 20 as the date of Heraclius' death, says that the siege of Alexandria lasted for nine months after that event, having begun five months before: and yet adds that the city fell on 1st Muḥarram, A. H. 20! This however is a slip, for several pages later Suyûṭî remarks that 'the first capture of Alexandria was in A. H. 21, the second A. H. 25.' He cites Ibn Ḳutaibah, as quoted by Al Kuda'î, for the statement that 'Amr returned from Alexandria (i.e. to Babylon) in Dhû 'l Ḳa'dah, A. H. 20 (Oct.–Nov. 641).

So much for the chief Arabic authorities. Their discrepancies are obviously great and hard to reconcile. But it is easy to mark some of the sources of the confusion which prevails among these writers, and has puzzled and misled modern historians. Probably no other period of the same brevity has so many natural pitfalls for the chronologer. Here, as in the case of the Persian conquest, we have a period of some three years, and a date is loosely given for the conquest, when in one case it represents the invasion, in another the completed subjugation, of the country. Further, the name 'Miṣr' most unfortunately denotes both the town of Memphis close to Babylon on the south and also the whole country of Egypt. Consequently the 'capture of Memphis' and 'the capture of

Egypt' are often impossible to distinguish. Then the capture of Babylon was a different event from the capture of Miṣr: but the two localities practically adjoined, and the confusion of the events was almost inevitable. Lastly, Alexandria was captured not once, but twice; and even the earliest Arab chroniclers, who wrote 200 years afterwards, found the tradition much bedimmed and the order of events forgotten. Accordingly their mistakes and contradictions must be pronounced more deplorable than surprising.

But an entirely new light has been cast on both the history and the chronology of the conquest by the work of John, the Coptic bishop of Nikiou. John was one of the bishops attending the consecration of the Patriarch Isaac in 690 A.D. (see infra, pp. 548–50), and was probably born about the time of the invasion; but he must have heard every incident recounted by eyewitnesses. His evidence therefore is of extreme value, as far as it goes, though unfortunately parts of the history are entirely wanting, while others are in such lamentable disorder that the sense cannot be followed. But notwithstanding the state of the Ethiopic MS., it gives some fresh dates of remarkable precision, and these dates give fixed bases for the construction of a scientific chronology.

We have already seen that for the time of the Persian conquest there is a blank in John's history. The gap reaches from the accession of Heraclius to thirty years beyond, from 610 to 640 about. The entry of the Arabs into Egypt is not recorded: and when the story is resumed, Theodore, commander-in-chief of the Roman forces in Egypt, had just heard of the defeat and death of John, general of the militia, in the Fayûm. The Roman troops then concentrated at the fortress of Babylon with the intention of giving battle to the Arabs before the inundation. The Nile begins to rise about Midsummer, and reaches its full height at the autumnal equinox: so that the engagement at Heliopolis may be set down to July or August. If now we follow Ibn 'Abd al Ḥakam, Balâdhurî, and Ṭabarî in placing the entry of the Saracens in December, 639, we have the battle of Heliopolis in July or August, 640: and it may well be that the reinforcements of the Saracen army were first seen from the towers of Babylon on June 6, a day which from Severus and others is proved to have a strong hold on Coptic tradition, but which cannot be associated with any decisive event in the conquest.

Mr. Brooks is clearly right in regarding chapters cxiv and cxv of John's history as out of place. The heading of chapter cxv runs, 'How the Muslims got possession of Miṣr in the fourteenth year of the lunar cycle, and took the citadel of Babylon in the fifteenth year,' although unfortunately the corresponding narrative has dropped out of the body of the text. In chapter cxvi the death of Heraclius is dated 'in the thirty-first year of his reign, in the Egyptian month of Yakâtit, which answers to the Roman month of February, in the fourteenth year of the cycle and the year 357 of Diocletian.' The fall of the fortress of Babylon is said in ch. cxvii to have happened on Easter Monday, and in cxviii the capture of Nikiou is dated the following 'Sunday, 18 Genbot in the fifteenth year of the cycle.' Mr. Brooks, following Zotenberg, remarks that of these dates the only one which we can control—that for the death of Heraclius—is absolutely accurate, since we know that Heraclius died on Feb. 11, 641; and that this fact is a strong presumption for the accuracy of the other dates. But both authors, in spite of this assertion, find themselves compelled to demonstrate that the other dates are only partially correct. Thus speaking of the cycle years named in the heading of ch. cxv Mr. Brooks says, 'I cannot think that much confidence is to be placed in these dates' (p. 439); and again he proves that when the 18 Genbot fell on a Sunday it was not in the fifteenth year of the indiction, as John states; that in short we must alter John's date, which would give May 13, 642, to May 13, 641. In other words, part of John of Nikiou's evidence has to be explained away.

Now I venture to think that this is quite needless. The

mistake arises from a misunderstanding of John's cycle, which John's critics wrongly identify with the indiction. But John himself clearly calls it the *lunar cycle*, and he is not referring to the indiction—which doubtless had fallen into disuse in Egypt when he wrote—but to the Dionysian cycle of nineteen years, which continues in use to the present day, and in which the numbers are commonly called the Golden Numbers. Zotenberg says that this cycle was not used for civil purposes; but, the indiction being obsolescent in Egypt, John was more than justified in using the ecclesiastical reckoning, with which as a learned bishop he must have been quite familiar. We may now set out his statements thus:—

(1) Capture of the town of Miṣr, fourteenth year of cycle.

(2) Death of Heraclius, fourteenth year of cycle on Feb. 11, 641.

(3) Capture of citadel of Babylon, fifteenth year of cycle, Easter Monday, i.e. April 9, 641.

(4) Capture of Nikiou, fifteenth year of cycle, May 13, 641.

This table shows that, if John is correctly reported, the year of the cycle he employs changes between Feb. 11 and April 9. But this is precisely the case: for the Dionysian lunar cycle began on March 23 (S. Butcher on the *Ecclesiastical Calendar*, p. 73, and Bond's *Handybook of Dates*, p. 218); and the fourteenth year of the cycle extends from March 23, 640, to March 22, 641, the fifteenth year similarly from March 23, 641, to March 22, 642. If my theory be sound, the exactitude of John's chronology is completely vindicated; not only is there nothing which requires explaining away, but our confidence in the writer's dates is greatly strengthened.

I may add that the indiction, as used in Egypt before the conquest, had become worse than useless for historical purposes, because, as Wilcken shows (*Hermes*, 19, pp. 293 seq.), instead of commencing with 1 Thoth, the Egyptian new year's day, and so corresponding with a calendar year, it was reckoned sometimes from the day of the reigning

Emperor's accession, and sometimes from various other days through the summer, on a system, or want of system, which no one can understand. There is the more reason, therefore, to credit a capable writer like John with the use of a notation of fixed and unimpeachable value.

There is one other passage in John's story which gives a cycle date and which may seem to tell against my theory. In ch. cxxi we read, 'In the second year of the lunar cycle, there arrived John from Damietta . . . who assisted the Muslims in order to prevent them from destroying the city.' This year would run from March 23, 646–7; so that the event must have happened after Manuel's rebellion, of which there is not a word in the Chronicle. Nevertheless I think the date is correct. The existence of another gap here at the end of the history is no matter for surprise. The alternative is to take the year of the indiction, which would be 643–4. But this is practically impossible, because in that year there is no record of any event which would have inclined the Arabs to the destruction of Alexandria; whereas by all accounts Manuel's revolt and the Roman reoccupation of Alexandria took place about November, 645; his forces were not crushed till some months later; and the recapture of the city by the Arabs almost certainly happened after March 23 in 646. We know too that on the recapture a great part of the city perished in the flames, and that 'Amr actually did destroy part of the walls, so that he may well have contemplated the destruction of the whole city. Moreover, Zotenberg appears in his translation to have omitted an important word; for where he renders 'Après avoir pris possession d'Alexandrie, il ('Amr) fit dessécher le canal de la ville,' Dr. Charles renders, 'When he seized the city of Alexandria, he *often* had the canal emptied'; and these words show that, in writing the paragraph in which the date occurs, the writer's mind was travelling considerably beyond the first capture, which, as we shall see, occurred in 642. The date at issue, therefore, fits in with my theory of the Dionysian lunar cycle, which I venture to regard as established.

We now come to a date of great importance and some perplexity, that of the Patriarch Cyrus' return from Constantinople to Alexandria. Cyrus had been recalled from Egypt by Heraclius about mid November, 640, after the first abortive treaty for the surrender of Babylon; and he seems to have been sent into exile. Restored to favour by Heraclius' successor, Constantine III, he was to have been sent back to Egypt, when after a reign of one hundred days the Emperor died in May, 641. Heraclonas came to the throne, but the revolt of Valentine secured in the same summer the association of the Emperor's half-brother, Constans, in the purple. About the same time Cyrus was dispatched with reinforcements to Egypt, and he was at Rhodes—probably taking in stores at the arsenal—early in September. Theodore, the commander-in-chief for Egypt, was also at Rhodes, and throwing off his allegiance to Martina at the instigation of Valentine, wished to sail for Pentapolis, but was landed at Alexandria with Cyrus at dawn on 17 Maskaram (Thoth), the feast of the Holy Cross, i.e. September 14.

Such is the narrative formed from the sadly dislocated story of John of Nikiou, and it is confirmed by the statement of Nicephorus that Cyrus was sent back by Heraclonas. But now comes in one of those unfortunate *ex post facto* prophecies, so common in Coptic writers, which would make it necessary to fix the date of Cyrus' arrival at Easter. Directly after his arrival John relates (ch. cxx) that in the celebration at the great church of Caesarion *on Easter Day* the deacon at the mass chose another chant instead of the proper one, 'This is the day which the Lord hath made,' &c. (Ps. cxviii. 24–26); the change was considered very ill-omened, and the word of the priests went abroad that Cyrus would never see another Easter. And when Cyrus subsequently died on Holy Thursday, 25 Magabit—three days before the following Easter—the people pointed to the accomplishment of the prophecy. Mr. Brooks shows with convincing clearness that 25 Magabit (Phamenoth) is March 21, not April 2 as Zotenberg reckons; and further, that as in 642 Easter Day fell on March 24, in that year, and that year only, Holy Thursday coincided with 25 Magabit; so that 'the death of Cyrus is fixed beyond possibility of doubt to Thursday, March 21, 642.' It follows that the Easter on which Cyrus is by this tale supposed to have returned was the Easter of 641, which fell on April 8.

Put briefly now John's assertions would be as follows:—

(1) Cyrus landed September 14, after the death of Heraclius, or 641.

(2) He celebrated at Easter, 641, the day of his return.

(3) He died March 21, 642.

These assertions are obviously inconsistent. Zotenberg makes no doubt that Cyrus landed on Sept. 14, and thinks it is very strange that his return should be celebrated by a solemn service seven months later. But he accepts the strangeness, and puts Cyrus' death off to 643. Mr. Brooks takes another view. Proving conclusively that Cyrus died on the Thursday before Easter, 642, he argues that Zotenberg is wrong in making the return of Theodore and the return of Cyrus coincide, and he dates the arrival of Cyrus Easter, 641. He sees the difficulty of rejecting John's statement that the return of Cyrus occurred after the death of Constantine III, and the concurrent testimony of Nicephorus; but he inclines to the view that John's text is here faulty. Finally he says, 'Whether indeed Cyrus actually returned before Easter, 641, must be left an open question, but that John means to represent him as having done so I can feel no doubt; it is of course possible that the chronology has been altered for the purpose of bringing in the prophecy' (l. c. p. 441).

I cannot quite agree with either of these views. On the one hand Zotenberg's date for Cyrus' death is absolutely untenable[1]; and on the other I think Mr. Brooks is wrong in separating the return of Cyrus from the return of Theodore, which latter event occurred on Sept. 14, 641. Mr. Brooks

[1] Pereira, in his *Vida do Abba Daniel* (p. 18), adopts Zotenberg's chronology without examination, just as he adopts Amélineau's for the date of Isaac (p. 29).

says that the two events are 'entirely distinct'; but the text reads thus: 'He (Theodore) entered Alexandria on the night of the seventeenth day of Maskaram, on the festival of the Holy Cross. And all the inhabitants of Alexandria, men and women, old and young, went out to meet the Patriarch Cyrus, rejoicing and giving thanks for the arrival of the Patriarch of Alexandria. And Theodore betook himself secretly with the Patriarch to the church of the Tabionnesiotes, and closed the door.' In face of this language it seems to me plainly impossible to suppose that the two men arrived at different times, or that, when Theodore arrived, Cyrus had already been upwards of five months in Alexandria. Moreover, if Cyrus returned at Easter, 641, other difficulties follow. Not only must we reject John's whole account of the events at Constantinople after Heraclius' death, or at least Cyrus' part in them, as well as the evidence of Nicephorus, but we must reject a further very clear statement of John's. For after relating the solemn service at the Caesarion, he says that Cyrus *then* went to Babylon. Mr. Brooks accepts this, and adds that Babylon 'had just then fallen into the hands of the Arabs,' having been captured, as he proves, April 9, 641. Yet on the next page he shows that the capitulation of Alexandria which Cyrus agreed upon with 'Amr at Babylon, and which admittedly was the object of Cyrus' visit to Babylon, took place in the month between Oct. 12 and Nov. 10, 641. How can these statements be reconciled? Moreover, we know from John and from other sources that 'Amr left Babylon almost directly after its capture, and was already at Nikiou by May 13, so that there is no room left for the visit and the negotiations of Cyrus. Moreover, to date the capitulation of Alexandria in this interval would be, as Mr. Brooks would acknowledge, to dislocate the whole chronology.

Holding then with Zotenberg that Cyrus landed with Theodore on Holy Cross Day, i.e. Sept. 14, 641, and holding with Mr. Brooks that Cyrus died the Holy Thursday following, i.e. March 21, 642, one has to reconcile this position with John's evidence. A study of the context will give the key to the problem. For on examination it becomes transparently clear that the festival at which Cyrus' return was celebrated, when the wrong chant was used, *was not Easter at all, but the Exaltation of the Cross*, i. e. the festival of the day on which, as I contend, Cyrus landed. For (1) we are told in so many words that Cyrus' sermon was all about the Cross[1]; and that he specially carried in procession from the convent of the Tabionnesiotes that portion of the Holy Rood or that Cross which the general John had brought to Cyrus before his exile. These details are quite pointless if the festival was Easter, but full of point if it was Holy Cross Day. Further, just as a few lines earlier Theodore is shown to have repaired immediately on landing to the convent of the Tabionnesiotes in company with Cyrus, so here Cyrus is represented as having come from the convent of the Tabionnesiotes to the Caesarion for the so-called Easter service. If it had been really at Easter, this coincidence about the convent is meaningless; while if, as I contend, it was the Exaltation service, the coincidence is a simple necessity. On landing he went to the convent, and from the convent he came in procession to the Caesarion. Finally, the chant 'This is the day' &c. is used on all despotic days and during the days of festival—فى الاعياد السيديه وكامل أيام لفطر—but I am unable to discover whether its liturgical use furnishes any clear evidence either for or against Easter. On the whole, however, I cannot doubt that the service which Cyrus attended on his arrival was that of the Exaltation,

[1] Zotenberg has missed the sense of the passage. He renders, 'Il fit ouvrir (?) la citerne dans laquelle se trouvait la Sainte-Croix qu'il avait reçue avant son exil du général Jean.' The query is his; but Dr. Charles' version is, 'Now he *extolled highly the well in which the holy cross had been found*, which he had received previously to his exile from the general John.' Cyrus was obviously recounting the story of the Invention of the Cross, and all doubt must vanish when it is remembered that with the Eastern Church the Invention and the Exaltation of the Cross were always celebrated on one and the same day, September 14.

or in other words that his arrival took place on September 14, 641.

But if this is so, what becomes of the prophecy? My answer is twofold: (1) that it may still stand for what it is worth. For if it was made at the Exaltation service, it referred either to the anniversary of that same festival or to the next Easter: and in either case it came true. But (2) the rational explanation is that on Cyrus' return the people saw signs of illness or change upon him, and coloured the incident of the chant with their own foreboding. 'He will never see another Easter' was the language of the forecast. Some years later the fact of his death just before Easter became the central fact in the story, the terms of which were then altered at a time when the precise details of what passed were forgotten. Because Cyrus did not see another Easter, the origin of the forecast was thus loosely assigned, regardless of chronology, to the previous Easter. Accordingly it was natural that the words 'on the day of the Holy Resurrection' should be interpolated in John's text, where indeed they look wholly out of place[1]. They are almost certainly some scribe's note, which has been embodied in the text; and if they are removed, every perplexity disappears, and the order of events which was confused and obscure becomes clear and luminous.

John's next statement now follows quite naturally. Shortly after Holy Cross Day, Cyrus repaired to Babylon to seek an interview with 'Amr, whose return from his somewhat barren campaign in the Delta is fixed by Ibn Ḳutaibah in Dhû 'l Ḳa'dah, A.H. 20 (Oct. 12—Nov. 10, 641). This would give the date of Cyrus' visit as towards the end of October; so that it would be impossible to fix the date of the treaty as early as Oct. 17 with Mr. Brooks. Even if 'Amr had reached Babylon early in Dhû 'l Ḳa'dah, which is not stated, several days must have been spent in negotiating,

[1] 'Lorsque—le jour de la Sainte-Résurrection—on commença à célébrer la messe, au lieu de chanter le psaume du jour,' &c. (Zotenberg).

and I cannot think the treaty was concluded much before the end of Dhû 'l Ḳa'dah—in fact I would place the date of capitulation arranged by Cyrus on Nov. 8 precisely. The terms included an armistice of eleven months—within which time the Roman troops were bound to evacuate the city of Alexandria. Mr. Brooks chooses Oct. 17, because it gives eleven months exactly to Sept. 17, 642, which he shows to be the date of the evacuation. But there is no reason to think that the Byzantine army would stay to the last day of the armistice, when once they were ready to sail: and if the eleven months counted from Nov. 8 by Arab reckoning, the time would expire on Sept. 29. Mr. Brooks urges that his date (Oct. 17) 'exactly agrees with the statement of Ibn 'Abd al Ḥakam that the siege lasted nine months after Heraclius' death.' Heraclius died on Sunday, Feb. 11, 641; so that even by Arab reckoning we get into November. On the other hand, Maḳrîzî says that the capture of Alexandria took place nine months and five days after the death of Heraclius. Now Feb. 11 in 641=23 Ṣafar, and nine months and five days added give 28 Dhû 'l Ḳa'dah, which corresponds to Thursday, Nov. 8.

This I think is the true date. As Mr. Brooks observes, the treaty cannot have been later than November, because Cyrus on his return to Alexandria from Babylon requested Theodore to submit it to the Emperor Heraclius, i. e. Heraclonas, whose death occurred within that month. But it is an interesting question whether the Arab writers, while correctly giving the interval between the death of Heraclius I and the surrender of Alexandria, dated his death Feb. 11, or March 11. Theophanes and Cedrenus both give, though wrongly, March 11 as the date; and possibly this may have misled Muslim historians. For it is curious to remark that if we calculate the nine months and five days from March 11, or 22 Rabi' I, we come to 27 Dhû 'l Ḥijjah, or Dec. 7. Now this Dec. 7 was a Friday and comes very close to the 1 Muḥarram (Dec. 10) which is so firmly fixed in Arab tradition as the day of the fall of Alexandria.

Mr. Brooks shows with great force that John's remaining dates give, when rightly interpreted, July 14, 642, as the date of the enthronement of Peter, the successor of Cyrus in the Melkite Patriarchate, and Sept. 17 of the same year as the date on which the city was evacuated by the imperial forces (p. 443). I may add that the return of Benjamin from his exile in Upper Egypt took place in the year 644, though probably nearer the end than the beginning[1].

But I am bound to disagree with Mr. Brooks in one or two suggestions which he makes. He quotes Eutychius, Ibn 'Abd al Ḥakam, and Makîn as concurring in fixing the duration of the siege of Alexandria at fourteen months; and he accordingly dates the commencement of the siege about the end of August, 640. He also quotes Eutychius as stating that the siege of Babylon lasted seven months, which, as Babylon fell April 9, 641, would give early in September, 640, for the commencement of the siege of Babylon: so that the two fortified places would have been besieged practically together. Now on military grounds alone this is quite impossible. 'Amr never had troops enough to invest the two fortresses at once. Nor is there any direct authority to warrant Mr. Brooks' deduction. On the contrary the authority is all against it. John himself makes 'Amr quit Babylon after the capture on April 9, 641, and seize Nikiou a month later: and if we take Jumâdā I as the mean between Rabi' I, given by Al Kindî and Yâḳût, and Jumâdā II given by the writer cited in Maḳrîzî, this exactly tallies with John's account. From Nikiou 'Amr's army marched on northwards, and it is quite possible that they established a leaguer of Alexandria at the end of June or early in July, 641. This therefore, and not August or September, 640, must be the point from which the fourteen months' siege is to be counted, if the statement of Eutychius, Ibn 'Abd al Ḥakam, and Makîn

[1] Amélineau puts the return of Benjamin in 641 (*Vie du Patriarche Isaac*, p. xiv), but this allows an exile of ten years only, instead of the thirteen agreed on by practically all the authorities.

is accepted. In other words, the period of fourteen months is to be reckoned *backwards from the actual occupation of the city* at the end of September, 642, and not from the date of the treaty in 641.

This conclusion brings us into almost exact agreement with Ṭabarî, who says that the siege lasted five months *before the capitulation*: and it would be just four-and-a-half months by Arab reckoning from July 1 to November 8. This coincidence seems to confirm both my dates, and at the same time it suggests an explanation of the widely different terms assigned by different writers for the duration of the siege. Obviously some authorities reckoned from the investment up to the treaty of surrender, others up to the actual evacuation of the city. Suyûṭî's statement which I have quoted above seems a confusion between Ṭabarî and Eutychius, and is an obvious blunder. Al Yaʿḳûbî, Balâdhurî, Ibn Khaldûn, and other writers who give three months as the duration of the siege, clearly mean that three months elapsed before the treaty; and if to this period we add the eleven months of the armistice, we again get fourteen months between the first appearance of the Arabs before the city and its occupation. Thus, although these several accounts somewhat differ, the discrepancies can be nearly reconciled and that in a striking manner.

Similarly I must demur to Mr. Brooks' assertion that 'the interval of eleven months' (i.e. the period of the armistice) 'was occupied by 'Amr in an invasion of Pentapolis.' I admit that John's text, as it stands, lends colour to this view, because the short paragraph in which the invasion is mentioned is placed just before that recounting the death of Cyrus. But there is a second account of Cyrus' death later; and the disorder of the whole chapter is so obvious that the argument from order is by no means conclusive. Military reasons surely would have forbidden 'Amr from undertaking a distant expedition before he was in possession of Alexandria, the only possible base for such an enterprise. Ibn al Athîr here is decisive as to the date, which he puts in A.H. 22: and however the other Arabic writers vary the date, they are agreed (see Eutychius and Yâḳût) that Barca was occupied a year subsequently to the capture of Alexandria. I put the expedition to Pentapolis accordingly in the winter following the evacuation of Alexandria. The Muslim year A. H. 22 began on Nov. 30 in 642; and if the expedition started soon after the turn of the year, we have an easy explanation of the fact that the date varies between A. H. 21 and A. H. 22 in the Arab authorities.

I have no doubt that 'Amr was fully occupied at Babylon, possibly in arranging for the complete subjugation or submission of Upper Egypt, certainly in reopening the canal of Trajan. From Balâdhurî we know that the year of famine in Arabia was A. H. 21 (begins Dec. 10, 641): and Ibn al Athîr says that in this year, i. e. probably August or September of 642, 'Amr sent corn to Medina by the canal which he had dug out. The canal could only be cleaned out in winter at low Nile, and could only be navigated in summer at high Nile: in the winter of 640–1 'Amr was busy with the siege of Babylon; so that the excavation must be assigned to the winter of 641–2, as Ibn al Athîr implies. The same authority quite definitely states that the date of 'Amr's invasion of Barca was A. H. 22, which ran from Nov. 30, 642, to Nov. 20, 643.

I set out the dates, then, as follows:—

(1) 'Amr's army at Al 'Arîsh . . . Dec. 12, 639.

The day comes from Ibn 'Abd al Ḥakam, but Balâdhurî, Ṭabarî, Yâḳût, and Makîn are in practical agreement about the date of the invasion.

(2) Pelusium captured . . . . . . circa Jan. 20, 640.

Eutychius, Yâḳût, &c. agree that the town was taken after a siege of one month.

(3) 'Amr's raid into the Fayûm . . May, 640.

John of Nikiou is the sole authority for this.

(4) Arrival of Arab reinforcements . June 6, 640.

This is on the authority of Severus, but doubtful.

(5) Battle of Heliopolis . . . . . July, 640:

followed by the occupation of the town of Miṣr.

(6) Siege of the fortress of Babylon begun . . . . Sept. 640.

Ibn 'Abd al Ḥakam and Eutychius agree on this.

(7) Treaty made by Cyrus, the Muḳauḳas, but denounced and disowned by Heraclius . . . . Oct. 640.

(8) Surrender of Babylon . . . . April 9, 641.

The day comes from John of Nikiou. This date represents the 'conquest of Egypt,' or rather 'conquest of Miṣr,' which the best authorities, according to Maḳrîzî, put in A. H. 20. These authorities include Ibn Ḳutaibah, Eutychius, Yâḳût, Abû 'l Maḥâsin, Ibn Kathîr, Waḳidî, Abû Ma'shar, &c., though they do not all agree in their interpretation of the phrase, some taking it to mean the fall of Babylon, others the fall of Alexandria. But Ṭabarî gives the date for the fall of Babylon as Rabi' II, A. H. 20 (March 20 to April 17, 641), and so is in complete harmony with John of Nikiou.

(9) Nikiou captured . . . . May 13, 641.
(10) Alexandria attacked . . . . . . End of June, 641.
(11) Return of Cyrus . . . . Sept. 14, 641.
(12) Capitulation of Alexandria . . Nov. 8, 641.
(13) Excavation of Trajan's canal . . Winter, 641–2.
(14) Death of Cyrus. . . . . March 21, 642.
(15) Enthronement of Cyrus' successor July 14, 642.
(16) Evacuation of Alexandria by the Romans . . . . Sept. 17, 642.
(17) Expedition to Pentapolis . . . Winter, 642–3.
(18) Return of Benjamin . . . . . . Autumn of 644.
(19) Revolt of Manuel . . . . End of 645.
(20) Recapture of Alexandria by the Arabs . . . . Summer, 646.

Though this chronology comes in an appendix to my history, I was forced to work it out before writing the narrative, as the order of events obviously depended on the settlement of dates. It has been a very difficult problem or set of problems. and I have been obliged to show the working in great detail, much as I regret the length of this essay. My table of dates differs in several material points from Mr. Brooks' list, but in closing the subject I cannot but again acknowledge the debt which students owe to his researches.

APPENDIX E

ON THE AGE OF 'AMR IBN AL 'AṢĪ

THERE is some discrepancy among the Arab authorities on the subject of 'Amr's age at the time of his death, though their agreement upon the date of that event is nearly unanimous. It may be taken for granted that he died on the Yûm al Fiṭr A. H. 43, corresponding to January 6, 664. His age at that time is variously given as ninety, seventy-three, and seventy. I believe the last number to be correct, or at any rate ninety to be wrong.

In the calculations which follow I assume that the Arab writers have reckoned by Arab years, and I therefore make a rough allowance for the difference in the length of the year on the two systems.

The ninth-century Ibn Ḳutaibah in his account of 'Amr (ed. Wüstenfeld, pp. 145 seq.) says that he died at the age of seventy-three in A. H. 42 or 43, though some say 51. He adds that his son 'Abdallah died at the age of seventy-two in A. H. 65, and was only twelve years younger than his father. Now if this were true, 'Abdallah would have been born c. 615 A. D., and therefore 'Amr about 603: consequently 'Amr at his death in 664 would have been about sixty-three. Ibn Ḳutaibah therefore is quite inconsistent.

Ibn Khallikân gives 'Amr's age as ninety, following Waḳidî.

Ibn al Ḥajar quotes Yahyâ ibn Bakîr as saying that 'Amr lived to be ninety years old, and he adds that 'Amr was seven years old when Omar was born. Suyûṭî agrees with this, saying that 'Amr died at the age of ninety in

A. H. 43. Now Omar's death took place on 26 Dhû 'l Ḥijjah, A. H. 23 = Nov. 3, 664, at the age of fifty-five. Omar therefore was born c. 590 A. D.; and if 'Amr were seven years old at that time, he was born c. 583 A. D. In other words 'Amr was not ninety but eighty when he died. There is, however, some discrepancy about Omar's age at death. Ibn Ḳutaibah (p. 91), while strongly affirming that fifty-five is the correct age, alleges that Waḳidî on the authority of 'Âmir ibn Sa'd gives sixty-three. If the age of sixty-three be taken, Omar's birth would fall c. 682 and 'Amr's c. 575 A. D.; and 'Amr in 664 would be well over ninety by Arab reckoning. It follows also that at the time of the conquest he would be sixty-four or sixty-five by European reckoning. This seems very improbable.

Nawawî, however, who affirms that the 'Îd al Fiṭr of A. H. 43 is the right date for 'Amr's death against all others which are assigned for it, also avers that 'Amr's age at death was seventy (ed. Wüstenfeld, p. 478). This would place 'Amr's birth about the year 595, and would make him consequently some forty-four years old at the time of the conquest.

We have therefore to choose between the two statements that the commander of the Arab forces at the time of the invasion was forty-four and that he was sixty-four. *A priori* there cannot be much doubt on the subject. A fiery and impetuous character could scarcely have been predicated of a man so far beyond middle life, nor can 'Amr be imagined to have played the part he did, both during the conquest and subsequently in Egypt and in Syria, at the more advanced age. If, for example, 'Amr was ninety at the end of 663, he was about eighty-five at the battle of Siffîn in 658—a battle in which he is known to have shown the most amazing activity and personal prowess. This alone is something like a *reductio ad absurdum* of the statement. But it is extremely easy to see how it arose. For nothing is simpler than to mistake seventy for ninety in copying in the Arabic, and nothing is more natural than that سبعين or seventy should have been corrupted into تسعين or ninety. And it is the later authorities who give the higher number. We may conclude then that 'Amr died at the age of seventy.

APPENDIX F

ON THE DATES OF THE COPTIC PATRIARCHS AFTER BENJAMIN IN THE SEVENTH CENTURY

QUESTIONS connected with the conquest made it necessary at times to refer to the successors of Benjamin, and some importance attaches to their chronology. Not the least of such questions is the date at which John of Nikiou's history was written. The evidence as usual is indirect, but it turns mainly on the date of the Patriarch Isaac, at whose consecration John was present. Isaac was third in succession from Benjamin, the two intervening Patriarchs being Agatho and John of Samanûd: but as it seems possible to ascertain the date of Isaac's consecration exactly, it will be easier from that fixed point to work backwards for the others.

The chief source of information is the Coptic 'Life of Isaac' which has been published with a translation by Amélineau (*Histoire du Patriarche Copte Isaac*). The writer in an interesting preface asserts that the Coptic document merely avers that Isaac died on 9 Athor (which is Nov. 5, not Nov. 6 as stated): 'À cette date se bornent toutes les indications chronologiques, c'est-à-dire qu'elle ne nous apprend absolument rien.' But because Makîn gives A. H. 69 as the year of his death, Amélineau concludes that Isaac died Nov. 6, 688. Von Gutschmid gives the date Nov. 5, 692.

But Amélineau is wrong in saying that the Coptic document gives no other indication for the chronology. He has overlooked a very material statement. For on p. 50 we read that Isaac was consecrated 'on 8 Khoiak, *which was a Sunday'*—the proper day for the ceremony. Now about this period the 8 Khoiak fell on a Sunday only in the years 684 and 690: of these years 684 is quite impossible, consequently Isaac was consecrated on 8 Khoiak (or Dec. 4), 690. This then is the date at which John of Nikiou was present. Severus makes the term of Isaac's pontificate vary between two years nine months and three years in different MSS.; but knowing that Isaac died on Nov. 5, if we now assign Nov. 5, 693, as the date of Isaac's death, we get a term of two years eleven months, which is the exact term assigned by Makrîzî.

It would be easy to follow Amélineau's preface, and to show how entirely he has mistaken the period at which Isaac was born, and which he places before the Arab conquest. Indeed he makes Isaac about eighteen at the time of the conquest (which he puts in 640), and dates his birth 622. To this conclusion he is largely led by the fact that Isaac as a boy was placed with a relative Menesôn, who was ⲡⲭⲁⲣⲧⲟⲗⲁⲣⲓⲟⲥ ϧⲁ ⲣⲁⲧϥ ⲛⲅⲉⲱⲣⲅⲓⲟⲥ ⲉϥⲟⲓ ⲛⲉⲡⲁⲣⲭⲟⲥ ⲉϯⲭⲱⲣⲁ ⲛⲧⲉ ⲭⲏⲙⲓ, or registrar to George, eparch of the land of Egypt. This title is distinctly curious, as showing how the forms of Byzantine government persisted after the conquest: but that they did so remain is not for a moment in doubt, inasmuch as in the same document reference is made to an official who is actually called ⲡⲓⲁⲩⲅⲟⲩⲥⲧⲁⲗⲓⲟⲥ, or the Augustal (p. 73), and that in direct connexion with the 'king of the Saracens,' 'Abd al 'Azîz, who is mentioned by name a few pages earlier (pp. 43 and 64). The occurrence of the title therefore is far from proving that Isaac's boyhood was spent under Byzantine rule. Indeed his flight into the desert at a time when he was hardly out of his boyhood is conclusively proved to have taken place after the conquest, because we find his parents directly afterwards consulting a Coptic Archbishop at Alexandria. This cannot have happened between the years 631 and 644, since there was no Coptic Archbishop in the city during that period: nor can it have been previous to 631, because soon after his flight Isaac is found talking to a country priest, of whom, the story says (p. 12), 'many testify that he was a confessor, and had been set before the judgement-seat of Cyrus, and had received many stripes for the confession of the faith'[1]; and this language proves that the persecution of Cyrus, which lasted from 631 to 641, was over. It follows that the parents' appeal to the Archbishop must have been subsequent to 644, and consequently that the Archbishop was Benjamin.

There is little or nothing to show in what decade this appeal took place, about 650 or 660 or 670. I incline to the first decade, because I attach weight to the continual assertions of Isaac's youth — therein disagreeing with Amélineau, who for example sees no difficulty in interpreting 'jeune garçon' as a middle-aged man, although it is given in strict antithesis to 'vieillard' (pp. 25–6). If the period in question were about 657, Isaac was born about 640, and was about 53 when he died. The Patriarch to whom he acted as secretary for a time was doubtless Agatho, though the only Patriarch mentioned by name is John of Samanûd (p. 42), who nominated Isaac to the succession. I may further note that if Amélineau's chronology were right, i. e. if Isaac had been born in 622, then the ten years of the great persecution, i. e. 631 to 641, would coincide with Isaac's ninth to nineteenth year. But during the whole of this time, as I have said, there was no Coptic Archbishop at Alexandria, as the story demands: whereas if, as I contend, Isaac was born circa 640, and fled into the desert circa 657, then the story runs naturally; because Benjamin had been back in Alexandria for thirteen years at that date—during in fact the greater part of Isaac's boyhood.

Having now fixed the date of Isaac's consecration and death, we know that his predecessor John of Samanûd, after a reign of nine years, died on a certain 1 Khoiak, or Nov. 27. This would naturally be Nov. 27, 690; but we

[1] Amélineau's translation, 'qu'on le fit monter sur le tribunal de Cyrus,' does not bring out the pluperfect form of the Coptic original, ⲉⲁⲩⲧⲁϩⲟϥ, as Mr. Crum tells me.

should have to admit that Isaac was consecrated exactly a week after the death of his predecessor, whereas the Coptic Biography contains a long account of the dissensions which followed on the vacancy, and the efforts made to secure the election of one George, who claimed to have been rightfully nominated. The archdeacon, however, forbade the consecration of George, and subsequently on the arrival of a commission from the Saracen ruler, the bishops were summoned to lay the matter before him at Babylon. George's life failed to bear the necessary scrutiny: people flocked from all parts of the country to hear 'Abd al 'Azîz's decision: and when it was given at their wish in favour of Isaac, there were dances and rejoicings from Babylon to Alexandria (pp. 44–9). It is obvious that all this must have taken a long time: so that we are forced, while maintaining that Isaac was enthroned on 8 Khoiak, 690, to throw back the death of John of Samanûd to 1 Khoiak (or Nov. 27), 689. In other words, there was a year's vacancy. This inference is confirmed by the *Chronicon Orientale*, which asserts that John died on 1 Khoiak which was a Saturday. We have seen that in 690 8 Khoiak was Sunday; therefore 1 Khoiak in that year was also Sunday: but 1 Khoiak fell on a Saturday, as required, in 689.

Allowing now nine years to John's pontificate, we get back to 680 for its commencement. His predecessor Agatho died on Oct. 13, so that the term corresponds very closely. John died therefore on Oct. 13, 680, after a period of office which is given as nineteen years. But we have already seen that Benjamin died on 8 Tûbah, or Jan. 3, 662; and the interval amounts to eighteen years and something under ten months—a close approximation. The chronology thus dovetails with nicety.

The table of chronology may now be set out. I have followed in the main the data given by Severus; and these taken in conjunction with Isaac's Biography and other authorities seem to fit so well together as almost to preclude the chance of error. Von Gutschmid, while agreeing on the dates for the death of Benjamin and the death of Agatho, differs in putting the death of John of Samanûd on May 2, 689 (*Kleine Schriften*, ii. 500), for which there is not adequate authority: moreover, he puts the consecration of Isaac in Feb. 690, and his death Nov. 5, 692—dates which are conclusively refuted by the Coptic Biography. The true dates seem to stand as follows:—

Patriarch.	Date of Consecration.	Term of office.	Date of death.
Benjamin . . .	Jan. 623 .	39 years .	Jan. 3, 662.
Agatho	Jan. 662 .	19 " .	Oct. 13, 680.
John of Samanûd	Oct. 680 .	9 " .	Nov. 27, 689.
	(One year's vacancy.)		
Isaac	Dec. 4, 690	3 " .	Nov. 5, 693.
Simon	Jan. 694 .	7½ " .	July 18, 701.

The dates for Simon, and the explanation of the delay in his appointment, may be found in Renaudot.

INDEX

THE TREATY OF MIṢR IN ṬABARĪ

AN ESSAY IN HISTORICAL CRITICISM

BY

A. J. BUTLER, D.Litt.

FELLOW OF BRASENOSE COLLEGE

OXFORD

AT THE CLARENDON PRESS

CHIEF REFERENCES AND ABBREVIATIONS

1. Ṭabarī, *Annales*. Ed. De Goeje. (Lugd. Bat., 1879, &c. 8vo.) . . . . *De Goeje.*
2. *The First Mohammadan Treaties with Christians*. By Stanley Lane-Poole, in *Proceedings of the Royal Irish Academy*. Vol. XXIV. Sec. C, no. 13 . . *P.R.I.A.*
3. *Al Maḳrīzī: Livre des Admonitions etc. ou Description Historique et Topographique de l'Égypte*: traduit par M. Paul Casanova: 3me partie. (*Mémoires de l'Institut Français d'Archéologie Orientale du Caire*: Tome iii, 1906.) . . . *Casanova.*
4. *Annali dell' Islam* per Leone Caetani, Principe di Teano. t. iv. (Milano, 1911) fol. . . . . *Caetani.*
5. *History of the Patriarchs of the Coptic Church* in *Patrologia Orientalis*. t. i, fasc. 4 . *Hist. Pat.*
6. *The Churches and Monasteries of Egypt*. Evetts and Butler (Anecdota Oxoniensia). Oxford, 1895 . . . . . . *Abū Ṣāliḥ.*
7. *The Arab Conquest of Egypt*. By A. J. Butler. (Oxford, 1902.) . . . . . *Arab Conquest.*

THE TREATY OF MIṢR IN ṬABARĪ

In returning to the very obscure and difficult subject of the Mohammedan conquest of Egypt, I desire generally to correct any important error proved against my former work [1] by well-founded criticism, to deal with, and if possible overthrow, certain objections which seem to be ill-founded, and to set out revised conclusions based on later reflection and research.

But the scope of this essay must be limited: and I cannot hope or pretend to give here such a list of corrections and additions as would be required if a second edition of *Arab Conquest* were demanded. No such demand is likely to come in my lifetime: and, the wider field of travel being forbidden, all I can do is to select some area which seems rich in opportunities for the kind of excursion which I propose. Such an area seems to be provided by the traditions which Ṭabarī has recorded in his great work, and to which I have not hitherto devoted the detailed study which possibly they merit, and in particular by the Treaty of Miṣr.[2]

[1] *The Arab Conquest of Egypt.* Oxford, Clarendon Press, 1902.

[2] The reference is to de Goeje's well-known edition of Ṭabarī. I have been justly criticized for using Zotenberg's edition, and that

It may tend to clearness if these various traditions—or the chief of them—are set out in the order of Ṭabarī, although that does not correspond to any order of chronology. As a rule a rough paraphrase or mere outline will suffice: where questions of importance arise, a literal translation will be given: and for the actual treaty the Arabic text must accompany its English rendering. The traditions are mainly seven in number—A, B, C, D, E, F, G—which I will give, each with its exordium.

A. *Ibn Isḥāḳ says, as said Ibn Ḥumaid, that Salamah said on his authority, that:*

Omar after subjugating the whole of Syria wrote to 'Amr ibn al 'Aṣī to march to Egypt with his army. So he set out, and captured Bāb al Yūn (Babylon) in the year A.H. 20. There is a difference of opinion concerning the date of the taking of Alexandria, some giving the year as A.H. 25.

B.[1] *Ibn Ḥumaid says that Salamah says thus, on the authority of Ibn Isḥāḳ, who says that Al Ḳāsim (an Egyptian) ibn Ḳuzman told him—on the authority of Ziyād ibn Jazū, who said he was in 'Amr's army when he took Miṣr and Alexandria—the following story:*

We took Alexandria in the Caliphate of Othman in the year A.H. 21 or 22.

error will not be here repeated: nor would it avail to explain the reason for using Zotenberg originally.

[1] De Goeje, pp. 2580–83. Ibn Ḥumaid died 248 A.H., and Salamah after 190 A.H.

After the capture of Bāb al Yūn we captured gradually those villages of the Delta which were between us and Alexandria, one after another, till we reached Balhīb. Our prisoners had already reached Mecca, Medina, and Yemen at the time when we reached Balhīb: when the commander of Alexandria sent to 'Amr, saying, 'I have already paid tribute to Persian and Roman,[1] whom I hate more than you Arabs. I will pay you tribute, if you please, provided that you restore the prisoners of Egypt whom you have taken.'

'Amr answered, proposing in effect an armistice[2] till he could consult Omar and get his reply upon the question: and this was agreed. They stayed at Balhīb till Omar's answer came, when 'Amr read it out. It refused to restore the prisoners who were already in Arab lands, as impracticable, but offered to allow all prisoners in 'Amr's custody a free choice between Christianity and Islam. These terms were accepted by the commander of Alexandria.

Thereupon the captives were all mustered, and each one had to pronounce in presence of the Arab army and a large gathering of Christians. Every decision was followed by shouts on one side or the other, the Arab cheers being louder than the cheers

[1] How could any Roman governor of Alexandria speak of having paid tribute to the Romans? That would imply that he was in revolt against the emperor. There is further no evidence whatever to connect any one occupying the position of governor or commander at this time with the period of Persian domination in Egypt.

[2] This may be a reminiscence of the eleven months' armistice recorded by John of Nikiou.

when a village is taken. The Arabs claimed that the great majority chose Islam.

Al Ḳāsim (the contemporary soldier) says: 'Among the prisoners was 'Abdallah ibn 'Abd ar Raḥmān abū Maryām, who in my lifetime became chief of the Banū Zubaid. When we gave him the choice between Islam and Christianity, though his father, mother, and brothers were among the Christians, he chose Islam, and we transferred him to us. Then his father, mother, and brothers sprang out upon him, assailing us with abuse, and they tore his garments. But he became our chief, as you may see this day.'

'After this Alexandria surrendered and we entered it. . . . He who thinks otherwise, viz. that Alexandria and the cities round about were not brought under tribute, and that there was no treaty with the inhabitants, by Allah he is a liar.'

Note. This tradition claims to be derived from a soldier of the conquest. It insists that Alexandria was surrendered under treaty, and it has some points of correspondence with the history of John of Nikiou. But it begins with the capture of Babylon and says nothing about any treaty there.

C.[1] *Ṭabarī writes that Saif says in the letter which As Sarī wrote to me (Ṭabarī) that Shu'aib informed him on [Ibn Isḥāḳ's] authority and that of Ar Rabīa' and that of Abū 'Uthmān and that of Abū Hārithah*, as follows:

[1] De Goeje, p. 2584.

Omar remained at Jerusalem after making the treaty of peace there, and sent ʻAmr to Egypt. He also sent Zubair in support.

Note. Here the authorities go back from Sarī, contemporary with Ṭabarī, to Abū ʻUthmān, who died some seventy to eighty years after the subjugation of Egypt. It is obvious that very many links in this chain of tradition are missing: nor is there anything to show what documentary evidence, if any, was available to Sarī when he made his communication in writing, or to what extent he relied on mere oral tradition.

D. *As Sarī has written to me on the authority of of Shuʻaib on the authority of Saif, who says Abū ʻUthmān has told us on the authority of Khālid ibn Miʻdān and ʻUbādah,*[1] as follows:

"ʻAmr set out to Egypt after Omar returned to Medina,[2] and marched till he came to Bāb al Yūn. Zubair followed, and they joined forces. Here Abū Maryām, the katholikos of Miṣr, met them, with him being the bishop [Abū Maryām] and the officials, he [the katholicos] having been sent by Al Muḳauḳis to protect their country.'

There was fighting then between these people and ʻAmr, who proposed a parley, details of which are given by Ṭabarī.[3] But the dialogue is too lengthy for useful quotation, and the next words seem to

[1] Khālid died 102 or 103 A.H., and ʻUbādah 118 A.H.

[2] This obviously disagrees with C.

[3] pp. 2585–6.

record a story of treachery as follows: 'Quite suddenly a raid was made on 'Amr and Zubair at night by Farkab. 'Amr was prepared, and met him: he and all his followers were killed.' Ibn al Athīr says 'the tribune was killed', which implies that Farkab was the military tribune.[1] But the story is very confused, and continues thus:

''Amr and Zubair marched straight for 'Ain Shams: in it were a large number of them (the enemy). 'Amr sent Abrahah ibn as Sabbāḥ to Al Faramā, and 'Aūf ibn Mālik to Alexandria, and he encamped against it. Then each of them said to the men of his city, "If you capitulate, you shall have the status of protection at our hands,"'[2]—and so forth.

Note. This tradition like the last appears to hang upon the evidence of Ṭabarī's contemporary Sarī, and a weak chain behind him. The same is true of the following traditions, E and F.

E. *As Sarī has written to me (Ṭabarī) on the authority of Shu'aib, on the authority of Saif, on the authority of Abū 'Uthmān and Abū Hārithah, that these two said as follows:*

'When 'Amr encamped against the people at 'Ain Shams, the rule was between the Copts and the Nubians. Zubair came with him. Then said the people of Miṣr to their king, "Why do you go out

[1] Ibn al Athīr distinctly says that the tribune was called *Arṭabūn*, which, as I have shown, should be read *Aretion*. *Arab Conquest*, p. 215, n. 2.

[2] The parley with these two cities by envoys sent during the Arab march to Babylon is clearly legendary.

against a people which has smitten Chosroes and Caesar (Heraclius) and vanquished them in their countries? Make terms with the people and get a treaty from them and do not expose yourself to them nor us to them."'

'And this was on the fourth day.'

What is meant by the fourth day is not clear: probably the fourth day of a truce, which seems to be referred to above (pp. 2586–7). Fighting followed: Zubair mounted the wall of the fortress and descended among them by force, while the people from within the fortress are described as issuing out of the gate to make terms with 'Amr.

The terms of the treaty of peace are now given textually: and—

'All the people of Miṣr accepted this treaty, and the horses were collected: 'Amr founded Fusṭāṭ, and the Muslims stayed there. Abū Maryam and Abū Maryām appeared and spoke to 'Amr about the prisoners captured after the battle' (? Heliopolis).

Then follows the well-known story of the Muslim meal and the Egyptian banquet, with other matter neither clear nor important.

F. *As Sarī*[1] *has written to me on the authority of Shu'aib on the authority of Saif on the authority of Abū Sa'īd ar Rabīa' ibn an Numān on the authority of 'Amr ibn Shu'aib*, as follows:

'When 'Amr and Al Muḳauḳis met at 'Ain Shams and their cavalry began to fight', there were signs of insubordination in the Muslim ranks, and the Muslims

[1] p. 2592.

were very hard pressed for a while, though in the end they won a complete victory. . . . 'Miṣr was captured during the first Rabīʿ in the year 16 and the sovereignty of Islam rose therein.'

G. *ʿAlī ibn Saḥl*[1] *informs me saying, Al Walīd ibn Muslim has related that Ibn Lahīʿah told him on the authority of Yazīd ibn Ḥabīb that:*

'When the Muslims had conquered Egypt, they sent an expedition to Egyptian Nubia':—and the expedition clearly was a failure.

[1] p. 2593.

HAVING now sketched out the main traditions with which we are concerned, I come to a discussion of the treaty. The tradition in which it occurs depends on the letter of Ṭabarī's contemporary Sarī, who got it from Shu'aib, Shu'aib from Saif (who died about 180 A. H.), and he from Abū 'Uthmān (who died about 100 A. H.). But these narrators can hardly have repeated the text of the treaty, which Sarī professes to give and which he may have got from an independent source. It is even possible that he or some informant may have seen an original document or a copy. On the other hand, there are certain obscurities and difficulties, both in the form and in the substance of the treaty, which suggest that it has suffered from a process of handing down, whether by word of mouth or by written record. Dr. Stanley Lane-Poole thinks that, broadly speaking, the treaty bears on its face the seal of its own authenticity: but the words giving the total of the poll-tax and the method of its payment, as well as some other points, seem by their uncertainty to denote at least the hand of a copyist. We know that some early treaties were preserved: Omar is said to have had a box full of them. They were probably executed in duplicate, so that one copy at least remained with the conquered people: and in this case either the original or a copy may conceivably have been seen by Ṭabarī, or rather by Sarī his informant, 300 years later. But it requires a somewhat robust faith to believe, as Dr. Lane-Poole seems to believe, in the verbal inspiration of the text.

However, if the Treaty of Miṣr is genuine, I must grant that Ṭabarī associates it very closely with the fall of Babylon and not with the surrender of Alexandria. Consequently, if Ṭabarī is right, I was wrong, as Dr. Lane-Poole alleges,[1] in calling it the Treaty of Alexandria and in identifying it with the very important Treaty of Alexandria given by John of Nikiou.

I propose, however, to reserve this question of the genuineness of the treaty in Ṭabarī to a later stage in the argument: to take Ṭabarī's version of events as it stands: and to discuss

i. The time and place of the treaty:
ii. The parties to the treaty:
iii. The meaning of the treaty:
iv. The authenticity of the treaty:
and v. The identity of Al Muḳauḳis.

I. *The moment at which the treaty was made and the place.*

On these matters there is little room for doubt, if Ṭabarī is to be believed. Ṭabarī's story is as follows. There had been at some point a parley between the belligerents and a truce for four or five days, which ended in the decision of the Romans to reject the Muslim terms: and there is some evidence that the truce was broken on the fourth day treacherously. Fighting was renewed: but how long the siege lasted after this rupture Ṭabarī does not record. Victory, however, determined in favour of the Arabs at a moment when Zubair scaled the walls and

[1] *P.R.I.A.*, p. 240.

fought his way down into the fortress. At the same moment tokens of surrender had been made, and some of the defenders were on their way out to arrange a capitulation. Zubair and his victorious following joined the envoys of the garrison, and accompanied them through the fortress gate to 'Amr's presence. Thereupon the brief but solemn treaty of peace was drawn up and attested by Zubair himself and his two sons, 'Abdallah and Muḥammad. Such is the somewhat unconvincing story.

There can be no question that the incident is described as relating to the surrender of the Castle of Babylon or Ḳaṣr ash Shama'. Dr. Lane-Poole in his account of the matter remarks [1] that Ṭabarī does not name the fortress or city wall which Zubair scaled. True; but other Muslim writers leave no shadow of doubt. They name the fortress Babylon: they give the point at which the assault was made: and Zubair's scaling-ladder was long preserved at Fusṭāṭ as a relic of the siege. Moreover, Dr. Lane-Poole himself, in citing Maḳrīzī's account, says [2]:—'Fighting with the garrison of Babylon was accordingly renewed: but finally Al Muḳauḳis persuaded the people that resistance was hopeless, and 'Amr's terms were accepted.' He urges, however, that 'the capture of the fort, الحصن, must be distinguished from the fall of the castle, القصر, i.e. Babylon. He bases this conclusion upon the supposed discrepancy between the date given by John of Nikiou for the surrender of the fortress of Babylon, i.e. 9 April, 641 (which date is unimpeachable), and Maḳrīzī's statement that the negotiations between

[1] *P.R.I.A.*, p. 242. [2] *P.R.I.A.*, p. 245.

'Amr and Al Muḳauḳis began at Rauḍah at the time of high Nile, which would be about six months earlier. But I think the discrepancy does not lie here. We know that the negotiations failed and the war continued: but there is no warrant for compressing the duration of the renewed struggle into a few days instead of six months. The endeavour is made in order to identify the negotiations as described by Maḳrīzī with the four days' truce mentioned by Ṭabarī. But this truce almost certainly occurred shortly after the arrival of the reinforcements under Zubair.[1] It is true that just before this event the fact is recorded that ''Amr set out for Egypt and marched till he came to Bāb al Yūn': but this, taken as a general description of the march, is not inconsistent with the insertion of detail which follows, nor with the fact (which seems established) that Zubair joined 'Amr's army before it had reached Babylon. I therefore regard this parley and the four days' truce as a quite distinct incident from the Rauḍah negotiations at the time of high Nile, and as having occurred some weeks earlier, and prior to 'Amr's arrival at Babylon. So I disagree with Dr. Lane-Poole's statement where he says[2]: 'According to Ṭabarī, after the Arabs had reached Babylon, there came to meet them on the part of Al Muḳauḳis a patriarch (*gāthalīḳ* catholicus) and a bishop. . . . This was before reinforcements had reached the Muslims.' On the contrary, Ṭabarī says[3]: 'Zubair followed, and they joined forces. *Here* Abū Maryam, the katholikos of Miṣr, met them,

[1] Trad. D above, pp. 11–12. [2] *P.R.I.A.*, p. 241.
[3] De Goeje, p. 2584.

with him being the bishop,' and again [1] "'Amr and Zubair marched straight for 'Ain Shams'.

But the accounts, both in Ṭabarī and in Maḳrīzī, are so wanting in clearness and precision that the construction of any continuous narrative or orderly sequence of events must admittedly be largely a matter of remote inference or even conjecture.

Dr. Lane-Poole, however, in order to uphold his theory has to connect the treaty, not with the fall of Babylon, i.e. Ḳaṣr ash Shama', but with the fall of a fort on the ridge of rocky ground to the south, on which, according to Strabo, there stood in his day a fort originally erected by the Persians some 500 years earlier. This attempt to deprive Trajan's fortress of its well-known name of Babylon assumes the survival of the old original Persian fort in the seventh century, an assumption which rests upon no proof whatever, but is contradicted by explicit evidence of the Arab historians. It might suffice to say that Abu 'l Maḥāsin definitely calls the fortress Ḳaṣr ash Shama',[2] while Maḳrīzī agrees with other writers in stating that the fortress was opposite the island of Rauḍah, as Dr. Lane-Poole himself admits.[3] No other fortress but Trajan's (or Ḳaṣr ash Shama') corresponds in any way with this description, and the suggested identification of the fortress in Ṭabarī with the *Istabl Antār* [4] is altogether impossible. Indeed, it is a mistake into which no one familiar

[1] De Goeje, p. 2586.

[2] *Annales*, edd. Juynboll et Matthes, vol. i, p. 8 (Lugd. Bat., 1855–61).

[3] *P.R.I.A.*, p. 244.

[4] This identification occurs in Dr. Lane-Poole's *Cairo Fifty Years Ago*, pp. 146–7, to which he refers (Murray, 1896).

with the topography of the region could possibly fall; and Lane's evidence proves at most the existence of a Roman embankment at the foot of the ridge. There is not a single trace of any ancient building upon the ridge. Severus, too, expressly says[1]: 'The Arabs . . . arrived at a fortress built of stone, situated between Upper Egypt and the Delta and called Babylon. . . . Then the Arabs called that place, namely the fortress, Bablūn al Fusṭāṭ and that is its name to this day.' Severus uses the terms قصر and حصن indifferently, and I venture to say that there is no warrant whatever for distinguishing them. Dr. Lane-Poole says[2]: 'The capture of the fort, الحصن, must evidently be distinguished from the fall of the castle القصر. . . . Maḳrīzī mentions another fortress besides Ḳaṣr ash Shamaʿ . . . and this other fortress which was situated on a rocky hill to the south-east of Ḳaṣr ash Shamaʿ, and was within the city, was particularly called the fortress or palace قصر of Babylon.' What is the authority for this statement? It may rest on the mistaken evidence of Al Kuḍāʿī, which Maḳrīzī cites, but admits to be at variance with the much higher authority of Ibn ʿAbd al Ḥakam.[3]

But M. Casanova, in his learned edition of Maḳrīzī lends countenance to a theory at once similar and dissimilar to that of Dr. Lane-Poole. Commenting on the statement in Maḳrīzī's text that the Muslims laid siege to Bāb al Yūn, in which were Romans, Copts, and the Muḳauḳis, Casanova

[1] Brit. Mus. MS., 26100, p. 105.
[2] *P. R. I. A.*, p. 245.
[3] See M. Casanova's *Maḳrīzī*, part iii, p. 109 (Imprimerie de l'Institut Français au Caire, 1906).

writes :—'Cette tradition, en effet, semble en contradiction avec la première. Mais il est à remarquer qu'il s'agit cette fois de Bāb alioûn, et puisque ce nom subsiste encore, il faut en conclure qu'il y a eu deux sièges distincts, celui de Ḳaṣr ach Cham' et celui de Bāb alioûn'[1]: and he goes on to say that Strabo's description excludes the Ḳaṣr ash Shama', while it fits the height of the modern Bablûn, 'qui est très escarpée du côté du Nil', thus assuming the existence of the old fort at the conquest. So he makes two sieges and two forts: but whereas Dr. Lane-Poole says that the ḥiṣn was Ḳaṣr ash Shama', while the ḳaṣr was on the rocky ridge, Casanova says that the ḥiṣn was the fortified enclosure of the town, while 'le ḳaṣr désigne tout particulièrement la forteresse de Babylone'. But I confess that I find his reasoning hard to follow. For at one moment he says that Ḳaṣr ash Shama', '*qui représentait la ville*, fut prise de vive force,' and the next that 'le ḥiṣn répondrait mieux à la ville même': and when he charges me with failing to see the difference between the two forts[2] and the two Arab traditions, and of error in describing Ḳaṣr ash Shama' as 'the Roman fortress of Babylon', I stand not only impenitent but more convinced than ever that my description is correct, that the name Babylon was applied to Ḳaṣr ash Shama' as well as to the town of Miṣr, that Bāb al Yūn or Bāb aliūn is a mere blunder for 'Babylon',

[1] Casanova, p. 121 n.

[2] Casanova, p. 121 n. I pointed out the difference between Strabo's fort and Ḳaṣr ash Shama' built by Trajan, at least twenty years before Casanova's work was published, viz., in my *Ancient Coptic Churches*, vol. i, pp. 171–4. The charge against me therefore is not very well founded.

and that in all the hazy and confused statements about the fortress made by the Arab historians, the reference is to Ḳaṣr ash Shama' and not to the early Persian fort, *of which no trace remained at the conquest.*

For Maḳrīzī himself definitely calls the fortress ḥiṣn.[1] He identifies the site, rightly or wrongly, with that of an early Persian fort, which, he says, lay in ruins 500 years before the Romans rebuilt it.[2] Moreover, he quotes Ibn 'Abd al Ḥakam in the same connexion as saying that 'the Persians founded the fortress (ḥiṣn) which is to-day at Fusṭāṭ Miṣr': and he further cites Al Ḳuḍā'ī as remarking of the Ḳaṣr ash Shama' that it was begun by the Persians, but finished by the Romans, *who held it till the Arab conquest.*

Now two things are clear from this: (1) that at the date of the conquest, i.e. some seven centuries after Strabo's time, all trace of the original Persian fort had vanished, and (2) that Arab writers identify, however mistakenly, the site of the two fortresses, the Persian and the Roman, and not only fail to distinguish them, but are not conscious that any question of a distinction could arise. That Zubair's exploit is connected with Ḳaṣr ash Shama' by them, is certain: and if, as Casanova urges, the fortress in question were Strabo's fortress on the steep ridge,

[1] Casanova, p. 121.

[2] This, of course, is wrong. Something at least of the old Persian fort survived in Strabo's time, and Ḳaṣr ash Shama' was built by Trajan. Yet it is quite possible, indeed very probable, that Trajan found Persian remains, whether of temple or fort, on the site of Ḳaṣr ash Shama', as the stories of Murtaḍī and Yāḳūt indicate.

the incident of 'Ubādah,[1] which turns on Roman horsemen issuing from the fortress gate and being chased back to it, would be impossible even of invention—it would be too ludicrous. Maḳrīzī, however, not only connects the fortress of the conquest with the island of the arsenal or Rauḍah, but he says that boats were moored against this fortress. It is absolutely impossible to apply such a description to any fortress but Ḳaṣr ash Shama': [2] that it was true of Ḳaṣr ash Shama' is proved by the whole tenor of the Arab stories of the siege, and the proof has been confirmed and rendered visible lately by the excavations which have revealed the channel or waterway and small quay at the very foot of the Iron Gate of the fortress. Lastly, I would urge that even if a detached fort existed on the ridge, the capture of such a secondary position could not be the determining factor in the operations round Miṣr, so long as the huge and immensely powerful fortress erected by Trajan—the fortress in which the Roman commander had his head-quarters—still defied the Muslim arms.

Both the military exigencies of the case, therefore, and the records of the Arab historians point to Ḳaṣr ash Shama' as that castle of Babylon which they represent as capitulating under the Treaty of Miṣr. Indeed the evidence of their intention is so

[1] Casanova, p. 119.

[2] Casanova remarks, in objecting to my contention :—'Il serait étrange qu'une forteresse fût en plaine et immédiatement dominée par une hauteur.' To this I reply, that the strangeness does not alter the fact, and that it would be much more strange if boats were moored to a fortress on the top of a hill.

overwhelming, that any other theory is untenable: although I must assert with emphasis that the question what the Arab historians intended to represent is totally different from the question whether their representation of the facts is correct. And while I think Ṭabarī's opinion very clear, I think it no less mistaken, as will be shown.

II. *The Parties to the Treaty.*

Granted that the treaty is genuine, it bears its own witness to the fact that it was made between 'Amr, the commander of the Arab forces, and the people of Miṣr in general.

It is also clear that, according to Ṭabarī, the treaty was made on the side of the people of Miṣr by plenipotentiaries who came out of the fortress, in other words by the defenders of the fortress. Unfortunately in the early Muslim treaties it was not the practice for both parties to set their hand to the instrument. The signing, sealing, and delivering was all done by the Muslims: and the treaty is rather a grant of security and protection conditional upon terms to be observed than a deed of mutual covenants solemnly entered into and executed between two parties. Hence in this case there is nothing in the document to show who actually negotiated the treaty on behalf of the people of Miṣr, and the question can only be settled by external evidence.

Dr. Lane-Poole says boldly:[1] 'It is abundantly evident that this is a treaty with the Copts, not with the Romans. . . . The people of Miṣr, not the Roman army of occupation, still less the emperor

[1] *P.R.I.A.*, p. 239.

Heraclius, were the contracting parties on the other side. As there is no indication in the treaty itself that the Romans were consulted in the matter, we must conclude that this treaty was made behind their backs; that it was a compact between the Copts and the Arabs without the authority of the Roman garrison, though these last had the option of accepting the same terms.' Again,[1] 'It was, as is evident, a treaty with the Copts of the city of Miṣr as against the Romans:' once more:[2] 'Ṭabarī's story fits perfectly with the contents of the treaty, which is thus shown to be a treaty with the Egyptian people against the wish of the Roman army of occupation:' and finally,[3] 'In each story' (i.e. Ṭabarī's and Maḳrīzī's) 'it is essentially a treaty with the Copts, not with the Romans.'

Now what is the justification for all this? It is neither more nor less than the fact that to the *people of Miṣr* was conveyed the grant of security under the treaty. Starting with that fact, Dr. Lane-Poole lays down the proposition that the people of Miṣr were Copts: he then argues that the Copts were hostile to the Romans, and that consequently the treaty was made in favour of the Copts: and he concludes that the treaty, being in favour of the Copts, was not only 'without the authority of the Romans', but 'against the Romans' and 'behind their backs'. Such is the logical process, which now has to be examined.

Who were the people of Miṣr? In the first place, as Dr. Lane-Poole remarks, the term *Miṣr* has a double meaning—the capital city and the country of Egypt

[1] p. 241. [2] p. 243. [3] p. 245.

—and we do not even know for certain which was intended. But he adduces the analogy of other early Muslim treaties—those of Damascus, Lydda, and Jerusalem—and argues that the practice of the Arabs was to make a treaty, upon the capture of a chief town, with the townsfolk. Accordingly Miṣr in the present case should be taken as meaning the city of Miṣr, which lay over and spread beyond the region now miscalled Old Cairo, though it seems to have been identified loosely at times with the ancient Memphis [1] and its environs on both banks of the Nile. How far the city of Miṣr extended at the time of the conquest, and what fortifications it had besides Ḳaṣr ash Shamaʿ, cannot be known. But there is evidence that it extended somewhat widely. The outpost of ʿUmm Dunain (the Tendounias of John of Nikiou) lay at a point now represented by the Esbekiah in Cairo, and the very ancient churches in the Ḥārat ar Rūm and Ḥārat az Zuwailah were apparently considered within the old city of Miṣr, as Abū Ṣāliḥ [2] seems to indicate; and the same writer also describes the city of ʿAin Shams as lying outside the city of Miṣr. But there is no evidence of any wide circumvallation: for the battle of ʿAin Shams and the fall of Tendounias seem to have been followed quickly by the Arab occupation of Miṣr and the siege of the formidable fortress of Babylon.[3] Here the resistance of the Romans was concentrated: but it is quite

[1] Maḳrīzī, *Sultans Mamlouks,* t. ii, p. 119 (ed. Quatremère, Paris, 1845).

[2] pp. 86–7, and notes: but the matter is not clear of doubt.

[3] Note that John of Nikiou in his chapter-headings clearly distinguishes the capture of Miṣr from the fall of Babylon.

certain that there was also a large population in the city of Miṣr.

Of what race or creed was this population? The answer is plain—Egyptian—though there was doubtless some small admixture of Jews, Arabs, Berbers, and Nubians. But it must be remembered that the Egyptians at this time, though all Christian, were of two races and two creeds, viz. by race either Copts or Graeco-Romans (Byzantines), by creed either monophysites or melkites. But the racial cleavage by no means coincided with the religious division: in other words a Roman might hold the Coptic form of faith, and a Copt might hold the melkite (or Roman or Chalcedonian) form.

Now if there is one thing indisputable in all this tangled story, it is that for the ten years preceding the time of the Arab invasion, and at that time, the Copts suffered the severest persecution at the hands of Cyrus, the nominee of Heraclius as patriarch of Alexandria and governor-general of Egypt. It is certain also that the Copts had neither bishop nor leader in the city of Miṣr, since their patriarch and all their prominent men had been driven into exile into the mountains and deserts. Whatever the relative number of the Copts might have been—even if they were as numerous at this military centre as the Romans and Roman sympathizers—it is not conceivable that there should have existed then in the city of Miṣr a body of Copts in a position to enter upon a treaty with the victorious Arabs.

Apart from this, however, one must not exaggerate the distinction between Copt and Roman. It must be remembered that the Graeco-Romans at this time were not an alien army of occupation, as Dr. Lane-Poole seems to imagine them. The country had been Graeco-Roman for 700 years, and for centuries longer if we date the mixture of race, as is right, to the early Greek settlements and trace it through Ptolemaic times. It was the Hellenes, and not the Italians, who contributed and maintained that element of the population which came to be called in later times Roman or Byzantine. And during all those centuries there had been a continuous mingling of the two races; so that although the Egyptian racial type probably prevailed by reason of that unchangeable and invincible vitality which has ever marked it, yet the dominant civilization of the country at this time was Hellenic, whether called Byzantine or Graeco-Roman; and from Pelusium to Barca, from Alexandria to Syene and Meroe, the land was covered with cities bearing Graeco-Roman names—cities in which the arts, the architecture, the language and the letters were far more Graeco-Roman than Coptic.

Nor is there any reason to think that the city of Miṣr or city of Babylon, as it was also called,[1] presented any exception to the rule.

To say therefore that by the term *people of Miṣr* only the Copts could be meant, is to make a quite baseless and unwarranted assumption.

But there are other obvious objections. A good

[1] Ptolemy, for example, calls it City of Babylon; so does Palladius. It is frequently so called in the Aphrodito papyri, and the name may be traced onwards to the middle ages. Thus Sir J. Mandeville speaks of Egypt as 'the land of Babylon', and the term 'Soldan', 'Suldan', or 'Sowdone' (i. e. Sultan) 'of Babylon', was commonly used in English, and its analogue in continental, literature up to the sixteenth century to denote the ruler of Egypt.

deal of the confusion caused by the use of the term *Copts* in the Arab historians springs from the fact that the term did not originally bear the precise and limited meaning which it now bears in common parlance. There is no doubt that at the time of the conquest the Arabs frequently used the term *Copts* as synonymous with *Egyptians*, i. e. as denoting the people of Egypt generally, and that a distinction between the Coptic and the Graeco-Roman elements in the population was not ordinarily present to their minds. Of course if a special reinforcement of imperial troops entered Egypt at any time by order of Heraclius, those troops would be called distinctively Roman by the Arabs, and are perhaps so referred to in the Treaty of Miṣr, in which—be it remarked—the Copts are not even mentioned. But that the Graeco-Roman inhabitants, as well as the Coptic, were often included under the term *Copts* is unquestionable.

This fact explains much that is otherwise inexplicable. For instance, Dr. Lane-Poole quotes Maḳrīzī as saying that Al Muḳauḳis 'left the fortress of Babylon in company with the leaders of the Copts', and crossed to the island of Rauḍah. Whoever Al Muḳauḳis was, he was the Roman governor of Egypt: and it is certain from John of Nikiou that the Copts within the fortress during the siege were actually in prison, and were barbarously treated by the Romans. Again Ṭabarī records a representation in favour of peace made *by the people of Miṣr to their king* (ملكهم). This *king* cannot possibly mean Heraclius, who is called *Caesar* in the same passage, and can only mean *ruler*, i. e. the viceroy Al

Muḳauḳis. And that meaning is placed beyond doubt by the words of Mas'ūdī,[1] who calls Al Muḳauḳis king of Miṣr and lord of the Copts, and says that he used to spend part of the year in Alexandria, part in the city of Menf or Memphis, part in Ḳaṣr ash Shama'. Now it is clearly ridiculous to speak of Al Muḳauḳis as king or ruler of the Copts as opposed to the Romans, or in any other sense than as ruler of the *Egyptians*. Indeed that supposition is refuted by Dr. Lane-Poole's own words, where he gives Maḳrīzī's story as follows: [2]

'Fearing that the fortresses would fall, he (Al Muḳauḳis) opened negotiations with the Arabs. He urged that the *Romans* were far more numerous and better equipped than the Muslims. . . . But Al Muḳauḳis could obtain no modification of the terms. Fighting with the garrison of Babylon was accordingly renewed: but finally Al Muḳauḳis persuaded the people that resistance was hopeless, and 'Amr's terms were accepted—a poll-tax of two dinars a head, &c.'

Clearly here Al Muḳauḳis was speaking as representative not of Copts but of Romans. I need not labour the point: but I pass on to another of even greater importance. If the treaty is genuine, it was a military convention between belligerents marking the surrender of a great Roman stronghold: and it is sheer absurdity to imagine that the Copts, who had no separate existence as a belligerent party, could have arranged such a convention in their own favour 'behind the backs of the Romans' and 'against the Romans'.

[1] ii. 412, ed. Barbier de Meynard. [2] *P. R. I. A.*, p. 244.

To put the matter quite plainly, I would ask the following questions :—

(1) Is it denied that Al Muḳauḳis was himself a Roman as distinguished from a Copt, and was Roman governor of Egypt ?

(2) Is it denied that the military governor of the fortress of Babylon was a Roman in the same sense ? [1]

(3) Is it denied that the garrison of the fortress was Roman and under Roman officers to the exclusion of Copts ?

(4) Is it denied that the defenders of the fortress capitulated and entered into the Treaty of Miṣr ?

On one and all of these points denial is impossible, whether regard be had to Dr. Lane-Poole's own admissions or to the whole evidence of Coptic and Arabic chronicles.

But if this is so, if the Treaty of Miṣr was negotiated by the Roman commander or ruler and the Roman defenders of the besieged fortress of Babylon on behalf of the people of Miṣr ; how is it possible to maintain that the treaty was made 'with the Copts and not with the Romans', 'behind the backs of the Romans', 'between the Copts and the Arabs without the authority of the Roman garrison', and finally that it was 'a treaty with the Copts of the city of Miṣr as against the Romans' ? Clearly such a theory is absolutely untenable ; and if there is any truth in Ṭabarī's story, the treaty was made with the Romans on behalf of the people of Miṣr, whether Graeco-Roman or Coptic.

[1] Dr. Lane-Poole is wrong in calling the governor of the fortress Aretion (p. 242). I do not know what his authority for this statement is: but it would seem that Aretion was the tribune killed in the night attack upon the Arabs. v. supra, p. 12, n. 1.

III. *The Meaning of the Treaty*

It remains now to give the text of the treaty and to consider its interpretation. Dr. Lane-Poole points out very justly its close correspondence with the earlier treaty, which was granted by the Caliph Omar at the capitulation of Jerusalem, and he remarks that 'Amr ībn al 'Aṣī, who made the Treaty of Miṣr, was present and subscribed the Treaty of Jerusalem as witness: moreover the two treaties 'contain not only practically identical clauses but even absolutely identical words and phrases': 'Amr therefore modelled the Treaty of Miṣr on the Treaty of Jerusalem. I propose further to follow Dr. Lane-Poole in setting out both the treaties, though on the comparison I shall have to base some conclusions quite at variance with his.

The Arabic text is as follows (De Goeje, p. 2588):

بسم الله الرحمن الرحيم هذا ما اعطى عمرو بن العاصى
اهل مصر من الامان على انفسهم وملّتهم واموالهم
وكنائسهم وصُلُبهم وبرّهم وبحرهم لا يُدخل عليهم شىء
من ذلك ولا يُنتقَص ولا يساكنهم النوب وعلى اهل
مصر ان يعُطوا الجزيه اذا اجتمعوا على هذا الصلح
وانتهتْ زيادة نهرهم خمسين الف الف وعليهم ما جني
لصوتُهم فان ابى احد منهم ان يجيب رفع عنهم
من الجزاء بقدرهم وذمّتنا ممن ابى بريئة وان نقص
نهرهم من غايته اذا انتهى رُفع عنهم بقدر ذلك ومن

دخل في صلحهم من الروم والنوب فله مثل ما لهم
وعليه مثل ما عليهم ومن ابى واختار الذهاب فهو
آمن حتّى يبلغ مأمنه او يخرج من سلطاننا عليهم ما
عليهم اثلاثًا في كل ثلث جباية ثلث ما عليهم

على ما في هذا الكتاب عهدُ الله وذمّته وذمّة رسوله
وذمّة الخليفة امير المؤمنين وذمّة المؤمنين وعلى النوبة
الذين استجابوا ان يعينوا بكذا وكذا رأسًا وكذا وكذا
فرسًا على ان لا يُغزوا ولا يمنعوا من تجارة صادرة ولا
واردة شهد بذلك الزبير وعبد الله ومحمد ابناه
وكتب وردان وحَضَرَ

One may translate as follows:

In the name of God, the Merciful, the Compassionate.

1. This is what 'Amr ibn al 'Aṣī granted the people of Miṣr—to wit, security for their persons and their religion and their property, their churches and their crosses, their land and their water. In none of these things shall there be any encroachment nor any abatement of their rights.[1]

[1] Dr. Lane-Poole translates doubtfully 'There shall not be taken from them anything of this nor diminished'. He quotes De Sacy's rendering: 'On n'attentera à leurs droits relativement à aucune de ces choses et on ne leur fera éprouver aucun tort,' *Mémoires de l'Institut* (Acad. des Inscriptions et Belles-Lettres), v. 35. Caetani renders, 'In niuna di queste cose entrerà (il governo Arabo) e nulla sarà tolto' (*Annali dell' Islam*, vol. iv, p. 304). I am following Caetani in numbering the clauses of the treaty for the sake of convenience, just as he follows my numbering for the Treaty of Alexandria given by John of Nikiou.

2. The Nubians[1] shall not settle among them.

3. The people of Miṣr are bound to pay the poll-tax, if they agree upon this treaty of peace and the inundation of their river has reached full level—fifty millions.

4. They are responsible for any acts of their brigands.

5. If any of them refuse [the terms of the treaty], the total of the poll-tax shall be reduced for them in proportion ; and we are free of obligation to protect those who refuse.

6. If their river does not rise to its usual level, then the sum [of taxation] shall be reduced for them in proportion.

7. Whosoever of the Romans or the Nubians enters into their treaty, for him are the same rights as for them (i. e. the people of Miṣr) and the same obligations.

8. Whosoever refuses [these terms] and chooses to depart, he shall be safe until he reaches his own place of security or quits our dominion.

9. The tribute imposed is to be paid by three equal instalments, one-third at each payment.

10. For what is written in this treaty stands the pledge and warranty of God, the warranty of His Prophet, the warranty of the Caliph, the Commander of the Faithful, and the warranty of the Faithful.

11. For the Nubians who come under this treaty, it is prescribed that they shall furnish so

[1] I totally reject Dr. Lane-Poole's translation of *garrisons*, with which Caetani dallies needlessly, though he decides against it in the end. My reasons will be given below.

many head (of cattle) and so many horses; and in return [1] they shall not be plundered nor hindered in their trade, coming or going.

Witnesses, Az Zubair and 'Abdallah and Muḥammad,[2] his sons. Wardān wrote the treaty, and there were present ... (so and so—names omitted).

Such is the Treaty of Miṣr. I now give the Treaty of Jerusalem, mainly in Dr. Lane-Poole's translation:

In the name of God the Compassionate, the Merciful.

1. This is what the servant of God, Omar, Commander of the Faithful, gave to the people of Jerusalem in pledge of security. He gave them security for their persons and their goods and their churches and their crosses, and its [3] sick and its sound, and all of their religion: their churches shall not be impoverished or destroyed: nor shall [aught] of it be diminished, neither of its appurtenances nor of its crosses nor of anything of its provisions. And they shall not be forced against their faith, and not one of them shall be harmed.

2. None of the Jews shall dwell with them in Jerusalem.

3. The people of Jerusalem are bound to pay the poll-tax as the people of Madain (Ctesiphon) pay it.

4. They are bound to expel the Romans and brigands from [the city].

[1] The Arabic على ان denotes the other side of the bargain: i.e. they gain immunity from plunder and freedom to trade.

[2] No son of Zubair named Muḥammad is known to history.

[3] The use of pronouns here and elsewhere is irregular, but the sense is generally clear.

5. Whosoever [of the Romans, &c.] goes away, shall be safe in person and property until they reach their own place of safety; and whoever remains shall be safe and under the same obligation as the people of Jerusalem to pay the poll-tax.

6. Whosoever of the people of Jerusalem prefers to take his goods and to depart along with the Romans, and leave their churches and crosses, they shall be safe in person until they reach their own place of security.

7. Whosoever of the people of the country was in Jerusalem before the fighting, if he wish to settle, on him are binding the same terms as on the people of Jerusalem, the poll-tax; and if he wishes to depart with the Romans or to return to his own people [he may do so].

8. Nothing shall be taken from them (i.e. the people of the treaty) until the harvest is gathered.

9. For what is in this treaty stands the pledge and warranty of God, the warranty of His Prophet, the warranty of the Caliph, and the warranty of the Faithful, provided that they pay the due amount of the poll-tax.

Witnesses, Khālid ibn Walīd, 'Amr ibn al 'Aṣī, 'Abd ar Raḥmān ibn 'Aūf, and Mu'awīah ibn Abī Sufiān.

Though on the whole I have taken Dr. Lane-Poole's translation, I have thought it better to arrange and number the clauses, and in cl. 1 to 6 I have made verbal changes; but in cl. 7 and 8 I have given what I think is the right translation in correction of Dr. Lane-Poole's rendering, which seems to miss the sense completely—indeed to make no sense at all. He renders:

'And whoso of the people of the land was in it [Jerusalem] before the fighting, if he wish to settle, on him is binding the like as what [is binding] on the people of Jerusalem, a poll-tax, and if he wishes to depart with the Romans or to return to his own people, nothing shall be taken from them [i. e. in poll-tax] until the harvest is reaped.'

Either the words 'and if he wishes to depart with the Romans or to return to his own people' are redundant and should go out of the text; or after them must be understood words like 'he is free to do so'; or, as I think better, the text must be rendered in the way I have rendered it. In any case a break is required before the words about the collection of the poll-tax, which must be marked off and stand apart, because they obviously apply not to those who depart, *but to all who come under the treaty*. And this provision for collecting the tribute after harvest clearly corresponds to the provision in the Egyptian treaty for the collection after high Nile.

Returning now to the Treaty of Miṣr, one may note that the first clause grants security for the persons, property, and religion of the Christians, thus agreeing with the first clause in the Treaty of Jerusalem.

In cl. 2 I read a similar agreement: for just as the Treaty of Jerusalem prohibits the Jews from dwelling in the Holy City, so the Treaty of Miṣr prohibits the Nubians from settling in Miṣr. But Dr. Lane-Poole will have none of this agreement. He destroys the obvious correspondence by banishing the Nubians altogether from the treaty, reading the Arabic نوب (which means *Nubians*) as نُوَب and giving it the entirely novel meaning of *garrisons*:[1] so that he renders cl. 2, 'The garrisons shall not settle among them.' I shall try to show that this rendering is not only wrong but impossible.

Of course I admit that the analogy between the case of the Jews at Jerusalem and that of the Nubians in Egypt at the date of the respective treaties is not very striking. When the Treaty of Jerusalem was concluded, it was but twenty years since the Christians had suffered the massacre by thousands of their women and children, and the plunder and destruction of their churches, at the hands of the Persians; and they remembered that in all this work the Jews had sided with the Persians and had goaded them on to deeds of ferocity. The Christians, therefore, had good reason to bargain for the expulsion of the Jews from the city. Now it cannot be shown that the people of Miṣr had the same reason to bargain for the exclusion of the Nubians from their city; but it can be shown that they had quite sufficient reason to claim protection against the Nubians, and to debar Nubians from settling in the country. Nothing more is required for my argument.

[1] On the mere question of grammar نوب may be accented as نُوَب, but there is no authority for its use in the sense of *garrisons* at so early a date, even if it was ever used with that extended meaning. It means literally *times* or *turns*, and so *turns-about*, 'à tour de rôle,' and then in later usage something like a change of guard, or finally a guard-post subject to relief at stated times. But Dozy, whom Dr. Lane-Poole cites in support of his rendering, is altogether against it: q. v.

Dr. Lane-Poole refers to Ṭabarī's statement (or rather tradition) that 'when the Arabs reached 'Ain Shams, the rule was between the Copts and the Nubians',[1] and contends that it is unintelligible: whereas if it be rendered 'between the Copts and the garrisons', and if the garrisons are identified with the Romans, then all is lucid.

Now in the first place I see no difficulty whatever in accepting the obvious sense, 'between the Copts and the Nubians.' One has only to remember that politically Nubia at this time was a powerful and populous kingdom under its own rulers and practically independent of the Roman dominion: while geographically it was conterminous and continuous with Egypt and formed an essential part of the Nile country, with undefined frontiers, or frontiers defined only at a single frontier post, Syene. Nubia even to-day is called the Egyptian Sudan, and what is more likely than that it was pictured in the mind of the early Arab historians as part of Egypt? Indeed, that Ṭabarī so looked upon Nubia is absolutely proved by his own language in this very account of the conquest of Egypt; for he says later—'When the Muslims had conquered Egypt, they sent an expedition against *Egyptian Nubia*.'[2] This corresponds to our phrase the Egyptian Sudan. Clearly to Ṭabarī then as to us Nubia formed part of Egypt: and he or his informant might say with perfect accuracy that the rule in Egypt was divided between the Egyptians and the Nubians.[3]

[1] See Trad. E, p. 12 supra.

[2] p. 2593. See Trad. G, p. 14 supra.

[3] There is abundant evidence to show that in Roman times even

It may be asked, were the relations between Nubia and Egypt proper at this time such as to justify the expression? Upon this point Dr. Lane-Poole makes a most astounding statement. 'We read', he says, 'nothing in history about Nubian influence or Nubian settlements in Egypt at least since the Ethiopian dynasty of thirteen hundred years before.'[1] *Aliquando bonus dormitat Homerus*; but of all the extraordinary statements ever made by a scholar and historian surely this is one of the strangest and the farthest from the truth.

In making it Dr. Lane-Poole apparently is thinking of the Meroitic dynasty of about 750 B.C., when Nubia was the centre of a great empire, in which Egypt was a mere province. But then and through a long series of reigns 'the culture and religion of the royal family and of the priests was derived from Egypt'.[2] The Meroitic era proper began in the third century B.C., when the king Ergamenes threw off the bondage of the Egyptian religion and adopted Hellenic culture, as Diodorus relates. Friendly relations with the Ptolemies generally prevailed, and we read of Blemmyes or Nubians born in Egypt and holding much the same position as Greeks born in Egypt.[3] 'One of the last acts of Cleopatra was to send Caesarion and her two

the Thebaid was constantly distinguished from Egypt, and that Egypt was described as divided into three provinces, called Egypt proper, the Thebaid, and Libya. See *Accad. dei Lincei*, *Rendiconti*, 1903, p. 315, and the classical authorities there quoted.

[1] *P.R.I.A.*, p. 236.

[2] *Oxford Excavations in Nubia: Catalogue of Exhibition of Antiquities*, pp. 1, 2 (Oxford, Holywell Press, 1911).

[3] *Karanōg, the Romano-Nubian Cemetery*, by C. Leonard

children by Antony down to the south in the hope that in Aethiopia they would find shelter.'[1]

But we are concerned mainly with the Roman empire in Egypt. Has Dr. Lane-Poole never heard of Cornelius Gallus at Philae in 29 B.C.? of Queen Candace's expedition to Elephantine? of Gaius Petronius's victories in Nubia and annexation as far as Primis or Ḳaṣr Ibrīm? About A.D. 250 the Blemmyes invaded Egypt and were not driven back till A.D. 261 by Julius Aemilianus. They soon returned, and actually occupied Coptos and Ptolemaïs in the Thebaid by a settlement which lasted till their expulsion by Probus in A.D. 276. A few years later Diocletian had the sense to abandon the country south of Syene, and at the same time he transferred the troublesome Nobatae and Noubae from the oasis of Khargah to Nubia, and agreed to pay tribute to both the Blemmyes and the Nobatae. Peace was thus secured for a long time; but in the days of Constantine raids as far north as Sabenna are mentioned. In the fourth century the edict of Theodosius united Nobatae and Blemmyes against the Shenouti and the Coptic Christians of Upper Egypt; and from this time onwards they are constantly found raiding Upper Egypt and the Thebaid[2] and harrying the Christians; while in the middle of the fifth century 'the Blemmyes were now more than raiders; they were definitely settled in the Thebaid and assumed

Woolley and D. Randall-MacIver, text, p. 88 (University Museum, Philadelphia, 1910), and references to the Rylands Papyri there quoted.

[1] *Karanōg*, p. 85.

[2] See *Egyptian Exploration Fund Report*, 1903–4: *Christian Egypt*, p. 81. The MS. of Shenouti in the Cairo Museum (8006 in Crum's Catalogue) shows that these invasions were frequent.

in a measure its civil government; the Roman troops that had garrisoned the frontier were prisoners in their hands, and Ptolemais seems to have been the regular base from which their forces terrorized the country to the north'.[1] Maximinus crushed these Nubians in A.D. 453 and concluded a peace which lasted more or less till the time of Justinian; but an extant letter, dated about A.D. 540, to John, Prefect of the East, from a landholder in Upper Egypt complains of two invasions by the Blemmyes in three years. Then followed the well-known missions of Justinian and Theodora which evangelized the Nobatae, whose king Silko warred against the Blemmyes and destroyed them. But Christianity did not change the habits of the Nubians. About A.D. 580 Aristomachus was sent by Tiberius II to chastise the Nubians;[2] and in the time of the emperor Maurice we find either Nubian troops or troops from Nubia employed in Egypt proper.[3]

So all through the Roman dominion the relations of Egypt and Nubia were relations of continual hostility, of war and plunder, of invasion and counter-invasion.[4] And the Muslims in their turn found that the conquest of Nubia did not follow upon the con-

[1] *Karanōg*, p. 96.

[2] *John of Nikiou*, p. 525 (*Notices et Extraits des Manuscrits*, &c., t. xxiv, Paris, 1883). [3] Id., p. 531.

[4] See J. Leipoldt's article written as preface to Rudolph Haupt's *Katalog* 5 (Aegyptologie, &c.), pp. viii, ix (Halle a. S., 1905): 'Am allerhässlichsten benahmen sich aber die reichen Herren, wenn ein Einfall der Egoosh (Nubier) drohte. In diesen Zeiten höchster Gefahr pflegten alle nordwärts zu fliehen . . . Die ägyptische Regierung schon im vierten und fünften Jahrhundert recht machtlos war: nicht einmal ihre Soldaten hatte sie in der Gewalt, und die Verhinderung von Nubiereinfällen gelang ihr nur selten.'

quest of Egypt; for Ṭabarī himself relates the failure of the expedition which 'Amr made against Nubia, as soon as Egypt was subjugated.

I claim therefore to have shown that, during the whole of the thirteen hundred years in which Dr. Lane-Poole alleges that Nubian influence and Nubian settlements were unknown in Egypt, the tide of war had rolled over the land between Nubia and Egypt, ebbing and flowing at irregular intervals but with ceaseless recurrence; that Nubia was a thorn in the side of the Romans all through their dominion in Egypt, as it was a thorn in the side of the Muslims long after they had conquered Egypt; and that, so far from Nubian settlements being unknown in Egypt, it had been the regular policy and practice of the Nubians to crown a successful invasion by a settled occupation in Upper Egypt. It was therefore perfectly natural that at the time of the Arab invasion the people of Miṣr should bargain for protection against Nubian settlements.

If this is not enough to prove that *Nūb* in the treaty has its ordinary sense of *Nubians*, let us consider the consequences of adopting Dr. Lane-Poole's rendering *garrisons*. I have already taken the broad ground that, as the Roman Empire had been established in Egypt for at least seven hundred years, it is a mistake to speak of Egypt in A.D. 640 as a country held by alien Roman 'garrisons' and an alien 'Roman army of occupation'. Such phrases fly in the face of history.[1] But further: if 'Amr

[1] The Roman army in Egypt was largely recruited from the native inhabitants: see *The Garrison of Egypt under the Roman Empire*, by Mr. Cheeseman in *Karanōg*, pp. 106–14.

meant *garrisons*, why did not he use the common Arabic word for *garrison*, حرسيه ? Again, if the Romans in Egypt are described as garrisons in the Treaty of Miṣr, why are they not so described, and why is the term *Nūb* not used, in the Treaty of Jerusalem? And if the term *garrisons* in the Treaty of Miṣr is equivalent to *Romans*, why does that treaty speak of 'Romans *and* garrisons', thus making a distinction between them? But the climax of absurdity is reached when we come to the last clause (11) in the treaty, which provides that the 'garrisons' are to furnish so many head of cattle or sheep[1] and so many horses, and are to receive in return full freedom for trade to and from Egypt. What can this mean if the 'garrisons' are the Romans?

Dr. Lane-Poole sees the difficulty. 'The last clause relating to the garrisons', he remarks, 'is not very intelligible,' and he proceeds to quote what he calls Weil's translation as follows: 'And (it is binding) on the *garrisons* who consent (to this treaty) that they shall help the Muslims with so many men and so many horses that they (*the Nūb*) be not hindered from trade, coming or going.' Notice that Dr. Lane-Poole takes upon himself to substitute 'garrisons' for Weil's 'Nubians', and yet does not hesitate to change that inconvenient word back to 'Nūb' or Nubians in his own gloss explaining the pronoun 'they'! We may correct this procedure, and see what results. The clause will then run, according to the *garrisons* theory, as follows: 'The

[1] This rendering is more probably correct than 'head of men', i. e. soldiers.

garrisons who come under this treaty are bound to furnish so many head (of cattle or men) and so many horses, so that the garrisons may trade freely, coming and going'—which is very like nonsense. Dr. Lane-Poole argues that 'the clause may be understood to provide for a limited escort of friendly Romans to protect the caravans trading between Egypt and Syria; but such a provision appears extremely improbable'. Not only improbable, but impossible: it is the *reductio ad absurdum* of the *garrisons* theory.

But if, as I contend, *Nūb* means *Nubians*, then it is the Nubians in Egypt who have to furnish cattle and horses (possibly a contingent of horse and foot) and who are to be protected in their trade across the desert to Nubia. The trade in ivory and other products of the Sudan was much the same then as now, and as much exposed to danger from Beduin and brigands.[1] The Arabs too were strangers to the country, and they may have foreseen the requirement of a corps of local guides to aid in patrolling the southern and western deserts. So interpreted therefore the provision in the treaty is both intelligible and natural. Last but not least, the other Muslim historians who quote or comment on the

[1] Juvenal, for example, mentions the ivory trade: 'Dentibus ex illis quos mittit porta Syenes.' See also *England in the Sudan*, by Yakūb Pasha Artīn, p. 8 (Macmillan, 1911): 'All these temples and fortresses, whose ruins alone remain, could not have been constructed in deserts such as we see to-day. There must have existed from remotest times a considerable trade, at least a transport trade, between the Sudan and Egypt. Certain it is that there were wars both of a defensive and of an aggressive nature from at least the time of the twelfth dynasty.'

treaty never doubt for a moment that *Nūb* means *Nubians.* Thus Ibn al Athīr says, 'In this treaty even the Romans and Nubians inhabiting Egypt were included as forming part of the population of the country.'[1]

So much for the strange theory of the 'garrisons'.

It remains to notice one or two other points in the treaty. Clause 2 seems to fix the total amount of poll-tax, 'provided that the people of Miṣr accept the treaty and the river reaches its full level,' at 50,000,000—but the coin is not specified. I can hardly think Dr. Lane-Poole correct in taking this as *dirhems.* The evidence of practically all the Arab writers agrees that the tax was stated in *dinars*—two dinars a head, old men, women, and children being excluded. Clearly, however, 50,000,000 dinars cannot have been intended: that would imply 25,000,000 able-bodied men in the population, which is absurd. But if 5,000,000 be substituted for 50,000,000 by a very slight change in the text (خمسة for خمسين), that would imply a taxable population of 2,500,000, which might be a fair rough estimate of numbers for the whole of Egypt at the time of the treaty. But whichever way the total of tribute be taken (dirhems or dinars), a great difficulty arises: because it is certain that any such total must refer not to a section but to the whole population of Egypt. In other words, 'the people of Miṣr' in this clause must mean, not the people of the city of Miṣr, but the people of Egypt. Yet

[1] Ibn al Athīr, *Chronicon quod perfectissimum inscribitur,* ed. C. J. Tornberg, Leyden, 1868–74, p. 441.

we have seen that it was the people of the city who were parties to the treaty; and اهل مصر cannot mean two different things in the same document. The only solution is to regard the numeral 50,000,000 (or 5,000,000) as a marginal gloss which has crept into the text. This solution commends itself the more as there is no total of poll-tax specified in the Treaty of Jerusalem. Caetani (p. 309) says that the omission of any capitation tax is one of the points in favour of the treaty, because under Omar the two dinars per head was not known—only a lump sum being fixed. It also seems *a priori* most unlikely that the Arab commander would bind himself to accept an off-hand estimate furnished by the Romans, who would have every motive for reducing the total. It must further be remembered that Ṭabarī's words immediately following the treaty run :—'So the people of Miṣr, all of them, entered into those covenants and accepted the treaty, and the horses were collected.' It is quite certain that the whole population of *Egypt* did not enter upon this treaty. Moreover, the collection of horses is recorded as an incident in close connexion with the acceptation of the treaty; and whether it refers to horses which the Nubians had to furnish, or, as seems more probable, to horses at once available and supplied by the people of the city, it shows the limited scope of the treaty at the moment. It obviously cannot refer to a collection of horses from all quarters of Egypt: for it is absolutely beyond question that, at the time when the Treaty of Miṣr was concluded, the Muslims had effected next to nothing in Upper Egypt, while the whole of the Delta was still Roman and could not be described as coming under the treaty. Ṭabarī's own words[1] make doubt on this point impossible, apart from the overwhelming evidence of other Arab writers and of John of Nikiou: and Dr. Lane-Poole virtually agrees.[2] Everything therefore seems to support the theory that the '50,000,000', which hangs very loosely on the text, is a gloss which should be removed.

One other point. The position of cl. 11 is curious and obviously suggests some kind of afterthought. Yet if this provision were a mere interpolation by a later writer, why should it be placed between the warranty clause and the attestation clause? It would have been more natural, and just as easy, for an interpolator to insert his fictitious addition somewhere in the body of the treaty. Indeed it might be argued, that the abnormal position of the clause is actually a point in its favour: though the same cannot be said of its obscurity.

Leaving, however, all criticism of the text, one may now sum up the conclusions reached about the treaty. It was a treaty made not with the Copts but with the Romans: it concerned primarily the population of the city of Miṣr, whom it ruled out as belligerents and brought under tribute, giving in return protection and religious liberty: it secured to the Arabs possession of the largest city in Egypt after Alexandria: it released their forces for the campaign

[1] See Tradition B, p. 9 supra.

[2] *P.R.I.A.*, p. 235: 'At the time of the treaty only a small part of the country was subdued, and most of the country was in Roman hands.'

in the Delta: and it gave to the still unconquered towns and provinces of Upper and Lower Egypt a model of the conditions under which the Muslims were ready to grant peace together with security for life, property, and religion.

IV. *The Authenticity of the Treaty.*

Up to this point I have assumed the genuineness of the treaty, with some reserve, in order to deal with Dr. Lane-Poole's arguments as founded on that assumption. But while Dr. Lane-Poole regards the treaty as textually accurate and unquestionably authentic, it must not be concealed that other oriental scholars regard it as for the most part spurious. Contrast the almost sacrosanct regard in which Dr. Lane-Poole holds the document with what Wellhausen says of the whole Saifian traditions.[1] Indeed, Wellhausen in his brief study of the conquest, written before my work and Dr. Lane-Poole's article, does not directly mention this treaty; while Caetani, the latest, fullest, and most searching writer on the subject, definitely decides that both the Treaty of Jerusalem and the Treaty of Miṣr are in the main apocryphal.[2]

The truth probably lies somewhat short of this extreme opinion. But one thing is certain: either the Treaty of Miṣr is spurious or its historical setting is wrong. It is absolutely impossible that the treaty as it stands can have been concluded by Al Muḳauḳis upon the surrender of Babylon and by him referred

[1] *Skizzen und Vorarbeiten*, vi. 94. See also his general remarks on the early Mohammedan writings in iv. of the same series.

[2] Caetani, pp. 300, 306–8.

to Heraclius. Every modern authority agrees that John of Nikiou's evidence upon the date of the surrender is final. That date is 9 April, 641, and at that date Al Muḳauḳis was not in Egypt and Heraclius was dead.

If, therefore, the treaty is genuine, it must have got into a wrong context. For in its present form it cannot possibly be identified with the Treaty of Alexandria, which John of Nikiou records: and alternatively, if it can be identified as a confused reminiscence of that treaty, the text cannot be regarded as authentic. To what then could it relate, if genuine? John of Nikiou shows clearly that the capture of the city of Miṣr was anterior to the fall of Babylon, though all details of that capture are lost with the lost chapter of which the heading alone remains. Balādhurī also makes it clear that in the conquest of Egypt there were two treaties,[1] one merely local and temporary, the other marking the final triumph of the Arabs and settling the terms for the surrender of the country by the Romans. If Ṭabarī's treaty can be identified with the minor treaty recorded by Balādhurī, it would not run counter to anything in John of Nikiou, and in spite of some

[1] Caetani, p. 251, where Balādhurī is quoted, and Caetani comments as follows: 'In questa tradizione si osservino due cose: in primo luogo che s'ignora il nome di al Muqawqis e che lo si chiama il signore di Alyūnah senz' altre specificazioni. Si parla poi di due trattati ben distinti, e qui noi scorgiamo memoria dei due trattati, l'uno concluso alla presa di Babilonia con il signore della fortezza (Saḥib Alyūnah), e l'altro non specificato ulteriormente, ma senza dubbio quello di Alessandria, stipulato da Ciro.'

The term *Al Yūnah* comes of course from Bab-al-yūn (Gate of Al Yūn), the form of Babylon which Arab writers got from a mistaken etymology.

difficulties might claim at least a measure of authenticity.

But the conclusions of Caetani are too important to pass over lightly. Dr. Lane-Poole, he remarks,[1] does not avail himself of the precious information of Balādhurī: he ignores Wellhausen's criticisms and he regards all the authorities as of equal value. We find Saif displaying very imperfect knowledge of events in Egypt as in Syria, and arbitrarily filling the gaps with elements in part only good and flung together in wild disorder. The treaty, therefore, appears in bad company, and we may suspect that the text of the treaty is as disordered as the text of the narrative. The last article, no. 11, is a rock on which the theory of absolute authenticity must split. Nubians in the treaty are an anachronism, and this article must be an interpolation taken from a subsequent treaty between Arabs and Nubians after the conquest of Upper Egypt. 'Hence the treaty', continues Caetani, 'is not the authentic text of the Treaty of Miṣr, but a text in which authorities of the Persian school are mingled with elements, in part ancient and perhaps contemporary with the conquest, of different provenance.' He proceeds to argue that article 2 cannot be of the time of the conquest: apart, however, from articles 2 and 11 the treaty has some genuine character. Moreover, the omission of the amount of the poll-tax per head is against it: but while some of the conditions recall those of the treaty of Alexandria as given by John of Nikiou, the main terms for the surrender of Egypt have little or nothing in common.

[1] Id., p. 308.

Finally he concludes that the Treaty of Jerusalem and Treaty of Miṣr are both mainly apocryphal, though parts may be taken from ancient and authentic documents. In both we have to note the intermixture of authentic conditions with apocryphal and with others which, being common to all treaties, have no special value. 'Generally these two treaties are artificial compositions of a later age with elements of various origin and diverse value. The historian must not ignore them, but must not found upon their slender support any important conclusion.'[1]

Such is Caetani's opinion. I do not agree with his sweeping judgement, nor does it seem founded so much upon argument as upon assertion. The articles 2 and 11, which are cited in condemnation of the Treaty of Miṣr as anachronistic, I have already shown above to be justified historically; and though I agree that the sum total of the poll-tax given in the treaty must be wrong, no great stress can be laid upon an error in arithmetic in Arab documents. It seems to me also that both the points of agreement and the points of difference in the two treaties (Jerusalem and Miṣr) suggest a higher measure of authenticity in the text than Caetani is disposed to admit, although I fully concur with him in thinking the whole narrative in Ṭabarī, or in the Saifian tradition, hopelessly disordered.

Beyond that, sure ground does not lie. Wellhausen accuses Saif of filling the gaps in his narrative with idle romancing (Kannegiesserei) and calls his narrative legendary. But the story of Zubair's escalade, for example, which Caetani would place

[1] Caetani, p. 310.

in that category, seems well enough attested, though the setting is doubtful. On the whole I am unable to accept Caetani's criticisms except in so far as I have here admitted their justice, or to base upon them any subversive modifications of the general narrative of events as set out in my eighteenth chapter of the *Arab Conquest of Egypt*.

But while I am disposed to think the treaty possibly in its main outline authentic, I confess that its exact position in the history is exceedingly difficult to determine. I have already shown that Ṭabarī intended beyond all question to associate the treaty with the surrender of Babylon, i.e. Ḳaṣr ash Sham'a: Balādhurī seems also to associate his first treaty with the surrender of Babylon or Ḳaṣr ash Sham'a. It is reasonable to suppose, and unreasonable to doubt, that these two treaties refer to the same event. Either then the Treaty of Miṣr must be regarded as that made in October at the time of high Nile—the abortive treaty which I have described in the *Arab Conquest*[1]—or it must be taken as relating to the capitulation of the city of Miṣr, as opposed to that of the fortress of Babylon—the capitulation which is barely recorded in a chapter-heading by John of Nikiou, but of which the whole description and detail are lost. The balance of evidence is perhaps in favour of the latter hypothesis: but no historian has yet issued from that inextricable labyrinth which the Arab writers have built around the central facts of the conquest with a key to its mysteries.

[1] p. 262.

V. *The Identity of Al Muḳauḳis.*

In dealing above with the parties to the treaty I have mentioned Al Muḳauḳis many times without diverting the argument to discuss the question of his identity. But Dr. Lane-Poole challenges my identification of him with Cyrus, the imperial patriarch and viceroy, and it is time to take up the challenge. Though most competent scholars both in Europe and in Egypt have accepted my theory at least in part, I have no wish to take shelter under their authority, or to regard it as outweighing Dr. Lane-Poole's criticisms: which I now proceed to examine.

After citing my evidence on the Coptic side (Severus, the Synaxarium, the Life of Samuel of Ḳalamūn) Dr. Lane-Poole says:

'Supposing these translations to be accurate, and supposing the MSS., which are chiefly late, to be faithful transcripts of early authoritative documents—a matter which I am not qualified to decide—these extracts taken together show that Cyrus and the Muḳauḳis were one and the same person in the opinion of the writers. This can hardly be contested. The only question is whether the writers were authoritative.'[1] 'The whole question turns on the relative credibility of two or three Coptic authorities and the whole series of Arabic historians.[2] If we had nothing but these Coptic and Ethiopic data to

[1] *P.R.I.A.*, p. 250. [2] Id., p. 252.

go upon, the identification might perhaps be taken as proved. But when we look at the long series of Arabic writers, not only those who survive, but many who are cited by survivors but whose original writings are lost, and when we fail to find the slightest hint that any one of them suspected Al Muḳauḳis and Cyrus to be the same person, I confess that their evidence, negative as it is, seems to me overwhelming. How is it that not one of them says that Al Muḳauḳis was a priest, much less an archbishop? Why do they give him the name of George, son of Mīnā, or son of Ḳurḳub, if his real name was Cyrus?[1] Why does Abū Ṣaliḥ, who was a Christian, and wrote about A. D. 1200, state that Heraclius placed the government of Egypt under "George, the son of Mīnā, Al Muḳauḳis", and also cite the book of Janāḥ for the fact that "the bishop of the Romans at Miṣr and Alexandria was named Cyrus"? How is it that not a single historian of Egypt, Muslim or Christian, has said in so many words "Al Muḳauḳis was a title or nickname given to the patriarch Cyrus"?'[2]

I have set out these extracts at some length because I am anxious to present Dr. Lane-Poole's argument fairly and fully. Briefly, then, he seeks to discredit the very positive evidence from Coptic sources, and he sets against it the negative results from Arabic sources—the silence and the confusion on the subject among Arabic historians.

Now first of all as to the Arabic writers. Of course this negative argument has a good deal of

[1] جرجس George, and قيروس Cyrus are not very unlike.

[2] Id., p. 253.

plausibility about it, but it does not prove much more than that among Arabic historians there exists on the question the greatest uncertainty and perplexity, and in their statements they show the greatest inconsistency: the one is the result of the other. But if there is anything certain, it is that the Arab writers caught the name Al Muḳauḳis by hearsay or tradition one from another without understanding it; that the name prevailed among them to the exclusion, or the confusion, of the personal name of the official to whom it belonged; and that the name was a vague title of non-Arabic origin denoting the ruler of Egypt. They call the ruler of Egypt in the time of Mohammed Al Muḳauḳis, and they call the ruler of Egypt at the time of the conquest Al Muḳauḳis. It matters little for my argument whether the name was first used by the Arabs in connexion with Mohammed's mission and applied by analogy to the governor-general at the time of the conquest; or whether (as I think) it was first heard at the time of the conquest and applied by error to the governor-general who received Mohammed's mission. In either case the term denoted the viceroy of the Roman emperor or the governor-general in Egypt. Seeing the consequences which would flow from an admission of this fact, Dr. Lane-Poole tries to escape them in the following manner:

'Such is Dr. Butler's positive evidence. The coincidences upon which he also relies are the statements on the one hand that Cyrus, on the other that Al Muḳauḳis, was governor of Egypt under Heraclius; the statements of the Greek historians and John of Nikiou that Cyrus made peace with the Arabs, and those of the Arabic historians that Al Muḳauḳis made peace with them. But these coincidences may be explained by the hypothesis that Al Muḳauḳis was the sub-governor who made the peace, and Cyrus the patriarch and supreme governor who accepted his subordinate's arrangement and reported it to the emperor.' [1]

In order, therefore, to avoid the identification of Al Muḳauḳis with Cyrus, Dr. Lane-Poole has to identify him, not with the governor-general of Egypt, but with some sub-governor: and this hypothesis he further develops to the conclusion that 'So far as the Arabic evidence goes, except for his name, Al Muḳauḳis may have been Theodore', i. e. the military governor at Alexandria. Clearly if the Muḳauḳis's name was Theodore, he was not 'George, son of Mīnā': but the fact is that 'George, son of Mīnā' fits no person and fits no theory in this strange eventful chronicle, and must be regarded as erroneous. But let us examine the Arabic writers' evidence, and see in what language they describe Al Muḳauḳis. Now dealing first with Ṭabarī, it cannot be denied that he distinguishes in one tradition [2] between Al Muḳauḳis and the *katholikos of Miṣr*. The question is what the latter phrase means. The term *katholikos* is not and never was a term rightly applicable to any church dignitary in Egypt. It is an Armenian, or Syrian, or Nestorian term, made familiar to Ṭabarī in Ṭabaristān or in Baghdad, and misapplied to Egypt. No doubt it means 'metropolitan', *but it does not necessarily*

[1] *P.R.I.A.*, p. 252.

[2] See Tradition D supra, p. 11.

mean 'patriarch'.[1] Further, we have seen that *Miṣr* has the double sense of *Egypt* and the *city of Miṣr.* It follows that the phrase *katholikos of Miṣr*, for which Dr. Lane-Poole and others usually give the impossible rendering *patriarch of Egypt*, may mean nothing more or less than *metropolitan of the city of Miṣr.* That there was a metropolitan of Miṣr distinct from the patriarch is probable: for it is known that there was a bishop of Miṣr, and the title frequently occurs in Coptic history.[2] There was also a bishop of Babylon, or 'bishop of the Castle of Babylon',[3] a bishop of Memphis, a bishop of Ḥulwān; and the bishop of Miṣr doubtless had precedence over all bishops in the locality. Moreover, the title of metropolitan was given to the bishop of Damietta; and it is difficult to conceive that the bishop of Miṣr—the capital city after Alexandria—was of less importance and lower dignity, as would be the case, if he had not the rank of metropolitan. I may add that I have spoken of *patriarch of Egypt* as an impossible rendering, because it is an impossible title. The patriarch was patriarch of Alexandria: that was the invariable title. Such a title as *patriarch of Miṣr* or *patriarch of Egypt* is absolutely unknown, and to use it is as

[1] Al Bīrūnī, speaking of the melkite Syrian Christians, defines Katholikos thus: Arabic *Jāthalīk.* The residence of the katholikos of the Melkites in Muslim countries is Baghdad. He is *under the patriarch of Antioch* (ed. C. E. Sachau, London, 1879, pp. 283–4). So the katholikos of the Armenian Church was appointed originally from Caesarea, and had not even the specific rank of metropolitan. To-day there are four katholikoi in Armenia.

[2] See for example, *Abū Ṣaliḥ*, pp. 92, 121, 138.

[3] *Arab Conquest*, p. 173.

absurd as to speak of the archbishop of England. On the other hand, the title *metropolitan of Miṣr* does not rest on mere conjecture. I have found it actually used about A.D. 750, when one Theodore is described as the metropolitan bishop of Miṣr.[1]

If this explanation is adopted, all difficulty arising from the distinction between the katholikos and Al Muḳauḳis vanishes: they were two different persons, and no one has ever contended that the bishop of Miṣr was Al Muḳauḳis. And the difficulty about the name Abū Maryām also vanishes. I would no longer say that the name is impossible—an erroneous assertion in which Dr. Lane-Poole follows me:[2] all I would say is that it is doubtful in this context. I would point out—what has not been noticed before, I think—that the same name is given to the Christian pervert at Balhīb in Ṭabarī's own story of the surrender of Alexandria—'Abdallah 'Abd ar Raḥmān *Abū Maryām*, where the forenames are clearly the Islamic additions.[3] The name therefore is possible: but the fact that we have Abū Maryām the metropolitan, Abū Maryām the bishop, and again Abū Maryām the pervert, unquestionably establishes a confusion which renders the whole of this nomenclature very uncertain. But if it was the metropolitan of Miṣr and another bishop who met 'Amr, there is nothing inconsistent with my theory in Ṭabarī's statement that they were sent by Al Muḳauḳis and returned to him: indeed the story then fits together admirably.[4]

[1] تادرس المترانوس اسقف مصر in *Hist. Pat.* (*Patr. Orient.* t. v. fasc. 1), p. 106.

[2] *P.R.I.A.*, p. 243.

[3] See Trad. B, p. 10, supra.

[4] I should say that I have frankly abandoned the explanation of

Before quitting Ṭabarī, however, I must point out a discrepancy in his evidence. For whereas in the one tradition he says that when 'Amr, reinforced by Zubair, met Abū Maryam and Abū Maryām, they fought with him;[1] in the other he says 'When 'Amr and Al Muḳauḳis met at 'Ain Shams, their armies began to fight'.[2] That these two statements refer to one and the same incident, does not in my opinion admit of reasonable doubt. It is one more illustration of the necessity of considering the various traditions in Ṭabarī in their isolation as well as in their union. But if the incident is the same, and if one tradition alleges that it was the katholikos of Miṣr, while another alleges that it was Al Muḳauḳis, whose meeting with 'Amr was followed by the battle at 'Ain Shams, or the battle of Heliopolis, then it follows that the Muḳauḳis may be identified with the katholikos of Miṣr, and the katholikos of Miṣr may be the metropolitan of Egypt, or in other words the Patriarch Cyrus. In that case, however, the tradition which separates Cyrus from Al Muḳauḳis must be so far mistaken. And it must be remembered that equal authority cannot attach to inconsistent traditions. One must choose between them on a balance of evidence.

the name Abū Maryām which I gave in the *Arab Conquest* (p. 513). It cannot be identified with the name Benjamin. Historically it is certain that Benjamin was in retreat in the desert till after the Muslim power was established in Egypt: and philologically I accept Caetani's objection that the names *Ibn Yāmīn* and *Maryām* were both so well known to the Arabs that confusion between them is very improbable. I may add that the very name Abū Maryām is found, in the Aphrodito papyri (MS. 1448, Brit. Mus. Catalogue), dating from about A.D. 700.

[1] p. 2584. [2] p. 2592.

Ṭabarī's testimony, however, rightly interpreted, not only harmonizes rather than clashes with my theory, but actually supports it. I may add that there is not a word in his whole story suggesting or justifying the identification of Al Muḳauḳis with any subordinate officer of the empire whatever.

Let us now see whether other Arabic historians bear out Dr. Lane-Poole's contention. There is an important passage in Ibn ʿAbd al Ḥakam (*c.* A.D. 850) which, so far as I know, has not been noticed in this connexion :

فوجّه هرقل ملك الروم كما نتى شيبج من اهل مصر المقوقس اميراً على مصر وجمل اليه حربها وجبايه خراجها ونزل الاسكندريه[1]

Which means that Heraclius, the Roman emperor, deputed Al Muḳauḳis as viceroy over Egypt with full military power and with control of the revenue or taxes. What can such a position mean but one of supreme authority ? In naming Al Muḳauḳis as controller of the revenue Ibn ʿAbd al Ḥakam is not only supported by Eutychius[2] (A.D. 876–939) among Arabic writers, but he is in most remarkable agreement with the seventh-century Coptic document,[3] which in recounting the visit of **ⲡⲕⲁⲩⲭⲓⲟⲥ ⲡⲉⲡⲥⲉⲩⲧⲟⲁⲣⲭⲏⲉⲡⲓⲥⲕⲟⲡⲟⲥ** (i.e. the Muḳauḳis, the

[1] This is in the part published by Karle, p. 55 of the Arabic text (Göttingen, 1856, 4to).

[2] For quotation and reference see below, p. 80.

[3] *MSS. Copt.*, Clar. Press, p. 5, published in Amélineau's *Vie de Samuel de Ḳalamīm.* See *Arab Conquest*, p. 518 ; but I did not know of the passage in Ibn ʿAbd al Ḥakam when that page was written.

sham archbishop), to the monastery of Ḳalamūn makes the archbishop claim the title of 'controller of the revenue of the land of Egypt'. Such a coincidence must carry great weight. Now this same incident is also recounted in the Arabic version of Coptic Synaxarium,[1] and there the person who tried to make Samuel confess the Chalcedonian or melkite form of belief is called definitely Al Muḳauḳis—a clear proof that пкаυχιос is the Coptic original of المقوقس — and one MS. adds to the name Al Muḳauḳis 'the patriarch'. The person then who claimed the title of Controller of the Revenue is proved by these two Coptic documents to be the Muḳauḳis just as Ibn 'Abd al Ḥakam alleges, and is also proved to be the melkite archbishop and patriarch—or Cyrus.

But there is a further striking correspondence

[1] *Synaxaire Arabe Jacobite*, par René Basset, in Patrol. Orient. . iii. fasc. 3, p. 406. The authority of this Arabic version has been impugned by Dr. Lane-Poole on the ground of its lateness. The truth is that it embodies traditions and records from the earliest times, with late additions. I may perhaps give one example proving its remarkable accuracy. On p. 326 of t. i, in Basset's edition, is an account of an eclipse which occurred in 958 of the era of the Martyrs (29 Aug. 1241–28 Aug. 1242), and which, being on 6th October, fell in 1241, and not, as Basset says, in 1242. The description of the eclipse is such as to preclude any other than a total eclipse, and the writer clearly depicts totality at Alexandria. When I asked the astronomers to verify the statement, I was told that Oppolzer's chart shows the line of totality along the north of Asia Minor, and therefore far away from Alexandria. But the description of totality at Alexandria was so unmistakable, that I had the matter referred to Greenwich Observatory, where a rough calculation was made, correcting Oppolzer, and showing the line of totality as passing through Alexandria. Thus the historical accuracy of this record in the *Synaxarium* is completely vindicated.

between Ibn 'Abd al Ḥakam and another quite independent authority. The Arabic historian makes two statements about Al Muḳauḳis, the one emphasizing his military, the other his fiscal authority. On the fiscal side, we have clear confirmation from Coptic documents; on the military side I now give a curious confirmation from a seventh-century Syriac document which has not very long come to light. The *Chronicon Anonymum,* translated and edited by Guidi and published among the Chronica Minora,[1] was written in the seventh century shortly after the subjugation of Egypt, and it declares that the Arabs were deterred at first from the invasion because the frontiers of Egypt were defended with a large and powerful army *by the patriarch of Alexandria.* Such a statement would sound almost incredible, if it stood alone: how could an archbishop control these purely military measures? But if the patriarch at this time was Cyrus, as is not denied, and if Cyrus was Al Muḳauḳis, then the assertion of the very early Syriac document exactly tallies with Ibn 'Abd al Ḥakam's description of the viceroy as clothed with full military power.

So much, then, for Ibn 'Abd al Ḥakam. It is obviously impossible to deny that he represents Al Muḳauḳis as sent to Egypt by Heraclius with

[1] *Corpus Script. Hist. Orient.—Scriptores Syri*: Ser. iii, t. iv, p. 31 'Potiti sunt Arabes tota regione Syriae et Palestinae. Aegyptum quoque ingredi in animo erat, sed non valuerunt: *custodiebantur enim fines exercitu magno et vi, a patriarcha Alexandrino*'. Guidi remarks that the Chronicle as it stands may be dated with certainty A.D. 670–80, though parts seem older, and that it was the work of a Nestorian monk.

full civil and military power; that such a description cannot conceivably apply to any subordinate official; and that the evidence of this Arabic writer is most remarkably confirmed by independent Coptic and Syriac documents almost or actually contemporary with the conquest.

Al Balādhurī (A.D. 806–93) is not very definite about Al Muḳauḳis. But he represents him as having concluded peace with 'Amr under a treaty which Heraclius repudiated—presumably the treaty of Miṣr; as subsequently in command at Alexandria during the siege; and as again negotiating with 'Amr for the surrender of that city. There is no word in this writer to support the assumption that the Muḳauḳis was a subordinate official: indeed Balādhurī's account is in close agreement with John of Nikiou's account of Cyrus.

Al Y'aḳūbī (died A.D. 873), who was not an Egyptian, makes the Muḳauḳis conclude peace with 'Amr—a peace which Heraclius repudiated.

Ibn al Athīr (A.D. 1160–1232) seems to follow Ṭabarī; but he describes Abū Maryam, who was sent by Al Muḳauḳis to meet 'Amr, as *katholikos of Memphis*, clearly showing that he understood the expression *katholikos of Miṣr* as referring to the bishop of the city of Miṣr and not to the patriarch of Alexandria. There is therefore nothing inconsistent in Ibn al Athīr's evidence with the theory identifying Al Muḳauḳis with Cyrus. I may add that bishop and archbishop were not very clearly distinguished by Arab writers. Thus Abu 'l Maḥāsin, who speaks of Abū Maryam as katholikos of Miṣr, also speaks of Benjamin as bishop of

Alexandria. So the phrase *bishop of Rome* is not unknown in history. But Ibn al Athīr represents the Muḳauḳis as ordering battle to be given at 'Ain Shams on the advice of the military tribune; as negotiating later at Alexandria; and as making peace with the Arabs. This Arabic historian then in no way countenances the theory that the Muḳauḳis could be a subordinate officer.

Yaḳūt (A.D. 1178–1229) makes the Muḳauḳis the author of the peace on behalf of Copts and Romans and subject to the emperor's approval—evidence that he was in the writer's opinion viceroy of Egypt.

Al Makīn (A.D. 1205–73) says that Al Muḳauḳis was 'governor of Egypt in the name of Heraclius', i.e. viceroy.

Ibn Duḳmāḳ (*c.* A.D. 1350–1406) cites Ibn Wahb as quoting Al Laith ibn S'ad as follows: 'Al Muḳauḳis, the Roman, who was viceroy (ملك) of Egypt, made terms of peace with 'Amr.'

Maḳrīzī (A.D. 1365–1442) quotes Yazīd ibn Abī Ḥabīb as saying that 'Al Muḳauḳis, the Roman, being governor of Egypt, made peace with 'Amr'; and 'the fort', i.e. Babylon, 'was commanded by Al U'airig under the authority of the Muḳauḳis'; and of the Muḳauḳis again 'he governed the country for the emperor Heraclius'. He also made the Treaty of Miṣr, which the emperor repudiated, 'reproaching *his representative* with imitating the cowardice and meanness of the Egyptians,' &c. There is no shadow of doubt that Al Maḳrīzī regarded Al Muḳauḳis as viceroy of Egypt.

Abu 'l Maḥāsin (A.D. 1411–69) says that 'the

commander of Ḳaṣr ash Shamʻa (i. e. fortress of
Babylon) was 'Ughairig, who was subordinate
to Al Muḳauḳis'.[1] The same writer says again,
'Then began the siege of the fortress, which was
commanded by Al Mandafūr[2] *on behalf of Al
Muḳauḳis*, ibn Ḳarḳab al Yunānī.' Again he speaks
of 'the principal Egyptians with their governor
Al Muḳauḳis'. There was no question of an inferior
official in the judgement of Abu 'l Maḥāsin.

With him As Suyūṭī (A.D. 1445–1505) is in general
agreement: 'The emperor Heraclius repudiated the
agreement made by Al Muḳauḳis with the Arabs,'
and so forth.

In order to meet Dr. Lane-Poole's statement that,
so far as the Arabic evidence goes, Al Muḳauḳis
might be 'sub-governor' or some official under the
governor-general of Egypt, I have reviewed the
evidence and selected definitions of his authority
and position from the principal Arabic historians
from Ibn ʻAbd al Ḥakam down to As Suyūṭī. And
what is the result? They one and all either describe
him as مَلِك king or viceroy, and امِير, prince or
governor-general, or else they describe his office in
terms which cannot possibly apply to any but the
supreme authority in Egypt. The Arabic historians,
therefore, can only be taken to prove that the
Muḳauḳis was Heraclius' viceroy in Egypt; and
they totally fail to support any theory which would

---

[1] Two MSS. give the name of the Muḳauḳis as جُرَيْج or جُرَيْج
ibn Mīnā. Clearly the name has been transferred from the commander of the fortress to the Muḳauḳis by error.

[2] Probably μανδάτωρ, as I have shown. See *Arab Conquest*,
p. 513.

assign to him any subordinate position. He was ruler of the country, deputed by the emperor, exactly as Ibn 'Abd al Ḥakam alleges.

So much seems fairly established. But if Dr. Lane-Poole was driven to the theory that Al Muḳauḳis held a subordinate position as the only way of avoiding the identification of Al Muḳauḳis with Cyrus, and if that theory has been proved totally irreconcilable with the evidence of the Arabic historians on which he relied, then Dr. Lane-Poole's position has become altogether untenable.

But his argument had two divisions—one, that the Arabic evidence told against the identification of Cyrus with the Muḳauḳis, the other that the Coptic evidence was unworthy of credit. On the first I have rebutted his contention: I now will deal with his attempt to discredit the Coptic authorities. It is quite true that I said in the *Arab Conquest of Egypt*[1] that the historical value of certain Coptic documents which I named is not very great; but the saying is quoted somewhat unfairly against me. The reason I gave was that the writers, 'where they might have told us so much, furnish only a few scanty and incidental allusions to contemporary history'; but it is obviously most unjust to reject the historical material which Coptic authorities do afford on the ground that they do not afford more. In these documents the allusions to matters of history are clearly unstudied, and when they relate to contemporary events, they are of unquestionable value. I have already dwelt on the Bodleian seventh-century Coptic MS. recounting the visit of

[1] Pref. p. x.

the melkite archbishop to the monastery of Ḳalamūn, and I have shown how it agrees with the story of the same event (in which the visitor is called Al Muḳauḳis) in the Arabic Synaxarium. Is this evidence to be rejected? On the contrary, I have shown that the identification of Cyrus as military ruler of Egypt is further confirmed by the seventh-century Syriac document, and I may now add that there is a distinct precedent for the union of the supreme secular and ecclesiastical power in a single person to be found in the sixth century. For Justinian offered the patriarchate of Alexandria coupled with the viceroyalty to Theodosius, if only he would accept the tome of Leo;[1] and, this being so, there is clearly nothing remarkable in the fact that Heraclius united both offices in the person of Cyrus.[2] Both these statements are made by, or at least occur in, Severus: whose history with its later additions is a compilation the value of which is now admitted by scholars. I spoke somewhat slightingly of it, no doubt;[3] but I spoke on imperfect acquaintance with the work, which then existed only in MS., but has since been in large part published. Mr. Evetts, who is editing the text with a translation, thus speaks of the work: '*L'Histoire des Patriarches d'Alexandrie* est le *Liber Pontificalis* de l'Église Copte. La première partie est une compilation faite . . . par Sévère, évêque d'El Eshmounein dans la Haute-Égypte, d'après des documents grecs et coptes qu'il a trouvés dans les monastères de son pays et qu'il a traduits

[1] *Hist. Pat.*, p. 462. [2] Id., p. 489.
[3] *Arab Conquest*, Pref., p. xiv.

avec l'aide de quelques clercs. . . . Dès le septième siècle et surtout dès l'époque de la conquête arabe, l'histoire des patriarches devient beaucoup plus complète et plus intéressante. *Nous avons ici une série de vraies biographies écrites par des auteurs contemporains.*' With this verdict no one who has carefully studied the work of Severus can fail to agree; but as I have not seen any reasoned discussion of the question, I may venture to give some of the grounds which justify a high estimate of Severus' authority as a historian.[1]

From the earliest times the records of the Coptic Church seem to have been written mainly in the form of biographies, and to have been preserved in the library of the well-known monastery of Macarius at Waḍī Naṭrūn. No better place of security could have been found than within the walls of this remote convent fortress in the desert; and here were stored the MSS. on which Severus founded his history. A note dated June 1, A.D. 1081, and added to the text runs as follows[2]: 'Here ends the sixteenth chapter wherein the history of the fathers is completed as far as Abba Simon, the forty-second patriarch. . . . Hereafter will follow that which we have translated from the documents in the monastery of St. Macarius, viz. the history of the patriarchs from Michael the Last to Sinuthius the First. We

[1] Renaudot in his preface has some remarks on the value of Severus, and gives reasons for not publishing the whole text; but he does not deal with the internal evidence which the text affords for its historic authenticity (*Historia Patriarcharum Alexandrinorum*, Paris, 1713, 4to).

[2] *Hist. Pat. Alex.* in *Patrol. Orient.*, t. v, fasc. 1, p. 47.

also translated in this monastery the lives of nine other patriarchs in the year 796 of the Martyrs (A.D. 1080). This is written by Apacyrus the deacon and Michael, son of Apater, of Damanhūr, through the grace of God which enabled us to find the histories in the monastery of St. Macarius, with the help of the brother Theodore, the steward, son of Paul, on Sunday the 6th of B'aūnah in the year 797 of the righteous martyrs. We have compared the MSS. one with another and found them corresponding to our copies, and so we assured ourselves of their authenticity.'

This is a record of the careful and conscientious study of original sources, and the same process can be traced nearly four centuries earlier. For we learn from another passage[1] that events up to the time of Chalcedon and Dioscorus (*c.* A.D. 450) were 'written down in the twelfth part of the histories of the Church'. Next, for the chronicle from Cyril down to Alexander 'we may consult the teacher and scribe George, archdeacon and secretary to the patriarch Simon' (A.D. 689–701), who also wrote his history at the monastery of St. Macarius; and the writer adds, 'Therefore I, the vile sinner, beg you to pray the Lord Christ for me that he may loose the bond of my feeble tongue and open my darkened heart and give me knowledge of words, so that I may be able to show forth what you, my brethren and my father, ask of me, not as a teacher and guide above you but *as a scholar*, *since I saw that of which I have written with mine own eyes* and its importance imposes an obligation upon me, besides

[1] *Hist. Pat.*, pp. 90–93.

what I heard from friends older than myself such as I could trust and believe.[1] . . . Indeed the Lord Christ knows that *we have added nothing to the facts*, having related what took place down to the death of the blessed father Theodore, patriarch of Alexandria, and the affairs of state in his days to the end of the seventeenth chapter of the history, completed above,' i. e. to A.D. 743. 'Now . . . we will write the eighteenth chapter of the history of the Church,' the historian proceeds, while to an assertion which he makes a few lines lower he adds, 'as we witnessed with our own eyes many times'; and again, 'They set up a king called Kyriakos (in Nubia) who has remained king to the day on which I write this history.'[2] Here is clear proof of a contemporary writer in the eighth century of our era. The writer was the secretary to Mūsā, bishop of Wasīm, near Gīzah, who constantly writes in the first person—e.g. 'we attended at the palace', 'there was with us Abba Theodore, bishop of Miṣr,' &c.—and he gives textually an extract of the patriarch Michael's memorandum (on the subject of the monastery of Mīnā by Mariūṭ) which was presented to 'Abd al Malik's secretary.[3] On the other hand he defends an omission of certain incidents by saying, 'I have related these matters

[1] This bears a close resemblance to the well-known passage in Thucydides i. 22 τὰ δ' ἔργα τῶν πραχθέντων . . . οὐκ ἐκ τοῦ παρατυχόντος πυνθανόμενος ἠξίωσα γράφειν, οὐδ' ὡς ἐμοὶ ἐδόκει, ἀλλ' οἷς τε αὐτὸς παρῆν καὶ παρὰ τῶν ἄλλων ὅσον δυνατὸν ἀκριβείᾳ περὶ ἑκάστου ἐπεξελθών. It would have been well if Ṭabarī and other Arabic writers had shown the same critical spirit and the same regard for historical accuracy.

[2] *Hist. Pat.*, p. 143.

[3] Id., p. 122.

in the book of his (Michael's) biography apart from this history.'[1] But he again records historical events—the death of Marwān: 'they impaled Marwān head downwards, having taken him prisoner: and we were witnesses of this event.'[2]

In the seventh century the biographer of John III (A.D. 677–86), in recounting the story of John's last journey to Alexandria says, 'the writer of this history was with him, for he was his spiritual son,' and he gives many graphic details such as a contemporary writer alone could furnish.

Further, many historical allusions which occur in Severus and can be controlled, are obviously correct. Thus in the account of Simon I we read, 'On a Sunday news came to the Amīr that the army of the Romans had risen against the prince Justinian and deposed him, and had appointed Leontius in his stead.'[3] Simon's patriarchate is dated A.D. 689–701 or rather 700, and Justinian II was deposed in A.D. 695. Again, 'Meanwhile the Roman monarchy was like a children's game.[4] For when the Romans had deposed Justinian their prince, they made Leo (or Leontius) their ruler in his place. But Leo was put to death before he had completed the third year of his reign, and after him reigned Apeimarus (called Tiberius). . . . After him reigned Philippicus. Then after two years Anastasius was made prince of the Romans and is still reigning. [By saying *still* the writer means at the time of composing the history.[5]]'

[1] *Hist. Pat.*, p. 114. [2] Id., p. 187. [3] Id., p. 35.

[4] Such as that known as *King of the Castle*.

[5] *Hist. Pat.*, p. 57. The words in square brackets are a note by

One other instance must suffice. When the tyrant Ḳurrah was governor of Egypt, we are told that he exercised the most violent extortion, seizing and confiscating private property, estates, revenues, and endowments, till the people were reduced to abject poverty, 'and men began to flee from place to place, but no place would harbour them.' For Ḳurrah sent his agent, 'who collected the fugitives from every place, and brought them back, and bound them and punished them.'[1] These events are recorded as happening in the patriarchate of Alexander II (A.D. 705–30). Now this account has been absolutely confirmed by the recently discovered Aphrodito papyri, where precisely the same story of the fugitives may be gathered from the Greek documents, which are dated A.D. 708–10.[2] This coincidence of the two versions is exceedingly strong evidence for the historical accuracy of the *History of the Patriarchs.*

It is no doubt difficult at times to distinguish the real author of any particular story in this work, for the reason that the biographies and other documents embodied in the history were written by several hands during the life or just after the death of the successive patriarchs; and the *ego* of the writer is constantly changing. Thus the compiler who says, at the end of the life of Michael I, 'he

the translator or editor of the original Greek or Coptic record. Mr. Evetts ascribes the note to Mauhūb.

[1] *Hist. Pat.*, p. 64.

[2] See two articles by Mr. H. I. Bell, (1) *The Aphrodito Papyri* in *Journal of Hellenic Studies*, vol. xxviii, p. 98 (1908), and (2) *Translations of the Greek Aphrodito Papyri in the British Museum* in *Der Islam*, Bd. ii, Heft 2/3, p. 270 (Strassburg, 1911).

remained on the evangelical throne, according to the statement which we found in the library of the monastery of St. Macarius, twenty-three years and a half' [1] (to A.D. 768), cannot be the same as the writer who speaks of Anastasius as Roman emperor still reigning, though he is doubtless the author of the comment on the word *still*. But the fact that the various MSS. found in the library were copied *verbatim et litteratim*, and that they go back to the earliest times and are contemporary for the most part with the events recorded, gives a very high value to the work. Of course, miraculous and fabulous elements as well as mistakes are found, just as they are found in all the Arab historians; but there would be little early history of any sort left, if every record tainted with legendary matter or error were rejected. And on the whole I say without fear that the general credibility of the patriarchal chronicles on matters of history is established beyond question.

This has been a rather long digression; but it was necessary to rebut Dr. Lane-Poole's assertion impugning Severus' authority. He makes a great point of the apparent admission by Severus that he did not know Greek or Coptic. This confession of ignorance is certainly made by the writer of the third preface to the history; but there is strong evidence that Severus' name was attached by the error of a copyist to that preface, which Severus cannot have written.[2] There proves therefore on examination to

[1] *Hist. Pat.*, p. 215.

[2] The share of Severus in the editorship of these histories is difficult to determine. If the third preface were written by him, it

be little or no warrant for the belief that Severus was ignorant of Greek and Coptic, and every warrant for the belief that his history was a careful compilation founded upon authentic documents. It is accordingly wrong to discredit his evidence; indeed, I am not aware of a single Arab historian whose work can be shown to be based in the same way upon a continuous series of written records, and records, for the most part, of contemporary writers. The Arab historians recount a great many traditions of early times, but they very seldom cite or even mention original documents.[1] In other words, Coptic history is based on a much more scientific and solid foundation of MS. authority.

These considerations justify such an estimate of the historical value of Severus' work, that its evidence on the question of Al Muḳauḳis' identity cannot be

would mean that his collection went down to his own times, i. e. at least to A.D. 977, and that it included some biographies, composed by himself, of patriarchs his contemporaries. But the author or compiler of the ten biographies from Michael III (A.D. 881) to Sinuthius II (died A.D. 1047) was Michael, bishop of Tīnnis; and in these Severus had no hand. It seems probable, according to the best opinion, that Severus' own work was the collection and compilation of the lives of the first forty-two patriarchs from St. Mark to Simon I, and that this is the work referred to as the *Book of Biographies* in the list of Severus' works given in the Life of Philotheus (A.D. 981–1005); and also the work which about a hundred years later was discovered at the monastery of the Lady at Nahyā by Mauhūb, as he relates in his preface to the twenty-sixth chapter of the *History of the Patriarchs*, a chapter not yet published (Paris MS. 302, p. 135).

[1] Of course, it is common enough for one Arab writer to quote another, e. g. Maḳrīzī cites Ibn 'Abd al Ḥakam and others. But Ibn 'Abd al Ḥakam does not enlighten us with regard to his original MS. sources.

lightly set aside. Let us see then what Severus says—or rather the biographer of the patriarch Benjamin.

'Heraclius appointed Cyrus, governor of Egypt, to be both patriarch and governor together.' When Cyrus came to Alexandria Benjamin was warned and fled to a desert monastery in Upper Egypt, where he remained in hiding for ten years, and 'these were the years', he says, 'during which Heraclius and Al Muḳauḳis reigned over Egypt.' He again speaks of Al Muḳauḳis as having driven him away, and speaks of Cyrus as 'the misbelieving governor of Alexandria, who was both governor and patriarch under the Romans'.[1] This language establishes the identity of Cyrus and Al Muḳauḳis very clearly, and, as I have shown,[2] it completely agrees with the language of the Arabic Synaxarium[3] —'Al Muḳauḳis was head of the faith of Chalcedon, and had been made governor and patriarch over Egypt',—and with the Ethiopic Synaxarium, 'Al Muḳauḳis, i. e. the governor and archbishop of the city of Alexandria and all the land of Egypt.'[1] I have also shown the exact correspondence of the language with that of the contemporary Bodleian MS., which makes the Muḳauḳis hold the two offices of archbishop (or patriarch) and controller of finance in Egypt; and I have shown how a nearly contem-

[1] *Hist. Pat.*, pp. 490, 491, 495.

[2] *Arab Conquest*, p. 521.

[3] The fact that the story of Benjamin at Ḳalamūn and the visit of Al Muḳauḳis is confirmed by the contemporary Bodleian MS., is good evidence for the authority of the Synaxarium on this question.

porary Syriac MS., the *Chronicon Anonymum*, makes the patriarch of Alexandria responsible for the military defences of Egypt against the Arabs; while on the other hand the Arab historian Ibn 'Abd al Ḥakam describes the viceroy of Heraclius in Egypt as possessing full military power and as controller of finance, and calls him Al Muḳauḳis.

The Greek historians also use language tending to the same conclusion. Nicephorus[1] says that Heraclius sent Marianus to Alexandria to act in concert with Cyrus, the patriarch of Alexandria, and to settle together some arrangement with regard to the Arabs; and again he speaks of Cyrus as bishop of Alexandria.[2]

Theophanes is more explicit. He says, 'on the death of George (melkite or Chalcedonian patriarch) Cyrus was sent as bishop to Alexandria,'[3] and speaking of the Arabs he says: 'They invaded Egypt. Now Cyrus was charged before the emperor with having made over the gold of Egypt to the Arabs, and the emperor sent an angry message for his recall.'[4]

The facts to which these Greek writers testify are as follows. Both agree that Cyrus was patriarch of

[1] Nicephorus Constantinopolitanus, *De Rebus post Mauricium gestis*, *Corp. Script. Hist. Byzant.*, p. 28 παραγγείλας ὡς ἀνακοινοῦσθαι Κύρῳ τῷ Ἀλεξανδρείας ἱεράρχῃ καὶ ὡς ἂν κοινῇ βουλεύσοιντο τὰ πρὸς τοὺς Σαρακηνοὺς διάδοιντο.

[2] Id. ib., p. 30.

[3] See *Corp. Script. Hist. Byzant.*, *Theophanes*, t. i, p. 507.

[4] Id. ib., p. 518 Στρατεύουσι κατ' Αἰγύπτου. κατηγορεῖτο δὲ ὁ Κῦρος ἐπὶ τοῦ βασιλέως ὡς τὸ χρυσίον τῆς Αἰγύπτου τοῖς Σαρακηνοῖς δούς. καὶ ἀποστείλας μετ' ὀργῆς τοῦτον μετεπέμψατο.

Alexandria. Nicephorus also represents Marianus,[1] the military commander, as sent by Heraclius under orders to act with Cyrus in reference to the Arabs—a statement which implies that Cyrus had secular as well as ecclesiastical authority in Egypt; while Theophanes asserts that Cyrus, having undertaken to pay tribute to the Arabs, was angrily recalled by Heraclius. This again implies that Cyrus was armed with secular power as Heraclius' viceroy, and the allusion is clearly to the treaty of Miṣr made by Cyrus and its angry repudiation by the emperor.[2]

[1] The names Marinus and Marianus are both given in Theophanes, but to separate persons; and I cannot help wondering whether these names lie concealed under the Arabic Abū Maryam and Abū Maryām. Marianus also is found in the biography of Benjamin in Severus. It is of course true that these Graeco-Roman names are given to generals and not to bishops, as in Ṭabarī's story; but the confusion is quite possible. The name Aretianus is also found, and some confusion with Aretion certainly exists here; while Arrianus seems to be another variant.

[2] Caetani (pp. 244–5) has a long note criticizing what he calls my reconstruction of the conquest in connexion with this incident. He is persuaded that the Copts, literally so called as distinct from the Romans, entered into the treaty of Miṣr—a view which I have endeavoured to refute above—and he remarks: 'Non è logico che i Copti, nel fare un trattato con gli Arabi, si riserbassero di sentire il parere ed avere l'approvazione di Eraclio. È chiaro che Eraclio l'avrebbe respinto. Nel testo di Ibn 'Abd al Ḥakam si parla d'un solo trattato e non di due. Ciro al principio dell' assedio di Babilonia era forse in Alessandria, e le fonti bizantine ignorano questo trattato respinto da Eraclio e la deposizione di Ciro per effetto di esso.' Apart from the fallacious assumption that the Copts, as such, were in a position to make any treaty, it seems a sufficient answer to say that the learned Italian writer must have forgotten Theophanes. For the rest, I cannot agree that the recall of Cyrus was caused by his general mismanagement of the war, or by a sudden outburst of wrath on Heraclius' part, or that his

But how closely this evidence of the Greek historians tallies with that of the Arab writers in all but this one point—that the Arabs use the term *Al Muḳauḳis* where the Greeks write *Cyrus*! For the Arab writers agree generally that the treaty with 'Amr was made by Al Muḳauḳis, that it had to be submitted by him for approval to Heraclius, and that Heraclius repudiated it with anger; and though they do not mention the recall of Al Muḳauḳis, the recall of Cyrus is confirmed by the contemporary writer John of Nikiou.

It remains briefly to notice the testimony of two Christian Arabic historians—Abū Ṣāliḥ, and Sa'īd ibn al Bāṭrīḳ or Eutychius. Abū Ṣāliḥ, while agreeing that Al Muḳauḳis was made governor of Egypt by Heraclius,[1] also says that the ten years of banishment suffered by the patriarch Benjamin were the ten years during which Al Muḳauḳis was ruling in Egypt.[2] I do not blink the fact that Abū Ṣāliḥ makes the Muḳauḳis bear the name of George, son of Mīnā,[3] and that other writers give

mission to Egypt after Heraclius' death proves that he was not regarded as a traitor. It merely proves that the surrender advocated by Cyrus was no longer thought impossible. One more point. Yāḳūt expressly says that though the Muḳauḳis generally resided at Alexandria, yet that he was at Babylon at the time of the siege, as Caetani (p. 254) records: how then can Caetani justify the assertion that he was *perhaps* at Alexandria?

[1] Caetani, p. 81. [2] Id., p. 230.

[3] I have not much to alter in the views expressed by me in the *Arab Conquest* (pp. 522–3), though I doubt now whether Al 'Arāj (which means 'the cripple') was suggested in any way by Jurīj or Juraij. It looks more like a nickname to which we have no further clue; while Juraij doubtless, as Caetani remarks, corresponds to Gregory rather than to George. In that case it = Ḳarḳar. Caetani,

other names; but it is sufficient to say that no name whatever is attached to the title in any early authority, and that a name first occurring five or six centuries after the death of Al Muḳauḳis cannot stand for a moment against the cumulative force of the arguments identifying Al Muḳauḳis with Cyrus. Abū Ṣāliḥ the Armenian then agrees with the Coptic and Greek and with the Egyptian historians as to the office which Al Muḳauḳis held, and he agrees with Severus that Al Muḳauḳis was the Chalcedonian persecutor of the Copts who drove Benjamin into exile.

Eutychius (A.D. 876–939) wrote about three centuries before Abū Ṣāliḥ, and it must be remembered that he was not merely a Chalcedonian himself, but actually melkite patriarch in Egypt. He says, 'After the flight of George, Cyrus became patriarch of Alexandria. He was a Maronite, of the same creed as Heraclius';[1] but in another place[2] he says:

و كان العامل على الخراج بمصر المقوقس من قبل هركل الملك

The controller of the revenue in Egypt on behalf of the emperor Heraclius was Al Muḳauḳis, 'who was', he adds, 'a Jacobite (or Copt) hating the Romans, but not daring to betray his Jacobite opinions, lest he should be put to death by the Romans'!

Of course Eutychius as melkite patriarch was anxious to remove from the memory of Cyrus the

p. 91: cf. also his note on p. 94 with reference to my explanation of the term Ḳarḳar.

[1] *Eutychii Annales*, ed. Pococke, t. ii, p. 267 (Oxon., 1654, 4to).

[2] Id. ib., p. 302.

odium of the surrender of Egypt to the Arabs; but he is driven to strange shifts. Thus having declared that Cyrus came as patriarch on Heraclius' appointment to Alexandria, he avers on the same page that there was no melkite patriarch of Alexandria for ninety-seven years after the flight of George—a very daring perversion of history. Apparently, therefore, Eutychius at once refuses to recognize Cyrus as melkite patriarch and at the same time charges Al Muḳauḳis with being a Copt at heart. The very charge is an admission that Al Muḳauḳis was professedly a melkite: and though Eutychius does not say that Cyrus and Al Muḳauḳis were one, this coincidence is very significant; while his further statement that Al Muḳauḳis was made controller of the revenue by Heraclius brings him into line with Ibn 'Abd al Ḥakam and with the Bodleian Coptic MS. Like the Arab writers too Eutychius represents Al Muḳauḳis as present in the fortress of Babylon at the siege, as retiring to Rauḍah, as negotiating with 'Amr, and as concluding peace by the Treaty of Miṣr. But I attribute Eutychius' failure to identify Cyrus with Al Muḳauḳis in terms rather to ignorance than to disingenuousness—an ignorance which leads him to speak of Al Muḳauḳis as alive at the time of Manuel's rebellion.[1]

[1] Ibn 'Abd al Ḥakam has been quoted as supporting this statement; but the fact is that there was no one alive at the date of Manuel's rebellion (A. D. 645) to whom the name could apply, and Arab writers persistently confuse the peaceful surrender of Alexandria by the Muḳauḳis with its subsequent recapture from the rebel Manuel.

I have now shown what an extraordinary concurrence and convergence of evidence there is from original and sometimes contemporary documents—Greek, Coptic, Syriac, and Arabic—establishing the identity of Al Muḳauḳis with Cyrus, Patriarch of Alexandria, Controller of the Revenues, and Governor-General of Egypt at the time of the conquest. It is no answer to say that the title Al Muḳauḳis is sometimes given by Arab historians to this or that person who cannot have been Cyrus. I admit the fact, but totally deny the conclusion that, because the term is misapplied in particular cases and bestowed on different persons, therefore it does not properly belong to any single person. That seems to be Caetani's argument.[1] But the truth rather is that while the Arab historians for the most part wrote with only a vague notion of the Muḳauḳis as

[1] p. 342. 'Nella narrazione della resa di Babilonia presso le fonti Arabi noi crediamo perciò possibile che sotto il nome di Al Muqawqis siano da intendersi due persone distinte e diverse, le quali nullo hanno che fare con Ciro ossia il comandante militare greco che consegnò la rocca di Babilonia, e un qualche vescovo copto che ottenne un accordo provvisorio per la protezione delli Copti sino alla fine della campagna contro i Greci. Siccome Ciro infine riappare sicuramente nei cronisti musulmani come Al Muqawqis alla resa di Alessandria, è evidente che sotto un solo nome si ascondono per lo meno tre persone distinte.' Again on pp. 244–5 he speaks of my 'erroneous theory that Al Muḳauḳis is always Cyrus'. That of course is an unfair presentment of the case. I admit fully that actions and situations are ascribed by Arab historians to an Al Muḳauḳis who cannot always be Cyrus; but their erroneous application of the name does not render my theory erroneous. But I hope it is not presumptuous to say, in differing from Caetani, that I have the profoundest respect and admiration for his monumental *Annali dell' Islam* and the amazing amount of scholarly labour and research which it contains.

governor of Egypt, they not unnaturally represent him at times as concerned in actions or incidents in which he had no direct part or presence. They were undeniably bewildered on the subject of his name and personality, and thus make mistakes about it. But the problem remains amid their discrepancies to discover the true personality—to identify the real Muḳauḳis. No Arab writer has said or could say that there were three different persons all rightly bearing that title: nor is it logical to argue that the existence of discrepancies renders the riddle of the title insoluble. It is the business of historical criticism to sift discrepancies and to get at the underlying truth. And I venture to think that an impartial survey of the evidence establishes beyond question the conclusion that Al Muḳauḳis must be identified with Cyrus and with no one else.

INDEX

BABYLON OF EGYPT

A STUDY IN THE HISTORY OF OLD CAIRO

BY

A. J. BUTLER, D.Litt.

FELLOW OF BRASENOSE COLLEGE

OXFORD

AT THE CLARENDON PRESS

TABLE OF CONTENTS

Chapter I.

Chapter II.

Chapter III.

BABYLON OF EGYPT

CHAPTER I

ALTHOUGH a good deal depends upon the meaning to be attached to the term Babylon in the Arab chronicles of Egypt, and although oriental scholars have given some attention to the subject,[1] I am not aware that any comprehensive study of the question has been made with a view either to define the proper usage of the term in the seventh century of our era or to examine critically those misunderstandings and misapplications of the term, which originated with Arab authors, but have been followed with too ready acquiescence by at least some modern historians.

Of course all are agreed that the name finds its local habitation somewhere in the region of Ancient Miṣr, now called Old Cairo : but the expression Babylon is often narrowed in historical writings to denote either the Roman fortress built by Trajan and called Ḳaṣr ash Shamaʿ, or else a fort in the neighbourhood of Ḳaṣr ash Shamaʿ but not identical with it; and upon these interpretations are based

[1] Quatremère (*Mém.*, i. 45 seq.), Amélineau in his *Géographie de l'Égypte à l'époque copte*, and Casanova in *Noms coptes du Caire*, as well as in his edition of Maḳrîzî and other works, have dealt with some aspects of the question, and to them I render all due acknowledgement.

conclusions seriously affecting both the history and the topography of the Arab conquest.

On the contrary I shall show, or aim at showing, in this essay that for many centuries before the conquest Babylon was the recognized name of a town or city of great importance: that the term was so understood at the time of the conquest: and that this usage prevailed for some centuries after the conquest. At the same time it will be made clear that, owing to that strange dualism of nomenclature which the normal coexistence of different languages in Egypt renders so common there, the usage of the term cannot be sharply distinguished from other names of the same town or locality: but that in fact the primeval name of ⲭⲏⲙⲓ, the ancient name of Miṣr (which was also adopted by the Arabs), the name of Memphis, the old capital, the Greek name Letopolis, and finally the name Fusṭâṭ, bestowed on the place by the Arabs, are all used more or less interchangeably with Babylon at different epochs by various writers, Coptic, Greek, or Arabic.

I cannot pretend to say what is the earliest mention of Babylon in history. But it is sufficient for my purpose to begin with Diodorus Siculus, whose account of Egypt may probably be dated about 50 B.C. He relates [1] that a number of prisoners were brought from Asiatic Babylon by Sesostris to carry out his public works in Egypt, and were driven by the hardships of their task to revolt. Thereupon they seized a strong position on the Nile, carried on war against the Egyptians, and harried

[1] i. 55.

the country round: but they were finally amnestied, and they founded a settlement on the spot which they called Babylon. Ctesias, he adds, gives a different account, alleging that Babylon was founded by some of those who came to Egypt with Semiramis.

Both Sesostris and Semiramis are so remote and so legendary that these stories have little importance except as testifying to the tradition that the name Babylon in Egypt had a real historical origin —which Pauly denies.[1]

Diodorus is said to have travelled in Egypt. Strabo certainly visited that country in 24–25 B.C., and saw at Babylon a fortified position held by one of three Roman legions then garrisoning Egypt.[2] He confirms the tradition ascribing the foundation of this Babylon to a revolt of Babylonians, and in another passage he even applies the term Babylonians to the people of the place.[3] But I have discussed Strabo's evidence so fully elsewhere[4] that I need not repeat my argument here: I am satisfied, however—and most scholars agree—that the Roman encampment at that time must have been on the elevated plateau which lies to the south of Ḳaṣr ash Shamaʿ, and which was called later by the Arabs Ar Raṣad. But the camp in that position was dependent, as Strabo shows, for its water supply upon a series of water-wheels which raised it from the Nile: and machinery of this kind was obviously

[1] *Real-Encyclopädie*, s.v. Babylon. [2] *Geog.*, xvii. 35.

[3] 'The Babylonians opposite Memphis,' *κῆβον δὲ Βαβυλώνιοι οἱ κατὰ Μέμφιν* (sc. *τιμῶσι*), xvii. 812.

[4] *Ancient Coptic Churches*, i. 172.

open to destruction by any hostile force. It was clearly this consideration which made Trajan erect Ḳaṣr ash Shamaʿ on the flat, close to the river bank, with an inlet for boats from the Nile to the southern gate of the fortress, and he made up for the loss of advantage in position by the immense strength and the height of the walls and towers of the new castle.[1]

Josephus, writing perhaps about A. D. 80, and speaking of the Israelite exodus, says that the Hebrews journeyed *κατὰ Λητοῦς πόλιν, ἔρημον τότε οὖσαν· Βαβυλὼν γὰρ ὕστερον κτίζεται ἐκεῖ, Καμβύσου καταστρεφομένου τὴν Αἴγυπτον.*[2] What does *ἔρημον* mean? There seems no record of Letopolis as a name of Babylon in later times: and there are only two possible interpretations of the word. Either it means that the place was mere desert at the time of the exodus, that the city of Letopolis subsequently arose there, and that Babylon later occupied the same site; or that Letopolis was an old Egyptian city then abandoned. The latter supposition must be nearer the truth, since it is well known that Pharaonic monuments existed on the spot, and some of them lasted till long after the Arab occupation.

However, Josephus's account would give about 525 B.C. as the date for the foundation of Babylon: and inasmuch as it tends to confirm Strabo's account by suggesting a true historical origin for the name, it supplies a further argument against Pauly's theory. For Pauly contends that Babylon was merely a fanciful name given on the analogy of

[1] The walls were originally at least 60 feet high.

[2] *Ant.*, ii. 15 (315).

scores of other Greek town-names in Egypt. But how can this theory be reconciled with the fact that in this instance the already existing and quite classical Greek name of Letopolis was discontinued, being superseded by a name of non-Greek origin like Babylon? Surely it is more reasonable to suppose that such a change was made by Persians during a Persian occupation of Egypt, whether under Cambyses, as suggested by Josephus, or under Nebuchadnezzar, as alleged by John of Nikiou and several writers. Indeed the strength of this tradition which gives a Babylonian origin to the fortress, if not to the town, indicates that it rests on a historical basis, and is no mere myth or legend.

We now pass to a very definite and interesting notice of the town or city of Babylon by Ptolemy.[1] He not only indicates the geographical position of Babylon in proximity to Heliopolis, but adds the very important remark that the River of Trajan (the well-known Amnis Trajanus, or canal connecting the Nile and the Red Sea) flows through Heroon Polis and the city of Babylon. Now although the course of the Nile has varied in the region of Cairo even during historical times, the old alignment of the eastern bank is fairly well known. It is certain, for instance, that the channel between the island of Rauḍah and Ḳaṣr ash Shama' was much wider than at present. Nâṣir-i-Khusrau,[2] who visited the place about A.D. 1047, says that this channel was spanned by a bridge of 36 barges: while Idrîsî, about a century later, gives the number as 30. Moreover, in A.D. 642, the mosque which

[1] *Geog.*, iv. 5.

[2] Ed. Schefer, p. 153.

'Amr then founded, and of which the site has never changed, stood on the river bank. Abû Ṣalîḥ,[1] too, records that the church of Mînâ in the Ḥamrâ formerly stood on the bank of the Nile: while from John of Nikiou it is clear, as I have elsewhere pointed out,[2] that the eastward trend of the Nile continued as far north at least as Maḳs, and that the quays of Maḳs lay close to the modern Ezbekîah. On these and the like data a definite line can be drawn for the right bank of the river from the rocky headland south of Ḳaṣr ash Shama' through the region now called Old Cairo and Cairo: and the point where the canal of Trajan took off from the river can be determined with tolerable accuracy. But the physical conformation of the ground is such as to render it improbable that any great variation of the alignment took place between the era of Ptolemy and the Arab invasion: in other words, the mouth of the canal upon the Nile had not then shifted much from its old position, though undoubtedly after the seventh century the land encroached so rapidly upon the eastern shore of the Nile that the canal mouth had to be pushed further and further to the west as the water receded.

But the fact of cardinal importance is that Ptolemy describes the canal as flowing *through the city of Babylon*—not by it, or near it, but through it: so that the canal divided the city, just as later it divided Miṣr al Ḳadîmah (or Old Cairo) and Cairo itself up to the present century. It follows beyond

[1] Ed. Evetts and Butler, p. 104.
[2] *Arab Conquest of Egypt*, p. 217 n.

all question that in Ptolemy's time the name Babylon denoted a city which lay both north and south of the canal of Trajan, and that it could not be limited to any town, still less to any point or post, south of the canal.

That Babylon was a city, therefore, and that it was widespread and intersected by the canal, are the two facts which the evidence of Ptolemy established irrefutably.

For Ptolemy, it must be remembered, was a native of Egypt: he spent most of his life in Alexandria: and as his last recorded observation is dated A.D. 151, and he is said to have lived to the age of 78, it is clear that both the construction of Ḳaṣr ash Shama' by Trajan and his excavation of the canal must have taken place in Ptolemy's lifetime. Ptolemy, therefore, wrote with local knowledge, as a contemporary historian as well as geographer, when he called Babylon a city.[1]

I may add that the northward extension of the city is fully confirmed by Arab writers. Thus Ibn Duḳmâḳ[2] says: 'Al Maṭarîah, called also 'Ain Shams (or Heliopolis). There were wonderful remains there, especially the two obelisks famous in all countries. The city in ancient times was very long and wide and *contiguous to Ancient Miṣr* on the site of the present Fusṭâṭ.' Inasmuch as Miṣr and Fusṭâṭ are more or less identical with Babylon, this passage corroborates the statement that Babylon

[1] His words are:—Ηρώων πόλις δι' ἧς καὶ Βαβυλῶνος πόλεως Τραιανὸς ποταμὸς ῥεῖ.

[2] Part V, p. 43.

reached far enough northward to come into touch with the suburbs of Heliopolis. Al Ḳudâ'î, too, seems to record a gate of Ancient Miṣr considerably northward of the city's recognized limits, when he speaks of 'a place called Munyat Ḥarb near the gate of Ancient Miṣr, on the spot, it is said, where Cairo now stands'.[1]

But to resume the sequence of historical evidence. In the *Itinerarium Antonini* of the second century we find the place designated Babylonia, the order being Babylonia, Heliu, Scenas Veteranorum, Vicum Judaeorum, Thou, Heroon, Serapiu, Clysmon. It should of course be noted (1) that there is no sort of confusion here between Babylon and Heliopolis; and (2) that Babylonia, Heliu, and Heroon are all Greek forms in a familiar language which suppresses the complement πόλις; and (3) that in the Greek form Babylonia, the accent would lie upon the penultimate, and that this accent determined the Arab pronunciation (as usual in such cases), so that Babylonia transliterates into the Bâb al Lûnîah of Arab history.

About the year A.D. 303 we read that Apa Tîl was taken by forcible conscription and enrolled in the garrison of the fortress of Babylon:[2] and the same document records that the governor of Egypt, Arianus, came to Babylon and ordered all the soldiers there to worship idols.

In the *Notitia Dignitatum Imperii* are two entries of interest as follows:—

[1] Quoted by Ibn Khallikân: ed. de Slane, ii. 603.

[2] MSS. Copt. Vat. 66, fol. 158, quoted by Quatremère.

Legio quinta Macedonica[1]*—Memphi:*
Legio tertia decima gemina—Babylonia:

which show that in the time of Arcadius and Honorius not only were Memphis and Babylon clearly distinguished, but each was garrisoned by a legion.

Of about the same date is the mention of Babylon by St. Jerome,[2] who speaks of Hilarion's journey from Pelusium to that city: and by Rufinus, who says that there were great numbers of anchorites in the region of Memphis and Babylon.

Among the *Oxyrhynchus Papyri* is a document[3] dated A. D. 303, in which the comarchs, or village headmen, record the expenses of three workmen 'sent to Babylon' from the village of Tampeti.

Pegôsh,[4] in the well-known story, was taken on his journey from Pelusium to Babylon.

[1] Casanova, in *Noms Coptes*, pp. 81 seq., devotes several pages to the question why the name Macedonia was sometimes applied to Miṣr according to the testimony of certain Arab writers. He can give no confident explanation of the fact, but suggests a rather elaborate ancient Egyptian etymology for the word Macedonia. I cannot help thinking that a much simpler solution of the difficulty may be found in this statement of the *Notitia Dignitatum*. Given the fact that the Macedonian legion was stationed at Memphis, nothing is more natural than to suppose that the regiment, in recollection of their place of origin or the scene of their titular triumphs, gave the name Macedonia to the district about them, just as Babylonians originally named the city of Babylon after their home in Asia. In giving the name of Macedonia to Miṣr, the Arabs intended the region about Memphis and Babylon, as Casanova justly supposes, and not the country of Egypt.

[2] Life of Hilarion, in Rosweyde's *Vitae Patrum*, i. 62.

[3] Part VI, p. 206.

[4] Revillout, *Actes et Contrats* (1876), no. 55: and *Musée Guimet*, xvii. 1 (Vita Pachomii, § 1).

Apollinaris Sidonius in his letter to Agricola about Theodoric says that 'the tables were covered with cloths of Babylon',[1] thus proving that the city then, as later, was famous for its textiles.

Babylon is incidentally mentioned by Palladius, when the writer, speaking of the mount of St. Antony, remarks: *ἐκάθητο δὲ μεταξὺ Βαβυλῶνος καὶ Ἡρακλέους*—a passage definitely ranking Babylon as a city about the year A.D. 400.[2]

That Babylon was the seat of a bishopric is certain. Zosimus, bishop of Babylon, is mentioned by John Moschus,[3] as appointed by the patriarch Apollinaris, probably in the fourth century: Cyrus, bishop of Babylon, is named in the Acts of the Council of Ephesus and in the first Act of the Council of Chalcedon (A.D. 451): and a bishop of Babylon is again recorded in the time of Benjamin—seventh century. Now it is clear that a bishop cannot derive his title from a fort, and must derive it from a city.

[1] Hamilton Jackson's *Shores of the Adriatic: The Italian Side*, p. 256.

[2] Ed. Dom C. Butler, p. 63, xxi. and note. The mount is at Pispir on the Nile, not that by the Red Sea.

[3] *Pratum Spirituale* (*Vitae Patrum*, x. 676). But this patriarch, Apollinaris, though twice mentioned by John Moschus, is not in Renaudot or in the usual lists of patriarchs.

CHAPTER II

ALTHOUGH it may not be quite consistent with the chronological order which I am following, I may here examine the evidence of M. Amélineau and Mr. Crum. The former remarks[1] under the word Kîmé ⲕⲏⲙⲉ that while the term usually denotes Northern or Lower Egypt, it seems also to be used as the name of a town, like مصر in Arabic. This town he takes to be Memphis, and he refers to Revillout's *Actes et Contrats*, pp. 104, 105, 106, 109: adding, however, that these passages are too fragmentary to found any serious thesis upon. The Synaxar, he proceeds, speaks of a town which it calls Miṣr al Ḳadîmah, and also of a town of Miṣr, 'which cannot be Cairo, because that town was built long after the persecution of Diocletian'. That surely is a strange remark. Of course the truth is that Miṣr was the earlier name, and that the epithet Ḳadîmah was added only in later times, when the place had to be distinguished from the new town in the vicinity, viz. Miṣr al Ḳâhirah or Cairo. In the time of Diocletian there was only the one name Miṣr, though beyond reasonable doubt it was applied to Memphis as well as to Babylon.[2]

Indeed, M. Amélineau himself goes on to point

[1] *Géog. copte*, pp. 223–5.

[2] Champollion thinks it improbable that the name Miṣr, whatever its origin, was in vogue among native Egyptians.

out that in the Acts of Apatîr[1]: 'le castrum de Babylone est rendu en arabe par مصر': and in the history of Timotheus the martyr, who belonged to Miṣr al Ḳadîmah, and suffered under Diocletian, Miṣr again is equivalent to the Castle of Babylon. I would rather say equivalent to Babylon, although the association of the place with a strong fortress naturally caused the town to be spoken of as the Fortress of Babylon.

But the *scalae* give other equivalents. Thus, in MSS. Copt. Bib. Nat., No. 43, we find

ⲙⲉⲛⲃⲉ منف مصر القديمة
ⲃⲁⲃⲩⲗⲟⲛ بابلون مصر

No. 44 ⲕⲩⲡⲧⲟⲛ ⲙⲉⲛⲃⲉ مصر[2]

Nos. 50, 53, 54, 55

ⲱⲛ ⲛⲉⲙ ⲃⲁⲃⲩⲗⲱⲛ مصر وعين شمس

No. 54 ⲙⲉϥⲓ منف وهى مصر القديمة

In the Bodleian Codex Mareschalchus, and also in Lord Crawford's MS., the same ⲱⲛ ⲛⲉⲙ ⲃⲁⲃⲩⲗⲱⲛ = مصر و عين شمس occurs: while in the British Museum Codex Orientalis we have with ⲱⲛ ⲛⲉⲙ ⲃⲁⲃⲩⲗⲱⲛ the Arabic مصر وهى عين شمس—a variation which identifies Babylon with ʿAin Shams, and both with Miṣr: also ⲓⲗⲓⲟⲩ = عين شمس و هى مصر القديمة.[3]

In the list of bishoprics[4] we have ⲙⲓⲟⲧ ⲃⲁⲥⲟⲩⲗⲱⲛ = ⲡⲉⲧⲫⲣⲏ = عين شمس.

[1] Hyvernat, *Actes des Martyrs*, p. 91.

[2] Quatremère quotes no. 44, fol. 79, as giving to Fusṭâṭ the name of Babylon: by Fusṭâṭ he may mean Miṣr. (*Mém.*, i. 48.)

[3] Most of these equivalents are taken from the *scalae* given by Amélineau in App. III to his *Géog. copte*.

[4] Id., App. IV.

ⲉⲓⲗⲏⲟⲩ = ⲧⲁⲃⲃⲩⲗⲱⲛ ⲃⲁⲑⲓ = (*sic*) مصر الكرشى مجتمعة.

ⲡⲁⲗⲓⲛ ⲫⲩⲥⲧⲁⲧⲱⲛ ⲕⲉⲡⲓⲧⲱ ⲃⲁⲃⲩⲗⲱⲛ = بابلون (*sic*) مصر مشطاط.

While in another list the Arabic is more correct :

ⲉⲓⲗⲏⲟⲩ ⲃⲁⲑⲁⲓ = الكرسين مجتمعة.

These correspondences prove that Ôn—variously called Iliou, Eilêou,[1] Heliopolis, and ʻAin Shams—is closely coupled with Babylon,[2] indeed identified with

[1] It is obvious that these Coptic forms account for the ⲗⲓⲟⲩⲓ which puzzled Champollion (*L'Égypte sous les Pharaons*, ii. 35) as well as Quatremère (*Mém.*, i. 49), and which Amélineau (*Géog. copte*, p. 541) regards as the original name of the locality called Fusṭâṭ by the Arabs on the strength of an equivalent ⲗⲓⲟⲩⲓ = القاهرة. There seems no evidence to support this conclusion, and I think it quite mistaken. Surely Lioui is a mere variant of Iliou, which again, like Eilêou, is taken from the Greek Ἡλίου, the πόλις being often omitted in such words, as in the *Itinerarium Antonini*, cited above (p. 12). The confusion of Lioui or ʻAin Shams with Babylon, Fusṭâṭ, and Cairo is plain enough from the quotations I have given, and the identification of Lioui with Cairo amounts to precisely the same thing as the identification of ʻAin Shams with Babylon—an error or an exaggeration frequent in Arab writers.

[2] This coupling of Ôn with Babylon in the list of bishoprics gives the clue to the meaning of the Arabic phrase 'the two sees united', which Amélineau has missed somewhat strangely (op. cit., p. 540). He says: 'Il y avait là deux sièges réunis, celui de Fostât et celui de Babylone, et ils étaient réunis dans une ville qui se nommait Eilêou': and he goes on to remark that Lioui can only mean Cairo, appealing to the word Lûnîah, which Abû Ṣâliḥ gives as equivalent to Fusṭâṭ, in confirmation or his view. Thus he argues that Lûnîah is a wrong reading for Lûîah. In fact it is a totally different word, arising, as I have shown, from the false etymology which split up Babilonia or Babilûnîah into Bâb al Lûnîah. Moreover, it is on the one hand impossible to suppose that the Arab settlement of Fusṭâṭ was ever erected into a bishop's see, and on the other certain that there was an ancient see of Babylon; certain also that the still more ancient metropolis of

Babylon, with Miṣr, and with Fusṭâṭ: and the fact that all these several identifications are made shows how hazy were the topographical limits of the several cities, and how names survived in disregard and confusion of such limits, despite historical changes and the long passage of time.

On the whole subject of these correspondences one may refer to M. Casanova's *Noms coptes du Caire*,[1] with most of which I cordially agree. Thus he remarks:[2] 'Ainsi pour les Coptes aucune différence entre 'Ain Chams, le Caire, Fosṭâṭ et Babylone. Tous ces noms se confondent et s'échangent': and again, 'Le nom de Babylone s'étend jusqu'au delà du Caire, jusqu'à l'ancienne Héliopolis'.

But obviously in these *scalae* or lists the use of the term Fusṭâṭ and of the epithet Ḳadîmah applied to Miṣr before Cairo was founded, requires to be explained. The explanation seems simple enough. Such usage is clearly anachronistic, though the

Heliu was the seat originally of a bishopric. This proposition, which I first laid down as a theory based on inherent probability, I have now proved as fact by the discovery of a passage in John Moschus (cap. 124) as follows:—'Tenensque nos Papa Alexandrinus beatissimus Apollinaris omnes tres fecit episcopos: unum quidem Heliopoleos, alium Leontopoleos, me vero in Babylonem misit' (*Vitae Patrum*, x. 676). John Moschus is not speaking of himself, and the exact date of Apollinaris's patriarchate I do not know: but there is no question that the two separate sees of Heliopolis and Babylon existed simultaneously. Nor can it be doubted that, as Heliopolis sank down and decayed, while Babylon advanced in importance, it became necessary to unite the two sees. It was equally natural that the name of Babylon should ultimately prevail in the combination, as it did prevail. But the 'two sees united' of the *scalae* were Babylon and Heliopolis, not Babylon and Fusṭâṭ.

[1] pp. 38 seq. [2] p. 41.

anachronisms cannot have existed in the original lists, but represent additions or alterations made by copyists, as the changes of time rendered further equivalents necessary.

To return to M. Amélineau. There is one remark of his which needs some qualifying. He argues that the name ⲕⲏⲙⲉ was given first to Memphis, but that in after time as Memphis declined, *that city* was called Miṣr al Ḳadîmah. Despite the precise identification of Memphis with Miṣr al Ḳadîmah in the *scalae* quoted above, I do not think it true to say that the site of Memphis was commonly called Miṣr al Ḳadîmah. It is not alleged that such a use of the name to denote Memphis as opposed to Babylon is unknown: for ʻAbd al Latîf, in a passage describing the ruins of Memphis, calls the site Miṣr al Ḳadîmah, and all doubt of his meaning is removed, because he defines the place as in the region or province of Jîzah. But such usage is rare and exceptional. Miṣr al Ḳadîmah, it must be remembered, is a term of Arab origin, and when it arose—in the seventh century or later—Memphis had practically disappeared as the capital, and the Miṣr of the Arab historians undoubtedly lay on the eastern bank of the Nile. Indeed, M. Amelineau's proposition is rather the converse of the truth. For it is quite certain that Arab writers often transferred the name of Memphis to Miṣr al Ḳadîmah: they imagined, in fact, that Memphis had occupied the site of Babylon. This I take to be the true explanation of the correspondence between the two cities given in the *scalae*, in which Miṣr is rather called Memphis than Memphis called Miṣr. The Arabs had little knowledge of

Memphis, but it was easy for them to transpose the site, or to extend the boundaries, of ancient Memphis to the ancient city of Miṣr on the other side of the river.

Apart from this, however, M. Amélineau's final conclusion is that the name **ⲕⲏⲙⲉ** was given to three different towns in Egypt, viz. (1) to Memphis; (2) to Babylon after the Persian conquest and during the Roman period; and (3) to Fusṭâṭ and Cairo: and this conclusion, with certain reserves as to the chronological divisions, seems sound.

But apparently the word **ⲕⲏⲙⲉ** is used in contexts in which it is both impossible to translate it by Lower Egypt and difficult to render it as a city, whether Memphis or Miṣr. Thus in Mr. Crum's *Coptic Ostraka* **ⲕⲏⲙⲉ** occurs in no. 385, and a note elsewhere[1] refers to a phrase in Revillout's *Actes et Contrats*, 56, viz. 'in the monastery or without in Kême', whence it is argued that Kême must mean the valley, and cannot mean Babylon, because Babylon is mentioned in the same text; and Mr. Crum cites Stern's opinion that Kême in the Jeremias papyri from Memphis means Upper Egypt. Reference is also made to the story of Pegôsh, who in his journey from Pelusium was made to avoid Panau lest he should be rescued before reaching Kême, and who was taken to Babylon and thence to Antinoe. Here again Mr. Crum alleges that Kême must be identified with Upper Egypt; while Sir F. G. Kenyon, on the same evidence, suggests that Kême is an intermediate district—Middle Egypt.

On this I would remark that all difficulty would disappear, at least in regard to the quotation from

[1] Id., p. 73.

Revillout and the story of Pegôsh, if Kême is understood to mean Memphis. The fear was that the prisoner Pegôsh might be rescued in the Delta before he could reach Memphis on his journey southward: accordingly he was taken direct—no doubt over the desert—to Babylon, where he would naturally be made to cross to the western bank by the bridge of boats or by ferry, and so to Memphis and Antinoe. To hold this hypothesis at least is easier than to reconcile M. Amélineau's statement that Kême usually means Lower Egypt with Mr. Crum's view that it means Upper Egypt, or Sir F. G. Kenyon's that it means something between the two.

The confusion between Memphis and Babylon had not arisen among Coptic writers of this period. I have shown that somewhat earlier each of the two cities had its own Roman legion, and the distinction between them is made clear by many passages in Coptic MSS.[1] Yet it must be remembered that, just as Miṣr is used to denote both the city of Miṣr and the country of Egypt, so Kême or Khêmi was also used ambiguously. Thus in the life of Pachomius,[2] in a phrase which definitely contrasts Egypt with the Thebaid, the word for Egypt is ⲭⲏⲙⲓ; while in the Coptic Apocrypha,[3] where the arch-

[1] Thus in Hyvernat's *Actes des Martyrs*, p. 94, we have ⲧⲁⲙⲙⲱⲟⲩ ⲛ̄ⲧⲉ ⲙⲉⲙϥⲓ for the village of Tammôou, near Memphis, on the western bank (v. Amélineau, *Géog. copte*, p. 477): and ⲉⲡⲓⲕⲁⲥⲧⲣⲟⲛ ⲛ̄ⲧⲉ ⲃⲁⲃⲩⲗⲱⲛ, pp. 91 and 93. The latter phrase Hyvernat curiously renders 'au champ de Babylone', but surely it means to the fortress of Babylon.

[2] *An. Mus. Guimet*, xvii, p. 1.

[3] Ed. Wallis Budge, p. 105.

bishop of Alexandria 'sent festal letters southward throughout all Kême', obviously Kême denotes neither Lower Egypt nor Upper Egypt exclusively, but the whole of Egypt within the archbishopric. But such instances illustrate the flexible character of these Coptic terms, and prove that no very rigid conclusion as to the precise meaning of Kême or Khêmi can be based upon any particular text or passage. It was an elastic term.

CHAPTER III

Returning now from this digression to the sequence of authorities upon the use of the word Babylon, I come to Zosimus, who wrote probably *c.* A.D. 450. In describing the defeat and death of Probus in the campaign against Zenobia's occupation of Egypt, he relates that the Roman general seized *τὸ πρὸς τῇ Βαβυλῶνι ὄρος*[1]—the mountain near Babylon. What mountain was in the writer's mind? There are only two alternatives: either it was some part of Mount Muḳaṭṭam, such as the place where the citadel of Cairo now stands,—and this fulfils the condition of commanding the route to Syria better than any other; or it was that other elevation called by the Arabs Ar Raṣad or Jabal Jûyûshî—that elevation with which both M. Casanova and Mr. Guest associate specially the name Babylon. But the language of Zosimus renders it quite impossible that he can have regarded the name Babylon as attaching to either mount. For whichever hill he had in mind, it was *near* Babylon, and so was not Babylon. In thus clearly distinguishing it from Babylon, he proved not only that neither hill could be called Babylon, but also that Babylon was the name of the city and not of a mount.

[1] *Corp. Script. Hist. Byzant.* (ed. Bekker, Bonnae), lib. i, c. 44.

We now come to John of Nikiou, whose important evidence requires close examination. His account is as follows: 'Trajan went to Egypt and there built a fortress with a powerful and impregnable citadel having an abundant supply of water, and he named it Babylon of Egypt. This fortress had originally been founded by Nebuchadnezzar, king of the Medes and Persians, who called it the Fortress of Babylon. It was at the time when he had become king of Egypt by the will of God, and when after the destruction of Jerusalem he had exiled the Jews, who stoned the prophet of God at Thebes in Egypt and committed many crimes. Thereupon Nebuchadnezzar came in person to Egypt with a large army, conquered the country—for the Jews had rebelled against him—and called the fortress after the name of his own capital, viz. Babylon. As for Trajan, he raised the circuit walls and enlarged the other buildings of the fortress. He also had a small canal excavated for carrying Nile water to Clysma and connecting the Nile with the Red Sea. This he called the canal of Trajan.'[1]

Now there are two main points to notice in this narrative.

(1) The site of Trajan's fortress (which is unquestionably Ḳaṣr ash Shama'), is absolutely identified by John of Nikiou with the site of a Persian fortress dating from the reign of Nebuchadnezzar. John betrays no consciousness whatever that the original Babylonian fort may have occupied a different site from that of Trajan's stronghold: and his evidence must be taken to prove that at the

[1] Ed. Zotenberg, pp. 413–14.

time of the Arab conquest all trace of a Persian fort on Ar Raṣad had disappeared—a conclusion which is singularly borne out by other Egyptian writers. Thus Eutychius, who wrote *c.* A.D. 920, and who was a native of Old Cairo, strongly retains the Persian tradition: but he alleges[1] that King Artaxerxes Ochus 'built at Fusṭâṭ Miṣr the fortress which is now called Ḳaṣr ash Shama'.'

(2) The original foundation of the fortress is associated with a rebellion. But while Strabo makes out that the rebels were Babylonians who built the first fortress in aid of their revolt, John of Nikiou declares that it was Nebuchadnezzar who built the fortress in order to secure the country after he had crushed a rebellion of the Jews. I confess that John's story, though written so long after Strabo's, has the greater air of probability. The date of Nebuchadnezzar's invasion of Egypt is about 567 B.C.

But passing on from this question for the moment, one must note further that all through the cited passage it is the *Fortress of Babylon* which is spoken of. Upon this M. Amélineau remarks: 'Puis, dans un grand nombre de passages, il est parlé de la ville de Babylone avec une confusion incroyable, que ne fait (*sic*) qu'augmenter les notes du traducteur.' I cannot understand this remark. M. Amélineau refers in a foot-note to five passages, but in no single one of them does the expression 'town of Babylon' occur. On pp. 555, 556, and 562 the term is 'the citadel of Babylon': on pp. 557 and 559, 'Babylon of Egypt': on pp. 562 and 566 it is 'the citadel of Babylon of

[1] Ann., i. 67.

Egypt': on p. 575 the patriarch Cyrus went 'to Babylon' simply: and on p. 577 we read that the victorious Arabs forced the Egyptians to clear out Trajan's canal (which had become choked up) in order to bring the Nile water from 'Babylon of Egypt' to the Red Sea. The text, therefore, of John of Nikiou does not present any trace of that incredible confusion on the subject of Babylon which M. Amélineau discovers there.

However, I fully grant, and indeed insist strongly on the point, that, although there is no confusion whatever in John of Nikiou's language as it stands, the word Babylon is used in some of these passages to denote a town or city. But I hold that this is due to no error on the part of writer or translator, but is deliberately intended by John of Nikiou. When he says that Cyrus went to Babylon, and that the canal was cleaned out so as to make a waterway from Babylon to the Red Sea, it is quite clear that Babylon denotes a city: and we get back again to the statement of Ptolemy that the city of Babylon lay across the canal of Trajan. So when John speaks of the 'fortress of Babylon', he means either the fortified city of Babylon, or simply the fortress in Babylon, i.e. Ḳaṣr ash Shamaʿ, which formed the citadel of Babylon: and the term 'Babylon of Egypt' corresponds to the Coptic ⲃⲁⲃⲩⲗⲱⲛ ⲛ̄ⲧⲉ ⲭⲏⲙⲓ and is used generally as equivalent to the city.

Much is made of the distinction which John appears to draw between Babylon and Miṣr in the chapter-heading CXIV (CXV), which runs: 'How the Muslims gained possession of Miṣr in the 14th year of the lunar cycle, and took possession of the citadel of Babylon in the 15th year.'[1] The difference of expression is undeniable: but if it can be shown that Miṣr and Babylon were convertible terms, as I believe, then the difference has no deeper cause than mere avoidance of tautology. It seems to me that the proof of my contention lies in the very next chapter-heading CXV (CXVI): for it tells 'Of the return of the patriarch Cyrus from exile and his departure *to Miṣr* to pay tribute to the Muslims'. Now in the chapter which bears the corresponding number in the text there is nothing at all about these events. The discrepancy is explained by the fact that the text is notoriously disordered. But in chapters CXIX and CXX, on the other hand, we have an unmistakeable recital of the very events to which chapter-heading CXV refers. For there[2] is the record of Cyrus's return from exile, followed by an account of the ceremonies and services which he attended at Alexandria: and immediately afterwards come the words: 'Cyrus then journeyed *to Babylon* to treat for peace with the Muslims, and offered to pay them tribute if they would put an end to the war in Egypt.'[3] Here the correspondence between the title of the chapter and the actual narrative of the text is so close and so certain that it cannot be questioned: but Cyrus is described in the one as going to Miṣr to pay tribute to the Muslims and in the other as going to Babylon to pay tribute to the Muslims. Whence it follows that John of Nikiou did regard Miṣr and Babylon as meaning the same thing, and also that he did speak of Babylon as a city.

[1] p. 357. [2] p. 572. [3] p. 575.

John of Nikiou's date is roughly the latter part of the seventh century, and similar use of the word Babylon to denote the city is found in another authentic Coptic document of about the same date—the Life of the patriarch Isaac. In that story the bishops summoned from Alexandria by 'Abd al 'Azîz 'arrived at Babylon'. Then we read that the bishops and 'a number of people from Babylon and Alexandria'[1] met in the church of St. Sergius, which still exists in the fortress of Ḳaṣr ash Shama': and when Isaac's consecration as patriarch was accomplished, it was celebrated by an outburst of joy and festivity 'from Babylon to Alexandria'. Nothing could more decisively establish the meaning of Babylon as city of Babylon than this coupling of the two capitals, Babylon and Alexandria, together.

So in the Memphitic codex,[2] which contains the same history, the term Babylon occurs three times on a single page denoting the city. The date of Isaac's consecration was A.D. 690, as I have shown elsewhere.[3]

A little later both Greek and Arabic papyri[4] are found constantly using the term Babylon, especially in connexion with payment of taxes or delivery of corn at the city, which had become the capital under Muslim rule, to the neglect of Alexandria. Thus in A.D. 708 Ḳurrah orders the people of Ashfûḥ to pay their tax or tribute quarterly at Babylon. An Arabic

[1] *Histoire du patriarche copte Isaac*, par E. Amélineau: Paris, 1890, pp. 45, 46.

[2] Zoega, *Cat. Codd. Copt.*, p. 110.

[3] *Arab Conquest of Egypt*, p. 552.

[4] *Papyri Schott-Reinhardt*, i, p. 86 (Heidelberg, 1906).

text contains an order for delivery of produce at the granaries of Babylon, and I may note here in passing that the Arabic form of the word is Bâb al Yûn باب اليون.[1] With this compare the *ἀμὶρ τοῦ σίτου Βαβυλῶνος*, quoted from Wessely by Becker,[2] which corresponds to the Roman *praefectus annonae*. A similar order seems referred to in the eighth-century Greek papyrus in the Khedivial Library at Cairo, where the expression occurs *καθολικῶν ὁρρίων Βαβυλῶνος*.[3] Many like allusions are found in the Aphrodito papyri in the British Museum.[4] Thus nos. 1335 and 1407 speak of the corn-stores at Babylon and delivery of wheat 'for the Muḥajirûn of Fusṭâṭ'. In nos. 1371 and 1376 Rauḍah is described as 'the island of Babylon'. In no. 1378 mention is made of a palace being built *at Fusṭâṭ* near the river for the Amîr al Mû'minîn, and materials are ordered to be delivered 'in Babylon for the said palace'. This use of Babylon and Fusṭâṭ in the same document is curious: but the form in the Greek is *φοσσάτου*, which occurs also in no. 1379 and in the Schott-Reinhardt papyri.[5] In nos. 1386, 1387, and 1404, granaries at Babylon are again named, while in no. 1379 we read of a granary being built at Fusṭâṭ. In the account of tribute from the village of Aphrodito, no. 1411, after payments in respect of various field apportionments comes the item 'from the men

[1] Id. ib., p. 98.

[2] Id. ib., p. 45.

[3] *Studia Sinaitica*, no. XII, p. 1 (1907).

[4] Translated by Mr. H. I. Bell in *Der Islam*, June and November, 1911, March and October, 1912.

[5] p. 90. The Coptic ⲫⲱⲥⲁⲧⲟⲛ occurs in the Catalogue of the Rylands Papyri, p. 173.

who are at Babylon', which possibly refers to workmen sent there from Aphrodito: as in no. 1414 we read of skilled workmen employed on the palace of the Amîr al Mû'minîn and at the dockyards in Babylon: and again in no. 1433 mention is made of one workman 'for the building of the fortress of Babylon'—which must refer to some sort of repair. In the same interesting document a 'carpenter for work ordered by the Amîr at Babylon', material for the Amîr's palace at Babylon, a 'currier for the Amîr's tent which is being made at Babylon', and a 'shift of iron-workers at Babylon', may be noted: and the *carabi* or vessels being built 'in the island of Babylon' are three times named in this papyrus and as many times in no. 1434, and again in no. 1435. Two other uses of the term Babylon in the eighth century may be found in Mr. Crum's *Rechtsurkunden aus Djême*,[1] and there are many instances in the British Museum Catalogue of Coptic MSS. The frequent recurrence of Babylon in these documents of daily life, and the total absence in them of any corresponding Arabic name, show how familiar and widespread was the use of the term to denote a capital city. The same may be said of the references in the Papyrus Rainer.[2]

These instances are more than enough to prove that in popular parlance the term Babylon was used to denote the whole region covered by the term Miṣr at that time and later by Miṣr al Ḳadîmah. They prove also, I think, that at that date the dis-

[1] Nos. 5. 21 and 93. 17 (Leipzig, 1912).

[2] For 1887, p. 58.

tinction between Babylon and Fusṭâṭ amounted only to this—that Fusṭâṭ was a mere quarter in the city: in other words, the term Fusṭâṭ had not then won its way to acceptance as the definite designation of any Muslim town. I have already shown that the supposed connexion between the name Fusṭâṭ and the tent of 'Amr is mainly legendary; that Fusṭâṭ is a word foreign to the Arabic;[1] that its origin is to be found in the Byzantine *φόσσατον* or *φοσσᾶτον*, which signifies a camp; and that the Arabs probably caught the name in the first instance from the Romans at Babylon, who naturally spoke of the region north of the fortress where 'Amr pitched his standard as 'the camp'. This explanation of the term has now been generally accepted. From it there follows the conclusion that the area covered by the name Fusṭâṭ was originally a very restricted one—that in fact, as I have said elsewhere, the town of Fusṭâṭ was not laid out on any large scale with a definite plan of making it the Muslim capital.

There is no question that the first fixed settlement centred about the region marked by the Mosque of 'Amr, and that the Muslim town gradually spread eastward and southward from that point. But the evidence of the papyri shows that even sixty or seventy years after the conquest the name Fusṭâṭ had not acquired that wider significance which it attained in later times, when it became equivalent to Miṣr. When one finds, for example, in the Aphrodito papyri the use of both terms Fusṭâṭ and Babylon together, one is bound to infer that Babylon is still

[1] *Arab Conquest of Egypt*, pp. 339–40, and notes.

the general term for the city, while Fusṭâṭ denotes merely the particular locality in which the Arabs were quartered. This conclusion is in general agreement with that of Becker,[1] who says, 'As far as we know from papyri, Babylon and Fusṭâṭ were still distinguished at the end of the first century (A.H.). ... In Fusṭâṭ lived the Muḥâjirûn ... there their Khiṭâṭ were marked out, and the seat of the administration'. So also Mr. Guest in his well-known article on the Foundation of Fusṭâṭ:[2]

'Speaking generally one may say that the foundation of Fusṭâṭ probably did not mean much more than the making permanent of the camp already on the site': and again, 'The busy commercial town described by Ibn Ḥauqal,[3] with its crowded markets and blocks of buildings, some containing as many as two hundred people, belongs to the tenth century. This state must have been reached gradually. A long straggling colony of mean houses and hovels, or more likely of huts and booths, such as one may see nowadays attached to some town to which semi-nomad Arabs resort; arranged irregularly in groups in loose order concentrated to some extent about the Mosque of 'Amr as the focus formed by the centre of authority ... this is the picture that our accounts of Fusṭâṭ in the days of 'Amr enable us to draw.'

In what way and at what times the first Muslim settlements spread, and Fusṭâṭ advanced to a civic

[1] *Encyclopaedia of Islam*, s.v. Babylon.

[2] *J. R. A. S.*, January, 1907.

[3] Also, I may add, by Nâṣir-i-Khusrau. See Schefer's well-known edition of the Sefer Nameh.

dignity and importance which enabled it in Muslim acceptation to rival the ancient name of Miṣr, and to supersede that of Babylon,—these are questions with which this essay has little concern. But in Mr. Guest's admirable article, and the well-known studies of MM. Casanova and Salmon upon the topography of Cairo, will be found the principal information available. My purpose has been merely to show that at the time of the conquest the term Babylon denoted the same thing as Miṣr, just as Fusṭâṭ afterwards denoted the same thing as Miṣr; and that consequently it must be a pure anachronism to limit the meaning of the term Babylon, as used in the early historians, to that point in the topography of Old Cairo where the name Bâblûn happens to linger to-day, or indeed to any point in the wide area of the city.

Yet it is certain, as Becker says, that the original distinction between Fusṭâṭ and Babylon became lost, the name Babylon tending to fall out of vogue with the Arabs, while it survived in Coptic usage. I cannot agree with him, however, when he avers that the application of the term Babylon was *extended* by the Copts, who 'occasionally used Babylon to describe the whole of the great series of towns from Ḳaṣr ash Shama' through Fusṭâṭ or Cairo to Maṭarîah—Heliopolis'. What proof is there of any such extension? Becker's suggestion is indeed the exact converse of the truth, which is that, in using the term in its wider significance, the Copts were merely maintaining with their wonted conservatism the custom and habit of antiquity: whereas the Arabs did undoubtedly extend the use of the term Fusṭâṭ (which first applied to a mere section of Babylon) to denote the whole city, until the name Babylon was narrowed and fell into abeyance and disappeared from the popular language.

The entire history of the usage of the word from the time of Ptolemy onwards shows that the area covered by the name in Roman times already extended far enough to embrace the whole of that 'great series of towns' not merely from Ḳaṣr ash Shama', but from Ar Raṣad in the south to the northern limits of Fusṭâṭ and Cairo. Any extension of the name Babylon, therefore, took place *before* and not after the Arab conquest; and when Ptolemy speaks of Trajan's canal as 'flowing through Babylon city', he implies that the city extended north as well as south of the canal.

What, then, was the line of the canal, and where was its mouth on the Nile, in A. D. 640? I have already stated that these questions admit of fairly precise answers, thanks to the scholarly labours of M. Casanova and of Mr. Guest. It is needless here to recapitulate their results: indeed, of M. Casanova's great work on the topography of Fusṭâṭ only a part at present has been published. But, besides the plan at the end of his *Noms Coptes*, he gives a sketch showing where the canal of Trajan took off from the Nile,[1] and gives the authorities upon which it is

[1] *Essai de reconstitution topographique de la ville de Fousṭâṭ ou Miṣr*, par P. Casanova (Inst. Franç. d'Arch. Orient., 1913), croquis no. 26, p. 78. See also his *Noms Coptes*, p. 99, 'Les Déplacements du Nil': and Prince Caetani's *Annali dell' Islam*, vol. iv, p. 568, though this last plan is very rough and sketchy. Another small plan may be found in *The Story of Cairo*, by S. Lane-Poole, p. 256.

founded; and Mr. Guest[1] has drawn a rough plan of Fusṭâṭ in A.D. 642, in which the mouth of the canal is just north of the church of Mârî Mînâ. Until M. Casanova has published his complete map uniting his detail sketches of the topography, I am unable to say how minutely the two authorities agree: but judging from his *Essai* and from the very definite statement in his edition of Maḳrîzî[2] there seems little room for divergence of opinion. In any case the difference cannot be material for my purpose, which is merely to show that, unless and until Ptolemy's explicit evidence is discredited or rather disproved, the city of Babylon, spreading on both sides of Trajan's canal, must in those days have occupied northwards a considerable area now included in modern Cairo.

And of this wide-spreading city the Arab historians have some clear traditions remaining. Thus Al Baladhurî and Al Ḥazimî both speak of an earlier town on the site occupied by Fusṭâṭ:[3] but almost the only precise statement with regard to the older city of Babylon to be found in Arab writings is that the most thickly populated part of the township was the region known to the Arabs as Al Ḥamrâ al Ḳuṣwâ. But this isolated statement made by Ibn Duḳmâḳ[4] is of singular

[1] *Miṣr in the Fifteenth Century*, by A. R. Guest and E. T. Richmond: in *J. R. A. S.*, 1903.

[2] *Description historique et géographique de l'Égypte:* trad. par P. Casanova, pp. 307–8 (Inst. Franç. d'Arch. Orient., 1906).

[3] *J. R. A. S.*, January, 1907, Guest's article on the 'Foundation of Fusṭâṭ', p. 63, Al Ḥazimî is cited by Maḳrîzî (i. 287), but his date is uncertain.

[4] iv. 91, as quoted by Guest, loc. cit.

interest and importance, because a glance at the map furnished by Mr. Guest[1] will show that Al Ḥamrâ al Ḳuṣwâ was the most northern quarter of Fusṭâṭ, lying between Kôm al Aḥmar and Jabal Yashkur, towards the mouth of Trajan's canal, *by which it was intersected.* In other words, this casual remark of Ibn Duḳmâḳ provides a very singular confirmation of Ptolemy's statement that the canal of Trajan flowed through the city of Babylon.

Differing from Mr. Guest, I venture to think that great weight must be attached to this piece of information, which seems to fit in with all the facts and to serve for correction of some erroneous conclusions. Thus it contradicts my former theory that at the time of the conquest it was Ar Raṣad and the adjacent locality[2] which were mainly occupied by the town of Miṣr or Babylon. But being thus in conflict with Ibn Duḳmâḳ, I must admit that he is right, and I am wrong; and though I still hold that the town—or at least the name—of Babylon originated upon Ar Raṣad, I accept literally Ibn Duḳmâḳ's statement that in Roman times it centred much further north and lay across the canal of Trajan. This at once makes it easier to understand the settled tradition that the confines of Babylon and of Heliopolis were almost in touch, and it clears up John of Nikiou's statement that the city of Miṣr not only fell long before the fall of the fortress, but fell without offering any marked resistance. Indeed, one can now realize how this main part of the city blocked the path of the advancing Arabs, and had

[1] loc. cit. after p. 83.

[2] *Arab Conquest of Egypt*, p. 245.

to be captured before 'Amr could pitch his camp against the walls of the fortress.[1]

[1] The name Ḥamrâ is supposed to denote a Roman settlement by the 'red' complexion which the Arabs associated with the Romans: and Ibn Duḳmâḳ elsewhere (iv. 5) explains the term by saying that the three Ḥamrâs were settled by those Romans who had embraced Islam in Syria, and had accompanied 'Amr in his march on Egypt. It may be questioned whether 'Amr carried with him enough Romans to settle so wide a district, and whether the name is not rather in reminiscence of the conquered Romans on the spot. But this etymology may be quite fanciful: and Abû Ṣâliḥ (p. 102) explains the name otherwise by saying that it refers to a red standard which was set up by the Arabs at the conquest. On the other hand, Goldziher, in *Byzantinische Zeitschrift* for October, 1903, points out that it was a common practice with the Arabs to designate non-Arab western folk as 'red', i.e. fair-complexioned, and he refers to a note of his own.

I may add that Europeans were also called by the Arabs the 'fair' or 'tawny' race, Banû al Aṣfar: see, for example, Ibn Khallikân (ed. de Slane), vol. iv, p. 8, the curious passage with its play on colour, p. 371, and note 6 on p. 590.

CHAPTER IV

THERE is no want of additional evidence in Arab writers, though they are not as explicit as might be desired. Thus Maḳrîzî quotes Ibn Sa'îd as saying, on the authority of the Kitâb al Kamaîm—'As for Fusṭâṭ Miṣr, its buildings originally joined those of 'Ain Shams. Islam arose. There was (at Miṣr) a fortress round which were dwelling-places. It was against this fortress that 'Amr camped, and he pitched his tent on the site of the mosque called after him.' This, of course, identifies the fortress absolutely with Ḳaṣr ash Shama': it also shows that Miṣr or Babylon extended from Ḳaṣr ash Shama' northwards as well as west and south. In the account quoted by Maḳrîzî of the Khiṭṭat Ahl ar Râyah [1] it is probable that the houses and gardens [2] already existing to the north of the fortress were apportioned to the Muslims: moreover, this passage gives additional confirmation of the identity of the fortress which 'Amr besieged with Ḳaṣr ash Shama'. Ibn Duḳmâḳ [3] cites the same tradition from the Kitâb al Mughrib of Ibn Sa'îd, and in much the same language. So Abû Ṣâliḥ, in speaking of 'the city of Miṣr and outside it the city of 'Ain Shams', [4]

[1] Casanova, pp. 143–4.

[2] Vide *Arab Conquest of Egypt*, p. 243.

[3] Part IV, p. 3.

[4] Ed. Evetts and Butler, p. 86. I have followed the Arabic

seems to refer to them as closely adjoining, and he also implies that they were founded together. In curious correspondence with Abû Ṣâliḥ is the geographer Idrîsî, who says, 'Ancient Miṣr was also called 'Ain Shams';[1] and again, 'The town of Miṣr bears in the Greek language the name of Banbilûnah بنبلونه',[2] or Babylon. From these two passages taken together it is obvious that Idrîsî regarded the city of Miṣr as having extended far to the north of the town as he found it *c.* A.D. 1150,[3] and that in his day the name of Babylon still survived, and was not the name of a fort or of any particular spot in Miṣr, but the name of the city itself, though a name not then prevalent in use by the Arabs.

Abû Ṣâliḥ, whose date may be given roughly as A.D. 1200, confirms Idrîsî—with a strange difference—for he remarks, 'The name of Miṣr in Frankish Roman (or Greek) is Babylon the Fortress',[4] a sen-

rather more literally than in the English translation on that page. Only one obelisk now marks the site of Heliopolis: but 'Abd al Latîf, speaking of 'Ain Shams in his day, tells of marvellous images, immense statues of hewn stone—colossi thirty cubits high, some standing on pedestals, some seated on thrones or seats of massive construction—and countless obelisks mostly overthrown and broken. He adds that one of the city gates 'remains to this day': ed. Pococke, pp. 109 seq. The passage gives an impressive idea of the size and splendour of the city which contained these monuments.

[1] Ed. Joubert (Paris, 1836), i. 301.

[2] Id. ib., p. 302. The first ن is clearly a copyist's error.

[3] Idrîsî describes the town in his day as surrounded on all sides by gardens, plantations, sugar-canes, &c. At the time of the Arab conquest the plain north of the fortress is described by Maḳrîzî as covered with gardens and convents: but I think Idrîsî is the only writer who gives the information that the site of the Mosque of 'Amr was originally occupied by a Coptic church, which 'Amr seized and converted into a mosque (p. 303).

[4] p. 86.

tence which at once extends and limits the meaning quite inconsistently. But in another place Abû Ṣâliḥ shows clearly that in his opinion the name Babylon applied to the whole town at the conquest, where, speaking of 'Amr's arrival, he says, 'Al Fusṭâṭ was then called Al Lûnîah'.[1] This, as I have shown above, is merely a mutilated form of the word Babylonia, which in the Greek would be pronounced Babilunîa, and which the Arabs understood as Bâb al Lûnîah, or gate of Lûnîah, Lûnîah being the city. Abû Ṣâliḥ proceeds to speak of the Governor of Al Lûnîah after the conquest demanding the poll-tax from the people—just as we find in the Aphrodito papyri that the people are ordered to deliver their tribute in money or kind at Babylon.

But this form Babylonia—which explains Idrîsî's Banbilûnah and Abû Ṣâliḥ's Lûnîah, and which dates (as I have shown) at least as early as the *Itinerarium Antonini*, persisted quite unaltered in Italian usage, and practically identical in European usage, far into the Middle Ages. Of this fact there is abundant evidence in the treaties and letters edited by Michele Amari[2] from the archives of Florence. Thus the grant of a warehouse at Babilonia is twice recorded in the treaties of A.D. 1154.[3] In the contemporary version of a treaty between Pisa and Egypt, Saladin is described as 'king of Babilonia';[4] the treaty is executed at Babilonia (Sept. 25, A.D. 1173), and witnessed by 'Marcus, Patriarch of Alexandria, of Babilonia, of Nubia, and of Saba', and the phrase

[1] p. 74.

[2] *I Diplomi Arabi del R. Archivio Fiorentino*, Firenze, 1863.

[3] pp. 243 and 248. [4] p. 257.

'Sultan of Babilonia of Egypt' or 'Sultan, lord of Babilonia' frequently occurs,[1] with dates ranging from A.D. 1207 to 1434. But in all these instances the Arabic text of the treaties is not given—only an Italian or Latin version: and whether the term *Babilonia* corresponds to Bâblûn or to Miṣr in the Arabic cannot be absolutely determined. More probably the word was Miṣr: for I do not think that a Coptic patriarch at any time would have styled himself 'patriarch of the city of Babylon' in writing his titles, whereas 'patriarch of Alexandria and of Egypt, Nubia', &c., would not have been irregular.[2] It might seem, therefore, that where Miṣr in the sense of Egypt occurred in these treaties, the Pisan and Florentine envoys misunderstood and took it in the narrower sense of the city of Miṣr, which city was familiarly known as Babylon to western peoples from the days of the crusaders.[3] On the other hand, it is beyond question that sometimes in these documents Babilonia stands, and was meant to stand, for the city and not the country: where, for example, the concession of a warehouse at Babylon is recorded, the allusion plainly is to Cairo or Old Cairo.

Beyond vague and rather baseless conjecture, there is nothing to explain how or why Babylon became almost synonymous with Egypt in western parlance. But this much at least is certain: if Babylon has not been the familiar name of a great and famous city, it

[1] pp. 280, 344, 357, 468. See also p. 287, and Appendix, p. 15.

[2] See *Ancient Coptic Churches*, ii. 302.

[3] See, for example, *Devise des chemins de Babiloine* in *Archives de l'Orient Latin*, t. 11, p. 89 (Paris, 1884), and Abû Ṣâliḥ, p. 86, n. 6.

would never have been identified with, or used as the symbol of, Egypt itself. And it must be remembered that this identification is not confined to western or foreign nations. In a well-known Coptic document of the year A.D. 1210 we find a sovereign of Egypt [1] described as ruler 'of Babylon of Egypt, Phoenicia, Syria, &c.', which, as M. Casanova remarks, is like describing the king of Great Britain as 'king of London, Wales, Ireland, and Scotland'. But he propounds the theory that the Coptic document is a translation from an Arabic orginal; then for the Coptic ⲃⲁⲃⲩⲗⲱⲛ ⲛⲧⲉ ⲭⲏⲙⲓ he supposes that ديار مصر stood in the Arabic text, and that the Copt translator, 'ignorant les finesses de la langue Arabe, a cru que "les maisons" désignaient une ville et non une contrée', and so rendered by ⲃⲁⲃⲩⲗⲱⲛ ⲛⲧⲉ ⲭⲏⲙⲓ instead of ⲭⲏⲙⲓ alone. This is certainly ingenious, but there is one strong objection against it. Surely it is very difficult to believe that in the thirteenth century a Cairene Copt would know Coptic better than Arabic, or would so far ignore the niceties of Arabic as to misunderstand the familiar phrase ديار مصر. Ibn Khallikân, who was born just about the date of this document, and wrote his Biographies about A.D. 1260, numbers Coptic among the extinct written languages: [2] and although this assertion is exaggerated, or should at least be confined to Lower Egypt,[3] yet it is far more

[1] Casanova shows reason for regarding Saladin as the sovereign referred to. *Notes sur un texte Copte du XIIIe siècle*, par P. Casanova (Le Caire, 1901).

[2] In the Life of Ibn Bawwâb in vol. ii, p. 285.

[3] According to Abû Ṣâliḥ, at the opening of the thirteenth century, Coptic was still spoken in Upper Egypt. Thus speaking

probable that the author of the story of John of Phanidjoit's martyrdom was ignorant of the precise value of the Coptic form which he was employing, and that, as he found ⲭⲏⲙⲓ (in the sense of country) and ⲃⲁⲃⲩⲗⲱⲛ ⲛ̄ⲧⲉ ⲭⲏⲙⲓ (in the sense of city) both rendered by Miṣr in Arabic, he confused the two or thought them equivalent. Of course it may be held that the Copts by this time had extended the meaning of Babylon from city to country, like the westerns, in forgetfulness of the original limitation of the term. But M. Amélineau shows[1] that in this very document the word ⲭⲏⲙⲓ is used both for Cairo and for Egypt without ⲃⲁⲃⲩⲗⲱⲛ.[2] Clearly the elements of confusion existed: and it was this confusion which made Babylon a synonym for Egypt.

Nor is the definite recognition of this synonym wanting in Arabic writers. Thus Maḳrîzî[3] quotes 'Abd al Malik Ibn Hishâm as saying: 'Bâblîûn is a name denoting Egypt', and Al Ḳuḍâ'î (*ob.* A. D. 1062) as saying: 'Outside Fusṭâṭ is the Ḳaṣr known as

of Udrunkah, he says: 'The Christians living there are learned in their religion and in expounding the Coptic language' (p. 315); and again, of the same place: 'The inhabitants . . . understand the Coptic language, which is the means of communication there both for children and adults, and they are able to explain it in Arabic' (p. 343). More curious is another remark: 'The Christian women of Upper Egypt and their children can hardly speak anything but the Sahidic dialect of Coptic; they have, however, also a perfect knowledge of the Greek language' (p. 317). Unless *Greek* here is an error for *Arabic*, the last statement is almost incredible: the idea of Coptic women in Upper Egypt possessing a perfect knowledge of Greek is absurd.

[1] *Géog. copte*, p. 539.

[2] See also Casanova, *Noms Coptes*, pp. 49–51.

[3] *Khiṭâṭ*, i. 287.

Bâb Lîûn (Babylon) on the hill. Lîûn is the name of the country of Egypt in the language of the negroes and of the Greeks'. Again, in the compendium of Yaḳût called Marâṣid al Iṭṭilâ'[1] we find it stated that 'Babylon is a general name for Egypt in the language of the ancients and a special name for Fusṭâṭ'—very remarkable testimony.

I have now endeavoured to trace the history and meaning of the term Babylon of Egypt from pre-Christian times down to the fifteenth century of our era, and have shown that while originally it denoted a settlement of no great size, the town advanced to become the second metropolis of Egypt, outlasting the more ancient cities of Heliopolis and Memphis: that for centuries before and for a long time after the conquest of Egypt by the Arabs, Babylon was the name of a great city: and that when the Arab designation Fusṭâṭ so far prevailed that the term Babylon passed out of vogue in the popular language, such nevertheless was the renown of Babylon that the name was used as a symbol and synonym for Egypt itself throughout Europe.

The evidence is strong and continuous, and the conclusion it carries seems to me irresistible. It is this: that when Arab historians, of whom the earliest wrote some centuries after the conquest, speak of Babylon as if it were this or that particular fort or building or locality in Ancient Miṣr, they speak erroneously.

That they do so speak, however, is undeniable: and this fact has yet to be considered. Two things

[1] Ed. Juynboll, i. 113.

are certain: first that the Arab settlement called Fusṭâṭ gradually spread all over the site of Babylon or Miṣr, so as to encompass Ḳaṣr ash Shamaʿ on every side; and next that all the Roman and other ancient remains of Babylon disappeared under this process with the single exception of that great fortress. It is clear, too, that the conquerors tended more and more to apply the name Fusṭâṭ, which reminded them of their first encampment in Egypt, to the spreading Arab town; and that of the two coexisting ancient names for the locality they preferred Miṣr[1] with its simply Arabicized form to the puzzling Babylon or Babylonia, with its misleading suggestions Gate of Yûn or Ôn, Gate of Lîûn, and Gate of Lûnîah. But it is perfectly natural that as the Roman remains vanished, so the Roman name Babylon became more and more divorced from the Arab town and more and more strictly confined and limited to the fortress of Ḳaṣr ash Shamaʿ, which challenged time and change, and stood as the one enduring monument of the Roman dominion.

That this explanation fits the facts better than any other, I have no doubt: nor do I doubt that where an Arab writer speaks of Babylon in connexion with the conquest, he means either the city of Babylon or else Ḳaṣr ash Shamaʿ: but in most cases the consciousness that Babylon was a great city at the conquest had been lost when the chronicles were written. I hold, therefore, that the expression Fortress of Babylon, which I have applied to Ḳaṣr ash Shamaʿ, is correct in both senses, i.e. whether

[1] Idrîsî uses the terms Miṣr and Fusṭâṭ indifferently with a slight preference for Miṣr.

used—analogously to Tower of London—to denote the ancient fortress of the city, or used in the sense of Babylon the Fortress.

But it will be said that Arab writers sometimes localize the name Babylon to a point which is outside the fortress and which therefore must be distinguished from the fortress. This is apparently true: and it must be granted that more than one such point is mentioned. For instance, Ibn Duḳmâḳ has the following passage:[1] '*Kanîsat as S'aîdah.* This church is on the skirt of Kôm ibn Ghurâb among the potteries near Bâb al Yûn (Babylon). *Kanîsat Abû Ḳîr.* This church adjoins the last near Bâb al Yûn. *Ḳanîsah known as Santâdur* (*Tâdrus*). This church, too, adjoins the two preceding near Bâb al Yûn. All three are in one place.'

There can be no doubt that the writer here refers to the three still existing churches which I have elsewhere described.[2] The first is now called the 'Church of Al 'Adra by Babylon of the Steps', and the others Abû Ḳîr wa Yuḥannâ and Tâdrus; so that the names subsist unchanged to this day.[3]

[1] iv. 107. [2] *Ancient Coptic Churches*, i. 250 seq.

[3] Casanova in *Noms Coptes* (p. 30) cites this passage and also a corresponding passage from Maḳrîzî, which gives, however, a church of Abû Mînâ instead of Abû Ḳîr. Either Maḳrîzî is mistaken and is thinking of the Abû Mînâ (or Mârî Mînâ) which lies north of Ḳaṣr ash Shama': or if this other church of St. Menas existed when he wrote, it has completely disappeared. Probably there is a textual error as Casanova supposes. But on the same page Casanova quotes from Amélineau a passage in the Synaxarium which alleges that the bodies of SS. Barbara and Juliana were laid in a church of Abû Ḳîr. Now I find that the text of the Synaxarium as given by Basset does not agree with this: it says that 'The bodies of the two saints were laid in a church outside the city of Ghalâlîyâ, and the body of St. Barbara is to-day in the

But the question is what does Ibn Duḳmâḳ mean when he speaks of these churches as *near Babylon?* Can it possibly imply that the name Babylon was then specialized to denote a place identical with the locality in which the name Bâblûn is still preserved? I think not. These churches are not said to be *in* Babylon, but *near* Babylon: consequently the place at which they stood and still stand was *not* Babylon. If it is argued that the name must have belonged to the spot, because it is there still, I answer that the title of the church to-day is not 'Church of Babylon' but '*Church of the Virgin by Bâblûn of the Steps*'. That is the official title, and Dair Bâblûn is a mere popular abbreviation of the name of the convent: which is still, therefore, properly described

city of Miṣr in the church of Abû Ḳîr' (*Patr. Or.*, t. III, fasc. iii, 2, p. 404). Casanova rightly observes that this church has nothing to do with Abû Ḳîr on the north coast (as Amélineau supposes), but must be either the church in Dair Tâdrus or else a church in Ḳaṣr ash Shama': and he cites Eutychius in favour of the latter locality. I have already shown (*Ancient Coptic Churches*, i. 249) that there is no evidence for such a church in Ḳaṣr ash Shama' to corroborate Eutychius. But if it were true, it is certain that this church was destroyed: and I think it far more probable that a new church dedicated to St. Barbara was erected, with or without her relics, than that the existing church of St. Barbara was originally called Abû Ḳîr and has changed its dedication, as Casanova supposes. But it is not even certain that Eutychius meant to say that the church was *inside* the Ḳaṣr: his language might be interpreted merely to be a loose description of the existing Abû Ḳîr as by the entrance of the Ḳaṣr. For Ibn Duḳmâḳ (ii. 26) speaks of the gate which is on the eastern side of the fortress, and was called the Iron Gate, as the gate by which the whole of Ḳaṣr ar Rûm is entered, Ḳaṣr ar Rûm being of course another name for Ḳaṣr ash Shama'. This gate, therefore, was specially recognized as the entrance of the Roman fortress: it is the one still remaining, and Dair Bâblûn is very near it.

not as Babylon or in Babylon, but near Babylon. Babylon is a name belonging not to the site but to the vicinity: and the actual proximity of this group of churches to Ḳaṣr ash Shama' fully explains all that needs explanation in the title.[1] Accordingly neither Ibn Duḳmâḳ nor the modern name of the place can be held to prove any such use of the term Babylon as would necessarily distinguish it from Ḳaṣr ash Shama'.

But the passage from Al Ḳudâ'î cited by Maḳrîzî, which describes the Ḳaṣr called Babylon as outside Fusṭâṭ and on a hill, would seem to imply that a Fortress of Babylon existed in the eleventh century which was not Ḳaṣr ash Shama', but was on a hill: and that consequently an ancient building still remained upon the height, which is taken to be Ar Raṣad. Indeed, Al Ḳudâ'î goes on to say, 'A little of it remains built in stone at the extremity of the

[1] The term 'of the Steps' remains puzzling. It might perhaps refer to the steps which have been brought to light by the south gate of Ḳaṣr ash Shama'—the nearest point of the fortress. But it may be possible to get a little closer to the true explanation. It is pointed out by Guest and Richmond in *J. R. A. S.*, 1903 (p. 804), that 'there seems to have been a gate in the town wall of Miṣr which was called Gate of Bâblûn', and reference is made to *Khiṭaṭ*, ii. 517, l. 12. The position of this wall or section of the wall was, according to the writers, south of Ḳaṣr ash Shama', and it ran east and west near Dair Tâdrus and Dair Bâblûn. The tradition that this wall was part of the ancient circuit wall of Babylon city may well have lingered on, so that the gate in it became known as the Gate of Babylon, just as the fortress within was called Fortress of Babylon. And assuming that the line of the wall is correctly indicated, the wall must have risen near the two convents; and there may well have been steps inside leading up to the gate. This is merely conjectural: but it seems that, in explaining the origin of the name Bâblûn in Dair Bâblûn, one may trace it to a point even nearer than the fortress.

mount (*jabal*), and at the present day there is a mosque on it'.

Maḳrîzî comments upon this as follows: 'This is obviously an express assertion that Ḳaṣr Bâb al Yûn is not the same as Ḳaṣr ash Shama': for Ḳaṣr ash Shama' is in the interior of Fusṭâṭ, and this Ḳaṣr Bâb al Yûn, according to Al Ḳudâ'î, is on the hill known as Ash Sharaf, and Ash Sharaf is outside Fusṭâṭ. But it is contrary to what Ibn 'Abd al Ḥakam says in his Futûh Miṣr'.

Maḳrîzî therefore refutes Al Ḳudâ'î upon the evidence of Ibn 'Abd al Ḥakam, and believes that Babylon and Ḳaṣr ash Shama' are identical.

Moreover, Maḳrîzî is fully aware that the Babylon of Ibn 'Abd al Ḥakam and the Ḳaṣr ash Shama' of Al Ḳudâ'î were one and the same. For he puts side by side the description of the fortress as it is given by each of the two writers: (i) Ibn 'Abd al Ḥakam says: 'The Persians had begun the building of the fortress called Babylon, that is the fortress which is now in Fusṭâṭ: but when the armies of Persia were defeated and driven out of Syria by the Romans, the latter finished the building of the stronghold, and reoccupied it. Egypt then remained under Roman rule until God conquered it for the Muslims'.[1] The corresponding passage of Al

[1] There is no doubt whatever that this refers to Ḳaṣr ash Shama'. Professor C. C. Torrey, of Yale, who is editing the unpublished MS. of Ibn 'Abd al Ḥakam, has been kind enough to give me the benefit of his complete knowledge of the text, and he writes as follows:—' This statement of Ibn 'Abd al Ḥakam agrees with what he says everywhere else. According to his account in the Futûh Miṣr, the ultimate stronghold of the Greeks, *the* "fortress" where the decisive battle was fought was باب اليون ... Babylon is the

Ḳudâ'î occurs in that writer's description of Ḳaṣr ash Shama', and is as follows:—(ii) 'It is said that the Persians when they overcame the Romans and ruled Syria as their masters, and also got possession of Egypt, began the building of this fortress and constructed a fire-temple in it. It was not completed, however, by their hands: but when they were conquered by the Romans, the latter finished the building and fortified it. They then remained in it till the time of the [Muslim] conquest.' It is clear, therefore, that what Ibn 'Abd al Ḥakam calls Babylon, Al Ḳudâ'î calls Ḳaṣr ash Shama', and that Al Ḳudâ'î in putting the fortress called Babylon in quite another place is in glaring contradiction with Ibn 'Abd al Ḥakam.

On the other hand it is fair to remember that Ibn Duḳmâḳ seems to confirm Al Ḳudâ'î when he remarks[1] that Al Ḥâkim built the mosque of Ar Raṣad on the *sharaf* near the remains of the

fortress on the river bank, connected with the island by a pontoon bridge, over which the Muḳauḳis made his escape, emerging from the castle by the southern gate. In the passage in which Ibn 'Abd al Ḥakam first mentions the fortress in his account of the conquest, it might seem that he makes a distinction between a more comprehensive fortification (الحصن) and a smaller citadel (القصر)... But the fact is... that Ibn 'Abd al Ḥakam here uses the term الحصن loosely, referring to the whole settlement at this strategic point. In the sequel, in speaking of the actual siege, he uses the terms الحصن and القصر interchangeably without any distinction whatever.' My thanks are also due to Professor Torrey for some of the information which I have embodied in the text above.

[1] Part IV, 58. Ibn Khallikân also, in his Life of Al Ḥâkim (ed. de Slane, iii. 457), records the completion of a mosque on Ar Raṣad called Jâmi' al Fîlah, which was begun by Al Afdal in A.D. 1104. Guest refers to Maḳrîzî's *Khiṭâṭ*, ii. 451. (*J.R.A.S.*, January, 1907, p. 72.)

Ḳaṣr known as Babylon—in the year A.D. 1012. But I think the significance of this passage is merely that the *sharaf* was near the remains of Ḳaṣr ash Shama', and that such destruction of the circuit wall to the north of the fortress as had then taken place justified Ibn Duḳmâḳ in speaking of its 'remains'. Yet Maḳrîzî[1] himself elsewhere identifies the hill of Babylon with one near Zain al 'Âbidîn—perhaps that on which the citadel of Cairo now stands—proof that he is rather at sea in the matter, and can place the hill north as readily as south of Ḳaṣr ash Shama'; indeed, in yet another passage[2] he puts Babylon again to the north, but near Maḳs. His evidence, therefore, is too contradictory to support any very definite conclusion. But it may even be that Al Ḳudâ'î also, in placing Babylon outside Fusṭâṭ and in speaking of some remains in the *jabal* together with a mosque, is not thinking of Ar Raṣad at all, but of Al Muḳaṭṭam, as the site of the ancient Babylon.

[1] *Khiṭâṭ*, i. 298. See Casanova's edition, p. 148, and his note. He inclines to think that Maḳrîzî's text here must be corrupt.

[2] Id., ii. 452. See Guest and Richmond's Article on Miṣr in *J.R.A.S.*, 1903, p. 807.

CHAPTER V

APART from these confused statements, there seems to be no evidence for the existence of any ancient remains upon Ar Raṣad, nor of the name Babylon as a particular name attaching to that elevation. Upon one of the citations from Ibn 'Abd al Ḥakam made by Maḳrîzî, M. Casanova in his edition of the latter writer [1] propounds a theory that Ḳaṣr ash Shama' and Babylon were distinct, and that there were two separate sieges—one of Ḳaṣr ash Shama' and one of Babylon. But the very text which he quotes contains the refutation of this theory: because, while Ibn 'Abd al Ḥakam is describing the siege of a fortress which he expressly calls Babylon, he makes the Muḳauḳis quit the fortress by its south gate and cross to the island of Rauḍah.[2] The south gate of Ḳaṣr ash Shama' is the one remaining to-day, and the quay is still there at which boats were moored, as the story requires, for crossing to the island, which lay opposite the fortress: and these details, which are so exactly conformable with the topography and the structure of Ḳaṣr ash Shama', are totally at variance with any theory which places Babylon upon an elevated rock

[1] p. 120, n. 4.

[2] Casanova admits that the arsenal proves the island to be Rauḍah: id., p. 121, note 1. The arsenal of Rauḍah is frequently mentioned in Arab history.

like Ar Raṣad. I have dealt with this question elsewhere,[1] and must refer to the argument there.

But there are one or two other pieces of evidence which may be added. That Maḳrîzî himself regards the fort (*ḥiṣn*) which 'Amr besieged as Ḳaṣr ash Shama' is clear from the words in his chapter called 'The site of Al Fusṭâṭ before Islam'. They are to the effect that the *only building* there was 'a fortress called to-day Ḳaṣr ash Shama' and Al Mu'allaḳah', a fortress which then looked on to the Nile, though he adds that convents and churches were scattered all over the plain around.[2] Nothing could be less ambiguous.

And that this fortress was the only fortress apart from 'Umm Dûnain mentioned, or correctly mentioned, in Arab histories of the conquest, can be proved by other evidence. I have already dealt above with John of Nikiou's distinction between the capture of the city of Miṣr and the capture of the citadel of Babylon, and have shown that the distinction as regards the names is accidental, and the names might be reversed. John might just as well have said the city of Babylon and the citadel of Miṣr. But there is, so far as I am aware, no trace in Arab writers of any consciousness that there was any struggle around Ar Raṣad, still less that at the conquest a fortress there existed which could be called the citadel. For consider: if M. Casanova's theory were true—if the fortress of Babylon really were placed on Ar Raṣad—then we should have this strange result, that there stood upon that height a building so vast and so

[1] *The Treaty of Miṣr in Ṭabari*, pp. 19 seq. (Oxford, 1913.)

[2] Ed. Casanova, pp. 104–5.

strong that Ḳaṣr ash Shama' with all its huge walls and towers—its powerful and impregnable defences, as John of Nikiou calls them—was comparatively easy of capture, indeed fell almost without a blow, while a siege of seven months was necessary to reduce the stronghold on Ar Raṣad. For if Babylon were on Ar Raṣad, that story would be required, and that alone could be founded on John of Nikiou's narrative.

But that story is obviously unhistorical. Archaeology, too, is against it. For Trajan's fortress withstood the shocks of time in the main unbroken for more than thirteen centuries,[1] while no one has ever been able to point out any authentic ancient remains whatever upon Ar Raṣad. There is, however, one piece of evidence which might be cited against this statement, and which must be examined.

In *Cairo Fifty Years Ago*[2] the common misunderstandings about Babylon are exemplified, e.g. 'The Egyptian Babylon was situated on a rocky hill called in Arabic *ash Sharaf*': Ḳaṣr ash Shama' 'was on the north-west of Babylon', while the other fortress 'was upon the hill, and this being *within* the town was particularly called by the Arabs "the Fortress or Palace of Babylon" (Ḳaṣr Bâbelyûn), though it is clear that Ḳaṣr ash Shama' was the chief fortress or defence of Babylon'. But the writer, Lane, goes on to say that the building now used as

[1] See my plan in *Arab Conquest of Egypt*, p. 240. This plan has been reproduced by Caetani in his *Annali dell' Islam*, vol. iv, p. 272, who also gives some photographs on pp. 184 and 256.

[2] Ed. S. Lane-Poole, 1896, p. 146. I have reason to think that Dr. Lane-Poole would no longer agree with the opinions here quoted.

a powder magazine upon the hill was named Iṣtabl Anṭâr, and that 'this was probably what the Arabs called "Ḳaṣr Bâbelyûn".' No proof at all is given to support this opinion, and there is nothing at present to show that the 'massive walls' of this magazine on Ar Raṣad are not of Arab construction. The nature of the building unfortunately debarred me, as it has debarred others, from examining it and studying its construction: and it may be that some traces of Roman or even earlier architecture may be discovered there whenever a proper survey is permitted and carried out. But against this possibility must be weighed the evidence of Pococke, who wrote a hundred years before Lane, and who carefully studied the remains on the spot. He gives a sketch of what he calls 'Jebel Jehusi, the Old Babylon',[1] i.e. Ar Raṣad, a sketch which conveys a fair idea of Strabo's rocky ridge; but all he shows upon the eastern end of the hill, where the powder magazine now stands, is a small round building like a low tower. There is nothing whatever corresponding to the large rectangular building with which the traveller is familiar: and though it is possible that this building lay outside Pococke's field of view, the inference rather is that the building was not standing there at the time of Pococke's visit *c.* A.D. 1740. Indeed, the silence of Pococke confirms this inference from the picture. He believes that the hill is the site of the ancient Babylonian settlement—indeed, that the city of Babylon centred about the hill; and he proceeds to say:

[1] *Description of the East*, vol. i, p. 25, pl. viii. See also the photographs in *Annali dell' Islam*, vol. iv, facing p. 168.

'On the top of the hill is the uninhabited convent of St. Michael, to which a priest goes every Sunday to officiate. The town of Babylon, probably in time, extended down to the plain' [from the hill]: 'for to the north of that part of the hill which sets out toward the river' (i.e. the rocky ridge) 'are remains of a very extensive building, which I conjecture might be a sort of castrum for the Roman legion which was at Babylon. It is called Ḳaṣr Kieman, &c.' Now of this Ḳaṣr Kieman[1] Pococke gives a plan absolutely and incontrovertibly identifying it with Ḳaṣr ash Shamaʻ; indeed, in a note he remarks, 'I found some called this place Casrkeshemeh.' Pococke, therefore, knows of no fortress of Babylon upon the hill. He mentions and sketches Strabo's rocky ridge or Ar Raṣad: he mentions, sketches, and plans out Ḳaṣr ash Shamaʻ; but he is totally silent as regards the existence of any building upon Ar Raṣad except an abandoned or nearly abandoned Coptic convent. But if the ancient remains which Lane imagined he saw in 1840 were really ancient, and if they represented the Babylonian fortress of antiquity, they must have been in better preservation and more conspicuous a hundred years earlier at the time of Pococke's visit, and Pococke could never have passed them over in

[1] The name is probably a corruption of the Coptic ⲛⲧⲉ ϫⲏⲙⲓ. In my *Ancient Coptic Churches,* i. 176, I have perhaps done some injustice to Pococke's plan of Ḳaṣr ash Shamaʻ. It is true that he did not measure the angles &c. of the circuit wall, and so produces a neat parallelogram instead of a very irregular figure: but the second pair of round towers which he indicates may have existed, and the general extent of the remains which he saw may be given with rough accuracy.

total silence. Lane's evidence upon the subject must therefore be regarded as mistaken.

Moreover, it is no exaggeration to say that the Arab historians, with the slight exceptions given above, are hardly conscious that there can be any question of a difference between the site of the ancient Persian fortress and the site of the Roman fortress of Ḳaṣr ash Shama'. To them the site of Ḳaṣr ash Shama' is also the site of the Babylonian fortress.

I have admitted and do not doubt that the original Persian fortress was actually built upon Ar Raṣad. But the Arab writers so persistently identify the site of the original fortress with Ḳaṣr ash Shama' that they are proved not to have suspected any difference between the sites: and this again proves that no ancient fortress can have existed upon Ar Raṣad in Arab times. When Trajan built Ḳaṣr ash Shama', in lieu of the Persian stronghold upon Ar Raṣad, for the Roman legion quartered at Babylon, the Persian fortress was either dismantled or perished subsequently by natural decay; and the period of more than 500 years which elapsed between the construction of Ḳaṣr ash Shama' and the invasion of the Arabs fully suffices to account for the total disappearance of the Persian fort. Vague traditions of its former existence survived in Babylon, and some echo of these traditions was caught by the Arabs: but their writers were driven irresistibly to identify the vanished castle of the Persians with the still standing castle of the Romans, that castle which 'Amr had conquered with so much difficulty.

Some further proofs of this may be given.

I have already dwelt upon John of Nikiou's evidence showing that this early Coptic historian definitely calls Ḳaṣr ash Shama' by the name Babylon, and definitely assigns its origin to Nebuchadnezzar and its reconstruction to Trajan; whence one must argue that, if the Persian fort on Ar Raṣad had been in existence when John wrote in the seventh century, it would have been quite impossible for him to allege that it was the same fort which Trajan rebuilt. The Arab writers may have got their information from John's history: but if so, they see no reason for doubting his account of the matter. Thus Maḳrîzî[1] repeats the same story. Ḳaṣr ash Shama', he says, was founded after the devastation of Egypt by Nebuchadnezzar, though other opinions are held as to the date of its construction and the name of the founder. He goes on to say that it (the Persian fort) lay in ruins for 500 years, and hardly a vestige of it remained: until the Romans, having conquered Egypt from the Greeks, sent Arjalîs (? Archelaus), who rebuilt the fortress upon the old foundations, which he discovered.[2] According to Ibn Sa'îd it was Kasharjûsh, the Persian, who built Ḳaṣr ash Shama': others say Artaxerxes, or a king of Egypt named Ḳastû, who built a temple of fire on the bank of the Nile. I will not repeat Ibn 'Abd al Ḥakam's evidence. Al Ḳudâ'î in his chapter 'on the Fortress of Ḳaṣr ash Shama'' gives much the same story, but adds that the temple of fire is the building still called in his day the 'Dome of Smoke': and this account

[1] Ed. Casanova, p. 107.

[2] This is quoted from Al Waḳidî: see Hamaker's edition, Notes, pp. 90 seq. Arjalîs might be Trajan's engineer or general.

seems to stand in opposition to Al Ḳudâ'î's other account cited above, which places Babylon on the *sharaf* or cliff.[1]

So, again, the Marâṣid al Iṭṭilâ'[2] alleges that Ḳaṣr ash Shama' was a castle, on the site of Fusṭâṭ in Egypt, built by the Persians and completed by the Romans. Severus[3] knows nothing of a fort on Ar Raṣad. His words are: 'Then the Arabs crossed the hills (the desert) until they arrived at a fortress built of stone situated between Upper and Lower Egypt and called Babylon. And here they pitched their tents, that they might prepare to fight a battle with the Romans. Then the Arabs called that place, namely the fortress, Bâblûn al Fusṭâṭ (perhaps Bâblûn of Al Fusṭâṭ), and that is its name to this day'. The fact that the camp was pitched before the fortress proves that it was Ḳaṣr ash Shama', and that fortress Severus says was called Babylon at the time he wrote. And Mas'ûdî, speaking with apparent reason,[4] carries the name Ḳaṣr ash Shama' back to the date of the conquest, when he says that Al

[1] See Casanova's *Maḳrîzî*, pp. 107–9. The article in the *J.R.A.S.*, for 1903, says (p. 807) that 'Maḳrîzî, despite the conflicting statements of his predecessors, realized that the ancient Babylonian fortress was not the same as Ḳaṣr ash Shama', but it is evident that he had not identified its remains': and the writers go on to explain Maḳrîzî's own inconsistencies. But their words which I have given appear to assume that remains of the Babylonian fortress existed in Maḳrîzî's time, and this assumption does not seem well warranted.

[2] ii. 221. [3] Brit. Mus. MS. Or. 26100, p. 105.

[4] I have elsewhere expressed the opinion that the name Ḳaṣr ash Shama' probably arose from the Coptic ⲕⲁⲥⲧⲣⲟⲛ ⲛ̄ⲧⲉ ⲭⲏⲙⲓ. See Abû Ṣâliḥ, p. 72, n. 4. I may add that it is sometimes called (e.g. by Ibn Duḳmâḳ) Ḳaṣr ar Rûm, and that this name seems rightly held by Casanova to lie underneath the Coptic ⲕⲉϣⲣⲱⲙⲓ.

Muḳauḳis spent part of the year in Ḳaṣr ash Shama', which to-day is known under the same name in the middle of Fusṭâṭ:[1] and his whole account proves incontestably that this fortress of Al Yûnah (or Lûnîah as he elsewhere calls it), by which he means Babylon, must be identified with Ḳaṣr ash Shama'. Abû Ṣâliḥ[2] says that the people of Fusṭâṭ dug a moat against the Arabs; that Fusṭâṭ then was called Al Lûnîah (or Babylon); and that 'Amr, when he had received reinforcements, took the fortress: moreover, he speaks of 'the governor of Al Lûnîah or Fusṭâṭ' after the conquest. It would clearly be impossible to speak of the *governor of Babylon* as governor of the conquered city, if Babylon were a mere fort on Ar Raṣad. On the other hand, Abû Ṣâliḥ does mention two forts built by Khûsh (or Artaxerxes Ochus), king of the Persians, viz. Ḳaṣr ash Shama' and another on the other side of the Nile.[3] But inasmuch as he alleges that the king (Ochus) 'used to alight at both forts from his boat', Abû Ṣâliḥ obviously has no idea of any fort upon a considerable elevation like Ar Raṣad. Indeed, the context leaves no shadow of doubt that this second Persian fort was at Jîzah, on the western bank of the river. The notice is interesting, because it proves that the Persians saw the military necessity

[1] Ed. de Goeje, p. 213.

[2] p. 74.

[3] p. 177: 'There is a church of Mark the Evangelist and Apostle in the fort built by Khûsh, king of the Persians, at the same time as Ḳaṣr ash Shama'.' This church of St. Mark was at Jîzah. But from Ibn Duḳmâḳ (iv. 126) one is driven to conclude that the fort at Jîzah also had disappeared, because, in A.D. 642, a fort was seen to be necessary, and the Arabs at first refused to build one as ordered by Omar.

of fortifying both banks of the Nile at the apex of the Delta, just as subsequently the Romans stationed one legion at Memphis and one at Babylon, and the Arabs in turn placed a strong garrison at Jîzah after the conquest as well as at Babylon.[1] But the very fact that Abû Ṣâliḥ, while he mentions two fortresses founded by the Persians, does not mention or betray any knowledge of a Persian fortress upon Ar Raṣad, must be taken as one more proof that no ancient remains existed there in Abû Ṣâliḥ's time, and that the very tradition of Strabo's fortress was unknown to him.

Finally, Eutychius,[2] who has a similar tradition of Artaxerxes Ochus, mentions only one fortress as built by him, and that fortress he expressly identifies with Ḳaṣr ash Shama'.

It would be easy to produce other passages from Arab annals and to show that where the name Babylon is applied to a fortress, it is of Ḳaṣr ash Shama' that the writer is thinking in every case, and that there is no testimony whatever for the existence of any fortress upon Ar Raṣad in Arab times. In all these Arab authors, wherever the Persian tradition is given, it is associated with Ḳaṣr ash Shama' and not with Ar Raṣad.[3] Indeed, so strong and so one-sided is the evidence of this association, that I should be inclined to question Strabo's story

[1] See *Arab Conquest of Egypt*, p. 431.

[2] Migne, *Patr. Gr.*, cxi, p. 967.

[3] It may be mentioned that Suyûtî speaks of a Ḳaṣr Fâris, or Persian Fort, outside the walls of Alexandria (Ḥusn al Muḥâḍarah, pt. I, p. 65, Cairo ed.): but there is nothing to show whether this fort was older than the time of Chosroes.

of the 'rocky ridge reaching down to the Nile', were it not that such a ridge exists to-day, and after a careful survey on the spot I am bound to admit that the description of Strabo must have been absolutely accurate, and that the Persian fortress existed there at the time of Strabo's visit to Egypt.

But this admission in no way weakens the evidence upon which I found the conclusion that at the time of the Arab conquest the Persian fortress recorded by Strabo had either vanished altogether or lay in ruins. Any remains which then existed were too insignificant either to bear part in the Roman defences of Babylon or to impress the imagination of Coptic or Arab historians.

To sum up. It seems established

(1) that on the site of Ancient Miṣr or Old Cairo there originally existed in Pharaonic times a city of some importance, marked by Egyptian monuments, (such as the Surîyat abî al Ḥôl or Doxy of the Sphinx,) some of which survived to the days of Al Ḥâkim:

(2) that in the sixth century before our era there was a Babylonian military settlement made and a fortress erected upon the rocky height which the Arabs later called Ar Raṣad:

(3) that from this settlement the name Babylon spread over the adjacent region, and became the normal designation of a great town extending far enough northward of Ar Raṣad to touch with its outlying suburbs the southern environs of the mighty but decaying city of Heliopolis:

(4) that when Trajan, wishing to strengthen his hold upon the apex of the Delta, resolved to build a

powerful fortress as the citadel of Babylon, he abandoned the site of the Persian fort upon Ar Raṣad and planted his citadel upon the bank of the Nile, so as to secure an unfailing water supply for the garrison and free communication by river between the garrison and the rest of Egypt: and this fortress was called the Castle of Babylon, or the Castle of Khêmi, and that the Arabic form of the name was Ḳaṣr ash Shama':

(5) that the Persian fort on Ar Raṣad thenceforward fell into decay and oblivion, so that at the Arab conquest, five and a half centuries later, only vague traditions of its existence survived:

(6) that the name of Babylon, which the Arabs found applied to the city otherwise called Miṣr was gradually displaced by the new name Fusṭâṭ of Arab origin; and as the name Fusṭâṭ grew and prevailed to designate the city, so the name Babylon fell into disfavour and disuse, until at the time when the Arab chronicles began to be written it had become practically restricted to the fortress of Ḳaṣr ash Shama', yet curiously prevailed in Europe to denote the whole country of Egypt:

(7) and that, finally, even the limited use of the name tended to disappear in Egypt in more modern times, as the association of the term Babylon with the fortress was weakened or severed; so that to-day it is not among the ruins of Ḳaṣr ash Shama', but in the little Coptic convent called Dair Bâblûn near the southern gate of the fortress, that there lingers the name of the great city which succeeded Memphis as the capital of Middle Egypt.

INDEX

OTHER TITLES IN THIS HARDBACK REPRINT PROGRAMME FROM SANDPIPER BOOKS LTD (LONDON) AND POWELLS BOOKS (CHICAGO)

ISBN 0–19–	Author	Title
8143567	ALFÖLDI A.	The Conversion of Constantine and Pagan Rome
6286409	ANDERSON George K.	The Literature of the Anglo-Saxons
8228813	BARTLETT & MacKAY	Medieval Frontier Societies
8111010	BETHURUM Dorothy	Homilies of Wulfstan
8114222	BROOKS Kenneth R.	Andreas and the Fates of the Apostles
8203543	BULL Marcus	Knightly Piety & Lay Response to the First Crusade
8216785	BUTLER Alfred J.	Arab Conquest of Egypt
8148348	CAMPBELL J.B.	The Emperor and the Roman Army 31 BC to 235 AD
826643X	CHADWICK Henry	Priscillian of Avila
826447X	CHADWICK Henry	Boethius
8219393	COWDREY H.E.J.	The Age of Abbot Desiderius
8148992	DAVIES M.	Sophocles: Trachiniae
825301X	DOWNER L.	Leges Henrici Primi
8154372	FAULKNER R.O.	The Ancient Egyptian Pyramid Texts
8221541	FLANAGAN Marie Therese	Irish Society, Anglo-Norman Settlers, Angevin Kingship
8143109	FRAENKEL Edward	Horace
8201540	GOLDBERG P.J.P.	Women, Work and Life Cycle in a Medieval Economy
8140215	GOTTSCHALK H.B.	Heraclides of Pontus
8266162	HANSON R.P.C.	Saint Patrick
8224354	HARRISS G.L.	King, Parliament and Public Finance in Medieval England to 1369
8581114	HEATH Sir Thomas	Aristarchus of Samos
8140444	HOLLIS A.S.	Callimachus: Hecale
8212968	HOLLISTER C. Warren	Anglo-Saxon Military Institutions
8223129	HURNARD Naomi	The King's Pardon for Homicide – before AD 1307
8140401	HUTCHINSON G.O.	Hellenistic Poetry
8142560	JONES A.H.M.	The Greek City
8218354	JONES Michael	Ducal Brittany 1364–1399
8271484	KNOX & PELCZYNSKI	Hegel's Political Writings
8225253	LE PATOUREL John	The Norman Empire
8212720	LENNARD Reginald	Rural England 1086–1135
8212321	LEVISON W.	England and the Continent in the 8th century
8148224	LIEBESCHUETZ J.H.W.G.	Continuity and Change in Roman Religion
8141378	LOBEL Edgar & PAGE Sir Denys	Poetarum Lesbiorum Fragmenta
8241445	LUKASIEWICZ, Jan	Aristotle's Syllogistic
8152442	MAAS P. & TRYPANIS C.A.	Sancti Romani Melodi Cantica
8148178	MATTHEWS John	Western Aristocracies and Imperial Court AD 364–425
8223447	McFARLANE K.B.	Lancastrian Kings and Lollard Knights
8226578	McFARLANE K.B.	The Nobility of Later Medieval England
8148100	MEIGGS Russell	Roman Ostia
8148402	MEIGGS Russell	Trees and Timber in the Ancient Mediterranean World
8142641	MILLER J. Innes	The Spice Trade of the Roman Empire
8147813	MOORHEAD John	Theoderic in Italy
8264259	MOORMAN John	A History of the Franciscan Order
8116020	OWEN A.L.	The Famous Druids
8131445	PALMER, L.R.	The Interpretation of Mycenaean Greek Texts
8143427	PFEIFFER R.	History of Classical Scholarship (vol 1)
8111649	PHEIFER J.D.	Old English Glosses in the Epinal-Erfurt Glossary
8142277	PICKARD–CAMBRIDGE A.W.	Dithyramb Tragedy and Comedy
8269765	PLATER & WHITE	Grammar of the Vulgate
8213891	PLUMMER Charles	Lives of Irish Saints (2 vols)
820695X	POWICKE Michael	Military Obligation in Medieval England
8269684	POWICKE Sir Maurice	Stephen Langton
821460X	POWICKE Sir Maurice	The Christian Life in the Middle Ages
8225369	PRAWER Joshua	Crusader Institutions
8225571	PRAWER Joshua	The History of The Jews in the Latin Kingdom of Jerusalem
8143249	RABY F.J.E.	A History of Christian Latin Poetry
8143257	RABY F.J.E.	A History of Secular Latin Poetry in the Middle Ages (2 vols)
8214316	RASHDALL & POWICKE	The Universities of Europe in the Middle Ages (3 vols)
8148380	RICKMAN Geoffrey	The Corn Supply of Ancient Rome
8141076	ROSS Sir David	Aristotle: Metaphysics (2 vols)
8141092	ROSS Sir David	Aristotle: Physics
8264178	RUNCIMAN Sir Steven	The Eastern Schism
814833X	SALMON J.B.	Wealthy Corinth
8171587	SALZMAN L.F.	Building in England Down to 1540
8218362	SAYERS Jane E.	Papal Judges Delegate in the Province of Canterbury 1198–1254
8221657	SCHEIN Sylvia	Fideles Crucis

8148135	SHERWIN WHITE A.N.	The Roman Citizenship
8113927	SISAM, Kenneth	Studies in the History of Old English Literature
8642040	SOUTER Alexander	A Glossary of Later Latin to 600 AD
8222254	SOUTHERN R.W.	Eadmer: Life of St. Anselm
8251408	SQUIBB G.	The High Court of Chivalry
8212011	STEVENSON & WHITELOCK	Asser's Life of King Alfred
8212011	SWEET Henry	A Second Anglo-Saxon Reader—Archaic and Dialectical
8148259	SYME Sir Ronald	History in Ovid
8143273	SYME Sir Ronald	Tacitus (2 vols)
8200951	THOMPSON Sally	Women Religious
8201745	WALKER Simon	The Lancastrian Affinity 1361–1399
8161115	WELLESZ Egon	A History of Byzantine Music and Hymnography
8140185	WEST M.L.	Greek Metre
8141696	WEST M.L.	Hesiod: Theogony
8148542	WEST M.L.	The Orphic Poems
8140053	WEST M.L.	Hesiod: Works & Days
8152663	WEST M.L.	Iambi et Elegi Graeci
822799X	WHITBY M. & M.	The History of Theophylact Simocatta
8206186	WILLIAMSON, E.W.	Letters of Osbert of Clare
8114877	WOOLF Rosemary	The English Religious Lyric in the Middle Ages
8119224	WRIGHT Joseph	Grammar of the Gothic Language